ELEMENTARY NUMERICAL ANALYSIS
An Algorithmic Approach

International Series in Pure and Applied Mathematics

G. Springer
Consulting Editor

Ahlfors: *Complex Analysis*
Bender and Orszag: *Advanced Mathematical Methods for Scientists and Engineers*
Buck: *Advanced Calculus*
Busacker and Saaty: *Finite Graphs and Networks*
Cheney: *Introduction to Approximation Theory*
Chester: *Techniques in Partial Differential Equations*
Coddington and Levinson: *Theory of Ordinary Differential Equations*
Conte and de Boor: *Elementary Numerical Analysis: An Algorithmic Approach*
Dennemeyer: *Introduction to Partial Differential Equations and Boundary Value Problems*
Dettman: *Mathematical Methods in Physics and Engineering*
Hamming: *Numerical Methods for Scientists and Engineers*
Hildebrand: *Introduction to Numerical Analysis*
Householder: *The Numerical Treatment of a Single Nonlinear Equation*
Kalman, Falb, and Arbib: *Topics in Mathematical Systems Theory*
McCarty: *Topology: An Introduction with Applications to Topological Groups*
Moore: *Elements of Linear Algebra and Matrix Theory*
Moursund and Duris: *Elementary Theory and Application of Numerical Analysis*
Pipes and Harvill: *Applied Mathematics for Engineers and Physicists*
Ralston and Rabinowitz: *A First Course in Numerical Analysis*
Ritger and Rose: *Differential Equations with Applications*
Rudin: *Principles of Mathematical Analysis*
Shapiro: *Introduction to Abstract Algebra*
Simmons: *Differential Equations with Applications and Historical Notes*
Simmons: *Introduction to Topology and Modern Analysis*
Struble: *Nonlinear Differential Equations*

ELEMENTARY NUMERICAL ANALYSIS
An Algorithmic Approach

Third Edition

S. D. Conte
Purdue University

Carl de Boor
University of Wisconsin—Madison

INTERNATIONAL STUDENT EDITION

McGRAW-HILL INTERNATIONAL BOOK COMPANY

Auckland   Bogotá   Guatemala   Hamburg   Johannesburg   Lisbon
London   Madrid   Mexico   New Delhi   Panama   Paris   San Juan
São Paulo   Singapore   Sydney   Tokyo

ELEMENTARY NUMERICAL ANALYSIS
An Algorithmic Approach

INTERNATIONAL STUDENT EDITION

This book was set in Times Roman by Science Typographers, Inc. The
editors were Carol Napier and James S. Amar; the production supervisor
was Phil Galea. The drawings were done by Fine Line Illustrations, Inc.

Library of Congress Cataloging in Publication Data

Conte, Samuel Daniel, date
    Elementary numerical analysis.

    (International series in pure and applied
mathematics)
    Includes index.
    1. Numerical analysis—Data processing.
I. de Boor, Carl, joint author. II. Title.
QA297.C65   1980   519.4   79-24641
ISBN 0-07-012447-7

When ordering this title use ISBN 0-07-066228-2

TOSHO PRINTING CO., LTD. TOKYO JAPAN

CONTENTS

*Sections marked with an asterisk may be omitted without loss of continuity.

PREFACE

This is the third edition of a book on elementary numerical analysis which is designed specifically for the needs of upper-division undergraduate students in engineering, mathematics, and science including, in particular, computer science. On the whole, the student who has had a solid college calculus sequence should have no difficulty following the material. Advanced mathematical concepts, such as norms and orthogonality, when they are used, are introduced carefully at a level suitable for undergraduate students and do not assume any previous knowledge. Some familiarity with matrices is assumed for the chapter on systems of equations and with differential equations for Chapters 8 and 9. This edition does contain some sections which require slightly more mathematical maturity than the previous edition. However, all such sections are marked with asterisks and all can be omitted by the instructor with no loss in continuity.

This new edition contains a great deal of new material and significant changes to some of the older material. The chapters have been rearranged in what we believe is a more natural order. Polynomial interpolation (Chapter 2) now precedes even the chapter on the solution of nonlinear systems (Chapter 3) and is used subsequently for some of the material in all chapters. The treatment of Gauss elimination (Chapter 4) has been simplified. In addition, Chapter 4 now makes extensive use of Wilkinson's backward error analysis, and contains a survey of many well-known methods for the eigenvalue-eigenvector problem. Chapter 5 is a new chapter on systems of equations and unconstrained optimization. It contains an introduction to steepest-descent methods, Newton's method for nonlinear systems of equations, and relaxation methods for solving large linear systems by iteration. The chapter on approximation (Chapter 6) has been enlarged. It now treats best approximation and good approximation by polynomials, also approximation by trigonometric functions, including the Fast Fourier Transforms, as well as least-squares data fitting, orthogonal polynomials, and curve fitting by splines. Differentiation and integration are now treated in Chapter 7, which contains a new section on adaptive quadrature. Chapter 8 on ordinary differential equations contains considerable new material and some new sections. There is a new section on step-size control in Runge-Kutta methods and a new section on stiff differential equations as well as an extensively revised section on numerical instability. Chapter 9 contains a brief introduction to collocation as a method for solving boundary-value problems.

This edition, as did the previous one, assumes that students have access to a computer and that they are familiar with programming in some procedure-oriented language. A large number of algorithms are presented in the text, and FORTRAN programs for many of these algorithms have been provided. There are somewhat fewer complete programs in this edition. All the programs have been rewritten in the FORTRAN 77 language which uses modern structured-programming concepts. All the programs have been tested on one or more computers, and in most cases machine results are presented. When numerical output is given, the text will indicate which machine (IBM, CDC, UNIVAC) was used to obtain the results.

The book contains more material than can usually be covered in a typical one-semester undergraduate course for general science majors. This gives the instructor considerable leeway in designing the course. For this, it is important to point out that only the material on polynomial interpolation in Chapter 2, on linear systems in Chapter 4, and on differentiation and integration in Chapter 7, is required in an essential way in subsequent chapters. The material in the first seven chapters (exclusive of the starred sections) would make a reasonable first course.

We take this opportunity to thank those who have communicated to us misprints and errors in the second edition and have made suggestions for improvement. We are especially grateful to R. E. Barnhill, D. Chambless, A. E. Davidoff, P. G. Davis, A. G. Deacon, A. Feldstein, W. Ferguson, A. O. Garder, J. Guest, T. R. Hopkins, D. Joyce, K. Kincaid, J. T. King, N. Krikorian, and W. E. McBride.

S. D. Conte
Carl de Boor

INTRODUCTION

This book is concerned with the practical solution of problems on computers. In the process of problem solving, it is possible to distinguish several more or less distinct phases. The first phase is *formulation*. In formulating a mathematical model of a physical situation, scientists should take into account beforehand the fact that they expect to solve a problem on a computer. They will therefore provide for specific objectives, proper input data, adequate checks, and for the type and amount of output.

Once a problem has been formulated, numerical methods, together with a preliminary error analysis, must be devised for solving the problem. A numerical method which can be used to solve a problem will be called an *algorithm*. An algorithm is a complete and unambiguous set of procedures leading to the solution of a mathematical problem. The selection or construction of appropriate algorithms properly falls within the scope of *numerical analysis*. Having decided on a specific algorithm or set of algorithms for solving the problem, numerical analysts should consider all the sources of error that may affect the results. They must consider how much accuracy is required, estimate the magnitude of the round-off and discretization errors, determine an appropriate step size or the number of iterations required, provide for adequate checks on the accuracy, and make allowance for corrective action in cases of nonconvergence.

The third phase of problem solving is *programming*. The programmer must transform the suggested algorithm into a set of unambiguous step-by-step instructions to the computer. The first step in this procedure is called *flow charting*. A flow chart is simply a set of procedures, usually in logical block form, which the computer will follow. It may be given in graphical or procedural statement form. The complexity of the flow will depend upon the complexity of the problem and the amount of detail included. However, it should be possible for someone other than the programmer to follow the flow of information from the chart. The flow chart is an effective aid to the programmer, who must translate its major functions into a program, and, at the same time, it is an effective means of communication to others who wish to understand what the program does. In this book we sometimes use flow charts in graphical form, but more often in procedural statement form. When graphical flow charts are used, standard conventions are followed, whereas all procedural statement charts use a self-explanatory ALGOL-like statement language. Having produced a flow chart, the programmer must transform the indicated procedures into a set of machine instructions. This may be done directly in machine language, in an assembly language, or in a procedure-oriented language. In this book a dialect of FORTRAN called FORTRAN 77 is used exclusively. FORTRAN 77 is a new dialect of FORTRAN which incorporates new control statements and which emphasizes modern structured-programming concepts. While FORTRAN IV compilers are available on almost all computers, FORTRAN 77 may not be as readily available. However, conversion from FORTRAN 77 to FORTRAN IV should be relatively straightforward.

A procedure-oriented language such as FORTRAN or ALGOL is sometimes called an *algorithmic* language. It allows us to express a mathematical algorithm in a form more suitable for communication with computers. A FORTRAN procedure that implements a mathematical algorithm will, in general, be much more precise than the mathematical algorithm. If, for example, the mathematical algorithm specifies an iterative procedure for finding the solution of an equation, the FORTRAN program must specify (1) the accuracy that is required, (2) the number of iterations to be performed, and (3) what to do in case of nonconvergence. Most of the algorithms in this book are given in the normal mathematical form and in the more precise form of a FORTRAN procedure.

In many installations, each of these phases of problem solving is performed by a separate person. In others, a single person may be responsible for all three functions. It is clear that there are many interactions among these three phases. As the program develops, more information becomes available, and this information may suggest changes in the formulation, in the algorithms being used, and in the program itself.

ELEMENTARY NUMERICAL ANALYSIS
An Algorithmic Approach

Polynomial : one or more terms containing constants, variables + exponents (but not if a term contains division by a variable)

$\nearrow$ (not -ve !)
$0, 1, 2, 3 \ldots$

eg $4xy^2 + 2x - 5$ ✓

but not $\dfrac{2}{x}$ or $2x^{-2}$

Integral coefficients means the coefficients of the polynomial are integers.

+/- whole numbers

$(\ldots -3, -2, -1, 0, 1, 2, 3 \ldots)$

NUMBER SYSTEMS AND ERRORS

In this chapter we consider methods for representing numbers on computers and the errors introduced by these representations. In addition, we examine the sources of various types of computational errors and their subsequent propagation. We also discuss some mathematical preliminaries.

1.1 THE REPRESENTATION OF INTEGERS

In everyday life we use numbers based on the decimal system. Thus the number 257, for example, is expressible as

$$257 = 2 \cdot 100 + 5 \cdot 10 + 7 \cdot 1$$
$$= 2 \cdot 10^2 + 5 \cdot 10^1 + 7 \cdot 10^0$$

We call 10 the **base** of this system. Any integer is expressible as a polynomial in the base 10 with integral coefficients between 0 and 9. We use the notation

$$N = (a_n a_{n-1} \cdots a_0)_{10}$$
$$= a_n 10^n + a_{n-1} 10^{n-1} + \cdots + a_0 10^0 \qquad (1.1)$$

to denote any positive integer in the base 10. There is no intrinsic reason to use 10 as a base. Other civilizations have used other bases such as 12, 20, or 60. Modern computers read pulses sent by electrical components. The state of an electrical impulse is either *on* or *off*. It is therefore convenient to represent numbers in computers in the **binary** system. Here the base is 2, and the integer coefficients may take the values 0 or 1.

A nonnegative integer N will be represented in the binary system as

$$N = (a_n a_{n-1} \cdots a_1 a_0)_2$$
$$= a_n 2^n + a_{n-1} 2^{n-1} + \cdots + a_1 2^1 + a_0 2^0 \tag{1.2}$$

where the coefficients a_k are either 0 or 1. Note that N is again represented as a polynomial, but now in the base 2. Many computers used in scientific work operate internally in the binary system. Users of computers, however, prefer to work in the more familiar decimal system. It is therefore necessary to have some means of converting from decimal to binary when information is submitted to the computer, and from binary to decimal for output purposes.

Conversion of a binary number to decimal form may be accomplished directly from the definition (1.2). As examples we have

$$(11)_2 = 1 \cdot 2^1 + 1 \cdot 2^0 = 3$$
$$(1101)_2 = 1 \cdot 2^3 + 1 \cdot 2^2 + 0 \cdot 2^1 + 1 \cdot 2^0 = 13$$

The conversion of integers from a base β to the base 10 can also be accomplished by the following algorithm, which is derived in Chap. 2.

Algorithm 1.1 Given the coefficients $a_n, \ldots, a_0$ of the polynomial

$$p(x) = a_n x^n + a_{n-1} x^{n-1} + \cdots + a_1 x + a_0 \tag{1.3}$$

and a number β. Compute recursively the numbers $b_n, b_{n-1}, \ldots, b_0$:

$$b_n := a_n$$
$$b_{n-1} := a_{n-1} + b_n \beta$$
$$b_{n-2} := a_{n-2} + b_{n-1} \beta$$
$$b_{n-3} := a_{n-3} + b_{n-2} \beta$$
$$\cdots \cdots \cdots \cdots \cdots \cdots \cdots$$
$$b_0 := a_0 + b_1 \beta$$

Then $b_0 = p(\beta)$.

Since, by the definition (1.2), the binary integer $(a_n a_{n-1} \cdots a_0)_2$ represents the value of the polynomial (1.3) at $x = 2$, we can use Algorithm 1.1, with $\beta = 2$, to find the decimal equivalents of binary integers.

Thus the decimal equivalent of $(1101)_2$ computed using Algorithm 1.1 is

$$b_3 = 1$$
$$b_2 = 1 + 1 \cdot 2 = 3$$
$$b_1 = 0 + 3 \cdot 2 = 6$$
$$b_0 = 1 + 6 \cdot 2 = 13$$

and the decimal equivalent of $(10000)_2$ is

$$b_4 = 1$$
$$b_3 = 0 + 1 \cdot 2 = 2$$
$$b_2 = 0 + 2 \cdot 2 = 4$$
$$b_1 = 0 + 4 \cdot 2 = 8$$
$$b_0 = 0 + 8 \cdot 2 = 16$$

Converting a decimal integer N into its binary equivalent can also be accomplished by Algorithm 1.1 if one is willing to use *binary* arithmetic. For if $N = (a_n a_{n-1} \cdots a_0)_{10}$, then by the definition (1.1), $N = p(10)$, where $p(x)$ is the polynomial (1.3). Hence we can calculate the binary representation for N by translating the coefficients $a_n, \ldots, a_0$ into binary integers and then using Algorithm 1.1 to evaluate $p(x)$ at $x = 10 = (1010)_2$ in binary arithmetic. If, for example, $N = 187$, then

$$187 = (187)_{10} = 1 \cdot 10^2 + 8 \cdot 10^1 + 7 \cdot 10^0$$
$$= (1)_2(1010)_2^2 + (1000)_2(1010)_2^1 + (111)_2(1010)_2^0$$

and using Algorithm 1.1 and binary arithmetic,

$$b_2 = (1)_2$$
$$b_1 = (1000)_2 + (1)_2(1010)_2 = (1000)_2 + (1010)_2 = (10010)_2$$
$$b_0 = (111)_2 + (10010)_2(1010)_2 = (111)_2 + (10110100)_2 = (10111011)_2$$

Therefore $187 = (10111011)_2$.

Binary numbers and binary arithmetic, though ideally suited for today's computers, are somewhat tiresome for people because of the number of digits necessary to represent even moderately sized numbers. Thus eight binary digits are necessary to represent the three-decimal-digit number 187. The **octal** number system, using the base 8, presents a kind of compromise between the computer-preferred binary and the people-preferred decimal system. It is easy to convert from octal to binary and back since three binary digits make one octal digit. To convert from octal to binary, one merely replaces all octal digits by their binary equivalent; thus

$$(347)_8 = (011 \quad 100 \quad 111)_2 = (11100111)_2$$

Conversely, to convert from binary to octal, one partitions the binary digits in groups of three (starting from the right) and then replaces each three-group by its octal digit; thus

$$(10111011)_2 = (010 \quad 111 \quad 011)_2 = (273)_8$$

If a decimal integer has to be converted to binary by hand, it is usually fastest to convert it first to octal using Algorithm 1.1, and then from octal to binary. To take an earlier example,

$$187 = (187)_{10} = (1)_8(12)_8^2 + (10)_8(12)_8^1 + (7)_8(12)_8^0$$

Hence, using Algorithm 1.1 [with 2 replaced by $10 = (12)_8$, and with *octal* arithmetic],

$$b_2 = (1)_8$$
$$b_1 = (10)_8 + (1)_8(12)_8 = (22)_8$$
$$b_0 = (7)_8 + (22)_8(12)_8 = (7)_8 + (264)_8 = (273)_8$$

Therefore, finally,

$$187 = (273)_8 = (010111011)_2$$

EXERCISES

1.1-1 Convert the following binary numbers to decimal form:
$(1010)_2$ $(100101)_2$ $(10000001)_2$

1.1-2 Convert the following decimal numbers to binary form:
82, 109, 3433

1.1-3 Carry out the conversions in Exercises 1.1-1 and 1.1-2 by converting first to octal form.

1.1-4 Write a FORTRAN subroutine which accepts a number to the base BETIN with the NIN digits contained in the one-dimensional array NUMIN, and returns the NOUT digits of the equivalent in base BETOUT in the one-dimensional array NUMOUT. For simplicity, restrict both BETIN and BETOUT to 2, 4, 8, and 10.

1.2 THE REPRESENTATION OF FRACTIONS

If x is a positive real number, then its **integral** part x_I is the largest integer less than or equal to x, while

$$x_F = x - x_I$$

is its **fractional** part. The fractional part can always be written as a *decimal fraction*:

$$x_F = \sum_{k=1}^{\infty} b_k 10^{-k} \tag{1.4}$$

where each b_k is a nonnegative integer less than 10. If $b_k = 0$ for all k greater than a certain integer, then the fraction is said to *terminate*. Thus

$$\tfrac{1}{4} = 0.25 = 2 \cdot 10^{-1} + 5 \cdot 10^{-2}$$

is a terminating decimal fraction, while

$$\tfrac{1}{3} = 0.333 \cdots = 3 \cdot 10^{-1} + 3 \cdot 10^{-2} + 3 \cdot 10^{-3} + \cdots$$

is not.

If the integral part of x is given as a decimal integer by

$$x_I = (a_n a_{n-1} \cdots a_0)_{10}$$

while the fractional part is given by (1.4), it is customary to write the two representations one after the other, separated by a point, the "decimal point":

$$x = (a_n a_{n-1} \cdots a_0.b_1 b_2 b_3 \cdots)_{10}$$

Completely analogously, one can write the fractional part of x as a *binary* fraction:

$$x_F = \sum_{k=1}^{\infty} b_k 2^{-k}$$

where each b_k is a nonnegative integer less than 2, i.e., either zero or one. If the integral part of x is given by the binary integer

$$x_I = (a_n a_{n-1} \cdots a_0)_2$$

then we write

$$x = (a_n a_{n-1} \cdots a_0.b_1 b_2 b_3 \cdots)_2$$

using a "binary point."

The binary fraction $(.b_1 b_2 b_3 \cdots)_2$ for a given number x_F between zero and one can be calculated as follows: If

$$x_F = \sum_{k=1}^{\infty} b_k 2^{-k}$$

then

$$2x_F = \sum_{k=1}^{\infty} b_k 2^{-k+1} = b_1 + \sum_{k=1}^{\infty} b_{k+1} 2^{-k}$$

Hence b_1 is the integral part of $2x_F$, while

$$(2x_F)_F = 2x_F - b_1 = \sum_{k=1}^{\infty} b_{k+1} 2^{-k}$$

Therefore, repeating this procedure, we find that b_2 is the integral part of $2(2x_F)_F$, b_3 is the integral part of $2(2(2x_F)_F)_F$, etc.

If, for example, $x = 0.625 = x_F$, then

$$2(0.625) = 1.25 \qquad \text{so } b_1 = 1$$

$$2(0.25) = 0.5 \qquad \text{so } b_2 = 0$$

$$2(0.5) = 1.0 \qquad \text{so } b_3 = 1$$

and all further b_k's are zero. Hence

$$0.625 = (.101)_2$$

This example was rigged to give a terminating binary fraction. Unhappily, not every terminating decimal fraction gives rise to a terminating binary fraction. This is due to the fact that the binary fraction for

$x_F = 10^{-1} = 0.1$ is not terminating. We have

$$2(0.1) = 0.2 \quad \text{so } b_1 = 0$$
$$2(0.2) = 0.4 \quad \text{so } b_2 = 0$$
$$2(0.4) = 0.8 \quad \text{so } b_3 = 0$$
$$2(0.8) = 1.6 \quad \text{so } b_4 = 1$$
$$2(0.6) = 1.2 \quad \text{so } b_5 = 1$$

and now we are back to a fractional part of 0.2, so that the digits cycle. It follows that

$$0.1 = (.0 \quad 0011 \quad 0011 \cdots)_2$$

The procedure just outlined is formalized in the following algorithm.

Algorithm 1.2 Given x between 0 and 1 and an integer β greater than 1. Generate recursively $b_1, b_2, b_3 \ldots$ by

$$c_0 := x$$
$$b_1 := (\beta c_0)_I, \quad c_1 := (\beta c_0)_F$$
$$b_2 := (\beta c_1)_I, \quad c_2 := (\beta c_1)_F$$
$$\cdots \cdots \cdots \cdots \cdots \cdots$$

Then
$$x = (.b_1 b_2 b_3 \cdots)_\beta = \sum_{k=1}^{\infty} b_k \beta^{-k}$$

We have stated this algorithm for a general base β rather than for the specific binary base $\beta = 2$, for two reasons. If this conversion to binary is carried out with pencil and paper, it is usually faster to convert first to octal, i.e., use $\beta = 8$, and then to convert from octal to binary. Also, the algorithm can be used to convert a binary (or octal) fraction to decimal, by choosing $\beta = 10$ and using binary (or octal) arithmetic.

To give an example, if $x = (.101)_2$, then, with $\beta = 10 = (1010)_2$ and binary arithmetic, we get from Algorithm 1.2

$$10(.101)_2 = (110.010)_2 \quad \text{so } b_1 = (110)_2 = 6, \quad c_1 = (.01)_2$$
$$10(.01)_2 = (10.10)_2 \quad \text{so } b_2 = (10)_2 = 2, \quad c_2 = (.1)_2$$
$$10(.1)_2 = (101.)_2 \quad \text{so } b_3 = (101)_2 = 5, \quad c_3 = 0$$

Hence subsequent b_k's are zero. This shows that

$$(.101)_2 = 0.625$$

confirming our earlier calculation. Note that if x_F is a terminating binary fraction with n digits, then it is also a terminating decimal fraction with n digits, since

$$(.1)_2 = 0.5$$

EXERCISES

1.2-1 Convert the following binary fractions to decimal fractions:
  $(.1100011)_2$ $(.11111111)_2$

1.2-2 Find the first 5 digits of .1 written as an octal fraction, then compute from it the first 15 digits of .1 as a binary fraction.

1.2-3 Convert the following octal fractions to decimal:
  $(.614)_8$ $(.776)_8$
Compare with your answer in Exercise 1.2-1.

1.2-4 Find a binary number which approximates π to within 10^{-3}.

1.2-5 If we want to convert a decimal integer N to binary using Algorithm 1.1, we have to use *binary* arithmetic. Show how to carry out this conversion using Algorithm 1.2 and *decimal* arithmetic. (*Hint:* Divide N by the appropriate power of 2, convert the result to binary, then shift the "binary point" appropriately.)

1.2-6 If we want to convert a terminating binary fraction x to a decimal fraction using Algorithm 1.2, we have to use *binary* arithmetic. Show how to carry out this conversion using Algorithm 1.1 and *decimal* arithmetic.

1.3 FLOATING-POINT ARITHMETIC

Scientific calculations are usually carried out in floating-point arithmetic. An n-digit floating-point number in base β has the form

$$x = \pm (.d_1 d_2 \cdots d_n)_\beta \beta^e \qquad (1.5)$$

where $(.d_1 d_2 \cdots d_n)_\beta$ is a β-fraction called the **mantissa**, and e is an integer called the **exponent**. Such a floating-point number is said to be **normalized** in case $d_1 \neq 0$, or else $d_1 = d_2 = \cdots = d_n = 0$.

For most computers, $\beta = 2$, although on some, $\beta = 16$, and in hand calculations and on most desk and pocket calculators, $\beta = 10$.

The precision or length n of floating-point numbers on any particular computer is usually determined by the word length of the computer and may therefore vary widely (see Fig. 1.1). Computing systems which accept FORTRAN programs are expected to provide floating-point numbers of two different lengths, one roughly double the other. The shorter one, called **single precision**, is ordinarily used unless the other, called **double precision**, is specifically asked for. Calculation in double precision usually doubles the storage requirements and more than doubles running time as compared with single precision.

Figure 1.1 Floating-point characteristics.

Computer	β	n	$M = -m$
IBM 7094	2	27	2^7
Burroughs 5000 Series	8	13	2^6
IBM 360/370	16	6	2^6
CDC 6000 and Cyber Series	2	48	2^{10}
DEC 11/780 VAX	2	24	2^7
Hewlett Packard 67	10	10	99

The exponent e is limited to a range

$$m < e < M \tag{1.6}$$

for certain integers m and M. Usually, $m = -M$, but the limits may vary widely; see Fig. 1.1.

There are two commonly used ways of translating a given real number x into an n β-digit floating-point number $fl(x)$, rounding and chopping. In **rounding**, $fl(x)$ is chosen as the normalized floating-point number nearest x; some special rule, such as symmetric rounding (rounding to an even digit), is used in case of a tie. In **chopping**, $fl(x)$ is chosen as the nearest normalized floating-point number *between* x and 0. If, for example, two-decimal-digit floating-point numbers are used, then

$$fl\left(\tfrac{2}{3}\right) = \begin{cases} (0.67)10^0 & \text{rounded} \\ (0.66)10^0 & \text{chopped} \end{cases}$$

and

$$fl(-838) = \begin{cases} -(0.84)10^3 & \text{rounded} \\ -(0.83)10^3 & \text{chopped} \end{cases}$$

On some computers, this definition of $fl(x)$ is modified in case $|x| \geq \beta^M$ (**overflow**) or $0 < |x| \leq \beta^{m-n}$ (**underflow**), where m and M are the bounds on the exponents; either $fl(x)$ is not defined in this case, causing a stop, or else $fl(x)$ is represented by a special number which is not subject to the usual rules of arithmetic when combined with ordinary floating-point numbers.

The difference between x and $fl(x)$ is called the **round-off error**. The round-off error depends on the size of x and is therefore best measured relative to x. For if we write

$$fl(x) = x(1 + \delta) \tag{1.7}$$

where $\delta = \delta(x)$ is some number depending on x, then it is possible to *bound δ independently* of x, at least as long as x causes no overflow or underflow. For such an x, it is not difficult to show that

$$|\delta| < \tfrac{1}{2}\beta^{1-n} \qquad \text{in rounding} \tag{1.8}$$

while

$$-\beta^{1-n} < \delta \leq 0 \qquad \text{in chopping} \tag{1.9}$$

See Exercise 1.3-3. The maximum possible value for $|\delta|$ is often called the **unit roundoff** and is denoted by u.

When an arithmetic operation is applied to two floating-point numbers, the result usually fails to be a floating-point number of the same length. If, for example, we deal with two-decimal-digit numbers and

$$x = (0.20)10^1 = 2 \qquad y = (0.77)10^{-6} \qquad z = (0.30)10^1 = 3$$

then
$$x + y = (0.200000077)10^1 \qquad x \cdot y = (0.154)10^{-5}$$

$$\frac{x}{z} = (0.666 \cdots)10^0$$

Hence, if ω denotes one of the arithmetic operations (addition, subtraction, multiplication, or division) and ω^* denotes the floating-point operation of the same name provided by the computer, then, however the computer may arrive at the result $x\omega^*y$ for two given floating-point numbers x and y, we can be sure that usually

$$x\omega^*y \neq x\omega y$$

Although the floating-point operation ω^* corresponding to ω may vary in some details from machine to machine, ω^* is usually constructed so that

$$x\omega^*y = fl(x\omega y) \tag{1.10}$$

In words, the floating-point sum (difference, product, or quotient) of two floating-point numbers usually equals the floating-point number which represents the exact sum (difference, product, or quotient) of the two numbers. Hence (unless overflow or underflow occurs) we have

$$x\omega^*y = (x\omega y)(1 + \delta) \qquad \text{for some } \delta \text{ with } |\delta| \leq u \tag{1.11a}$$

where u is the unit roundoff. In certain situations, it is more convenient to use the equivalent formula

$$x\omega^*y = (x\omega y)/(1 + \delta) \qquad \text{for some } \delta \text{ with } |\delta| \leq u \tag{1.11b}$$

Equation (1.11) expresses the basic idea of backward error analysis (see J. H. Wilkinson [24]†). Explicitly, Eq. (1.11) allows one to interpret a floating-point result as the result of the corresponding ordinary arithmetic, but performed on slightly perturbed data. In this way, the analysis of the effect of floating-point arithmetic can be carried out in terms of ordinary arithmetic.

For example, the value of the function $f(x) = x^{2^n}$ at a point x_0 can be calculated by n squarings, i.e., by carrying out the sequence of steps

$$x_1 := x_0^2, x_2 := x_1^2, \ldots, x_n := x_{n-1}^2$$

with $f(x_0) = x_n$. In floating-point arithmetic, we compute instead, according to Eq. (1.11a), the sequence of numbers

$$\hat{x}_1 = x_0^2(1 + \delta_1), \hat{x}_2 = (\hat{x}_1)^2(1 + \delta_2), \ldots, \hat{x}_n = (\hat{x}_{n-1})^2(1 + \delta_n)$$

†Numbers in brackets refer to items in the references at the end of the book.

with $|\delta_i| \leq u$, all i. The computed answer is, therefore,

$$\hat{x}_n = x_0^{2^n}(1 + \delta_1)^{2^{n-1}} \cdots (1 + \delta_{n-1})^2(1 + \delta_n)$$

To simplify this expression, we observe that, if $|\delta_1|, \ldots, |\delta_r| \leq u$, then

$$(1 + \delta_1) \cdots (1 + \delta_r) = (1 + \delta)^r$$

for some δ with $|\delta| \leq u$ (see Exercise 1.3-6). Also then

$$(1 + \delta)^r = (1 + \eta)^{r+1}$$

for some η with $|\eta| \leq u$. Consequently,

$$\hat{x}_n = x_0^{2^n}(1 + \delta)^{2^n} = f(x_0(1 + \delta))$$

for some δ with $|\delta| \leq u$. In words, the computed value $\hat{x}_n$ for $f(x_0)$ is the exact value of $f(x)$ at the perturbed argument $x = x_0(1 + \delta)$.

We can now gauge the effect which the use of floating-point arithmetic has had on the accuracy of the computed value for $f(x_0)$ by studying how the value of the (exactly computed) function $f(x)$ changes when the argument x is perturbed, as is done in the next section. Further, we note that this error is, in our example, comparable to the error due to the fact that we had to convert the initial datum x_0 to a floating-point number to begin with.

As a second example, of particular interest in Chap. 4, consider calculation of the number s from the equation

$$a_1 b_1 + \cdots + a_r b_r + a_{r+1} s = c \tag{1.12}$$

by the formula $\qquad s = \left(c - \sum_{k=1}^{r} a_k b_k \right) / a_{r+1}$

If we obtain s through the steps

$$s_0 := c$$
$$s_i := s_{i-1} - a_i b_i, \qquad i = 1, \ldots, r$$
$$s := s_r / a_{r+1}$$

then the corresponding numbers computed in floating-point arithmetic satisfy

$$\hat{s}_0 = c$$
$$\hat{s}_i = \left[\hat{s}_{i-1} - a_i b_i (1 + \delta) \right](1 + \delta), \qquad i = 1, \ldots, r$$
$$\hat{s} = \hat{s}_r / \left[a_{r+1}(1 + \delta) \right]$$

Here, we have used Eqs. (1.11a) and (1.11b), and have not bothered to distinguish the various δ's by subscripts. Consequently,

$$a_{r+1}(1 + \delta)\hat{s} = \hat{s}_r$$

$$= \hat{s}_{r-1}(1 + \delta) - a_r b_r(1 + \delta)^2$$

$$= \hat{s}_{r-2}(1 + \delta)^2 - a_{r-1}b_{r-1}(1 + \delta)^3 - a_r b_r(1 + \delta)^2$$

$$\vdots$$

$$= \hat{s}_0(1 + \delta)^r - a_1 b_1(1 + \delta)^{r+1} - \cdots - a_r b_r(1 + \delta)^2$$

This shows that the computed value $\hat{s}$ for s satisfies the perturbed equation

$$a_1 b_1(1 + \delta)^{r+1} + \cdots + a_r b_r(1 + \delta)^2 + a_{r+1}(1 + \delta)\hat{s} = c(1 + \delta)^r$$

$$(1.13)$$

Note that we can reduce all exponents by 1 in case $a_{r+1} = 1$, that is, in case the last division need not be carried out.

EXERCISES

1.3-1 The following numbers are given in a decimal computer with a four-digit normalized mantissa:

(a) $0.4523 \cdot 10^4$ (b) $0.2115 \cdot 10^{-3}$ (c) $0.2583 \cdot 10^1$

Perform the following operations, and indicate the error in the result, assuming symmetric rounding:

    a. $(a) + (b) + (c)$ d. $(a) - (b) - (c)$
    b. $(a)/(c)$ e. $(a)(b)/(c)$
    c. $(a) - (b)$ f. $(b)/(c) \cdot (a)$

1.3-2 Let $fl(x)$ be given by chopping. Show that $fl(-x) = -fl(x)$, and that $fl(\beta^r x) = \beta^r fl(x)$ (unless overflow or underflow occurs).

1.3-3 Let $fl(x)$ be given by chopping and let $\delta = \delta(x)$ be such that $fl(x) = x(1 + \delta)$. (If $x = 0$, pick $\delta = 0$.) Show that then δ is bounded as in (1.9).

1.3-4 Give examples to show that most of the laws of arithmetic fail to hold for floating-point arithmetic. (*Hint:* Try laws involving three operands.)

1.3-5 Write a FORTRAN FUNCTION FL(X) which returns the value of the n-decimal-digit floating-point number derived from X by rounding. Take n to be 4 and check your calculations in Exercise 1.3-1. [Use ALOG10(ABS(X)) to determine e such that $10^{e-1} \leq |x| < 10^e$.]

1.3-6 Let $U = \{1 + \delta : |\delta| \leq u\}$. Show that for all $\alpha_1, \ldots, \alpha_r \in U$, there exists $\alpha \in U$ so that $\alpha_1 \alpha_2 \cdots \alpha_r = \alpha^r$. Show also that $a_1 \alpha_1 + a_2 \alpha_2 + \cdots a_r \alpha_r = (a_1 + a_2 + \cdots + a_r)\alpha$ for some $\alpha \in U$, provided $a_1, a_2, \ldots, a_r$ all have the same sign.

1.3-7 Carry out a backward error analysis for the calculation of the scalar product $s = a_1 b_1 + a_2 b_2 + \cdots + a_n b_n$. Redo the analysis under the assumption that double-precision accumulation is used. This means that the double-precision results of each multiplication are retained and added to the sum in double precision, with the resulting sum rounded only at the end to single precision.

1.4 LOSS OF SIGNIFICANCE AND ERROR PROPAGATION; CONDITION AND INSTABILITY

If the number x^* is an approximation to the exact answer x, then we call the difference $x - x^*$ the **error** in x^*; thus

$$\text{Exact} = \text{approximation} + \text{error} \qquad (1.14)$$

The **relative error** in x^*, as an approximation to x, is defined to be the number $(x - x^*)/x$. Note that this number is close to the number $(x - x^*)/x^*$ if it is at all small. [Precisely, if $\alpha = (x - x^*)/x$, then $(x - x^*)/x^* = \alpha/(1 - \alpha)$.]

Every floating-point operation in a computational process may give rise to an error which, once generated, may then be amplified or reduced in subsequent operations.

One of the most common (and often avoidable) ways of increasing the importance of an error is commonly called **loss of significant digits**. If x^* is an approximation to x, then we say that x^* approximates x to r significant β-digits provided the absolute error $|x - x^*|$ is at most $\frac{1}{2}$ in the rth significant β-digit of x. This can be expressed in a formula as

$$|x - x^*| \leq \tfrac{1}{2}\beta^{s-r+1} \qquad (1.15)$$

with s the largest integer such that $\beta^s \leq |x|$. For instance, $x^* = 3$ agrees with $x = \pi$ to one significant (decimal) digit, while $x^* = \frac{22}{7} = 3.1428 \cdots$ is correct to three significant digits (as an approximation to π). Suppose now that we are to calculate the number

$$z = x - y$$

and that we have approximations x^* and y^* for x and y, respectively, available, each of which is good to r digits. Then

$$z^* = x^* - y^*$$

is an approximation for z, which is also good to r digits unless x^* and y^* agree to one or more digits. In this latter case, there will be cancellation of digits during the subtraction, and consequently z^* will be accurate to fewer than r digits.

Consider, for example,

$$x^* = (0.76545421)10^1 \qquad y^* = (0.76544200)10^1$$

and assume each to be an approximation to x and y, respectively, correct to seven significant digits. Then, in eight-digit floating-point arithmetic,

$$z^* = x^* - y^* = (0.12210000)10^{-3}$$

is the *exact* difference between x^* and y^*. But as an approximation to $z = x - y$, z^* is good only to three digits, since the fourth significant digit of z^* is derived from the eighth digits of x^* and y^*, both possibly in error.

Hence, while the *error* in z^* (as an approximation to $z = x - y$) is at most the sum of the errors in x^* and y^*, the *relative* error in z^* is possibly 10,000 times the relative error in x^* or y^*. Loss of significant digits is therefore dangerous only if we wish to keep the relative error small.

Such loss can often be avoided by anticipating its occurrence. Consider, for example, the evaluation of the function

$$f(x) = 1 - \cos x$$

in six-decimal-digit arithmetic. Since $\cos x \approx 1$ for x near zero, there will be loss of significant digits for x near zero if we calculate $f(x)$ by first finding $\cos x$ and then subtracting the calculated value from 1. For we cannot calculate $\cos x$ to more than six digits, so that the error in the calculated value may be as large as $5 \cdot 10^{-7}$, hence as large as, or larger than, $f(x)$ for x near zero. If one wishes to compute the value of $f(x)$ near zero to about six significant digits using six-digit arithmetic, one would have to use an alternative formula for $f(x)$, such as

$$f(x) = 1 - \cos x = \frac{1 - \cos^2 x}{1 + \cos x} = \frac{\sin^2 x}{1 + \cos x}$$

which can be evaluated quite accurately for small x; else, one could make use of the Taylor expansion (see Sec. 1.7) for $f(x)$,

$$f(x) = \frac{x^2}{2} - \frac{x^4}{24} + \cdots$$

which shows, for example, that for $|x| \le 10^{-3}$, $x^2/2$ agrees with $f(x)$ to at least six significant digits.

Another example is provided by the problem of finding the roots of the quadratic equation

$$ax^2 + bx + c = 0 \tag{1.16}$$

We know from algebra that the roots are given by the quadratic formula

$$x = \frac{-b \pm \sqrt{b^2 - 4ac}}{2a} \tag{1.17}$$

Let us assume that $b^2 - 4ac > 0$, that $b > 0$, and that we wish to find the root of smaller absolute value using (1.17); i.e.,

$$x_1 = \frac{-b + \sqrt{b^2 - 4ac}}{2a} \tag{1.18}$$

If $4ac$ is small compared with b^2, then $\sqrt{b^2 - 4ac}$ will agree with b to several places. Hence, given that $\sqrt{b^2 - 4ac}$ will be calculated correctly only to as many places as are used in the calculations, it follows that the numerator of (1.18), and therefore the calculated root, will be accurate to fewer places than were used during the calculation. To be specific, take the equation

$$x^2 + 111.11x + 1.2121 = 0 \qquad (1.19)$$

Using (1.18) and five-decimal-digit floating-point chopped arithmetic, we calculate

$$b^2 = 12{,}345$$
$$b^2 - 4ac = 12{,}340$$
$$\sqrt{b^2 - 4ac} = 111.09$$
$$x_1 = \frac{-b + \sqrt{b^2 - 4ac}}{2a} = -0.01000$$

while in fact,
$$x_1 = -0.010910$$

is the correct root to the number of digits shown. Here too, the loss of significant digits can be avoided by using an alternative formula for the calculation of the absolutely smaller root, viz.,

$$x_1 = \frac{-2c}{b + \sqrt{b^2 - 4ac}} \qquad (1.20)$$

Using this formula, and five-decimal-digit arithmetic, we calculate

$$x_1 = -0.010910$$

which is accurate to five digits.

Once an error is committed, it contaminates subsequent results. This **error propagation** through subsequent calculations is conveniently studied in terms of the two related concepts of *condition* and *instability*.

The word **condition** is used to describe the sensitivity of the function value $f(x)$ to changes in the argument x. The condition is usually measured by the maximum relative change in the function value $f(x)$ caused by a unit relative change in the argument. In a somewhat informal formula,

condition of f at $x =$

$$\max\left\{ \left| \frac{f(x) - f(x^*)}{f(x)} \right| \Big/ \left| \frac{x - x^*}{x} \right| : \quad |x - x^*| \text{ "small"} \right\}$$

$$\approx \left| \frac{f'(x)x}{f(x)} \right| \quad (1.21)$$

The larger the condition, the more ill-conditioned the function is said to be. Here we have made use of the fact (see Sec. 1.7) that

$$f(x) - f(x^*) \approx f'(x)(x - x^*)$$

i.e., the change in argument from x to x^* changes the function value by approximately $f'(x)(x - x^*)$.

If, for example,

$$f(x) = \sqrt{x}$$

then $f'(x) = \frac{1}{2}/\sqrt{x}$, hence the condition of f is, approximately,

$$\left| \frac{f'(x)x}{f(x)} \right| = \frac{\left[\frac{1}{2}/\sqrt{x} \right] x}{\sqrt{x}} = \frac{1}{2}$$

This says that taking square roots is a well-conditioned process since it actually reduces the relative error. By contrast, if

$$f(x) = \frac{10}{1 - x^2}$$

then $f'(x) = 20x/(1 - x^2)^2$, so that

$$\left| \frac{f'(x)x}{f(x)} \right| = \left| \frac{\left[20x/(1 - x^2)^2 \right] x}{10/(1 - x^2)} \right| = \frac{2x^2}{|1 - x^2|}$$

and this number can be quite large for $|x|$ near 1. Thus, for x near 1 or -1, this function is quite ill-conditioned. It very much magnifies relative errors in the argument there.

The related notion of **instability** describes the sensitivity of a numerical process for the calculation of $f(x)$ from x to the inevitable rounding errors committed during its execution in finite precision arithmetic. The precise effect of these errors on the accuracy of the computed value for $f(x)$ is hard to determine except by actually carrying out the computations for particular finite precision arithmetics and comparing the computed answer with the exact answer. But it is possible to estimate these effects roughly by considering the rounding errors one at a time. This means we look at the individual computational steps which make up the process. Suppose there are n such steps. Denote by x_i the output from the ith such step, and take $x_0 = x$. Such an x_i then serves as input to one or more of the later steps and, in this way, influences the final answer $x_n = f(x)$. Denote by f_i the function which describes the dependence of the final answer on the intermediate result x_i. In particular, f_0 is just f. Then the total process is unstable to the extent that one or more of these functions f_i is ill-conditioned. More precisely, the process is unstable to the extent that one or more of the f_i's has a much larger condition than $f = f_0$ has. For it is the condition of f_i which gauges the relative effect of the inevitable rounding error incurred at the ith step on the final answer.

To give a simple example, consider the function

$$f(x) = \sqrt{x + 1} - \sqrt{x}$$

for "large" x, say for $x \approx 10^4$. Its condition there is

$$\left| \frac{f'(x)x}{f(x)} \right| = \frac{1}{2} \frac{|1/\sqrt{x + 1} - 1/\sqrt{x}|x}{\sqrt{x + 1} - \sqrt{x}} = \frac{1}{2} \frac{x}{\sqrt{x + 1}\sqrt{x}} \approx \frac{1}{2}$$

which is quite good. But, if we calculate $f(12345)$ in six-decimal arithmetic, we find

$$f(12345) = \sqrt{12346} - \sqrt{12345}$$
$$= 111.113 - 111.108 = 0.005$$

while, actually, $f(12345) = 0.00450003262627751 \cdots$

So our calculated answer is in error by 10 percent. We analyze the computational process. It consists of the following four computational steps:

$$\begin{aligned}
x_0 &:= 12345 \\
x_1 &:= x_0 + 1 \\
x_2 &:= \sqrt{x_1} \\
x_3 &:= \sqrt{x_0} \\
x_4 &:= x_2 - x_3
\end{aligned}$$
(1.22)

Now consider, for example, the function f_3, i.e., the function which describes how the final answer x_4 depends on x_3. We have

$$f_3(t) = x_2 - t$$

hence its condition is, approximately,

$$\left| \frac{f_3'(t)t}{f_3(t)} \right| = \left| \frac{t}{x_2 - t} \right|$$

This number is usually near 1, i.e., f_3 is usually well-conditioned *except* when t is near x_2. In this latter case, f_3 can be quite badly conditioned. For example, in our particular case, $t \approx 111.11$ while $x_2 - t \approx 0.005$, so the condition is $\sim 22{,}222$, or more than 40,000 times as big as the condition of f itself.

We conclude that the process described in (1.22) is an unstable way to evaluate f. Of course, if you have read the beginning of this section carefully, then you already know a stable way to evaluate this function, namely by the equivalent formula

$$f(x) = \frac{1}{\sqrt{x+1} + \sqrt{x}}$$

In six-decimal arithmetic, this gives

$$f(12345) = \frac{1}{\sqrt{12346} + \sqrt{12345}} = \frac{1}{222.221} = 0.00450002$$

which is in error by only 0.0003 percent. The computational process is

$$x_0 := 12345$$
$$x_1 := x_0 + 1$$
$$x_2 := \sqrt{x_1}$$
$$x_3 := \sqrt{x_0} \qquad (1.23)$$
$$x_4 := x_2 + x_3$$
$$x_5 := 1/x_4$$

Here, for example, $f_3(t) = 1/(x_2 + t)$, and the condition of this function is, approximately,

$$\left| \frac{f_3'(t)t}{f_3(t)} \right| = \left| \frac{t}{x_2 + t} \right| \approx \frac{1}{2}$$

for $t \approx x_2$, which is the case here. Thus, the condition of f_3 is quite good; it is as good as that of f itself.

We will meet other examples of large instability, particularly in the discussion of the numerical solution of differential equations.

EXERCISES

1.4-1 Find the root of smallest magnitude of the equation

$$x^2 + 0.4002 \cdot 10^0 x + 0.8 \cdot 10^{-4} = 0$$

using formulas (1.18) and (1.20). Work in floating-point arithmetic using a four- (decimal-) place mantissa.

1.4-2 Estimate the error in evaluating $f(x) = (\cos x)\exp(10x^2)$ around $x = 2$ if the absolute error in x is 10^{-6}.

1.4-3 Find a way to calculate
(a) $f(x) = \dfrac{x - \sin x}{\tan x}$
(b) $f(x) = (\alpha + x)^n - \alpha^n$,
(c) $f(x) = \sin(\alpha + x) - \sin \alpha$
(d) $f(x) = x - \sqrt{x^2 - \alpha}$

correctly to the number of digits used when x is near zero for (a)–(c), very much larger than α for (d).

1.4-4 Assuming a computer with a four-decimal-place mantissa, add the following numbers first in ascending order (from smallest to largest) and then in descending order. In doing so round off the partial sums. Compare your results with the correct sum $x = 0.107101023 \cdot 10^5$.

$0.1580 \cdot 10^0$	$0.6266 \cdot 10^2$	$0.8999 \cdot 10^4$
$0.2653 \cdot 10^0$	$0.7555 \cdot 10^2$	
$0.2581 \cdot 10^1$	$0.7889 \cdot 10^3$	
$0.4288 \cdot 10^1$	$0.7767 \cdot 10^3$	

1.4-5 A dramatically unstable way to calculate $f(x) = e^x$ for negative x is provided by its Taylor series (1.36). Calculate e^{-12} by evaluating the Taylor series (1.36) at $x = -12$ and compare with the accurate value $e^{-12} = 0.00000\ 61442\ 12354 \cdots$. [*Hint:* By (1.36), the difference between e^x and the partial sum $s_n = \sum_0^n x^j/j!$ is less than the next term $|x^{n+1}/(n+1)!|$ in absolute value, in case x is negative. So, it would be all right to sum the series until $s_n = s_{n+1}$.]

1.4-6 Explain the result of Exercise 1.4-5 by comparing the condition of $f(x) = e^x$ near $x = -12$ with the condition of some of the functions f_i involved in the computational process. Then find a stable way to calculate e^{-12} from the Taylor series (1.36). (*Hint:* $e^{-x} = 1/e^x$.)

1.5 COMPUTATIONAL METHODS FOR ERROR ESTIMATION

This chapter is intended to make the student aware of the possible sources of error and to point out some techniques which can be used to avoid these errors. In appraising computer results, such errors must be taken into account. Realistic estimates of the total error are difficult to make in a practical problem, and an adequate mathematical theory is still lacking. An appealing idea is to make use of the computer itself to provide us with such estimates. Various methods of this type have been proposed. We shall discuss briefly five of them. The simplest method makes use of **double precision**. Here one simply solves the same problem twice—once in single precision and once in double precision. From the difference in the results an estimate of the total round-off error can then be obtained (assuming that all other errors are less significant). It can then be assumed that the same accumulation of roundoff will occur in other problems solved with the same subroutine. This method is extremely costly in machine time since double-precision arithmetic increases computer time by a factor of 8 on some machines, and in addition, it is not always possible to isolate other errors.

A second method is **interval arithmetic**. Here each number is represented by two machine numbers, the maximum and the minimum values that it might have. Whenever an operation is performed, one computes its maximum and minimum values. Essentially, then, one will obtain two solutions at every step, the true solution necessarily being contained within the range determined by the maximum and minimum values. This method requires more than twice the amount of computer time and about twice the storage of a standard run. Moreover, the usual assumption that the true solution lies about midway within the range is not, in general, valid. Thus the range might be so large that any estimate of the round-off error based upon this would be grossly exaggerated.

A third approach is **significant-digit** arithmetic. As pointed out earlier, whenever two nearly equal machine numbers are subtracted, there is a danger that some significant digits will be lost. In significant-digit arithmetic an attempt is made to keep track of digits so lost. In one version only the significant digits in any number are retained, all others being discarded. At the end of a computation we will thus be assured that all digits retained are significant. The main objection to this method is that some information is lost whenever digits are discarded, and that the results obtained are likely to be much too conservative. Experimentation with this technique is still going on, although the experience to date is not too promising.

A fourth method which gives considerable promise of providing an adequate mathematical theory of round-off-error propagation is based on a **statistical approach**. It begins with the assumption that round-off errors are independent. This assumption is, of course, not valid, because if the same problem is run on the same machine several times, the answers will always be the same. We can, however, adopt a stochastic model of the propagation of round-off errors in which the local errors are treated as if they were random variables. Thus we can assume that the local round-off errors are either uniformly or normally distributed between their extreme values. Using statistical methods, we can then obtain the standard deviation, the variance of distribution, and estimates of the accumulated round-off error. The statistical approach is considered in some detail by Hamming [1] and Henrici [2]. The method does involve substantial analysis and additional computer time, but in the experiments conducted to date it has obtained error estimates which are in remarkable agreement with experimentally available evidence.

A fifth method is **backward error analysis**, as introduced in Sec. 1.3. As we saw, it reduces the analysis of rounding error effects to a study of perturbations in exact arithmetic and, ultimately, to a question of condition. We will make good use of this method in Chap. 4.

1.6 SOME COMMENTS ON CONVERGENCE OF SEQUENCES

Calculus, and more generally analysis, is based on the notion of convergence. Basic concepts such as derivative, integral, and continuity are defined in terms of convergent sequences, and elementary functions such as $\ln x$ or $\sin x$ are defined by convergent series. At the same time, numerical answers to engineering and scientific problems are never needed *exactly*. Rather, an approximation to the answer is required which is accurate "to a certain number of decimal places," or accurate to within a given tolerance ε.

It is therefore not surprising that many numerical methods for finding the answer α of a given problem merely produce (the first few terms of) a sequence $\alpha_1, \alpha_2, \alpha_3, \ldots$ which is shown to converge to the desired answer.

To recall the definition:

A sequence $\alpha_1, \alpha_2, \ldots$ of (real or complex) numbers converges to α if and only if, for all $\varepsilon > 0$, there exists an integer $n_0(\varepsilon)$ such that for all $n \geq n_0$, $|\alpha - \alpha_n| < \varepsilon$.

Hence, if we have a numerical method which produces a sequence $\alpha_1, \alpha_2, \ldots$ converging to the desired answer α, then we can calculate α to any desired accuracy merely by calculating α_n for "large enough" n.

From a computational point of view, this definition is unsatisfactory for the following reasons: (1) It is often not possible (without knowing the answer α) to know when n is "large enough." In other words, it is difficult to get hold of the function $n_0(\varepsilon)$ mentioned in the definition of convergence. (2) Even when some knowledge about $n_0(\varepsilon)$ is available, it may turn out that the required n is too large to make the calculation of α_n feasible.

Example The number $\pi/4$ is the value of the infinite series

$$\sum_{i=0}^{\infty} \frac{(-1)^i}{2i+1} = 1 - \sum_{j=1}^{\infty} \frac{2}{16j^2 - 1}$$

Hence, with

$$\alpha_n = 1 - \sum_{j=1}^{n} \frac{2}{16j^2 - 1} \qquad n = 1, 2, \ldots$$

the sequence $\alpha_1, \alpha_2, \ldots$ is monotone-decreasing to its limit $\pi/4$. Moreover,

$$0 \leq \alpha_n - \pi/4 \leq \frac{1}{4n+3} \qquad n = 1, 2, \ldots$$

To calculate $\pi/4$ correct to within 10^{-6} using this sequence, we would need $10^6 \leq 4n + 3$, or roughly, $n = 250{,}000$. On a computer using eight-decimal-digit floating-point arithmetic, round-off in the calculation of $\alpha_{250{,}000}$ is probably much larger than 10^{-6}. Hence $\pi/4$ could not be computed to within 10^{-6} using this sequence (except, perhaps, by adding the terms from smallest to largest).

To deal with these problems, some notation is useful. Specifically, we would like to measure how fast sequences converge. As with all measuring, this is done by comparison, with certain standard sequences, such as

$$\left.\begin{array}{l} 1/n \\ 1/n^r \\ r^n \\ 1/(\ln n) \end{array}\right\} \qquad n = 1, 2, 3, \ldots$$

The comparison is made as follows: one says that α_n **is of order** β_n (or α_n is big-oh of β_n), and writes

$$\alpha_n = \mathcal{O}(\beta_n) \tag{1.24}$$

in case

$$|\alpha_n| \leq K|\beta_n| \tag{1.25}$$

for some constant K and all sufficiently large n. Thus

$$\left.\begin{array}{l} 1/n \\ 10{,}000/n \\ 10/n - 40/n^2 + e^{-n} \\ 1/n^2 \end{array}\right\} = \mathcal{O}(1/n)$$

Further, if it is possible to choose the constant K in (1.25) arbitrarily small as soon as n is large enough; that is, should it happen that

$$\lim_{n \to \infty} \alpha_n/\beta_n = 0$$

then one says that α_n **is of higher order than** β_n (or α_n is little-oh of β_n), and writes

$$\alpha_n = o(\beta_n) \tag{1.26}$$

Thus

$$\left.\begin{array}{l} 1/n^2 \\ 1/(n \ln n) \end{array}\right\} = o(1/n)$$

while $\sin(1/n) \neq o(1/n)$.

The order notation appears customarily only on the right-hand side of an equation and serves the purpose of describing the essential feature of an error term without bothering about multiplying constants or other detail. For instance, we can state concisely the unsatisfactory state of affairs in the earlier example by saying that

$$1 - \sum_{j=2}^{n} 1/(j^2 - 1) = \pi/4 + \mathcal{O}(1/n)$$

but also

$$1 - \sum_{j=2}^{n} 1/(j^2 - 1) \neq \pi/4 + o(1/n)$$

i.e., the series converges to $\pi/4$ as fast as $1/n$ (goes to zero) but no faster. A convergence order or rate of $1/n$ is much too slow to be useful in calculations.

Example If $\alpha_n = \alpha + o(1)$, then, by definition,

$$\lim_{n \to \infty} \frac{\alpha_n - \alpha}{1} = 0$$

Hence $\alpha_n = \alpha + o(1)$ is just a fancy way of saying that the sequence $\alpha_1, \alpha_2, \ldots$ converges to α.

Example If $|r| < 1$, then the geometric series $\sum_{i=0}^{\infty} r^i$ sums to $1/(1 - r)$. With $s_n = \sum_{i=0}^{n} r^i$, we have $s_n = (1 - r^{n+1})/(1 - r) = 1/(1 - r) - r^{n+1}/(1 - r)$. Thus

$$s_n = \frac{1}{1 - r} + \mathcal{O}(r^n)$$

Further, if $\bar{r} > |r|$, then

$$s_n = \frac{1}{1 - r} + o(\bar{r}^n)$$

Hence, whenever $\alpha_n = \alpha + \mathcal{O}(r^n)$ for some $|r| < 1$, we say that the convergence is (at least) geometric, for it is then (at least) of the same order as the convergence of the geometric series.

Although it is better to know that $\alpha_n = \alpha + \mathcal{O}(\beta_n)$ than to know nothing, knowledge about the order of convergence becomes quite useful only when we know more precisely that

$$\alpha_n = \alpha + \beta_n + o(\beta_n)$$

This says that for "large enough" n, $\alpha_n \approx \alpha + \beta_n$. To put it differently,

$$\alpha_n = \alpha + \beta_n + o(\beta_n)$$
$$= \alpha + \beta_n + \beta_n o(1)$$
$$= \alpha + \beta_n (1 + \varepsilon_n)$$

where $\varepsilon_1, \varepsilon_2, \ldots$ is a sequence converging to zero. Although we cannot *prove* that a certain n is "large enough," we can *test the hypothesis* that n is "large enough" by comparing $\alpha_{k+1} - \alpha_k$ with $\beta_{k+1} - \beta_k$. If

$$\frac{|\alpha_{k+1} - \alpha_k|}{|\beta_{k+1} - \beta_k|} \approx 1$$

for k near n, say for $k = n - 2, n - 1, n$, then we accept the hypothesis that n is "large enough" for

$$\alpha_n \approx \alpha + \beta_n$$

to be true, and therefore accept $|\beta_n|$ as a good estimate of the error $|\alpha - \alpha_n|$.

Example Let $p > 1$. Then the series $\sum_j 1/(p^j + 1)$ converges to its limit α like the geometric series $\sum_j 1/p^j$, i.e.,

$$\alpha_n = \sum_{j=1}^n 1/(p^j + 1) = \alpha + \mathcal{O}(1/p^{n+1})$$

To get a more precise statement, consider

$$\beta_n = \sum_{j=n+1}^\infty 1/p^j = (1/p^{n+1})/(1 - 1/p) = 1/[p^n(p - 1)]$$

Then

$$\alpha_n = \alpha - \sum_{j=n+1}^\infty 1/(p^j + 1) = \alpha - \beta_n + \sum_{j=n+1}^\infty [1/p^j - 1/(p^j + 1)]$$
$$= \alpha - \beta_n + o(\beta_n)$$

since

$$0 \le \sum_{j=n+1}^\infty [1/p^j - 1/(p^j + 1)] = \sum_{j=n+1}^\infty 1/(p^j(p^j + 1)) \le \sum_{j=n+1}^\infty (1/p^2)^j$$
$$= \mathcal{O}((1/p^2)^{n+1})$$

For the ratios, we find

$$\left|\frac{\alpha_{n+1} - \alpha_n}{\beta_{n+1} - \beta_n}\right| = p^{n+1}/(p^{n+1} + 1)$$

which is, e.g., within $1/10$ of 1 for $n = 3$ and $p = 2$. Thus, $\beta_3 = 1/8 = 0.125$ is then a good indication of the error in $\alpha_3 = 0.64444\ 44444$. In fact, $\alpha = 0.76449\ 9780$; the error in α_3 is therefore $0.12005 \cdots$.

This notation carries over to functions of a real variable. If

$$\lim_{h \to 0} T(h) = A$$

we say that the convergence is $\mathcal{O}(f(h))$ provided

$$\frac{|T(h) - A|}{|f(h)|} \leq K$$

for some finite constant K and all small enough h. If this holds for all $K > 0$, that is, if

$$\lim_{h \to 0} \frac{T(h) - A}{f(h)} = 0$$

then we call the convergence $o(f(h))$.

Example For h "near" zero, we have

$$\frac{\sin h}{h} = 1 - (\tfrac{1}{3!})h^2 + (\tfrac{1}{5!})h^4 - \cdots = 1 + \mathcal{O}(h^2)$$

$$= 1 - \tfrac{1}{6}h^2 + o(h^2)$$

Hence, for all $\gamma < 2$, $\qquad \dfrac{\sin h}{h} = 1 + o(h^\gamma)$

Example If the function $f(x)$ has a zero of order γ at $x = \xi$, then

$$f(\xi + h) = \mathcal{O}(h^\gamma) \quad \text{but} \quad f(\xi + h) \neq o(h^\gamma)$$

Rules for calculating with the order symbols are collected in the following lemma.

Lemma 1.1 If $\alpha_n = \alpha + \mathcal{O}(f(n))$, $\lim_{n \to \infty} f(n) = 0$, and c is a constant, then

$$c\alpha_n = c\alpha + \mathcal{O}(f(n))$$

If also $\beta_n = \beta + \mathcal{O}(g(n))$, and $g(n) = \mathcal{O}(f(n))$, then

$$\alpha_n + \beta_n = \alpha + \beta + \mathcal{O}(f(n)) \quad \text{and} \quad \alpha_n \beta_n = \alpha\beta + \mathcal{O}(f(n))$$

$$(1.27)$$

If, further, $\beta \neq 0$, then also

$$\frac{\alpha_n}{\beta_n} = \frac{\alpha}{\beta} + \mathcal{O}(f(n))$$

while if $\alpha = \beta = 0$, then

$$\alpha_n \beta_n = \mathcal{O}(f(n)g(n))$$

Finally, all statements remain true if $\mathcal{O}$ is replaced by o throughout.

The approximate calculation of a number α via a sequence $\alpha_1, \alpha_2, \ldots$ converging to α always involves an act of faith regardless of whether or not the order of convergence is known. Given that the sequence is known to converge to α, practicing numerical analysts ascertain that n is "large enough" by making sure that, for small values of i, α_{n-i} differs "little enough" from α_n. If they also know that the convergence is $\beta_n + o(\beta_n)$, they check whether or not the sequence behaves accordingly near n. If they also know that α satisfies certain equations or inequalities—α might be the sought-for solution of an equation—they check that α_n satisfies these equations or inequalities "well enough." In short, practicing numerical analysts make sure that n satisfies all conditions they can think of which are necessary for n to be "large enough." If all these conditions are satisfied, then, lacking sufficient conditions for n to be "large enough," they accept α_n on faith as a good enough approximation to α. In a way, numerical analysts use all means at their disposal to distinguish a "good enough" approximation from a bad one. They can do no more (and should do no less).

It follows that numerical results arrived at in this way should not be mistaken for final answers. Rather, they should be questioned freely if subsequent investigations throw any doubt upon their correctness.

The student should appreciate this as another example of the basic difference between numerical analysis and analysis. Analysis became a precise discipline when it left the restrictions of practical calculations to deal entirely with problems posed in terms of an abstract model of the number system, called the *real numbers*. This abstract model is designed to make a precise and useful definition of limit possible, which opens the way to the abstract or symbolic solution of an impressive array of practical problems, once these problems are translated into the terms of the model. This still leaves the task of translating the abstract or symbolic solutions back into practical solutions. Numerical analysis assumes this task, and with it the limitations of practical calculations from which analysis managed to escape so elegantly. Numerical answers are therefore usually tentative and, *at best*, known to be accurate only to within certain bounds.

Numerical analysis is therefore not merely concerned with the *construction* of numerical methods. Rather, a large portion of numerical analysis consists in the derivation of useful *error bounds*, or *error estimates*, for the numerical answers produced by a numerical algorithm. Throughout this book, the student will meet this preoccupation with error bounds so typical of numerical analysis.

EXERCISES

1.6-1 The number ln 2 may be calculated from the series

$$\ln 2 = 1 - \tfrac{1}{2} + \tfrac{1}{3} - \tfrac{1}{4} + \cdots$$

It is known from analysis that this series converges and that the magnitude of the error in any partial sum is less than the magnitude of the first neglected term. Estimate the number of terms that would be required to calculate ln 2 to 10 decimal places.

1.6-2 For h near zero it is possible to write

$$\frac{\tan h}{h} = 1 + \mathcal{O}(h^\gamma)$$

and

$$\frac{\tan h}{h} = 1 + o(h^\delta)$$

Find the values of γ and δ for which these equalities hold.

1.6-3 Try to calculate, on a computer, the limit of the sequence

$$\alpha_n = (\tan 8^{-n} - \sin 8^{-n}) \cdot 8^{3n} \qquad n = 0, 1, 2, \ldots$$

Theoretically, what is $\alpha = \lim_{n \to \infty} \alpha_n$ and what is the order of convergence of the sequence?

1.7 SOME MATHEMATICAL PRELIMINARIES

It is assumed that the student is familiar with the topics normally covered in the undergraduate analytic geometry and calculus sequence. These include elementary notions of real and complex number systems; continuity; the concept of limits, sequences, and series; differentiation and integration. For Chap. 4, some knowledge of determinants is assumed. For Chaps. 8 and 9, some familiarity with the solution of ordinary differential equations is also assumed, although these chapters may be omitted.

In particular, we shall make frequent use of the following theorems.

Theorem 1.1: Intermediate-value theorem for continuous functions Let $f(x)$ be a continuous function on the interval $[a, b]$. If $f(\underline{x}) \leq \alpha \leq f(\bar{x})$ for some number α and some $\underline{x}, \bar{x} \in [a, b]$, then

$$\alpha = f(\xi) \qquad \text{for some } \xi \in [a, b]$$

This theorem is often used in the following form:

Theorem 1.2 Let $f(x)$ be a continuous function on $[a, b]$, let $x_1, \ldots, x_n$ be points in $[a, b]$, and let $g_1, \ldots, g_n$ be real numbers all *of one sign*. Then

$$\sum_{i=1}^{n} f(x_i) g_i = f(\xi) \sum_{i=1}^{n} g_i \qquad \text{for some } \xi \in [a, b]$$

To indicate the proof, assume without loss of generality that $g_i \geq 0$, $i = 1, \ldots, n$. If $f(\underline{x}) = \min_i f(x_i)$ and $f(\overline{x}) = \max_i f(x_i)$, then

$$f(\underline{x}) \sum_{i=1}^{n} g_i = \sum_{i=1}^{n} f(\underline{x})g_i \leq \sum_{i=1}^{n} f(x_i)g_i \leq \sum_{i=1}^{n} f(\overline{x})g_i = f(\overline{x}) \sum_{i=1}^{n} g_i$$

Hence $\alpha = \sum_i f(x_i)g_i$ is a number between the two values $f(\underline{x})\sum_i g_i$ and $f(\overline{x})\sum_i g_i$ of the continuous function $f(x)\sum_i g_i$, and the conclusion follows from Theorem 1.1.

One proves analogously the corresponding statement for *infinite* sums or *integrals*:

Theorem 1.3: Mean-value theorem for integrals Let $g(x)$ be a nonnegative or nonpositive integrable function on $[a, b]$. If $f(x)$ is continuous on $[a, b]$, then

$$\int_a^b f(x)g(x)\, dx = f(\xi) \int_a^b g(x)\, dx \qquad \text{for some } \xi \in [a, b] \quad (1.28)$$

Warning The assumption that $g(x)$ is of one sign is essential in Theorem 1.3, as the simple example $f(x) = g(x) = x$, $[a, b] = [-1, 1]$ shows.

Theorem 1.4 Let $f(x)$ be a continuous function on the closed and bounded interval $[a, b]$. Then $f(x)$ "assumes its maximum and minimum values on $[a, b]$"; i.e., there exist points $\underline{x}$ and $\overline{x}$ in $[a, b]$ such that

$$\text{for all } x \in [a, b]: \qquad f(\underline{x}) \leq f(x) \leq f(\overline{x})$$

Theorem 1.5: Rolle's theorem Let $f(x)$ be continuous on the (closed and finite) interval $[a, b]$ and differentiable on (a, b). If $f(a) = f(b) = 0$, then

$$f'(\xi) = 0 \qquad \text{for some } \xi \in (a, b)$$

The proof makes essential use of Theorem 1.4. For by Theorem 1.4, there are points $\underline{x}, \overline{x}$ in $[a, b]$ such that, for all $x \in [a, b]$, $f(\underline{x}) \leq f(x) \leq f(\overline{x})$. If now neither $\underline{x}$ nor $\overline{x}$ is in (a, b), then $f(x) \equiv 0$, and every $\xi \in (a, b)$ will do. Otherwise, either $\underline{x}$ or $\overline{x}$ is in (a, b), say, $\overline{x} \in (a, b)$. But then $f'(\overline{x}) = 0$, since

$$0 \leq \lim_{h \to 0-} \frac{f(\overline{x}) - f(\overline{x} + h)}{-h} = f'(\overline{x}) = \lim_{h \to 0+} \frac{f(\overline{x} + h) - f(\overline{x})}{h} \leq 0$$

$f(\overline{x})$ being the *biggest value* achieved by $f(x)$ on $[a, b]$.

An immediate consequence of Rolle's theorem is the following theorem.

Theorem 1.6: Mean-value theorem for derivatives If $f(x)$ is continuous on the (closed and finite) interval $[a, b]$ and differentiable on (a, b), then

$$\frac{f(b) - f(a)}{b - a} = f'(\xi) \qquad \text{for some } \xi \in (a, b) \qquad (1.29)$$

One gets Theorem 1.6 from Theorem 1.5 by considering in Theorem 1.5 the function

$$F(x) = f(x) - f(a) - \frac{f(b) - f(a)}{b - a}(x - a)$$

instead of $f(x)$. Clearly, $F(x)$ vanishes both at a and at b.

It follows directly from Theorem 1.6 that if $f(x)$ is continuous on $[a, b]$ and differentiable on (a, b), and c is some point in $[a, b]$, then for all $x \in [a, b]$

$$f(x) = f(c) + (x - c)f'(c + \theta(x - c)) \qquad \text{for some } \theta \in (0, 1) \tag{1.30}$$

The fundamental theorem of calculus provides the more precise statement: If $f(x)$ is continuously differentiable, then for all $x \in [a, b]$

$$f(x) = f(c) + \int_c^x f'(s) \, ds \tag{1.31}$$

from which (1.30) follows by the mean-value theorem for integrals (1.28), since $f'(x)$ is continuous. More generally, one has the following theorem.

Theorem 1.7: Taylor's formula with (integral) remainder If $f(x)$ has $n + 1$ continuous derivatives on $[a, b]$ and c is some point in $[a, b]$, then for all $x \in [a, b]$

$$f(x) = f(c) + f'(c)(x - c) + \frac{f''(c)(x - c)^2}{2!} + \cdots$$

$$+ \frac{f^{(n)}(c)(x - c)^n}{n!} + R_{n+1}(x) \tag{1.32}$$

where

$$R_{n+1}(x) = \frac{1}{n!} \int_c^x (x - s)^n f^{(n+1)}(s) \, ds \tag{1.33}$$

One gets (1.32) from (1.31) by considering the function

$$F(x) = f(x) + f'(x)(c - x) + \frac{f''(x)(c - x)^2}{2!} + \cdots + \frac{f^{(n)}(x)(c - x)^n}{n!}$$

instead of $f(x)$. For, $F'(x) = f^{(n+1)}(x)(c - x)^n/n!$; hence by (1.31),

$$F(x) = F(c) + \frac{1}{n!} \int_c^x (c - s)^n f^{(n+1)}(s) \, ds$$

But since $F(c) = f(c)$, this gives

$$f(c) = F(x) + \frac{1}{n!} \int_x^c (c - s)^n f^{(n+1)}(s) \, ds$$

which is (1.32), after the substitution of x for c and of c for x.

Actually, $f^{(n+1)}(x)$ need not be continuous for (1.32) to hold. However, if in (1.32), $f^{(n+1)}(x)$ is continuous, one gets, using Theorem 1.3, the more familiar but less useful form for the remainder:

$$R_{n+1}(x) = \frac{f^{(n+1)}(\xi)(x-c)^{n+1}}{(n+1)!} \qquad \text{where } \xi = c + \theta(x-c) \quad (1.34)$$

By setting $h = x - c$, (1.32) and (1.34) take the form

$$f(c+h) = f(c) + hf'(c) + \frac{h^2}{2!}f''(c) + \cdots + \frac{h^n}{n!}f^{(n)}(c)$$

$$+ \frac{h^{n+1}}{(n+1)!}f^{(n+1)}(c + \theta h) \qquad \text{for some } \theta \in (0, 1) \quad (1.35)$$

Example The function $f(x) = e^x$ has the Taylor expansion

$$e^x = 1 + x + \frac{x^2}{2!} + \cdots + \frac{x^n}{n!} + \frac{x^{n+1}e^\xi}{(n+1)!}$$

$$\text{for some } \xi \text{ between 0 and } x \qquad (1.36)$$

about $c = 0$. The expansion of $f(x) = \ln x = \log_e x$ about $c = 1$ is

$$\ln x = (x-1) - \frac{(x-1)^2}{2} + \frac{(x-1)^3}{3} - \frac{(x-1)^4}{4} + \cdots$$

$$- \frac{(-1)^n(x-1)^n}{n} + \frac{(-1)^n(x-1)^{n+1}\xi^{-(n+1)}}{n+1}$$

where $0 < x \le 2$, and ξ is between 1 and x.

A similar formula holds for functions of several variables. One obtains this formula from Theorem 1.7 with the aid of

Theorem 1.8: Chain rule If the function $f(x, y, \ldots, z)$ has continuous first partial derivatives with respect to each of its variables, and $x = x(t), y = y(t), \ldots, z = z(t)$ are continuously differentiable functions of t, then $g(t) = f(x(t), y(t), \ldots, z(t))$ is also continuously differentiable, and

$$g'(t) = \frac{\partial f}{\partial x}x'(t) + \frac{\partial f}{\partial y}y'(t) + \cdots + \frac{\partial f}{\partial z}z'(t)$$

From this theorem, one obtains an expression for $f(x, y, \ldots, z)$ in terms of the value and the partial derivatives at $(a, b, \ldots, c)$ by introducing the function

$$g(t) = f(a + t(x-a), b + t(y-b), \ldots, c + t(z-c))$$

and then evaluating its Taylor series expansion around $t = 0$ at $t = 1$. For example, this gives

Theorem 1.9 If $f(x, y)$ has continuous first and second partial derivatives in a neighborhood D of the point (a, b) in the (x, y) plane, then

$$f(x, y) = f(a, b) + f_x(a, b)(x - a) + f_y(a, b)(y - b) + R_2(x, y)$$

$$(1.37)$$

for all (x, y) in D, where

$$R_2(x, y) = \frac{f_{xx}(\xi, \eta)(x - a)^2}{2} + f_{xy}(\xi, \eta)(x - a)(y - b)$$

$$+ \frac{f_{yy}(\xi, \eta)(y - b)^2}{2}$$

for some $(\xi, \eta) \in D$ depending on (x, y), and the subscripts on f denote partial differentiation.

For example, the expansion of $e^{x \sin y}$ about $(a, b) = (0, 0)$ is

$$e^{x \sin y} = 1 + 0 \cdot x + 0 \cdot y + R_2(x, y) \tag{1.38}$$

Finally, in the discussion of eigenvalues of matrices and elsewhere, we need the following theorem.

Theorem 1.10: Fundamental theorem of algebra If $p(x)$ is a polynomial of degree $n \geq 1$, that is,

$$p(x) = a_0 + a_1 x + a_2 x^2 + \cdots + a_n x^n$$

with $a_0, \ldots, a_n$ real or complex numbers and $a_n \neq 0$, then $p(x)$ has at least one zero; i.e., there exists a complex number ξ such that $p(\xi) = 0$.

This rather deep theorem should not be confused with the straightforward statement, "A polynomial of degree n has at most n zeros, counting multiplicity," which we prove in Chap. 2 and use, for example, in the discussion of polynomial interpolation.

EXERCISES

1.7-1 In the mean-value theorem for integrals, Theorem 1.3, let $f(x) = e^x$, $g(x) = x$, $[a, b] = [0, 1]$. Find the point ξ specified by the theorem and verify that this point lies in the interval $(0, 1)$.

1.7-2 In the mean-value theorem for derivatives, Theorem 1.6, let $f(x) = x^2$. Find the point ξ specified by the theorem and verify that this point lies in the interval (a, b).

1.7-3 In the expansion (1.36) for e^x, find n so that the resulting power sum will yield an approximation correct to five significant digits for all x on $[0, 1]$.

1.7-4 Use Taylor's formula (1.32) to find a power series expansion about $c = 0$ for $\sin(\pi x/2)$. Find an expression for the remainder, and from this estimate the number of terms that would be needed to guarantee six-significant-digit accuracy for $\sin(\pi x/2)$ for all x on the interval $[-1, 1]$.

1.7-5 Find the remainder $R_2(x, y)$ in the example (1.38) and determine its maximum value in the region D defined by $[0 \le x \le \pi/2, 0 \le y \le \pi/2]$.

1.7-6 Prove that the remainder term in (1.35) can also be written

$$\frac{h^{n+1}}{(n+1)!} f^{(n+1)}(c) + o(h^{n+1})$$

[if $f^{(n+1)}(x)$ is continuous at $x = c$].

1.7-7 Illustrate the statement in Exercise 1.7-6 by calculating, for $f(x) = e^x$, $c = 0$,

$$R_3(h) = e^h - \left(1 + h + \frac{h^2}{2}\right) \quad \text{and} \quad \frac{h^3}{3!} f^{(3)}(0) = \frac{h^3}{3!}$$

for various values of h, for example, for $h = 2^{-k}$, $k = 1, 2, 3, \ldots$, and comparing $R_3(h)$ with $(h^3/3!)f^{(3)}(0)$.

1.7-8 Prove Theorem 1.9 from Theorems 1.7 and 1.8.

1.7-9 Prove Euler's formula

$$e^{i\theta} = \cos \theta + i \sin \theta$$

(with $i = \sqrt{-1}$), by comparing the power series for e^x, evaluated at $x = i\theta$, with the sum of the power series for $\cos \theta$ and i times the one for $\sin \theta$.

INTERPOLATION BY POLYNOMIALS

Polynomials are used as the basic means of approximation in nearly all areas of numerical analysis. They are used in the solution of equations and in the approximation of functions, of integrals and derivatives, of solutions of integral and differential equations, etc. Polynomials owe this popularity to their simple structure, which makes it easy to construct effective approximations and then make use of them.

For this reason, the representation and evaluation of polynomials is a basic topic in numerical analysis. We discuss this topic in the present chapter in the context of polynomial interpolation, the simplest and certainly the most widely used technique for obtaining polynomial approximations. More advanced methods for getting good approximations by polynomials and other approximating functions are given in Chap. 6. But it will be shown there that even best polynomial approximation does not give appreciably better results than an appropriate scheme of polynomial interpolation.

Divided differences serve as the basis of our treatment of the interpolating polynomial. This makes it possible to deal with osculatory (or Hermite) interpolation as a special limiting case of polynomial interpolation at distinct points.

2.1 POLYNOMIAL FORMS

In this section, we point out that the customary way to describe a polynomial may not always be the best way in calculations, and we propose alternatives, in particular the Newton form. We also show how to evaluate a polynomial given in Newton form. Finally, in preparation for polynomial interpolation, we discuss how to count the zeros of a polynomial.

A **polynomial** $p(x)$ **of degree** $\leq n$ is, by definition, a function of the form

$$p(x) = a_0 + a_1 x + a_2 x^2 + \cdots + a_n x^n \tag{2.1}$$

with certain coefficients $a_0, a_1, \ldots, a_n$. This polynomial has **(exact) degree** n in case its leading coefficient a_n is nonzero.

The **power form** (2.1) is the standard way to specify a polynomial in mathematical discussions. It is a very convenient form for differentiating or integrating a polynomial. But, in various specific contexts, other forms are more convenient.

Example 2.1: The power form may lead to loss of significance If we construct the power form of the straight line $p(x)$ which takes on the values $p(6000) = 1/3$, $p(6001) = -2/3$, then, in five-decimal-digit floating-point arithmetic, we will obtain $p(x) = 6000.3 - x$. Evaluating this straight line, in the same arithmetic, we find $p(6000) = 0.3$ and $p(6001) = -0.7$, which recovers only the first digit of the given function values, a loss of four decimal digits.

A remedy of sorts for such loss of significance is the use of the **shifted power form**

$$p(x) = a_0 + a_1(x - c) + a_2(x - c)^2 + \cdots + a_n(x - c)^n \tag{2.2}$$

If we choose the **center** c to be 6000, then, in the example, we would get $p(x) = 0.33333 - (x - 6000.0)$, and evaluation in five-decimal-digit floating-point arithmetic now provides $p(6000) = 0.33333$, $p(6001) = -0.66667$; i.e., the values are as correct as five digits can make them.

It is good practice to employ the shifted power form with the center c chosen somewhere in the interval $[a, b]$ when interested in a polynomial on that interval. A more sophisticated remedy against loss of significance (or illconditioning) is offered by an expansion in Chebyshev polynomials or other orthogonal polynomials; see Sec. 6.3.

The coefficients in the shifted power form (2.2) provide derivative values, i.e.,

$$a_i = p^{(i)}(c)/i! \qquad i = 0, \ldots, n$$

if $p(x)$ is given by (2.2). In effect, the shifted power form provides the **Taylor expansion** for $p(x)$ around the center c.

A further generalization of the shifted power form is the **Newton form**

$$\begin{aligned}
p(x) = a_0 &+ a_1(x - c_1) + a_2(x - c_1)(x - c_2) \\
&+ a_3(x - c_1)(x - c_2)(x - c_3) + \cdots \\
&+ a_n(x - c_1)(x - c_2) \cdots (x - c_n)
\end{aligned} \tag{2.3}$$

This form plays a major role in the construction of an interpolating polynomial. It reduces to the shifted power form if the **centers** $c_1, \ldots, c_n$ all equal c, and to the power form if the centers $c_1, \ldots, c_n$ all equal zero. The following discussion on the evaluation of the Newton form therefore applies directly to these simpler forms as well.

It is inefficient to evaluate each of the $n + 1$ terms in (2.3) separately and then sum. This would take $n + n(n + 1)/2$ additions and $n(n + 1)/2$ multiplications. Instead, one notices that the factor $(x - c_1)$ occurs in all terms but the first; that is,

$$p(x) = a_0 + (x - c_1)\{a_1 + a_2(x - c_2) + a_3(x - c_2)(x - c_3)$$
$$+ \cdots + a_n(x - c_2)(x - c_3) \cdots (x - c_n)\}$$

Again, each term between the braces but the first contains the factor $(x - c_2)$; that is,

$$p(x) = a_0 + (x - c_1)\{a_1 + (x - c_2)[a_2 + a_3(x - c_3)$$
$$+ \cdots + a_n(x - c_3) \cdots (x - c_n)]\}$$

Continuing in this manner, we obtain $p(x)$ in **nested form**:

$$p(x) = a_0 + (x - c_1)\{a_1 + (x - c_2)[a_2 + (x - c_3)\langle a_3 + \cdots$$
$$+ (x - c_{n-1})(a_{n-1} + (x - c_n)a_n) \cdots \rangle]\}$$

whose evaluation for any particular value of x takes $2n$ additions and n multiplications. If, for example, $p(x) = 1 + 2(x - 1) + 3(x - 1)(x - 2) + 4(x - 1)(x - 2)(x - 3)$, and we wish to compute $p(4)$, then we calculate as follows:

$$p(4) = 1 + (4 - 1)\{2 + (4 - 2)[3 + (4 - 3)\langle 4 \rangle]\}$$
$$= 1 + (4 - 1)\{2 + (4 - 2)[7]\}$$
$$= 1 + (4 - 1)\{16\}$$
$$= 49$$

This procedure is formalized in the following algorithm.

Algorithm 2.1: Nested multiplication for the Newton form Given the $n + 1$ coefficients $a_0, \ldots, a_n$ for the Newton form (2.3) of the polynomial $p(x)$, together with the centers $c_1, \ldots, c_n$. Given also the number z.

$$a_n' := a_n$$

For $i = n - 1, n - 2, \ldots, 0$, do:
$$a_i' := a_i + (z - c_{i+1})a_{i+1}'$$

Then, $a_0' = p(z)$. Moreover, the auxilliary quantities $a_1', \ldots, a_n'$ are of independent interest. For, we have

$$p(x) = a'_0 + a'_1(x - z) + a'_2(x - z)(x - c_1)$$
$$+ a'_3(x - z)(x - c_1)(x - c_2)$$
$$+ \cdots + a'_n(x - z)(x - c_1)(x - c_2) \cdots (x - c_{n-1}) \quad (2.4)$$

i.e., $a'_0, \ldots, a'_n$ are also coefficients in the Newton form for $p(x)$, but with centers $z, c_1, c_2, \ldots, c_{n-1}$.

We prove the assertion (2.4). From the algorithm,

$$a_n = a'_n$$
$$a_i = a'_i + a'_{i+1}(c_{i+1} - z) \qquad i = n - 1, n - 2, \ldots, 0$$

Substituting these expressions into (2.3), we get

$$p(x) = a_0 + a_1(x - c_1) + a_2(x - c_1)(x - c_2)$$
$$+ \cdots + a_n(x - c_1) \cdots (x - c_n)$$

$$= a'_0 + a'_1(c_1 - z)$$
$$+ [a'_1 + a'_2(c_2 - z)](x - c_1)$$
$$+ [a'_2 + a'_3(c_3 - z)](x - c_1)(x - c_2)$$

$$\vdots$$

$$+ [a'_{n-1} + a'_n(c_n - z)](x - c_1) \cdots (x - c_{n-1})$$
$$+ a'_n(x - c_1) \cdots (x - c_{n-1})(x - c_n)$$

$$= a'_0 + a'_1(x - z) + a'_2(x - z)(x - c_1)$$
$$+ \cdots + a'_n(x - z)(x - c_1) \cdots (x - c_{n-1})$$

which proves (2.4).

Aside from producing the value of the polynomial (2.3) at any particular point z economically, the nested multiplication algorithm is useful in changing from one Newton form to another. Suppose, for example, that we wish to express the polynomial

$$p_2(x) = 1.5709 + 0.0006(x - 1) + 0.00012(x - 1)(x - 4)$$

in terms of powers of x, that is, in the Newton form with all centers equal to zero. Then, applying Algorithm 2.1 with $z = 0$ (and $n = 2$), we get

$$a'_2 = a_2 = 0.00012$$
$$a'_1 = a_1 + (z - c_2)a'_2 = 0.0006 + (0 - 4)(0.00012) = 0.00012$$
$$a'_0 = a_0 + (z - c_1)a'_1 = 1.5709 + (0 - 1)(0.00012) = 1.57078$$

Hence

$$p_2(x) = 1.57078 + 0.00012(x - 0) + 0.00012(x - 0)(x - 1)$$

Applying Algorithm 2.1 to this polynomial, again with $z = 0$, gives

$$a_2' = a_2 = 0.00012$$

$$a_1' = a_1 + (z - c_2)a_2' = 0.00012 + (0 - 1)(0.00012) = 0.0$$

$$a_0' = a_0 + (z - c_1)a_1' = 1.57078 + (0 - 0)(0.0) = 1.57078$$

Therefore

$$p_2(x) = 1.57078 + 0.0(x - 0) + 0.00012(x - 0)(x - 0)$$

$$= 1.57078 + 0.00012x^2$$

In this simple example, we can verify this result quickly by multiplying out the terms in the original expression.

$$p_2(x) = 1.5709 + 0.0006(x - 1) + 0.00012(x^2 - 5x + 4)$$

$$= [1.5709 - 0.0006 + (0.00012)(4)]$$

$$+ [0.0006 + (0.00012)(-5)]x + 0.00012x^2$$

$$= 1.57078 + 0.00012x^2$$

Repeated applications of the Nested Multiplication algorithm are useful in the evaluation of derivatives of a polynomial given in Newton form (see Exercises 2.1-2 through 2.1-5). The algorithm is also helpful in establishing the following basic fact.

Lemma 2.1 If $z_1, \ldots, z_k$ are distinct zeros of the polynomial $p(x)$, then

$$p(x) = (x - z_1)(x - z_2) \cdots (x - z_k)r(x)$$

for some polynomial $r(x)$.

To prove this lemma, we write $p(x)$ in power form (2.1), i.e., in Newton form with all centers equal to zero, and then apply Algorithm 2.1 once, to get

$$p(x) = p(z) + (x - z)q(x)$$

[since $a_0' = p(z)$], with $q(x) = a_1' + a_2'x + \cdots + a_n'x^{n-1}$, a polynomial of degree $< n$. In effect, we have divided $p(x)$ by the linear polynomial $(x - z)$; $q(x)$ is the quotient polynomial and the number $p(z)$ is the remainder. Now pick specifically $z = z_1$. Then, by assumption, $p(z_1) = 0$, i.e.,

$$p(x) = (x - z_1)q(x)$$

This finishes the proof in case $k = 1$. Further, for $k > 1$, it follows that $z_2, \ldots, z_k$ are necessarily zeros of $q(x)$, since $p(x)$ vanishes at these points while the linear polynomial $x - z_1$ does not, by assumption. Hence, induction on the number k of zeros may now be used to complete the proof.

Corollary If $p(x)$ and $q(x)$ are two polynomials of degree $\leq k$ which agree at the $k + 1$ distinct points $z_0, \ldots, z_k$, then $p(x) = q(x)$ identically.

Indeed, their difference $d(x) = p(x) - q(x)$ is then a polynomial of degree $\leq k$, and can, by Lemma 2.1, be written in the form

$$d(x) = (x - z_0) \cdots (x - z_k)r(x)$$

with $r(x)$ some polynomial. Suppose that $r(x) = c_0 + \cdots + c_m x^m$ for some coefficients $c_0, \ldots, c_m$ with $c_m \neq 0$. Then

$$k \geq \text{degree } d = k + 1 + m$$

which is nonsense. Hence, $r(x) = 0$ identically, and so $p(x) = q(x)$.

This corollary gives the answer, "At most one," to the question "How many polynomials of degree $\leq k$ are there which take on specified values at $k + 1$ specified points?"

These considerations concerning zeros of polynomials can be refined through the notion of multiplicity of a zero. This will be of importance to us later on, in the discussion of osculatory interpolation. We say that the point z is a zero of **(exact) multiplicity** j, or **of order** j, of the function $f(x)$ provided

$$f(z) = f'(z) = \cdots = f^{(j-1)}(z) = 0 \neq f^{(j)}(z)$$

Example
For instance, the polynomial

$$(x - z)^j$$

has a zero of multiplicity j at z. It is reasonable to count such a zero j times since it can be thought of as the limiting case of the polynomial

$$(x - z_1) \cdots (x - z_j)$$

with j distinct, or simple, zeros as all these zeros come together, or coalesce, at z.

As another example, for $0 < A < 1$, the function $\sin x - Ax$ has three (simple) zeros in the interval $-\pi < x < \pi$ which converge to the number 0 as $A \to 1$. Correspondingly, the (limiting) function $\sin x - x$ has a triple zero at 0.

With this notion of multiplicity of a zero, Lemma 2.1 can be strengthened as follows.

Lemma 2.2 If $z_1, \ldots, z_k$ is a sequence of zeros of the polynomial $p(x)$ counting multiplicity, then

$$p(x) = (x - z_1)(x - z_2) \cdots (x - z_k)r(x)$$

for some polynomial $r(x)$.

See Exercise 2.1-6 for a proof of this lemma. Note that the number z could occur in the sequence $z_1, \ldots, z_k$ as many as j times in case z is a zero of $p(x)$ of order j.

From the lemma 2.2, we get by the earlier argument the

Corollary If $p(x)$ and $q(x)$ are two polynomials of degree $\leq k$ which agree at $k + 1$ points $z_0, \ldots, z_k$ in the sense that their difference $r(x) = p(x) - q(x)$ has the $k + 1$ zeros $z_0, \ldots, z_k$ (counting multiplicity), then $p(x) = q(x)$ identically.

EXERCISES

2.1-1 Evaluate the cubic polynomial $p(x) = (x - 99\pi)(x - 100\pi)(x - 101\pi)$ at $x = 314.15$. Then use nested multiplication to obtain $p(x)$ in power form, and evaluate that power form at $x = 314.15$. Compare!

2.1-2 Let $p(x) = a_0 + (x - c_1)(a_1 + \cdots + (x - c_n)(a_n) \cdots)$ be a polynomial in Newton form. Prove: If $c_1 = c_2 = \cdots = c_{r+1}$, then $p^{(j)}(c_1) = j!a_j, j = 0, \ldots, r$. [*Hint:* Under these conditions, $p(x)$ can be written

$$p(x) = \sum_{j=0}^{r} a_j(x - c_1)^j + (x - c_1)^{r+1}q(x)$$

with $q(x)$ some polynomial. Now differentiate.]

2.1-3 Find the first derivative of

$$p(x) = 3 - (x - 1)(4 - (x + 1)\{5 - x[6 - (x + 2)]\})$$

at $x = 2$. [*Hint:* Apply Algorithm 2.1 twice to obtain the Newton form for $p(x)$ with centers 2, 2, 1, -1; then use Exercise 2.1-2.]

2.1-4 Find also the second derivative of the polynomial $p(x)$ of Exercise 2.1-3 at $x = 2$.

2.1-5 Find the Taylor expansion around $c = 3$ for the polynomial of Exercise 2.1-3. [*Hint:* The Taylor expansion for a polynomial around a point c is just the Newton form for this polynomial with centers $c, c, c, c, \ldots$.]

2.1-6 Prove Lemma 2.2. [*Hint:* By Algorithm 2.1, $p(x) = (x - z_1)q(x)$. Now, to finish the proof by induction on the number k of zeros in the given sequence, prove that $z_2, \ldots, z_k$ is necessarily a sequence of zeros (counting multiplicity) of $q(x)$. For this, assume that the number z occurs exactly j times in the sequence $z_2, \ldots, z_k$ and distinguish the cases $z = z_1$ and $z \neq z_1$. Also, use the fact that $p^{(j)}(x) = (x - z_1)q^{(j)}(x) + jq^{(j-1)}(x)$.]

2.1-7 Prove that, in the language of the corollary to Lemma 2.2, the Taylor polynomial $\sum_{i=0}^{j-1} f^{(i)}(a)(x - a)^i/i!$ agrees with the function $f(x)$ j-fold at the point $x = a$ (i.e., a is a j-fold zero of their difference).

2.1-8 Suppose someone gives you a FUNCTION F(X) which supposedly returns the value at X of a specific polynomial of degree $< r$. Suppose further that, on inspection, you find that the routine does indeed return the value of *some* polynomial of degree $< r$ (e.g., you find only additions/subtractions and multiplications involving X and numerical constants in that subprogram, with X appearing as a factor less than r times). How many function values would you have to check before you could be sure that the routine does indeed do what it is supposed to do (assuming no rounding errors in the calculation)?

2.1-9 For each of the following power series, exploit the idea of nested multiplication to find an efficient way for their evaluation. (You will have to assume, of course, that they are to be summed only over $n \leq N$, for some a priori given N.)

(a) $e^x = \sum_n x^n/n!$

(b) $\ln x = 2\sum_{n \text{ odd}} \dfrac{1}{n}\left(\dfrac{x - 1}{x + 1}\right)^n$

(c) $\sin^{-1} x = \sum_{n \text{ odd}} \dfrac{1 \cdot 3 \cdots (n - 2)}{2 \cdot 4 \cdots (n - 1)} x^n/n$

2.2 EXISTENCE AND UNIQUENESS OF THE INTERPOLATING POLYNOMIAL

Let $x_0, x_1, \ldots, x_n$ be $n + 1$ distinct points on the real axis and let $f(x)$ be a real-valued function defined on some interval $I = [a, b]$ containing these points. We wish to construct a polynomial $p(x)$ of degree $\leq n$ which interpolates $f(x)$ at the points $x_0, \ldots, x_n$, that is, satisfies

$$p(x_i) = f(x_i) \qquad i = 0, \ldots, n$$

As we will see, there are many ways to write down such a polynomial. It is therefore important to remind the reader at the outset that, by the corollary to Lemma 2.1, *there is at most one polynomial of degree $\leq n$ which interpolates $f(x)$ at the $n + 1$ distinct points $x_0, \ldots, x_n$.*

Next we show that *there is at least one polynomial of degree $\leq n$ which interpolates $f(x)$ at the $n + 1$ distinct points $x_0, x_1, \ldots, x_n$.* For this, we employ yet another polynomial form, the **Lagrange form**

$$p(x) = a_0 l_0(x) + a_1 l_1(x) + \cdots + a_n l_n(x) \tag{2.5}$$

with
$$l_k(x) = \prod_{\substack{i=0 \\ i \neq k}}^{n} \frac{x - x_i}{x_k - x_i} \qquad k = 0, \ldots, n \tag{2.6}$$

the **Lagrange polynomials for the points** $x_0, \ldots, x_n$. The function $l_k(x)$ is the product of n linear factors, hence a polynomial of exact degree n. Therefore, (2.5) does indeed describe a polynomial of degree $\leq n$. Further, $l_k(x)$ vanishes at x_i for all $i \neq k$ and takes the value 1 at x_k, i.e.,

$$l_k(x_i) = \begin{Bmatrix} 1, i = k \\ 0, i \neq k \end{Bmatrix} \qquad i = 0, \ldots, n$$

This shows that

$$p(x_i) = \sum_{k=0}^{n} a_k l_k(x_i) = a_i \qquad i = 0, \ldots, n$$

i.e., the coefficients $a_0, \ldots, a_n$ in the Lagrange form are simply the values of the polynomial $p(x)$ at the points $x_0, \ldots, x_n$. Consequently, for an arbitrary function $f(x)$,

$$p(x) = \sum_{k=0}^{n} f(x_k) l_k(x) \tag{2.7}$$

is a polynomial of degree $\leq n$ which interpolates $f(x)$ at $x_0, \ldots, x_n$. This establishes the following theorem.

Theorem 2.1 Given a real-valued function $f(x)$ and $n + 1$ distinct points $x_0, \ldots, x_n$, there exists exactly one polynomial of degree $\leq n$ which interpolates $f(x)$ at $x_0, \ldots, x_n$.

Equation (2.7) is called the **Lagrange formula** for the interpolating polynomial.

As a simple application, we consider the case $n = 1$; i.e., we are given $f(x)$ and two distinct points x_0, x_1. Then

$$l_0(x) = \frac{x - x_1}{x_0 - x_1} \qquad l_1(x) = \frac{x - x_0}{x_1 - x_0}$$

and

$$p(x) = f(x_0)l_0(x) + f(x_1)l_1(x) = f(x_0)\frac{x - x_1}{x_0 - x_1} + f(x_1)\frac{x - x_0}{x_1 - x_0}$$

$$= \frac{f(x_0)(x - x_1) - f(x_1)(x - x_0)}{x_0 - x_1} = f(x_0) + \frac{f(x_1) - f(x_0)}{x_1 - x_0}(x - x_0)$$

This is the familiar case of *linear interpolation* written in some of its many equivalent forms.

Example 2.2 An integral related to the complete elliptic integral is defined by

$$K(k) = \int_0^{\pi/2} \frac{dx}{[1 - (\sin k)^2 \sin^2 x]^{1/2}} \tag{2.8}$$

From a table of values of these integrals we find that, for various values of k measured in degrees,

$$K(1) = 1.5709$$
$$K(4) = 1.5727$$
$$K(6) = 1.5751$$

Find $K(3.5)$, using a second-degree interpolating polynomial.

We have

$$l_0(3.5) = \frac{(3.5 - 4)(3.5 - 6)}{(1 - 4)(1 - 6)} = \frac{1.25}{15} = 0.08333$$

$$l_1(3.5) = \frac{(3.5 - 1)(3.5 - 6)}{(4 - 1)(4 - 6)} = \frac{-6.25}{-6} = 1.04167$$

$$l_2(3.5) = \frac{(3.5 - 1)(3.5 - 4)}{(6 - 1)(6 - 4)} = \frac{-1.25}{10} = -0.12500$$

Then

$$K(3.5) \approx (1.5709)(0.08333) + (1.5727)(1.04167) + (1.5751)(-0.12500)$$
$$= 1.57225$$

This approximation is in error in the last place.

The Lagrange form (2.7) for the interpolating polynomial makes it easy to show the existence of an interpolating polynomial. But its evaluation at a point x takes at least $2(n + 1)$ multiplications/divisions and $(2n + 1)$ additions and subtractions *after* the denominators of the Lagrange polynomials have been calculated once and for all and divided into the corresponding function values. This is to be compared with n multiplications and n additions necessary for the evaluation of a polynomial of degree n in power form by nested multiplication (see Algorithm 2.1).

A more serious objection to the Lagrange form arises as follows: In practice, one is often uncertain as to how many interpolation points to use. Hence, with $p_j(x)$ denoting the polynomial of degree $\leq j$ which interpolates $f(x)$ at $x_0, \ldots, x_j$, one calculates $p_0(x), p_1(x), p_2(x), \ldots$, increasing the number of interpolation points, and hence the degree of the interpolating polynomial until, so one hopes, a satisfactory approximation $p_k(x)$ to $f(x)$ has been found. In such a process, use of the Lagrange form seems wasteful since, in calculating $p_k(x)$, no obvious advantage can be taken of the fact that one already has $p_{k-1}(x)$ available. For this purpose and others, the Newton form of the interpolating polynomial is much better suited.

Indeed, write the interpolating polynomial $p_n(x)$ in its Newton form, using the interpolation points $x_0, \ldots, x_{n-1}$ as centers, i.e.,

$$p_n(x) = A_0 + A_1(x - x_0) + A_2(x - x_0)(x - x_1)$$
$$+ \cdots + A_n(x - x_0) \cdots (x - x_{n-1}) \qquad (2.9)$$

For any integer k between 0 and n, let $q_k(x)$ be the sum of the first $k + 1$ terms in this form,

$$q_k(x) = A_0 + A_1(x - x_0) + A_2(x - x_0)(x - x_1)$$
$$+ \cdots + A_k(x - x_0) \cdots (x - x_{k-1})$$

Then every one of the remaining terms in (2.9) has the factor $(x - x_0)$ $\cdots (x - x_k)$, and we can write (2.9) in the form

$$p_n(x) = q_k(x) + (x - x_0) \cdots (x - x_k)r(x)$$

for some polynomial $r(x)$ of no further interest. The point is that this last term $(x - x_0) \cdots (x - x_k)r(x)$ vanishes at the points $x_0, \ldots, x_k$, hence $q_k(x)$ itself must already interpolate $f(x)$ at $x_0, \ldots, x_k$ [since $p_n(x)$ does]. Since $q_k(x)$ is also a polynomial of degree $\leq k$, it follows that $q_k(x) = p_k(x)$; i.e., $q_k(x)$ must be the unique polynomial of degree $\leq k$ which interpolates $f(x)$ at $x_0, \ldots, x_k$.

This shows that the Newton form (2.9) for the interpolating polynomial $p_n(x)$ can be built up step by step as one constructs the sequence $p_0(x), p_1(x), p_2(x), \ldots$, with $p_k(x)$ obtained from $p_{k-1}(x)$ by addition of the next term in the Newton form (2.9), i.e.,

$$p_k(x) = p_{k-1}(x) + A_k(x - x_0) \cdots (x - x_{k-1})$$

It also shows that the coefficient A_k in the Newton form (2.9) for the interpolating polynomial is the leading coefficient, i.e., the coefficient of x^k, in the polynomial $p_k(x)$ of degree $\leq k$ which agrees with $f(x)$ at $x_0, \ldots, x_k$. This coefficient depends only on the values of $f(x)$ at the points $x_0, \ldots, x_k$; it is called **the kth divided difference of $f(x)$ at the points** $x_0, \ldots, x_k$ (for reasons given in the next section) and is denoted by

$$f[x_0, \ldots, x_k]$$

With this definition, we arrive at the **Newton formula** for the interpolating polynomial

$$p_n(x) = f[x_0] + f[x_0, x_1](x - x_0) + f[x_0, x_1, x_2](x - x_0)(x - x_1) +$$
$$\cdots + f[x_0, x_1, \ldots, x_n](x - x_0)(x - x_1) \cdots (x - x_{n-1})$$

This can be written more compactly as

$$p_n(x) = \sum_{i=0}^{n} f[x_0, \ldots, x_i] \prod_{j=0}^{i-1} (x - x_j) \tag{2.10}$$

if we make use of the convention that

$$\prod_{m=r}^{s} a_m = \begin{cases} a_r a_{r+1} \cdots a_s & \text{for } r \leq s \\ 1 & \text{for } r > s \end{cases}$$

For $n = 1$, (2.10) reads

$$p_1(x) = f[x_0] + f[x_0, x_1](x - x_1)$$

and comparison with the formula $p_1(x) = f(x_0) + [f(x_1) - f(x_0)]/[x_1 - x_0]$ obtained earlier therefore shows that

$$f[x_0] = f(x_0)$$

$$f[x_0, x_1] = [f(x_1) - f(x_0)]/(x_1 - x_0) = \frac{f(x_0) - f(x_1)}{x_0 - x_1} \tag{2.11}$$

The first divided difference, at any rate, is a ratio of differences.

EXERCISES

2.2-1 Prove that $f[x_0, x_1, \ldots, x_n] = \sum_{i=0}^{n} f(x_i)/w'(x_i)$, with $w(x) = (x - x_0)(x - x_1) \cdots (x - x_n)$. [*Hint:* Find the leading coefficient of the polynomial (2.7).]

2.2-2 Calculate the limit of the formula for $f[x_0, x_1, \ldots, x_n]$ given in Exercise 2.2-1 as $x_2 \to x_1$, while all other points remain fixed.

2.2-3 Prove that the polynomial of degree $\leq n$ which interpolates $f(x)$ at $n + 1$ distinct points is $f(x)$ itself in case $f(x)$ is a polynomial of degree $\leq n$.

2.2-4 Prove that the kth divided difference $p[x_0, \ldots, x_k]$ of a polynomial $p(x)$ of degree $\leq k$ is independent of the interpolation points $x_0, x_1, \ldots, x_k$.

2.2-5 Prove that the kth divided difference of a polynomial of degree $< k$ is 0.

2.3 THE DIVIDED-DIFFERENCE TABLE

Higher-order divided differences may be constructed by the formula

$$f[x_0, \ldots, x_k] = \frac{f[x_1, \ldots, x_k] - f[x_0, \ldots, x_{k-1}]}{x_k - x_0} \tag{2.12}$$

whose validity may be established as follows.

Let $p_i(x)$ be the polynomial of degree $\leq i$ which agrees with $f(x)$ at $x_0, \ldots, x_i$, as before, and let $q_{k-1}(x)$ be the polynomial of degree $\leq k - 1$ which agrees with $f(x)$ at the points $x_1, \ldots, x_k$. Then

$$p(x) = \frac{x - x_0}{x_k - x_0} q_{k-1}(x) + \frac{x_k - x}{x_k - x_0} p_{k-1}(x) \qquad (2.13)$$

is a polynomial of degree $\leq k$, and one checks easily that $p(x_i) = f(x_i)$, $i = 0, \ldots, k$. Consequently, by the uniqueness of the interpolating polynomial, we must have $p(x) = p_k(x)$. Therefore

$$
\begin{aligned}
f[x_0, \ldots, x_k] &= \text{leading coefficient of } p_k(x) && \text{by definition} \\
&= \frac{\text{leading coef. of } q_{k-1}(x)}{x_k - x_0} && \text{by (2.13)} \\
&\quad - \frac{\text{leading coef. of } p_{k-1}(x)}{x_k - x_0} \\
&= \frac{f[x_1, \ldots, x_k] - f[x_0, \ldots, x_{k-1}]}{x_k - x_0} && \text{by definition}
\end{aligned}
$$

which proves the important formula (2.12).

Example 2.3 Solve Example 2.2 using the Newton formula.

In this example, we have to determine the polynomial $p_2(x)$ of degree ≤ 2 which satisfies

$$p_2(1) = 1.5709 \qquad p_2(4) = 1.5727 \qquad p_2(6) = 1.5751$$

By (2.11) we can calculate

$$K[1, 4] = \frac{1.5709 - 1.5727}{1 - 4} = 0.0006$$

$$K[4, 6] = \frac{1.5727 - 1.5751}{4 - 6} = 0.0012$$

Therefore, by (2.12),

$$K[1, 4, 6] = \frac{0.0006 - 0.0012}{1 - 6} = 0.00012$$

and (2.10) now gives

$$p_2(x) = 1.5709 + 0.0006(x - 1) + 0.00012(x - 1)(x - 4)$$

Substituting into this the value $x = 3.5$, we obtain

$$p_2(3.5) = 1.5709 + (0.0006)(2.5) + (0.00012)(2.5)(-0.5) = 1.57225$$

which agrees with the result obtained in Example 2.2.

Equation (2.12) shows the kth divided difference to be a difference quotient of $(k - 1)$st divided differences, justifying their name. Equation (2.12) also allows us to generate all the divided differences needed for the Newton formula (2.10) in a simple manner with the aid of a so-called *divided-difference table*.

Such a table is depicted in Fig. 2.1, for $n = 4$.

The entries in the table are calculated, for example, column by column, according to the following algorithm.

Algorithm 2.2: Divided-difference table Given the first two columns of the table, containing $x_0, x_1, \ldots, x_n$ and, correspondingly, $f[x_0], f[x_1], \ldots, f[x_n]$.

For $k = 1, \ldots, n$, do:

For $i = 0, \ldots, n - k$, do:

$$f[x_i, \ldots, x_{i+k}] := \frac{f[x_{i+1}, \ldots, x_{i+k}] - f[x_i, \ldots, x_{i+k-1}]}{x_{i+k} - x_i}$$

If this algorithm is carried out by hand, the following directions might be helpful. Draw the two diagonals from the entry to be calculated through its two neighboring entries to the left. If these lines terminate at $f[x_i]$ and $f[x_j]$, respectively, divide the difference of the two neighboring entries by the corresponding difference $x_j - x_i$ to get the desired entry. This is illustrated in Fig. 2.1 for the entry $f[x_1, \ldots, x_4]$.

When the divided-difference table is filled out, the coefficients $f[x_0, \ldots, x_i]$, $i = 0, \ldots, n$, for the Newton formula (2.10) can be found at the head of their respective columns.

For reasons of storage requirements, and because the DO variables in many FORTRAN dialects can only increase, one would use a somewhat modified version of Algorithm 2.2 in a FORTRAN program. First, for the evaluation of the Newton form according to Algorithm 2.1, it is more convenient to use the form

$$p_n(x) = \sum_{i=0}^{n} f[x_i, \ldots, x_n] \prod_{j=i+1}^{n} (x - x_j)$$

Figure 2.1 Divided-difference table.

x_i	$f[\ ] = f(\ )$	$f[,]$	$f[,,]$	$f[,,,]$	$f[,,,,]$
x_0	$f[x_0]$				
		$f[x_0, x_1]$			
$x_1 - -f[x_1]$			$f[x_0, x_1, x_2]$		
		$f[x_1, x_2]$		$f[x_0, x_1, x_2, x_3]$	
x_2	$f[x_2]$		$f[x_1, x_2, x_3]$		$f[x_0, x_1, x_2, x_3, x_4]$
		$f[x_2, x_3]$		$f[x_1, x_2, x_3, x_4]$	
x_3	$f[x_3]$		$f[x_2, x_3, x_4]$		
		$f[x_3, x_4]$			
$x_4 - -f[x_4]$					

i.e., to use the Newton formula with centers $x_n, x_{n-1}, \ldots, x_1$. For then the value $v = p_n(z)$ can be calculated, according to Algorithm 2.1, by

$$v := f[x_0, \ldots, x_n]$$
For $i = 1, \ldots, n$, do:
$$v := f[x_i, \ldots, x_n] + (z - x_i)v$$

Second, since we are then only interested in the numbers $f[x_i, \ldots, x_n]$, $i = 0, \ldots, n$, it is not necessary to store the entire divided-difference table (requiring a two-dimensional array in which roughly half the entries would not be used anyway, because of the triangular character of the divided-difference table). For if we use the abbreviation

$$d_{ij} = f[x_i, \ldots, x_{i+j}]$$

then the calculations of Algorithm 2.2 read

For $k = 1, \ldots, n$, do:
$\quad$ For $i = 0, \ldots, n - k$, do:
$$d_{ik} := (d_{i+1, k-1} - d_{i, k-1})/(x_{i+k} - x_i)$$

In particular, the number $d_{i, k-1}$ is not used any further once d_{ik} has been calculated, so that we can safely store d_{ik} over $d_{i, k-1}$.

Algorithm 2.3: Calculation of the coefficients for the Newton formula
Given the $n + 1$ distinct points $x_0, \ldots, x_n$ and, correspondingly, the numbers $f(x_0), \ldots, f(x_n)$, with $f(x_i)$ stored in d_i, $i = 0, \ldots, n$.

For $k = 1, \ldots, n$, do:
$\quad$ For $i = 0, \ldots, n - k$, do:
$$d_i := (d_{i+1} - d_i)/(x_{i+k} - x_i)$$

Then $d_i = f[x_i, \ldots, x_n]$, $i = 0, \ldots, n$.

Example 2.4 Let $f(x) = (1 + x^2)^{-1}$. For $n = 2, 4, \ldots, 16$, calculate the polynomial $p_n(x)$ of degree $\leq n$ which interpolates $f(x)$ at the $n + 1$ equally spaced points

$$x_i = i\frac{10}{n} - 5 \qquad i = 0, \ldots, n$$

Then estimate the maximum interpolation error

$$E_n = \max_{-5 \leq x \leq 5} |f(x) - p_n(x)| \qquad n = 2, 4, \ldots, 16$$

on the interval $[-5, 5]$ by computing

$$E_n \approx \max_i |f(y_i) - p_n(y_i)|$$

where

$$y_i = \frac{i}{10} - 5 \qquad i = 0, \ldots, 100$$

The FORTRAN program below uses Algorithms 2.1 and 2.3 to solve this problem.

FORTRAN PROGRAM FOR EXAMPLE 2.4

```
C   PROGRAM FOR EXAMPLE 2.4
        INTEGER I,J,K,N,NP1
        REAL D(17),ERRMAX,H,PNOFY,X(17),Y
C   POLYNOMIAL INTERPOLATION AT EQUALLY SPACED POINTS TO THE FUNCTION
        F(Y)  =  1./(1. + Y*Y)
C
        PRINT 600
  600 FORMAT('1    N',5X,'MAXIMUM ERROR')
        DO 40 N=2,16,2
        NP1 = N+1
        H = 10./FLOAT(N)
        DO 10 I=1,NP1
            X(I) = FLOAT(I-1)*H - 5.
            D(I) = F(X(I))
   10    CONTINUE
C            CALCULATE DIVIDED DIFFERENCES BY ALGORITHM 2.3
        DO 20 K=1,N
            DO 20 I=1,NP1-K
                D(I) = (D(I+1) - D(I))/(X(I+K) - X(I))
   20    CONTINUE
C            ESTIMATE MAXIMUM INTERPOLATION ERROR ON (-5,5)
        ERRMAX = 0.
        DO 30 J=1,101
            Y = FLOAT(J-1)/10. - 5.
C            CALCULATE PN(Y) BY ALGORITHM 2.1
            PNOFY = D(1)
            DO 29 K=2,NP1
                PNOFY = D(K) + (Y - X(K))*PNOFY
   29        CONTINUE
            ERRMAX = MAX(ABS(F(Y) - PNOFY), ERRMAX)
   30    CONTINUE
        PRINT 630, N,ERRMAX
  630    FORMAT(I5,E18.7)
   40 CONTINUE
                                                        STOP
        END
```

COMPUTER OUTPUT FOR EXAMPLE 2.4

N	MAXIMUM ERROR
2	6.4615385E − 01
4	4.3813387E − 01
6	6.1666759E − 01
8	1.0451739E + 00
10	1.9156431E + 00
12	3.6052745E + 00
14	7.1920080E + 00
16	1.4051542E + 01

Note how the interpolation error soon *increases* with increasing degree even though we use more and more information about the function $f(x)$ in our interpolation process. This is because we have used uniformly spaced interpolation points; see Exercise 6.1-12 and Eq. (6.20).

EXERCISES

2.3-1 From a table of logarithms we obtain the following values of $\log x$ at the indicated tabular points.

x	$\log x$
1.0	0.0
1.5	0.17609
2.0	0.30103
3.0	0.47712
3.5	0.54407
4.0	0.60206

Form a divided-difference table based on these values.

2.3-2 Using the divided-difference table in Exercise 2.3-1, interpolate for the following values: $\log 2.5$, $\log 1.25$, $\log 3.25$. Use a third-degree interpolating polynomial in its Newton form.

2.3-3 Estimate the error in the result obtained for $\log 2.5$ in Exercise 2.3-2 by computing the next term in the interpolating polynomial. Also estimate it by comparing the approximation for $\log 2.5$ with the sum of $\log 2$ and the approximation for $\log 1.25$.

2.3-4 Derive the formula

$$f[x_0, \ldots, x_j] = f[x_1, \ldots, x_{j+1}] + (x_0 - x_{j+1})f[x_0, \ldots, x_{j+1}]$$

Then use it to interpret the Nested Multiplication Algorithm 2.1, applied to the polynomial (2.10), as a way to calculate $p[z, x_0, \ldots, x_{n-1}]$, $p[z, x_0, \ldots, x_{n-2}]$, $\ldots, p[z, x_0]$ and $p[z]$, i.e., as a way to get another diagonal in the divided difference table for $p(x)$.

2.3-5 By Exercise 2.2-3, the polynomial of degree $\leq k$ which interpolates a function $f(x)$ at $x_0, \ldots, x_k$ is $f(x)$ itself if $f(x)$ is a polynomial of degree $\leq k$. This fact may be used to check the accuracy of the *computed* interpolating polynomial. Adapt the FORTRAN program given in Example 2.4 to carry out such a check as follows: For $n = 4, 8, 12, \ldots, 32$, find the polynomial $p_n(x)$ of degree $\leq n$ which interpolates the function $f_n(x) = \prod_{j=1}^{n}(x - j - \frac{1}{3})$ at $0, 1, 2, \ldots, n$. Then estimate $E_n = \max_{x_0 \leq x \leq x_n}|f_n(x) - p_n(x)|$ by $\max |f_n(y_i) - p_n(y_i)|$, where the y_i's are a suitably large number of points in $[0, n]$.

2.3-6 Prove that the first derivative $p_2'(x)$ of the parabola interpolating $f(x)$ at $x_0 < x_1 < x_2$ is equal to the straight line which takes on the value $f[x_{i-1}, x_i]$ at the point $(x_{i-1} + x_i)/2$, for $i = 1, 2$. Generalize this to describe $p_n'(x)$ as the interpolant to data $\{\xi_i, f[x_i, x_{i+1}]\}$, for appropriate ξ_i in $x_i \leq x \leq x_{i+1}$ in case $p_n(x)$ interpolates $f(x)$ at $x_0 < x_1 < \cdots < x_n$.

*2.4 INTERPOLATION AT AN INCREASING NUMBER OF INTERPOLATION POINTS

Consider now the problem of estimating $f(x)$ at a point $x = \bar{x}$, using polynomial interpolation at distinct points $x_0, x_1, x_2, \ldots$. With $p_k(x)$ the polynomial of degree $\leq k$ which interpolates $f(x)$ at $x_0, \ldots, x_k$, we calculate successively $p_0(\bar{x}), p_1(\bar{x}), p_2(\bar{x}), \ldots$ until, so we hope, the difference between $p_{k+1}(\bar{x})$ and $p_k(\bar{x})$ is sufficiently small. The Newton form for the interpolating polynomial

$$p_k(x) = \sum_{i=0}^{k} f[x_0, \ldots, x_i]\psi_i(x)$$

with $\quad\quad \psi_i(x) = (x - x_0) \cdots (x - x_{i-1})$

is expressly designed for such calculations. If we know $p_k(\bar{x})$, $\psi_k(\bar{x})$, and $f[x_0, \ldots, x_{k+1}]$, then we can calculate $p_{k+1}(\bar{x})$ by

$$p_{k+1}(\bar{x}) = p_k(\bar{x}) + f[x_0, \ldots, x_{k+1}]\psi_k(\bar{x})(\bar{x} - x_k)$$

Algorithm 2.4: Interpolation using an increasing number of interpolation points Given distinct points $x_0, x_1, x_2, \ldots$ and the values $f(x_0), f(x_1), f(x_2), \ldots$ of a function $f(x)$ at these points. Also, given a point $\bar{x}$.

$f[x_0] := f(x_0), p_0(\bar{x}) := f(x_0), \psi_0(\bar{x}) := 1$
For $k = 0, 1, 2, \ldots$, until satisfied, do:

> $f[x_{k+1}] := f(x_{k+1})$
> For $i = k, \ldots, 0$, do:
>
> > $f[x_i, \ldots, x_{k+1}] := \dfrac{f[x_{i+1}, \ldots, x_{k+1}] - f[x_i, \ldots, x_k]}{x_{k+1} - x_i}$
>
> $\psi_{k+1}(\bar{x}) := \psi_k(\bar{x})(\bar{x} - x_k)$
> $p_{k+1}(\bar{x}) := p_k(\bar{x}) + f[x_0, \ldots, x_{k+1}]\psi_{k+1}(\bar{x})$

This algorithm generates the entries of the divided-difference table for $f(x)$ at $x_0, x_1, x_2, \ldots$ a diagonal at a time. During the calculation of $p_{k+1}(\bar{x})$, the upward diagonal emanating from $f[x_{k+1}]$ is calculated up to and including the number $f[x_0, \ldots, x_{k+1}]$, using the number $f[x_{k+1}] = f(x_{k+1})$ and the previously calculated entries $f[x_k], f[x_{k-1}, x_k]$, $\ldots, f[x_0, \ldots, x_k]$ in the preceding diagonal. Hence, even if only the most recently calculated diagonal is saved (in a FORTRAN program, say), the algorithm provides incidentally the requisite coefficients for the Newton form for $p_{k+1}(x)$ with centers $x_{k+1}, \ldots, x_1$:

$$p_{k+1}(x) = \sum_{i=0}^{k+1} f[x_i, \ldots, x_{k+1}] \prod_{j=i+1}^{k+1} (x - x_j) \quad\quad (2.14)$$

Example 2.5 We apply Algorithm 2.4 to the problem of Examples 2.2 and 2.3, using $x_0 = 1$, $x_1 = 4$, $x_2 = 6$, and in addition, $x_3 = 0$. For this example, $\bar{x} = 3.5$. We get $p_0(\bar{x}) = K[x_0] = 1.5709$ and $\psi_0(\bar{x}) = 1$. Next, with $K[x_1] = 1.5727$, we get $K[x_0, x_1] = 0.0006$, and with $\psi_1(\bar{x}) = (\bar{x} - x_0)\psi_0(\bar{x}) = 2.5$, we get $p_1(\bar{x}) = 1.5709 + 0.0015 = 1.5724$.

Adding the point $x_2 = 6$, we have $K[x_2] = 1.5751$; hence $K[x_1, x_2] = 0.0012$, $K[x_0, x_1, x_2] = 0.00012$; therefore, as $\psi_2(\bar{x}) = (-0.5)(2.5) = -1.25$,

$$p_2(\bar{x}) = 1.5724 - 0.00015 = 1.57225$$

the number calculated earlier in Example 2.3. To check the error for this approximation to $K(3.5)$, we add the point $x_3 = 0$. With $K[x_3] = 1.5708$, we compute $K[x_2, x_3] = 0.000717$, $K[x_1, x_2, x_3] = 0.000121$, $K[x_0, x_1, x_2, x_3] = -0.000001$, and get, with $\psi_3(\bar{x}) = (-2.5)(-1.25) = 3.125$, that

$$p_3(\bar{x}) = 1.57225 - 0.000003$$

indicating that 1.5722 or 1.5723 is probably the value of $K(3.5)$ to within the accuracy of the given values of $K(x)$.

These calculations, if done by hand, are conveniently arranged in a table as shown in Fig. 2.2, which also shows how Algorithm 2.4 gradually builds up the divided-difference table.

We have listed below a FORTRAN FUNCTION, called TABLE, which uses Algorithm 2.4 to interpolate in a given table of abscissas and ordinates X(I), F(I), I = 1, ..., NTABLE, with F(I) = f(X(I)), and X(1) < X(2) < $\cdots$, in order to find a good approximation to $f(x)$ at x = XBAR. The program generates p_0(XBAR), p_1(XBAR), ... , until

$$|p_k(\text{XBAR}) - p_{k-1}(\text{XBAR})| \le \text{TOL}$$

where TOL is a given error requirement, or until $k + 1$ = min(20, NTABLE), and then returns the number p_k(XBAR). The sequence $x_0, x_1, x_2, \ldots$ of points of interpolation is chosen from the tabular points X(1), X(2), ..., X(NTABLE) as follows: If X(I) < XBAR $\le$ X(I + 1), then x_0 = X(I + 1), x_1 = X(I), x_2 = X(I + 2), x_3 = X(I - 1), ..., except near the beginning or the end of the given table, where eventually only points to the right or to the left of XBAR are used. To protect the program (and the user!) against an unreasonable choice for TOL, the program should be modified so as to terminate also if and when the successive differences $|p_{k+1}(\text{XBAR}) - p_k(\text{XBAR})|$ begin to *increase* as k increases. (See also Exercise 2.4-1.)

Figure 2.2

k	$p_k(\bar{x})$	$\psi_k(\bar{x})$	x_k	$K[\ ]$	$K[,]$	$K[,,]$	$K[,,,]$
0	1.5709	1.	1	1.5709			
	+ 15				0.0006		
1	1.5724	2.5	4	1.5727		0.00012	
	− 15				0.0012		−0.000001
2	1.57225	−1.25	6	1.5751		0.000121	
	− 3				0.000717		
3	1.572247	3.125	0	1.5708			

FORTRAN SUBPROGRAM FOR INTERPOLATION IN A FUNCTION TABLE

```
      REAL FUNCTION TABLE (XBAR, X, F, NTABLE, TOL, IFLAG )
C  RETURNS AN INTERPOLATED VALUE  TABLE  AT  XBAR  FOR THE FUNCTION
C  TABULATED AS (X(I),F(I)), I=1,...,NTABLE.
      INTEGER IFLAG,NTABLE,   J,NEXT,NEXTL,NEXTR
      REAL F(NTABLE),TOL,X(NTABLE),XBAR,   A(20),ERROR,PSIK,XK(20)
C******  I N P U T  ******
C  XBAR  POINT AT WHICH TO INTERPOLATE .
C  X(I), F(I), I=1,...,NTABLE  CONTAINS THE FUNCTION TABLE .
C     A S S U M P T I O N ...  X IS ASSUMED TO BE INCREASING.
C  NTABLE  NUMBER OF ENTRIES IN FUNCTION TABLE.
C  TOL  DESIRED ERROR BOUND .
C******  O U T P U T  ******
C  TABLE  THE INTERPOLATED FUNCTION VALUE .
C  IFLAG  AN INTEGER,
C     = 1 , SUCCESSFUL EXECUTION ,
C     = 2 , UNABLE TO ACHIEVE DESIRED ERROR IN 20 STEPS,
C     = 3 , XBAR LIES OUTSIDE OF TABLE RANGE. CONSTANT EXTRAPOLATION IS
C           USED.
C******  M E T H O D  ******
C  A SEQUENCE OF POLYNOMIAL INTERPOLANTS OF INCREASING DEGREE IS FORMED
C  USING TABLE ENTRIES ALWAYS AS CLOSE TO  XBAR  AS POSSIBLE. EACH IN-
C  TERPOLATED VALUE IS OBTAINED FROM THE PRECEDING ONE BY ADDITION OF A
C  CORRECTION TERM (AS IN THE NEWTON FORMULA). THE PROCESS TERMINATES
C  WHEN THIS CORRECTION IS LESS THAN  TOL  OR, ELSE, AFTER  20  STEPS.
C
C           LOCATE  XBAR  IN THE X-ARRAY.
      IF (XBAR .GE. X(1) .AND. XBAR .LE. X(NTABLE)) THEN
         DO 10 NEXT=2,NTABLE
            IF (XBAR .LE. X(NEXT))      GO TO 12
   10    CONTINUE
      END IF
      IF (XBAR .LT. X(1)) THEN
         TABLE = F(1)
      ELSE
         TABLE = F(NTABLE)
      END IF
      PRINT 610,XBAR
  610 FORMAT(E16.7,' NOT IN TABLE RANGE.')
      IFLAG = 3
                                RETURN
   12 XK(1) = X(NEXT)
      NEXTL = NEXT-1
      NEXTR = NEXT+1
      A(1) = F(NEXT)
      TABLE = A(1)
      PSIK = 1.
C       USE ALGORITHM 2.4, WITH THE NEXT XK ALWAYS THE TABLE
C       ENTRY NEAREST   XBAR   OF THOSE NOT YET USED.
      KP1MAX = MIN(20,NTABLE)
      DO 20 KP1=2,KP1MAX
         IF (NEXTL .EQ. 0) THEN
            NEXT = NEXTR
            NEXTR = NEXTR+1
         ELSE IF (NEXTR .GT. NTABLE) THEN
            NEXT = NEXTL
            NEXTL = NEXTL-1
         ELSE IF (XBAR - X(NEXTL) .GT. X(NEXTR) - XBAR) THEN
            NEXT = NEXTR
            NEXTR = NEXTR+1
         ELSE
            NEXT = NEXTL
            NEXTL = NEXTL-1
         END IF
         XK(KP1) = X(NEXT)
         A(KP1) = F(NEXT)
         DO 13 J=KP1-1,1,-1
            A(J) = (A(J+1) - A(J))/(XK(KP1) - XK(J))
   13    CONTINUE
```

```
C           FOR I=1,...,KP1,  A(I)  NOW CONTAINS THE DIV.DIFF. OF
C           F(X) OF ORDER  K-I  AT  XK(I),...,XK(KP1).
            PSIK = PSIK*(XBAR - XK(KP1-1))
            ERROR = A(1)*PSIK
C                 TEMPORARY PRINTOUT
            PRINT 613,KP1,XK(KP1),TABLE,ERROR
   613      FORMAT(I10,3E17.7)
            TABLE = TABLE + ERROR
            IF (ABS(ERROR) .LE. TOL)  THEN
               IFLAG = 1
                                           RETURN
            END IF
   20  CONTINUE
       PRINT 620,KP1MAX
  620  FORMAT(' NO CONVERGENCE IN ',I2,' STEPS.')
       IFLAG = 2
                                           RETURN
       END
```

EXERCISES

2.4-1 The FORTRAN function TABLE given in the text terminates as soon as $|p_{k+1}(XBAR)$
$- p_k(XBAR)| \le$ TOL. Show that this does not guarantee that the value $p_{k+1}(XBAR)$
returned by TABLE is within TOL of the desired number $f(XBAR)$ by the following
examples:

(a) $f(x) = x^2$; for some I, $X(I) = -10$, $X(I + 1) = 10$, XBAR = 0, TOL = 10^{-5}.

(b) $f(x) = x^3$; for some I, $X(I) = -100$, $X(I + 1) = 0$, $X(I + 2) = 100$, XBAR =
-50, TOL = 10^{-5}.

2.4-2 Iterated linear interpolation is based on the following observation attributable to
Neville: Denote by $p_{i,j}(x)$ the polynomial of degree $\le j - i$ which interpolates $f(x)$ at the
points $x_i, x_{i+1}, \ldots, x_j, i \le j$. Then

$$p_{ij}(x) = \frac{x - x_i}{x_j - x_i} p_{i+1, j-1}(x) + \frac{x_j - x}{x_j - x_i} p_{i, j-1}(x)$$

Verify this identity. [*Hint:* We used such an identity in Sec. 2.3; see Eq. (2.13).]

2.4-3 Iterated linear interpolation (continued). The identity of Neville's established in Exercise
2.4-2 allows one to generate the entries in the following triangular table

$$f(x_0) = p_{00}(\bar{x})$$

$$p_{01}(\bar{x})$$

$$f(x_1) = p_{11}(\bar{x}) \qquad\qquad p_{02}(\bar{x})$$

$$p_{12}(\bar{x})$$

$$f(x_2) = p_{22}(\bar{x}) \qquad\qquad \vdots \quad \vdots \quad p_{0n}(\bar{x})$$

$$\vdots \qquad\qquad p_{n-2, n}(\bar{x})$$

$$\vdots \quad \vdots \quad p_{n-1, n}(\bar{x})$$

$$f(x_n) = p_{nn}(\bar{x})$$

column by column, by repeatedly carrying out what looks like linear interpolation, to reach
eventually the desired number $p_{0n}(\bar{x})$, the value at $\bar{x}$ of the interpolating polynomial which
agrees with $f(x)$ at the $n + 1$ points $x_0, \ldots, x_n$. This is **Neville's Algorithm. Aitken's Algorithm**
is different in that one generates instead a triangular table whose jth column consists of the

numbers

$$p_{0, 1, \ldots, j, j+1}(\bar{x})$$
$$p_{0, 1, \ldots, j, j+2}(\bar{x})$$
$$p_{0, 1, \ldots, j, n}(\bar{x})$$

with $p_{0, 1, \ldots, j, r}(x)$ (for $r > j$) the polynomial of degree $\leq j + 1$ which agrees with $f(x)$ at the points $x_0, x_1, \ldots, x_j$, and x_r.

Show by an operations count that Neville's algorithm is more expensive than Algorithm 2.4. (Also, observe that Algorithm 2.4 provides, at no extra cost, a Newton form for the interpolating polynomial for subsequent evaluation at other points, while the information generated in Neville's or Aitken's algorithm is of no help for evaluation at other points.)

2.4-4 In **inverse interpolation** in a table, one is given a number $\bar{y}$ and wishes to find the point $\bar{x}$ so that $f(\bar{x}) = \bar{y}$, where $f(x)$ is the tabulated function. If $f(x)$ is (continuous and) strictly monotone-increasing or -decreasing, this problem can always be solved by considering the given table $x_i, f(x_i)$, $i = 0, 1, 2, \ldots$ to be a table $y_i, g(y_i)$, $i = 0, 1, 2, \ldots$ for the inverse function $g(y) = f^{-1}(y) = x$ by taking $y_i = f(x_i)$, $g(y_i) = x_i$, $i = 0, 1, 2, \ldots$, and to interpolate for the unknown value $g(\bar{y})$ in this table. Use the FORTRAN function TABLE to find $\bar{x}$ so that $\sin \bar{x} = 0.6$.

2.5 THE ERROR OF THE INTERPOLATING POLYNOMIAL

Let $f(x)$ be a real-valued function on the interval $I = [a, b]$, and let $x_0, \ldots, x_n$ be $n + 1$ distinct points in I. With $p_n(x)$ the polynomial of degree $\leq n$ which interpolates $f(x)$ at $x_0, \ldots, x_n$, the *interpolation error* $e_n(x)$ of $p_n(x)$ is given by

$$e_n(x) = f(x) - p_n(x) \tag{2.15}$$

Let now $\bar{x}$ be any point different from $x_0, \ldots, x_n$. If $p_{n+1}(x)$ is the polynomial of degree $\leq n + 1$ which interpolates $f(x)$ at $x_0, \ldots, x_n$ and at $\bar{x}$, then $p_{n+1}(\bar{x}) = f(\bar{x})$, while by (2.10),

$$p_{n+1}(x) = p_n(x) + f\left[x_0, \ldots, x_n, \bar{x}\right] \prod_{j=0}^{n} (x - x_j)$$

It follows that

$$f(\bar{x}) = p_{n+1}(\bar{x}) = p_n(\bar{x}) + f\left[x_0, \ldots, x_n, \bar{x}\right] \prod_{j=0}^{n} (\bar{x} - x_j)$$

Therefore,

For all $\bar{x} \neq x_0, \ldots, x_n$: $\qquad e_n(\bar{x}) = f\left[x_0, \ldots, x_n, \bar{x}\right] \prod_{j=0}^{n} (\bar{x} - x_j)$

$$\tag{2.16}$$

showing the error to be "like the next term" in the Newton form.

We cannot evaluate the right side of (2.16) without knowing the number $f(\bar{x})$. But as we now prove, the number $f[x_0, \ldots, x_n, \bar{x}]$ is closely related to the $(n + 1)$st derivative of $f(x)$, and using this information, we can at times estimate $e_n(\bar{x})$.

Theorem 2.2 Let $f(x)$ be a real-valued function, defined on $[a, b]$ and k times differentiable in (a, b). If $x_0, \ldots, x_k$ are $k + 1$ distinct points in $[a, b]$, then there exists $\xi \in (a, b)$ such that

$$f[x_0, \ldots, x_k] = \frac{f^{(k)}(\xi)}{k!} \qquad (2.17)$$

For $k = 1$, this is just the mean-value theorem for derivatives (see Sec. 1.7). For the general case, observe that the error function $e_k(x) = f(x) - p_k(x)$ has (at least) the $k + 1$ distinct zeros $x_0, \ldots, x_k$ in $I = [a, b]$. Hence, if $f(x)$, and therefore $e_k(x)$, is k times differentiable on (a, b), then it follows from Rolle's theorem (see Sec. 1.7) that $e'(x)$ has at least k zeros in (a, b); hence $e''(x)$ has at least $k - 1$ zeros in (a, b), and continuing in this manner, we finally get that $e_k^{(k)}(x)$ has at least one zero in (a, b). Let ξ be one such zero. Then

$$0 = e_k^{(k)}(\xi) = f^{(k)}(\xi) - p_k^{(k)}(\xi)$$

On the other hand, we know that, for any x,

$$p_k^{(k)}(x) = f[x_0, \ldots, x_k]k!$$

since, by definition, $f[x_0, \ldots, x_k]$ is the leading coefficient of $p_k(x)$, and (2.17) now follows.

By taking $a = \min_i x_i$, $b = \max_i x_i$, it follows that the unknown point ξ in (2.17) can be assumed to lie somewhere between the x_i's.

If we apply Theorem 2.2 to (2.16), we get Theorem 2.3.

Theorem 2.3 Let $f(x)$ be a real-valued function defined on $[a, b]$ and $n + 1$ times differentiable on (a, b). If $p_n(x)$ is the polynomial of degree $\leq n$ which interpolates $f(x)$ at the $n + 1$ distinct points $x_0, \ldots, x_n$ in $[a, b]$, then for all $\bar{x} \in [a, b]$, there exists $\xi = \xi(\bar{x}) \in (a, b)$ such that

$$e_n(\bar{x}) = f(\bar{x}) - p_n(\bar{x}) = \frac{f^{(n+1)}(\xi)}{(n + 1)!} \prod_{j=0}^{n} (\bar{x} - x_j) \qquad (2.18)$$

It is important to note that $\xi = \xi(\bar{x})$ depends on the point $\bar{x}$ at which the error estimate is required. This dependence need not even be continuous. As we have need in Chap. 7 to integrate and differentiate $e_n(x)$ with respect to x, we usually prefer for such purposes the formula (2.16). For, as we show in' Sec. 2.7, $f[x_0, \ldots, x_n, x]$ is a well-behaved function of x.

The error formula (2.18) is of only limited practical utility since, in general, we will seldom know $f^{(n+1)}(x)$, and we will almost never know the point ξ. But when a *bound* on $|f^{(n+1)}(x)|$ is known over the entire interval $[a, b]$, then we can use (2.18) to obtain a (usually crude) bound on the error of the interpolating polynomial in that interval.

Example 2.6 Find a bound for the error in linear interpolation.

The linear polynomial interpolating $f(x)$ at x_0 and x_1 is

$$p_1(x) = f(x_0) + f[x_0, x_1](x - x_0) = \frac{(x_1 - x)f(x_0) + (x - x_0)f(x_1)}{x_1 - x_0}$$

Equation (2.18) then yields the error formula

$$f(\bar{x}) - p_1(\bar{x}) = (\bar{x} - x_0)(\bar{x} - x_1)\frac{f''(\xi)}{2!}$$

where ξ depends on $\bar{x}$. If $\bar{x}$ is a point between x_0 and x_1, then ξ lies between x_0 and x_1. Hence, if we know that $|f''(x)| \leq M$ on $[x_0, x_1]$, then

$$|f(\bar{x}) - p_1(\bar{x})| \leq |(\bar{x} - x_0)(\bar{x} - x_1)|\frac{M}{2}$$

The maximum value of $|(\bar{x} - x_0)(\bar{x} - x_1)|$ for $\bar{x} \in [x_0, x_1]$ occurs at $\bar{x} = (x_0 + x_1)/2$; hence is $(x_1 - x_0)^2/4$. It follows that, for any $\bar{x} \in [x_0, x_1]$,

$$|f(\bar{x}) - p_1(\bar{x})| \leq (x_1 - x_0)^2\frac{M}{8}$$

Example 2.7 Determine the spacing h in a table of equally spaced values of the function $f(x) = \sqrt{x}$ between 1 and 2, so that interpolation with a second-degree polynomial in this table will yield a desired accuracy.

By assumption, the table will contain $f(x_i)$, with $x_i = 1 + ih$, $i = 0, \ldots, N$, where $N = (2 - 1)/h$. If $\bar{x} \in [x_{i-1}, x_{i+1}]$, then we approximate $f(\bar{x})$ by $p_2(\bar{x})$, where $p_2(x)$ is the quadratic polynomial which interpolates $f(x)$ at x_{i-1}, x_i, x_{i+1}. By (2.18), the error is then

$$f(\bar{x}) - p_2(\bar{x}) = (\bar{x} - x_{i-1})(\bar{x} - x_i)(\bar{x} - x_{i+1})\frac{f'''(\xi)}{3!}$$

for some ξ in (x_{i-1}, x_{i+1}). Since we do not know ξ, we can merely estimate $f'''(\xi)$,

$$|f'''(\xi)| \leq \max_{1 \leq x \leq 2} |f'''(x)|$$

One calculates $f'''(x) = \frac{3}{8}x^{-5/2}$; hence $|f'''(\xi)| \leq \frac{3}{8}$. Further,

$$\max_{x \in [x_{i-1}, x_{i+1}]} |(x - x_{i-1})(x - x_i)(x - x_{i+1})| = \max_{y \in [-h, h]} |(y + h)y(y - h)|$$

$$= \max_{y \in [-h, h]} |y(y^2 - h^2)|$$

using the linear change of variables $y = x - x_i$. Since the function $\psi(y) = y(y^2 - h^2)$ vanishes at $y = -h$ and $y = h$, the maximum of $|\psi(y)|$ on $[-h, h]$ must occur at one of the extrema of $\psi(y)$. These extrema are found by solving the equation $\psi'(y) = 3y^2 - h^2 = 0$, giving $y = \pm h/\sqrt{3}$. Hence

$$\max_{x \in [x_{i-1}, x_{i+1}]} |(x - x_{i-1})(x - x_i)(x - x_{i+1})| = \frac{2h^3}{3\sqrt{3}}$$

We are now assured that, for any $\bar{x} \in [1, 2]$,

$$|f(\bar{x}) - p_2(\bar{x})| \leq \frac{(2h^3/[3\sqrt{3}])(3/8)}{6} = \frac{h^3}{24\sqrt{3}}$$

if $p_2(x)$ is chosen as the quadratic polynomial which interpolates $f(x) = \sqrt{x}$ at the three tabular points nearest $\bar{x}$. If we wish to obtain seven-place accuracy this way, we would have to choose h so that

$$\frac{h^3}{24\sqrt{3}} < 5 \cdot 10^{-8}$$

giving $h \approx 0.0128$, or $N \approx 79$.

The function $\psi_{n+1}(x) = \Pi_{j=0}^{n}(x - x_j)$ which appears in (2.18) depends, of course, strongly on the placement of the interpolation points. It is possible to choose these points for given n in the given interval $a \leq x \leq b$ in such a way that $\max|\psi_{n+1}(x)|$ there is as small as possible. This choice of points, the so-called Chebyshev points, is discussed in some detail in Sec. 6.1. For the common choice of equally spaced interpolation points, the local maxima of $|\psi_{n+1}(x)|$ increase as one moves from the middle of the interval toward its ends, and this increase becomes more pronounced with increasing n (see Fig 2.3). In view of (2.18), it is therefore advisable (at least when interpolating to uniformly spaced data) to make use of the interpolating polynomial only near the middle data points. The interpolant becomes less reliable as one approaches the leftmost or rightmost data point. Of course, going beyond them is even worse. Such an undertaking is called **extrapolation** and should only be used with great caution.

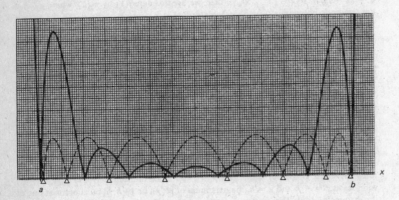

Figure 2.3 The function $|\psi_{n+1}(x)|$ for $n = 8$ and (a) equally spaced interpolation points (solid); (b) Chebyshev points for the same interval (dotted).

EXERCISES

2.5-1 A table of values of $\cos x$ is required so that linear interpolation will yield six-decimal-place accuracy for any value of x in $[0, \pi]$. Assuming that the tabular values are to be equally spaced, what is the minimum number of entries needed in the table?

2.5-2 The function defined by

$$f(x) = \int_{0}^{x} \sin s^2 \, ds$$

has been tabulated for equally spaced values of x with step $h = 0.1$. What is the maximum error encountered if cubic interpolation is to be used to calculate $f(\bar{x})$ for $\bar{x}$ any point on the interval $[0, \pi/2]$?

2.5-3 Prove: If the values $f(x_0), \ldots, f(x_n)$ are our *only* information about the function $f(x)$, then we can say *nothing* about the error $e_n(\bar{x}) = f(\bar{x}) - p_n(\bar{x})$ at a point $\bar{x} \neq x_0, \ldots, x_n$; that is, the error may be "very large" or may be "very small." [*Hint:* Consider interpolation at $x_0, x_1, \ldots, x_n$ to the function $f(x) = K(x - x_0) \cdots (x - x_n)$, where K is an unknown constant.] What does this imply about programs like the FUNCTION TABLE in Sec. 2.4 or Algorithm 2.4?

2.5-4 Use (2.18) to give a *lower* bound on the interpolation error $|f(\bar{x}) - p_n(\bar{x})|$ when $f(x) = \ln x$, $n = 3$, $x_0 = 1$, $x_1 = \frac{4}{3}$, $x_2 = \frac{5}{3}$, $x_3 = 2$, and $\bar{x} = \frac{3}{2}$.

2.6 INTERPOLATION IN A FUNCTION TABLE BASED ON EQUALLY SPACED POINTS

Much of engineering and scientific calculation uses functions such as $\sin x$, e^x, $J_n(x)$, $\text{erf}(x)$, etc., which are defined by an infinite series, or as the solution of a certain differential equation, or by similar processes involving limits, and can therefore, in general, not be evaluated in a finite number of steps. Computer installations provide subroutines for the evaluation of such functions which use approximations to these functions either by polynomials or by ratios of polynomials. But before the advent of high-speed computers, the only tool for the use of such functions in calculations was the *function table*. Such a table contains function values $f(x_i)$ for certain points $x_0, \ldots, x_n$, and the user has to interpolate (literally, "polish by filling in the cracks," therefore also "falsify") the given values whenever the value of $f(x)$ at a point not already listed is desired. Polynomial interpolation was initially developed to facilitate this process. Since in such tables $f(x)$ is given at a usually increasing sequence of *equally spaced* points, certain simplifications in the calculation of the interpolating polynomial can be made, which we discuss in this section.

Throughout this section, we assume that $f(x)$ **is tabulated for** $x = a(h)b$; that is, we have the numbers $f(x_i)$, $i = 0, \ldots, N$, available, where

$$x_i = a + ih \qquad i = 0, \ldots, N, \text{ with } N = \frac{b - a}{h} \tag{2.19}$$

It is convenient to introduce a linear change of variables

$$s = s(x) = \frac{x - x_0}{h} \qquad \text{so that} \qquad x = x(s) = x_0 + sh \tag{2.20}$$

and to abbreviate

$$f(x) = f(x_0 + sh) = f_s \tag{2.21}$$

This has the effect of standardizing the situation to one where $f(x)$ is known at the first $N + 1$ nonnegative integers, thus simplifying notation. It should be noted that the *linear* change of variables (2.20) carries polynomials of degree n in x into polynomials of degree n in s.

To calculate the polynomial of degree $\leq n$ which interpolates $f(x)$ at $x_k, \ldots, x_{k+n}$, we need not calculate in this case a *divided-difference* table. Rather, it is sufficient to calculate a *difference* table. To make this precise, we introduce the **forward difference** .

$$\Delta^i f_s = \begin{cases} f_s & i = 0 \\ \Delta(\Delta^{i-1} f_s) = \Delta^{i-1} f_{s+1} - \Delta^{i-1} f_s & i > 0 \end{cases} \qquad (2.22)$$

The forward difference is related to the divided difference in the following way.

Lemma 2.3 For all $i \geq 0$

$$f[x_k, \ldots, x_{k+i}] = \frac{1}{i! h^i} \Delta^i f_k \qquad (2.23)$$

Since both sides of (2.23) are defined by induction on i, the proof of Lemma 2.3 has to be by induction. For $i = 0$, (2.23) merely asserts the validity of the conventions

$$f[x_k] = f(x_k) = f_k = \Delta^0 f_k$$

and is therefore true. Assuming (2.23) to hold for $i = n \geq 0$, we have

$$f[x_k, \ldots, x_{k+n+1}] = \frac{f[x_{k+1}, \ldots, x_{k+n+1}] - f[x_k, \ldots, x_{k+n}]}{x_{k+n+1} - x_k}$$

$$= \frac{\Delta^n f_{k+1} / (n! h^n) - \Delta^n f_k / (n! h^n)}{(n+1)h}$$

$$= \frac{\Delta^{n+1} f_k}{(n+1)! h^{n+1}}$$

showing (2.23) to hold, then, for $i = n + 1$ too.

With this, the polynomial of degree $\leq n$ interpolating $f(x)$ at $x_k, \ldots, x_{k+n}$ becomes

$$p_n(x) = \sum_{i=0}^{n} \frac{1}{i! h^i} \Delta^i f_k \prod_{j=0}^{i-1} (x - x_{k+j}) \qquad (2.24)$$

In terms of s, we have

$$x - x_{k+j} = x_0 + sh - [x_0 + (k+j)h] = (s - k - j)h$$

Hence

$$p_n(x) = p_n(x_0 + sh) = \sum_{i=0}^{n} \Delta^i f_k \prod_{j=0}^{i-1} \frac{s - k - j}{j + 1}$$

A final definition shortens this expression still further. For real y and for i a nonnegative integer, we define the **binomial function**

$$\binom{y}{i} = \begin{cases} 1 & i = 0 \\ \displaystyle\prod_{j=0}^{i-1} \frac{y-j}{j+1} = \frac{(y)(y-1)\cdots(y-i+1)}{1\cdot 2\cdots i} & i > 0 \end{cases} \quad (2.25)$$

The word "binomial" is justified, since (2.25) is just the binomial coefficient $\binom{y}{i}$ whenever y is an integer. With this, (2.24) takes the simple form

$$p_n(x_0 + sh) = \sum_{i=0}^{n} \Delta^i f_k \binom{s-k}{i}$$

$$= f_k + (s-k)\Delta f_k + \frac{(s-k)(s-k-1)}{2}\Delta^2 f_k$$

$$+ \cdots + \frac{(s-k)\cdots(s-k-n+1)}{n!}\Delta^n f_k \quad (2.26)$$

which goes under the name of **Newton forward-difference formula** for the polynomial of degree $\leq n$ which interpolates $f(x)$ at $x_k + ih$, $i = 0, \ldots, n$.

If in (2.26) we set $k = 0$, which is customary, the Newton forward-difference formula becomes

$$\boxed{p_n(x_0 + sh) = \sum_{i=0}^{n} \Delta^i f_0 \binom{s}{i}} \quad (2.27)$$

If s is an integer between zero and n, then this formula reads

$$f_s = p_n(x_0 + sh) = \sum_{j=0}^{n} \binom{s}{j}\Delta^j f_0 = \sum_{j=0}^{s} \binom{s}{j}\Delta^j f_0 \quad (2.28)$$

The striking similarity with the binomial theorem

$$(a + b)^s = \sum_{j=0}^{s} \binom{s}{j} a^j b^{s-j}$$

is not accidental. If we introduce the **forward-shift** operator

$$E f_i = f_{i+1} \quad \text{all } i$$

then we can write $\Delta + 1 = E$, i.e., then

$$(\Delta + 1)f_i = (f_{i+1} - f_i) + f_i = f_{i+1} = E f_i$$

Therefore

$$f_s = E^s f_0 = (\Delta + 1)^s f_0 = \sum_{j=0}^{s} \binom{s}{j}\Delta^j 1^{s-j} f_0 = \sum_{j=0}^{s} \binom{s}{j}\Delta^j f_0$$

which is (2.28).

We resist the temptation to delve now into the vast operational calculus for differences based on formulas like $\Delta + 1 = E$, but do derive one formula of immediate use. Since $\Delta = E - 1$, we get from the binomial theorem that

$$\Delta^s = (E - 1)^s = \sum_{j=0}^{s} \binom{s}{j} E^j (-1)^{s-j}$$

or

$$\Delta^s f_i = \sum_{j=0}^{s} (-1)^{s-j} \binom{s}{j} f_{i+j} \tag{2.29}$$

The coefficients $\Delta^j f_k$ for (2.26) are conveniently read off a (*forward-*) *difference table* for $f(x)$. Such a table is shown in Fig. 2.4. According to (2.22), each entry is merely the difference between the entry to the left below and the entry to the left above. The differences which appear in (2.27) lie along the diagonal marked ① in Fig. 2.4.

Difference tables are used to check the smoothness of a tabulated function, to detect isolated errors and to decide on the degree of the

Figure 2.4 Forward-difference table.

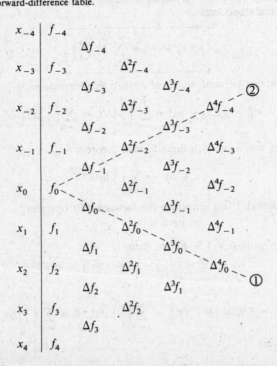

interpolating polynomial appropriate for the table. We illustrate these points in the following example.

Example 2.8 From a book of interplanetary coordinates, we have copied (incorrectly, to make a point) the x coordinate of Mars in a heliocentric coordinate system at the dates given. These coordinates are given at intervals of 10 days, and have been obtained by astronomers by various means. In Fig. 2.5, we have constructed a (forward-) difference table for these data.

The first three differences are of constant sign; hence, the first two are monotone. Third- and higher-order differences show a pronounced oscillatory behavior. If we believe the tabulated function to be smooth, i.e., to be slowly varying, then this behavior of the higher differences must be the effect of error.

Suppose the error in the ith function value is ε_i, all i. Then the table in Fig. 2.5 contains the numbers $\Delta^s(f_i + \varepsilon_i)$ and these differ from the supposedly slowly varying correct numbers $\Delta^s f_i$ by the amount $\Delta^s \varepsilon_i$. From (2.29), we have

$$\Delta^s \varepsilon_i = \sum_{j=0}^{s} \binom{s}{j}(-1)^{s-j}\varepsilon_{i+j} \tag{2.30}$$

and so

$$|\Delta^s \varepsilon_i| \le \sum_{j=0}^{s} \binom{s}{j}|\varepsilon_{i+j}| \le \varepsilon \sum_{j=0}^{s} \binom{s}{j} = \varepsilon(1+1)^s = \varepsilon 2^s$$

with $\varepsilon := \max_j |\varepsilon_j|$. If the tabulated values are accurately rounded values, then $\varepsilon \le 0.000005$ and the errors in the fourth differences should therefore be no bigger than 8 units in the last place. Yet the errors are much larger if we ascribe the oscillatory behavior to error.

Figure 2.5 Heliocentric, equatorial x coordinate of Mars (somewhat erroneous).

t	$x = f(t)$	Δf	$\Delta^2 f$	$\Delta^3 f$	$\Delta^4 f$	$\Delta^5 f$	$\Delta^6 f$
1,250.5	1.39140						
		−1444					
1,260.5	1.37696		−1469				
		−2913		55			
1,270.5	1.34783		−1414		−3		
		−4327		52		97	
1,280.5	1.30456		−1362		94		−302
		−5689		146		−205	
1,290.5	1.24767		−1216		−111		408
		−6905		35		203	
1,300.5	1.17862		−1181		92		−311
		−8086		127		−108	
1,310.5	1.09776		−1054		−16		128
		−9140		111		20	
1,320.5	1.00636		−943		4		
		−10083		115			
1,330.5	0.90553		−828				
		−10911					
1,340.5	0.79642						

A closer inspection of these fourth differences reveals *systematic* behavior in the oscillations. If we subtract the average value 10 of the column of fourth differences from each entry in that column, then we get the sequence

$$-13 \quad 84 \quad -121 \quad 82 \quad -26 \quad -6$$

whose pattern suggests to the experienced that a mistake of about 20 units in the last place was committed in the table entry corresponding to the -121 above, i.e., in the entry 1.24767, for $t = 1,290.5$. Indeed, a solitary change by -20 units in the last place of that entry would change the column of fourth differences by

$$-20 \quad 80 \quad -120 \quad 80 \quad -20 \quad 0$$

according to (2.30), and thus account for essentially all the oscillations in that column.

To summarize: Isolated errors in a function table are signaled by systematic oscillations in the higher differences. By comparing these oscillations around the (local) average with those generated by a single error according to (2.30), an estimate of the error can be made and the table corrected.

Figure 2.6 Heliocentric, equatorial x coordinate of Mars.

t	$x = f(t)$	Δf	$\Delta^2 f$	$\Delta^3 f$	$\Delta^4 f$	$\Delta^5 f$	$\Delta^6 f$
1,250.5	1.39140						
		-1444					
1,260.5	1.37696		-1469				
		-2913		55			
1,270.5	1.34783		-1414		17		
		-4327		72		-3	
1,280.5	1.30456		-1342		14		-2
		-5669		86		-5	
1,290.5	⌐1.24787		-1256		9		8
		-6925		95		3	
1,300.5	1.17862		-1161		12		-11
		-8086		107		-8	
1,310.5	1.09776		-1054		4		8
		-9140		111		0	
1,320.5	1.00636		-943		4		
		-10083		115			
1,330.5	0.90553		-828				
		-10911					
1,340.5	0.79642						

In our example, correction of $f(1,290.5)$ to 1.24787 produces the difference table in Fig. 2.6. Now even the fourth differences are of one sign. The fifth differences oscillate, but they are smaller in size than the maximum error of $16 = 2^5/2$ units possible because of rounding in the function values. We conclude that the fifth differences consist essentially of noise due to the rounding in the function values and that interpolation by a fourth-degree polynomial should give satisfactory (and defensible) results.

Because of the former importance of function tables, a rather large body of material concerning interpolation in function tables has been developed over the centuries. Difference operators other than the forward-difference operator Δ (such as the forward shift E) have been introduced to provide a compact notation for various forms for the interpolating polynomial, all of which differ only in the order in which interpolation points appear. These forms have been associated with the names of Newton, Gauss, Bessel, Stirling, Gregory, Everett, etc., often by tradition rather than by historical fact. A complete treatment of these forms can be found in Hildebrand [5].

We choose not to discuss these forms. We feel that Algorithm 2.4 and the FORTRAN subprogram TABLE discussed in Sec. 2.4 are sufficient equipment for the few occasions the student is likely to make use of tables.

EXERCISES

2.6-1 Prove that a solitary error in a function table leaves the average of the first few difference columns unchanged.

2.6-2 The values of $f(x)$ given below are those of a certain polynomial of degree 4. Form a difference table, and from this table find $f(5)$. (See Exercise 2.6-6.)

x	0	1	2	3	4
$f(x)$	1	5	31	121	341

2.6-3 Form a difference table for the following data, and estimate the degree of the interpolating polynomial needed to produce interpolated values correct to the number of significant figures given.

x	$f(x)$
1.0	1.5709
2.0	1.5713
3.0	1.5719
4.0	1.5727
5.0	1.5738
6.0	1.5751
7.0	1.5767
8.0	1.5785
9.0	1.5805

2.6-4 Using the difference table in Fig. 2.6 find
 (a) $f(1252.5)$ (b) $f(1332.5)$
In each case estimate the error.

2.6-5 Prove that if $p_n(x)$ is a polynomial of degree n with leading coefficient a_n, and x_0 is an arbitrary point, then

$$\Delta^n p_n(x_0) = a_n n! h^n$$

and
$$\Delta^{n+1}p_n(x_0) = 0$$

[*Hint:* Use the definition (2.22) of the forward-difference operator Δ. Else, use Lemma 2.1 and (2.17).]

2.6-6 Let $x_i = x_0 + ih$, $i = 0, 1, 2, \ldots$, and assume that you know the numbers $\Delta^0 p_n(x_n)$, $\Delta^1 p_n(x_{n-1}), \ldots, \Delta^n p_n(x_0)$ for a certain polynomial $p_n(x)$ of degree $\leq n$. Show how to get from this information the values $p_n(x_{n+1})$, $p_n(x_{n+2}), \ldots$, using just n additions per value. [*Hint:* By Exercise 2.6-5, $\Delta^n p_n(x_i)$ does not depend on i, while for all i, j, $\Delta^j p_n(x_i) = \Delta^j p_n(x_{i-1}) + \Delta^{j+1} p_n(x_{i-1})$, by definition of the forward difference.] This method is useful for graphing polynomials. What is its connection with Algorithm 2.1?

2.6-7 Make what simplifications you can in the Lagrange form of the interpolating polynomial when the data points are equally spaced.

2.6-8 Derive the Newton backward-difference formula

$$p_n(x_0 + sh) = \sum_{i=0}^{n} (-)^i \Delta^i f_{-i} \cdot \binom{-s}{i}$$

for use near the right end of a table. It uses the differences along the diagonal marked ② in Fig. 2.4.

*2.7 THE DIVIDED DIFFERENCE AS A FUNCTION OF ITS ARGUMENTS AND OSCULATORY INTERPOLATION

We have so far dealt with divided differences only in their role as coefficients in the Newton form for the interpolating polynomial, i.e., as constants to be calculated from the given numbers $f(x_i)$, $i = 0, \ldots, n$. But the appearance of the *function* $g_n(x) = f[x_0, x_1, \ldots, x_n, x]$ in the error term (2.18) for polynomial interpolation makes it necessary to understand how the divided difference $f[x_0, \ldots, x_k]$ behaves as one or all of the points $x_0, \ldots, x_k$ vary.

We begin by extending the definition of the kth divided difference $f[x_0, \ldots, x_k]$ to all choices of $x_0, \ldots, x_k$; i.e., we drop the requirement that the points $x_0, \ldots, x_k$ be pairwise distinct. Since, to recall, the kth divided difference $f[x_0, \ldots, x_k]$ of f at the points $x_0, \ldots, x_k$ is defined as the leading coefficient (i.e., the coefficient of x^k) in the polynomial $p_k(x)$ of degree $\leq k$ which agrees with $f(x)$ at the $k + 1$ points $x_0, \ldots, x_k$, we must then explain what we mean by the phrase "$p_k(x)$ agrees with $f(x)$ at the points $x_0, \ldots, x_k$," in case some of these points coincide.

Here is our definition of that phrase. We say that **the two functions** $f(x)$ **and** $g(x)$ **agree at the points** $x_0, \ldots, x_k$ in case

$$f^{(j)}(z) = g^{(j)}(z) \qquad \text{for } j = 0, 1, \ldots, m - 1$$

for every point z which occurs m times in the sequence $x_0, \ldots, x_k$. In effect, $f(x)$ and $g(x)$ agree at the points $x_0, \ldots, x_k$ if their difference has the zeros $x_0, \ldots, x_k$, counting multiplicity (see Sec. 2.1).

Example $f(x)$ and $g(x)$ agree at the points 2, 1, 2, 4, 2, 5, 4 in case

$$f(1) = g(1), \quad f(2) = g(2), \quad f'(2) = g'(2), \quad f''(2) = g''(2)$$
$$f(4) = g(4), \quad f'(4) = g'(4), \quad f(5) = g(5)$$

The Taylor polynomial

$$\hat{p}_n(x) = \sum_{j=0}^{n} f^{(j)}(c)(x - c)^j / j! \tag{2.31}$$

agrees with $f(x)$ at the point c $n + 1$ times, according to this definition.

For
$$(d/dx)^i (x - c)^j |_{x=c} = \left\{ \begin{array}{ll} j! & i = j \\ 0 & i \neq j \end{array} \right\}$$

and therefore

$$\hat{p}_n^{(i)}(c) = f^{(i)}(c) \qquad i = 0, \ldots, n$$

One speaks of **osculatory interpolation** whenever the interpolating polynomial has higher than first-order contact with $f(x)$ at an interpolation point (*osculum* is the Latin word for "kiss").

It does make good sense to talk about *the* polynomial of degree $\leq k$ which agrees with a given function $f(x)$ at $k + 1$ points since, by the corollary to Lemma 2.2 (in Sec. 2.1), two polynomials of degree $\leq k$ which agree at $k + 1$ points (distinct or not, but counting multiplicity) must be identical. If this interpolating polynomial $p_k(x)$ of degree $\leq k$ to $f(x)$ at $x_0, \ldots, x_k$ exists, then its leading coefficient is, by definition, the kth divided difference $f[x_0, \ldots, x_k]$, hence

$$p(x) = p_k(x) - f[x_0, \ldots, x_k](x - x_0) \cdots (x - x_{k-1})$$

is a polynomial of degree $\leq k - 1$. Since $(x - x_0) \cdots (x - x_{k-1})$ agrees with the zero function at $x_0, \ldots, x_{k-1}$, it follows that $p(x)$ agrees at $x_0, \ldots, x_{k-1}$ with $p_k(x)$, hence with $f(x)$, i.e., $p(x)$ must be *the* polynomial of degree $\leq k - 1$ which agrees with $f(x)$ at $x_0, \ldots, x_{k-1}$. Induction on n therefore establishes the Newton formula

$$p_n(x) = \sum_{j=0}^{n} f[x_0, \ldots, x_j] \prod_{i=0}^{j-1} (x - x_i) \tag{2.32}$$

for the polynomial of degree $\leq n$ which agrees with $f(x)$ at $x_0, \ldots, x_n$. This formula is, of course, indistinguishable from the formula (2.10), which is the whole point of this section.

Finally, we should like to make certain that, for every choice of interpolation points $x_0, \ldots, x_k$ and function $f(x)$, there exists a polynomial of degree $\leq k$ which agrees with the function $f(x)$ at these points. This we cannot guarantee, for $f(x)$ may not have as many derivatives as we are required to match by the coincidences among the x_i's. But, if $f(x)$ has enough derivatives, then we can prove the existence of the interpolating polynomial $p_k(x)$ by induction on k and gain a useful formula [essentially (2.12) again] for the divided difference in the bargain.

Theorem 2.4 If $f(x)$ has m continuous derivatives and no point occurs in the sequence $x_0, \ldots, x_n$ more than $m + 1$ times, then there exists exactly one polynomial $p_n(x)$ of degree $\leq n$ which agrees with $f(x)$ at $x_0, \ldots, x_n$.

For the proof of existence, we may as well assume that the sequence of interpolation points is nondecreasing,

$$x_0 \leq \cdots \leq x_n$$

For $n = 0$, there is nothing to prove. Assume the statement correct for $n = k - 1$ and consider it for $n = k$. There are two cases.

Case $x_0 = x_k$. Then $x_0 = \cdots = x_k$ and we must have $m \geq k$, by assumption; i.e., $f(x)$ has at least k continuous derivatives. Then the Taylor polynomial $\hat{p}_k(x)$ for $f(x)$ around the center $c = x_0$ does the job, as already remarked earlier; see (2.31). Note that its leading coefficient is the number $f^{(k)}(x_0)/k!$, thus

$$f[x_0, \ldots, x_k] = f^{(k)}(x_0)/k! \qquad \text{if } x_0 = x_1 = \cdots = x_k \qquad (2.33)$$

Case $x_0 < x_k$. Then, by induction hypothesis, we can find a polynomial $p_{k-1}(x)$ of degree $\leq k - 1$ which agrees with $f(x)$ at $x_0, \ldots, x_{k-1}$, and a polynomial $q_{k-1}(x)$ of degree $\leq k - 1$ which agrees with $f(x)$ at $x_1, \ldots, x_k$. The polynomial

$$p_k(x) = \frac{x - x_0}{x_k - x_0} q_{k-1}(x) + \frac{x_k - x}{x_k - x_0} p_{k-1}(x) \qquad (2.34)$$

is then of degree $\leq k$, and we claim that it is the required polynomial; i.e., $p_k(x)$ agrees with $f(x)$ at $x_0, \ldots, x_k$. We have

$$p_k^{(j)}(x) = \frac{x - x_0}{x_k - x_0} q_{k-1}^{(j)}(x) + \frac{x_k - x}{x_k - x_0} p_{k-1}^{(j)}(x) + j \frac{q_{k-1}^{(j-1)}(x) - p_{k-1}^{(j-1)}(x)}{x_k - x_0}$$

$$(2.35)$$

Suppose $z = x_i = \cdots = x_{i+r}$. If $z = x_0$, then $q_{k-1}^{(j)}(z) = f^{(j)}(z) = p_{k-1}^{(j)}(z)$ for $j = 0, \ldots, r - 1$, and also $p_{k-1}^{(r)}(z) = f^{(r)}(z)$ (since $z < x_k$), thus from (2.35),

$$p_k^{(j)}(z) = 0 \cdot q_{k-1}^{(j)}(z) + f^{(j)}(z) + j[f^{(j-1)}(z) - f^{(j-1)}(z)]/(x_k - x_0)$$

$$= f^{(j)}(z) \qquad \text{for } j = 0, \ldots, r$$

The argument for the case $z = x_k$ is analogous. Finally, if $z \neq x_0, x_k$, then $q_{k-1}^{(j)}(z) = f^{(j)}(z) = p_{k-1}^{(j)}(z)$ for $j = 0, \ldots, r$ and so, from (2.35),

$$p_k^{(j)}(z) = \frac{z - x_0}{x_k - x_0} f^{(j)}(z) + \frac{x_k - z}{x_k - x_0} f^{(j)}(z) + j \frac{f^{(j-1)}(z) - f^{(j-1)}(z)}{x_k - x_0}$$

$$= f^{(j)}(z) \qquad \text{for } j = 0, \ldots, r$$

This proves the statement for $n = k$.

On comparing leading coefficients on both sides of (2.34), we get again the formula (2.12), i.e.,

$$f\left[x_0, \ldots, x_k\right] = \left(f\left[x_1, \ldots, x_k\right] - f\left[x_0, \ldots, x_{k-1}\right]\right) / \left(x_k - x_0\right)$$

$$\text{if } x_k \neq x_0 \tag{2.36}$$

Having extended the definition of $f[x_0, \ldots, x_k]$ to arbitrary choices of $x_0, \ldots, x_k$, we now consider how $f[x_0, \ldots, x_k]$ depends on these points $x_0, \ldots, x_k$. These considerations will make clear that the extended definition was motivated by continuity considerations.

We begin with the observation that $f[x_0, \ldots, x_k]$ is a *symmetric* function of its arguments; that is, $f[x_0, \ldots, x_k]$ depends only on the numbers $x_0, \ldots, x_k$ and not on the order in which they appear in the argument list. This is obvious since the entire interpolating polynomial $p_k(x)$ does not depend on the order in which we write down the interpolation points. This implies that we may assume without loss that the arguments $x_0, \ldots, x_k$ of $f[x_0, \ldots, x_k]$ are in increasing order whenever it is convenient to do so.

Next we show that $f[x_0, \ldots, x_k]$ is a *continuous* function of its arguments.

Theorem 2.5 Assume that $f(x)$ is n times continuously differentiable on $[a, b]$, and let $y_0, \ldots, y_n$ be points in $[a, b]$, distinct or not. Then
  (i) There exists $\xi \in [\min_i y_i, \max_i y_i]$ such that $f[y_0, \ldots, y_n] = f^{(n)}(\xi)/n!$
  (ii) If, for each r, $x_0^{(r)}, \ldots, x_n^{(r)}$ are $n + 1$ points in $[a, b]$, and $\lim_{r \to \infty} x_i^{(r)} = y_i$, $i = 0, \ldots, n$, then

$$\lim_{r \to \infty} f\left[x_0^{(r)}, \ldots, x_n^{(r)}\right] = f\left[y_0, \ldots, y_n\right]$$

The proof is by induction on n. For $n = 0$, all assertions are trivially true. Assume the statements correct for $n = k - 1$, and consider $n = k$.

We first prove (ii) in case not all $n + 1$ points $y_0, \ldots, y_n$ are the same. Then, assuming without loss that $y_0 \leq \cdots \leq y_n$, we have $y_0 < y_n$ and therefore $x_0^{(r)} < x_n^{(r)}$ for all large r, and so, by (2.36),

$$\lim_{r \to \infty} f\left[x_0^{(r)}, \ldots, x_n^{(r)}\right] = \lim_{r \to \infty} \frac{f\left[x_1^{(r)}, \ldots, x_n^{(r)}\right] - f\left[x_0^{(r)}, \ldots, x_{n-1}^{(r)}\right]}{x_n^{(r)} - x_0^{(r)}}$$

$$= \frac{\lim f\left[x_1^{(r)}, \ldots, x_n^{(r)}\right] - \lim f\left[x_0^{(r)}, \ldots, x_{n-1}^{(r)}\right]}{y_n - y_0}$$

$$= \frac{f\left[y_1, \ldots, y_n\right] - f\left[y_0, \ldots, y_{n-1}\right]}{y_n - y_0}$$

The last equality is by induction hypothesis. But this last expression equals $f[y_0, \ldots, y_n]$, by (2.36), which proves (ii) for this case.

Next, we prove (i). If $y_0 = y_1 = \cdots = y_n$, then (i) is just a restatement of (2.33). Otherwise, we may assume that

$$y_0 \le y_1 \le \cdots \le y_n$$

and then $y_0 < y_n$. But then we may find, for all r, $x_0^{(r)} < \cdots < x_n^{(r)}$ in $[a, b]$ so that $\lim_{r \to \infty} x_i^{(r)} = y_i$, $i = 0, \ldots, n$. By Theorem 2.2, we can find then $\xi^{(r)} \in [x_0^{(r)}, x_n^{(r)}]$ so that

$$f\left[x_0^{(r)}, \ldots, x_n^{(r)}\right] = f^{(n)}(\xi^{(r)})/n! \qquad \text{for } r = 1, 2, 3, \ldots$$

But then, by (ii) just proved for this case,

$$f\left[y_0, \ldots, y_n\right] = \lim_{r \to \infty} f\left[x_0^{(r)}, \ldots, x_n^{(r)}\right] = \lim_{r \to \infty} f^{(n)}(\xi^{(r)})/n!$$
$$= f^{(n)}(\xi)/n!$$

for some $\xi \in [\lim x_0^{(r)}, \lim x_n^{(r)}] = [y_0, y_n]$, by the continuity of $f^{(n)}(x)$, which proves (i).

Finally, to prove (ii) in the case that $y_0 = y_1 = \cdots = y_n$, we now use (i) to conclude the existence of $\xi^{(r)} \in [\min_i x_i^{(r)}, \max_i x_i^{(r)}]$ so that $f[x_0^{(r)}, \ldots, x_n^{(r)}] = f^{(n)}(\xi^{(r)})/n!$ for all r. But then, since $y_0 = \cdots = y_n$ and $\lim x_i^{(r)} = y_i$, all i, we have $\lim \xi^{(r)} = y_0$ and so, with (2.36) and the continuity of $f^{(n)}(x)$,

$$f\left[y_0, \ldots, y_n\right] = f^{(n)}(y_0)/n! = \lim f^{(n)}(\xi^{(r)})/n! = \lim f\left[x_0^{(r)}, \ldots, x_n^{(r)}\right]$$

This proves both (i) and (ii) for $n = k$ and for all choices of $y_0, \ldots, y_n$ in $[a, b]$.

We conclude this section with some interesting consequences of Theorem 2.5. It follows at once that the function

$$g_n(x) = f\left[x_0, \ldots, x_n, x\right]$$

which appears in the error term for polynomial interpolation is defined for all x and is a *continuous* function of x if $f(x)$ is sufficiently smooth. Thus it follows that

$$f(x) = \sum_{i=0}^{n} f\left[x_0, \ldots, x_i\right] \prod_{j=0}^{i-1} (x - x_j) + f\left[x_0, \ldots, x_n, x\right] \prod_{j=0}^{n} (x - x_j)$$

$$(2.37)$$

for all x, and not only for $x \ne x_0, \ldots, x_n$ [see (2.16)], and also for all $x_0, \ldots, x_n$, distinct or not, in case $f(x)$ has enough derivatives.

Further, if $f(x)$ is sufficiently often differentiable, then $g_n(x)$ is differentiable. For by the definition of derivatives,

$$g_n'(x) = \lim_{h \to 0} g_n\left[x, x + h\right]$$

if this limit exists. On the other hand,

$$g_n\left[x, x + h\right] = f\left[x_0, \ldots, x_n, x, x + h\right] \underset{h \to 0}{\to} f\left[x_0, \ldots, x_n, x, x\right]$$

by Theorem 2.5. Hence

$$\frac{d}{dx} f\left[x_0, \ldots, x_n, x\right] = f\left[x_0, \ldots, x_n, x, x\right] \tag{2.38}$$

Finally, it explains our definition of osculatory interpolation as *repeated* interpolation. For it shows that the interpolating polynomial at points $x_0, \ldots, x_n$ converges to the interpolating polynomial at points $y_0, \ldots, y_n$ as $x_i \rightarrow y_i$, all i. Thus, k-fold interpolation at a point is the limiting case as we let k distinct interpolation points coalesce. The student is familiar with this phenomenon in the case $n = 1$ of linear interpolation. In this case, the straight line $p_1(x) = f(x_0) + f[x_0, x_1](x - x_0)$ is a secant to (the graph of) $f(x)$ which goes over into the tangent $\hat{p}_1(x) = f(y) + (x - y)f'(y)$ as both x_0 and x_1 approach the point y, and $\hat{p}_1(x)$ agrees with $f(x)$ in value *and* slope at $x = y$.

Example 2.9 With $f(x) = \ln x$, calculate $f(1.5)$ by cubic interpolation, using $f(1) = 0$, $f(2) = 0.693147, f'(1) = 1, f'(2) = 0.5$.

In this case, the four interpolation points are $y_0 = y_1 = 1$, $y_2 = y_3 = 2$. We calculate

$$f[y_0, y_1] = f'(y_0) = 1 \quad f[y_1, y_2] = 0.693147 \quad f[y_2, y_3] = f'(y_2) = 0.5$$

$$f[y_0, y_1, y_2] = \frac{0.693147 - 1}{2 - 1} = -0.306853$$

$$f[y_1, y_2, y_3] = \frac{0.5 - 0.693147}{2 - 1} = -0.193147$$

$$f[y_0, y_1, y_2, y_3] = \frac{-0.193147 + 0.306853}{2 - 1} = 0.113706$$

The complete divided-difference table is written as follows:

y_i	$f[\ ]$	$f[,]$	$f[,,]$	$f[,,,]$
1	0.0			
		1.0		
1	0.0		-0.306853	
		0.693147		0.113706
2	0.693147		-0.193147	
		0.5		
2	0.693147			

With this

$$p_3(x) = 0. + (1.)(x - 1) + (-0.306853)(x - 1)^2 + (0.113706)(x - 1)^2(x - 2)$$

is the cubic polynomial which agrees with $\ln x$ in value *and* slope at the two points $x = 1$ and $x = 2$. The osculatory character of the approximation of $\ln x$ by $p_3(x)$ is evident from Fig. 2.7. Using Algorithm 2.1 to evaluate $p_3(x)$ at 1.5, we get

$$\ln 1.5 \approx p_3(1.5) = 0.409074$$

With $e_3(x) = f(x) - p_3(x)$ the error, we get from (2.37) and Theorem 2.5(i) the estimate

$$|e_3(1.5)| \leq \frac{1}{4!} \max_{1 \leq \xi \leq 2} |f^{(4)}(\xi)|(1.5 - 1)^2(1.5 - 2)^2 = 0.015625$$

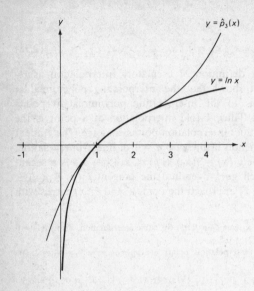

Figure 2.7 Osculatory interpolation.

Since $\ln 1.5 = 0.405465$, the error is actually only 0.00361. This shows once again that the uncertainty about the location of ξ makes error estimates based on (2.18) rather conservative—to put it nicely.

We conclude this section with a FORTRAN program which calculates the coefficients for the Newton form of $p_n(x)$ and then evaluates $p_n(x)$ at a given set of equally spaced points.

```
C   CONSTRUCTION OF THE NEWTON FORM FOR THE POLYNOMIAL OF DEGREE
C   .LE. N , WHICH AGREES WITH  F(X)  AT Y(I), I=1,...,NP1.
C   SOME OR ALL OF THE INTERPOLATION POINTS MAY COINCIDE, SUBJECT
C   ONLY TO THE FOLLOWING RESTRICTIONS.
C   (1) IF  Y(I) = Y(I+K),   THEN  Y(I) = Y(I+1) = ... = Y(I+K) .
C   (2) IF ALSO  Y(I-1) .NE. Y(I) , OR IF   I = 1 , THEN
C       F(I+J) = VALUE OF J-TH DERIVATIVE OF  F(X)  AT  X = Y(J),
C                                                   J=0,...,K.
C
      INTEGER I,J,K,N,NPOINT,NP1
      REAL DX,DY,F(30),FLAST,PNOFX,REALK,X,Y(30)
      READ 500,NP1,(Y(I),F(I),I=1,NP1)
  500 FORMAT(I2/(2F10.3))
C              CONSTRUCT DIVIDED DIFFERENCES
      N = NP1 - 1
      DO 10 K=1,N
         REALK = K
         FLAST = F(1)
         DO 9 I=1,NP1-K
            DY = Y(I+K) - Y(I)
            IF (DY .EQ. 0.) THEN
               F(I) = F(I+1)/REALK
            ELSE
               F(I) = (F(I+1) - FLAST)/DY
               FLAST = F(I+1)
            END IF
    9    CONTINUE
```

```
           F(NP1-K+1) = FLAST
    10 CONTINUE
C          CALCULATE PN(X) FOR VARIOUS VALUES OF X.
        READ 501,NPOINT,X,DX
   501 FORMAT(I3/2F10.3)
        DO 30 J=1,NPOINT
           PNOFX = F(1)
           DO 29 I=2,NP1
              PNOFX = F(I) + (X - Y(I))*PNOFX
    29     CONTINUE
           PRINT 629,J,X,PNOFX
   629     FORMAT(I10,2E20.7)
           X = X + DX
    30 CONTINUE
                                    STOP
        END
```

The calculation of divided differences corresponds to Algorithm 2.3 if all interpolation points are distinct. If some interpolation points coincide, the input must contain values of derivatives of the interpolant. Specifically, the input is assumed to consist of the array of interpolation points $Y(I)$, $I = 1, \ldots, NP1 = n + 1$, together with an array of numbers $F(I)$, $I = 1, \ldots, NP1$. For simplicity of programming, the sequence of interpolation points is assumed to satisfy the restriction that

$$\text{if } Y(I) = Y(I + K), \text{ then } Y(I) = Y(I + 1) = \cdots = Y(I + K)$$

i.e., all repeated interpolation points appear together. With this restriction, it is further assumed that, for each I,

$$F(I) = f^{(j)}(Y(I)) \quad \text{if} \quad Y(I) = Y(I - j) \neq Y(I - j - 1)$$

Thus, with $f(x) = 1/x$, $n = 6$, the following input would be correct, in the sense that it would produce the polynomial of degree ≤ 6, which interpolates $f(x) = 1/x$ at the given $Y(I)$, $I = 1, \ldots, 7$.

I	1	2	3	4	5	6	7
Y(I)	2.	2.	2.	1.	4.	4.	5.
F(I)	0.5	−0.25	0.25	1.	0.25	−0.0625	0.2

The student is encouraged to take an example like this and trace through the calculations in the FORTRAN program. The following flow chart describing the calculations of the divided differences might help in this endeavor.

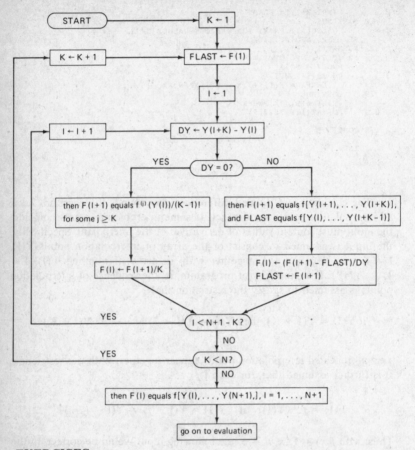

EXERCISES

2.7-1 For $f(x) = e^x$ calculate $f(0.5)$, using quadratic interpolation, given that $f(0) = 1$, $f'(0) = 1$, $f(1) = 2.7183$. Compare with the correctly rounded result $f(0.5) = 1.6487$.

2.7-2 For $f(x) = \sinh x$ we are given that

$$f(0) = 0 \qquad f'(0) = 1 \qquad f(1) = 1.1752 \qquad f'(1) = 1.5431$$

Form a divided-difference table and calculate $f(0.5)$ using cubic interpolation. Compare the result with $\sinh 0.5 = 0.5211$.

2.7-3 A function $f(x)$ has a double zero at z_1 and a triple zero at z_2. Determine the form of the polynomial of degree ≤ 5 which interpolates $f(x)$ twice at z_1, three times at z_2, and once at some point z_3.

2.7-4 Find the coefficients a_0, a_1, a_2, a_3 for the cubic polynomial $p_3(x) = a_0 + a_1(x - y) + a_2(x - y)^2 + a_3(x - y)^3$, so that

$$p_3(y) = f_y \qquad p_3'(y) = f_y' \qquad p_3(z) = f_z \qquad p_3'(z) = f_z'$$

where $y, z, f_y, f_y', f_z, f_z'$ are given numbers (and $y \neq z$).

2.7-5 Get a simple expression for $p_3[(y + z)/2]$ in terms of the given numbers $y, z, f_y, f'_y, f_z, f'_z$, where $p_3(x)$ is the polynomial determined in Exercise 2.7-4.

2.7-6 Let $f(x)$ and $g(x)$ be smooth functions. Prove that $f(x)$ agrees with $g(x)$ k-fold at the point $x = c$ if and only if $f(x) = g(x) + \mathcal{O}(|x - c|^k)$ for x near c.

2.7-7 Let $g(x) = f[x_0, \ldots, x_k, x]$. Prove that

$$g[y_0, \ldots, y_n] = f[x_0, \ldots, x_k, y_0, \ldots, y_n]$$

(use induction).

2.7-8 Use Exercise 2.7-7 to prove that if $g(x) = f[x_0, \ldots, x_k, x]$, then

$$n + 1 \text{ times}$$
$$g^{(n)}(x) = n! f[x_0, \ldots, x_k, \overbrace{x, \ldots, x}]$$

2.7-9 Let $f(x) = g(x)h(x)$. Prove that

$$f[x_0, \ldots, x_k] = \sum_{i=0}^{k} g[x_0, \ldots, x_i] h[x_i, \ldots, x_k]$$

(use induction; else identify the right side as the leading coefficient of a polynomial of degree $\leq k$ which interpolates $g(x)h(x)$ at $x_0, \ldots, x_k$). What well known calculus formula do you obtain from this in case $x_0 = \cdots = x_k$?

THE SOLUTION OF NONLINEAR EQUATIONS

One of the most frequently occurring problems in scientific work is to find the roots of equations of the form

$$f(x) = 0 \qquad (3.1)$$

i.e., zeros of the function $f(x)$. The function $f(x)$ may be given explicitly, as, for example, a polynomial in x or as a transcendental function. Frequently, however, $f(x)$ may be known only implicitly; i.e., a rule for evaluating $f(x)$ for any argument may be known, but its explicit form is unknown. Thus $f(x)$ may represent the value which the solution of a differential equation assumes at a specified point, while x may represent an initial condition of the differential equation. In rare cases it may be possible to obtain the exact roots of (3.1), an illustration of this being a factorable polynomial. In general, however, we can hope to obtain only approximate solutions, relying on some computational technique to produce the approximation. Depending on the context, "approximate solution" may then mean either a point x^*, for which (3.1) is "approximately satisfied," i.e., for which $|f(x^*)|$ is "small," or a point x^* which is "close to" a solution of (3.1). Unfortunately the concept of an "approximate solution" is rather fuzzy. An approximate solution obtained on a computer will almost always be in error due to roundoff or instability or to the particular arithmetic used. Indeed there may be many "approximate solutions" which are equally valid even though the required solution is unique.

To illustrate the uncertainties in root finding we exhibit below in Fig. 3.1 a graph of the function

$$P_6(x) = (1 - x)^6 = 1 - 6x + 15x^2 - 20x^3 + 15x^5 - 6x^5 + x^6$$

This function has of course the single zero $x = 1$. A FORTRAN program was written to evaluate $P_6(x)$ in its expanded form. This program was used to evaluate $P_6(x)$ at a large number of points $x_1 < x_2 < \cdots < x_N$ near $x = 1$ on a CDC 6500 computer. A Calcomp plotter was then used to produce the piecewise straight-line graph presented in Fig. 3.1. From the graph we see that $P_6(x)$ has many apparent zeros since it has many sign changes. These apparent zeros range from 0.994 to 1.006. Thus use of the expanded form of $P_6(x)$ to estimate the zero at $x = 1$ leads to apparently acceptable estimates which are correct to only 2 decimal digits, even though the CDC 6500 works in 14-digit floating-point arithmetic. The reason for this behavior can be traced to round-off error and significant-digit cancellation in the FORTRAN calculation of $P_6(x)$. This example illustrates some of the dangers in root finding.

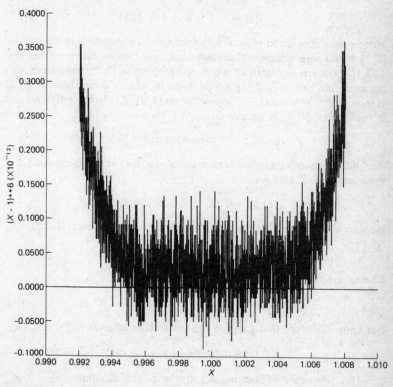

Figure 3.1

In the remainder of this chapter we shall consider various iterative methods for finding approximations to simple roots of (3.1). Special attention will be given to polynomial equations because of their importance in engineering applications.

3.1 A SURVEY OF ITERATIVE METHODS

In this section, we introduce some elementary iterative methods for finding a solution of the equation

$$f(x) = 0 \qquad (3.1)$$

and illustrate their use by applying them to the simple polynomial equation

$$x^3 - x - 1 = 0 \qquad (3.2)$$

for which $f(x) = x^3 - x - 1$.

For this example, one finds that

$$f(1) = -1 < 0 < 5 = f(2) \qquad (3.3)$$

Hence, since $f(x)$ is continuous, $f(x)$ must vanish somewhere in the interval $[1, 2]$, by the intermediate-value theorem for continuous functions (see Sec. 1.7). If $f(x)$ were to vanish at two or more points in $[1, 2]$, then, by Rolle's theorem (see Sec. 1.7), $f'(x)$ would have to vanish somewhere in $[1, 2]$. Hence, since $f'(x) = 3x^2 - 1$ is positive on $[1, 2]$, $f(x)$ has exactly one zero in the interval $[1, 2]$. If we call this zero ξ, then

$$\xi \approx 1.5 \text{ with absolute error } \leq 0.5$$

To find out more about this zero, we evaluate $f(x)$ at the midpoint 1.5 of the interval $[1, 2]$ and get

$$f(1.5) = 0.875 > 0 > -1 = f(1)$$

Hence we now know that the zero ξ lies in the smaller interval $[1, 1.5]$; i.e.,

$$\xi \approx 1.25 \text{ with absolute error } \leq 0.25$$

Checking again at the midpoint 1.25, we find

$$f(1.25) = -0.296 \cdots < 0 < 0.875 = f(1.5)$$

and know therefore that ξ lies in the yet smaller interval $[1.25, 1.5]$; i.e.,

$$\xi \approx 1.375 \text{ with absolute error } \leq 0.125$$

This procedure of locating a solution of the equation $f(x) = 0$ in a sequence of intervals of decreasing size is known as the **bisection** method.

Algorithm 3.1: Bisection method Given a function $f(x)$ continuous on the interval $[a_0, b_0]$ and such that $f(a_0)f(b_0) \leq 0$.

For $n = 0, 1, 2, \ldots,$ until satisfied, do:

> Set $m = (a_n + b_n)/2$
>
> If $f(a_n)f(m) \leq 0$, set $a_{n+1} = a_n$, $b_{n+1} = m$
>
> Otherwise, set $a_{n+1} = m$, $b_{n+1} = b_n$
>
> Then $f(x)$ has a zero in the interval $[a_{n+1}, b_{n+1}]$

We shall frequently state algorithms in the above concise form. For students familiar with the ALGOL language, this notation will appear quite natural. Further, we have used here the phrase "until satisfied" in order to stress that this description of the algorithm is *incomplete*. A user of the algorithm must specify precise termination criteria. These will depend in part on the specific problem to be solved by the algorithm. Some of the many possible termination criteria are discussed in the next section.

At each step of the bisection algorithm 3.1, the length of the interval known to contain a zero of $f(x)$ is reduced by a factor of 2. Hence each step produces one more correct binary digit of the root ξ of $f(x) = 0$. After 20 steps of this algorithm applied to our example and starting as we did with $a_0 = 1$, $b_0 = 2$, one gets

$$1.3247175 \cdots = a_{20} \leq \xi \leq b_{20} = 1.3247184 \cdots$$

$$f(a_{20}) = (-1.857 \cdots)10^{-6} < 0 < (2.209 \cdots)10^{-6} = f(b_{20})$$

Clearly, with enough effort, one can always locate a root to any desired accuracy with this algorithm. But compared with other methods to be discussed, the bisection method converges rather slowly.

One can hope to get to the root faster by using more fully the information about $f(x)$ available at each step. In our example (3.2), we started with the information

$$f(1) = -1 < 0 < 5 = f(2)$$

Since $|f(1)|$ is closer to zero than is $|f(2)|$ the root ξ is likely to be closer to 1 than to 2 [at least if $f(x)$ is "nearly" linear]. Hence, rather than check the midpoint, or average value, 1.5 of 1 and 2, we now check $f(x)$ at the weighted average

$$w = \frac{|f(2)| \cdot 1 + |f(1)| \cdot 2}{|f(2)| + |f(1)|} \tag{3.4}$$

Note that since $f(1)$ and $f(2)$ have opposite sign, we can write (3.4) more simply as

$$w = \frac{f(2) \cdot 1 - f(1) \cdot 2}{f(2) - f(1)} \tag{3.5}$$

This gives for our example

$$w = \frac{5 \cdot 1 + 1 \cdot 2}{6} = 1.166666 \cdots$$

and

$$f(w) = -0.578703 \cdots < 0 < 5 = f(2)$$

Hence ξ lies in $[1.166666 \cdots, 2]$. Repeating the process for this interval, we get

$$w = \frac{5 \cdot (1.166666 \cdots) + (0.578703 \cdots) \cdot 2}{5.578703 \cdots} = 1.253112 \cdots$$

$$f(w) = -0.285363 \cdots < 0 < 5 = f(2)$$

Consequently, $f(x)$ has a zero in the interval $[1.253112 \cdots, 2]$. This algorithm is known as the **regula falsi**, or **false-position**, method.

> **Algorithm 3.2: Regula falsi** Given a function $f(x)$ continuous on the interval $[a_0, b_0]$ and such that $f(a_0)f(b_0) < 0$.
>
> For $n = 0, 1, 2, \ldots$, until satisfied, do:
>
> Calculate $w = [f(b_n)a_n - f(a_n)b_n]/[f(b_n) - f(a_n)]$
>
> If $f(a_n)f(w) \leq 0$, set $a_{n+1} = a_n$, $b_{n+1} = w$
>
> Otherwise, set $a_{n+1} = w$, $b_{n+1} = b_n$

After 16 steps of this algorithm applied to our example and starting as we did with $a_0 = 1$, $b_0 = 2$, one gets

$$1.3247174 \cdots = a_{16} \leq \xi \leq b_{16} = 2$$

$$f(a_{16}) = (-1.95 \cdots)10^{-6} < 0 < 5 = f(b_{16})$$

Hence, although the regula falsi produces a point at which $|f(x)|$ is "small" somewhat faster than does the bisection method, it fails completely to give a "small" interval in which a zero is known to lie.

A glance at Fig. 3.2 shows the reason for this. As one verifies easily, the weighted average

$$w = \frac{f(b_n)a_n - f(a_n)b_n}{f(b_n) - f(a_n)}$$

is the point at which the straight line through the points $\{a_n, f(a_n)\}$ and $\{b_n, f(b_n)\}$ intersects the x axis. Such a straight line is a secant to $f(x)$, and in our example, $f(x)$ is concave upward and increasing (in the interval $[1, 2]$ of interest); hence the secant is always above (the graph of) $f(x)$. Consequently, w always lies to the left of the zero (in our example). If $f(x)$ were concave downward and increasing, w would always lie to the right of the zero.

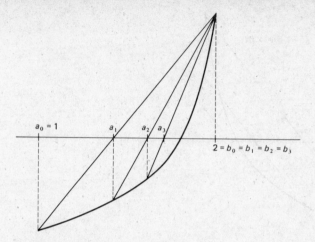

Figure 3.2 Regula falsi.

The regula falsi algorithm can be improved in several ways, two of which we now discuss. The first one, called **modified regula falsi**, replaces secants by straight lines of ever-smaller slope until w falls to the opposite side of the root. This is shown graphically in Fig. 3.3.

Algorithm 3.3: Modified regula falsi Given $f(x)$ continuous on $[a_0, b_0]$ and such that $f(a_0)f(b_0) < 0$.

Set $F = f(a_0)$, $G = f(b_0)$, $w_0 = a_0$

For $n = 0, 1, 2, \ldots$, until satisfied, do:

Calculate $w_{n+1} = (Ga_n - Fb_n)/(G - F)$

If $f(a_n)f(w_{n+1}) \leq 0$, set $a_{n+1} = a_n$, $b_{n+1} = w_{n+1}$, $G = f(w_{n+1})$

If also $f(w_n)f(w_{n+1}) > 0$, set $F = F/2$

Otherwise, set $a_{n+1} = w_{n+1}$, $F = f(w_{n+1})$, $b_{n+1} = b_n$

If also $f(w_n)f(w_{n+1}) > 0$, set $G = G/2$

Then $f(x)$ has a zero in the interval $[a_{n+1}, b_{n+1}]$

If the modified regula falsi is applied to our example with $a_0 = 1$, $b_0 = 2$, then after six steps, one gets

$$1.32471795 \cdots = a_6 \leq \xi \leq b_6 = 1.32471796 \cdots$$

$$f(a_6) = (-1.736 \cdots)10^{-8} < 0 < (1.730 \cdots)10^{-8} = f(b_6)$$

which shows an impressive improvement over the bisection method.

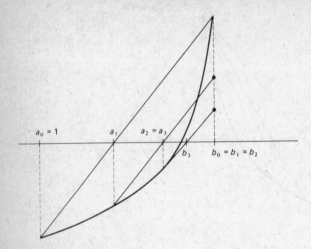

Figure 3.3 Modified regula falsi.

A second, very popular modification of the regula falsi, called the **secant** method, retains the use of secants throughout, but may *give up the* **bracketing** *of the root*.

Algorithm 3.4: Secant method Given a function $f(x)$ and two points x_{-1}, x_0.

For $n = 0, 1, 2, \ldots$, until satisfied, do:

Calculate $x_{n+1} = [f(x_n)x_{n-1} - f(x_{n-1})x_n]/[f(x_n) - f(x_{n-1})]$

If the second method is applied to our example with $x_{-1} = 1$, $x_0 = 2$, then after six steps one gets

$$x_6 = 1.3247179 \cdots, \qquad f(x_6) = (3.458 \cdots)10^{-8}$$

Apparently, the secant method locates quite rapidly a point at which $|f(x)|$ is "small," but gives, in general, no feeling for how far away from a zero of $f(x)$ this point might be. Also, $f(x_n)$ and $f(x_{n-1})$ need not be of opposite sign, so that the expression

$$x_{n+1} = \frac{f(x_n)x_{n-1} - f(x_{n-1})x_n}{f(x_n) - f(x_{n-1})} \tag{3.6}$$

is prone to round-off-error effects. In an extreme situation, we might even have $f(x_n) = f(x_{n-1})$, making the calculation of x_{n+1} impossible. Although this does not cure the trouble, it is better to calculate x_{n+1} from the equivalent expression

$$x_{n+1} = x_n - f(x_n)\frac{x_n - x_{n-1}}{f(x_n) - f(x_{n-1})} \qquad (3.7)$$

in which x_{n+1} is obtained from x_n by adding the "correction term"

$$\frac{-f(x_n)}{[f(x_n) - f(x_{n-1})]/(x_n - x_{n-1})} \qquad (3.8)$$

The student will recognize the ratio $[f(x_n) - f(x_{n-1})]/(x_n - x_{n-1})$ as a first divided difference of $f(x)$ and from (2.10) as the slope of the secant to $f(x)$ through the points $\{x_{n-1}, f(x_{n-1})\}$ and $\{x_n, f(x_n)\}$. Furthermore from (2.17) we see that this ratio is equal to the slope of $f(x)$ at some point between x_{n-1} and x_n if $f(x)$ is differentiable. It would be reasonable therefore to replace this ratio by the value of $f'(x)$ at some point "near" x_n and x_{n-1}, given that $f'(x)$ can be calculated.

If $f(x)$ is differentiable, then on replacing in (3.7) the slope of the secant by the slope of the tangent at x_n, one gets the iteration formula

$$x_{n+1} = x_n - \frac{f(x_n)}{f'(x_n)} \qquad (3.9)$$

of **Newton's** method.

Algorithm 3.5: Newton's method Given $f(x)$ continuously differentiable and a point x_0.

> For $n = 0, 1, 2, \ldots$, until satisfied, do:
> Calculate $x_{n+1} = x_n - f(x_n)/f'(x_n)$

If this algorithm is applied to our example with $x_0 = 1$, then after four steps, one gets

$$x_4 = 1.3247181 \cdots \qquad f(x_4) = (9.24 \cdots)10^{-7}$$

Finally, we mention **fixed-point iteration**, of which Newton's method is a special example. If we set

$$g(x) = x - \frac{f(x)}{f'(x)} \qquad (3.10)$$

then the iteration formula (3.9) for Newton's method takes on the simple form

$$x_{n+1} = g(x_n) \qquad (3.11)$$

If the sequence $x_1, x_2, \cdots$ so generated converges to some point ξ, and $g(x)$ is continuous, then

$$\xi = \lim_{n \to \infty} x_{n+1} = \lim_{n \to \infty} g(x_n) = g\left(\lim_{n \to \infty} x_n\right) = g(\xi) \qquad (3.12)$$

or $\xi = g(\xi)$, that is, ξ is then a fixed point of $g(x)$. Clearly, if ξ is a fixed point of the iteration function $g(x)$ for Newton's method, then ξ is a solution of the equation $f(x) = 0$. Now, for a given equation $f(x) = 0$, it is possible to choose various iteration functions $g(x)$, each having the property that a fixed point of $g(x)$ is a zero of $f(x)$. For each such choice, one may then calculate the sequence $x_1, x_2, \cdots$ by

$$x_{n+1} = g(x_n) \qquad n = 0, 1, 2, \cdots$$

and hope that it converges. If it does, then its limit is a solution of the equation $f(x) = 0$. We discuss fixed-point iteration in more detail in Secs. 3.3 and 3.4.

Example 3.1 The function $f(x) = x - 0.2 \sin x - 0.5$ has exactly one zero between $x_0 = 0.5$ and $x_1 = 1.0$, since $f(0.5)f(1.0) < 0$, while $f'(x)$ does not vanish on $[0.5, 1]$. Locate the zero correct to six significant figures using Algorithms 3.1, 3.3, 3.4, and 3.5.

The following calculations were performed on an IBM 7094 computer in single-precision 27-binary-bit floating-point arithmetic.

	Algorithm 3.1		Algorithm 3.3		Algorithm 3.4	Algorithm 3.5
n	x_n	ε_n	x_n	ε_n	x_n	x_n
-1					1.	
0	0.75	$3 \cdot 10^{-1}$	0.75	$3 \cdot 10^{-1}$	0.5	0.5
1	0.625	$2 \cdot 10^{-1}$	0.80606124	$2 \cdot 10^{-1}$	0.61212248	0.61629718
2	0.5625	$6 \cdot 10^{-2}$	0.61534080	$3 \cdot 10^{-3}$	0.61549349	0.61546820
3	0.59375	$3 \cdot 10^{-2}$	0.61701328	$2 \cdot 10^{-3}$	0.61546816	0.61546816
4	0.609375	$2 \cdot 10^{-2}$	0.61701363	$2 \cdot 10^{-3}$		
5	0.6171875	$8 \cdot 10^{-3}$	0.61546816	0		
6	0.61328125	$4 \cdot 10^{-3}$				
...	....	......				
10	0.61547852	$4 \cdot 10^{-4}$				
...	....	......				
19	0.61546850	$5 \cdot 10^{-7}$				

In Algorithms 3.1 and 3.3, x_n is the midpoint between the lower and the upper bounds, a_n and b_n, after n iterations, while the ε_n gives the corresponding bound on the error in x_n provided by the algorithm. Note the rapid and systematic convergence of Algorithms 3.4 and 3.5. The bisection method converges very slowly but steadily, while the modified regula falsi method seems to converge "in jumps," although it does obtain the correct zero rather quickly.

EXERCISES

3.1-1 Find an interval containing the real positive zero of the function $f(x) = x^2 - 2x - 2$. Use Algorithms 3.1 and 3.2 to compute this zero correct to two significant figures. Can you estimate how many steps each method would require to produce six significant figures?

3.1-2 For the example given in the text, carry out two steps of the modified regula falsi (Algorithm 3.3).

3.1-3 The polynomial $x^3 - 2x - 1$ has a zero between 1 and 2. Using the secant method (Algorithm 3.4), find this zero correct to three significant figures.

3.1-4 In Algorithm 3.1 let M denote the length of the initial interval $[a_0, b_0]$. Let $\{x_0, x_1, x_2, \ldots\}$ represent the successive midpoints generated by the bisection method. Show that

$$|x_{i+1} - x_i| = \frac{M}{2^{i+2}}$$

Also show that the number I of iterations required to guarantee an approximation to a root to an accuracy ε is given by

$$I > -2 - \frac{\log(\varepsilon/M)}{\log 2}$$

3.1-5 The bisection method can be applied whenever $f(a)f(b) < 0$. If $f(x)$ has more than one zero in (a, b), which zero does Algorithm 3.1 usually locate?

3.1-6 With $a = 0$, $b = 1$, each of the following functions changes sign in (a, b), that is, $f(a)f(b) < 0$. What point does the bisection Algorithm 3.1 locate? Is this point a zero of $f(x)$?

$$f(x) = (3x - 1)^{-1} \qquad f(x) = \cos 10x \qquad f(x) = \begin{cases} 1 & x \geq 0.3 \\ -1 & x < 0.3 \end{cases}$$

3.1-7 The function $f(x) = e^{2x} - e^x - 2$ has a zero on the interval $[0, 1]$. Find this zero correct to four significant digits using Newton's method (Algorithm 3.5).

3.1-8 The function $f(x) = 4 \sin x - e^x$ has a zero on the interval $[0, 0.5]$. Find this zero correct to four significant digits using the secant method (Algorithm 3.4).

3.1-9 Using the bisection algorithm locate the smallest positive zero of the polynomial $p(x) = 2x^3 - 3x - 4$ correct to three significant digits.

3.2 FORTRAN PROGRAMS FOR SOME ITERATIVE METHODS

When the algorithms introduced in the preceding section are used in calculations, the vague phrase "until satisfied" has to be replaced by precise termination criteria. In this section, we discuss some of the many possible ways of terminating iteration in a reasonable way and give translations of Algorithms 3.1 and 3.3, into FORTRAN.

FORTRAN SUBROUTINE FOR THE BISECTION ALGORITHM 3.1

```
        SUBROUTINE BISECT ( F, A, B, XTOL, IFLAG )
C****** I N P U T ******
C  F  NAME OF FUNCTION WHOSE ZERO IS SOUGHT. NAME MUST APPEAR IN AN
C       E X T E R N A L  STATEMENT IN THE CALLING PROGRAM.
C  A,B  ENDPOINTS OF THE INTERVAL WHEREIN A ZERO IS SOUGHT.
C  XTOL  DESIRED LENGTH OF OUTPUT INTERVAL.
C****** O U T P U T ******
C  A,B  ENDPOINTS OF INTERVAL KNOWN TO CONTAIN A ZERO OF  F  .
```

```
C   IFLAG   AN INTEGER,
C           = -1, FAILURE SINCE  F  HAS SAME SIGN AT INPUT POINTS A AND B
C           = 0 , TERMINATION SINCE  ABS(A-B)/2 .LE. XTOL
C           = 1 , TERMINATION SINCE  ABS(A-B)/2 IS SO SMALL THAT ADDITION
C               TO  (A+B)/2  MAKES NO DIFFERENCE .
C****** M E T H O D ******
C   THE BISECTION ALGORITHM 3.1 IS USED, IN WHICH THE INTERVAL KNOWN TO
C   CONTAIN A ZERO IS REPEATEDLY HALVED .
C
        INTEGER IFLAG
        REAL A,B,F,XTOL,    ERROR,FA,FM,XM
        FA = F(A)
        IF (FA*F(B) .GT. 0.)  THEN
            IFLAG = -1
            PRINT 601,A,B
  601       FORMAT(' F(X) IS OF SAME SIGN AT THE TWO ENDPOINTS',2E15.7)
                                            RETURN
        END IF
C
        ERROR = ABS(B-A)
C       DO WHILE  ERROR .GT. XTOL
    6   ERROR = ERROR/2.
        IF (ERROR .LE. XTOL)            RETURN
        XM = (A+B)/2.
C                   CHECK FOR UNREASONABLE ERROR REQUIREMENT
        IF (XM + ERROR .EQ. XM) THEN
            IFLAG = 1
                                        RETURN
        END IF
        FM = F(XM)
C               CHOOSE NEW INTERVAL
        IF (FA*FM .GT. 0.) THEN
            A = XM
            FA = FM
        ELSE
            B = XM
        END IF
                                    GO TO 6
        END
```

The following program makes use of this subroutine to find the root of Eq. (3.2), discussed in the preceding section.

```
C  MAIN PROGRAM FOR TRYING OUT BISECTION ROUTINE
      INTEGER IFLAG
      REAL A,B,ERROR,XI
      EXTERNAL FF
      A = 1.
      B = 2.
      CALL BISECT ( FF, A, B, 1.E-6, IFLAG )
      IF (IFLAG .LT. 0)              STOP
      XI = (A+B)/2.
      ERROR = ABS(A-B)/2.
      PRINT 600, XI,ERROR
  600 FORMAT(' THE ZERO IS ',E15.7,' PLUS/MINUS ',E15.7)
                                    STOP
      END
      REAL FUNCTION FF(X)
      REAL X
      FF = -1. - X*(1. - X*X)
      PRINT 600,X,FF
  600 FORMAT(' X, F(X) = ',2E15.7)
                                    RETURN
      END
```

We now comment in some detail on the subroutine BISECT above. We have dropped the subscripts used in Algorithm 3.1. At any stage, the variables A and B contain the current lower and upper bound for the root to be found, the initial values being supplied by the calling program. In particular, the midpoint

$$XM = \frac{A + B}{2}$$

is always the current best estimate for the root, its absolute difference from the root always being bounded by

$$ERROR = \frac{|A - B|}{2}$$

Iteration is terminated once

$$ERROR \leq XTOL$$

where XTOL is a given absolute error bound. The calling program then uses the current value of A and B to estimate the root. In addition to A, B and XTOL, the calling program is also expected to supply the FORTRAN name of the function $f(x)$ whose zero is to be located. Since the assumption that $f(A)$ and $f(B)$ are of opposite sign is essential to the algorithm, there is an initial test for this condition. If $f(A)$ and $f(B)$ are not of opposite sign, the routine immediately terminates. The output variable IFLAG is used to signal this unhappy event to the calling program.

The subroutine never evaluates the given function more than once for the same argument, but rather saves those values which might be needed in subsequent steps. This is a reasonable policy since the routine might well be used for functions whose evaluation is quite costly. Finally, the routine has some protection against an unreasonable error requirement: Suppose, for simplicity, that all calculations are carried out in four-decimal-digit floating-point arithmetic and that the bounds A and B have already been improved to the point that

$$A = 131.6 \quad \text{and} \quad B = 131.7$$

so that

$$ERROR = \frac{B - A}{2} = 0.05$$

Then

$$XM = \frac{A + B}{2} = \frac{263.3}{2} = 131.6, \text{ or } 131.7$$

depending on how rounding to four decimal places is done. In any event,

$$XM = A \quad \text{or} \quad XM = B$$

so that, at the end of this step, neither A nor B has changed. If now the given error tolerance XTOL were less than 0.05, then the routine would never terminate, since $|B - A|/2$ would never decrease below 0.05. To avoid such an infinite loop due to an unreasonable error requirement (unreasonable since it requires the bounds A and B to be closer together than is possible for two floating-point numbers of that precision to be without coinciding), the routine calculates the current value of ERROR as follows. Initially,

$$ERROR = |B - A|$$

At the beginning of each step, ERROR is then halved, since that is the reduction in error per step of the bisection method. The routine terminates, once ERROR is so small that its floating-point addition to the current value of XM does not change XM.

Next we consider the modified regula falsi algorithm 3.3. In contrast to the bisection method, the modified regula falsi is not guaranteed to produce as small an interval containing the root as is possible with the finite-precision arithmetic used (see Exercise 3.2-1). Hence additional termination criteria must be used for this algorithm.

FORTRAN PROGRAM USING THE MODIFIED REGULA FALSI ALGORITHM 3.3

```
         SUBROUTINE MRGFLS ( F, A, B, XTOL, FTOL, NTOL, W, IFLAG )
C******  I N P U T  ******
C   F  NAME OF FUNCTION WHOSE ZERO IS SOUGHT. NAME MUST APPEAR IN AN
C         E X T E R N A L  STATEMENT IN THE CALLING PROGRAM .
C   A,B  ENDPOINTS OF INTERVAL WHEREIN ZERO IS SOUGHT.
C   XTOL  DESIRED LENGTH OF OUTPUT INTERVAL
C   FTOL  DESIRED SIZE OF  F(W)
C   NTOL  NO MORE THAN  NTOL  ITERATION STEPS WILL BE CARRIED OUT.
C******  O U T P U T  ******
C   A,B  ENDPOINTS OF INTERVAL CONTAINING THE ZERO .
C   W   BEST ESTIMATE OF THE ZERO .
C   IFLAG  AN INTEGER,
C      =-1, FAILURE, SINCE  F  HAS SAME SIGN AT INPUT POINTS  A, B .
C      = 0, TERMINATION BECAUSE  ABS(A-B) .LE. XTOL .
C      = 1, TERMINATION BECAUSE  ABS(F(W)) .LE. FTOL .
C      = 2, TERMINATION BECAUSE  NTOL  ITERATION STEPS WERE CARRIED OUT .
C******  M E T H O D  ******
C   THE MODIFIED REGULA FALSI ALGORITHM 3.3 IS USED. THIS MEANS THAT,
C   AT EACH STEP, LINEAR INTERPOLATION BETWEEN THE POINTS   (A,FA)  AND
C   (B,FB)  IS USED, WITH  FA*FB .LT. 0 ,TO GET A NEW POINT  (W,F(W))
C   WHICH REPLACES ONE OF THESE IN SUCH A WAY THAT AGAIN  FA*FB .LT. 0.
C   IN ADDITION, THE ORDINATE OF A POINT STAYING IN THE GAME FOR MORE
C   THAN ONE STEP IS CUT IN HALF AT EACH SUBSEQUENT STEP.
C
         INTEGER IFLAG,NTOL,   N
         REAL A,B,F,FTOL,W,XTOL,    FA,FB,FW,SIGNFA,PRVSFW
         FA = F(A)
         SIGNFA = SIGN(1., FA)
         FB = F(B)
         IF (SIGNFA*FB .GT. 0.) THEN
            PRINT 601,A,B
  601       FORMAT(' F(X) IS OF SAME SIGN AT THE TWO ENDPOINTS',2E15.7)
            IFLAG = -1
                                            RETURN
         END IF
C
         W = A
         FW = FA
         DO 20 N=1,NTOL
```

```
C                        CHECK IF INTERVAL IS SMALL ENOUGH.
      IF (ABS(A-B) .LE. XTOL) THEN
         IFLAG = 0
                                           RETURN
      END IF
C                        CHECK IF FUNCTION VALUE AT  W  IS SMALL ENOUGH .
      IF (ABS(FW) .LE. FTOL) THEN
         IFLAG = 1
                                           RETURN
      END IF
C                        GET NEW GUESS  W   BY LINEAR INTERPOLATION .
      W = (FA*B - FB*A)/(FA - FB)
      PRVSFW = SIGN(1.,FW)
      FW = F(W)
C                               CHANGE TO NEW INTERVAL
      IF (SIGNFA*FW .GT. 0.) THEN
         A = W
         FA = FW
         IF (FW*PRVSFW .GT. 0.)  FB = FB/2.
      ELSE
         B = W
         FB = FW
         IF (FW*PRVSFW .GT. 0.)  FA = FA/2.
      END IF
   20 CONTINUE
      PRINT 620,NTOL
  620 FORMAT(' NO CONVERGENCE IN ',I5,' ITERATIONS')
      IFLAG = 2
                                           RETURN
      END
```

First, the routine terminates if the newly computed function value is no bigger in absolute value than a given tolerance FTOL. This brings in the point of view that an "approximate root" of the equation $f(x) = 0$ is a point x at which $|f(x)|$ is "small." Also, since the routine repeatedly divides by function values, such a termination is necessary in order to avoid, in extreme cases, division by zero.

Second, the routine terminates when more than a given number NTOL of iteration steps have been carried out. In a way, NTOL specifies the amount of computing users are willing to invest in solving their problems. Use of such a termination criterion also protects users against unreasonable error requirements and programming errors, and against the possibility that they have not fully understood the problem they are trying to solve. Hence such a termination criterion should be used with any iterative method.

As in the routine for the bisection method, the subroutine MRGFLS returns an integer IFLAG which indicates why iteration was terminated, and the latest value of the bounds A and B for the desired root. Finally, as with the bisection routine, the routine never evaluates the given function more than once for the same argument.

Algorithms 3.4 and 3.5 for the secant method and Newton's method, respectively, do not necessarily bracket a root. Rather, both generate a sequence $x_0, x_1, x_2, \ldots$, which, so one hopes, converges to the desired root ξ of the given equation $f(x) = 0$. Hence both algorithms should be viewed primarily as finding points at which $f(x)$ is "small" in absolute value; iteration is terminated when the newly computed function value is absolutely less than a given FTOL.

The iteration may also be terminated when successive iterates differ in absolute value by less than a given number XTOL. It is customary therefore to use one or both of the following termination criteria for either the secant or Newton's method:

$$|f(x_n)| \leq \text{FTOL} \quad \text{or} \quad |x_n - x_{n-1}| \leq \text{XTOL} \tag{3.13}$$

If the size of the numbers involved is not known in advance, it is usually better to use *relative* error requirements, i.e., to terminate if

$$\frac{|f(x_n)|}{\text{FSIZE}} \leq \text{FTOL} \quad \text{or} \quad |x_n - x_{n-1}| \leq \text{XTOL}*|x_n| \tag{3.14}$$

where FSIZE is an estimate of the magnitude of $f(x)$ in some vicinity of the root established during the iteration.

In Sec. 1.6 we discussed the danger of concluding that a given sequence has "converged" just because two successive terms in the sequence differ by "very little." Such a criterion is nevertheless commonly used in routines for the secant and Newton methods. For one thing, such a criterion is necessary in the secant method to avoid division by zero. Also, in both methods, the difference between the last two iterates calculated is a rather conservative bound for the error in the most recent iterate once the iterates are "close enough" to the root. To put it naively: If successive iterates do not differ by much, there is little reason to go on iterating. Subroutines for the Newton and secant methods are not included in the text but are left as exercises for the student.

Example 3.2a Find the real positive root of the equation

$$x^3 - x - 1 = 0$$

The results for Algorithms 3.1, 3.3, 3.4, and 3.5 are given in the following table, which parallels the table in Example 3.1.

	Bisection		Modified regula falsi		Secant	Newton
n	x_n	ε_n	x_n	ε_n	x_n	x_n
					1.0	
0	1.5	$5 \cdot 10^{-1}$	1.5	$5 \cdot 10^{-1}$	2.0	1.0
1	1.25	$3 \cdot 10^{-1}$	1.5833333	$4 \cdot 10^{-1}$	1.1666667	1.5
2	1.375	$1 \cdot 10^{-1}$	1.6616541	$3 \cdot 10^{-1}$	1.2531120	1.3478261
3	1.3125	$6 \cdot 10^{-2}$	1.3249256	$2 \cdot 10^{-3}$	1.3372064	1.3252004
4	1.34375	$3 \cdot 10^{-2}$	1.3256293	$9 \cdot 10^{-4}$	1.3238501	1.3247182
5	1.328125	$2 \cdot 10^{-2}$	1.3256305	$9 \cdot 10^{-4}$	1.3247079	1.3247180
6	1.3203125	$8 \cdot 10^{-3}$	1.3247180	$4 \cdot 10^{-9}$	1.3247180	
...	....	......				
10	1.3247070	$5 \cdot 10^{-4}$				
...	....	......				
20	1.3247180	$5 \cdot 10^{-7}$				

Example 3.2b The so-called biasing problem in electronic circuit design requires the solution of an equation of the form $f(v) = 50I(e^{qv} - 1) + v - 20$ where v represents the voltage, I is a measure of current, and q is a parameter relating the electron charge and the absolute temperature. In a typical engineering problem this equation would need to be solved for various values of the parameters I and q to see how the smallest positive zero of $f(v)$ changes as the parameters change.

Using Newton's method find the smallest positive zero of $f(v)$ under two different sets of parameter values $(I, q) = (10^{-8}, 40)$ and $(I, q) = (10^{-6}, 20)$. Set XTOL $= 10^{-8}$ and FTOL $= 10^{-7}$.

The results using the indicated starting values are given below.

$I = 10^{-8}, q = 40$		$I = 10^{-6}, q = 20$	
XN	FXN	XN	FXN
0.35000000	$-1.0486984E + 00$	0.55000000	$1.5436571E + 00$
0.39186072	$1.6002561E + 00$	0.52464183	$3.2740616E - 01$
0.37948785	$3.3539839E - 01$	0.51580645	$2.6559725E - 02$
0.37525497	$2.6518162E - 02$	0.51495562	$2.1750479E - 04$
0.37485947	$2.0554242E - 04$	0.51494853	$1.4904231E - 08$
0.37485636	$1.2605184E - 08$		

In this example a poor selection of starting values will lead to divergence.

EXERCISES

3.2-1 Try to find the root $x = 1.3333$ of the equation $(x - 1.3333)^3 = 0$ to five places of accuracy using the modified regula falsi algorithm 3.3 and starting with the interval $[1, 2]$. Why does the method fail in this case to give a "small" interval containing the root?

3.2-2 Because of the use of the product FA*FM in the subroutine BISECT, overflow or underflow may occur during the execution of this subroutine, even though the function values FA and FM are well-defined floating-point numbers. Repair this flaw in the subroutine, using the FORTRAN function SIGN. Also, is it necessary to update the value of FA each time A is changed?

3.2-3 Prove that the function $f(x) = e^x - 1 - x - x^2/2$ has exactly one zero, namely, $\xi = 0$. (*Hint:* Use the remainder in a Taylor expansion for e^x around 0.) Then evaluate the FORTRAN function

$$F(X) = EXP(X) - 1. - X - X*X/2$$

for various values of the argument X "near" zero to show that this function has many sign changes, hence many zeros, "near" X $= 0$. What can you conclude from these facts, specifically, as regards the bisection method, and more generally, as regards the (theoretical) concept of a "zero of a function"?

3.2-4 Suppose you are to find that root of the equation $\tan x = x$ which is closest to 50, using the secant method and nine-decimal-digit floating-point arithmetic. Would it be "reasonable" to use the termination criterion $|f(x_n)| \leq 10^{-8}$?

3.2-5 Binary search The problem of table lookup consists in finding, for given X, an integer I such that X lies between TABLE (I) and TABLE (I + 1), where TABLE is a given one-dimensional array containing an increasing (or a decreasing) sequence. Write a FORTRAN subprogram which utilizes the bisection method to carry out this search efficiently. How many times does your routine compare X with an entry of TABLE if TABLE has n entries?

3.2-6 Write a subroutine for the secant method based on the form (3.7). Allow for termination using either of the relative error criteria (3.14). Also in computing the relative error $|x_n - x_{n-1}| \leq \text{XTOL} \cdot |x_n|$ do not recompute the difference $x_n - x_{n-1}$ but rather use the correction from the previous iteration.

3.2-7 Write a subroutine for Newton's method. Be sure to provide an exit in the event that $f'(x_n) = 0$. In addition to the termination criteria (3.13) or (3.14), provision for termination should also be made in the event of nonconvergence after a given number NTOL of iterations.

3.2-8 Find the smallest positive root of each of the following equations to maximum precision on your computer using Algorithms 3.1, 3.3, 3.4 and 3.5. Compare your results, the number of iterations required and the accuracy attained.

(a) $e^{-x} - \sin x = 0$

(b) $x - e^{-x^2} = 0$

(c) $x^3 - x - 2 = 0$

3.2-9 Solve the equation in Example 3.2b by Newton's method using the parameter values $(I, q) = (10^{-7}, 30)$. Try to solve this equation using various starting values between 0 and 4 and note the effect on convergence or divergence.

3.3 FIXED-POINT ITERATION

In Sec. 3.1, we mentioned fixed-point iteration as a possible method for obtaining a root of the equation

$$f(x) = 0 \qquad (3.15)$$

In this method, one derives from (3.15) an equation of the form

$$x = g(x) \qquad (3.16)$$

so that any solution of (3.16), i.e., any **fixed point** of $g(x)$, is a solution of (3.15). This may be accomplished in many ways. If, for example,

$$f(x) = x^2 - x - 2 \qquad (3.17)$$

then among possible choices for $g(x)$ are the following:

(a) $g(x) = x^2 - 2$

(b) $g(x) = \sqrt{2 + x}$

(c) $g(x) = 1 + \dfrac{2}{x}$ $\qquad (3.18)$

(d) $g(x) = x - \dfrac{x^2 - x - 2}{m}$ $\qquad$ for some nonzero constant m

Each such $g(x)$ is called an **iteration function** for solving (3.15) [with $f(x)$ given by (3.17)]. Once an iteration function $g(x)$ for solving (3.15) is chosen, one carries out the following algorithm.

Algorithm 3.6: Fixed-point iteration Given an iteration function $g(x)$ and a starting point x_0

> For $n = 0, 1, 2, \ldots$, until satisfied, do:
>
> Calculate $x_{n+1} = g(x_n)$

For this algorithm to be useful, we must prove:

(i) For the given starting point x_0, we can calculate successively $x_1, x_2, \ldots$.
(ii) The sequence $x_1, x_2, \ldots$ converges to some point ξ.
(iii) The limit ξ is a fixed point of $g(x)$, that is, $\xi = g(\xi)$.

The example of the real-valued function

$$g(x) = -\sqrt{x}$$

shows that (i) is not a trivial requirement. For in this case, $g(x)$ is defined only for $x \geq 0$. Starting with any $x_0 > 0$, we get $x_1 = g(x_0) < 0$; hence we cannot calculate x_2. To settle (i), we make the following assumption.

Assumption 3.1 There is an interval $I = [a, b]$ such that, for all $x \in I$, $g(x)$ is defined and $g(x) \in I$; that is, the function $g(x)$ maps I into itself.

It follows from this assumption, by induction on n, that if $x_0 \in I$, then for all n, $x_n \in I$; hence $x_{n+1} = g(x_n)$ is defined and is in I.

We discussed (iii) already, in Sec. 3.1. For we proved there that (iii) holds if $g(x)$ is continuous. Hence, to settle (iii), we make Assumption 3.2.

Assumption 3.2 The iteration function $g(x)$ is continuous on $I = [a, b]$.

We note that Assumptions 3.1 and 3.2 together imply that $g(x)$ *has a fixed point in* $I = [a, b]$. For if either $g(a) = a$ or $g(b) = b$, this is obviously so. Otherwise, we have $g(a) \neq a$ and $g(b) \neq b$. But by Assumption 3.1, both $g(a)$ and $g(b)$ are in $I = [a, b]$; hence $g(a) > a$ and $g(b) < b$. This implies that the function $h(x) = g(x) - x$ satisfies $h(a) > 0$, $h(b) < 0$. Since $h(x)$ is continuous on I, by Assumption 3.2, $h(x)$ must therefore vanish somewhere in I, by the intermediate-value theorem for continuous functions (see Sec. 1.7). But this says that $g(x)$ has a fixed point in I, and proves the assertion.

For the discussion of (ii) concerning convergence, it is instructive to carry out the iteration graphically. This can be done as follows. Since $x_n = g(x_{n-1})$, the point $\{x_{n-1}, x_n\}$ lies on the graph of $g(x)$. To locate

$\{x_n, x_{n+1}\}$ from $\{x_{n-1}, x_n\}$, draw the straight line through $\{x_{n-1}, x_n\}$ parallel to the x axis. This line intersects the line $y = x$ at the point $\{x_n, x_n\}$. Through this point, draw the straight line parallel to the y axis. This line intersects the graph $y = g(x)$ of $g(x)$ at the point $\{x_n, g(x_n)\}$. But since $g(x_n) = x_{n+1}$, this is the desired point $\{x_n, x_{n+1}\}$. In Fig. 3.4, we have carried out the first few steps of fixed-point iteration for four typical cases. Note that ξ is a fixed point of $g(x)$ if and only if $y = g(x)$ and $y = x$ intersect at $\{\xi, \xi\}$.

As Fig. 3.4 shows, fixed-point iteration may well fail to converge, as it does in Fig. 3.4a and d. Whether or not the iteration converges [given that $g(x)$ has a fixed point] seems to depend on the slope of $g(x)$. If the slope of $g(x)$ is too large in absolute value, near a fixed point ξ of $g(x)$, then we cannot hope for convergence to that fixed point. We therefore make Assumption 3.3.

Assumption 3.3 The iteration function is differentiable on $I = [a, b]$. Further, there exists a nonnegative constant $K < 1$ such that

$$\text{for all } x \in I \qquad |g'(x)| \leq K$$

Note that Assumption 3.3 implies Assumption 3.2, since a differentiable function is, in particular, continuous.

Theorem 3.1 Let $g(x)$ be an iteration function satisfying Assumptions 3.1 and 3.3. Then $g(x)$ has exactly one fixed point ξ in I, and starting with any point x_0 in I, the sequence $x_1, x_2, \ldots$ generated by fixed-point iteration of Algorithm 3.6 converges to ξ.

To prove this theorem, recall that we have already proved the existence of a fixed point ξ for $g(x)$ in I. Now let x_0 be any point in I. Then, as we remarked earlier, fixed-point iteration generates a sequence $x_1, x_2, \ldots$ of points all lying in I, by Assumption 3.1. Denote the error in the nth iterate by

$$e_n = \xi - x_n \qquad n = 0, 1, 2, \ldots$$

Then since $\xi = g(\xi)$ and $x_n = g(x_{n-1})$, we have

$$e_n = \xi - x_n = g(\xi) - g(x_{n-1}) = g'(\eta_n)e_{n-1} \qquad (3.19)$$

for some η_n between ξ and x_{n-1} by the mean-value theorem for derivatives (see Sec. 1.7). Hence by Assumption 3.3,

$$|e_n| \leq K|e_{n-1}|$$

It follows by induction on n that

$$|e_n| \leq K|e_{n-1}| \leq K^2|e_{n-2}| \leq \cdots \leq K^n|e_0|$$

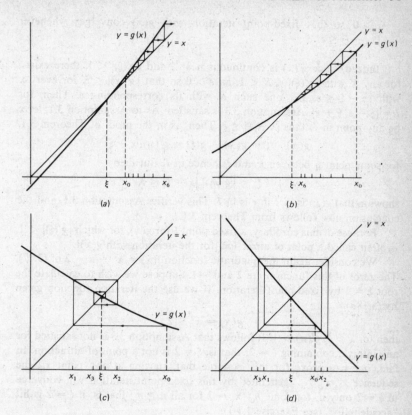

Figure 3.4 Fixed-point iteration.

Since $0 \leq K < 1$, we have $\lim_{n\to\infty} K^n = 0$; therefore

$$\lim_{n\to\infty} |e_n| = \lim_{n\to\infty} K^n |e_0| = 0$$

regardless of the initial error e_0. But this says that $x_1, x_2, \ldots$ converges to ξ. It also proves that ξ is the only fixed point of $g(x)$ in I. For if, also, ζ is a fixed point of $g(x)$ in I, then with $x_0 = \zeta$, we should have $x_1 = g(x_0) = \zeta$; hence $|e_0| = |e_1| \leq K|e_0|$. Since $K < 1$, this then implies $|e_0| = 0$, or $\zeta = \xi$. This completes the proof.

It is often quite difficult to verify Assumption 3.1. In such a situation, the following weaker statement may at least assure success if the iteration is started "sufficiently close" to the fixed point.

Corollary If $g(x)$ is continuously differentiable in some open interval containing the fixed point ξ, and if $|g'(\xi)| < 1$, then there exists an

$\varepsilon > 0$ so that fixed-point iteration with $g(x)$ converges whenever $|x_0 - \xi| \leq \varepsilon$.

Indeed, since $g'(x)$ is continuous near ξ and $|g'(\xi)| < 1$, there exists, for any K with $|g'(\xi)| < K < 1$, an $\varepsilon > 0$ so that $|g'(x)| \leq K$ for every x with $|x - \xi| \leq \varepsilon$. Fix one such K with its corresponding ε. Then, for $I = [\xi - \varepsilon, \xi + \varepsilon]$, Assumption 3.3 is satisfied. As to Assumption 3.1, let x be any point in I, thus $|x - \xi| \leq \varepsilon$. Then, as in the proof of Theorem 3.1,

$$g(x) - \xi = g(x) - g(\xi) = g'(\eta)(x - \xi)$$

for some point η between x and ξ, hence in I. But then

$$|g(x) - \xi| \leq |g'(\eta)| \, |x - \xi| \leq K\varepsilon < \varepsilon$$

showing that $g(x)$ is in I if x is in I. This verifies Assumption 3.1, and the conclusion now follows from Theorem 3.1.

Because of this corollary, a fixed point ξ for $g(x)$, for which $|g'(\xi)| < 1$, is often called a **point of attraction** [for the iteration with $g(x)$].

We consider again the quadratic function $f(x) = x^2 - x - 2$ of (3.17). The zeros of this function are 2 and -1. Suppose we wish to calculate the root $\xi = 2$ by fixed-point iteration. If we use the iteration function given by (3.18a),

$$g(x) = x^2 - 2$$

then for $x > \frac{1}{2}, g'(x) > 1$. It follows that Assumption 3.3 is not satisfied for any interval containing $\xi = 2$; that is, $\xi = 2$ is not a point of attraction. In fact, one can prove for this example that, starting at any point x_0, the sequence $x_1, x_2, \ldots$ generated by this fixed-point iteration will converge to $\xi = 2$ only if, for some n_0, $x_n = 2$ for all $n \geq n_0$; that is, if $\xi = 2$ is hit "accidentally" (see Exercise 3.3-1).

On the other hand, if we choose (3.18b), then

$$g(x) = \sqrt{2 + x} \qquad \text{hence} \qquad g'(x) = \frac{1}{2\sqrt{2 + x}}$$

Now $x \geq 0$ implies $g(x) \geq 0$ and $0 \leq g'(x) \leq 1/\sqrt{8} < 1$, while, for example, $x \leq 7$ implies $g(x) = \sqrt{2 + x} \leq \sqrt{2 + 7} = 3$. Hence, with $I = [0, 7]$, both Assumptions 3.1 and 3.3 are satisfied, and any $x_0 \in [0, 7]$ leads, therefore, to a convergent sequence. Indeed, if we take $x_0 = 0$, then

$$x_1 = \sqrt{2} \qquad\qquad = 1.41421$$

$$x_2 = \sqrt{3.41421} = 1.84775$$

$$x_3 = \sqrt{3.84775} = 1.96157$$

$$x_4 = \sqrt{3.96157} = 1.99036$$

$$x_5 = \sqrt{3.99036} = 1.99759$$

which clearly converges to the root $\xi = 2$.

As a more realistic example, we consider the transcendental equation

$$f(x) = x - 2 \sin x = 0 \tag{3.20}$$

The most natural rearrangement here is

$$x = 2 \sin x$$

so that $g(x) = 2 \sin x$. An examination of the curves $y = g(x)$ and $y = x$ shows that there is a root between $\pi/3$ and $2\pi/3$. Further,

$$\text{if } \frac{\pi}{3} \le x \le \frac{2\pi}{3} \quad \text{then } \sqrt{3} \le g(x) \le 2$$

Hence if $\pi/3 \le a \le \sqrt{3}$ and $2 \le b \le 2\pi/3$, then Assumption 3.1 is satisfied. Finally, $g'(x) = 2 \cos x$ strictly decreases from 1 to -1 as x increases from $\pi/3$ to $2\pi/3$. It follows that Assumption 3.3 is satisfied whenever $\pi/3 < a \le \sqrt{3}$, $2 \le b < 2\pi/3$. In conclusion, fixed-point iteration with $g(x) = 2 \sin x$ converges to the unique solution of (3.20) in $[\pi/3, 2\pi/3]$ whenever $x_0 \in (\pi/3, 2\pi/3)$.

Example 3.3 Write a program which uses fixed-point iteration to find the smallest positive zero of the function $f(x) = e^{-x} - \sin x$.

The first step is to select an iteration function and an initial value which will lead to a convergent iteration. We rewrite $f(x) = 0$ in the form

$$x = x + e^{-x} - \sin x =: g(x)$$

Now since $f(0.5) = 0.127 \cdots$ and $f(0.7) = -0.147 \cdots$ the smallest positive zero lies in the interval $I = [0.5, 0.7]$. To verify that $g(x)$ is a convergent iteration function we note that with

$$g'(x) = 1 - e^{-x} - \cos x$$

$g'(0.5) = -0.48 \cdots$, $g'(0.7) = -0.26 \cdots$ and since $g'(x)$ is a monotone function on I, we have $|g'(x)| < 1$ for $x \in I$. It can similarly be verified that $0.5 < g(x) < 0.7$ for all $x \in I$. Hence fixed-point iteration will converge if x_0 is chosen in I.

The program below was run on a CDC 6500. Note that successful termination of this program requires that both of the following error tests be satisfied

$$|x_n - x_{n-1}| < \text{XTOL}|x_n|$$
$$|f(x_n)| < \text{FTOL}$$

The program also terminates if the convergence tests are not satisfied within 20 iterations.

```
C   PROGRAM FOR EXAMPLE 3.3
      INTEGER J
      REAL ERROR,FTOL,XNEW,XOLD,XTOL,Y
C   THIS PROGRAM SOLVES THE EQUATION
C       EXP(-X) = SIN(X)
C   BY FIXED POINT ITERATION, USING THE ITERATION FUNCTION
        G(X) = EXP(-X) - SIN(X) + X
C
      DATA XTOL, FTOL / 1.E-8, 1.E-8 /
      PRINT 600
  600 FORMAT(9X,'XNEW',12X,'F(XNEW)',10X,'ERROR')
      XOLD = .6
      Y = G(XOLD) - XOLD
      PRINT 601, XOLD,Y
```

```
601 FORMAT(3X,3E16.8)
    DO 10 J=1,20
        XNEW = G(XOLD)
        Y = G(XNEW) - XNEW
        ERROR = ABS(XNEW - XOLD)/ABS(XNEW)
        PRINT 601, XNEW,Y,ERROR
        IF (ERROR .LT. XTOL .OR. ABS(Y) .LT. FTOL) STOP
        XOLD = XNEW
 10 CONTINUE
    PRINT 610
610 FORMAT(' FAILED TO CONVERGE IN 20 ITERATIONS')
                                              STOP
    END
```

OUTPUT FOR EXAMPLE 3.3

XN	F(XN)	ERROR
6.00000000E − 01	−1.58308373E − 02	
5.84169163E − 01	6.06240576E − 03	2.70997483E − 02
5.90231568E − 01	−2.35449276E − 03	1.02712326E − 02
5.87877076E − 01	9.09583240E − 04	4.00507667E − 03
5.88786659E − 01	−3.52118178E − 04	1.54484349E − 03
5.88434541E − 01	1.36203144E − 04	5.98398213E − 04
5.88570744E − 01	−5.27011849E − 05	2.31413378E − 04
5.88518043E − 01	2.03892661E − 05	8.95489706E − 05
5.88538432E − 01	−7.88865463E − 06	3.46438992E − 05
5.88530543E − 01	3.05208415E − 06	1.34039851E − 05
5.88533595E − 01	−1.18084550E − 06	5.18591321E − 06
5.88532415E − 01	4.56865632E − 07	2.00642389E − 06
5.88532871E − 01	−1.76760146E − 07	7.76278869E − 07
5.88532695E − 01	6.83880224E − 08	3.00340402E − 07
5.88532763E − 01	−2.64591478E − 08	1.16200876E − 07
5.88532737E − 01	1.02369739E − 08	4.49578182E − 08
5.88532747E − 01	−3.96065403E − 09	1.73940600E − 08
5.88532743E − 01	1.53236357E − 09	6.72970888E − 09

EXERCISES

3.3-1 Verify that the iteration

$$x_{i+1} = x_i^2 - 2$$

will converge to the solution $\xi = 2$ of the equation

$$x^2 - x - 2 = 0$$

only if, for some n_0, all iterates x_n with $n \geq n_0$ are equal to 2, i.e., only "accidentally."

3.3-2 For each of the following equations determine an iteration function (and an interval I) so that the conditions of Theorem 3.1 are satisfied (assume that it is desired to find the smallest positive root):

(a) $x^3 - x - 1 = 0$ (b) $x - \tan x = 0$ (c) $e^{-x} - \cos x = 0$

3.3-3 Write a program based on Algorithm 3.6 and use this program to calculate the smallest roots of the equations given in Exercise 3.3-2.

3.3-4 Determine the largest interval I with the following property: For all $x_0 \in I$, fixed-point iteration with the iteration function

$$g(x) = x(2 - ax)$$

converges, when started with x_0. Are Assumptions 3.1 and 3.3 satisfied for your choice of I? What numbers are possible limits of this iteration? Can you think of a good reason for using this particular iteration? Note that the interval depends on the constant a.

3.3-5 Same as Exercise 3.3-4, but with $g(x) = (x + a/x)/2$.

3.3-6 The function $g(x) = \sqrt{1 + x^2}$ satisfies Assumption 3.1 for $I = (-\infty, \infty)$, and Assumption 3.3 on any finite interval, yet fixed-point iteration with this iteration function does not converge. Why?

3.3-7 The equation $e^x - 4x^2 = 0$ has a root between $x = 4$ and $x = 5$. Show that we cannot find this root using fixed point iteration with the "natural" iteration function

$$x = \tfrac{1}{2} e^{x/2}$$

Can you find an iteration function which will correctly locate this root?

3.3-8 The equation $e^x - 4x^2 = 0$ also has a root between $x = 0$ and $x = 1$. Show that the iteration function $x = \tfrac{1}{2} e^{x/2}$ will converge to this root if x_0 is chosen in the interval $[0, 1]$.

3.4 CONVERGENCE ACCELERATION FOR FIXED-POINT ITERATION

In this section, we investigate the rate of convergence of fixed-point iteration and show how information about the rate of convergence can be used at times to accelerate convergence.

We assume that the iteration function $g(x)$ is continuously differentiable and that, starting with some point x_0, the sequence $x_1, x_2, \ldots$ generated by fixed-point iteration converges to some point ξ. This point ξ is then a fixed point of $g(x)$, and we have, by (3.19), that

$$e_{n+1} = \xi - x_{n+1} = g'(\eta_n) e_n \tag{3.21}$$

for some η_n between ξ and x_n, $n = 1, 2, \ldots$. Since $\lim_{n \to \infty} x_n = \xi$, it then follows that $\lim \eta_n = \xi$; hence

$$\lim_{n \to \infty} g'(\eta_n) = g'(\xi)$$

$g'(x)$ being continuous, by assumption. Consequently,

$$e_{n+1} = g'(\xi) e_n + \varepsilon_n e_n \tag{3.22}$$

where $\lim \varepsilon_n = 0$. Hence, if $g'(\xi) \neq 0$, then for large enough n,

$$e_{n+1} \approx g'(\xi) e_n \tag{3.23}$$

i.e., the error e_{n+1} in the $(n + 1)$st iterate depends (more or less) linearly on the error e_n in the nth iterate. We therefore say that $x_0, x_1, x_2, \ldots$ converges **linearly** to ξ.

Now note that we can solve (3.21) for ξ. For

$$\xi - x_{n+1} = g'(\eta_n)(\xi - x_n) \tag{3.24}$$

gives

$$\xi(1 - g'(\eta_n)) = x_{n+1} - g'(\eta_n)x_n$$
$$= [1 - g'(\eta_n)]x_{n+1} + g'(\eta_n)(x_{n+1} - x_n)$$

Therefore

$$\xi = x_{n+1} + \frac{g'(\eta_n)(x_{n+1} - x_n)}{1 - g'(\eta_n)} = x_{n+1} + \frac{x_{n+1} - x_n}{g'(\eta_n)^{-1} - 1} \qquad (3.25)$$

Of course, we do not know the number $g'(\eta_n)$. But we know that the ratio

$$r_n := \frac{x_n - x_{n-1}}{x_{n+1} - x_n} = \frac{x_n - x_{n-1}}{g(x_n) - g(x_{n-1})} = g'(\zeta_n)^{-1} \qquad (3.26)$$

for some ζ_n between x_n and x_{n-1}, by the mean-value theorem for derivatives. For large enough n, therefore, we have

$$r_n = \frac{1}{g'(\zeta_n)} \approx \frac{1}{g'(\xi)} \approx \frac{1}{g'(\eta_n)}$$

and then the point

$$\hat{x}_n = x_{n+1} + \frac{x_{n+1} - x_n}{r_n - 1} \qquad \text{with} \qquad r_n = \frac{x_n - x_{n-1}}{x_{n+1} - x_n} \qquad (3.27)$$

should be a very much better approximation to ξ than is x_n or x_{n+1}.

This can also be seen graphically. In effect we obtained (3.27) by solving (3.24) for ξ after replacing $g'(\eta_n)$ by the number $g[x_{n-1}, x_n]$ and calling the solution $\hat{x}_n$. Thus $\hat{x}_n - x_{n+1} = g[x_{n-1}, x_n](\hat{x}_n - x_n)$. Since $x_{n+1} = g(x_n)$, this shows that $\hat{x}_n$ is a fixed point of the straight line

$$s(x) = g(x_n) + g[x_{n-1}, x_n](x - x_n)$$

This we recognize as the linear interpolant to $g(x)$ at x_{n-1}, x_n. If now the slope of $g(x)$ varies little between x_{n-1} and ξ, that is, if $g(x)$ is approximately a straight line between x_{n-1} and ξ, then the secant $s(x)$ should be a very good approximation to $g(x)$ in that interval; hence the fixed point $\hat{x}_n$ of the secant should be a very good approximation to the fixed point ξ of $g(x)$; see Fig. 3.5.

In practice, we will not be able to prove that any particular x_n is "close enough" to ξ to make $\hat{x}_n$ a better approximation to ξ than is x_n or x_{n+1}. But we can test the hypothesis that x_n is "close enough" by checking the ratios r_{n-1}, r_n. If the ratios are approximately constant, we accept the hypothesis that the slope of $g(x)$ varies little in the interval of interest; hence we believe that the secant $s(x)$ is a good enough approximation to $g(x)$ to make $\hat{x}_n$ a very much better approximation to ξ than is x_n. In particular, we then accept $|\hat{x} - x_n|$ as a good estimate for the error $|e_n|$.

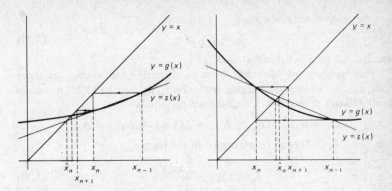

Figure 3.5 Convergence acceleration for fixed-point iteration.

Example 3.4 The equation

$$1.5x - \tan x = 0.1 \tag{3.28}$$

has a root $\xi = 0.20592169510 \cdots$. We choose the iteration function

$$g(x) = \frac{0.1 + \tan x}{1.5}$$

and starting with $x_0 = 0$, generate the sequence $x_1, x_2, \ldots$ by fixed-point iteration. Some of the x_n are listed in the table below. The sequence seems to converge, slowly but surely, to ξ. We also calculate the sequence of ratios r_n. These too are listed in the table.

n	x_n	$\hat{x}_n$	r_n	y_n
	0.0			0.0
1	0.0666667	0.2005954	1.4978	0.2005954
2	0.1111771	0.2024021	1.4879	0.2059125
3	0.1410916	0.2039180	1.4761	0.2059217
4	0.1613569	0.2048536	1.4659	
5	0.1751813	0.2053721	1.4579	
...	....	....	....	
10	0.2009941	0.2059055	1.4408	
15	0.2051206	0.2059213	1.4379	
20	0.2057911	0.2059217	1.4374	
25	0.2059004		1.4373	
30	0.2059182		1.4372	

Specifically, we find

$$r_1 = 1.4978 \cdots \qquad r_2 = 1.4879 \cdots \qquad r_3 = 1.4761 \cdots$$

which we think is "sufficiently" constant to conclude that, for all $n \geq 1$, $\hat{x}_n$ is a better approximation to ξ than is x_n. This is confirmed in the table, where we have also listed the $\hat{x}_n$.

Whether or not any particular $\hat{x}_n$ is a better approximation to ξ than is x_n, one can prove that the sequence $\hat{x}_1, \hat{x}_2, \ldots$ converges faster to ξ than does the original sequence $x_0, x_1, \ldots$; that is,

$$\hat{x}_n = \xi + o(e_n) \tag{3.29}$$

[See Sec. 1.6 for the definition of $o(\ )$.]

This process of deriving from a linearly converging sequence $x_0, x_1, x_2, \ldots$ a faster converging sequence $\hat{x}_1, \hat{x}_2, \ldots$ by (3.27) is usually called **Aitken's Δ^2 process.** Using the abbreviations

$$\Delta x_k = x_{k+1} - x_k \qquad \Delta^2 x_k = \Delta(\Delta x_k) = \Delta x_{k+1} - \Delta x_k$$

from Sec. 2.6, (3.27) can be expressed in the form

$$\hat{x}_n = x_{n+1} - \frac{(\Delta x_n)^2}{\Delta^2 x_{n-1}} \tag{3.30}$$

therefore the name "Δ^2 process." This process is applicable to any linearly convergent sequence, whether generated by fixed-point iteration or not.

Algorithm 3.7: Aitken's Δ^2 process Given a sequence $x_0, x_1, x_2, \ldots$ converging to ξ, calculate the sequence $\hat{x}_1, \hat{x}_2, \ldots$ by (3.30).

If the sequence $x_0, x_1, x_2, \ldots$ converges linearly to ξ, that is, if

$$\xi - x_{n+1} = K(\xi - x_n) + o(\xi - x_n) \qquad \text{for some } K \neq 0$$

then

$$\hat{x}_n = \xi + o(\xi - x_n)$$

Furthermore, if starting from a certain k on, the sequence $\Delta x_{k-1}/\Delta x_k, \Delta x_k/\Delta x_{k+1}, \ldots$ of difference ratios is approximately constant, then $\hat{x}_k$ can be assumed to be a better approximation to ξ than is x_k. In particular, $|\hat{x}_k - x_k|$ is then a good estimate for the error $|\xi - x_k|$.

If, in the case of fixed-point iteration, we decide that a certain $\hat{x}_k$ is a very much better approximation to ξ than is x_k, then it is certainly wasteful to continue generating x_{k+1}, x_{k+2}, etc. It seems more reasonable to start fixed-point iteration afresh with $\hat{x}_k$ as the initial guess. This leads to the following algorithm.

Algorithm 3.8: Steffensen iteration Given the iteration function $g(x)$ and a point y_0.

For $n = 0, 1, 2, \ldots$, until satisfied, do:

$x_0 := y_n$

Calculate $x_1 = g(x_0)$, $x_2 = g(x_1)$

Calculate $d = \Delta x_1$, $r = \Delta x_0/d$

Calculate $y_{n+1} = x_2 + d/(r - 1)$

One step of this algorithm consists of two steps of fixed-point iteration followed by one application of (3.27), using the three iterates available to get the starting value for the next step.

We have listed in the table above the y_n generated by this algorithm applied to Example 3.4. Already y_3 is accurate to all places shown.

EXERCISES

3.4-1 Assume that the error of a fixed-point iteration satisfies the recurrence relation

$$e_{n+1} = ke_n$$

for some constant k, $|k| < 1$. Find an expression for the number of iterations N required to reduce the initial error e_0 by a factor 10^{-m} ($m > 0$).

3.4-2 Fixed-point iteration applied to the equation

$$f(x) = 0.5 - x + 0.2 \sin x = 0$$

produced the successive approximations given in the following table:

k	x_k
0	0.5000 0000
1	0.5958 8511
2	0.6122 4830
3	0.6149 4176
4	0.6153 8219
5	0.6154 5412
6	0.6154 6587
7	0.6154 6779
8	0.6154 6810
9	0.6154 6815

Use the Aitken Algorithm 3.7 to compute an accelerated sequence $\hat{x}_k$ and the ratios r_k. From the ratios r_k calculate the approximate value of $g'(\xi)$.

3.4-3 Write a program to carry out Steffensen accelerated iteration (Algorithm 3.8). Use this program to compute the smallest positive zero of the function in Exercise 3.4-2 using the iteration function $g(x) = 0.5 + 0.2 \sin x$ and $x_0 = 0.5$.

3.4-4 In Sec. 3.3 we showed that the fixed-point iteration

$$x_{i+1} = \sqrt{2 + x_i}$$

produced the following sequence of approximations to the positive root of $f(x) = x^2 - x - 2$:

$$x_0 = 0 \qquad x_1 = 1.41421 \qquad x_2 = 1.84776$$
$$x_3 = 1.96157 \qquad x_4 = 1.99037 \qquad x_5 = 1.99759$$

Use Aitken's Algorithm 3.7 to accelerate this sequence and note the improvement in the rate of convergence to the root $\xi = 2$.

3.4-5 Consider the iteration function $g(x) = x - x^3$. Find the unique fixed point of $g(x)$. Prove that fixed-point iteration with this iteration function converges to the unique fixed point ξ of $g(x)$ if $x_0 \in (-1, 1)$. (*Hint:* Use the fact that if $x_n \leq x_{n+1} \leq x_{n+2} \leq \cdots \leq c$ for some constant c, then the sequence converges.) Is it true that, for some $k < 1$ and all n, $|e_n| \leq k|e_{n-1}|$?

*3.5 CONVERGENCE OF THE NEWTON AND SECANT METHODS

In the preceding section, we proved that the error e_n in the nth iterate x_n of fixed-point iteration satisfies

$$e_{n+1} \approx g'(\xi)e_n \tag{3.31}$$

for large enough n, provided $g(x)$ is continuously differentiable. Apparently, the smaller $|g'(\xi)|$, the more rapidly e_n goes to zero as $n \to \infty$. The convergence of fixed-point iteration should therefore be most rapid when $g'(\xi) = 0$.

If $g(x)$ is twice-differentiable, we get from Taylor's formula that

$$e_{n+1} = \xi - x_{n+1} = g(\xi) - g(x_n)$$
$$= -g'(\xi)(x_n - \xi) - \tfrac{1}{2}g''(\zeta_n)(x_n - \xi)^2$$

for some ζ_n between ξ and x_n, that is, that

$$e_{n+1} = g'(\xi)e_n - \tfrac{1}{2}g''(\zeta_n)e_n^2 \tag{3.32}$$

Hence, if $g'(\xi) = 0$ *and $g''(x)$ is continuous at ξ, then*

$$e_{n+1} \approx -\tfrac{1}{2}g''(\xi)e_n^2 \qquad \text{for large enough } n \tag{3.33}$$

In this case, e_{n+1} is (more or less) a quadratic function of e_n. We therefore say that, in this case, $x_1, x_2, \ldots$ converges **quadratically** to ξ.

Such an iteration function is obviously very desirable. The popularity of Newton's method can be traced to the fact that its iteration function

$$g(x) = x - \frac{f(x)}{f'(x)} \tag{3.34}$$

is of this kind.

Before proving that Newton's method converges quadratically (when it converges), we consider a simple example.

Example Finding the positive square root of a positive number A is equivalent to finding the positive solution of the equation $f(x) = x^2 - A = 0$. Then $f'(x) = 2x$, and substituting into (3.34), we obtain the iteration function

$$g(x) = x - \frac{x^2 - A}{2x} = \frac{1}{2}\left(x + \frac{A}{x}\right) \tag{3.35}$$

for finding the square root of A, leading to the iteration

$$x_{n+1} = \frac{1}{2}\left(x_n + \frac{A}{x_n}\right) \tag{3.36}$$

In particular, if $A = 2$ and $x_0 = 2$, the result of fixed-point iteration with (3.36) is as follows:

$$x_0 = 2.$$

$$x_1 = 1.5 \qquad\qquad r_1 = 6$$

$$x_2 = 1.41666666 \cdots \qquad r_2 = 34$$

$$x_3 = 1.41421568 \cdots \qquad r_3 = 1,154$$

$$x_4 = 1.41421356 \cdots \qquad r_4 = 1,331,714$$

$$x_5 = 1.41421356 \cdots$$

The sequence of iterates is evidently converging quite rapidly. The corresponding sequence $r_1, r_2, \ldots$ of ratios $r_n = \Delta x_{n-1} / \Delta x_n$ converges to ∞. Since, for convergent fixed-point iteration, $\lim_{n \to \infty} r_n^{-1} = g'(\xi)$, the example illustrates our assertion and shows the very desirable rapid convergence of Newton's method.

We could show the quadratic convergence of Newton's method by showing that if $f(\xi) = 0$ and $f'(\xi) \neq 0$, then the iteration function

$$g(x) = x - \frac{f(x)}{f'(x)}$$

of Newton's method is continuously differentiable in an open neighborhood of ξ, and $g'(\xi) = 0$. Consequently, by the corollary to Theorem 3.1, there exists $\varepsilon > 0$ such that fixed-point iteration with $g(x)$ converges to ξ for any choice of x_0 such that $|\xi - x_0| \leq \varepsilon$. But it seems more efficient to prove the quadratic convergence directly and at the same time establish a convergence proof of the secant method.

The error in Newton's method and in the secant method can be derived at the same time. Both methods interpolate the function $f(x)$ at two points, say α and β, by a straight line,

$$p(x) = f(\alpha) + f[\alpha, \beta](x - \alpha)$$

whose zero

$$\hat{\xi} = \alpha - f(\alpha)/f[\alpha, \beta]$$

is then taken as the next approximation to the actual zero of $f(x)$. In the secant method we take $\alpha = x_n$, $\beta = x_{n-1}$ and then produce $x_{n+1} = \hat{\xi}$ while in Newton's method we take $\alpha = \beta = x_n$.

In either case we know from (2.37) that

$$f(x) = f(\alpha) + f[\alpha, \beta](x - \alpha) + f[\alpha, \beta, x](x - \alpha)(x - \beta)$$

This equation holds for all x. If we now set $x = \xi$, the desired zero, then

$$0 = f(\xi) = f(\alpha) + f[\alpha, \beta](\xi - \alpha) + f[\alpha, \beta, \xi](\xi - \alpha)(\xi - \beta)$$

and therefore

$$f[\alpha, \beta](\xi - \alpha) = -f(\alpha) - f[\alpha, \beta, \xi](\xi - \alpha)(\xi - \beta)$$

Solving now for the ξ on the left side we obtain

$$\xi = \alpha - f(\alpha)/f[\alpha, \beta] - \frac{f[\alpha, \beta, \xi]}{f[\alpha, \beta]}(\xi - \alpha)(\xi - \beta)$$

or $\qquad \xi = \qquad \hat{\xi} \qquad - \dfrac{f[\alpha, \beta, \xi]}{f[\alpha, \beta]}(\xi - \alpha)(\xi - \beta)$ (3.37)

Equation (3.37) can now be used to obtain the error equations for the Newton and secant methods. For Newton's method we set $\alpha = \beta = x_n$, and recalling that $e_j = \xi - x_j$, $\hat{\xi} = x_{n+1}$, we obtain from (3.37)

$$e_{n+1} = -\frac{f[x_n, x_n, \xi]}{f[x_n, x_n]} e_n^2 \qquad (3.38)$$

Recalling also that $f[x_n, x_n] = f'(x_n)$ and that $f[x_n, x_n, \xi] = \frac{1}{2}f''(\eta_n)$ for some η_n between x_n and ξ, we can rewrite (3.38) as

$$e_{n+1} = -\frac{1}{2}\frac{f''(\eta_n)}{f'(x_n)} e_n^2 \qquad (3.38a)$$

This equation shows that Newton's method converges quadratically since e_{n+1} is approximately proportional to the square of e_n.

To establish the error equation for the secant method we set $\alpha = x_n$, $\beta = x_{n-1}$ in (3.37) and thus obtain

$$e_{n+1} = -\frac{f[x_{n-1}, x_n, \xi]}{f[x_{n-1}, x_n]} e_n e_{n-1} \qquad (3.39)$$

This equation shows that the error in the $(n + 1)$st iterate is approximately proportional to the product of the nth and $(n - 1)$st errors. Also since $f[x_{n-1}, x_n, \xi] = \frac{1}{2}f''(\zeta_n)$ and $f[x_{n-1}, x_n] = f'(\eta_n)$ for η_n, ζ_n some points between x_{n-1}, x_n and ξ, then for n large enough (3.39) becomes

$$e_{n+1} \approx -\frac{1}{2}\frac{f''(\xi)}{f'(\xi)} e_n e_{n-1} \qquad (3.39a)$$

To be more precise about the concept of **order of convergence**, we make the following definition:

Definition 3.1: Order of convergence Let $x_0, x_1, x_2, \ldots$ be a sequence which converges to a number ξ, and set $e_n = \xi - x_n$. If there exists a number p and a constant $C \neq 0$ such that

$$\lim_{n \to \infty} \frac{|e_{n+1}|}{|e_n|^p} = C$$

then p is called the **order of convergence** of the sequence and C is called the **asymptotic error constant**.

For fixed-point iteration in general based on $x = g(x)$ we have

$$\lim_{n \to \infty} \frac{|e_{n+1}|}{|e_n|} = |g'(\xi)|$$

so that the order of convergence is one and the asymptotic error constant is $|g'(\xi)|$. For Newton's method we see from (3.38a) that

$$\lim_{n \to \infty} \frac{|e_{n+1}|}{|e_n|^2} = \frac{1}{2} \left| \frac{f''(\xi)}{f'(\xi)} \right|$$

provided that $f'(\xi) \neq 0$, so that by the definition its order of convergence is 2 and the asymptotic error constant is $|f''(\xi)|/(2|f'(\xi)|)$.

To determine the order of convergence of the secant method we first note that from (3.39a)

$$|e_{n+1}| = c_n |e_n e_{n-1}| \quad \text{with} \lim_{n \to \infty} c_n = c_\infty = \tfrac{1}{2}|f''(\xi)/f'(\xi)| \quad (3.40)$$

We seek a number p such that

$$\lim_{n \to \infty} \frac{|e_{n+1}|}{|e_n|^p} = C$$

for some nonzero constant C.

Now from (3.40)

$$\frac{|e_{n+1}|}{|e_n|^p} = c_n |e_n|^{1-p} |e_{n-1}| = c_n \left(\frac{|e_n|}{|e_{n-1}|^p} \right)^\alpha \quad (3.41)$$

provided that $\alpha = 1 - p$ and also $\alpha p = -1$, i.e., provided that

$$p - p^2 = \alpha p = -1$$

The equation $p^2 - p - 1 = 0$ has the simple positive root $p = (1 + \sqrt{5})/2 = 1.618 \cdots$. With this choice of p and of $\alpha = -1/p$, we see that (3.41) defines a "fixed-point-like iteration"

$$y_{n+1} = c_n y_n^{-1/p}$$

where $\quad y_{n+1} = |e_{n+1}|/|e_n|^p \quad$ and $\lim_{n \to \infty} c_n = c_\infty$

It follows that y_n converges to the fixed point of the equation

$$x = c_\infty x^{-1/p}$$

whose solution is $c_\infty^{1/p}$ since $1 + 1/p = p$. This shows that for the secant method

$$\frac{|e_{n+1}|}{|e_n|^p} \approx \left| \frac{f''(\xi)}{2f'(\xi)} \right|^{1/p} \quad \text{for large } n \quad (3.42)$$

with $p = 1.618 \cdots$; i.e., the order of convergence of the secant method is $p = 1.618 \cdots$ and the asymptotic error constant is $|f''(\xi)/(2f'(\xi))|^{1/p}$.

This says that the secant method converges more rapidly than the usual fixed-point iteration but less rapidly than the Newton method.

Example 3.5 Using data from Example 3.2, verify the error formulas (3.39a) and (3.42) for the secant method.

In Example 3.2a we give the secant iterates for the positive root of $x^3 - x - 1 = 0$. In the table below we calculate $|e_n|$ and $|e_{n+1}|/|e_n e_{n-1}|$ for $n = 2, 3, 4$, assuming that the value of ξ correct to eight decimal digits is $\xi = 1.3247180$.

n	$|e_n|$	$|e_{n+1}|/|e_n e_{n-1}|$	$|e_{n+1}|/|e_n|^{1.618\cdots}$
1	0.1580513		1.41684
2	0.0716060	1.1034669	0.88969
3	0.0124884	0.9705400	1.04325
4	0.0008679	0.9318475	0.90778
5	0.0000101		

If we compute directly the constant $f''(\xi)/(2f'(\xi))$ we obtain $0.93188\cdots$, which agrees very closely with the ratio $|e_{n+1}/e_n e_{n-1}|$ for $n = 4$.

It can be shown directly that, if $f(\xi) = 0$, $f'(\xi) \neq 0$, and $f''(x)$ is twice continuously differentiable, then $g'(\xi) = 0$, where

$$g(x) = x - \frac{f(x)}{f'(x)}$$

is the Newton iteration function. It then follows by the corollary to Theorem 3.1 that if x_0 is chosen "close enough" to ξ, the Newton iteration will converge. The phrase "close enough" is not very precisely defined, and indeed Newton's method will frequently diverge or, when it does converge, converge to another zero than the one being sought. It would be desirable to establish conditions which guarantee convergence for any choice of the initial iterate in a given interval. One such set of conditions is contained in the following theorem.

Theorem 3.2 Let $f(x)$ be twice continuously differentiable on the closed finite interval $[a, b]$ and let the following conditions be satisfied:

(i) $f(a)f(b) < 0$
(ii) $f'(x) \neq 0$, $x \in [a, b]$
(iii) $f''(x)$ is either ≥ 0 or ≤ 0 for all $x \in [a, b]$
(iv) At the endpoints a, b

$$\frac{|f(a)|}{|f'(a)|} < b - a \qquad \frac{|f(b)|}{|f'(b)|} < b - a$$

Then Newton's method converges to the unique solution ξ of $f(x) = 0$ in $[a, b]$ for any choice of $x_0 \in [a, b]$.

Some comments about these conditions may be appropriate.

Conditions (i) and (ii) guarantee that there is one and only one solution in $[a, b]$. Condition (iii) states that the graph of $f(x)$ is either concave from above or concave from below, and furthermore together with condition (ii) implies that $f'(x)$ is monotone on $[a, b]$. Added to these, condition (iv) states that the tangent to the curve at either endpoint intersects the x axis within the interval $[a, b]$. A proof of this theorem will not be given here (see Exercise 3.5-7), but we do indicate why the theorem might be true. We assume without loss of generality that $f(a) < 0$. We can then distinguish two cases:

$$\text{Case } (a) \qquad f''(x) \geq 0$$
$$\text{Case } (b) \qquad f''(x) \leq 0$$

Case (b) reduces to case (a) if we replace f by $-f$. It therefore suffices to consider case (a). Here the graph of $f(x)$ has the appearance given in Fig. 3.6. From the graph it is evident that, for $x_0 > \xi$, the resulting iterates decrease monotonely to ξ, while, for $a \leq x_0 < \xi$, x_1 falls between ξ and b and then the subsequent iterates converge monotonely to ξ.

Example 3.6 Find an interval containing the smallest positive zero of $f(x) = e^{-x} - \sin x$ and which satisfies the conditions of Theorem 3.2 for convergence of Newton's method.

With $f(x) = e^{-x} - \sin x$, we have $f'(x) = -e^{-x} - \cos x$, $f''(x) = e^{-x} + \sin x$. We choose $[a, b] = [0, 1]$. Then since $f(0) = 1$, $f(1) = -0.47$, we have $f(a)f(b) < 0$ so

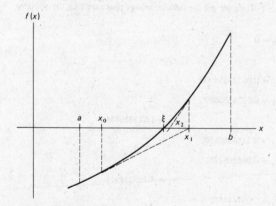

Figure 3.6 Newton convergence.

that condition (i) is satisfied. Since $f'(x) < 0$ for all $x \in [0, 1]$, condition (ii) is satisfied, and since $f''(x) > 0$ for all $x \in [0, 1]$, condition (iii) is satisfied. Finally since $f(0) = 1$, $f'(0) = -2$, we have $|f(0)|/|f'(0)| = \frac{1}{2} < b - a = 1$ and since $f(1) = -0.47 \cdots$, $f'(1) = 0.90 \cdots$, we have $|f(1)|/|f'(1)| = 0.52 \cdots < 1$, verifying condition (iv). Newton's iteration will therefore converge for any choice of x_0 in $[0, 1]$.

The conditions of Theorem 3.2 are also sufficient to establish convergence of the secant method although the modes of convergence may be quite different from those of Newton's method. If we assume again that $f'(x) > 0$ and $f''(x) \geq 0$ on the interval $[a, b]$ as shown in Fig. 3.6a, then there are essentially two different modes of convergence, depending upon where the initial points x_0 and x_1 are selected. In the first and simpler mode, if x_0 and x_1 are selected in the interval $[\xi, b]$, then convergence will be monotone from the right as in Newton's method. The student can verify this geometrically by drawing some typical curves meeting the conditions of Theorem 3.2.

If, however, we select one point, say x_0, in the interval $[\xi, b]$ and the point x_1 in the interval $[a, \xi]$, then the next iterate x_2 will lie also in the interval $[a, \xi]$ while the iterate x_3 will fall to the right of ξ. At this point we will again have two successive iterates, x_3 and x_2, which straddle the root ξ, and the entire sequence will be repeated. Convergence thus occurs in a waltz with an iterate on one side followed by two iterates on the other. See Fig. 3.6a for an illustration of this type of convergence.

Example 3.7 Examine the mode of convergence of the secant method as applied to the function $f(x) = e^x - 3$.

Obviously $f'(x) > 0$, $f''(x) > 0$ for all x. Furthermore, the endpoint conditions of Theorem 3.2 are satisfied, for example, in the interval $[0, 5]$. Hence, $f(x)$ has a zero in that interval, namely $\xi = \ln 3 = 1.098612289$, and we expect convergence if we select $x_0 = 0 < \xi$ and $x_1 = 5 > \xi$. Then we get the iterates below, thus verifying the waltzing mode of convergence:

$$x_0 = 0$$
$$x_1 = 5$$
$$x_2 = 0.06783654900$$
$$x_3 = 0.1324350609$$
$$x_4 = 1.813459843$$
$$x_5 = 0.7584862650$$
$$x_6 = 0.9868082782$$
$$x_7 = 1.119119918$$
$$x_8 = 1.097448653$$
$$x_9 = 1.098600396$$
$$x_{10} = 1.098612296$$

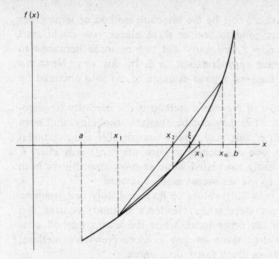

Figure 3.6a Secant convergence.

If we choose $x_0 = 3 > \xi$ and $x_1 = 2 > \xi$ instead, then we get the iterates

$$x_0 = 3$$
$$x_1 = 2$$
$$x_2 = 1.654309240$$
$$x_3 = 1.297433158$$
$$x_4 = 1.147393259$$
$$x_5 = 1.103265406$$
$$x_6 = 1.098724772$$
$$x_7 = 1.098612550$$
$$x_8 = 1.098612289$$

thus illustrating the monotone mode of convergence.

From a computational point of view, the accuracy attainable with Newton's method depends upon the accuracy to which $f(x)/f'(x)$ can be computed. It may happen, for example, that $f'(x)$, though it does not vanish, is very small near the zero. In this case, we can expect that any errors in $f(x)$ will be magnified when $f(x)/f'(x)$ is computed. In such cases, it will be difficult to obtain good accuracy.

There are two major disadvantages to Newton's method. First, one has to start "close enough" to a zero ξ of $f(x)$ to ensure convergence to ξ. (See Exercise 3.5-6 but also 3.3-4 and 3.3-5.) Since one usually does not know ξ, this might be difficult to do in practice, unless one has already obtained a good estimate $\hat{\xi}$ for ξ by some other method. If, for example, one has calculated an approximation $\hat{\xi}$ to ξ by the bisection method or some other iterative method which is good to two or three places, one might start Newton's method with $x_0 = \hat{\xi}$ and carry out two or three iterations to obtain quickly an accurate approximation to ξ. In this way, Newton's method is often used to **improve** a good estimate of the zero obtained by some other means.

A second disadvantage of Newton's method is the necessity to calculate $f'(x)$. In some cases, $f'(x)$ may not be available explicitly, and even when one can evaluate $f'(x)$, this may require considerable computational effort. In the latter case, one can decide to compute $f'(x_n)$ only every k steps, using the most recently calculated value at every step. But in both cases, it is usually better to use the **secant** method instead.

The secant method uses only values of $f(x)$, and only one function evaluation is required per step, while Newton's method requires two evaluations per step. On the other hand, when the secant method converges, it does not converge quite as fast as does Newton's method; although it usually converges much faster than linear.

The more rapid rate of convergence of Newton's method over the secant method is demonstrated in Example 3.2.

In this chapter we have considered six algorithms for finding zeros of functions. In comparing algorithms for use on computers one should take into account various criteria, the most important of which are assurances of convergence, the rate of convergence, and computational efficiency. No one method can be said to be always superior to another method. The bisection method, for example, while slow in convergence, is certain to converge when properly used, while Newton's method will frequently diverge unless the initial approximation is carefully selected. The term "computational efficiency" used above attempts to take into account the amount of work required to produce a given accuracy. Newton's method, although it generally converges more rapidly than the secant method, is not usually as efficient, because it requires the evaluation of both $f(x)$ and $f'(x)$ for each iteration. In cases where $f'(x)$ is available and easily computable, Newton's method may be more efficient than the secant method, but for a general-purpose routine, the secant method will usually be more efficient and should be preferred.

Algorithms 3.1 to 3.3 all have the advantage that they bracket the zero and thus guarantee error bounds on the root. Of these, Algorithm 3.2 (regula falsi) should never be used because it fails to produce a contracting interval containing the zero. In general, of these three, the modified regula falsi method (Algorithm 3.3) should be preferred.

Fixed-point iteration is effective when it converges quadratically, as in Newton's method. In general, fixed-point iteration converges only linearly, hence offers no real competition to the secant method or the modified regula falsi. Even with repeated extrapolation, as in the Steffensen iteration algorithm 3.8, convergence is at best only quadratic. Since one step of the Steffensen iteration costs two evaluations of the iteration function $g(x)$, Steffensen iteration is therefore comparable with Newton's method. But since the extrapolation part of one step of Steffensen iteration is the same as one step of the secant method applied to the function $f(x) = x - g(x)$, it would seem more efficient to forgo Steffensen iteration altogether, and just use the secant method on $f(x) = x - g(x)$.

The main purpose of discussing fixed-point iteration at all was to gain a simple model for an iterative procedure which can be analyzed easily. The insight gained will be very useful in the discussion of several equations in several unknowns, in Chap. 5.

EXERCISES

3.5-1 From the definition of fixed-point iteration with iteration function $g(x)$, we know that the error of the nth iterate satisfies

$$e_n = \xi - x_n = g(\xi) - g(x_{n-1})$$

We showed in the text that if $g'(\xi) = 0$ and $g''(x)$ is continuous at $x = \xi$, the iteration $x = g(x)$ converges quadratically. State conditions under which one can expect an iteration to converge cubically.

3.5-2 For Newton's method show that if $f(\xi) = 0$, $f'(\xi) \neq 0$ and if $f(x)$ is twice continuously differentiable, then $g'(\xi) = 0$. Also show that $g''(\xi) = f''(\xi)/f'(\xi)$.

3.5-3 For each of the following functions locate an interval containing the smallest positive zero and show that the conditions of Theorem 3.2 are satisfied.

  (a) $e^{-x} - x = 0$
  (b) $x^3 - x - 1 = 0$
  (c) $e^{-x^2} - \cos x = 0$

3.5-4 Solve each of the examples in Exercise 3.5-3 by both the secant method and Newton's method and compare your results.

3.5-5 If $x = \xi$ is a zero of $f(x)$ of order 2, then $f'(\xi) = 0$ and $f''(\xi) \neq 0$. Show that in this case Newton's method no longer converges quadratically [i.e., show that $g'(\xi) = \frac{1}{2} \neq 0$]. Also show that if $f'(\xi) = 0$, $f''(\xi) \neq 0$, and $f'''(x)$ is continuous in the neighborhood of ξ, the iteration

$$x_{n+1} = x_n - \frac{2f(x_n)}{f'(x_n)} =: g(x_n)$$

does converge quadratically. {*Hint:* For the calculation of $g'(\xi)$, use the fact that

$$\lim_{x \to \xi} \frac{f(x)f''(x)}{[f'(x)]^2} = \lim_{x \to \xi} \frac{f(x)}{[f'(x)]^2} \lim_{x \to \xi} f''(x)$$

and L'Hospital's rule.}

3.5-6 Find the root of the equation

$$x = \tan x$$

which is closest to 100, by Newton's method. (*Note:* Unless x_0 is very carefully chosen, Newton's method produces a divergent sequence.)

3.5-7 Supply the details of the proof of Theorem 3.2.

3.5-8 Prove that, under the conditions of Theorem 3.2, the secant method converges for any choice of x_0, x_1 in the interval $[a, b]$. Also show that the mode of convergence is either monotone or waltzing, depending on the location of two successive iterates. [*Hint:* Use the error equation (3.39) and proceed as in the proof for convergence of Newton's method.]

3.5-9 Show that if $x = \xi$ is a zero of $f(x)$ of multiplicity m the iteration

$$x_{n+1} = x_n - m \frac{f(x_n)}{f'(x_n)}$$

converges quadratically under suitable continuity conditions.

3.6 POLYNOMIAL EQUATIONS: REAL ROOTS

Although polynomial equations can be solved by any of the iterative methods discussed previously, they arise so frequently in physical applications that they warrant special treatment. In particular, we shall present some efficient algorithms for finding real and complex zeros of polynomials. In this section we discuss getting (usually rough) information about the location of zeros of a polynomial, and then give Newton's method for finding a real zero of a polynomial.

A polynomial of (exact) degree n is usually written in the form

$$p(x) = a_0 + a_1 x + a_2 x^2 + \cdots + a_n x^n \qquad a_n \neq 0 \qquad (3.43)$$

Before discussing root-finding methods, a few comments about polynomial roots may be in order. For $n = 2$, $p(x)$ is a quadratic polynomial and of course the zeros may be obtained explicitly by using the quadratic formula as we did in Chap. 1. There are similar, but more complicated, closed-form solutions for polynomials of degrees 3 and 4, but for $n \geq 5$ there are in general no explicit formulas for the zeros. Hence we are forced to consider iterative methods for finding zeros of general polynomials. The methods considered in this chapter can all be used to find real zeros and some can be adapted to find complex zeros. Often we are interested in finding all the zeros of a polynomial. A number of theorems from algebra are useful in locating and classifying the types of zeros of a polynomial.

First we have the fundamental theorem of algebra (see Theorem 1.10) which allows us to conclude that every polynomial of degree n with $a_n \neq 0$ has exactly n zeros, real or complex, if zeros of multiplicity r are counted r times. If the coefficients a_k of the polynomial $p(x)$ are all real and if $z = a + ib$ is a zero, then so is the number $\bar{z} = a - ib$. A useful method for determining the number of real zeros of a polynomial with real coefficients is **Descartes' rule of signs**. The rule states that the number n_p of positive zeros of a polynomial $p(x)$ is less than or equal to the number of variations v **in sign** of the coefficients of $p(x)$. Moreover, the difference $v - n_p$ is an even integer. To determine the number of sign variations, one simply counts the number of sign changes in the nonzero coefficients of $p(x)$. Thus if $p(x) = x^4 + 2x^2 - x - 1$; the number of sign changes is one and by Descartes' rule $p(x)$ has at most one positive zero, but since $v - n_p$

must be a nonnegative even integer, it must have exactly one positive zero. Similarly the number of negative real zeros of $p(x)$ is at most equal to the number of sign changes in the coefficients of the polynomial $p(-x) = -x^3 - 2x^2 - x - 1$; there are no sign changes in $p(-x)$ and hence there are no real negative zeros.

Example 3.8 Determine as much as you can about the real zeros of the polynomial

$$p(x) = x^4 - x^3 - x^2 + x - 1$$

Since there are three sign changes in the coefficients of $p(x)$, there are either three positive real zeros or one. Now $p(-x) = x^4 + x^3 - x^2 - x - 1$, and since there is only one sign change there must be one negative real zero. Thus we must have either three positive real zeros and one negative real zero, or one positive real zero, one negative real zero, and two complex conjugate zeros.

We now quote several theorems which give bounds on the zeros of polynomials. One of these states that if $p(x)$ is a polynomial with coefficients a_k as in (3.43), then $p(x)$ has at least one zero inside the circle defined by $\min\{\rho_1, \rho_n\}$ where

$$\rho_1 = n \frac{|a_0|}{|a_1|} \tag{3.44}$$

and

$$\rho_n = \sqrt[n]{\frac{|a_0|}{|a_n|}}$$

Example If the polynomial is

$$p(x) = x^5 - 3.7x^4 + 7.4x^3 - 10.8x^2 + 10.8x - 6.8 \tag{3.45}$$

then $a_5 = 1$, $a_1 = 10.8$, $a_0 = -6.8$. From (3.44) we get

$$\rho_1 = 5 \cdot \frac{6.8}{10.8} = 3.14 \cdots$$

$$\rho_n = \sqrt[5]{\frac{6.8}{1}} = 1.46 \cdots$$

Hence there must be at least one zero, real or complex, inside the circle $|x| \leq 1.46 \cdots$. Actually we consider this polynomial (3.45) in more detail in the next section where we show that the exact zeros are $1 \pm i$, $\pm \sqrt{2}\, i$, and 1.7.

A second useful theorem, attributable to Cauchy, allows us to establish bounds on the zeros of $p(x)$ as follows. If $p(x)$ is the polynomial (3.43), we define two new polynomials as follows:

$$P(x) = |a_n|x^n - |a_{n-1}|x^{n-1} - \cdots - |a_0| \tag{3.46}$$

$$Q(x) = |a_n|x^n + |a_{n-1}|x^{n-1} + \cdots + |a_1|x - |a_0| \tag{3.46a}$$

By Descartes' rule of signs, (3.46) has exactly one real positive zero R and (3.46a) has exactly one real positive zero r. The Cauchy theorem then states that all the zeros of $p(x)$ lie in the annular region

$$r \leq |x| \leq R$$

Example Consider again the polynomial (3.45). Then we have

$$P(x) = x^5 - 3.7x^4 - 7.4x^3 - 10.8x^2 - 10.8x - 6.8$$
$$Q(x) = x^5 + 3.7x^4 + 7.4x^3 + 10.8x^2 + 10.8x - 6.8$$

whose positive zeros are $R = 5.6 \cdots$, $r = 0.63 \cdots$ respectively. Hence all the zeros of $p(x)$ must satisfy

$$0.63 \cdots < |x| \leq 5.6 \cdots$$

A final theorem of this type states that if $p(x)$ is a polynomial of the form (3.43) and if

$$r := 1 + \max_{0 \leq k \leq n-1} \left| \frac{a_k}{a_n} \right|$$

then every zero of $p(x)$ lies in the circular region defined by $|x| \leq r$.

Example If we consider the polynomial (3.2),

$$p(x) = x^3 - x - 1$$

then $r = 1 + 1/1 = 2.0$ so that all zeros of $p(x)$ lie in a disk centered at the origin with radius 2. In Sec. 3.1 we found one real zero to be $\xi = 1.324 \cdots$. The other two zeros are complex but still inside the circle $|x| \leq 2$.

We now turn to the consideration of iterative methods for finding real zeros of polynomials. In any iterative method we shall have to evaluate the polynomial frequently and so this should be done as efficiently as possible. As shown in Chap. 2, the most efficient method for evaluating a polynomial is **nested multiplication** as described in Algorithm 2.1.

In Algorithm 2.1, the polynomial was assumed given in the Newton form (2.3) with centers $c_1, \ldots, c_n$. If the centers are all equal to zero, the Newton form (2.3) reduces to the standard power form (3.43). If now we are given a point z, Algorithm 2.1 for determining $p(z)$ specializes to

$$a_n' := a_n$$
$$a_{n-1}' := a_{n-1} + za_n'$$
$$\cdots \qquad\qquad (3.47)$$
$$a_1' := a_1 + za_2'$$
$$p(z) = a_0' := a_0 + za_1'$$

The auxiliary quantities $a_1', a_2', \ldots, a_n'$ are of independent interest for we have from (2.4), by again setting all the c_k to zero, that

$$p(x) = a'_0 + (x - z)\{a'_1 + a'_2 x + a'_3 x^2 + \cdots + a'_n x^{n-1}\}$$
$$= a'_0 + (x - z)q(x) \tag{3.48}$$

Hence, $a'_1, \ldots, a'_n$ are the coefficients of the quotient polynomial $q(x)$ obtained by dividing $p(x)$ by the linear polynomial $(x - z)$ and a'_0 is the remainder. In particular if we set $x = z$ in (3.48) we get anew that $p(z) = a'_0$.

Example 3.9: Converting a binary integer into a decimal integer In Sec. 1.1, we presented Algorithm 1.1 for converting a binary integer into a decimal integer. By convention, the binary integer

$$\alpha = (a_n a_{n-1} a_{n-2} \cdots a_0)_2$$

with the a_i either zero or one, represents the number

$$\alpha = a_n 2^n + a_{n-1} 2^{n-1} + \cdots + a_0 2^0$$

Its decimal equivalent can therefore be found by evaluating the polynomial

$$p(x) = a_0 + a_1 x + \cdots + a_n x^n$$

at $x = 2$, using the nested multiplication Algorithm 2.1. This shows Algorithm 1.1 to be a special case of Algorithm 2.1. As an application, the binary integer $\alpha = (110011)_2$ is converted to its decimal equivalent, as follows:

$$a'_5 = a_5 \qquad = 1$$
$$a'_4 = a_4 + 2a'_5 = 3$$
$$a'_3 = a_3 + 2a'_4 = 6$$
$$a'_2 = a_2 + 2a'_3 = 12$$
$$a'_1 = a_1 + 2a'_2 = 25$$
$$\alpha = a'_0 = a_0 + 2a'_1 = 51$$

Our immediate goal is to adapt Newton's method to the problem of finding real zeros of polynomials. To do this, we must be able to evaluate not only $p(x)$ but also $p'(x)$. To find $p'(x)$ at $x = z$, we differentiate (3.48) with respect to x and obtain

$$p'(x) = q(x) + q'(x)(x - z)$$

Hence, on setting $x = z$,

$$p'(z) = q(z)$$

Since $q(x)$ is itself a polynomial whose coefficients we know, we can apply Algorithm 2.1 once more to find $q(z)$, and therefore $p'(z)$. This gives the following algorithm.

Algorithm 3.9: Newton's method for finding real zeros of polynomials Given the $n + 1$ coefficients $a_0, \ldots, a_n$ of the polynomial $p(x)$ in

(3.43) and a starting point x_0.

For $m = 0, 1, \ldots$, until satisfied, do:

$$z := x_m, a'_n := a_n, a''_n := a'_n$$

For $k = n - 1, \ldots, 1$, do:

$$a'_k := a_k + za'_{k+1}$$

$$a''_k := a'_k + za''_{k+1}$$

$$a'_0 := a_0 + za'_1$$

$$x_{m+1} := x_m - a'_0/a''_1$$

Example 3.10 Find all the roots of the polynomial equation $p(x) = x^3 + x - 3 = 0$.

This equation has one real root and two complex roots. Since $p(1) = -1$ and $p(2) = 7$, the real root must lie between $x = 1$ and $x = 2$. We choose $x_0 = 1.1$ and apply Algorithm 3.9, carrying out all calculations on a hand calculator and retaining five places after the decimal point.

	$x_0 = 1.1$			$x_1 = 1.1 - (-0.569)/4.63 = 1.22289$	
k	a_k	a'_k	a''_k	a'_k	a''_k
3	1	1	1	1	1
2	0	1.1	2.2	1.22289	2.44578
1	1	2.21	4.63	2.49546	5.48638
0	-3	-0.569		0.05167	

	$x_2 = 1.22289 - a'_0/a''_1 = 1.21347$			$x_3 = 1.21347 - a'_0/a''_1 = 1.21341$	
k	a_k	a'_k	a''_k	a'_k	a''_k
3	1	1	1	1	1
2	0	1.21347	2.42694	1.21341	2.42682
1	1	2.47251	5.41753	2.47236	5.41709
0	-3	0.000317		-0.00001	

Note that a'_0 is approaching zero and that the a'_k are converging. No further improvement is possible in the solution or in the a'_k, considering the precision to which we are working. We therefore accept $x_3 = 1.21341$, which is correct to at least five significant figures, as the desired real root. To find the remaining complex roots, we apply the quadratic formula to the polynomial equation

$$x^2 + a'_2 x + a'_1 = x^2 + 1.21341x + 2.47236 = 0$$

This yields the results

$$x = \frac{-a'_2 \pm (a'^2_2 - 4a'_1)^{1/2}}{2}$$

$$= \frac{-1.21341 \pm 2.90122i}{2} = -0.60671 \pm 1.45061i$$

for the remaining roots. As a comparison, the zeros of this polynomial will be found again in Sec. 3.7, using a complex-root finder.

Example 3.11 Find the real positive root of the polynomial equation

$$x^5 - 3.7x^4 + 7.4x^3 - 10.8x^2 + 10.8x - 6.8 = 0$$

It is easily verified that the root lies between 1 and 2. We choose $x_0 = 1.5$. The FORTRAN program and machine results are given below. The exact root is 1.7, so that the machine result is correct to eight figures.

FORTRAN PROGRAM FOR EXAMPLE 3.11

```
C  NEWTON'S METHOD FOR FINDING A REAL ZERO OF A CERTAIN POLYNOMIAL.
C  THE COEFFICIENTS ARE SUPPLIED IN A DATA STATEMENT. A FIRST GUESS
C  X  FOR THE ZERO IS READ IN .
       PARAMETER N=6
       INTEGER J,K
       REAL A(N),B,C,DELTAX,X
       DATA A /-6.8, 10.8, -10.8, 7.4, -3.7, 1./
     1 READ 500, X
   500 FORMAT(E16.8)
       PRINT 601
   601 FORMAT('1NEWTONS METHOD FOR FINDING A REAL ZERO OF A POLYNOMIAL'
      *     //4X,'I',10X,'X',14X,'AP(0)',12X,'APP(1)'/)
       DO 10 J=1,20
          B = A(N)
          C = B
          DO 5 K=N,3,-1
             B = A(K-1) + X*B
             C = B + X*C
     5    CONTINUE
          B = A(1) + X*B
          PRINT 605,J,X,B,C
   605    FORMAT(I5,3(1PE17.7))
          DELTAX = B/C
          IF (ABS(DELTAX) .LT. 1.E-7 .OR. ABS(B) .LT. 1.E-7) STOP
          X = X - DELTAX
    10 CONTINUE
       PRINT 610
   610 FORMAT(' FAILED TO CONVERGE IN 20 ITERATIONS')
                                         GO TO 1
       END
```

COMPUTER RESULTS FOR EXAMPLE 3.11

I	X	AP	APP
1	1.5000000E 00	$-1.0625001E - 00$	3.7124998E 00
2	1.7861953E 00	7.2393334E $- 01$	9.6004875E 00
3	1.7107894E 00	8.0013633E $- 02$	7.5470622E 00
4	1.7001875E 00	1.3663173E $- 03$	7.2905675E 00
5	1.7000000E 00	4.7683716E $- 07$	7.2861013E 00
6	1.7000000E 00	$-1.1920929E - 07$	7.2860994E 00
7	1.7000000E 00	$-5.9604645E - 08$	7.2860998E 00

Although in the examples above we encountered no real difficulties in obtaining accurate solutions, the student is warned against assuming that polynomial root finding is without pitfalls. We enumerate some of the difficulties which may be encountered.

1. In Newton's method the accuracy of the zero is limited by the accuracy to which the correction term $p(x_i)/p'(x_i)$ can be computed. If, for example, the error in computing $p(x_i)$, due to roundoff or other causes, is ε, then the computed zero can be determined only up to the actual zero plus $\varepsilon/p'(x_i)$. Figure 3.1 shows dramatically the magnitude of possible errors. Substantial errors will also arise if $p(x)$ has a double zero at $x = \xi$ for then $p'(x)$ will vanish as $x_i \to \xi$ and any round-off errors in computing $p(x_i)$ will be magnified.

To illustrate the behavior of Newton's method around a double root, we consider the polynomial

$$p(x) = x^3 - 3x^2 + 4$$

which has a double zero at $x = 2$. Choosing $x_0 = 1.5$, we obtain, using the IBM 7094 (a machine with 27-binary-digit floating-point arithmetic), the results in Table 3.1.

The numbers after E indicate the exponents of 10. The underlined digits are known to be incorrect because of loss of significance in computing $p(x_i)$ and $p'(x_i)$. From this table we may make the following observations (see Exercise 3.5-5 in this connection):

a. The iterates are converging in spite of the fact that $p'(2) = 0$.

Table 3.1

i	x_i	$p(x_i)$	$p'(x_i)$	$p(x_i)/p'(x_i)$
0	1.5	0.625 E + 0	$-0.22499999E + 1$	$-0.27777778E + 0$
1	1.7777777	$0.13717422E + 0$	$-0.11851852E + 1$	$-0.11574074E + 0$
2	1.8935185	$0.32807648E - 1$	$-0.60487403E + 0$	$-0.54238810E - 1$
3	1.9477573	$0.80453157E - 2$	$-0.30526827E - 0$	$-0.26354902E - 1$
4	1.9741122	$0.19932091E - 2$	$-0.15331630E - 0$	$-0.13000633E - 1$
5	1.9871128	$0.49611926E - 3$	$-0.76824840E - 1$	$-0.64577974E - 2$
6	1.9935706	$0.12376904E - 3$	$-0.38452353E - 1$	$-0.32187638E - 2$
7	1.9967893	$0.30934811E - 4$	$-0.19232938E - 1$	$-0.16084287E - 2$
8	1.9983977	$0.77188015E - 5$	$-0.96056932E - 2$	$-0.80356526E - 3$
9	1.9992013	$0.19371510E - 5$	$-0.47900614E - 2$	$-0.40441045E - 3$
10	1.9996057	$0.47683716E - 6$	$-0.23651228E - 2$	$-0.20161200E - 3$
11	1.9998073	$0.11920929E - 6$	$-0.11558611E - 2$	$-0.10313461E - 3$
12	1.9999104	$0.59604645E - 7$	$-0.53713301E - 3$	$-0.11096813E - 3$
13	2.0000214	$0.29802322E - 7$	$+0.12850899E - 3$	$+0.23190846E - 3$
14	1.9997895	$0.14901161E - 6$	$-0.12628894E - 2$	$-0.11799259E - 3$
15	1.9999074	$0.59604645E - 7$	$-0.55501277E - 3$	$-0.10739328E - 3$

b. The rate of convergence is linear, not quadratic, as is normally the case for Newton's method. An examination of the corrections $p(x_i)/p'(x_i)$ shows that the error is being reduced by a factor of about $\frac{1}{2}$ with each iteration, up to iteration 12.

c. After iteration 13 we can expect no further improvement in the solution. This is because there are no correct figures left in $p(x_i)$, and at the same time $p'(x_i)$ is of the order of 10^{-3}. Thus the quotient $p(x_i)/p'(x_i)$ will produce an incorrect result in the fifth decimal place, making it impossible to improve the solution.

2. In some cases an improper choice of the initial approximation will cause convergence to a zero other than the one desired.

3. For some polynomials an improper choice of x_0 may lead to a divergent sequence. In Example 3.2, for instance, if we take $x_0 = 0$, we obtain the successive approximations $x_1 = -1$, $x_2 = -\frac{1}{2}$, $x_3 = -3$, $\dot{x}_4 = -2.04$, $x_5 = -1.40$, which certainly do not appear to be converging to the zero obtained before. An examination of the graph of the polynomial $p(x) = x^3 - x - 1$ (see Fig. 3.7) will help to explain this behavior. The successive iterates may oscillate indefinitely about the point $x = -\frac{1}{3}\sqrt{3}$ at which $p(x)$ has a maximum value.

4. Some polynomials, especially those of high degree, are very unstable, in the sense that small changes in the coefficients will lead to large changes in the zeros (see Example 3.12 below).

5. Once we have found a zero of a polynomial $p(x)$, the nested multiplication Algorithm (3.47) supplies us with the coefficients $a'_1, \ldots, a'_n$ of the polynomial $q(x)$ which has all the remaining zeros of $p(x)$ as zeros. To find these zeros it would therefore seem simpler to deal with the **reduced** or **deflated** polynomial $q(x)$ rather than with $p(x)$. But we can expect a loss of accuracy in the later zeros because the coefficients in the reduced polynomials will contain errors from incomplete convergence

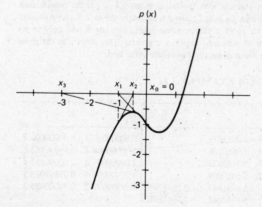

Figure 3.7

and from roundoff. To minimize such loss of accuracy, the zeros should be obtained in increasing order of magnitude (see Example 3.12). Also, the accuracy of a zero found from a reduced polynomial can be improved by iterating with the original polynomial.

Example 3.12 To illustrate some of the dangers in polynomial zero finding, we consider the two polynomials

$$x^7 - 28x^6 + 322x^5 - 1,960x^4 + 6,769x^3 - 13,132x^2 + 13,068x - 5,040 \quad (3.49)$$

and

$$x^5 - 15.5x^4 + 77.5x^3 - 155x^2 + 124x - 32 \quad (3.50)$$

We have used Newton's method (on a CDC 6500) to find all the zeros of these polynomials, working with the reduced polynomial at each stage, with roughly 10 percent error in the initial guess, and with the termination criterion $|x_i - x_{i-1}| < 10^{-7}|x_i|$.

The zeros of the first polynomial, (3.49), are 1, 2, 3, 4, 5, 6, and 7. Column A in the table below contains the approximations found, starting with the initial guesses 0.9, 1.9, 2.9, 3.9, 4.9, 5.9, and 6.9. The number of iterations required is listed after each zero.

The zeros in column B are those obtained when the coefficient of x^2 in (3.49) is replaced by $-13,133$, i.e., after a change of one unit in the fifth place of one coefficient is made. Only five zeros are found, and some of these differ from the corresponding zeros in column A in the second place. In order to confirm that these changes are not just due to roundoff, and to ascertain the fate of the two missing zeros, we also used Müller's method (to be discussed in the next section) which produced the seven zeros listed in column C. These are accurate to all places shown. Note that zeros 5 and 6 have been changed into a complex conjugate pair. Thus a change of $1/100$ of 1 percent in one of the coefficients has led to a change of 10 percent in some of the zeros. When the coefficients of a polynomial have been obtained experimentally, errors of this magnitude are easily encountered in the coefficients. We must, therefore, view with great caution zeros of polynomials of high degree found in this manner, especially when there is some doubt about the accuracy of the coefficients.

The zeros of the second polynomial, (3.50), are 0.5, 1, 2, 4, and 8. Starting with the initial guesses 0.45, 0.9, 1.8, 3.6, and 7.2, we computed the zeros in *ascending* order as shown in column D. Finally, in column E, we have listed the results of computing these zeros in *descending* order, i.e., starting with the initial guess 7.2 to get the zero 8, then using the reduced polynomial and the initial guess 3.6 to obtain the zero 4, etc. Although the first zero found is accurate to nine places, subsequent zeros are found only to six places. Moreover, the number of iterations required is greater. This illustrates the point that it is best to compute the zeros of smallest absolute value first.

COMPUTER RESULTS FOR EXAMPLE 3.12

A,	B	C		D	E
1.00000000 5	1.00139755 5	1.0013976		0.50000000 4	8.00000000 7
2.00000000 5	1.96892082 4	1.9689208		1.00000008 4	3.99999862 6
3.00000000 5	3.31832477 7	3.3183233		2.00000007 4	2.00000552 6
4.00000000 5	3.50505891 7	3.5050604		4.00000005 4	0.99999079 5
5.00000000 4		5.5731849	$+0.2641298i$	7.99999999 2	0.50000485 2
6.00000014 4		5.5731849	$-0.2641298i$		
6.99999993 2	7.05992816 40	7.0599281			

Maehly has proposed a way of using the reduced polynomial which avoids the difficulties illustrated above. Let $\xi_1, \ldots, \xi_k$ be k zeros of a polynomial which have already been found. To find the next zero, one carries out a Newton iteration on the reduced polynomial $\tilde{p}(x) = p(x)/(x - \xi_1)(x - \xi_2) \cdots (x - \xi_k)$, but one does not determine $\tilde{p}(x)$ by repeated synthetic division. Rather one leaves it in this form, in which case the iteration then becomes

$$x_{i+1} = x_i - \frac{\tilde{p}(x_i)}{\tilde{p}'(x_i)}$$

$$= x_i - \frac{p(x_i)}{p'(x_i) - \sum_{r=1}^{k} \frac{p(x_i)}{(x_i - \xi_r)}}$$

This technique appears to be quite effective in producing accurate successive zeros. See Exercise 3.6-7.

EXERCISES

3.6-1 Using Algorithm 3.9 and a hand calculator, find the real root of

$$x^3 + 2x - 1 = 0$$

correct to seven significant figures. Determine the remaining zeros from the reduced polynomial, using the quadratic formula. How accurate are these solutions?

3.6-2 Using Algorithm 3.9, find the real positive roots of the following polynomial equations:
  (a) $x^5 - 3x^3 + x^2 - 1 = 0$ (b) $x^3 + 3x - 1 = 0$

3.6-3 The polynomial $x^4 + 2.8x^3 - 0.38x^2 - 6.3x - 4.2$ has four real zeros. Find them, using Algorithm 3.9.

3.6-4 The polynomial

$$p(x) = x^8 - 170x^6 + 7{,}392x^4 - 39{,}712x^2 + 51{,}200$$

has the zeros ± 10, ± 8, ± 2, $\pm \sqrt{2}$. Find these zeros on a computer in ascending order of magnitude, choosing initial approximations within 10 percent of the exact solutions. Then change the coefficient of x^2 to $-39{,}710$, and solve the problem once again. Observe the change in the solutions.

3.6-5 Use Descartes' rule of signs and the theorems on polynomial zero bounds to find out as much as you can about the location and type of zeros of the polynomial

$$p(x) = x^4 - x^3 + x^2 - x + 1$$

3.6-6 The polynomial

$$p(x) = x^4 - 5.85x^2 + 6.3504$$

has a zero $\xi_1 = 1.2$. There is another real positive zero near $x = 2$. Use Maehly's technique to find this zero starting with $x_0 = 2$.

3.6-7 Write a program based on Maehly's method for finding successive real zeros of a polynomial $p(x)$.

3.6-8 Find the zeros of the polynomial in Example 3.12 using Maehly's method and compare with the results given in Example 3.12.

*3.7 COMPLEX ROOTS AND MÜLLER'S METHOD

The methods discussed up to this point allow us to find an isolated zero of a function once an approximation to that zero is known. These methods are not very satisfactory when all the zeros of a function are required or when good initial approximations are not available. For polynomial functions there are methods which yield an approximation to all the zeros simultaneously, after which the iterative methods of this chapter can be applied to obtain more accurate solutions. Among such methods may be mentioned the quotient-difference algorithm [2] and the method of Graeffe [5].

A method of recent vintage, expounded by Müller [6], has been used on computers with remarkable success. This method may be used to find any prescribed number of zeros, real or complex, of an arbitrary function. The method is iterative, converges almost quadratically in the vicinity of a root, does not require the evaluation of the derivative of the function, and obtains both real and complex roots even when these roots are not simple.

Moreover, the method is global in the sense that the user need not supply an initial approximation. In this section we describe briefly how the method is derived, omitting any discussion of convergence, and we discuss its use in finding both real and complex roots. We will especially emphasize the problem of finding complex zeros of polynomials with real coefficients since this problem is of great concern in many branches of engineering.

Müller's method is an extension of the secant method. To recall, in the secant method we determine, from the approximations x_i, x_{i-1} to a root of $f(x) = 0$, the next approximation x_{i+1} as the zero of the linear polynomial $p(x)$ which goes through the two points $\{x_i, f(x_i)\}$ and $\{x_{i-1}, f(x_{i-1})\}$. In Müller's method, the next approximation, x_{i+1}, is found as a zero of the *parabola* which goes through the three points $\{x_i, f(x_i)\}$, $\{x_{i-1}, f(x_{i-1})\}$, and $\{x_{i-2}, f(x_{i-2})\}$.

As shown in Chap. 2, the function

$$p(x) = f(x_i) + f[x_i, x_{i-1}](x - x_i) + f[x_i, x_{i-1}, x_{i-2}](x - x_i)(x - x_{i-1})$$

is the unique parabola which agrees with the function $f(x)$ at the three points x_i, x_{i-1}, x_{i-2}. Since

$$(x - x_i)(x - x_{i-1}) = (x - x_i)^2 + (x - x_i)(x_i - x_{i-1})$$

we can also write $p(x)$ in the form

$$p(x) = f(x_i) + (x - x_i)c_i + f[x_i, x_{i-1}, x_{i-2}](x - x_i)^2 \qquad (3.51)$$

with

$$c_i = f[x_i, x_{i-1}] + f[x_i, x_{i-1}, x_{i-2}](x_i - x_{i-1})$$

Thus any zero α of the parabola $p(x)$ satisfies

$$\alpha - x_i = \frac{-2f(x_i)}{c_i \pm \left\{ c_i^2 - 4f(x_i)f[x_i, x_{i-1}, x_{i-2}] \right\}^{1/2}} \qquad (3.52)$$

according to one version of the standard quadratic formula [see (1.20)]. If we choose the sign in (3.52) so that the denominator will be as large in magnitude as possible, and if we then label the right-hand side of (3.52) as h_{i+1}, then the next approximation to a zero of $f(x)$ is taken to be

$$x_{i+1} = x_i + h_{i+1}$$

The process is then repeated using x_{i-1}, x_i, x_{i+1} as the three basic approximations. If the zeros obtained from (3.52) are real, the situation is pictured graphically in Fig. 3.8. Note, however, that even if the zero being sought is real, we may encounter complex approximations because the solutions given by (3.52) may be complex. However, in such cases the complex component will normally be so small in magnitude that it can be neglected. In fact, in the subroutine given below, any complex components encountered in seeking a real zero can be suppressed.

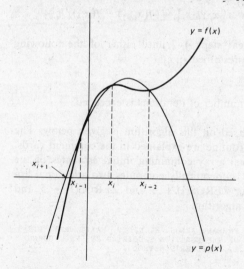

Figure 3.8

The sequence of steps required in Müller's method is formalized in Algorithm 3.10.

Algorithm 3.10: Müller's method

1. Let x_0, x_1, x_2 be three approximations to a zero ξ of $f(x)$. Compute $f(x_0)$, $f(x_1)$, $f(x_2)$.

2. Compute

$$h_2 := x_2 - x_1, h_1 := x_1 - x_0$$
$$f[x_2, x_1] = (f(x_2) - f(x_1))/h_2$$
$$f[x_1, x_0] = (f(x_1) - f(x_0))/h_1$$

3. Set $i = 2$
4. Compute

$$f[x_i, x_{i-1}, x_{i-2}] = (f[x_i, x_{i-1}] - f[x_{i-1}, x_{i-2}])/(h_i + h_{i-1})$$
$$c_i := f[x_i, x_{i-1}] + h_i f[x_i, x_{i-1}, x_{i-2}]$$

5. Compute

$$h_{i+1} := -2f(x_i)/\left(c_i \pm \sqrt{c_i^2 - 4f(x_i)f[x_i, x_{i-1}, x_{i-2}]}\right)$$

choosing the sign so that the denominator is largest in magnitude.
6. Set $x_{i+1} = x_i + h_{i+1}$
7. Compute

$$f(x_{i+1}) \quad \text{and} \quad f[x_{i+1}, x_i] = (f(x_{i+1}) - f(x_i))/h_{i+1}$$

8. Set $i = i + 1$ and repeat steps 4–7 until either of the following criteria is satisfied for prescribed $\varepsilon_1, \varepsilon_2$:
   (a) $|x_i - x_{i-1}| < \varepsilon_1|x_i|$
   (b) $|f(x_i)| < \varepsilon_2$
   or until the maximum number of iterations is exceeded.

A complete subroutine based on this algorithm is given below. The calling parameters for the subroutine are explained in the comment cards. ZEROS(I) is a one-dimensional array containing initial estimates of the desired zeros. The subroutine automatically computes two additional approximations to ZEROS(I) as ZEROS(I) + .5 and ZEROS(I) − .5 and then proceeds with the Müller algorithm.

```
      SUBROUTINE MULLER ( FN, FNREAL, ZEROS, N, NPREV, MAXIT, EP1, EP2 )
C DETERMINES UP TO  N   ZEROS OF THE FUNCTION SPECIFIED BY  FN , USING
C QUADRATIC INTERPOLATION, I.E., MUELLER'S METHOD .
      EXTERNAL FN
      LOGICAL FNREAL
      INTEGER MAXIT,N,NPREV,   KOUNT
      REAL EP1,EP2,    EPS1,EPS2
      COMPLEX ZEROS(N),   C,DEN,DIVDF1,DIVDF2,DVDF1P,FZR,FZRDFL
     *        ,FZRPRV,H,ZERO,SQR
C****** I N P U T  ******
C FN   NAME OF A SUBROUTINE, OF THE FORM  FN(Z, FZ)  WHICH, FOR GIVEN
C      Z , RETURNS  F(Z) . MUST APPEAR IN AN  E X T E R N A L  STATE-
C      MENT IN THE CALLING PROGRAM .
C FNREAL  A LOGICAL VARIABLE. IF .TRUE., ALL APPROXIMATIONS ARE TAKEN
C      TO BE REAL, ALLOWING THIS ROUTINE TO BE USED EVEN IF  F(Z)  IS
C      ONLY DEFINED FOR REAL  Z .
C ZEROS(1),....,ZEROS(NPREV)  CONTAINS PREVIOUSLY FOUND ZEROS (IF
```

```
C       NPREV .GT. 0).
C    ZEROS(NPREV+1),...,ZEROS(N)  CONTAINS FIRST GUESS FOR THE ZEROS TO BE
C       FOUND. (IF YOU KNOW NOTHING, 0  IS AS GOOD A GUESS AS ANY.)
C    MAXIT  MAXIMUM NUMBER OF FUNCTION EVALUATIONS ALLOWED PER ZERO.
C    EP1  ITERATION IS STOPPED IF ABS(H) .LT. EP1*ABS(ZR), WITH
C       H = LATEST CHANGE IN ZERO ESTIMATE  ZERO .
C    EP2  ALTHOUGH THE  EP1  CRITERION IS NOT MET, ITERATION IS STOPPED IF
C       ABS(F(ZERO)) .LT. EP2 .
C    N  TOTAL NUMBER OF ZEROS TO BE FOUND .
C    NPREV  NUMBER OF ZEROS FOUND PREVIOUSLY .
C******  O U T P U T  ******
C    ZEROS(NPREV+1), ..., ZEROS(N)  APPROXIMATIONS TO ZEROS .
C
C                   INITIALIZATION
      EPS1 = MAX(EP1, 1.E-12)
      EPS2 = MAX(EP2, 1.E-20)
C
      DO 100 I=NPREV+1,N
        KOUNT = 0
C               COMPUTE FIRST THREE ESTIMATES FOR ZERO AS
C                  ZEROS(I)+5., ZEROS(I)-.5, ZEROS(I)
    1   ZERO = ZEROS(I)
        H = .5
        CALL DFLATE(FN, ZERO+.5, I, KOUNT, FZR, DVDF1P, ZEROS, *1)
        CALL DFLATE(FN, ZERO-.5, I, KOUNT, FZR, FZRPRV, ZEROS, *1)
        HPREV = -1.
        DVDF1P = (FZRPRV - DVDF1P)/HPREV
        CALL DFLATE(FN, ZERO, I, KOUNT, FZR, FZRDFL, ZEROS, *1)
C       DO WHILE  KOUNT.LE.MAXIT OR  H  IS RELATIVELY BIG
C          OR  FZR = F(ZERO)  IS NOT SMALL
C          OR  FZRDFL = FDEFLATED(ZERO)  IS NOT SMALL OR NOT MUCH
C          BIGGER THAN ITS PREVIOUS VALUE  FZRPRV .
   40   DIVDF1 = (FZRDFL - FZRPRV)/H
        DIVDF2 = (DIVDF1 - DVDF1P)/(H + HPREV)
        HPREV = H
        DVDF1P = DIVDF1
        C = DIVDF1 + H*DIVDF2
        SQR = C*C - 4.*FZRDFL*DIVDF2
        IF (FNREAL .AND. REAL(SQR) .LT. 0.)  SQR = 0.
        SQR = SQRT(SQR)
        IF (REAL(C)*REAL(SQR)+AIMAG(C)*AIMAG(SQR) .LT. 0.) THEN
            DEN = C - SQR
        ELSE
            DEN = C + SQR
        END IF
        IF (ABS(DEN) .LE. 0.)  DEN = 1.
        H = -2.*FZRDFL/DEN
        FZRPRV = FZRDFL
        ZERO = ZERO + H
        IF (KOUNT .GT. MAXIT)        GO TO 99
C
   70   CALL DFLATE(FN, ZERO, I, KOUNT, FZR, FZRDFL, ZEROS, *1)
C                   CHECK FOR CONVERGENCE
        IF (ABS(H) .LT. EPS1*ABS(ZERO)) GO TO 99
        IF (MAX(ABS(FZR),ABS(FZRDFL)) .LT. EPS2)  GO TO 99
C                   CHECK FOR DIVERGENCE
        IF (ABS(FZRDFL) .GE. 10.*ABS(FZRPRV))  THEN
            H = H/2.
            ZERO = ZERO - H
                                    GO TO 70
        ELSE
                                    GO TO 40
        END IF
   99   ZEROS(I) = ZERO
  100 CONTINUE
                                    RETURN
      END
      SUBROUTINE DFLATE ( FN, ZERO, I, KOUNT, FZERO, FZRDFL, ZEROS, * )
C  TO BE CALLED IN   M U L L E R
      INTEGER I,KOUNT,  J
      COMPLEX FZERO,FZRDFL,ZERO,ZEROS(I),  DEN
```

```
      KOUNT = KOUNT + 1
      CALL FN(ZERO, FZERO)
      FZRDFL = FZERO
      IF (I .LT. 2)                          RETURN
      DO 10 J=2,I
         DEN = ZERO - ZEROS(J-1)
         IF (ABS(DEN) .EQ. 0.) THEN
            ZEROS(I) = ZERO*1.001
                                             RETURN 1
         ELSE
            FZRDFL = FZRDFL/DEN
         END IF
10    CONTINUE
                                             RETURN
      END
```

Müller's method, like the other algorithms described in this chapter, finds one zero at a time. To find more than one zero it uses a procedure known as **deflation**. If, for example, one zero ξ_1 has already been found, the routine calculates the next zero by working with the function

$$f_1(x) = \frac{f(x)}{x - \xi_1} \tag{3.53}$$

We already met this technique when solving polynomial equations by Newton's method, in which case the *deflated* or *reduced* function $f_1(x)$ was a by-product of the algorithm. In Müller's method, if r zeros $\xi_1, \ldots, \xi_r$ have already been found, the next zero is obtained by working with the deflated function

$$f_r(x) = \frac{f(x)}{(x - \xi_1)(x - \xi_2) \cdots (x - \xi_r)} \tag{3.54}$$

If no estimates are given, the routine always looks for zeros in order of increasing magnitude since this will usually minimize round-off-error growth. Also, all zeros found using deflated functions are tested for accuracy by substitution into the original function $f(x)$. In practice some accuracy may be lost when a zero is found using deflation. Approximate zeros found using deflation may be refined by using these approximate zeros as initial guesses in Newton's method applied to the original function. In applying the Müller subroutine, the user can specify the number of zeros desired. Some functions, for example, may have an infinite number of zeros, of which only the first few may be of interest.

Example 3.13 Bessel's function $J_0(x)$ is given by the infinite series

$$J_0(x) = 1 - \frac{x^2}{2^2 \cdot 1 \cdot 1} + \frac{x^4}{2^4 \cdot 2! \cdot 2!} - \frac{x^6}{2^6 \cdot 3! \cdot 3!} + \cdots$$

It is known that $J_0(x)$ has an infinite number of real zeros. Find the first three positive zeros, using Algorithm 3.10. The machine results given below were obtained on an IBM 7094 using a standard library subroutine for $J_0(x)$ based on the series given above. The values of $J_0(x)$ were computed to maximum accuracy.

The iterations were all started with the approximations $x_0 = -1$, $x_1 = 1$, $x_2 = 0$ and were continued until either of the following error criteria was satisfied:

(a) $\dfrac{|x_{i+1} - x_i|}{|x_{i+1}|} < 10^{-6}$

(b) $|J_0(x_i)| < 10^{-20}$

The converged values are correct to at least six significant figures. Note that the zeros are obtained in ascending order of magnitude.

COMPUTER RESULTS FOR EXAMPLE 3.13

Zero 1	Zero 2	Zero 3
− 0.09999999E 01	− 0.09999999E 01	− 0.09999999E 01
0.09999999E 01	0.09999999E 01	0.09999999E 01
0.	0.	0.
0.20637107E 01	0.36557332E 01	0.47983123E 01
0.23167706E 01	0.44416171E 01	0.59396663E 01
0.23970029E 01	0.50863190E 01	0.70758440E 01
0.24047983E 01	0.55024961E 01	0.88981197E 01
0.24048255E 01	0.55202182E 01	0.92976399E 01
0.24048255E 01	0.55200780E 01	0.86854592E 01
	0.55200780E 01	0.86529856E 01
		0.86537299E 01
		0.86537278E 01

All the following examples were run on a CDC 6500 computer using Algorithm 3.10. The error criteria for these examples were $\varepsilon_1 = \varepsilon_2 = 10^{-8}$, and all used the same starting values $(0.5, -0.5, 0.0)$ followed by deflation. Although the results are printed to 8 significant figures, one should recall that on a CDC 6500 the floating-point word length is 14 decimal digits. The output consists of the real and imaginary (if applicable) parts of the converged approximations to the roots, and the real and imaginary parts of the value of the function at those roots.

Example 3.14 Find all the zeros of the polynomial $p(x) = x^3 + x - 3$.

ROOT		F(ROOT)	
REAL PART	IMAGINARY PART	REAL PART	IMAGINARY PART
1.2134117E + 00	0.	− 4.2632564E − 14	0.
− 6.0670583E − 01	1.4506122E + 00	2.8421709E − 14	4.2632564E − 14
− 6.0670583E − 01	− 1.4506122E + 00	2.8421709E − 14	− 2.6290081E − 13

Compare these results with those obtained in Example 3.10, where we computed the solutions on a hand calculator. Note that since $p(x)$ has real coefficients, the complex roots occur in complex-conjugate pairs. Note as well that no estimates of the complex roots had to be provided. While Newton's method can be used to find complex roots, it must be supplied with a good estimate of that root, an estimate that may be difficult to obtain. Observe that the error in F(ROOT) is considerably smaller than 10^{-8} as required by the error criterion. In fact, in the last iteration, the error must have been reduced from something like 10^{-7} to 10^{-14}, indicating that the method converges almost quadratically.

Example 3.15 Find the zeros of the polynomial

$$f(x) = x^5 - 3.7x^4 + 7.4x^3 - 10.8x^2 + 10.8x - 6.8$$

This is Example 3.11 solved earlier by Newton's method. The exact zeros are $1 \pm i$, $\pm \sqrt{2} \, i$, and 1.7. The results below are correct to eight significant figures, even though there is a small real component to the pure-imaginary zeros $\pm \sqrt{2} \, i$.

ROOT		F(ROOT)	
REAL PART	IMAGINARY PART	REAL PART	IMAGINARY PART
1.0000000E + 00	−1.0000000E + 00	−2.8421709E − 14	2.8421709E − 14
1.0000000E + 00	1.0000000E + 00	1.4210855E − 13	−1.5631940E − 13
−9.0964472E − 12	1.4142136E + 00	−8.5330498E − 10	−1.2773698E − 09
8.3306265E − 11	−1.4142136E + 00	−8.5339025E − 10	−1.2785158E − 09
1.7000000E + 00	1.3036419E − 10	6.3431571E − 10	9.4984654E − 10

Example 3.16 Find the zeros of the polynomial

$$f(x) = x^7 - 28x^6 + 322x^5 - 1,960x^4 + 6,769x^3 - 13,132x^2 + 13,068 - 5,040$$

This example was treated by Newton's method in Example 3.12, where we had some difficulty in finding accurate solutions. The zeros are $x = 1, 2, 3, 4, 5, 6, 7$. The results below are remarkably accurate, although the long word length on the CDC 6500 is largely responsible for this. Note that although, in general, Müller's method seeks the zeros in ascending order of magnitude, in this case it did not succeed in doing so.

ROOT		F(ROOT)	
REAL PART	IMAGINARY PART	REAL PART	IMAGINARY PART
2.0000000E + 00	−2.6080092E − 16	−5.8207661E − 11	3.1296110E − 14
3.0000000E + 00	7.4093893E − 11	−7.8580342E − 10	3.5565069E − 09
1.0000000E + 00	−1.7030067E − 16	0.	−1.2261648E − 13
6.0000000E + 00	1.6284031E − 15	−1.0710210E − 08	−1.9540837E − 13
5.0000000E + 00	−7.2393906E − 13	2.4156179E − 09	−3.4749075E − 11
4.0000000E + 00	−2.3682266E − 10	2.0954758E − 09	8.5256156E − 09
7.0000000E + 00	−8.1000834E − 20	4.0745363E − 10	−5.8320601E − 17

Example 3.17 Find the zeros of the polynomial

$$f(x) = x^8 - 170x^6 + 7,392x^4 - 39,712x^2 + 51,200$$

This polynomial has the zeros ± 10, ± 2, ± 8, $\pm \sqrt{2}$. The program was run in the complex mode and produced the zeros correct to eight significant figures. This example shows that this algorithm is capable of handling polynomials of fairly high degree with good results (see Exercise 3.6-4).

ROOT		F(ROOT)	
REAL PART	IMAGINARY PART	REAL PART	IMAGINARY PART
$-1.4142136E + 00$	0.	$-2.3282064E - 10$	0.
$1.4142136E + 00$	0.	$-2.3283064E - 10$	0.
$2.0000000E + 00$	0.	0.	0.
$-2.0000000E + 00$	0.	0.	0.
$8.0000000E + 00$	0.	$2.9336661E - 08$	0.
$-8.0000000E + 00$	0.	$2.9336661E - 08$	0.
$1.0000000E + 01$	0.	$2.3352914E - 07$	0.
$-1.0000000E + 01$	0.	$1.8742867E - 07$	0.

EXERCISES

3.7-1 Use Müller's method to find the zeros, real or complex, of the following polynomials:
  (a) $x^7 - 1$
  (b) $x^4 - 7x^3 + 18x^2 - 20x + 8$
  (c) $x^6 + 2x^5 + x^4 + 3x^3 + 5x^2 + x + 1$

3.7-2 The equation $x - \tan x = 0$ has an infinite number of real roots. Use Müller's method to find the first three positive roots.

3.7-3 The Fresnel integral $C(x)$ is defined by the series

$$C(x) = \sum_{n=0}^{\infty} \frac{(-1)^n \left(\frac{\pi}{2}\right)^{2n}}{(2n)!\,(4n + 1)} x^{4n+1}$$

Find the first three real positive zeros of this function using Müller's method. Start by truncating the series with $n = 3$ and then increase n until you are satisfied that you have the correct zeros.

3.7-4 Bessel's function of order 1 is defined by the series

$$J_1(z) = \frac{z}{2} \sum_{k=0}^{\infty} \frac{(-z^2/4)^k}{k!\,(k + 1)!}$$

Find the first four zeros of this function proceeding as in Exercise 3.7-3.

FOUR

MATRICES AND SYSTEMS OF LINEAR EQUATIONS

Many of the problems of numerical analysis can be reduced to the problem of solving linear systems of equations. Among the problems which can be so treated are the solution of ordinary or partial differential equations by finite-difference methods, the solution of systems of equations, the eigenvalue problems of mathematical physics, least-squares fitting of data, and polynomial approximation. The use of matrix notation is not only convenient, but extremely powerful, in bringing out fundamental relationships. In Sec. 4.1 we introduce some simple properties of matrices which will be used in later sections. Some of the theorems and properties will be stated without proof.

4.1 PROPERTIES OF MATRICES

A system of m linear equations in n unknowns has the general form

$$
\begin{aligned}
a_{11}x_1 + a_{12}x_2 + \cdots + a_{1n}x_n &= b_1 \\
a_{21}x_1 + a_{22}x_2 + \cdots + a_{2n}x_n &= b_2 \\
\cdots\cdots\cdots\cdots\cdots\cdots\cdots\cdots\cdots\cdots\cdots \\
a_{m1}x_1 + a_{m2}x_2 + \cdots + a_{mn}x_n &= b_m
\end{aligned}
\tag{4.1}
$$

The **coefficients** a_{ij} $(i = 1, \ldots, m; j = 1, \ldots, n)$ and the **right sides** b_i $(i = 1, \ldots, m)$ are given numbers. The problem is to find, if possible, numbers x_j $(j = 1, \ldots, n)$ such that the m equations (4.1) are satisfied simultaneously. The discussion and understanding of this problem is greatly facilitated when use is made of the algebraic concepts of *matrix* and *vector*.

Definition of Matrix and Vector

A **matrix** is a rectangular array of (usually real) numbers arranged in rows and columns. The coefficients of (4.1) form a matrix, which we will call A. It is customary to display such a matrix A as follows:

$$A = \begin{bmatrix} a_{11} & a_{12} & \cdots & a_{1n} \\ a_{21} & a_{22} & \cdots & a_{2n} \\ \cdot & \cdot & \cdots & \cdot \\ a_{m1} & a_{m2} & \cdots & a_{mn} \end{bmatrix} \tag{4.2}$$

At times, we will write more briefly

$$A = (a_{ij}) \tag{4.3}$$

The matrix A in (4.2) has m **rows** and n **columns**, or A **is of order** $m \times n$, for short. The (i, j) **entry** a_{ij} of A is located at the intersection of the ith row and the jth column of A. If A is an $n \times n$ matrix, we say that A is a **square matrix of order** n. If a matrix has only one column, we call it a **column vector**, and a matrix having only one row is called a **row vector**. We denote column vectors by a single lowercase letter in bold type, to distinguish them from other matrices, and call them **vectors**, for short. Thus both the right-side constants b_i $(i = 1, \ldots, m)$ and the unknowns x_j $(j = 1, \ldots, n)$ form vectors,

$$\mathbf{b} = \begin{bmatrix} b_1 \\ b_2 \\ b_3 \\ \vdots \\ b_m \end{bmatrix} \qquad \mathbf{x} = \begin{bmatrix} x_1 \\ x_2 \\ x_3 \\ \vdots \\ x_n \end{bmatrix} \tag{4.4}$$

We say that $\mathbf{b}$ is an *m-vector*, and $\mathbf{x}$ is an *n*-vector.

Equality

If $A = (a_{ij})$ and $B = (b_{ij})$ are both matrices, then we say that A **equals** B, or $A = B$, provided A and B have the same order *and* $a_{ij} = b_{ij}$, all i and j.

Matrix Multiplication

In the terminology so far introduced, (4.1) states that the matrix A combined in a certain way with the one-column matrix, or vector, $\mathbf{x}$ should equal the one-column matrix, or vector, $\mathbf{b}$. The process of combining matrices involved here is called *matrix multiplication* and is defined, in general, as follows: Let $A = (a_{ij})$ be an $m \times n$ matrix, $B = (b_{ij})$ an $n \times p$ matrix; then *the matrix* $C = (c_{ij})$ *is the* (matrix) **product of** A **with** B (in that order), or $C = AB$, provided C is of order $m \times p$ and

$$c_{ij} = \sum_{k=1}^{n} a_{ik} b_{kj} \quad \text{for } i = 1, \ldots, m; j = 1, \ldots, p \qquad (4.5)$$

In words, the (i, j) entry of the product $C = AB$ of A with B is calculated by taking the n entries of row i of A and the n entries of column j of B, multiplying corresponding entries, and summing the resulting n products.

Example

$$\text{If } A = \begin{bmatrix} 3 & 0 & 2 \\ 1 & -2 & 0 \\ 0 & 1 & 1 \end{bmatrix} \quad \text{and} \quad B = \begin{bmatrix} 2 & 1 \\ 0 & 1 \\ 1 & 0 \end{bmatrix}, \quad \text{then} \quad AB = \begin{bmatrix} 8 & 3 \\ 2 & 3 \\ 1 & 1 \end{bmatrix}$$

The (2,1) entry of AB, for instance, is obtained by combining row 2 of A with column 1 of B:

$$1 \cdot 2 + 2 \cdot 0 + 0 \cdot 1 = 2$$

as indicated by the arrows.

With this definition of matrix product and the definitions (4.2) and (4.4), we can write our system of equations (4.1) simply as

$$A\mathbf{x} = \mathbf{b} \qquad (4.6)$$

At present, it looks as if this simplification was achieved at the cost of several definitions, one of them quite complicated, but the many advantages of matrix notation will become apparent in the course of this chapter.

Matrix multiplication does not at all behave like multiplication of numbers. For example, it is possible to form the product of the matrix A with the matrix B only when the number of columns of A equals the number of rows of B. Hence, even when the product AB is defined, the product of B with A need not be defined. Further, even when both AB and BA are defined, they need not be equal.

Example

$$\text{If } A = \begin{bmatrix} 2 & 1 \\ 1 & 3 \end{bmatrix} \quad \text{and} \quad B = \begin{bmatrix} 2 & 1 \\ 0 & 1 \end{bmatrix}, \quad \text{then} \quad AB = \begin{bmatrix} 4 & 3 \\ 2 & 4 \end{bmatrix} \neq \begin{bmatrix} 5 & 5 \\ 1 & 3 \end{bmatrix} = BA$$

On the other hand, *matrix multiplication is* **associative**: If A, B, C are matrices of order $m \times n$, $n \times p$, $p \times q$, respectively, then

$$(AB)C = A(BC) \qquad (4.7)$$

This can be seen as follows: Since A is of order $m \times n$, while B is of order $n \times p$, AB is defined and is of order $m \times p$; hence $(AB)C$ is defined and is of order $m \times q$. In the same way, one verifies that $A(BC)$ is defined and is also of order $m \times q$, so that at least one condition for equality is satisfied. Further,

$$(i,j) \text{ entry of } (AB)C = \sum_{k=1}^{p} \left[(i, k) \text{ entry of } AB \right] * c_{kj}$$

$$= \sum_{k=1}^{p} \left[\sum_{r=1}^{n} a_{ir} * b_{rk} \right] * c_{kj}$$

$$= \sum_{r=1}^{n} a_{ir} * \left[\sum_{k=1}^{p} b_{rk} * c_{kj} \right]$$

$$= \sum_{r=1}^{n} a_{ir} * \left[(r,j) \text{ entry of } BC \right]$$

$$= (i,j) \text{ entry of } A(BC)$$

proving that $(AB)C = A(BC)$. We will make repeated use of the special case when C is a vector (of appropriate order), that is

$$(AB)\mathbf{x} = A(B\mathbf{x})$$

Diagonal and Triangular Matrices

If $A = (a_{ij})$ is a square matrix of order n, then we call its entries $a_{11}, a_{22}, \ldots, a_{nn}$ the **diagonal** entries of A, and call all other entries **off-diagonal**. All entries a_{ij} of A with $i < j$ are called **superdiagonal**, all entries a_{ij} with $i > j$ are called **subdiagonal** (see Fig. 4.1).

If all off-diagonal entries of the *square* matrix A are zero, we call A a **diagonal matrix**. If all subdiagonal entries of the square matrix A are zero, we call A an **upper** (or right) **triangular matrix**, while if all superdiagonal entries of A are zero, then A is called **lower** (or left) **triangular**. Clearly, a matrix is diagonal if and only if it is both upper and lower triangular.

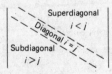

Superdiagonal
$i < j$
Diagonal $i = j$
Subdiagonal
$i > j$

Figure 4.1

Examples In the following examples, matrices A and C are diagonal; matrices A, B, C are upper-triangular and matrices A, C, and D are lower-triangular, and matrix E has none of these properties.

$$A = \begin{bmatrix} 1 & 0 & 0 \\ 0 & 1 & 0 \\ 0 & 0 & 1 \end{bmatrix} \qquad B = \begin{bmatrix} 0 & 1 & 2 \\ 0 & 3 & 1 \\ 0 & 0 & 4 \end{bmatrix} \qquad C = \begin{bmatrix} 0 & 0 & 0 \\ 0 & 0 & 0 \\ 0 & 0 & 0 \end{bmatrix}$$

$$D = \begin{bmatrix} 10 & 0 & 0 \\ 8 & 7 & 0 \\ 1 & 1 & 1 \end{bmatrix} \qquad E = \begin{bmatrix} 1 & 0 & 0 \\ 3 & 2 & 6 \\ 0 & 0 & 4 \end{bmatrix}$$

The Identity Matrix and Matrix Inversion

If a diagonal matrix of order n has all its diagonal entries equal to 1, then we call it the **identity matrix** of order n and denote it by the special letter I, or I_n if the order is important. The name identity matrix was chosen for this matrix because

$$I_n A = A \qquad \text{for all } n \times p \text{ matrices } A$$
$$B I_n = B \qquad \text{for all } m \times n \text{ matrices } B$$

The matrix I acts just like the number 1 in ordinary multiplication.

Division of matrices is, in general, not defined. However, for square matrices, we define a related concept, *matrix inversion*. We say that the *square* matrix A of order n is **invertible** provided there is a square matrix B of order n such that

$$AB = I = BA \tag{4.8}$$

The matrix $A = \begin{bmatrix} 1 & 1 \\ 0 & 1 \end{bmatrix}$, for instance, is invertible since

$$\begin{bmatrix} 1 & 1 \\ 0 & 1 \end{bmatrix}\begin{bmatrix} 1 & -1 \\ 0 & 1 \end{bmatrix} = \begin{bmatrix} 1 & 0 \\ 0 & 1 \end{bmatrix} = \begin{bmatrix} 1 & -1 \\ 0 & 1 \end{bmatrix}\begin{bmatrix} 1 & 1 \\ 0 & 1 \end{bmatrix}$$

On the other hand, the matrix $A = \begin{bmatrix} 1 & 2 \\ 2 & 4 \end{bmatrix}$ is not invertible. For if B were a matrix such that $BA = I$, then it would follow that

$$\begin{bmatrix} b_{11} + 2b_{12} & 2b_{11} + 4b_{12} \\ b_{21} + 2b_{22} & 2b_{21} + 4b_{22} \end{bmatrix} = BA = \begin{bmatrix} 1 & 0 \\ 0 & 1 \end{bmatrix}$$

Hence we should have $b_{11} + 2b_{12} = 1$ and, at the same time $2(b_{11} + 2b_{12}) = 2b_{11} + 4b_{12} = 0$, which is impossible.

We note that (4.8) can hold for at most one matrix B. For if

$$AB = I \qquad \text{and} \qquad CA = I$$

where B and C are square matrices of the same order as A, then

$$C = CI = C(AB) = (CA)B = IB = B$$

showing that B and C must then be equal. Hence, if A is invertible, then there exists exactly one matrix B satisfying (4.8). This matrix is called **the inverse of** A and is denoted by A^{-1}.

It follows at once from (4.8) that if A is invertible, then so is A^{-1}, and its inverse is A; that is,

$$(A^{-1})^{-1} = A \qquad (4.9)$$

Further, if both A and B are invertible square matrices of the same order, then their product is invertible and

$$(AB)^{-1} = B^{-1}A^{-1} \qquad (4.10)$$

Note the change in order! The proof of (4.10) rests on the associativity of matrix multiplication:

$$(AB)(B^{-1}A^{-1}) = A(BB^{-1})A^{-1} = AA^{-1} = I$$
$$(B^{-1}A^{-1})(AB) = B^{-1}(A^{-1}A)B = B^{-1}B = I$$

Example The matrix $A = \begin{bmatrix} 1 & 1 \\ 0 & 1 \end{bmatrix}$ has inverse $A^{-1} = \begin{bmatrix} 1 & -1 \\ 0 & 1 \end{bmatrix}$, while the matrix $B = \begin{bmatrix} 1 & 0 \\ 1 & 1 \end{bmatrix}$ has inverse $B^{-1} = \begin{bmatrix} 1 & 0 \\ -1 & 1 \end{bmatrix}$. Further, $AB = \begin{bmatrix} 2 & 1 \\ 1 & 1 \end{bmatrix}$. Hence by (4.10), $(AB)^{-1} = \begin{bmatrix} 1 & -1 \\ -1 & 2 \end{bmatrix} = B^{-1}A^{-1}$. On the other hand, $A^{-1}B^{-1} = \begin{bmatrix} 2 & -1 \\ -1 & 1 \end{bmatrix}$, and

$$(AB)(A^{-1}B^{-1}) = \begin{bmatrix} 2 & 1 \\ 1 & 1 \end{bmatrix}\begin{bmatrix} 2 & -1 \\ -1 & 1 \end{bmatrix} = \begin{bmatrix} 3 & -1 \\ 1 & 0 \end{bmatrix} \neq I$$

so that $A^{-1}B^{-1}$ cannot be the inverse of AB.

Matrix Addition and Scalar Multiplication

It is possible to multiply a matrix by a scalar ($=$ number) and to add two matrices of the same order in a reasonable way. First, if $A = (a_{ij})$ and $B = (b_{ij})$ are matrices and d is a number, we say that B is the **product** *of d with A*, or $B = dA$, provided B and A have the same order and

$$b_{ij} = da_{ij} \qquad \text{all } i \text{ and } j$$

Further, if $A = (a_{ij})$ and $B = (b_{ij})$ are matrices of the same order and $C = (c_{ij})$ is a matrix, we say that C is the **sum** *of A and B*, or $C = A + B$, provided C is of the same order as A and B and

$$c_{ij} = a_{ij} + b_{ij} \qquad \text{all } i \text{ and } j$$

Hence multiplication of a matrix by a number and addition of matrices is done entry by entry. The following rules regarding these operations, and also matrix multiplication, are easily verified: Assume that A, B, C are matrices such that all the sums and products mentioned below are defined, and let a, b be some numbers. Then

(i) $A + B = B + A$
(ii) $(A + B) + C = A + (B + C)$
(iii) $a(A + B) = aA + aB$
(iv) $(a + b)A = aA + bA$ (4.11)
(v) $(A + B)C = AC + BC$
(vi) $A(B + C) = AB + AC$
(vii) $a(AB) = (aA)B = A(aB)$
(viii) If $a \neq 0$ and A is invertible, then aA is invertible and $(aA)^{-1} = (1/a)A^{-1}$.

For the sake of illustration we now give a proof of (vi). With A an $m \times n$ matrix and B and C $n \times p$ matrices, both sides of (vi) are well-defined $m \times p$ matrices. Further,

$$(i,j)\text{entry of } A(B + C) = \sum_{k=1}^{n} a_{ik} * [(k,j) \text{ entry of } (B + C)]$$

$$= \sum_{k=1}^{n} a_{ik} * [b_{kj} + c_{kj}]$$

$$= \sum_{k=1}^{n} a_{ik}b_{kj} + \sum_{k=1}^{n} a_{ik}c_{kj}$$

$$= [(i,j) \text{ entry of } AB] + [(i,j) \text{ entry of } AC]$$

$$= (i,j) \text{ entry of } (AB + AC)$$

Finally, if the $m \times n$ matrix A has all its entries equal to 0, then we call it the **null matrix** of order $m \times n$ and denote it by the special letter O. A null matrix has the obvious property that

$$B + O = B \qquad \text{for all matrices } B \text{ of the same order}$$

Linear Combinations

The definition of sums of matrices and products of numbers with matrices makes it, in particular, possible to sum n-vectors and multiply n-vectors by numbers or scalars. If $\mathbf{x}^{(1)}, \ldots, \mathbf{x}^{(k)}$ are k n-vectors and $b_1, b_2, \ldots, b_k$ are k numbers, then the weighted sum

$$b_1\mathbf{x}^{(1)} + b_2\mathbf{x}^{(2)} + \cdots + b_k\mathbf{x}^{(k)}$$

is also an n-vector, called the **linear combination** of $\mathbf{x}^{(1)}, \ldots, \mathbf{x}^{(k)}$ with **weights**, or coefficients, $b_1, \ldots, b_k$.

Consider now, once more, our system of equations (4.1). For $j = 1, \ldots, n$, let $\mathbf{a}_j$ denote the jth column of the $m \times n$ coefficient matrix A; that is, $\mathbf{a}_j$ is the m-vector whose ith entry is the number a_{ij}, $i = 1, \ldots, m$.

Then we can write the m-vector $A\mathbf{x}$ as

$$A\mathbf{x} = x_1\mathbf{a}_1 + x_2\mathbf{a}_2 + \cdots + x_n\mathbf{a}_n$$

i.e., as a linear combination of the n columns of A with weights the entries of $\mathbf{x}$. The problem of solving (4.1) has therefore the equivalent formulation: Find weights $x_1, \ldots, x_n$ so that the linear combination of the n columns of A with these weights adds up to the right-side m-vector $\mathbf{b}$.

Consistent with this notation, we denote the jth column of the identity matrix I by the special symbol

$$\mathbf{i}_j$$

Clearly, $\mathbf{i}_j$ has all its entries equal to zero except for the jth entry, which is 1. It is customary to call $\mathbf{i}_j$ the jth **unit** vector. (As with the identity matrix, we do not bother to indicate explicitly the length or order of $\mathbf{i}_j$, it being understood from the context.) With this notation, we have

$$b_1\mathbf{i}_1 + b_2\mathbf{i}_2 + \cdots + b_n\mathbf{i}_n = \mathbf{b}$$

for every n-vector $\mathbf{b} = (b_i)$. Further, the jth column $\mathbf{a}_j$ of the matrix A can be obtained by multiplying A with $\mathbf{i}_j$; that is,

$$\mathbf{a}_j = A\mathbf{i}_j$$

Hence, if $C = AB$, then

$$C\mathbf{i}_j = (AB)\mathbf{i}_j = A(B\mathbf{i}_j)$$

so that the jth column of the product AB is obtained by multiplying the first factor A with the jth column of the second factor B.

Existence and Uniqueness of Solutions to (4.1)

In later sections, we will deal exclusively with linear systems which have a *square* coefficient matrix. We now justify this by showing that our system (4.1) cannot have exactly one solution for every right side unless the coefficient matrix is square.

Lemma 4.1 If $\mathbf{x} = \mathbf{x}_1$ is a solution of the linear system $A\mathbf{x} = \mathbf{b}$ then any solution $\mathbf{x} = \mathbf{x}_2$ of this system is of the form

$$\mathbf{x}_2 = \mathbf{x}_1 + \mathbf{y}$$

where $\mathbf{x} = \mathbf{y}$ is a solution of the **homogeneous** system $A\mathbf{x} = \mathbf{0}$.

Indeed, if both $\mathbf{x}_1$ and $\mathbf{x}_2$ solve $A\mathbf{x} = \mathbf{b}$, then

$$A(\mathbf{x}_2 - \mathbf{x}_1) = A\mathbf{x}_2 - A\mathbf{x}_1 = \mathbf{b} - \mathbf{b} = \mathbf{0}$$

i.e., then their difference $\mathbf{y} = \mathbf{x}_2 - \mathbf{x}_1$ solves the homogeneous system $A\mathbf{x} = \mathbf{0}$.

Example The linear system

$$x_1 + 2x_2 = 3$$
$$2x_1 + 4x_2 = 6$$

has the solution $x_1 = x_2 = 1$. The corresponding homogeneous system

$$x_1 + 2x_2 = 0$$
$$2x_1 + 4x_2 = 0$$

has the solution $x_1 = -2a$, $x_2 = a$, where a is an arbitrary scalar. Hence any solution of the original system is of the form $x_1 = 1 - 2a$, $x_2 = 1 + a$ for some number a.

The lemma implies the following theorem.

Theorem 4.1 The linear system $A\mathbf{x} = \mathbf{b}$ has at most one solution (i.e., the solution is unique if it exists) if and only if the corresponding homogeneous system $A\mathbf{x} = \mathbf{0}$ has only the "trivial" solution $\mathbf{x} = \mathbf{0}$.

Next we prove that we cannot hope for a unique solution unless our linear system has at least as many equations as unknowns.

Theorem 4.2 Any homogeneous linear system with fewer equations than unknowns has nontrivial (i.e., nonzero) solutions.

We have to prove that if A is an $m \times n$ matrix with

$$m < n$$

then we can find $\mathbf{y} \neq \mathbf{0}$ such that $A\mathbf{y} = \mathbf{0}$. This we do by induction on n. First, consider the case $n = 2$. In this case, we can have only one equation,

$$a_{11}x_1 + a_{12}x_2 = 0$$

and this equation has the nontrivial solution $x_1 = 0$, $x_2 = 1$, if $a_{12} = 0$; otherwise, it has the nontrivial solution $x_1 = a_{12}$, $x_2 = -a_{11}$. This proves our statement for $n = 2$. Let now $n > 2$, and assume it proved that any homogeneous system with less equations than unknowns and with less than n unknowns has nontrivial solutions; further, let $A\mathbf{x} = \mathbf{0}$ be a homogeneous linear system with m equations and n unknowns where $m < n$. We have to prove that this system has nontrivial solutions. This is certainly so if the nth column of A is zero, i.e., if $\mathbf{a}_n = \mathbf{0}$; for then the nonzero n-vector $\mathbf{x} = \mathbf{i}_n$ is a solution. Otherwise, some entry of $\mathbf{a}_n$ must be different from 0, say,

$$a_{in} \neq 0$$

In this case, we consider the $m \times (n - 1)$ matrix B whose jth column is

$$\mathbf{b}_j = \mathbf{a}_j - \frac{a_{ij}}{a_{in}}\mathbf{a}_n \qquad j = 1, \ldots, n - 1$$

If we can show that the homogeneous system

$$Bx = 0$$

has nontrivial solutions, then we are done. For if we can find numbers $x_1, \ldots, x_{n-1}$ not all zero such that

$$x_1 b_1 + x_2 b_2 + \cdots + x_{n-1} b_{n-1} = 0$$

then it follows from the definition of the b_j's that

$$x_1 a_1 + x_2 a_2 + \cdots + x_{n-1} a_{n-1} + \left(-\sum_{j=1}^{n-1} x_j \frac{a_{ij}}{a_{in}} \right) a_n = 0$$

thus providing a nontrivial solution to $Ax = 0$. Hence it remains only to show that $Bx = 0$ has nontrivial solutions. For this, note that for each j, the ith entry of b_j is

$$a_{ij} - \frac{a_{ij}}{a_{in}} a_{in} = 0$$

so that the ith equation of $Bx = 0$ looks like

$$0 \cdot x_1 + 0 \cdot x_2 + \cdots + 0 \cdot x_{n-1} = 0$$

and is therefore satisfied by any choice of $x_1, \ldots, x_{n-1}$. It follows that $x = y$ solves $Bx = 0$ if and only if $x = y$ solves the homogeneous system

$$\hat{B}x = 0$$

which we get from $Bx = 0$ by merely omitting the ith equation. But now $\hat{B}x = 0$ is a homogeneous linear system with $m - 1$ equations in $n - 1$ unknowns, hence with less equations than unknowns and with less than n unknowns. Therefore, by the induction hypothesis, $\hat{B}x = 0$ has nontrivial solutions, which finishes the proof.

Example Consider the homogeneous linear system $Ax = 0$ given by

$$x_1 + 2x_2 - x_3 = 0$$
$$x_1 - x_2 + x_3 = 0$$

so that $m = 2$, $n = 3$. Following the argument for Theorem 4.2, we construct a nontrivial solution as follows: Since $a_{23} \neq 0$, we pick $i = 2$ and get

$$b_1 = a_1 - \frac{a_{21}}{a_{23}} a_3 = \begin{bmatrix} 1 \\ 1 \end{bmatrix} - (1/1) \begin{bmatrix} -1 \\ 1 \end{bmatrix} = \begin{bmatrix} 2 \\ 0 \end{bmatrix}$$

$$b_2 = a_2 - \frac{a_{22}}{a_{23}} a_3 = \begin{bmatrix} 2 \\ -1 \end{bmatrix} - (-1/1) \begin{bmatrix} -1 \\ 1 \end{bmatrix} = \begin{bmatrix} 1 \\ 0 \end{bmatrix}$$

The smaller homogeneous system $Bx = 0$ is therefore

$$2x_1 + x_2 = 0$$
$$0x_1 + 0x_2 = 0$$

We can ignore the last equation and get, then, the homogeneous system $\hat{B}x = 0$ which consists of just one equation,

$$2x_1 + x_2 = 0$$

A nontrivial solution for this is $x_1 = 1$, $x_2 = -2$. Hence, with

$$x_3 = -[1(1/1) + (-2)(-1/1)] = -3$$

the 3-vector $\mathbf{x} = (x_j)$ is a nontrivial solution of the original system.

Next we prove that we cannot expect to get a solution to our linear system (4.1) for all possible choices of the right side $\mathbf{b}$ unless we have no more equations than unknowns.

Lemma 4.2 If A is an $m \times n$ matrix and the linear system $A\mathbf{x} = \mathbf{b}$ has a solution for every m-vector $\mathbf{b}$, then there exists an $n \times m$ matrix C such that

$$AC = I_m$$

Such a matrix C can be constructed as follows: By assumption, we can find a solution to the system $A\mathbf{x} = \mathbf{b}$ no matter what $\mathbf{b}$ is. Hence, choosing $\mathbf{b}$ to be the jth column of I, we can find an n-vector $\mathbf{c}_j$ such that

$$A\mathbf{c}_j = \mathbf{i}_j \quad j = 1, \ldots, m$$

But then, with C the $n \times m$ matrix whose jth column is $\mathbf{c}_j, j = 1, \ldots, m$, we get

$$(AC)\mathbf{i}_j = A(C\mathbf{i}_j) = A\mathbf{c}_j = \mathbf{i}_j = I\mathbf{i}_j \quad j = 1, \ldots, m$$

showing that the jth column of the product AC agrees with the jth column of $I, j = 1, \ldots, m$. But that says that $AC = I$.

Lemma 4.3 If B and C are matrices such that

$$BC = I$$

then the homogeneous system $C\mathbf{x} = \mathbf{0}$ has only the trivial solution $\mathbf{x} = \mathbf{0}$.

Indeed, if $C\mathbf{x} = \mathbf{0}$, then

$$\mathbf{x} = I\mathbf{x} = (BC)\mathbf{x} = B(C\mathbf{x}) = B\mathbf{0} = \mathbf{0}$$

Theorem 4.3 If A is an $m \times n$ matrix and the linear system $A\mathbf{x} = \mathbf{b}$ has a solution for every possible m-vector $\mathbf{b}$, then $m \leq n$.

For the proof, we get from Lemma 4.2 that

$$AC = I$$

for some $n \times m$ matrix C. But this implies by Lemma 4.3 that the homogeneous system $C\mathbf{x} = \mathbf{0}$ has only the trivial solution $\mathbf{x} = \mathbf{0}$. Therefore, by Theorem 4.2, C must have at least as many rows as columns, that is, $n \geq m$, which finishes the proof.

We now know that we cannot expect to get exactly one solution to our system (4.1) for every possible right side unless the system has exactly as many equations as unknowns, i.e., unless the coefficient matrix is square. We will therefore consider from now on only linear systems with a square coefficient matrix. For such square matrices, we prove a final theorem.

Theorem 4.4 Let A be an $n \times n$ matrix. Then the following are equivalent:

    (i) The homogeneous system $A\mathbf{x} = \mathbf{0}$ has only the trivial solution $\mathbf{x} = \mathbf{0}$.

    (ii) For every right-side $\mathbf{b}$, the system $A\mathbf{x} = \mathbf{b}$ has a solution.

    (iii) A is invertible.

First we prove that (i) implies (ii). Let $\mathbf{b}$ be a given n-vector. We have to prove that $A\mathbf{x} = \mathbf{b}$ has a solution. For this, let D be the $m \times (n + 1)$ matrix whose first n columns agree with those of A, while the $(n + 1)$st column is $\mathbf{b}$. Since D has more columns than rows, we can find, by Theorem 4.2, a nonzero $(n + 1)$-vector $\mathbf{y}$ such that $D\mathbf{y} = \mathbf{0}$, that is, such that

$$y_1\mathbf{a}_1 + y_2\mathbf{a}_2 + \cdots + y_n\mathbf{a}_n + y_{n+1}\mathbf{b} = \mathbf{0} \tag{4.12}$$

Clearly, the number y_{n+1} cannot be zero. For if y_{n+1} were zero, then as $\mathbf{y} \neq \mathbf{0}$, at least one of the numbers $y_1, \ldots, y_n$ would have to be nonzero, while at the same time

$$y_1\mathbf{a}_1 + \cdots + y_n\mathbf{a}_n = \mathbf{0}$$

But this would say that $A\mathbf{x} = \mathbf{0}$ admits the *nontrivial* solution $x_i = y_i$, $i = 1, \ldots, n$, which contradicts (i). Hence, since $y_{n+1} \neq 0$, we can solve (4.12) for $\mathbf{b}$ to get that

$$-\frac{y_1}{y_{n+1}}\mathbf{a}_1 - \cdots - \frac{y_n}{y_{n+1}}\mathbf{a}_n = \mathbf{b}$$

But this says that $A\mathbf{x} = \mathbf{b}$ has a solution, viz., the solution $x_i = -(y_i/y_{n+1})$, $i = 1, \ldots, n$, which proves (ii).

Next we prove that (ii) implies (iii). Assuming (ii), it follows with Lemma 4.2 that there exists an $n \times n$ matrix C such that

$$AC = I$$

Hence, by Lemma 4.3, the equation $C\mathbf{x} = \mathbf{0}$ has only the trivial solution $\mathbf{x} = \mathbf{0}$. This says that the $n \times n$ matrix C satisfies (i); hence, by the argument we just went through, C satisfies (ii); therefore, by Lemma 4.2, there exists an $n \times n$ matrix D such that

$$CD = I$$

But now we are done. For we showed earlier that if

$$AC = I = CD$$

with A, C, D square matrices, then C is invertible and

$$A = D = C^{-1}$$

Hence A is the inverse of an invertible matrix, therefore invertible.
Finally, Lemma 4.3 shows that (iii) implies (i).

Example We showed in an earlier example that the 2×2 matrix

$$A = \begin{bmatrix} 1 & 2 \\ 2 & 4 \end{bmatrix}$$

is not invertible and, in another example, that for this matrix the homogeneous system $Ax = 0$ has nontrivial solutions. By Theorem 4.4, the linear system $Ax = b$ should therefore not be solvable for some 2-vector b. Indeed, with $b = i_1$, we get the system

$$x_1 + 2x_2 = 1$$

$$2x_1 + 4x_2 = 0$$

which has no solution since the second equation demands that

$$2(x_1 + 2x_2) = 0$$

while the first equation demands that

$$2(x_1 + 2x_2) = 2$$

As a simple application of Theorem 4.4, we now prove that A *square and $AB = I$ implies $B = A^{-1}$ and $BA = I$.* Indeed, if A is of order $n \times n$, then $AB = I$ implies that B is of order $n \times n$, and that, for all n-vectors b, $A(Bb) = b$. But this says that we can solve $Ax = b$ for x no matter what b, hence A is invertible by Theorem 4.4, and that then $x = Bb$ is the solution, hence $Bb = A^{-1}b$ for all b, or $B = A^{-1}$. But then, finally, $BA = I$.

Linear Independence and Bases

Let $a_1, \ldots, a_n$ be n m-vectors, and let A be the $m \times n$ matrix whose jth column is a_j, $j = 1, \ldots, n$. We say that these m-vectors are **linearly independent**

if $x_1 a_1 + \cdots + x_n a_n = 0$ implies that $x_1 = \cdots = x_n = 0$

Otherwise, we call the vectors linearly dependent. Clearly, these n m-vectors are linearly independent if and only if the homogeneous system $Ax = 0$ has only the trivial solution $x = 0$. Hence we can infer from Theorem 4.2 that any set of more than m m-vectors must be linearly dependent.

Let $a_1, \ldots, a_n$ be linearly independent. If every m-vector b can be written as a linear combination of these n m-vectors, then we call $a_1, \ldots, a_n$ a **basis** (for all m-vectors). Clearly, $a_1, \ldots, a_n$ is a basis if and only if the linear system $Ax = b$ has exactly one solution for every m-vector b, that is, if and only if every m-vector can be written in exactly one way as a linear combination of the m-vectors $\mathbf{a}_1, \ldots, \mathbf{a}_n$. In particular, a basis (for all m-vectors) consists of exactly m m-vectors (that is, $n = m$), and the corresponding matrix is invertible.

Examples The vectors

$$\mathbf{a}_1 = \begin{bmatrix} 1 \\ 0 \\ 0 \end{bmatrix} \quad \mathbf{a}_2 = \begin{bmatrix} 0 \\ 1 \\ 0 \end{bmatrix}$$

are linearly independent; but they do not form a basis since there are only two 3-vectors. Further, every 2-vector can be written as a linear combination of the three 2-vectors

$$\mathbf{a}_1 = \begin{bmatrix} 1 \\ 0 \end{bmatrix} \quad \mathbf{a}_2 = \begin{bmatrix} 0 \\ 1 \end{bmatrix} \quad \mathbf{a}_3 = \begin{bmatrix} 1 \\ 1 \end{bmatrix}$$

but these three 2-vectors do not form a basis since they must be linearly dependent. Finally, the three 3-vectors

$$\mathbf{a}_1 = \begin{bmatrix} 1 \\ 0 \\ 0 \end{bmatrix} \quad \mathbf{a}_2 = \begin{bmatrix} 1 \\ 1 \\ 0 \end{bmatrix} \quad \mathbf{a}_3 = \begin{bmatrix} 1 \\ 1 \\ 1 \end{bmatrix}$$

do form a basis, since the corresponding matrix is invertible. To see this, it is, by Theorem 4.4, sufficient to prove that the system

$$x_1 + x_2 + x_3 = 0$$
$$x_2 + x_3 = 0$$
$$x_3 = 0$$

has only the trivial solution $x_1 = x_2 = x_3 = 0$. But that is obvious.

The Transposed Matrix

Finally, there is an operation on matrices which has no parallel in ordinary arithmetic, the formation of the transposed matrix. If $A = (a_{ij})$ and $B = (b_{ij})$ are matrices, we say that B *is the* **transpose** *of* A, or $B = A^T$, provided B has as many rows as A has columns and as many columns as A has rows and

$$b_{ij} = a_{ji} \quad \text{all } i \text{ and } j$$

In words, one forms the transpose A^T of A by "reflecting A across the diagonal."

If

$$A^T = A$$

then A is said to be **symmetric**.

The matrices

$$A = \begin{bmatrix} 1 & 3 & 2 \\ 3 & 0 & 4 \\ 2 & 4 & 5 \end{bmatrix} \quad B = \begin{bmatrix} 3 & -1 \\ 2 & 6 \\ 0 & 8 \end{bmatrix} \quad C = \begin{bmatrix} 3 & 4 & 7 \end{bmatrix}$$

have the transpose

$$A^T = \begin{bmatrix} 1 & 3 & 2 \\ 3 & 0 & 4 \\ 2 & 4 & 5 \end{bmatrix} \quad B^T = \begin{bmatrix} 3 & 2 & 0 \\ -1 & 6 & 8 \end{bmatrix} \quad C^T = \begin{bmatrix} 3 \\ 4 \\ 7 \end{bmatrix}$$

In particular, the transpose $\mathbf{b}^T$ of a column vector $\mathbf{b}$ is a row vector.

One easily verifies the following rules regarding transposition:

1. If A and B are matrices such that AB is defined, then $B^T A^T$ is defined and

$$(AB)^T = B^T A^T. \quad \text{Note the change in order!}$$

2. For any matrix A, $(A^T)^T = A$.
3. If the matrix A is invertible, then so is A^T, and $(A^T)^{-1} = (A^{-1})^T$.

To prove Rule 1, let A be an $m \times n$ matrix and B an $n \times p$ matrix so that AB is an $m \times p$ matrix and $(AB)^T$ is a $p \times m$ matrix. Then A^T is $n \times m$, B^T is $p \times n$; therefore the product $B^T A^T$ is well defined and a $p \times m$ matrix. Finally,

$$(i, j) \text{ entry of } (AB)^T = (j, i) \text{ entry of } AB$$

$$= \sum_{k=1}^{n} \left[(j, k) \text{ entry of } A \right] * \left[(k, i) \text{ entry of } B \right]$$

$$= \sum_{k=1}^{n} \left[(i, k) \text{ entry of } B^T \right] * \left[(k, j) \text{ entry of } A^T \right]$$

$$= (i, j) \text{ entry of } B^T A^T$$

As to Rule 3, we get from Rule 1 that

$$A^T (A^{-1})^T = (A^{-1} A)^T = I^T = I$$

$$(A^{-1})^T A^T = (A A^{-1})^T = I^T = I.$$

which proves Rule 3.

If $\mathbf{a}$ and $\mathbf{b}$ are n-vectors, then $\mathbf{b}^T \mathbf{a}$ is a 1×1 matrix or number, called the **scalar product** of $\mathbf{a}$ and $\mathbf{b}$ in case $\mathbf{a}$ and $\mathbf{b}$ are real vectors.

For matrices with complex entries (of interest in the discussion of eigenvalues), there is the related notion of the **conjugate transposed** or **Hermitian** A^H of the matrix A. For this, we recall that the conjugate $\bar{z}$ of a complex number z is obtained by changing the imaginary part of z to its negative. If $z \neq 0$, then $\bar{z}$ is the unique number α for which $\alpha z = |z|^2$. The Hermitian A^H is obtained from A just as the transposed A^T except that all entries of A^T are replaced by their complex conjugate. Thus $A^H = (b_{ij})$ in case

$$b_{ij} = \bar{a}_{ji} \quad \text{all } i, j$$

Hence, $A^H = A^T$ in case A is a real matrix. Note that, for n-vectors **a** and **b** with *complex* entries, the customary scalar product is the number $\mathbf{b}^H\mathbf{a}$, not $\mathbf{b}^T\mathbf{a}$, since it is $\mathbf{a}^H\mathbf{a}$ which then gives the square of the length of the vector **a**.

Permutations and Permutation Matrices

A **permutation of degree** n is any rearrangement of the first n integers; i.e., it is a sequence of n integers in which each integer between 1 and n appears at least once, hence at most once, therefore exactly once. There are many ways of writing a permutation of degree n. For our purposes, it is sufficient (and in a sense quite rigorous) to think of a permutation as an n-vector $\mathbf{p} = (p_i)$ with $p_i \in \{1, 2, \ldots, n\}$, all i, and $p_i \neq p_j$ for $i \neq j$. There are $n!$ permutations of degree n. A permutation **p** is said to be even or odd depending on whether the number of **inversions** in **p** is even or odd. Here the number of inversions in a permutation $\mathbf{p} = (p_i)$ is the number of instances an integer precedes a smaller one. For example, in the permutation **p** with $\mathbf{p}^T = [7, 2, 6, 3, 4, 1, 5]$,

7 precedes 2, 6, 3, 4, 1, 5	giving	6 inversions
2 precedes 1	giving	1 inversion
6 precedes 3, 4, 1, 5	giving	4 inversions
3 precedes 1	giving	1 inversion
4 precedes 1	giving	1 inversion
Hence **p** has altogether		13 inversions

Note that any interchange of two entries in a permutation changes the number of inversions by an *odd* amount.

A **permutation matrix of order** n is any $n \times n$ matrix P whose columns (rows) are a rearrangement or permutation of the columns (rows) of the identity matrix of order n. Precisely, the $n \times n$ matrix P is a permutation matrix if

$$P\mathbf{i}_j = \mathbf{i}_{p_j} \qquad j = 1, \ldots, n \tag{4.13}$$

for some permutation $\mathbf{p} = (p_i)$ of degree n.

Theorem 4.5 Let P be the permutation matrix satisfying (4.13). Then

(i) P^T is a permutation matrix, satisfying

$$P^T\mathbf{i}_{p_j} = \mathbf{i}_j \qquad j = 1, \ldots, n$$

Hence $P^TP = I$; therefore P is invertible, and $P^{-1} = P^T$.

(ii) If A is an $m \times n$ matrix, then AP is the $m \times n$ matrix whose jth column equals the p_jth column of A, $j = 1, \ldots, n$.

(iii) If A is an $n \times m$ matrix, then $P^T A$ is the $n \times m$ matrix whose ith row equals the p_ith row of A, $i = 1, \ldots, n$.

Example The matrix

$$P = \begin{bmatrix} 0 & 0 & 1 \\ 1 & 0 & 0 \\ 0 & 1 & 0 \end{bmatrix}$$

is the permutation matrix corresponding to the permutation $\mathbf{p}^T = [2 \quad 3 \quad 1]$ since $P\mathbf{i}_1 = \mathbf{i}_2$, $P\mathbf{i}_2 = \mathbf{i}_3$, and $P\mathbf{i}_3 = \mathbf{i}_1$. One has

$$P^T = \begin{bmatrix} 0 & 1 & 0 \\ 0 & 0 & 1 \\ 1 & 0 & 0 \end{bmatrix}$$

Hence $P^T\mathbf{i}_1 = \mathbf{i}_3$, $P^T\mathbf{i}_2 = \mathbf{i}_1$, $P^T\mathbf{i}_3 = \mathbf{i}_2$, illustrating (i) of Theorem 4.5. Further, one calculates, for example, that

$$AP = \begin{bmatrix} 1 & 2 & 3 \\ 4 & 5 & 6 \\ 7 & 8 & 9 \end{bmatrix} \begin{bmatrix} 0 & 0 & 1 \\ 1 & 0 & 0 \\ 0 & 1 & 0 \end{bmatrix} = \begin{bmatrix} 2 & 3 & 1 \\ 5 & 6 & 4 \\ 8 & 9 & 7 \end{bmatrix}$$

Hence column 2 of AP is column 3 $= p_2$ of A, illustrating (ii) of Theorem 4.5.

The Numerical Solution of Linear Systems

We will consider only linear systems

$$A\mathbf{x} = \mathbf{b}$$

which have one and only one solution for every right-side **b**. By Theorems 4.2 and 4.3, we must therefore restrict attention to those systems which have exactly as many equations as unknowns, i.e., for which the coefficient matrix A is square. For such systems, Theorem 4.4 tells us that A should be invertible in order that the system have exactly one solution for every right-side **b**. We will therefore assume that all linear systems under discussion have an invertible coefficient matrix.

A frequently quoted test for invertibility of a matrix is based on the concept of the **determinant**. The relevant theorem states that the matrix A is invertible if and only if $\det(A) \neq 0$. If $\det(A) \neq 0$, then it is even possible to express the solution of $A\mathbf{x} = \mathbf{b}$ in terms of determinants, by the so-called Cramer's rule. Nevertheless, determinants are not of *practical* interest for the solution of linear systems since the calculation of one determinant is, in general, of the same order of difficulty as solving the linear system. For this reason, we make no use of determinants in solving linear systems, nor do we attempt to define a determinant here. However, in Sec. 4.7, we do present a method for evaluating determinants (based on a direct method for solving linear systems) for use in another context.

Numerical methods for solving linear systems may be divided into two types, **direct** and **iterative**. Direct methods are those which, in the absence of round-off or other errors, will yield the exact solution in a finite number of elementary arithmetic operations. In practice, because a computer works with a finite word length, direct methods do not lead to exact solutions. Indeed, errors arising from roundoff, instability, and loss of significance may lead to extremely poor or even useless results. A large part of numerical analysis is concerned with why and how these errors arise, and with the search for methods which minimize the totality of such errors. The fundamental method used for direct solutions is *Gauss elimination*, but even within this class there are various choices of methods and these vary in computational efficiency and accuracy. Some of these methods will be examined in the next sections.

Iterative methods are those which start with an initial approximation and which, by applying a suitably chosen algorithm, lead to successively better approximations. Even if the process converges, we can only hope to obtain an approximate solution by iterative methods. Iterative methods vary with the algorithm chosen and in their rates of convergence. Some iterative methods may actually diverge; others may converge so slowly that they are computationally useless. The important advantages of iterative methods are the simplicity and uniformity of the operations to be performed, which make them well suited for use on computers, and their relative insensitivity to the growth of round-off errors.

Matrices associated with linear systems are also classified as **dense** or **sparse**. Dense matrices have very few zero elements, and the order of such matrices tends to be relatively small—perhaps of order 100 or less. It is usually most efficient to handle problems involving such matrices by direct methods. Sparse matrices have very few nonzero elements. They usually arise from attempts to solve differential equations by finite-difference methods. The order of such matrices may be very large, and they are ideally suited to solution by iterative methods which take advantage of the sparse nature of the matrix involved. Iterative methods for solving linear and nonlinear systems will be discussed in Chap 5.

EXERCISES

4.1-1 Let

$$A = \begin{bmatrix} 2 & 3 & 1 \\ 1 & -1 & 1 \\ 0 & 2 & 2 \end{bmatrix} \quad B = \begin{bmatrix} 1 & 2 & 1 \\ -1 & 2 & -1 \\ 2 & 0 & 2 \end{bmatrix} \quad C = \begin{bmatrix} 1 & 0 & 1 \\ 0 & 1 & 1 \\ 1 & 0 & 2 \end{bmatrix}$$

(a) Compute AB and BA and show that $AB \neq BA$.

(b) Find $(A + B) + C$ and $A + (B + C)$.

(c) Show that $A(BC) = (AB)C$.

(d) Verify that $(AB)^T = B^T A^T$.

4.1-2 Show that the following matrix A is not invertible (see Theorem 4.4):

$$A = \begin{bmatrix} 1 & 2 & 1 \\ 2 & -1 & -1 \\ 6 & 2 & 0 \end{bmatrix}$$

4.1-3 For the matrix A given below, find a permutation matrix P such that
(a) Postmultiplication of A by P interchanges the fourth and the first columns of A
(b) Premultiplication of A by P interchanges the third row and the first row of A

$$A = \begin{bmatrix} 4 & 1 & 2 & 1 \\ 3 & 2 & 1 & 1 \\ 1 & 2 & 0 & 1 \\ 1 & 1 & 0 & 1 \end{bmatrix}$$

4.1-4 In the matrix A in Exercise 4.1-3 find a sequence of permutation matrices which will transform A into the form

$$A' = \begin{bmatrix} 1 & 0 & 1 & 1 \\ 1 & 0 & 1 & 2 \\ 1 & 1 & 3 & 2 \\ 1 & 2 & 4 & 1 \end{bmatrix}$$

4.1-5 Write the following system in matrix form and identify the matrix A and the vector $\mathbf{b}$

$$\begin{aligned} 2x_1 + 3x_2 + 4x_3 + x_4 &= 1 \\ x_1 + 2x_2 + x_4 &= 0 \\ 2x_1 + 3x_2 + x_3 - x_4 &= 2 \\ x_1 - 2x_2 - x_3 - x_4 &= 3 \end{aligned}$$

4.1-6 Convince yourself that the notion of invertibility makes sense for *square* matrices only by proving the following: Let A be an $m \times n$ matrix; if B and C are $n \times m$ matrices such that $AB = I_m$ and $CA = I_n$, then $B = C = A^{-1}$; in particular, then $m = n$. [*Hint:* Prove first that $B = C$. Then show that $m =$ trace $(AB) =$ trace $(BA) = n$, where the **trace** of a square matrix is defined as the sum of its diagonal entries.]

4.1-7 Make use of Theorem 4.4 to prove that a permutation matrix is invertible.

4.1-8 Make use of Theorem 4.4 to prove that, if A and B are square matrices such that their product is invertible, then both A and B must be invertible.

4.1-9 Do the vectors

$$\begin{bmatrix} 1 \\ -1 \\ 0 \\ 0 \end{bmatrix} \begin{bmatrix} 0 \\ 1 \\ -1 \\ 0 \end{bmatrix} \begin{bmatrix} 0 \\ 0 \\ 1 \\ -1 \end{bmatrix} \begin{bmatrix} 1 \\ 0 \\ 0 \\ 1 \end{bmatrix}$$

form a basis?

4.1-10 Prove that the three vectors

$$\begin{bmatrix} 1 \\ 2 \\ 0 \end{bmatrix} \begin{bmatrix} 2 \\ 1 \\ 0 \end{bmatrix} \begin{bmatrix} \\ -1 \\ \end{bmatrix}$$

form a linearly independent set. Do they form a basis?

4.1-11 For each of the three operations with matrices, namely, addition of two matrices, multiplication of two matrices, and multiplication of a scalar with a matrix, write a FORTRAN subroutine which carries out the operation on appropriate input and returns the resulting matrix.

4.1-12 If $p(x) = c_0 + c_1 x + c_2 x^2 + \cdots + c_k x^k$ is a given polynomial and A is a given $n \times n$ matrix, then the matrix $p(A)$ is defined by

$$p(A) = c_0 A^0 + c_1 A^1 + c_2 A^2 + \cdots + c_k A^k$$

Here $A^0 = I$, $A^1 = A$, and for $j > 1$, $A^j = A(A^{j-1})$. Write an efficient FORTRAN subroutine with arguments N, KP1, A, C, PA, where N is the order of the matrix A, and PA is to contain, on return, the matrix $p(A)$, with C a one-dimensional array containing $C(i) = c_{i-1}$, $i = 1, \ldots, KP1$. Do not use any arrays in the subroutine other than the arrays A, C, and PA. (*Hint:* Remember Algorithm 2.1.)

4.1-13 Suppose there exists, for a given matrix A of order n, a polynomial $p(x)$ such that $p(0) \neq 0$, while $p(A)$ is the null matrix. Prove that A must be invertible.

4.1-14 Verify the rules stated in (4.11).

4.1-15 The **Vandermonde matrix** for the points $x_0, \ldots, x_n$ is, by definition, the matrix of order $n + 1$ given by $V = (x_i^j)_{i,j=0}^n$. The matrix plays a prominent role in some treatments of polynomial interpolation because it is the coefficient matrix in the linear system

$$\sum_{j=0}^{n} a_j x_i^j = f(x_i) \qquad i = 0, \ldots, n$$

for the power coefficients of the interpolating polynomial. Use the Lagrange polynomials (2.6) to construct the inverse for V in case $n = 3$. What is the relationship between the power form of the Lagrange polynomials for $x_0, \ldots, x_n$ and the entries of the inverse of V?

4.2 THE SOLUTION OF LINEAR SYSTEMS BY ELIMINATION

Let A be a given square matrix of order n, **b** a given n-vector. We wish to solve the linear system

$$A\mathbf{x} = \mathbf{b} \qquad (4.14)$$

for the unknown n-vector **x**. The solution vector **x** can be obtained without difficulty in case A is *upper-triangular* with *all* diagonal entries *nonzero*. For then the system (4.14) has the form

$$
\begin{aligned}
a_{11}x_1 + a_{12}x_2 + \cdots + a_{1,n-1}x_{n-1} + a_{1n}x_n &= b_1 \\
a_{22}x_2 + \cdots + a_{2,n-1}x_{n-1} + a_{2n}x_n &= b_2 \\
&\cdots\cdots\cdots\cdots\cdots\cdots\cdots\cdots \\
a_{n-1,n-1}x_{n-1} + a_{n-1,n}x_n &= b_{n-1} \\
a_{nn}x_n &= b_n
\end{aligned}
\qquad (4.15)
$$

In particular, the last equation involves only x_n; hence, since $a_{nn} \neq 0$, we must have

$$x_n = \frac{b_n}{a_{nn}}$$

Since we now know x_n, the second last equation

$$a_{n-1,n-1}x_{n-1} + a_{n-1,n}x_n = b_{n-1}$$

involves only one unknown, namely, x_{n-1}. As $a_{n-1,n-1} \neq 0$, it follows that

$$x_{n-1} = \frac{b_{n-1} - a_{n-1,n}x_n}{a_{n-1,n-1}}$$

With x_n and x_{n-1} now determined, the third last equation

$$a_{n-2,\,n-2}x_{n-2} + a_{n-2,\,n-1}x_{n-1} + a_{n-2,\,n}x_n = b_{n-2}$$

contains only one true unknown, namely, x_{n-2}. Once again, since $a_{n-2,\,n-2} \neq 0$, we can solve for x_{n-2},

$$x_{n-2} = \frac{b_{n-2} - a_{n-2,\,n-1}x_{n-1} - a_{n-2,\,n}x_n}{a_{n-2,\,n-2}}$$

In general, with $x_{k+1}, x_{k+2}, \ldots, x_n$ already computed, the kth equation can be uniquely solved for x_k, since $a_{kk} \neq 0$, to give

$$x_k = \frac{b_k - \displaystyle\sum_{j=k+1}^{n} a_{kj}x_j}{a_{kk}}$$

This process of determining the solution of (4.15) is called *back-substitution*.

Algorithm 4.1: Back-substitution Given the upper-triangular $n \times n$ matrix A with none of the diagonal entries equal to zero, and the n-vector **b**. The entries $x_n, x_{n-1}, \ldots, x_1$ of the solution **x** of $A\mathbf{x} = \mathbf{b}$ can then be obtained (in that order) by

$$\text{For } k = n, n-1, \ldots, 1, \text{ do}$$
$$x_k := \frac{b_k - \displaystyle\sum_{j=k+1}^{n} a_{kj}x_j}{a_{kk}}$$

Here, two remarks are in order: When $k = n$, then the summation $\sum_{j=k+1}^{n}$ reads $\sum_{j=n+1}^{n}$, which is interpreted as the sum over *no* terms and gives, by convention, the value 0. Also, we note the following consequence, almost evident from our description of back-substitution.

Theorem 4.6 An upper-triangular matrix A is invertible if and only if all its diagonal entries are different from zero.

Indeed, back-substitution shows that the linear system $A\mathbf{x} = \mathbf{b}$ has at most one solution for given **b**, in case all diagonal entries of A are nonzero; hence, by Theorem 4.4, A must be invertible. On the other hand, for each $j = 1, \ldots, n$, there exist $x_1, \ldots, x_j$ not all zero so that

$$a_{11}x_1 + \cdots + a_{1j}x_j = 0$$
$$\cdot \quad \cdot \quad \cdot \quad \cdot \quad \cdot \quad \cdot \quad \cdot \quad \cdot$$
$$a_{j-1,\,1}x_1 + \cdots + a_{j-1,\,j}x_j = 0$$

by Theorem 4.2. But then, if $a_{jj} = 0$, the vector $\mathbf{y} = [x_1 \cdots x_j 0 \cdots 0]^T$ is not the zero vector, yet satisfies $A\mathbf{y} = \mathbf{0}$, showing, by Theorem 4.4, that A is not invertible.

We are therefore justified in calling the vector $\mathbf{x}$ calculated by Algorithm 4.1 *the* solution of (4.15).

Example 4.1 Consider the following linear system:

$$
\begin{aligned}
2x_1 + 3x_2 - x_3 &= 5 \\
-2x_2 - x_3 &= -7 \\
-5x_3 &= -15
\end{aligned}
\tag{4.16}
$$

From the last equation, $x_3 = b_3/a_{33} = \frac{15}{5} = 3$. With this, from the second (last) equation, $x_2 = (b_2 - a_{23}x_3)/a_{22} = (-7 + 3)/(-2) = 2$. Hence, from the first equation, $x_1 = (b_1 - a_{12}x_2 - a_{13}x_3)/a_{11} = (5 - 3 \cdot 2 + 3)/2 = 1$.

If now the coefficient matrix A of the system $A\mathbf{x} = \mathbf{b}$ is not upper-triangular, we subject the system first to the method of elimination due to Gauss. This method is probably familiar to the student, from elementary algebra. Its objective is the transformation of the given system into an equivalent system with upper-triangular coefficient matrix. The latter system can then be solved by back-substitution.

We say that the two linear systems $A\mathbf{x} = \mathbf{b}$ and $\tilde{A}\mathbf{x} = \tilde{\mathbf{b}}$ are **equivalent** provided any solution of one is a solution of the other.

Theorem 4.7 Let $A\mathbf{x} = \mathbf{b}$ be a given linear system, and suppose we subject this system to a sequence of operations of the following kind:

   (i) Multiplication of one equation by a nonzero constant
   (ii) Addition of a multiple of one equation to another equation
   (iii) Interchange of two equations

If this sequence of operations produces the new system $\tilde{A}\mathbf{x} = \tilde{\mathbf{b}}$, then the systems $A\mathbf{x} = \mathbf{b}$ and $\tilde{A}\mathbf{x} = \tilde{\mathbf{b}}$ are equivalent. In particular, then, A is invertible if and only if $\tilde{A}$ is invertible.

See Exercise 4.2-11 for a proof.

Elimination is based on this theorem and the following observation: If $A\mathbf{x} = \mathbf{b}$ is a linear system and if, for some k and j, $a_{kj} \neq 0$, then we can eliminate the unknown x_j from any equation $i \neq k$ by adding $-(a_{ij}/a_{kj})$ times equation k to equation i. The resulting system $\tilde{A}\mathbf{x} = \tilde{\mathbf{b}}$ is equivalent to the original system.

In its simplest form, Gauss elimination derives from a given linear system $A\mathbf{x} = \mathbf{b}$ of order n a sequence of equivalent systems $A^{(k)}\mathbf{x} = \mathbf{b}^{(k)}$, $k = 0, \ldots, n - 1$. Here $A^{(0)}\mathbf{x} = \mathbf{b}^{(0)}$ is just the original system. The

$(k - 1)$st system has the following form:

$$a_{11}^{(k-1)}x_1 + a_{12}^{(k-1)}x_2 + \cdots + a_{1,k-1}^{(k-1)}x_{k-1} + a_{1k}^{(k-1)}x_k + \cdots + a_{1n}^{(k-1)}x_n = b_1^{(k-1)}$$

$$a_{22}^{(k-1)}x_2 + \cdots + a_{2,k-1}^{(k-1)}x_{k-1} + a_{2k}^{(k-1)}x_k + \cdots + a_{2n}^{(k-1)}x_n = b_2^{(k-1)}$$

$$\cdots \cdots \cdots \cdots \cdots \cdots \cdots \cdots \cdots$$

$$a_{k-1,k-1}^{(k-1)}x_{k-1} + a_{k-1,k}^{(k-1)} + \cdots + a_{k-1,n}^{(k-1)}x_n = b_{k-1}^{(k-1)}$$

$$a_{kk}^{(k-1)}x_k + \cdots + a_{kn}^{(k-1)}x_n = b_k^{(k-1)}$$

$$\cdots \cdots \cdots \cdots \cdots \cdots \cdots \cdots \cdots$$

$$a_{nk}^{(k-1)}x_k + \cdots + a_{nn}^{(k-1)}x_n = b_n^{(k-1)}$$

In words, the first k equations are already in upper-triangular form, while the last $n - k$ equations involve only the unknowns $x_k, \ldots, x_n$. From this, the kth system $A^{(k)}\mathbf{x} = \mathbf{b}^{(k)}$ is derived during the kth step of Gauss elimination as follows: The first k equations are left unchanged; further, if the coefficient $a_{kk}^{(k-1)}$ of x_k in equation k is not zero, then $m_{ik} = a_{ik}^{(k-1)}/a_{kk}^{(k-1)}$ times equation k is subtracted from equation i, thereby eliminating the unknown x_k from equation i, $i = k + 1, \ldots, n$. The resulting system $A^{(k)}\mathbf{x} = \mathbf{b}^{(k)}$ is clearly equivalent to $A^{(k-1)}\mathbf{x} = \mathbf{b}^{(k-1)}$, hence, by induction, to the original system; further, the kth system has its first $k + 1$ equations in upper-triangular form.

After $n - 1$ steps of this procedure, one arrives at the system $A^{(n-1)}\mathbf{x} = \mathbf{b}^{(n-1)}$, whose coefficient matrix is upper-triangular, so that this system can now be solved quickly by back-substitution.

Example 4.2 Consider the following linear system:

$$\begin{array}{lll} (a) & 2x_1 + 3x_2 - x_3 = 5 & \\ (b) & 4x_1 + 4x_2 - 3x_3 = 3 & \quad (4.17) \\ (c) & -2x_1 + 3x_2 - x_3 = 1 & \end{array}$$

To eliminate x_1 from equations (b) and (c), we add $-\frac{4}{2} = -2$ times equation (a) to equation (b), getting the new equation

$$0x_1 - 2x_2 - x_3 = -7$$

Also, adding $-(-2)/2 = 1$ times equation (a) to equation (c), we get the new equation (c),

$$0x_1 + 6x_2 - 2x_3 = 6$$

This gives the new system $A^{(1)}\mathbf{x} = \mathbf{b}^{(1)}$:

$$\begin{array}{lll} (a) & 2x_1 + 3x_2 - x_3 = 5 & \\ (b) & -2x_2 - x_3 = -7 & \quad (4.18) \\ (c) & 6x_2 - 2x_3 = 6 & \end{array}$$

completing the first step of Gauss elimination. In the second (and for this example, last) step, we eliminate x_2 from equation (c) by adding $-6/(-2) = 3$ times equation (b) to equation (c), getting the new equation (c),

$$0x_2 - 5x_3 = -15$$

hence the new and final system

$$2x_1 + 3x_2 - x_3 = 5$$
$$- 2x_2 - x_3 = -7 \qquad (4.19)$$
$$- 5x_3 = -15$$

By Theorem 4.7, this system is equivalent to the original system (4.17) but has an upper-triangular coefficient matrix; hence can be solved quickly by back-substitution, as we did in Example 4.1.

In the simple description of Gauss elimination just given, we used the kth equation to eliminate x_k from equations $k + 1, \ldots, n$ during the kth step of the procedure. This is of course possible only if, at the beginning of the kth step, the coefficient $a_{kk}^{(k-1)}$ of x_k in equation k is not zero. Unfortunately, it is not difficult to devise linear systems for which this condition is not satisfied. If, for example, the linear system $A\mathbf{x} = \mathbf{b}$ is

$$(a) \qquad x_2 + x_3 = 1$$
$$(b) \quad x_1 \qquad + x_3 = 1 \qquad (4.20)$$
$$(c) \quad x_1 + x_2 \qquad = 1$$

then it is impossible to use equation (a) to eliminate x_1 from the other equations. To cope with this difficulty and still end up with a triangular system equivalent to the given one, we have to allow at each step more freedom in the choice of the **pivotal equation** for the step, i.e., the equation which is used to eliminate one unknown from certain of the other equations.

In the system (4.20), for example, we could use equation (b) as the pivotal equation during the first step of elimination. In order to keep within our earlier format, we first bring equation (b) into the top position by interchanging it with (a). In this new ordering, the coefficient of x_1 in equation (a) is now nonzero and we can proceed as before, getting the new system $A^{(1)}\mathbf{x} = \mathbf{b}^{(1)}$:

(a) $x_1 + x_3 = 1$

(b) $x_2 + x_3 = 1$

(c) $x_2 - x_3 = 0$

From this, the second (and last) step of Gauss elimination proceeds without any further difficulty and yields the final upper triangular system

$$x_1 + x_3 = 1$$
$$x_2 + x_3 = 1$$
$$- 2x_3 = -1$$

whose solution, by back-substitution, gives $x_3 = x_2 = x_1 = \frac{1}{2}$.

This greater freedom in the choice of the pivotal equation is necessary not only because of the possibility of zero coefficients. Experience has shown that this freedom is also essential in combating rounding error effects (see Sec. 4.3). The additional work is quite small: At the beginning of the kth elimination step, one looks for a nonzero coefficient for x_k in equations $k, k + 1, \ldots, n$, and, if it is found in some equation $j > k$, one interchanges equations j and k.

Incidentally, *there must be such a nonzero coefficient in case A is invertible*. For otherwise our present linear system would contain the $n - k + 1$ equations

$$0 \cdot x_k + a_{i,k+1}^{(k-1)} x_{k+1} + \cdots + a_{in}^{(k-1)} x_n = b_i^{(k-1)} \qquad i = k, \ldots, n \tag{4.21}$$

which involve in effect only the $n - k$ unknowns $x_{k+1}, \ldots, x_n$. By Theorem 4.3, this subsystem (4.21) would therefore not be solvable for some right side; hence our whole present system would not be solvable for some right side, and therefore, by Theorem 4.4, the coefficient matrix of our present system would not be invertible. But since our present system is equivalent to the original system $A\mathbf{x} = \mathbf{b}$, it would then follow that A is not invertible. This proves our assertion.

When this process is carried out with the aid of a computer, the n original equations and the various changes made in them have to be recorded in some convenient and systematic way. Typically, one uses an $n \times (n + 1)$ working array or matrix which we will call W and which contains initially the coefficients and right side of the n equations $A\mathbf{x} = \mathbf{b}$. Whenever some unknown is eliminated from an equation, the changed coefficients and right side for this equation are calculated and stored in the working array W in place of the previous coefficients and right side. For reasons to be made clear below, we store the multiplier $m_{ik} = a_{ik}^{(k-1)}/a_{kk}^{(k-1)}$ (used to eliminate x_k from the ith equation) in w_{ik} in place of the number $a_{ik}^{(k)}$ since the latter is (supposed to be) zero anyway. We also record the row interchanges made with the aid of an integer array $\mathbf{p}$.

Algorithm 4.2: Gauss elimination Given the $n \times (n + 1)$ matrix W containing the matrix A of order n in its first n columns and the n-vector $\mathbf{b}$ in its last column.

> Initialize the n-vector $\mathbf{p}$ to have $p_i = i, i = 1, \ldots, n$
> For $k = 1, \ldots, n - 1$, do:
>> Find (the smallest) $i \geq k$ such that $w_{ik} \neq 0$
>> If no such i exists, signal that A is not invertible and stop
>> Otherwise, exchange the contents of p_k and p_i, and of rows k and i of W and continue
>> For $i = k + 1, \ldots, n$, do:
>>> $m := w_{ik} := w_{ik}/w_{kk}$
>>> For $j = k + 1, \ldots, n + 1$, do:
>>>> $w_{ij} := w_{ij} - m w_{kj}$
>
> If $w_{nn} = 0$, signal that A is not invertible and stop

Otherwise, the original system $A\mathbf{x} = \mathbf{b}$ is now known to be equivalent to the system $U\mathbf{x} = \mathbf{y}$, where U and $\mathbf{y}$ are given in terms of the final entries of W by

$$u_{ij} = \begin{cases} w_{ij} & i \le j \\ 0 & i > j \end{cases}, \qquad y_i = w_{i,n+1}, \qquad i = 1, \ldots, n \quad (4.22)$$

In particular, U is an upper-triangular matrix with all diagonal entries nonzero; hence Algorithm 4.1 can now be used to calculate the solution $\mathbf{x}$.

It is often possible to reduce the computational work necessary for solving $A\mathbf{x} = \mathbf{b}$ by taking into account special features of the coefficient matrix A, such as symmetry or sparseness. As an example we now discuss briefly the solution of tridiagonal systems.

We say that the matrix $A = (a_{ij})$ of order n is **tridiagonal** if

$$a_{ij} = 0 \qquad \text{whenever } |i - j| > 1$$

In words, A is tridiagonal if the only nonzero entries of A lie on the diagonal of A, a_{ii}, $i = 1, \ldots, n$, or the **subdiagonal** of A, $a_{i,i-1}$, $i = 2, \ldots, n$, or the **superdiagonal** of A, $a_{i,i+1}$, $i = 1, \ldots, n - 1$. Thus the following matrices are all tridiagonal.

$$\begin{bmatrix} 3 & 1 & 0 & 0 \\ 1 & 3 & 1 & 0 \\ 0 & 2 & 2 & 1 \\ 0 & 0 & 1 & 6 \end{bmatrix} \quad \begin{bmatrix} 1 & 0 & 0 & 0 \\ 0 & 1 & 0 & 0 \\ 0 & 0 & 1 & 0 \\ 0 & 0 & 1 & 0 \end{bmatrix} \quad \begin{bmatrix} 4 & 7 & 0 & 0 \\ 0 & 8 & 1 & 0 \\ 0 & 1 & 1 & 0 \\ 0 & 0 & 0 & 1 \end{bmatrix}$$

Assume that the coefficient matrix A of the linear system $A\mathbf{x} = \mathbf{b}$ is tridiagonal, and assume further that, for each k, we can use equation k as the pivotal equation during step k. Then, during the kth step of Algorithm 4.2, the variable x_k needs to be eliminated only from equation $k + 1$, $k = 1, \ldots, n - 1$. Further, during back-substitution, only x_{k+1} needs to be substituted into equation k in order to find x_k, $k = n - 1, \ldots, 1$. Finally, there is no need to store any of the entries of A known to be zero. Rather, only three vectors need to be retained, containing the subdiagonal, the diagonal, and the superdiagonal of A, respectively.

Consider now more specifically the following tridiagonal system of order n:

$$\begin{aligned} d_1 x_1 + c_1 x_2 \qquad\qquad\qquad\qquad &= b_1 \\ a_2 x_1 + d_2 x_2 + c_2 x_3 \qquad\qquad\quad &= b_2 \\ a_3 x_2 + d_3 x_3 + c_3 x_4 \qquad\quad &= b_3 \\ \ddots \qquad \ddots \qquad \ddots \qquad\qquad &\;\;\vdots \\ a_{n-1} x_{n-2} + d_{n-1} x_{n-1} + c_{n-1} x_n &= b_{n-1} \\ a_n x_{n-1} \quad + d_n x_n &= b_n \end{aligned}$$

Assuming $d_1 \neq 0$, we eliminate x_1 from the second equation, getting the new equation

$$d_2' x_2 + c_2 x_3 = b_2'$$

with $\qquad d_2' = d_2 - \dfrac{a_2}{d_1} c_1 \qquad b_2' = b_2 - \dfrac{a_2}{d_1} b_1$

Next, assuming $d_2' \neq 0$, we use this equation to eliminate x_2 from the third equation, getting the new equation

$$d_3' x_3 + c_3 x_4 = b_3'$$

with $\qquad d_3' = d_3 - \dfrac{a_3}{d_2'} c_2 \qquad b_3' = b_3 - \dfrac{a_3}{d_2'} b_2'$

Continuing in this manner, we eliminate, during step k, x_k from equation $k + 1$ (assuming that $d_k' \neq 0$), getting the new equation

$$d_{k+1}' x_{k+1} + c_{k+1} x_{k+2} = b_{k+1}'$$

with $\qquad d_{k+1}' = d_{k+1} - \dfrac{a_{k+1}}{d_k'} c_k \qquad b_{k+1}' = b_{k+1} - \dfrac{a_{k+1}}{d_k'} b_k'$

for $k = 1, 2, \ldots, n - 1$.

During back-substitution, we first get, assuming $d_n' \neq 0$,

$$x_n = \frac{b_n'}{d_n'}$$

and then, for $k = n - 1, \ldots, 1$,

$$x_k = \frac{b_k' - c_k x_{k+1}}{d_k'}$$

Algorithm 4.3: Elimination for tridiagonal systems Given the coefficients a_i, d_i, c_i and right-side b_i of the tridiagonal system

$$a_i x_{i-1} + d_i x_i + c_i x_{i+1} = b_i \qquad i = 1, \ldots, n \text{ (with } a_1 = c_n = 0\text{)}$$

For $k = 2, \ldots, n$, do:
$\left|\begin{array}{l} \text{If } d_{k-1} = 0, \text{ signal failure and stop} \\[4pt] \text{Otherwise, } m := \dfrac{a_k}{d_{k-1}} \text{ and continue} \\[6pt] d_k := d_k - m * c_{k-1} \\[4pt] b_k := b_k - m * b_{k-1} \end{array}\right.$

If $d_n = 0$, signal failure and stop

Otherwise, $x_n := \dfrac{b_n}{d_n}$ and continue

For $k = n - 1, \ldots, 1$, do:
$\left|\begin{array}{l} x_k := \dfrac{b_k - c_k * x_{k+1}}{d_k} \end{array}\right.$

Example 4.3 Solve the linear system

$$2x_1 \; - \; x_2 \qquad\qquad = 1$$
$$-x_{i-1} + 2x_i \; - \; x_{i+1} = 0 \qquad i = 2, \ldots, n-1$$
$$- \; x_{n-1} \; + 2x_n = 0$$

when $n = 10$.

The following FORTRAN program solves this problem. Note that we have translated Algorithm 4.3 into a subroutine called

$$\text{TRID(SUB, DIAG, SUP, B, N)}$$

where SUB, DIAG, SUP, B, are N-vectors which are expected to contain the coefficients and right side of the tridiagonal system

$$\text{SUB}(i)x_{i-1} + \text{DIAG}(i)x_i + \text{SUP}(i)x_{i+1} = B(i) \qquad i = 1, \ldots, N$$

[with SUB(1) and SUP(N) ignored]. The subroutine alters the contents of DIAG and returns the solution vector in B.

The exact solution of the given system is

$$x_i = \frac{n+1-i}{n+1} \qquad i = 1, \ldots, n$$

Hence the computed solution is in error in the sixth place after the decimal point. This program was run on an IBM 360.

```
C  FORTRAN PROGRAM FOR EXAMPLE 4.3
      PARAMETER N=10
      INTEGER I
      REAL A(N),B(N),C(N),D(N)
      DO 10 I=1,N
         A(I) = -1.
         D(I) = 2.
         C(I) = -1.
  10     B(I) = 0.
      B(1) = 1.
      CALL TRID ( A, D, C, B, N )
      PRINT 610, (I,B(I),I=1,N)
 610  FORMAT('1THE SOLUTION IS '/(I5,E15.7))
                                          STOP
      END
      SUBROUTINE TRID ( SUB, DIAG, SUP, B, N )
      INTEGER N,   I
      REAL B(N),DIAG(N),SUB(N),SUP(N)
C  THE TRIDIAGONAL LINEAR SYSTEM
C     SUB(I)*X(I-1) + DIAG(I)*X(I) + SUP(I)*X(I+1) = B(I), I=1,...,N
C  (WITH SUB(1) AND SUP(N) TAKEN TO BE ZERO) IS SOLVED BY FACTORIZATION
C  AND SUBSTITUTION. THE FACTORIZATION IS RETURNED IN  SUB , DIAG , SUP
C  AND THE SOLUTION IS RETURNED IN  B .
      IF (N .LE. 1) THEN
         B(1) = B(1)/DIAG(1)
                                          RETURN
      END IF
      DO 11 I=2,N
         SUB(I) = SUB(I)/DIAG(I-1)
         DIAG(I) = DIAG(I) - SUB(I)*SUP(I-1)
  11     B(I) = B(I) - SUB(I)*B(I-1)
      B(N) = B(N)/DIAG(N)
      DO 12 I=N-1,1,-1
  12     B(I) = (B(I) - SUP(I)*B(I+1))/DIAG(I)
                                          RETURN
      END
```

OUTPUT

THE SOLUTION IS
1   0.9090915E   00
2   0.8181832E   00
3   0.7272751E   00
4   0.6363666E   00
5   0.5454577E   00
6   0.4545485E   00
7   0.3636391E   00
8   0.2727295E   00
9   0.1818197E   00
10 0.9090990E −01

EXERCISES

4.2-1 One measure of the efficiency of an algorithm is the number of arithmetic operations required to obtain the solution. Show that Algorithm 4.2 applied to a system of order n requires $n(n - 1)/2$ divisions, $(n^3 - n)/3$ multiplications, and $(n^3 - n)/3$ additions.

4.2-2 Show that the back-substitution Algorithm 4.1 requires n divisions, $n(n - 1)/2$ multiplications, and $n(n - 1)/2$ additions.

4.2-3 On some machines, division is more time-consuming than multiplication. How would you modify Algorithm 4.2 for such a machine?

4.2-4 Calculate the number of additions and the number of multiplications necessary to multiply an $n \times n$ matrix with an n-vector.

4.2-5 How many additions, multiplications, and divisions are required in Algorithm 4.2 if only the final upper-triangular matrix U is desired?

4.2-6 Use elimination to show that the following system does not have a solution.

$$x_1 + 2x_2 + x_3 = 3$$
$$2x_1 + 3x_2 + x_3 = 5$$
$$3x_1 + 5x_2 + 2x_3 = 1$$

4.2-7 The execution time of a program incorporating Algorithm 4.2 is largely determined by the time spent in the innermost loop. For this reason, one would like to have that loop as efficient as possible. At the same time, FORTRAN stores arrays by columns and, on many machines, it is therefore much faster to deal with an array column by column rather than row by row.

For these reasons, reorganize Algorithm 4.2 in such a way that the innermost loop(s) run(s) over row indices, i.e., so that a column rather than a row is modified at a time.

4.2-8 Solve the following system by elimination. Round off all calculations to three significant digits.

$$0.21x_1 + 0.32x_2 + 0.12x_3 + 0.31x_4 = 0.96$$
$$0.10x_1 + 0.15x_2 + 0.24x_3 + 0.22x_4 = 0.71$$
$$0.20x_1 + 0.24x_2 + 0.46x_3 + 0.36x_4 = 1.26$$
$$0.61x_1 + 0.40x_2 + 0.32x_3 + 0.20x_4 = 1.53$$

Check your answers by substituting back into the original equations, and estimate their accuracy. Exact solution: $[1,1,1,1]$.

4.2-9 Use subroutine TRID to solve the linear system

$$-2(1 + h^2)x_1 + x_2 = 1$$
$$x_{i-1} - 2(1 + h^2)x_i + x_{i+1} = 0 \qquad i = 2, 3, \ldots, n - 1$$
$$x_{n-1} - 2(1 + h^2)x_n = 1$$

when $n = 30$ and $h = 0.1$.

4.2-10 Use Theorem 4.6 and the corollary to Lemma 2.1 to prove that every polynomial of degree $\leq n$ can be written in exactly one way in Newton form for given centers $c_1, \ldots, c_n$. (*Hint:* Consider the linear system for the coefficients in the Newton form for a polynomial which agrees with a given function at $c_1, \ldots, c_n, c_{n+1}$.)

4.2-11 Prove Theorem 4.7. (*Hint:* Prove first that any solution of $A\mathbf{x} = \mathbf{b}$ remains a solution of $\bar{A}\mathbf{x} = \bar{\mathbf{b}}$. Then show that any operation of the kind mentioned can be undone by an operation of the same kind, hence show that $A\mathbf{x} = \mathbf{b}$ can in turn be obtained from $\bar{A}\mathbf{x} = \bar{\mathbf{b}}$ by a sequence of such operations.)

4.3 THE PIVOTING STRATEGY

The elimination algorithm 4.2 presented in the preceding section calculates efficiently and with certainty the solution of any system $A\mathbf{x} = \mathbf{b}$, if all calculations are carried out in infinite-precision arithmetic. If, as is more usual, finite-precision arithmetic is used, it is not difficult to give examples for which Algorithm 4.2 produces completely erroneous answers.

In this section, we discuss briefly just one possible source for such a failure, an incorrect pivoting strategy. Here, we mean by **pivoting strategy** the scheme used to choose the pivotal equation (and, possibly even the pivotal column) at each elimination step.

Example 4.4 The solution of the system

$$0.0003x_1 + 1.566x_2 = 1.569$$
$$0.3454x_1 - 2.436x_2 = 1.018$$

is $x_1 = 10$, $x_2 = 1$. We use four-decimal floating arithmetic to solve this system by elimination, picking the first equation as the pivotal equation during the first (and only) step. We get the multiplier

$$m_{21} = 0.3454/0.0003 = 1,151.$$

Hence

$$a_{22}^{(1)} = -2.436 - (1,151.)(1.566) = -2.436 - 1,802. = -1,804.$$
$$b_2^{(1)} = 1.018 - (1,151.)(1.569) = 1.018 - 1,806. = -1,805.$$

This gives

$$x_2 = -1,805./-1,804. = 1.001$$

Hence, from the first equation,

$$x_1 = [1.569 - (1.566)(1.001)]/0.0003 = 3.333$$

A "plausible" explanation of this failure goes as follows: The *pivot* entry $a_{11} = 0.0003$ is "very small"; since the computations would break down if a_{11} were zero, it is not surprising that, in the environment of finite-precision arithmetic, the algorithm performs badly for a_{11} "near zero."

Of course, this explanation uses such undefined terms as "very small" and "near zero" and is therefore quite useless. In fact, by multiplying the first equation by an appropriate power of 10, we can make a_{11} as large as we wish *without changing the computed solution*. To see this, consider again the system of Example 4.4, but with the first equation multiplied by 10^m, where m is some integer:

$$0.0003 \cdot 10^m x_1 + 1.566 \cdot 10^m x_2 = 1.569 \cdot 10^m$$
$$0.3454 \quad x_1 - 2.436 \quad x_2 = 1.018$$

Using again the first equation as pivotal equation, and using four-decimal floating arithmetic, we get

$$m_{21} = \frac{0.3454}{0.0003 \cdot 10^m} = 1{,}151 \cdot 10^{-m}$$

Hence

$$a_{22}^{(1)} = -2.436 - (1{,}151 \cdot 10^{-m})(1.566 \cdot 10^m) = -1{,}804.$$
$$b_2^{(1)} = 1.018 - (1{,}151 \cdot 10^{-m})(1.569 \cdot 10^m) = -1{,}805.$$

which is the same result as before. Hence again $x_2 = 1.001$, and finally, $x_1 = (0.001 \cdot 10^m)/(0.0003 \cdot 10^m) = 3.333$.

Actually, the failure in this example is due to the fact that $|a_{11}|$ is small compared with $|a_{12}|$; thus a relatively small error due to roundoff in the computed x_2 led to a large variation of the computed x_1 from the correct x_1. This is confirmed if we use equation 2 as pivotal equation, where $|a_{22}/a_{21}| \approx 6$ as compared with $|a_{12}/a_{11}| \approx 5{,}220$. We get

$$m_{11} = \frac{0.0003}{0.3454} = 0.0008686$$

and the new first equation becomes

$$1.568 x_2 = 1.568$$

so that $x_2 = 1$, the correct answer, and finally, from the second equation, $x_1 = 10$. But even if roundoff had conspired to give $x_2 = 1.001$ (as it did in Example 4.4), the second equation would still give

$$x_1 = \frac{1.018 + 2.438}{0.3454} = 10.01$$

a good result.

It is much more difficult (if not impossible) to ascertain for a general linear system how various pivoting strategies affect the accuracy of the computed solution. A notable and important exception to this statement are the linear systems with positive definite coefficient matrix, that is, systems whose coefficient matrix satisfies

$$A = A^T \quad \text{and, for all } x \neq 0, \, x^T A x > 0$$

For such a system, the error in the computed solution due to rounding errors during elimination and back-substitution can be shown [41; p. 127] to be acceptably small if the trivial pivoting strategy of no interchanges is used. (See Exercise 4.4-9 for an efficient algorithm for this case.) But it is not possible at present to give a "best" pivoting strategy for a general linear system, nor is it even clear what such a term might mean.

For the sake of economy, the pivotal equation for each step must be selected on the basis of the current state of the system under consideration at the beginning of the step, i.e., without foreknowledge of the effect of the selection on later steps.

A currently accepted strategy is **scaled partial pivoting**. In this strategy, one calculates initially the "size" d_i of row i of A, for $i = 1, \ldots, n$. A convenient measure of this size is (see Sec. 4.5) the number

$$d_i = \max_{1 \leq j \leq n} |a_{ij}|$$

Then, at the beginning of the general, or kth, step of the elimination Algorithm 4.2, one picks as pivotal equation that one from the available $n - k$ candidates which has the absolutely largest coefficient of x_k relative to the size of the equation. In the terms of Algorithm 4.2, this means that the integer j is selected as the (usually smallest) integer between k and n for which

$$\frac{|w_{jk}|}{d_j} \geq \frac{|w_{ik}|}{d_i} \quad \text{for all } i = k, \ldots, n$$

Clearly, scaled partial pivoting selects the correct pivoting strategy for the system in Example 4.4, and is not thrown off by a rescaling of the equations.

It is possible to modify Algorithm 4.2 so as to leave not only the pivotal equation, but also the unknown to be eliminated open to choice. In this modification, one chooses two permutations, **p** and **q**, which designate the p_kth equation as the equation to be used during the kth step to eliminate x_{q_k}, $k = 1, \ldots, n - 1$. In **total pivoting**, pivotal equation and unknown are selected by looking for the absolutely largest coefficient of any of the $n - k$ unknowns in any of the $n - k$ candidate equations. Of course, such a strategy is much more expensive than scaled partial pivoting, hence is not often employed, even though it is admittedly superior to partial pivoting.

EXERCISES

4.3-1 Describe a modification of Algorithm 4.2 which incorporates total pivoting.

4.3-2 Give an example of a 2×2 linear system for which total pivoting gives more accurate results than scaled partial pivoting in four-decimal floating arithmetic. (*Hint:* Make both a_{11} and a_{21} "small" compared with a_{12} and a_{22}.)

4.3-3 Solve the following linear system, using four-decimal floating arithmetic, once with the first equation as pivotal equation and once with the second equation as pivotal equation, and finally with total pivoting.

$$0.1410 \cdot 10^{-2}x_1 + 0.4004 \cdot 10^{-1}x_2 = 0.1142 \cdot 10^{-1}$$

$$0.2000 \cdot 10^{0}x_1 + 0.4912 \cdot 10^{1}x_2 = 0.1428 \cdot 10^{1}$$

Compare with the exact answer $x_1 = 1.000$, $x_2 = 0.2500$.

4.3-4 Solve the system of Exercise 4.2-8, but using scaled partial pivoting, and compare with the results of Exercise 4.2-8.

4.4 THE TRIANGULAR FACTORIZATION

It is possible to visualize the elimination process of Algorithm 4.2 as deriving a **factorization** of the coefficient matrix A into three factors,

$$A = PLU$$

a permutation matrix P which accounts for the row interchanges made, a unit lower-triangular matrix L containing (in its interesting part) the multipliers used, and the final upper-triangular matrix U. This point of view leads to an efficient algorithm (**Choleski factorization**, see Exercise 4.4-9) in case A is a symmetric positive definite matrix. It is also of value in understanding the so-called **compact schemes** (associated with the names of Doolittle and Crout, see Exercise 4.4-8) which are advantageous in solving linear systems on desk (or pocket) calculators, since they reduce the number of intermediate results that have to be recorded. These schemes also permit the use of double-precision accumulation of scalar products (on some machines), for a reduction of rounding-error effects. Finally, the factorization point of view of elimination makes it easy to apply **backward error analysis** to the elimination process (as will be done in Sec. 4.6). For these reasons, we now exhibit the triangular factorization for A as generated by Algorithm 4.2.

Assume, to begin with, that no row interchanges occurred during execution of the algorithm and consider what happens to the ith equation. For $k = 1, 2, \ldots, i - 1$, the equation is transformed during the kth step from

$$a_{ik}^{(k-1)}x_k + a_{i,k+1}^{(k-1)}x_{k+1} + \cdots + a_{in}^{(k-1)}x_n = b_i^{(k-1)}$$

to

$$a_{i,k+1}^{(k)}x_{k+1} + \cdots + a_{in}^{(k)}x_n = b_i^{(k)}$$

by the prescription

$$a_{ij}^{(k)} = a_{ij}^{(k-1)} - m_{ik}a_{kj}^{(k-1)}$$

$$b_i^{(k)} = b_i^{(k-1)} - m_{ik}b_k^{(k-1)}$$

with the multiplier

$$m_{ik} = a_{ik}^{(k-1)}/a_{kk}^{(k-1)}$$

stored in the (i, k)-entry of the working array. Here, $a_{kj}^{(k-1)}$ and $b_k^{(k-1)}$ are the coefficients and right side of the pivotal equation for this step, hence are *in their final form*. This means, in terms of the output from Algorithm 4.2, i.e., in terms of the upper-triangular matrix U and the vector y produced in that algorithm, that

$$a_{kj}^{(k-1)} = u_{kj}, j = k, \ldots, n \quad \text{and} \quad b_k^{(k-1)} = y_k$$

Consequently,

$$\left.\begin{array}{l} m_{ik} = a_{ik}^{(k-1)}/u_{kk} \\ a_{ij}^{(k)} = a_{ij}^{(k-1)} - m_{ik}u_{kj}, j = k, \ldots, n \\ b_i^{(k)} = b_i^{(k-1)} - m_{ik}y_k \end{array}\right\} \quad k = 1, \ldots, i - 1$$

Since $a_{ij}^{(0)} = a_{ij}$, and $b_i^{(0)} = b_i$, we conclude that

$$m_{ik} = (a_{ik} - m_{i1}u_{1k} - m_{i2}u_{2k} - \cdots - m_{i,k-1}u_{k-1,k})/u_{kk}$$
$$k = 1, \ldots, i - 1$$

$$u_{ij} = a_{ij} - m_{i1}u_{1j} - m_{i2}u_{2j} - \cdots - m_{i,i-1}u_{i-1,j} \quad j = i, \ldots, n \quad (4.23)$$

and $$y_i = b_i - m_{i1}y_1 - m_{i2}y_2 - \cdots - m_{i,i-1}y_{i-1} \quad (4.24)$$

We now rewrite these equations so that the original data, A and **b**, appear on the right-hand side. Then we get

$$m_{i1}u_{1k} + \cdots + m_{ik}u_{kk} = a_{ik} \quad k = 1, \ldots, i - 1$$

$$m_{i1}u_{1j} + \cdots + m_{i,i-1}u_{i-1,j} + u_{ij} = a_{ij} \quad j = i, \ldots, n \quad (4.25)$$

and $$m_{i1}y_1 + \cdots + m_{i,i-1}y_{i-1} + y_i = b_i$$

Hence, if we let $L = (l_{ij})$ be the unit lower-triangular matrix given in terms of the final content of the work array W by

$$l_{ij} = \begin{cases} w_{ij} = m_{ij}, & i > j \\ 1, & i = j \\ 0, & i < j \end{cases} \quad (4.26)$$

then we can write these equations (for $i = 1, \ldots, n$) in matrix form simply as

$$LU = A$$

and

$$Ly = b$$

This demonstrates the triangular factorization, in case no interchanges occurred. If, on the other hand, interchanges did occur, then the final content of W would have been unchanged had we carried out these interchanges at the outset and then applied Algorithm 4.2 without any interchanges. This is so because all operations in the algorithm involve the subtraction of a certain multiple of one *row* from certain other *rows* in order to produce a zero in those other rows, and, for this, it does not matter in which order we have written down the rows. The only thing that matters is that, once a row has been used as pivotal row, it is not modified any further, and, for this, we must keep apart from the others those rows not yet used as pivotal rows.

Consequently, if interchanges do occur during execution of Algorithm 4.2, then the matrices L and U obtained by the algorithm satisfy

$$LU = P^{-1}A$$

for some appropriate permutation matrix P, i.e., then

$$PLU = A \tag{4.27}$$

and also
$$Ly = P^{-1}b \tag{4.28}$$

In terms of the vector $\mathbf{p}$ used in Algorithm 4.2 to record the interchanges made, the p_kth equation is used as pivot equation during the kth step. Hence P^{-1} should carry row p_k to row k, all k. This means that $Pi_k = i_{p_k}$, all k [see Theorem 4.5(iii)], if one really wanted to know. All that matters to us, though, is that, in terms of the output $\mathbf{p}$ from Algorithm 4.2,

$$P^{-1}\mathbf{b} = \left(b_{p_k}\right)_{k=1}^{n}$$

As a first application of the factorization point of view, we now look at the possibility of splitting the process of solving $A\mathbf{x} = \mathbf{b}$ into two phases, the *factorization phase* in which the triangular factors L and U (and a possibly different order $\mathbf{p}$ of the rows) are derived, and the *solving phase* during which one first solves the triangular system

$$Ly = P^{-1}\mathbf{b}\left(= \left(b_{p_k}\right)_1^n\right) \tag{4.29}$$

for $\mathbf{y}$ and then solves the triangular system

$$U\mathbf{x} = \mathbf{y}$$

for $\mathbf{x}$, by back-substitution. Note that the right-hand side $\mathbf{b}$ enters only the second phase. Hence, if the system is also to be solved for some other right-hand sides, only the second phase needs to be repeated.

According to (4.24), one solves (4.29) in Algorithm 4.2 by the steps

For $k = 1, \ldots, n$, do:
$$y_k := b_{p_k} - l_{k1}y_1 - \cdots - l_{k,k-1}y_{k-1}$$

In effect, this is like the back-substitution Algorithm 4.1 for solving $U\mathbf{x} = \mathbf{y}$ for $\mathbf{x}$, except that the equations are gone through from first to last, since L is *lower*-triangular.

We record the entire solving phase in the following:

Algorithm 4.4: Forward- and back-substitution Given the final contents of the first n columns of the working array W and the n-vector $\mathbf{p}$ of Algorithm 4.2 (applied to the system $A\mathbf{x} = \mathbf{b}$); also, given the right-side $\mathbf{b}$.

$$\text{For } k = 1, \ldots, n, \text{ do:}$$
$$\quad y_k := b_{p_k} - \sum_{j=1}^{k-1} w_{kj} y_j$$

$$\text{For } k = n, n-1, \ldots, 1, \text{ do:}$$
$$\quad x_k := \left(y_k - \sum_{j=k+1}^{n} w_{kj} x_j \right) / w_{kk}$$

The vector $\mathbf{x} = (x_i)$ now contains the solution of $A\mathbf{x} = \mathbf{b}$.

Note that, once again, both sums are sometimes empty.

The practical significance of the preceding discussion becomes clear when we count (floating-point) operations in Algorithms 4.2 and 4.4. By Exercise 4.2-2, it takes n divisions, $n(n-1)/2$ multiplications, and $n(n-1)/2$ additions to carry out the second loop in Algorithm 4.4. The first loop takes the same number of operations, except that no divisions are required. Hence Algorithm 4.4 takes

$$n^2 \text{ multiplications/divisions and } n(n-1) \text{ additions}$$

By Exercise 4.2-4, this is exactly the number of operations required to multiply an $n \times n$ matrix with an n-vector.

By contrast,

$$(n^3 - n)/3 \text{ multiplications/divisions and } n^3/3 + n^2/2 - n/6 \text{ additions}$$

are necessary to calculate the first n columns of the final contents of the working matrix W by Algorithm 4.2 (see Exercise 4.2-5). Hence the bulk of the work in solving $A\mathbf{x} = \mathbf{b}$ by elimination is needed to obtain the final content of the working matrix W, namely, $\mathcal{O}(\frac{1}{3}n^3)$ additions and the same number of multiplications/divisions, for large n. The subsequent forward- and back-substitution takes *an order of magnitude less* operations, namely, $\mathcal{O}(n^2)$ additions and the same number of multiplications, per right side. Hence we can solve $A\mathbf{x} = \mathbf{b}$ for many different right sides (once we know the final content of W) in the time it takes to calculate the final content of W.

In this accounting of the work, we have followed tradition and counted only floating-point operations. In particular, we have ignored index calculations, the cost of managing DO loops and other bookkeeping costs, since these latter calculations used to be much faster than floating-point operations. This is not the case anymore on today's computers, and this way of accounting the work done may give an inaccurate picture (see Exercise 4.2-7). On the other hand, just how the work (as measured by computing time required) depends on the bookkeeping aspect of a program varies strongly from computer to computer and is therefore hard to discuss in the generality of this textbook.

A FORTRAN subroutine, called SUBST, which incorporates the substitution Algorithm 4.4, follows.

```
      SUBROUTINE SUBST ( W, IPIVOT, B, N, X )
      INTEGER IPIVOT(N),   I,IP,J
      REAL B(N),W(N,N),X(N),   SUM
C****** I N P U T ******
C W, IPIVOT, N ARE AS ON OUTPUT FROM  F A C T O R , APPLIED TO THE
C    MATRIX  A  OF ORDER  N .
C B IS AN N-VECTOR, GIVING THE RIGHT SIDE OF THE SYSTEM TO BE SOLVED.
C****** O U T P U T ******
C X IS THE N-VECTOR SATISFYING  A*X = B .
C****** M E T H O D ******
C ALGORITHM 4.4 IS USED, I.E., THE FACTORIZATION OF  A  CONTAINED IN
C W  AND  IPIVOT  (AS GENERATED IN  FACTOR ) IS USED TO SOLVE  A*X = B
C FOR  X  BY SOLVING TWO TRIANGULAR SYSTEMS.
C
      IF (N .LE. 1) THEN
         X(1) = B(1)/W(1,1)
                                      RETURN
      END IF
      IP = IPIVOT(1)
      X(1) = B(IP)
      DO 15 I=2,N
         SUM = 0.
         DO 14 J=1,I-1
14          SUM = W(I,J)*X(J) + SUM
         IP = IPIVOT(I)
15       X(I) = B(IP) - SUM
C
      X(N) = X(N)/W(N,N)
      DO 20 I=N-1,1,-1
         SUM = 0.
         DO 19 J=I+1,N
19          SUM = W(I,J)*X(J) + SUM
20       X(I) = (X(I) - SUM)/W(I,I)
                                      RETURN
      END
```

Next, we give a FORTRAN subroutine called FACTOR, which uses the elimination Algorithm 4.2, with the pivoting strategy dictated by scaled partial pivoting, to calculate a triangular factorization (if possible) for a given $N \times N$ matrix A, storing the factorization in an $N \times N$ matrix W, and storing the pivoting strategy in an N-vector IPIVOT, ready for use in the subroutine SUBST given earlier. The user must provide an additional N-vector D as a working space needed to store the "size" of the rows of A. If there is no further need for the matrix A and storage is scarce, then A itself can be used for W in the argument list of the CALL statement (this is illegal in some FORTRAN dialects). The factorization will then replace the original matrix in the array A.

```
      SUBROUTINE FACTOR ( W, N, D, IPIVOT, IFLAG )
      INTEGER IFLAG,IPIVOT(N),  I,ISTAR,J,K
      REAL D(N),W(N,N),   AWIKOD,COLMAX,RATIO,ROWMAX,TEMP
C****** I N P U T ******
C  W ARRAY OF SIZE (N,N) CONTAINING THE MATRIX A  OF ORDER N  TO BE
C    FACTORED.
C  N  THE ORDER OF THE MATRIX
C****** W O R K   A R E A ******
C  D  A REAL VECTOR OF LENGTH N, TO HOLD ROW SIZES
C****** O U T P U T ******
C  W ARRAY OF SIZE (N,N) CONTAINING THE LU FACTORIZATION OF  P*A  FOR
C    SOME PERMUTATION MATRIX  P  SPECIFIED BY  IPIVOT .
C  IPIVOT  INTEGER VECTOR OF LENGTH  N  INDICATING THAT ROW IPIVOT(K)
C    WAS USED TO ELIMINATE  X(K) , K=1,...,N .
C  IFLAG   AN INTEGER,
C        = 1, IF AN EVEN NUMBER OF INTERCHANGES WAS CARRIED OUT,
C        = -1, IF AN ODD NUMBER OF INTERCHANGES WAS CARRIED OUT,
C        = 0, IF THE UPPER TRIANGULAR FACTOR HAS ONE OR MORE ZERO DIA-
C              GONAL ENTRIES.
C    THUS, DETERMINANT(A) = IFLAG*W(1,1)*...*W(N,N) .
C  IF IFLAG .NE. 0, THEN THE LINEAR SYSTEM A*X = B CAN BE SOLVED FOR
C    X BY A
C        CALL SUBST (W, IPIVOT, B, N, X )
C****** M E T H O D ******
C  THE PROGRAM FOLLOWS ALGORITHM 4.2, USING SCALED PARTIAL PIVOTING.
C
      IFLAG = 1
C           INITIALIZE IPIVOT, D
      DO 9 I=1,N
         IPIVOT(I) = I
         ROWMAX = 0.
         DO 5 J=1,N
    5       ROWMAX = AMAX1(ROWMAX,ABS(W(I,J)))
         IF (ROWMAX .EQ. 0.) THEN
            IFLAG = 0
            ROWMAX = 1.
         END IF
    9    D(I) = ROWMAX
      IF (N .LE. 1)                      RETURN
C           FACTORIZATION
      DO 20 K=1,N-1
C               DETERMINE PIVOT ROW, THE ROW  ISTAR .
      COLMAX = ABS(W(K,K))/D(K)
      ISTAR = K
      DO 13 I=K+1,N
         AWIKOD = ABS(W(I,K))/D(I)
         IF (AWIKOD .GT. COLMAX) THEN
            COLMAX = AWIKOD
            ISTAR = I
         END IF
   13    CONTINUE
      IF (COLMAX .EQ. 0.)  THEN
         IFLAG = 0
      ELSE
         IF (ISTAR .GT. K)  THEN
C              MAKE  K  THE PIVOT ROW  BY INTERCHANGING IT WITH
C                 THE CHOSEN ROW  ISTAR .
            IFLAG = -IFLAG
            I = IPIVOT(ISTAR)
            IPIVOT(ISTAR) = IPIVOT(K)
            IPIVOT(K) = I
            TEMP = D(ISTAR)
            D(ISTAR) = D(K)
            D(K) = TEMP
            DO 15 J=1,N
               TEMP = W(ISTAR,J)
               W(ISTAR,J) = W(K,J)
   15          W(K,J) = TEMP
         END IF
C              ELIMINATE  X(K)  FROM ROWS  K+1,...,N .
   16       DO 19 I=K+1,N
               W(I,K) = W(I,K)/W(K,K)
```

```
              RATIO = W(I,K)
              DO 19 J=K+1,N
                 W(I,J) = W(I,J) - RATIO*W(K,J)
   19         CONTINUE
          END IF
   20 CONTINUE
      IF (W(N,N) .EQ. 0.)    IFLAG = 0
                                         RETURN
      END
```

The preceding discussion points toward an efficient way to calculate the *inverse* for a given invertible matrix A of order n. As was pointed out in Sec. 4.1, for $j = 1, \ldots, n$, the jth column $A^{-1}\mathbf{i}_j$ of the inverse matrix A^{-1} is the solution of the linear system

$$A\mathbf{x} = \mathbf{i}_j$$

Hence, to calculate A^{-1}, one calls on FACTOR once, then solves each of the n systems $A\mathbf{x} = \mathbf{i}_j$, $j = 1, \ldots, n$, by Algorithm 4.4, that is, using SUBST. Therefore, once the elimination is carried out, it takes only $n \cdot n^2$ multiplications, and about the same number of additions, to find A^{-1}.

Having given this simple prescription for calculating the inverse of a matrix, we hasten to point out that *there is usually no good reason for ever calculating the inverse*. It does at times happen in certain problems that the entries of A^{-1} have some special physical significance. In the statistical treatment of the fitting of a function to observed data by the method of least squares, for example, the entries of a certain A^{-1} give information about the kinds and magnitudes of errors in the data. But whenever A^{-1} is needed merely to calculate a vector $A^{-1}\mathbf{b}$ (as in solving $A\mathbf{x} = \mathbf{b}$) or a matrix product $A^{-1}B$, A^{-1} should never be calculated explicitly. Rather, the substitution Algorithm 4.4 should be used to form these products. The reason for this exhortation is as follows: Calculating the vector $A^{-1}\mathbf{b}$ for given $\mathbf{b}$ amounts to finding the solution of the linear system $A\mathbf{x} = \mathbf{b}$. Once the triangular factorization for A has been calculated by Algorithm 4.2, the calculation of $A^{-1}\mathbf{b}$ can therefore be accomplished by Algorithm 4.4 in exactly the same number of multiplications and additions as it takes to form the product of A^{-1} with the vector $\mathbf{b}$, as was pointed out earlier. Hence, once the triangular factorization is known, no advantage for calculating $A^{-1}\mathbf{b}$ can be gained by knowing A^{-1} explicitly. (Since forming the product $A^{-1}B$ amounts to multiplying each column of B by A^{-1}, these remarks apply to calculating such matrix products as well.) On the other hand, a first step toward calculating A^{-1} is finding the triangular factorization for A, which is then followed by n applications of the substitution algorithm; hence calculating A^{-1} presents a considerable initial computational outlay when compared with the work of calculating $A^{-1}\mathbf{b}$. In addition, the matrix so computed is only an *approximate* inverse and is, in a sense, less accurate than the triangular factorization, since it is derived from the factorization by further calculations. Hence nothing can be gained, and accuracy can be lost, by using A^{-1} explicitly in the calculation of matrix products involving A^{-1}.

Below, we have listed a FORTRAN program for the calculation of the inverse of a given N × N matrix A. This program uses the subprograms FACTOR and SUBST mentioned earlier. Sample input and the resulting output are also listed. The following remarks might help in the understanding of the coding. The order N of the matrix A is part of the input to this program; hence it is not possible to specify the exact dimension of the matrix A during compilation. On the other hand, both FACTOR and SUBST expect matrices A and/or W of exact dimension N × N. In the FORTRAN program below, the matrix A is therefore stored in a one-dimensional array, making use of the FORTRAN convention that the (I,J) entry of a two-dimensional (N,M) array is the ((J − 1)*N + I) entry in an equivalent one-dimensional array. The same convention is followed in storing the entries of the Jth column of A^{-1} in the one-dimensional array AINV: the subroutine SUBST is given the ((J − 1)*N + 1) entry of AINV as the first entry of the N-vector called X in SUBST, into which the solution of the system $A\mathbf{x} = \mathbf{i}_j$ is to be stored.

FORTRAN PROGRAM FOR CALCULATING THE INVERSE OF A GIVEN MATRIX

```
C   PROGRAM FOR CALCULATING THE INVERSE OF A GIVEN MATRIX
C   CALLS  F A C T O R ,  S U B S T .
        PARAMETER NMAX=30,NMAXSQ=NMAX*NMAX
        INTEGER I,IBEG,IFLAG,IPIVOT(NMAX),J,N,NSQ
        REAL A(NMAXSQ),AINV(NMAXSQ),B(NMAX)
      1 READ 501, N
    501 FORMAT(I2)
        IF (N .LT. 1 .OR. N .GT. NMAX)     STOP
C                 READ IN MATRIX ROW BY ROW
        NSQ = N*N
        DO 10 I=1,N
     10    READ 510,  (A(J),J=I,NSQ,N)
    510 FORMAT(5E15.7)
C
        CALL FACTOR ( A, N, B, IPIVOT, IFLAG )
        IF (IFLAG .EQ. 0) THEN
           PRINT 611
    611    FORMAT('1MATRIX IS SINGULAR')
                                           GO TO 1
        END IF
        DO 21 I=1,N
     21    B(I) = 0.
        IBEG = 1
        DO 30 J=1,N
           B(J) = 1.
           CALL SUBST ( A, IPIVOT, B, N, AINV(IBEG) )
           B(J) = 0.
     30    IBEG = IBEG + N
        PRINT 630
    630 FORMAT('1THE COMPUTED INVERSE IS '//)
        DO 31 I=1,N
     31    PRINT 631, I, (AINV(J),J=I,NSQ,N)
    631 FORMAT('0ROW ',I2,8E15.7/(7X,8E15.7))
                                           GO TO 1
        END
```

SAMPLE INPUT

```
3
2.       3.      −1.
4.       4.      −3.
−2.      3.      −1.
```

RESULTING OUTPUT

THE COMPUTED INVERSE IS

ROW 1	0.2500000E 00	0.0		−0.2499999E	00
ROW 2	0.5000000E 00	−0.1999998E 00		0.9999996E	−01
ROW 3	0.1000000E 01	−0.6000000E 00		−0.2000000E	00

EXERCISES

4.4-1 Modify the FORTRAN program for the calculation of A^{-1} given in the text to obtain a program which solves the more general problem of calculating the product $C = A^{-1}B$, where A is a given (invertible) $n \times n$ matrix and B is a given $n \times m$ matrix.

4.4-2 Calculate the inverse of the coefficient matrix A of the system of Exercise 4.2-8; then check the accuracy of the computed inverse A_{comp}^{-1} by calculating $A_{\text{comp}}^{-1} A$ and AA_{comp}^{-1}.

4.4-3 Show that the matrix

$$A = \begin{bmatrix} 2 & 2 & 1 \\ 1 & 1 & 1 \\ 3 & 2 & 1 \end{bmatrix}$$

is invertible, but that A cannot be written as the product of a lower-triangular matrix with an upper-triangular matrix.

4.4-4 Prove that the sum and the product of two lower- (upper-) triangular matrices is lower- (upper-) triangular and that the inverse of a lower- (upper-) triangular matrix is lower- (upper-) triangular.

4.4-5 Prove that a triangular factorization is unique in the following sense: If A is invertible and $L_1 U_1 = A = L_2 U_2$, where L_1, L_2 are unit-lower-triangular matrices and U_1, U_2 are upper-triangular matrices, then $L_1 = L_2$ and $U_1 = U_2$. (*Hint:* Use Exercise 4.1-8 to prove that U_1, L_2 must be invertible; then show that $L_2^{-1}L_1 = U_2 U_1^{-1}$ must hold, which implies, with Exercise 4.4-4, that $L_2^{-1}L_1$ must be a diagonal matrix; hence, since both L_1 and L_2 have 1's on their diagonal, $L_2^{-1}L_1 = I$.)

4.4-6 Use the results of Exercise 4.4-5 to show that if A is symmetric ($A = A^T$) and has a triangular factorization, $A = LU$, then $U = DL^T$, with D the *diagonal* matrix having the same diagonal entries as U.

4.4-7 Prove: If the tridiagonal matrix A can be factored as $A = LU$, where L is lower-triangular and U is upper-triangular, then both L and U are also tridiagonal. Interpret Algorithm 4.3 as a way to factor tridiagonal matrices.

4.4-8 Compact schemes Construct the triangular factors L and U for A using Eqs. (4.23) in the form

$$l_{ij} = (a_{ij} - l_{i1}u_{1j} - \cdots - l_{i,j-1}u_{j-1,j})/u_{jj} \qquad \text{for } i > j$$

$$u_{ij} = a_{ij} - l_{i1}u_{1j} - \cdots - l_{i,i-1}u_{i-1,j} \qquad \text{for } i \leq j$$

to derive the interesting entries of L and U. In effect, the final content of the work array W is derived by carrying out, for each entry, all modifications at one time, thus avoiding the writing down of the various intermediate results. Of course, this has to be done in some systematic order. For l_{ij} (for $i > j$) cannot be calculated unless one already knows l_{ir} for $r < j$ and u_{rj} for $r \leq j$. Again, one must know already l_{ir} and u_{rj} for $r < i$ in order to calculate u_{ij} (for $i \leq j$).

(a) Devise an algorithm for the construction of L and U from A in this compact manner.

(b) Modify your algorithm to allow for scaled partial pivoting.

(c) If your algorithm is not already done this way, modify it so that the innermost loops run over row indices (see Exercise 4.2-7 for motivation).

4.4-9: Choleski's method If the matrix A of order n is real, symmetric ($A = A^T$), and positive definite (that is, $x^TAx > 0$ for all nonzero n-vectors x), then it is possible to factor A as LDL^T, where L is a real unit-lower-triangular matrix and $D = (d_{ij})$ is a (positive) diagonal matrix. Thus, from (4.23),

$$l_{ij} = (a_{ij} - l_{i1}l_{j1} - \cdots - l_{i,j-1}l_{j,j-1})/d_{jj} \qquad \text{for } i > j$$

while
$$d_{jj} = a_{jj} - l_{j1}^2 - \cdots - l_{j,j-1}^2$$

Write a FORTRAN subroutine based on these equations for the generation of (the interesting part of) L and D, and a subroutine for solving $Ax = b$ for x by substitution once L and D are known.

4.4-10 Show that Choleski's method is applicable whenever the matrix A is of the form BB^T with B an invertible matrix.

4.5 ERROR AND RESIDUAL OF AN APPROXIMATE SOLUTION; NORMS

Any computed solution of a linear system must, because of roundoff, be considered an approximate solution. In this section, we discuss the difficult problem of ascertaining the error of an approximate solution (without knowing the solution). In the discussion, we introduce and use norms as a convenient means of measuring the "size" of vectors and matrices.

If $\hat{x}$ is a computed solution for the linear system $Ax = b$, then its **error** is the difference

$$e = x - \hat{x}$$

This error is, of course, usually not known to us (for otherwise, we would know the solution x, making any further discussions unnecessary). But we can always compute the **residual** (error)

$$r = Ax - A\hat{x}$$

since Ax is just the right side b. The residual then measures how well $\hat{x}$

satisfies the linear system $A\mathbf{x} = \mathbf{b}$. If $\mathbf{r}$ is the zero vector, then $\hat{\mathbf{x}}$ is the (exact) solution; that is, $\mathbf{e}$ is then zero. One would expect each entry of $\mathbf{r}$ to be small, at least in a relative sense, if $\hat{\mathbf{x}}$ is a good approximation to the solution $\mathbf{x}$.

Example 4.5 Consider the simple linear system

$$1.01x_1 + 0.99x_2 = 2$$
$$0.99x_1 + 1.01x_2 = 2$$

whose unique solution $\mathbf{x}$ has the entries $x_1 = x_2 = 1$. The approximate solution $\hat{\mathbf{x}} = \begin{bmatrix} 1.01 \\ 1.01 \end{bmatrix}$ has error $\mathbf{e} = \begin{bmatrix} -0.01 \\ -0.01 \end{bmatrix}$ and residual $\mathbf{r} = \begin{bmatrix} -0.02 \\ -0.02 \end{bmatrix}$, so that a "small" residual (relative to the right side) corresponds to a relatively "small" error in this case. On the other hand, the approximate solution $\hat{\mathbf{x}} = \begin{bmatrix} 2 \\ 0 \end{bmatrix}$ has error $\mathbf{e} = \begin{bmatrix} -1 \\ 1 \end{bmatrix}$, but residual $\mathbf{r} = \begin{bmatrix} -0.02 \\ 0.02 \end{bmatrix}$, hence still a relatively "small" residual, while the error is now relatively "large." By taking a different right side, we can achieve the opposite effect. The linear system

$$1.01x_1 + 0.99x_2 = 2$$
$$0.99x_1 + 1.01x_2 = -2$$
(4.30)

has the unique solution $x_1 = 100$, $x_2 = -100$. The approximate solution $\hat{\mathbf{x}} = \begin{bmatrix} 101 \\ -99 \end{bmatrix}$ has error $\mathbf{e} = \begin{bmatrix} -1 \\ -1 \end{bmatrix}$, but residual $\mathbf{r} = \begin{bmatrix} -2 \\ -2 \end{bmatrix}$; hence the residual is now relatively "large," while the error is relatively "small" (only 1 percent of the solution).

As this example shows, the size of the *residual* $\mathbf{r} = \mathbf{b} - A\hat{\mathbf{x}}$ of an approximate solution $\hat{\mathbf{x}}$ is not always a reliable indicator of the size of the error $\mathbf{e} = \mathbf{x} - \hat{\mathbf{x}}$ in this approximate solution. Whether or not a "small" residual implies a "small" error depends on the "size" of the coefficient matrix and of its inverse, in a manner to be made precise below. For this discussion, we need a means of measuring the "size" of n-vectors and $n \times n$ matrices.

The absolute value provides a convenient way to measure the "size" of real numbers or even of complex numbers. It is much less certain how one should measure the size of an n-vector or an $n \times n$ matrix. There is certainly not any *one* way of doing this which is acceptable in all situations.

For example, a frequently used measure for the size of an n-vector $\mathbf{a}$ is the nonnegative number

$$\|\mathbf{a}\|_\infty = \max_{1 \leq i \leq n} |a_i|$$
(4.31)

Assume now that the computed solution $\hat{\mathbf{x}}$ to $A\mathbf{x} = \mathbf{b}$ is known to have six-place accuracy in this way of measuring size; i.e.,

$$\frac{\|\mathbf{x} - \hat{\mathbf{x}}\|_\infty}{\|\mathbf{x}\|_\infty} < 10^{-6}$$
(4.32)

Then this would indicate a very satisfactory computed solution in case the unknowns are, say, approximate values of the well-behaved solution of a certain differential equation. But if one of the unknowns happens to be your annual income while another is the gross national product, then (4.32) gives no hint as to whether or not **x** is a satisfactory computed solution (as far as you are concerned), since, with (4.32) holding, the error in your computed yearly income (even if received for only one year) might make you independently wealthy or put you in debt for life. A measure like

$$\|\mathbf{a}\| = \max\left\{ 10^{10}|a_1|, \max_{2 \le i \le n} |a_i| \right\}$$

(assuming your yearly income to be the first unknown) would give you much more information, as would certain measures of size which use several numbers (rather than just one nonnegative number) to describe the "size" of an n-vector.

For most situations, however, it suffices to measure the size of an n-vector by a *norm*. A norm retains certain properties of the absolute value for numbers. Specifically, a norm assigns to each n-vector **a** a real number $\|\mathbf{a}\|$, called **the norm of a**, subject to the following reasonable restrictions:

(i) For all n-vectors **a**, $\|\mathbf{a}\| \ge 0$, and $\|\mathbf{a}\| = 0$ if and only if $\mathbf{a} = \mathbf{0}$
(ii) For all n-vectors **a** and all numbers α, $\|\alpha\mathbf{a}\| = |\alpha| \|\mathbf{a}\|$ (4.33)
(iii) For any two n-vectors **a** and **b**, $\|\mathbf{a} + \mathbf{b}\| \le \|\mathbf{a}\| + \|\mathbf{b}\|$

The first restriction forces all n-vectors but the zero vector to have positive "length." The second restriction states, for example, that **a** and its negative $-\mathbf{a}$ have the same "length" and that the length of $3\mathbf{a}$ is three times the length of **a**. The third restriction is the **triangle inequality**, so called since it states that the sum of the lengths of two sides of a triangle is never smaller than the length of the third side.

The student is presumably familiar with the **euclidean** length or **norm**,

$$\|\mathbf{a}\|_2 = \sqrt{\mathbf{a}^T\mathbf{a}} = \sqrt{|a_1|^2 + |a_2|^2 + \cdots + |a_n|^2}$$

of the n-vector $\mathbf{a} = (a_i)$, at least for the case $n = 2$ or $n = 3$. But, for a reason made clear below, we prefer to use, in the numerical examples below, the **maximum norm** (4.31) as a way to measure the size or length of the n-vector **a**. It is not difficult to verify that (4.31) defines a norm, i.e., that $\|\mathbf{a}\| = \|\mathbf{a}\|_\infty$ satisfies the three properties of a norm listed in (4.33). As to (i), $\|\mathbf{a}\|_\infty$ is the maximum of nonnegative quantities, hence nonnegative; also, $\|\mathbf{a}\|_\infty = 0$ if and only if, for all i, $|a_i| = 0$, which is the same as saying that $\mathbf{a} = \mathbf{0}$. Further, if α is any scalar, then

$$\|\alpha\mathbf{a}\|_\infty = \max_i |\alpha a_i| = \max_i |\alpha| |a_i| = |\alpha| \max_i |a_i| = |\alpha| \|\mathbf{a}\|_\infty$$

proving (ii). Finally,

$$\|\mathbf{a} + \mathbf{b}\| = \max_i |a_i + b_i| \le \max_i (|a_i| + |b_i|)$$
$$\le \max_i |a_i| + \max_i |b_i| = \|\mathbf{a}\|_\infty + \|\mathbf{b}\|_\infty$$

proving (iii).

Other vector norms in frequent use include the 1-norm

$$\|\mathbf{a}\| = \|\mathbf{a}\|_1 = \sum_{i=1}^n |a_i|$$

and various instances of the weighted p-norm

$$\|\mathbf{a}\| = \|\mathbf{a}\|_{p,\,w} = \left(\sum_{i=1}^n |a_i|^p w_i \right)^{1/p}$$

where p is some number between 1 and ∞ and the numbers $w_1, \ldots, w_n$ are fixed positive quantities. The case $p = 2$, $w_i = 1$ (all i) leads to the familiar euclidean norm.

Once a vector norm is chosen, we then measure the corresponding size of an $n \times n$ matrix A by comparing the size of $A\mathbf{x}$ with the size of $\mathbf{x}$. Precisely, we define the corresponding **matrix norm** of A by

$$\|A\| = \max \frac{\|A\mathbf{x}\|}{\|\mathbf{x}\|} \tag{4.34}$$

where the maximum is taken over all (nonzero) n-vectors $\mathbf{x}$. It can be shown that this maximum exists for every $n \times n$ matrix A (and any choice of the vector norm). The matrix norm $\|A\|$ is characterized by the following two facts:

$$\text{For all } n\text{-vectors } \mathbf{x}, \ \|A\mathbf{x}\| \le \|A\| \, \|\mathbf{x}\|$$

and $\tag{4.35}$

$$\text{For some nonzero } n\text{-vector } \mathbf{x}, \ \|A\mathbf{x}\| \ge \|A\| \, \|\mathbf{x}\|$$

Of course, (4.35) implies at once that $\|A\mathbf{x}\| = \|A\| \, \|\mathbf{x}\|$ for any $\mathbf{x}$ with $\|A\mathbf{x}\| \ge \|A\| \, \|\mathbf{x}\|$. Further, the following properties can be shown to hold for the matrix norm (4.34):

(i) For all $n \times n$ matrices A: $\|A\| \ge 0$, and $\|A\| = 0$ if and only if $A = O$

(ii) For all $n \times n$ matrices A and all numbers α, $\|\alpha A\| = |\alpha| \, \|A\|$ $\tag{4.36}$

(iii) For any two $n \times n$ matrices A and B, $\|A + B\| \le \|A\| + \|B\|$

so that the term "norm" for the number $\|A\|$ is justified.

In addition,

(iv) For any two $n \times n$ matrices A and B, $\|AB\| \le \|A\| \, \|B\|$ $\tag{4.37}$

Finally, if the matrix A is invertible, then $\mathbf{x} = A^{-1}(A\mathbf{x})$; hence $\|\mathbf{x}\| \le \|A^{-1}\| \, \|A\mathbf{x}\|$. Combining this with (4.35), one gets

$$\text{For all } n\text{-vectors } \mathbf{x}, \quad \frac{\|\mathbf{x}\|}{\|A^{-1}\|} \le \|A\mathbf{x}\| \le \|A\| \, \|\mathbf{x}\| \qquad (4.38)$$

and both inequalities are *sharp*; i.e., each can be made an equality by an appropriate choice of a (nonzero) $\mathbf{x}$.

As it turns out, the matrix norm

$$\|A\|_2 = \max \frac{\|A\mathbf{x}\|_2}{\|\mathbf{x}\|_2}$$

based on the euclidean vector norm, is usually quite difficult to calculate, while the matrix norm

$$\|A\|_\infty = \max \frac{\|A\mathbf{x}\|_\infty}{\|\mathbf{x}\|_\infty}$$

based on the maximum norm, can be calculated quite easily, it being the number

$$\|A\|_\infty = \max_{1 \le i \le n} \sum_{j=1}^{n} |a_{ij}| \qquad (4.39)$$

To prove this, we have to show that the number $\|A\| = \max_i \Sigma_j |a_{ij}|$ satisfies the two statements in (4.35), i.e., that

$$\text{For all } n\text{-vectors } \mathbf{x}, \ \|A\mathbf{x}\|_\infty \le \left(\max_i \sum_{j=1}^{n} |a_{ij}| \right) \|\mathbf{x}\|_\infty$$

and

$$\text{For some nonzero } \mathbf{x}, \ \|A\mathbf{x}\|_\infty \ge \left(\max_i \sum_{j=1}^{n} |a_{ij}| \right) \|\mathbf{x}\|_\infty$$

But for an arbitrary $\mathbf{x}$,

$$\|A\mathbf{x}\|_\infty = \max_{1 \le i \le n} \left| \sum_{j=1}^{n} a_{ij} x_j \right| \le \max_{1 \le i \le n} \sum_{j=1}^{n} |a_{ij}| \, |x_j|$$

$$\le \max_{1 \le i \le n} \left(\left(\max_{1 \le j \le n} |x_j| \right) \sum_{j=1}^{n} |a_{ij}| \right) = \|\mathbf{x}\|_\infty \max_{1 \le i \le n} \sum_{j=1}^{n} |a_{ij}|$$

which proves the first statement. As to the second statement, let i_0 be an integer between 1 and n so that

$$\sum_{j=1}^{n} |a_{i_0 j}| = \max_{1 \le i \le n} \sum_{j=1}^{n} |a_{ij}|$$

and let $\mathbf{x}$ be an n-vector of max-norm 1 such that

$$a_{i_0 j} x_j = |a_{i_0 j}| \qquad j = 1, \ldots, n$$

e.g., take

$$x_j = \begin{cases} 1 & \text{if } a_{i_0 j} \geq 0 \\ -1 & \text{if } a_{i_0 j} < 0 \end{cases} \quad j = 1, \ldots, n$$

Then, for this clearly nonzero vector x, $\|x\|_\infty = 1$ and

$$\|Ax\|_\infty = \max_{1 \leq i \leq n} \left| \sum_{j=1}^{n} a_{ij} x_j \right| \geq \left| \sum_{j=1}^{n} a_{i_0 j} x_j \right|$$

$$= \sum_{j=1}^{n} |a_{i_0 j}| = \|x\|_\infty \left(\max_{1 \leq i \leq n} \sum_{j} |a_{ij}| \right)$$

which proves the second statement.

Example 4.5a For the coefficient matrix A of Example 4.5, one readily finds

$$\|A\|_\infty = \max\{|1.01| + |0.99|, |0.99| + |1.01|\} = 2$$

We have seen that

$$A \begin{bmatrix} 1 \\ 1 \end{bmatrix} = \begin{bmatrix} 2 \\ 2 \end{bmatrix} \quad \text{and} \quad A \begin{bmatrix} 100 \\ -100 \end{bmatrix} = \begin{bmatrix} 2 \\ -2 \end{bmatrix}$$

Hence

$$A \left(\begin{bmatrix} 1 \\ 1 \end{bmatrix} + \begin{bmatrix} 100 \\ -100 \end{bmatrix} \right) = \begin{bmatrix} 4 \\ 0 \end{bmatrix} \quad \text{and} \quad A \left(\begin{bmatrix} 1 \\ 1 \end{bmatrix} - \begin{bmatrix} 100 \\ -100 \end{bmatrix} \right) = \begin{bmatrix} 0 \\ 4 \end{bmatrix}$$

Therefore $A \begin{bmatrix} \frac{101}{4} & -\frac{99}{4} \\ -\frac{99}{4} & \frac{101}{4} \end{bmatrix} = \begin{bmatrix} 1 & 0 \\ 0 & 1 \end{bmatrix}$, showing that $A^{-1} = \begin{bmatrix} 25.25 & -24.75 \\ -24.75 & 25.25 \end{bmatrix}$.

Consequently, $\|A^{-1}\|_\infty = \max\{|25.25| + |-24.75|, |-24.75| + |25.25|\} = 50$.

For this example, then, (4.38) states that

$$\text{For all 2-vectors x, } 0.02\|x\|_\infty \leq \|Ax\|_\infty \leq 2\|x\|_\infty$$

Choosing $x = \begin{bmatrix} 1 \\ 1 \end{bmatrix}$, we get $Ax = \begin{bmatrix} 2 \\ 2 \end{bmatrix}$; hence $\|x\|_\infty = 1$, $\|Ax\|_\infty = 2$, and the second inequality becomes equality. Choosing $x = \begin{bmatrix} 100 \\ -100 \end{bmatrix}$, we get $Ax = \begin{bmatrix} 2 \\ -2 \end{bmatrix}$; hence $\|x\|_\infty = 100$ and $\|Ax\|_\infty = 2$, and the first inequality is an equality for this choice.

We now return to our discussion of the relationship between the *error* $e = x - \hat{x}$ in the approximate solution $\hat{x}$ of $Ax = b$ and the *residual* $r = b - A\hat{x}$. We have

$$r = Ax - A\hat{x} = A(x - \hat{x}) = Ae$$

Hence $e = A^{-1}r$. Therefore, remembering that $(A^{-1})^{-1} = A$, we get from (4.38)

$$\frac{\|r\|}{\|A\|} \leq \|e\| = \|A^{-1}r\| \leq \|A^{-1}\| \, \|r\| \tag{4.40}$$

This gives an upper and a lower bound on the **relative error** $\|e\|/\|x\|$ in terms of the **relative residual** $\|\mathbf{r}\|/\|\mathbf{b}\|$, namely

$$\frac{\|\mathbf{b}\|}{\|A\|\,\|\mathbf{x}\|}\cdot\frac{\|\mathbf{r}\|}{\|\mathbf{b}\|}\le\frac{\|\mathbf{e}\|}{\|\mathbf{x}\|}\le\frac{\|A^{-1}\|\,\|\mathbf{b}\|}{\|\mathbf{x}\|}\cdot\frac{\|\mathbf{r}\|}{\|\mathbf{b}\|} \tag{4.41}$$

Here, one can estimate $\|\mathbf{x}\|$ from a computed solution for the system $A\mathbf{x} = \mathbf{b}$. Else, use (4.40) in the special case $\hat{\mathbf{x}} = \mathbf{0}$, i.e.,

$$\frac{\|\mathbf{b}\|}{\|A\|}\le\|\mathbf{x}\|\le\|A^{-1}\|\,\|\mathbf{b}\|$$

to conclude from (4.41) that

$$\frac{1}{\|A\|\,\|A^{-1}\|}\cdot\frac{\|\mathbf{r}\|}{\|\mathbf{b}\|}\le\frac{\|\mathbf{e}\|}{\|\mathbf{x}\|}\le\|A^{-1}\|\,\|A\|\frac{\|\mathbf{r}\|}{\|\mathbf{b}\|} \tag{4.42}$$

The bounds (4.41) and (4.42) are *sharp* in the following sense. Whatever A and $\mathbf{x} \ne \mathbf{0}$ might be, there are nonzero choices for $\mathbf{e}$ or $\mathbf{r}$ for which one or the other of the inequalities in (4.41) becomes an equality. If one wants equality in one of the inequalities in (4.42), one would have to choose a particular $\mathbf{x}$ as well, but such choices are always possible.

Because of their importance, we state (4.41) and (4.42) in words: The relative error in an approximate solution for the linear system $A\mathbf{x} = \mathbf{b}$ can be as large as $\|A\|\,\|A^{-1}\|$ times, or, more precisely, as large as $\|A^{-1}\|\,\|\mathbf{b}\|/\|\mathbf{x}\|$ times, its relative residual, but it can also be as small as $1/(\|A\|\,\|A^{-1}\|)$ times, or, more precisely, as small as $\|\mathbf{b}\|/(\|A\|\,\|\mathbf{x}\|)$ times its relative residual. Hence, if $\|A\|\,\|A^{-1}\| \approx 1$, then the relative error and relative residual are always of the same size, and the relative residual can then be safely used as an estimate for the relative error. But the larger $\|A\|\,\|A^{-1}\|$ is, the less information about the relative error can be obtained from the relative residual.

The number $\|A\|\,\|A^{-1}\|$ is called the **condition number** of A and is at times abbreviated

$$\operatorname{cond}(A) = \|A\|\,\|A^{-1}\|$$

Note that the condition number $\operatorname{cond}(A)$ for A depends on the matrix norm used and can, for some matrices, vary considerably as the matrix norm is changed. On the other hand, the condition number is always at least 1, since for the identity matrix I, $\|I\| = \max\|\mathbf{x}\|/\|\mathbf{x}\| = 1$, and by (4.37), $\|I\| = \|AA^{-1}\| \le \|A\|\,\|A^{-1}\|$.

Example 4.6 We find from earlier calculations that, for the coefficient matrix A of Example 4.5, $\operatorname{cond}(A) = \|A\|_\infty\|A^{-1}\|_\infty = 2 \cdot 50 = 100$. Further, we saw in Example 4.5 that indeed the relative error of an approximate solution can be as large as 100 times its relative residual, but can also be just $\frac{1}{100}$ of its relative residual.

The bounds (4.41) and (4.42) require the number $\|A^{-1}\|$ which is not readily available. But, in typical situations, a good estimate for $\|\mathbf{e}\|$ is the number $\|\hat{\mathbf{e}}\|$, with $\hat{\mathbf{e}}$ the computed solution of the linear system $A\mathbf{e} = \mathbf{r}$. Since $\hat{\mathbf{x}}$ is usually obtained by Gauss elimination, a factorization for A is available and $\hat{\mathbf{e}}$ can therefore be obtained (by SUBST) with much less computational effort than was needed to obtain $\hat{\mathbf{x}}$. This presupposes that $\mathbf{r}$ is calculated in double precision. The vector $\hat{\mathbf{e}}$ so obtained is the first iterate in iterative improvement (Algorithm 4.5) discussed in the next section.

EXERCISES

4.5-1 Verify that

$$\|\mathbf{a}\| = \|\mathbf{a}\|_1 = \sum_{i=1}^{n} |a_i|$$

defines a norm for all n-vectors $\mathbf{a}$.

4.5-2 Prove that the matrix norm $\|A\|_1$ associated with the vector norm $\|\mathbf{a}\|_1$ of Exercise 4.5-1 can be calculated by

$$\|A\|_1 = \max_{1 \le j \le n} \sum_{i=1}^{n} |a_{ij}|$$

4.5-3 If we interpret a 2-vector $\mathbf{a}$ as a point in the plane with coordinates $\{a_1, a_2\}$, then its 2-norm $\|\mathbf{a}\|_2$ is the euclidean distance of this point from the origin. Further, the set of all vectors of euclidean norm 1 forms a circle around the origin of radius 1. Draw the "circle of radius 1 around the origin" when the distance of the "point" $\mathbf{a}$ is measured by (a) the 1-norm $\|\mathbf{a}\|_1$, (b) the norm $\|\mathbf{a}\|_{3/2}$, (c) the euclidean norm $\|\mathbf{a}\|_2$, (d) the norm $\|\mathbf{a}\|_4$, (e) the max-norm $\|\mathbf{a}\|_\infty$.

4.5-4 With the same interpretation of 2-vectors as points in the plane as used in Exercise 4.5-3, show that, for any two 2-vectors $\mathbf{a}$ and $\mathbf{b}$, the three "points" $\mathbf{0}$, $\mathbf{a}$, and $\mathbf{a} + \mathbf{b}$ are the vertices of a triangle with sides of (euclidean) length $\|\mathbf{a}\|_2$, $\|\mathbf{b}\|_2$, and $\|\mathbf{a} + \mathbf{b}\|_2$, and explain the term "triangle inequality" for property (iii) of norms [Eq. (4.33)].

4.5-5 Show that, for any 2-vectors $\mathbf{a}$ and $\mathbf{b}$ and any particular vector norm,

$$|\|\mathbf{a}\| - \|\mathbf{b}\|| \le \|\mathbf{a} - \mathbf{b}\|$$

4.5-6 Show that, for any 2-vectors $\mathbf{a}$ and $\mathbf{b}$, and any number λ between 0 and 1,

$$\|\lambda\mathbf{a} + (1 - \lambda)\mathbf{b}\| \le \max(\|\mathbf{a}\|, \|\mathbf{b}\|)$$

4.5-7 Show that the matrix norm $\|A\| = \max(\|A\mathbf{x}\|/\|\mathbf{x}\|)$ can also be calculated as

$$\|A\| = \max_{\|\mathbf{x}\| = 1} \|A\mathbf{x}\|$$

4.5-8 Prove all the statements in (4.36) regarding matrix norms.

4.5-9 Use Exercise 4.5-7 to calculate $\|A\|_2$, where

$$A = \begin{bmatrix} 3 & -5 \\ 6 & 1 \end{bmatrix}$$

(*Hint:* A 2-vector $\mathbf{x}$ has 2-norm $\|\mathbf{x}\|_2 = 1$ if and only if $x_1 = \cos\theta$, $x_2 = \sin\theta$ for some θ.)

4.5-10 Use Exercise 4.4-2 to calculate the condition number of the coefficient matrix A of the system of Exercise 4.2-8; then discuss relative error and relative residuals of the solutions calculated in Exercises 4.2-8 and 4.3-4 in terms of this condition number. Also, calculate $\hat{\mathbf{e}} = A^{-1}\mathbf{r}$ for these solutions (with $\mathbf{r}$ calculated in double precision), using just the substitution algorithm 4.4.

4.6 BACKWARD ERROR ANALYSIS AND ITERATIVE IMPROVEMENT

In the preceding Sec. 4.5, we used the condition number

$$\text{cond}(A) = \|A\| \, \|A^{-1}\| \tag{4.43}$$

of the coefficient matrix A of the linear system $A\mathbf{x} = \mathbf{b}$ as an $\mathbf{x}$-independent quantity in estimating the error of an approximate solution. To summarize: The condition number (4.43) provides a measure of how reliably the relative residual $\|\mathbf{b} - A\hat{\mathbf{x}}\|/\|\mathbf{b}\|$ of an approximate solution $\hat{\mathbf{x}}$ reflects the relative error $\|\mathbf{x} - \hat{\mathbf{x}}\|/\|\mathbf{x}\|$ of the approximate solution. The condition number is therefore a measure of how well we can hope to distinguish a "good" (approximate) solution from a "bad" one by looking at the residual error.

It is clearly quite difficult to calculate the condition number for a given matrix even if the matrix norm can be calculated relatively easily, since one must know A^{-1}. At times, $\text{cond}(A)$ can be *estimated* with the aid of the following theorem, which might also help to explain further the significance of the condition number.

Theorem 4.8 For any invertible $n \times n$ matrix A and any matrix norm, the condition number of A indicates the relative distance of A from the nearest noninvertible $n \times n$ matrix. Specifically,

$$\frac{1}{\text{cond}(A)} = \min\left\{ \frac{\|A - B\|}{\|A\|} \,\middle|\, B \text{ is not invertible} \right\}$$

A complete proof of this theorem is beyond the scope of this book (but see Exercise 4.6-5). We only show that

$$\frac{1}{\text{cond}(A)} \leq \inf\left\{ \frac{\|A - B\|}{\|A\|} \,\middle|\, B \text{ is not invertible} \right\}$$

i.e., that for any noninvertible $n \times n$ matrix B,

$$\frac{1}{\|A^{-1}\|} \leq \|A - B\| \tag{4.44}$$

Indeed, if B is not invertible, then by Theorem 4.4, there is a nonzero n-vector $\mathbf{x}$ such that $B\mathbf{x} = \mathbf{0}$. But then

$$\|A - B\| \, \|\mathbf{x}\| \geq \|(A - B)\mathbf{x}\| = \|A\mathbf{x} - B\mathbf{x}\| = \|A\mathbf{x}\| \geq \frac{\|\mathbf{x}\|}{\|A^{-1}\|}$$

using (4.38), and since $\mathbf{x} \neq \mathbf{0}$, we can divide by $\|\mathbf{x}\| \neq 0$ to obtain (4.44). The argument just given establishes the following useful corollary.

Corollary If A is invertible and B is a matrix such that

$$\|A - B\| < \frac{1}{\|A^{-1}\|}$$

then B is invertible.

To give an example, we find for the matrix

$$A = \begin{bmatrix} 1.01 & 0.99 \\ 0.99 & 1.01 \end{bmatrix}$$

of Example 4.5 that $\|A^{-1}\|_\infty \geq 1/0.02 = 50$, since the matrix $B = \begin{bmatrix} 1 & 1 \\ 1 & 1 \end{bmatrix}$ is not invertible, and $A - B = \begin{bmatrix} 0.01 & 0.01 \\ -0.01 & 0.01 \end{bmatrix}$ has max-norm $\|A - B\|_\infty$ $= 0.02$. Hence, since $\|A\|_\infty = 2$, we get that $\text{cond}(A) \geq 100$. A different example is provided by invertible triangular matrices. If A is triangular, we know from Theorem 4.6 that all diagonal entries of A are nonzero, and that replacing any diagonal entry of A by 0 makes A noninvertible. Consequently, if A is triangular, then

$$\text{cond}(A) \geq \frac{\|A\|_\infty}{\min_i |a_{ii}|}$$

The condition number also plays a role in the analysis of a further complication in solving linear systems. If the linear system $A\mathbf{x} = \mathbf{b}$ derives from a practical problem, we must expect the coefficients of this system to be subject to error, either because they result from other calculations or from physical measurement, or even only because of roundoff resulting from the conversion to a binary representation during read-in. Hence, assuming for the moment that the right side is accurate, we are, in fact, solving the linear system

$$\hat{A}\hat{\mathbf{x}} = \mathbf{b} \tag{4.45}$$

instead of $A\mathbf{x} = \mathbf{b}$, where $A = \hat{A} + E$, the matrix E containing the errors in the coefficients. Even if all calculations are carried out exactly, we still compute only the solution $\hat{\mathbf{x}}$ of (4.45) rather than the solution $\mathbf{x}$ of $A\mathbf{x} = \mathbf{b}$. Now, we have $\mathbf{x} = A^{-1}\mathbf{b}$; hence, assuming that (4.45) has a solution,

$$\mathbf{x} = A^{-1}\mathbf{b} = A^{-1}\hat{A}\hat{\mathbf{x}} = A^{-1}(A + \hat{A} - A)\hat{\mathbf{x}} = \hat{\mathbf{x}} + A^{-1}(\hat{A} - A)\hat{\mathbf{x}}$$

Therefore, with $\hat{A} - A = -E$,

$$\mathbf{x} - \hat{\mathbf{x}} = A^{-1}(-E)\hat{\mathbf{x}}$$

Hence

$$\|\mathbf{x} - \hat{\mathbf{x}}\| \leq \|A^{-1}\| \, \|E\| \, \|\hat{\mathbf{x}}\| = \|A^{-1}\| \, \|A\| \frac{\|E\|}{\|A\|} \|\hat{\mathbf{x}}\|$$

giving the final result

$$\frac{\|\mathbf{x} - \hat{\mathbf{x}}\|}{\|\hat{\mathbf{x}}\|} \le \text{cond}(A) \frac{\|E\|}{\|A\|} \tag{4.46}$$

In words, the change in the solution from $\mathbf{x}$ to $\hat{\mathbf{x}}$ relative to $\|\hat{\mathbf{x}}\|$ can be as large as $\text{cond}(A)$ times the relative change $\|E\|/\|A\|$ in the coefficient matrix. If the coefficients of the linear system $A\mathbf{x} = \mathbf{b}$ are known to be accurate only to about 10^{-s} (relative to the size of A) and $\text{cond}(A) \approx 10^t$, then there is no point in calculating the solution to a relative accuracy better than 10^{t-s}.

> **Example 4.7** Consider once more the linear system (4.30) in Example 4.5. We found earlier that $\text{cond}(A) = 100$ for its coefficient matrix A. By (4.46), a 1 percent change in the coefficients of the system could therefore change its solution drastically. Indeed, a 1 percent change (in the right direction) produces the linear system
>
> $$x_1 + x_2 = 2$$
> $$x_1 + x_2 = -2$$
>
> which has no solution at all, for the coefficient matrix now fails to be invertible.

The preceding analysis can be put to good use in gauging the effect of round-off errors incurred during elimination and back-substitution on the accuracy of the computed solution with the aid of backward error analysis. In this, we will make use of the terminology and notation introduced in Sec. 1.3.

Theorem 4.9 Suppose that, in order to obtain a factorization PLU for the nth order matrix A and, from this, the solution of the linear system $A\mathbf{x} = \mathbf{b}$, we use Algorithms 4.2 and 4.4, but employ floating point arithmetic with unit roundoff $u \le 0.01$, getting the computed factors P, $\hat{L}$, and $\hat{U}$ and the computed solution $\hat{\mathbf{x}}$. Then $\hat{\mathbf{x}}$ satisfies exactly the perturbed equation

$$(A + PE)\hat{\mathbf{x}} = \mathbf{b} \tag{4.47}$$

with
$$|E| \le u_n |P^{-1}A| + u_n(3 + u_n)|\hat{L}| \, |\hat{U}| \tag{4.48}$$

and
$$u_n := n(1.01)u$$

Here, we denote by $|B|$ the matrix obtained from $B = (b_{ij})$ by replacing all its entries by their absolute value,

$$|B| = (|b_{ij}|)$$

Also, we write

$$B \le C$$

for two matrices B and C in case B and C are of the same order and

$$b_{ij} \le c_{ij} \qquad \text{for all } i \text{ and } j$$

The theorem states that if n is not "too large" and if $|\hat{L}|\,|\hat{U}|$ is about the size of $|A|$, then we can account for the errors in the computed solution by adjustments in the equations of the same order of magnitude as are the changes we had to make merely to get the equations into the machine. In other words, the error in the computed solution caused by the use of floating-point arithmetic is then no worse than the error we had to accept from the outset because we were forced to round the entries of A to floating-point numbers.

Of course, should the matrix $|\hat{L}|\,|\hat{U}|$ be much larger than $|A|$, then the errors in the computed $\hat{x}$ may be much larger than those due to the conversion of the problem to machine floating-point numbers. Note that one could actually calculate the matrix $|\hat{L}|\,|\hat{U}|$ (at some expense) and go to higher-precision arithmetic in case the resulting bound on the perturbation matrix E exceeds the tolerance to which the entries of A are known to be accurate. But, more important, since the pivot order may materially affect the size of $|\hat{L}|\,|\hat{U}|$, we draw from Theorem 4.9 the important conclusion that *a pivoting strategy should try to keep the matrix $|\hat{L}|\,|\hat{U}|$ small.*

We now indicate the simple proof of Theorem 4.9, using the notation and terms introduced in Sec. 1.3. First, we deal with the interchanges made (as recorded in the permutation matrix P) by applying Algorithm 4.2 without interchanges to the matrix $A' := P^{-1}A$ (as we did in Sec. 4.4). Thus, we compute the interesting entries of the factors L and U according to (4.23) by

$$l_{ij} = \left(a'_{ij} - \sum_{k<j} l_{ik}u_{kj}\right)\Big/ u_{jj} \qquad i>j$$

$$u_{ij} = a'_{ij} - \sum_{k<i} l_{ik}u_{kj} \qquad i \leq j$$

Consequently, by Sec. 1.3, especially by comparison of (1.12) with (1.13), the entries $\hat{l}_{ij}$ and $\hat{u}_{ij}$ of the factors $\hat{L}$ and $\hat{U}$ as computed in floating-point arithmetic satisfy the perturbed equations

$$\hat{l}_{i1}\hat{u}_{1j}\varepsilon^{j} + \hat{l}_{i2}\hat{u}_{2j}\varepsilon^{j-1} + \cdots + \hat{l}_{ij}\hat{u}_{jj}\varepsilon = a'_{ij}\varepsilon^{j-1} \qquad i>j$$

$$\hat{l}_{i1}\hat{u}_{1j}\varepsilon^{i-1} + \hat{l}_{i2}\hat{u}_{2j}\varepsilon^{i-2} + \cdots + \hat{l}_{ii}\hat{u}_{ij} = a'_{ij}\varepsilon^{i-1} \qquad i \leq j$$

Here, each ε stands for some number of the form $(1 + \delta)$, with $|\delta| \leq u$, the unit roundoff. To simplify these equations, we next observe that for any such number ε and for any r, there exists δ with $|\delta| \leq (1.01)u$ so that

$$\varepsilon^{r} = 1 + r\delta$$

as long as $u \leq 0.01$. This shows that

$$\sum_{k} \hat{l}_{ik}\hat{u}_{kj} - a'_{ij}$$

$$= \begin{cases} a'_{ij}(j-1)\delta - \hat{l}_{i1}\hat{u}_{1j}j\delta - \cdots - \hat{l}_{ij}\hat{u}_{jj}\cdot 1\cdot\delta & i>j \\ a'_{ij}(i-1)\delta - \hat{l}_{i1}\hat{u}_{1j}(i-1)\delta - \cdots - \hat{l}_{ii}\hat{u}_{ij}\cdot 0\cdot\delta & i \leq j \end{cases}$$

and therefore
$$\hat{L}\hat{U} - A' = F \tag{4.49}$$
with
$$|F| \le u_n(|A'| + |\hat{L}|\,|\hat{U}|) \tag{4.50}$$
and $u_n = n(1.01)u$.

This shows that the computed factors $\hat{L}$ and $\hat{U}$ for A' are the exact factors for a perturbed matrix $A' + F$, with the error matrix F of the order of the roundoff in the entries of A, provided the matrix $|\hat{L}|\,|\hat{U}|$ is not much larger than $|A|$.

The computational steps used in Algorithm 4.4, i.e., in the solving phase, are rather similar to those above. One can, therefore, show in the same way that the computed vector $\hat{\mathbf{y}}$ satisfies exactly the perturbed lower-triangular system
$$(\hat{L} + G)\hat{\mathbf{y}} = \mathbf{b} \quad \text{with} \quad |G| \le u_n|\hat{L}|$$
while the computed solution $\hat{\mathbf{x}}$ satisfies exactly the perturbed linear system
$$(\hat{U} + H)\hat{\mathbf{x}} = \hat{\mathbf{y}} \quad \text{with} \quad |H| \le u_n|\hat{U}|$$
We conclude that the computed solution satisfies
$$(\hat{L} + G)(\hat{U} + H)\hat{\mathbf{x}} = \mathbf{b}$$
But now
$$
\begin{aligned}
(\hat{L} + G)(\hat{U} + H) &= \hat{L}\hat{U} + G\hat{U} + \hat{L}H + GH \\
&= A' + F + G\hat{U} + \hat{L}H + GH \\
&= A' + E
\end{aligned}
$$
where
$$
\begin{aligned}
|E| &\le |F| + |G|\,|\hat{U}| + |\hat{L}|\,|H| + |G|\,|H| \\
&\le u_n(|A'| + |\hat{L}|\,|\hat{U}|) + u_n|\hat{L}|\,|\hat{U}|(1 + 1 + u_n)
\end{aligned}
$$
which proves the theorem.

The bound (4.48) is conservative. If partial pivoting is used, then the bound
$$|E| \le nu|P^{-1}A| \tag{4.50a}$$
is often much more realistic. In any event, such a bound gives some insight into the effect of the precision used in the calculations on the accuracy of the computed solution. For we get, for example, from (4.46) and (4.50), that the error of the computed solution relative to the size of this solution is usually bounded as follows:
$$\frac{\|\mathbf{x} - \hat{\mathbf{x}}\|}{\|\hat{\mathbf{x}}\|} \le \text{cond}\,(A) \cdot n \cdot u \tag{4.51}$$

Quite loosely, the linear system $A\mathbf{x} = \mathbf{b}$ is often called **ill-conditioned** if $\text{cond}(A)$ is "large." Somewhat more to the point, one should say that the linear system is **ill-conditioned with respect to the precision used** if $\text{cond}(A)$ is about $1/u$, for then, by (4.51), a computed solution might well bear no resemblance to the (exact) solution of the system.

Example 4.8 Consider the linear system

$$0.24x_1 + 0.36x_2 + 0.12x_3 = 0.84$$
$$0.12x_1 + 0.16x_2 + 0.24x_3 = 0.52 \qquad (4.52)$$
$$0.15x_1 + 0.21x_2 + 0.25x_3 = 0.64$$

We attempt to solve this system by the elimination Algorithm 4.2, using two-decimal-digit floating-point arithmetic and scaled partial pivoting. The pivoting order turns out to be $\mathbf{p}^T = [1 \quad 2 \quad 3]$, and the final content of the working array is

$$\begin{bmatrix} 0.24 & 0.36 & 0.12 & 0.84 \\ 0.50 & -0.02 & 0.18 & 0.10 \\ 0.63 & 1.0 & -0.01 & 0.01 \end{bmatrix}$$

Continuing the calculations, we find by back-substitution the approximate solution $\hat{\mathbf{x}} = \begin{bmatrix} 25 \\ -14 \\ -1 \end{bmatrix}$. The residual is $\mathbf{r} = \begin{bmatrix} 0.0 \\ 0.0 \\ 0.08 \end{bmatrix}$. In fact, the solution is $\mathbf{x} = \begin{bmatrix} -3 \\ 4 \\ 1 \end{bmatrix}$, so that the computed solution $\hat{\mathbf{x}}$ is in error in the first significant digit.

The max-norm for the coefficient matrix A of this system is $\|A\|_\infty = 0.72$. Further, the matrix

$$B = \begin{bmatrix} 0.252 & 0.36 & 0.12 \\ 0.112 & 0.16 & 0.24 \\ 0.147 & 0.21 & 0.25 \end{bmatrix}$$

is noninvertible (its first column is 0.7 times its second column) while $\|A - B\|_\infty = 0.012$. Hence we get from Theorem 4.8 that

$$\text{cond}(A) \geq \frac{0.72}{0.012} \geq 60$$

This system is therefore very ill-conditioned with respect to the precision used, and the very large error in the computed solution is not surprising.

Next, we repeat the calculations, using three-decimal-digit floating-point arithmetic this time. Since $\text{cond}(A) \approx 60$, we still do not expect a very accurate computed solution. After Algorithm 4.2, the working matrix has the content

$$\begin{bmatrix} 0.24 & 0.36 & 0.12 & 0.84 \\ 0.5 & -0.02 & 0.18 & 0.10 \\ 0.625 & 0.75 & 0.04 & 0.04 \end{bmatrix} \qquad (4.53)$$

and back-substitution gives the computed solution $\hat{\mathbf{x}}^T = [-3 \quad 4 \quad 1]$; i.e., we get the (exact) solution, even though the system is still somewhat ill-conditioned with respect to the precision used. This becomes evident when we change the right side of (4.52) to $\mathbf{b} = \begin{bmatrix} 0.852 \\ 0.620 \\ 0.740 \end{bmatrix}$. Using the factorization (4.53), we calculate by Algorithm 4.4 the (approximate) solution $\hat{\mathbf{x}} = \begin{bmatrix} -3.30 \\ 4.05 \\ 1.53 \end{bmatrix}$ (still using three-decimal-digit floating-point arithmetic), which has residual $\mathbf{r} = \begin{bmatrix} 0.0024 \\ 0.0008 \\ 0.0020 \end{bmatrix}$. The exact solution is $\mathbf{x} = \begin{bmatrix} -3.6 \\ 4.25 \\ 1.55 \end{bmatrix}$; hence our computed solution has about 10 percent error, which is compatible with (4.51).

As this example shows, a large condition number relative to the precision used *may* lead to a relatively large error in the computed solution but is not guaranteed to do so.

Whether or not a given linear system is ill-conditioned with respect to the precision used can be conveniently ascertained [even without knowledge of cond(A)] during **iterative improvement**, which we now discuss. With $e = x - \hat{x}^{(1)}$ the (unknown) error in the approximate solution $\hat{x}^{(1)}$ for $Ax = b$, we found in Sec. 4.5 that

$$Ae = r \qquad (4.54)$$

where $r = b - A\hat{x}^{(1)}$ is the *computable* residual for $\hat{x}^{(1)}$. Here we have, then, a linear system whose solution is the error e and whose coefficient matrix agrees with the coefficient matrix of the original system. If $\hat{x}^{(1)}$ is obtained by the elimination Algorithm 4.2, we can solve (4.54) rather quickly by the substitution Algorithm 4.4. Let $\hat{e}^{(1)}$ be the (approximate) solution for (4.54) so computed. Then $\hat{e}^{(1)}$ will, in general, not agree with e. But at the very least, $\hat{e}^{(1)}$ should give an indication of the size of e. If $\|\hat{e}^{(1)}\| / \|\hat{x}^{(1)}\| \approx 10^{-s}$, we conclude that the first s decimal places of $\hat{x}^{(1)}$ probably agree with those of x. We would then also expect $\hat{e}^{(1)}$ to be that accurate an approximation to e. Hence we expect

$$\hat{x}^{(2)} = \hat{x}^{(1)} + \hat{e}^{(1)}$$

to be a better approximation to x than is $\hat{x}^{(1)}$. We can now, if necessary, compute the new residual $r = b - A\hat{x}^{(2)}$ and solve (4.54) again to obtain a new correction $\hat{e}^{(2)}$ and a new approximation $\hat{x}^{(3)} = \hat{x}^{(2)} + \hat{e}^{(2)}$ to x. The number of places in agreement in the successive approximations $\hat{x}^{(1)}, \hat{x}^{(2)}, \ldots$, as well as an examination of the successive residuals, should give an indication of the accuracy of these approximate solutions. One normally carries out this iteration until $\|\hat{e}^{(k)}\| / \|\hat{x}^{(k)}\| \approx 10^{-t}$ if t decimal places are carried during the calculations. The number of iteration steps necessary to achieve this end can be shown to increase with cond(A). When cond(A) is "very large," the corrections $\hat{e}^{(1)}, \hat{e}^{(2)}, \ldots$ may never decrease in size, thus signaling extreme ill-conditioning of the original system.

For the success of iterative improvement, it is absolutely mandatory that the residuals be computed as accurately as possible. If, as is usual, floating-point arithmetic is used, the residual should always be calculated in double-precision arithmetic.

Algorithm 4.5: Iterative improvement Given the linear system $Ax = b$ and the approximate solution $\hat{x}$.

Calculate $r = b - A\hat{x}$, using double-precision arithmetic
Use Algorithm 4.2 (or if possible, only Algorithm 4.4) to compute
    an (approximate) solution $\hat{e}$ of the linear system $Ae = r$
If $\|\hat{e}\| / \|\hat{x}\|$ is "small enough," stop and take $\hat{x} + \hat{e}$ as the solution
Otherwise, set $\hat{x} := \hat{x} + \hat{e}$ and repeat the procedure

Iterative improvement can be used whenever an approximate solution has been found by any means. It should always be used after an approximate solution has been found by elimination, since the corrections can then be calculated relatively cheaply by forward- and back-substitution. Also, the rate of convergence of the process (if any) gives a good indication of the condition of the system (with respect to the precision used).

Example 4.9 We apply iterative improvement to the approximate solution of (4.52) calculated in Example 4.8. The correctly computed residual is $r = \begin{bmatrix} 0.0 \\ 0.0 \\ 0.08 \end{bmatrix}$ rounded to two significant digits. Applying Algorithm 4.4 to this right side (using two-decimal-digit floating-point arithmetic), we get the correction $\hat{e}^{(1)} = \begin{bmatrix} 120 \\ -75 \\ -8 \end{bmatrix}$, which is of the same size as the computed solution. Hence we conclude that the given linear system is too ill-conditioned for the precision used and that a higher precision should be employed if we wish to calculate the solution of (4.52).

In Example 4.8 we also calculated an approximate solution $\hat{x} = \begin{bmatrix} -3.30 \\ +4.05 \\ 1.53 \end{bmatrix}$ for the linear system with the same coefficient matrix but a different right side, using three-decimal-digit floating-point arithmetic. The correctly computed residual is $r = \begin{bmatrix} 0.0024 \\ 0.0008 \\ 0.0020 \end{bmatrix}$.

Applying Algorithm 4.4 to this r as right side (using the same precision as before), we get the correction $\hat{e}^{(1)} = \begin{bmatrix} -0.3 \\ 0.2 \\ 0.02 \end{bmatrix}$, which is only 10 percent of the computed solution and gives the corrected solution $\hat{x}^{(2)} = \begin{bmatrix} -3.6 \\ 4.25 \\ 1.55 \end{bmatrix}$. The residual for this approximate solution turns out to be **0**, so that just one step of iterative improvement produces the (exact) solution in this example.

EXERCISES

4.6-1 Use Theorem 4.8 to estimate the condition number of the following matrix:

$$A = \begin{bmatrix} 7 & 8 & 9 \\ 8 & 9 & 10 \\ 9 & 10 & 8 \end{bmatrix}$$

4.6-2 Use iterative improvement on the computed solution in Exercise 4.3-4.

4.6-3 We say that a matrix A of order n is (strictly row) **diagonally dominant** if $|a_{ii}| > \sum_{j \neq i}|a_{ij}|$, $i = 1, \ldots, n$. Use the corollary to Theorem 4.8 to prove that a diagonally dominant matrix is invertible. (*Hint:* Write $A = DB$, where D is the diagonal matrix with diagonal entries equal to those of A; then show that $\|I - B\|_\infty < 1$.)

4.6-4 Estimate the condition number of the matrix of Exercise 4.6-1 by solving the linear system $Ax = b$ with (a) $b^T = [24, 27, 27]$, (b) $b^T = [24.1, 26.9, 26.9]$. Use iterative improvement.

4.6-5 Show that, for the particular matrix norm (4.39), a noninvertible matrix B for which equality holds in (4.44) can be constructed as follows: By (4.35), one can find x of norm 1 for which $\|A^{-1}\mathbf{x}\| = \|A^{-1}\| \|\mathbf{x}\|$. Now choose B as the matrix $A - \mathbf{x}\mathbf{z}^T$, with $\mathbf{z} = y_m^{-1}\mathbf{1}_m$, $\mathbf{y} = A^{-1}\mathbf{x}$, and m so chosen that $|y_m| = \|\mathbf{y}\|_\infty$.

4.6-6 Show that one can carry out the construction of Exercise 4.6-5 for a general norm provided one knows how to choose, for a given nonzero n-vector $\mathbf{y}$, an n-vector $\mathbf{z}$ so that, for all n-vectors $\mathbf{u}$, $\mathbf{z}^T\mathbf{u} \leq \|\mathbf{u}\|$ with equality if $\mathbf{u} = \mathbf{y}$. How would you choose $\mathbf{z}$ in case the norm is the 1-norm?

*4.7 DETERMINANTS

Although the student is assumed to be familiar with the concept of a determinant, we take this section to give the formal definition of determinants and give some of their elementary properties.

Associated with every square matrix A of numbers is a number called the determinant of the matrix and denoted by $\det(A)$. If $A = (a_{ij})$ is an $n \times n$ matrix, then the **determinant** of A is defined by

$$\det(A) = \sum_{\mathbf{p}} \sigma_{\mathbf{p}} a_{1,p_1} a_{2,p_2} \cdots a_{n,p_n} \tag{4.55}$$

where the sum is taken over all $n!$ permutations $\mathbf{p}$ of degree n, and $\sigma_{\mathbf{p}}$ is 1 or -1, depending on whether $\mathbf{p}$ is even or odd (see Sec. 4.1). Hence, if $n = 1$, then

$$\det(A) = \det[a_{11}] = a_{11}$$

while if $n = 2$

$$\det(A) = \det\begin{bmatrix} a_{11} & a_{12} \\ a_{21} & a_{22} \end{bmatrix} = a_{11}a_{22} - a_{12}a_{21} \tag{4.56}$$

Already, for $n = 3$, six products have to be summed, and for $n = 10$, over 3 million products, each with 10 factors, have to be computed and summed for the evaluation of the right side of (4.55). Hence the definition (4.55) is not very useful for the calculation of determinants. But we give below a list of rules regarding determinants which can be derived quite easily from the definition (4.55). With these rules, we then show how the determinant can be calculated, using the elimination Algorithm 4.2, in about $\mathcal{O}(n^3)$ [rather than $\mathcal{O}(n!)$] operations.

The determinant of a matrix is of importance because of the following theorem.

Theorem 4.10 Let A be an $n \times n$ matrix; then A is invertible if and only if $\det(A) \neq 0$.

We make use of this theorem in the next section, which concerns the calculation of eigenvalues and eigenvectors of a matrix.

For certain matrices, the determinant is calculated quite easily.

Rule 1 If $A = (a_{ij})$ is an upper- (lower-) triangular matrix, then

$$\det(A) = a_{11}a_{22} \cdots a_{nn}$$

i.e., the determinant is just the product of the diagonal entries of A.

For if A is, for example, upper-triangular and $\mathbf{p}$ is any permutation other than the identity permutation, then, for some i, we must have $p_i < i$, and the corresponding product $a_{1,p_1}a_{2,p_2} \cdots a_{n,p_n}$ contains, therefore, the *subdiagonal*, hence zero, entry a_{i,p_i} of A, and must be zero. Hence, if A is upper-triangular, then the only summand in (4.55) not guaranteed to be zero is the term $a_{11}a_{22} \cdots a_{nn}$ corresponding to the (even) identity permutation $\mathbf{p}^T = [1 \quad 2 \quad \cdots \quad n]$.

In particular,

$$\det(I) = 1 \tag{4.57}$$

One proves similarly a second rule.

Rule 2 If P is the $n \times n$ permutation matrix given by

$$P\mathbf{i}_j = \mathbf{i}_{p_j} \qquad j = 1, \ldots, n$$

with some permutation $\mathbf{p}$, then

$$\det(P) = \begin{cases} 1 & \text{if } \mathbf{p} \text{ is even} \\ -1 & \text{if } \mathbf{p} \text{ is odd} \end{cases}$$

Rule 3 If the matrix B results from the matrix A by the interchange of two columns (rows) of A, then $\det(B) = -\det(A)$.

Example

$$\det\begin{bmatrix} 1 & 4 \\ 2 & 3 \end{bmatrix} = 3 - 8 = -5 \quad \text{and} \quad \det\begin{bmatrix} 4 & 1 \\ 3 & 2 \end{bmatrix} = 8 - 3 = 5$$

Consequently, if two columns (rows) of the matrix A agree (so that their interchange leaves A unchanged), then $\det(A) = 0$.

Rule 4 If the matrix B is obtained from the matrix A by multiplying all entries of one column (row) of A by the same number α, then $\det(B) = \alpha \det(A)$.

Example

$$\det\begin{bmatrix} 3 \cdot 1 & 4 \\ 3 \cdot 2 & 3 \end{bmatrix} = 9 - 24 = -15 = 3(-5) = 3\det\begin{bmatrix} 1 & 4 \\ 2 & 3 \end{bmatrix}$$

Rule 5 Suppose that the three $n \times n$ matrices A_1, A_2, A_3 differ only in one column (row), say the jth, and the jth column (row) of A_3 is the vector sum of the jth column (row) of A_1 and the jth column (row) of A_2. Then

$$\det(A_1) + \det(A_2) = \det(A_3)$$

Example

$$\det\begin{bmatrix} 1 & 2 \\ 2 & 2 \end{bmatrix} + \det\begin{bmatrix} 1 & 2 \\ 1 & 1 \end{bmatrix} = (2 - 4) + (1 - 2) = 3 - 6 = \det\begin{bmatrix} 1 & 2 \\ 3 & 3 \end{bmatrix}$$

Rules 1 to 5 imply Theorems 4.11 and 4.12 below.

Theorem 4.11 If A and B are $n \times n$ matrices, then

$$\det(AB) = \det(A)\det(B)$$

Theorem 4.12 If A is an $n \times n$ matrix and $\mathbf{x} = (x_i)$ and $\mathbf{b}$ are n-vectors such that

$$A\mathbf{x} = \mathbf{b}$$

then, for $j = 1, \ldots, n$,

$$\det(A^{(j)}) = x_j\det(A) \qquad (4.58)$$

where $A^{(j)}$ is the matrix one gets on replacing the jth column of A by **b**.

If A is invertible, i.e., (by Theorem 4.10), if $\det(A) \neq 0$, then one can solve (4.58) for x_j, getting

$$x_j = \frac{\det(A^{(j)})}{\det(A)} \qquad j = 1, \ldots, n$$

This is **Cramer's rule** for the entries of the solution **x** of the linear system $A\mathbf{x} = \mathbf{b}$. Because of the difficulty of evaluating determinants, Cramer's rule is, in general, only of *theoretical interest*.

In fact, the fastest known way to calculate $\det(A)$ for an arbitrary $n \times n$ matrix A is to apply the elimination Algorithm 4.2 to the matrix A (ignoring the right side). We saw in Sec. 4.4 that this algorithm produces a factorization

$$A = PLU$$

of A into a permutation matrix P determined by the pivoting order **p**, a lower-triangular matrix L with all diagonal entries equal to 1, and the final upper-triangular coefficient matrix $U = (u_{ij})$, which has all the pivots on its diagonal. By Rule 1, $\det(L) = 1$, while by Rule 2, $\det(P) = 1$ or -1, depending on whether **p** is even or odd, i.e., depending on whether the number of interchanges made during the elimination is even or odd. Finally, again by Rule 1, $\det(U) = u_{11}u_{22} \cdots u_{nn}$. Hence

$$\det(A) = (-1)^i u_{11}u_{22} \cdots u_{nn} \qquad (4.59)$$

with i the number of interchanges during the elimination algorithm. Note that the FORTRAN program FACTOR returns this number $(-1)^i$ in IFLAG (in case A is found to be invertible), thus making it easy to calculate $\det(A)$ by (4.59) from the diagonal entries of the workarray W.

Of course, the elimination Algorithm 4.2 succeeds (at least theoretically) only when A is invertible. But if A is not invertible, then the algorithm will so indicate, in which case we know that $\det(A) = 0$, by Theorem 4.10.

Finally, if the matrix A has special properties, it is at times profitable to make use of the following rule.

Rule 6: *Expansion of a determinant by minors* The **minor** M_{ij} of the $n \times n$ matrix $A = (a_{ij})$ is, by definition, the determinant of the matrix of order $n - 1$ obtained from A by deleting the ith row and the jth column. One has

$$\text{For any } i, \det(A) = a_{i1}(-1)^{i+1}M_{i1} + a_{i2}(-1)^{i+2}M_{i2} + \cdots$$
$$+ a_{in}(-1)^{i+n}M_{in}$$

and

$$\text{For any } j, \det(A) = a_{1j}(-1)^{1+j}M_{1j} + a_{2j}(-1)^{2+j}M_{2j} + \cdots$$
$$+ a_{nj}(-1)^{n+j}M_{nj}$$

Rule 6 allows us to express a determinant of order n as a sum of determinants of order $n - 1$. By applying the rule recursively, we can eventually express $\det(A)$ as a sum of determinants of order 1. This rule is particularly useful for the calculation of $\det(A)$ when A is a sparse matrix, so that most of the summands drop out. For example, expanding in minors for the first row,

$$\det\begin{bmatrix} 0 & 1 & 0 \\ 1 & 0 & 0 \\ 0 & 0 & 1 \end{bmatrix} = 0 \det\begin{bmatrix} 0 & 0 \\ 0 & 1 \end{bmatrix} - 1 \det\begin{bmatrix} 1 & 0 \\ 0 & 1 \end{bmatrix} + 0 \det\begin{bmatrix} 1 & 0 \\ 0 & 0 \end{bmatrix}$$

$$= -1 \det\begin{bmatrix} 1 & 0 \\ 0 & 1 \end{bmatrix} = -1 \cdot 1 = -1$$

EXERCISES

4.7-1 Use Theorem 4.11 and Eq. (4.57) to prove that if A is invertible, then $\det(A) \neq 0$.

4.7-2 Use Theorems 4.12 and 4.4 to prove that if $\det(A) \neq 0$, then A is invertible.

4.7-3 Determine the number of arithmetic operations necessary to calculate the solution of a linear system of order 2 (*a*) by elimination and back-substitution, (*b*) by Cramer's rule.

4.7-4 If $n = 3$, then direct evaluation of (4.55) takes 12 multiplications and 5 additions. How many multiplications and additions does the evaluation of a determinant of order 3 take if expansion by minors (Rule 6) is used? How many multiplications/divisions and additions are necessary for the same task if elimination is used?

4.7-5 Prove: If the coefficient matrix of the linear system $A\mathbf{x} = \mathbf{b}$ is invertible, then it is always possible to reorder the equations (if necessary) so that the coefficient matrix of the reordered (equivalent) system has all diagonal entries nonzero. [*Hint:* By Theorem 4.10 at least one of the summands in (4.55) must be nonzero if A is invertible.]

4.7-6 Verify Rules 1 to 5 in case all matrices in question are of order 2. Try to prove Rules 4 and 5 for matrices of arbitrary order.

4.7-7 Prove Theorem 4.11 in case A and B are matrices of order 2.

4.7-8 Let A be a tridiagonal matrix of order n; for $p = 1, 2, \ldots, n$, let A_p be the $p \times p$ matrix obtained from A by omitting rows $p + 1, \ldots, n$ and columns $p + 1, \ldots, n$. Use Rule 6 to prove that, with $\det(A_0) = 1$,

$$\det(A_p) = a_{pp} \det(A_{p-1}) - a_{p,p-1}a_{p-1,p} \det(A_{p-2}) \qquad p = 2, 3, \ldots, n$$

Write a program for the evaluation of the determinant of a tridiagonal matrix based on this recursion formula.

*4.8 THE EIGENVALUE PROBLEM

Eigenvalues are of great importance in many physical problems. The stability of an aircraft, for example, is determined by the location in the complex plane of the eigenvalues of a certain matrix. The natural frequency of the vibrations of a beam are actually eigenvalues of an (infinite) matrix. Eigenvalues also occur naturally in the analysis of many mathematical problems because they are part of a particularly convenient and revealing way to represent a matrix (the Jordan canonical form and similar forms). For this reason, any system of first-order ordinary linear differential equations with constant coefficients can be solved in terms of the eigenvalues of its coefficient matrix. Again, the behavior of the sequence $A, A^2, A^3, \ldots$ of powers of a matrix is most easily analyzed in terms of the eigenvalues of A. Such sequences occur in the iterative solution of linear (and nonlinear) systems of equations.

For these and other reasons, we give in this section a brief introduction to the localization and calculation of eigenvalues. The state of the art is, unfortunately, much beyond the scope of this book. The encyclopedic book by J. H. Wilkinson [24] and the more elementary book by G. W. Stewart [23] are ready sources of information about such up-to-date methods as the QR method (with shifts), and for the many details omitted in the subsequent pages.

We say that the (real or complex) number λ is an **eigenvalue of the matrix** B provided for some nonzero (real or complex) vector $\mathbf{y}$,

$$B\mathbf{y} = \lambda\mathbf{y} \tag{4.60}$$

The n-vector $\mathbf{y}$ is then called an **eigenvector** of B belonging to the eigenvalue λ. We can write (4.60) in the form

$$(B - \lambda I)\mathbf{y} = \mathbf{0} \tag{4.61}$$

Since $\mathbf{y}$ is to be a nonzero vector, we see that λ is an eigenvalue of B if and only if the homogeneous system (4.61) has nontrivial solutions. Hence the following lemma is a consequence of Theorem 4.4.

Lemma 4.4 The number λ is an eigenvalue for the matrix B if and only if $(B - \lambda I)$ is not invertible.

Note that (4.60) or (4.61) determines an eigenvector for λ only up to scalar multiples. If $\mathbf{y}$ is an eigenvector belonging to λ, and $\mathbf{z}$ is a scalar multiple of $\mathbf{y}$, $\mathbf{z} = \alpha\mathbf{y}$, then $\mathbf{z}$ is also an eigenvector belonging to λ, since

$$B\mathbf{z} = B(\alpha\mathbf{y}) = \alpha(B\mathbf{y}) = \alpha(\lambda\mathbf{y}) = \lambda(\alpha\mathbf{y}) = \lambda\mathbf{z}$$

Examples The identity matrix I satisfies

$$Iy = y = 1y$$

for every vector y. Hence 1 is an eigenvalue of I, and every nonzero vector is an eigenvector for I belonging to 1. Since a vector can belong to only one eigenvalue (or none), it follows that 1 is the only eigenvalue of I.

The null matrix O has the number 0 as its one and only eigenvalue.

The matrix

$$B = \begin{bmatrix} 1 & 2 & 0 \\ 2 & 1 & 0 \\ 0 & 0 & -1 \end{bmatrix}$$

has the eigenvalue -1, since $Bi_3 = -i_3$. Also, $B(i_1 + i_2) = 3(i_1 + i_2)$, so that $\lambda = 3$ is also an eigenvalue for B. Finally, $B(i_1 - i_2) = -(i_1 - i_2)$, so that the eigenvalue -1 has the two linearly independent eigenvectors i_3 and $(i_1 - i_2)$.

If the matrix $B = (b_{ij})$ is upper-triangular, then λ is an eigenvalue of B if and only if $\lambda = b_{ii}$ for some i. For the matrix $(B - \lambda I)$ is then also upper-triangular; hence, by Theorem 4.6, $(B - \lambda I)$ is not invertible if and only if one of its diagonal entries is zero, i.e., if and only if $b_{ii} - \lambda = 0$ for some i. Hence the set of eigenvalues of a triangular matrix coincides with the set of numbers to be found on its diagonal.

Example 4.10 In particular, the only eigenvalue of the matrix

$$B = \begin{bmatrix} 0 & 0 & 1 \\ 0 & 0 & 0 \\ 0 & 0 & 0 \end{bmatrix}$$

is the number 0, and both i_1 and i_2 are eigenvectors for this B belonging to this eigenvalue. Any other eigenvector of B must be a linear combination of these two eigenvectors. For suppose that the nonzero 3-vector y $(= y_1 i_1 + y_2 i_2 + y_3 i_3)$ is an eigenvector for B (belonging therefore to the only eigenvalue 0). Then

$$0 = 0y = By = y_1 Bi_1 + y_2 Bi_2 + y_3 Bi_3$$
$$= 0 + 0 + y_3 Bi_3$$

Since $Bi_3 = i_1 \neq 0$, it follows that $y_3 = 0$, that is, $y = y_1 i_1 + y_2 i_2$, showing that y is a linear combination of the eigenvectors i_1 and i_2.

As an illustration of why eigenvalues might be of interest, we now consider briefly vector sequences of the form

$$z, Bz, B^2 z, B^3 z, \ldots \tag{4.62}$$

Such sequences occur in the various applications mentioned at the beginning of this section. We must deal with such sequences in Chap. 5, in the discussion of iterative methods for the solution of systems of equations.

Assume that the starting vector z in (4.62) can be written as a sum of eigenvectors of B, that is

$$z = y_1 + y_2 + \cdots + y_r, \tag{4.63}$$

where $$By_i = \lambda_i y_i \qquad i = 1, \ldots, r$$

The mth term in the sequence (4.62) then has the simple form

$$B^m z = \lambda_1^m y_1 + \lambda_2^m y_2 + \cdots + \lambda_r^m y_r \tag{4.64}$$

Hence the behavior of the *vector* sequence (4.62) is completely determined by the simple *numerical* sequences

$$\lambda_i^0, \lambda_i^1, \lambda_i^2, \lambda_i^3, \ldots \qquad i = 1, \ldots, r$$

It follows, for example, that

$$\lim_{m \to \infty} B^m z = 0 \qquad \text{if } |\lambda_i| < 1, \text{ for all } i \tag{4.65}$$

Assume further that the λ_i's are ordered by magnitude,

$$|\lambda_1| \geq |\lambda_2| \geq \cdots \geq |\lambda_r|$$

which can always be achieved by proper ordering of the y_i's. Further, we assume that

$$|\lambda_1| > |\lambda_2| \tag{4.66}$$

This assumption requires not only that λ_1 be different from all the other λ_i's [which can always be achieved by merely adding all y_i's in (4.63) which belong to λ_1, thereby getting just one eigenvector belonging to λ_1], but also that there be no other λ_i of the *same magnitude* as λ_1, and it is this part that makes (4.66) a nontrivial assumption.

Then, on dividing both sides of (4.64) by λ_1^m, we get that

$$(\lambda_1^{-1} B)^m z = y_1 + \sum_{i=2}^r \left(\frac{\lambda_i}{\lambda_1} \right)^m y_i \qquad m = 0, 1, 2, \ldots$$

By our assumptions,

$$\left| \frac{\lambda_i}{\lambda_1} \right| < 1 \qquad i = 2, \ldots, r$$

Hence we conclude that

$$\lim_{m \to \infty} (\lambda_1^{-1} B)^m z = y_1 \tag{4.67}$$

In words, if z can be written in the form (4.63) in terms of eigenvectors of B so that the eigenvalue λ_1 corresponding to y_1 is absolutely bigger than all the other eigenvalues, then a properly scaled version of $B^m z$ converges to y_1.

Example 4.11 We saw earlier that the matrix

$$B = \begin{bmatrix} 1 & 2 & 0 \\ 2 & 1 & 0 \\ 0 & 0 & -1 \end{bmatrix}$$

has the eigenvectors $z_1 = i_1 + i_2$, $z_2 = i_1 - i_2$, $z_3 = i_3$ with corresponding eigenvalues $\lambda_1 = 3$, $\lambda_2 = \lambda_3 = -1$. These eigenvectors are linearly independent (see Exercise 4.1-10), hence form a basis for all 3-vectors. It follows that every 3-vector can be written as a sum of eigenvectors of B. In particular, the vector z given by $z^T = [1 \ 2 \ 3]$ can be written

$$z = y_1 + y_2$$

where

$$y_1 = 1.5 z_1 \qquad y_2 = -0.5 z_2 + 3 z_3$$

Table 4.1

m	0	1	2	3	4	5
	1	5	13	41	121	365
$B^m \mathbf{z}$	2	4	14	40	122	364
	3	3	3	3	3	3
	1	1.0	1.00	1.000	1.000	1.000
$\mathbf{z}^{(m)}$	2	0.8	1.08	0.976	1.008	0.997
	3	0.6	0.23	0.073	0.025	0.008

In Table 4.1, we have listed $B^m \mathbf{z}$ and $\mathbf{z}^{(m)} = \alpha_m B^m \mathbf{z}$ for $m = 0, \ldots, 5$. $\mathbf{z}^{(m)}$ has been scaled to make its first entry equal to 1. Evidently, the $\mathbf{z}^{(m)}$ converge to the eigenvector $\mathbf{i}_1 + \mathbf{i}_2$ belonging to $\lambda_1 = 3$.

The **power method** for the calculation of the absolutely largest eigenvalue of a given matrix B is based on this illustration. One picks some vector $\mathbf{z}$, for example, $\mathbf{z} = \mathbf{i}_1$; generates the (first few) terms of the sequence (4.62); and calculates ratios of the form

$$\mathbf{u}^T B^{m+1} \mathbf{z} / (\mathbf{u}^T B^m \mathbf{z}) \tag{4.68}$$

as one goes along. From (4.64),

$$\frac{\mathbf{u}^T B^{m+1} \mathbf{z}}{\mathbf{u}^T B^m \mathbf{z}} = \frac{\lambda_1 \mathbf{u}^T \mathbf{y}_1 + (\lambda_2/\lambda_1)^{m+1} \mathbf{u}^T \mathbf{y}_2 + \cdots + (\lambda_r/\lambda_1)^{m+1} \mathbf{u}^T \mathbf{y}_r}{\mathbf{u}^T \mathbf{y}_1 + (\lambda_2/\lambda_1)^m \mathbf{u}^T \mathbf{y}_2 + \cdots + (\lambda_r/\lambda_1)^m \mathbf{u}^T \mathbf{y}_r}$$

therefore $(\mathbf{u}^T B^{m+1} \mathbf{z}) / (\mathbf{u}^T B^m \mathbf{z}) = \lambda_1 + \mathcal{O}\left((\lambda_2/\lambda_1)^m\right)$

provided $\mathbf{u}^T \mathbf{y}_1 \neq 0$ and provided $|\lambda_1| > |\lambda_2| \geq \cdots \geq |\lambda_r|$. Note that it pays to use the vector $\mathbf{u} = B^m \mathbf{z}$ in (4.68) in case B is symmetric, that is, $B = B^T$. The resulting ratio

$$(\mathbf{u}^T B \mathbf{u}) / (\mathbf{u}^T \mathbf{u})$$

is called the **Rayleigh quotient** (for $\mathbf{u}$ and B) and is easily seen to equal

$$(\mathbf{z}^T B^{2m+1} \mathbf{z}) / (\mathbf{z}^T B^{2m} \mathbf{z})$$

hence equals λ_1 to within $\mathcal{O}\left((\lambda_2/\lambda_1)^{2m}\right)$.

Example 4.12 From the sequence generated in Example 4.11, we obtain, with $\mathbf{u} = \mathbf{i}_1$, the sequence of ratios

$$5, 2.6, 3.1538 \cdots, 2.9512 \cdots, 3.0165 \cdots$$

while, with $\mathbf{u} = \mathbf{i}_2$, we get the sequence

$$2, 3.5, 2.8571 \cdots, 3.5 \quad , 2.9836 \cdots$$

Both sequences appear to converge to $3 = \lambda_1$. But, for $\mathbf{u} = \mathbf{i}_3$, we get the sequence

$$1, 1 \ , 1 \qquad , 1 \qquad , 1$$

which does not appear to converge to 3.

Since B is symmetric, we also calculate the sequence of Rayleigh quotients and find the ratios

$$1.5714 \cdots, 2.6 \quad , 2.9465 \cdots, 2.9939 \ldots, 2.9993 \cdots$$

This sequence gains roughly one digit per term which corresponds to the fact that it should agree with $3 = \lambda_1$ to within $\mathcal{O}((1/3)^{2m})$.

A clever variant of the power method is **inverse iteration**. Here one chooses, in addition to the starting vector $\mathbf{z}$ satisfying (4.63), a number p not equal to an eigenvalue of B and then forms the sequence

$$\mathbf{z}, \hat{B}\mathbf{z}, \hat{B}^2\mathbf{z}, \hat{B}^3\mathbf{z}, \ldots$$

with

$$\hat{B} = (B - pI)^{-1}$$

Note that, for each of the eigenvectors $\mathbf{y}_i$ of B in (4.63), $(B - pI)\mathbf{y}_i = B\mathbf{y}_i - p\mathbf{y}_i = (\lambda_i - p)\mathbf{y}_i$. Therefore,

$$(\lambda_i - p)^{-1}\mathbf{y}_i = (B - pI)^{-1}\mathbf{y}_i$$

This shows that $\mathbf{z}$ is also the sum of eigenvectors of $\hat{B} = (B - pI)^{-1}$, with corresponding eigenvalues $(\lambda_i - p)^{-1}$, $i = 1, \ldots, r$. If now p is quite close to one of the eigenvalues $\lambda_1, \ldots, \lambda_r$, say to λ_j, and not to any other, then $(\lambda_j - p)^{-1}$ will be quite large in absolute value compared with the other eigenvalues $(\lambda_i - p)^{-1}$, and our earlier discussion of the power method would then allow the conclusion that a suitably scaled version of the sequence $\mathbf{z}, \hat{B}\mathbf{z}, \hat{B}^2\mathbf{z}, \ldots$ converges quite fast to the eigenvector $\mathbf{y}_j$ corresponding to λ_j, while the corresponding ratios

$$\mathbf{u}^T\hat{B}^{m+1}\mathbf{z} / (\mathbf{u}^T\hat{B}^m\mathbf{z})$$

will converge equally fast to the number $(\lambda_j - p)^{-1}$. This makes inverse iteration a very effective method in the following situation: We have already obtained a good approximation to an eigenvalue of B and wish to refine this approximation and/or calculate a corresponding eigenvector.

As we described it, inverse iteration would require first the construction of the matrix $\hat{B} = (B - pI)^{-1}$. But, as discussed in Sec. 4.4, we do not construct such an inverse explicitly. Rather, with

$$\mathbf{z}^{(m)} := \hat{B}^m\mathbf{z} \qquad m = 0, 1, 2, \ldots$$

we note that

$$(B - pI)\mathbf{z}^{(m)} = \mathbf{z}^{(m-1)}$$

Consequently, once we have obtained a *PLU* factorization for the matrix $B - pI$, we obtain $\mathbf{z}^{(m)}$ from $\mathbf{z}^{(m-1)}$ by the substitution Algorithm 4.4, that is, in $\mathcal{O}(n^2)$ operations. This is no more expensive than the explicit calculation of the product $\hat{B}\mathbf{z}^{(m-1)}$ from $\hat{B}$, if we had it.

Here is a FORTRAN subroutine for carrying out inverse iteration. At the mth step, we have chosen $\mathbf{u} = B^m\mathbf{z}$, that is, we calculate the Rayleigh quotient at each step.

```
      SUBROUTINE INVITR ( B, N, EGUESS, VGUESS, W, D, IPIVOT,
     *                              EVALUE, VECTOR, IFLAG )
C     CALLS  F A C T O R , S U B S T .
      INTEGER IFLAG,IPIVOT(N),   I,ITER,ITERMX,J
      REAL B(N,N),D(N),EGUESS,EVALUE,VECTOR(N),VGUESS(N),W(N,N)
     *     ,EPSLON,EVNEW,EVOLD,SQNORM
C****** I N P U T ******
C  B  THE MATRIX OF ORDER  N  WHOSE EIGENVALUE/VECTOR IS SOUGHT.
C  N  ORDER OF THE MATRIX B .
C  EGUESS  A FIRST GUESS FOR THE EIGENVALUE.
C  VGUESS  N-VECTOR CONTAINING A FIRST GUESS FOR THE EIGENVECTOR.
C****** W O R K  A R E A ******
C  W  MATRIX OF ORDER  N
C  D  VECTOR OF LENGTH  N
C  IPIVOT  INTEGER VECTOR OF LENGTH  N
C****** O U T P U T ******
C  EVALUE  COMPUTED APPROXIMATION TO EIGENVALUE
C  VECTOR  COMPUTED APPROXIMATION TO EIGENVECTOR
C  IFLAG  AN INTEGER,
C         = 1 OR -1 (AS SET IN FACTOR), INDICATES THAT ALL IS WELL,
C         = 0 , INDICATES THAT SOMETHING WENT WRONG. SEE PRINTED ERROR
C              MESSAGE .
C****** M E T H O D ******
C  INVERSE ITERATION, AS DESCRIBED IN THE TEXT, IS USED.
C******
C  THE FOLLOWING T E R M I N A T I O N  P A R A M E T E R S  ARE SET
C  HERE, A TOLERANCE  E P S L O N  ON THE DIFFERENCE BETWEEN SUCCESSIVE
C  EIGENVALUE ITERATES, AND AN UPPER BOUND  I T E R M X  ON THE NUMBER
C  OF ITERATION STEPS.
      DATA EPSLON,ITERMX /.000001,20/
C
C                   PUT  B - (EGUESS)*IDENTITY   INTO  W
      DO 10 J=1,N
         DO 9 I=1,N
    9       W(I,J) = B(I,J)
   10    W(J,J) = W(J,J) - EGUESS
      CALL FACTOR ( W, N, D, IPIVOT, IFLAG )
      IF (IFLAG .EQ. 0)  THEN
         PRINT 610
  610    FORMAT(' EIGENVALUE GUESS TOO CLOSE.
     *            ,'NO EIGENVECTOR CALCULATED.')
                              RETURN
      END IF
C                       ITERATION STARTS HERE
      PRINT 619
  619 FORMAT(' ITER  EIGENVALUE      EIGENVECTOR COMPONENTS'/)
      EVOLD = 0.
      DO 50 ITER=1,ITERMX
C                       NORMALIZE CURRENT VECTOR GUESS
         SQNORM = 0.
         DO 20 I=1,N
   20       SQNORM = VGUESS(I)**2 + SQNORM
         SQNORM = SQRT(SQNORM)
         DO 21 I=1,N
   21       VGUESS(I) = VGUESS(I)/SQNORM
C    .            GET NEXT VECTOR GUESS
         CALL SUBST ( W, IPIVOT, VGUESS, N, VECTOR )
C                   CALCULATE RAYLEIGH QUOTIENT
         EVNEW = 0.
         DO 30 I=1,N
   30       EVNEW = VGUESS(I)*VECTOR(I) + EVNEW
         EVALUE = EGUESS + 1./EVNEW
C
         PRINT 630,ITER,EVALUE,VECTOR
  630    FORMAT(I3,E15.7,2X,3E14.7/(20X,3E14.7))
C                   STOP ITERATION IF CURRENT GUESS IS CLOSE TO
C                   PREVIOUS GUESS FOR EIGENVALUE
         IF ( ABS(EVNEW-EVOLD) .LE. EPSLON*ABS(EVNEW) )
     *                              RETURN
         EVOLD = EVNEW
         DO 50 I=1,N
```

```
   50        VGUESS(I) = VECTOR(I)
C
         IFLAG = 0
         PRINT 660,EPSLON,ITERMX
  660 FORMAT(' NO CONVERGENCE TO WITHIN',E10.4,' AFTER',I3,' STEPS.')
                                     RETURN
         END
```

Example 4.13 For the matrix B of Example 4.12, we use the above FORTRAN routine INVITR with $z = [1, 1, 1]^T$ and $p = 3.0165$, which is the best guess for $\lambda_1 = 3$ from the first sequence of ratios in Example 4.12.

ITER	EIGENVALUE	EIGENVECTOR COMPONENTS		
1	0.2991801 + 01	−0.3499093 + 02	−0.3499093 + 02	−0.1437446 + 00
2	0.3000000 + 01	0.4285478 + 02	0.4285478 + 02	0.7232219 − 03
3	0.3000000 + 01	−0.4285496 + 02	−0.4285496 + 02	−0.2971047 − 05
4	0.3000000 + 01	0.4285496 + 02	0.4285496 + 02	0.1220522 − 07

$$\text{EIGENVALUE} = 0.3000000 + 01$$
$$\text{EIGENVECTOR} =$$
$$0.4285496 + 02 \quad 0.4285496 + 02 \quad 0.1220522 - 07$$

The output shows very rapid convergence of the eigenvector (a gain of about two decimal places per iteration step), and an even more rapid convergence of the eigenvalue, because B is symmetric and a Rayleigh quotient was computed.

As an illustration of the fact that, in contrast to the power method itself, inverse iteration may be used for any eigenvalue, we also start with $z = [1,1,1]^T$ and $p = 0$, hoping to catch thereby an absolutely *smallest* eigenvalue of B.

ITER	EIGENVALUE	EIGENVECTOR COMPONENTS		
1	−0.9000000 + 01	0.1924501 + 00	0.1924501 + 00	−0.5773503 + 00
2	−0.1320000 + 01	0.1005038 + 00	0.1005038 + 00	0.9045340 + 00
3	−0.1033195 + 01	0.3658808 − 01	0.3658809 − 01	−0.9878783 + 00
4	−0.1003661 + 01	0.1232878 − 01	0.1232877 − 01	0.9986311 + 00
5	−0.1000406 + 01	0.4114594 − 02	0.4114604 − 02	−0.9998476 + 00
6	−0.1000045 + 01	0.1371724 − 02	0.1371714 − 02	0.9999831 + 00
7	−0.1000005 + 01	0.4572417 − 03	0.4572513 − 03	−0.9999981 + 00
8	−0.1000001 + 01	0.1524206 − 03	0.1524109 − 03	0.9999998 + 00
9	−0.1000000 + 01	0.5080043 − 04	0.5081010 − 04	−0.1000000 + 01

$$\text{EIGENVALUE} = -0.1000000 + 01$$
$$\text{EIGENVECTOR} =$$
$$0.5080043 - 04 \quad 0.5081010 - 04 \quad -0.1000000 + 01$$

The convergence is much slower since 0 is not particularly close to the eigenvalue -1, but we have convergence after nine iterations, with the computed eigenvector of the form $[0,0,1]^T$ (rather than of the more general form $[a, -a, b]^T$ possible for the eigenvalue -1 of B).

The power method and its variant, inverse iteration, are *not* universally applicable. First of all, complex arithmetic has to be used, in general, if complex eigenvalues are to be found. There are special tricks available to sneak up on a pair of complex conjugate eigenvalues of a real matrix B in real arithmetic. A more serious difficulty is the possibly very slow convergence when the next largest eigenvalue is very close in absolute value to the largest. While Aitken's Δ^2 process (Algorithm 3.7) can be used to accelerate convergence if there is some, there will be no convergence in general in the extreme case when $|\lambda_1| = |\lambda_2|$ while $\lambda_1 \neq \lambda_2$ (for example, when $\lambda_2 = \bar{\lambda}_1$). A remedy of sorts can at times be provided by an appropriate shift, that is, by working with the matrix $B - pI$ rather than B itself, so that $|\lambda_1 - p| > |\lambda_2 - p|$ (see Exercises 4.8-6 and 4.8-7).

Finally, the power method loses its theoretical support (as we gave it here) when we cannot write the starting vector z as a sum of eigenvectors of B. Since we do not know the eigenvectors of B, we can be sure that z can be written as a sum of eigenvectors of the $n \times n$ matrix B only if we know that *every* n-vector can be written as a sum of eigenvectors of B. But then we are asking, in effect, that B have enough eigenvectors to staff a basis. A basis for all n-vectors which consists entirely of eigenvectors for the $n \times n$ matrix B is called a **complete** set of eigenvectors for B. Clearly, if $z_1, \ldots, z_n$ is a complete set of eigenvectors for the $n \times n$ matrix B—hence a basis for all n-vectors—then any particular n-vector z can be written as a linear combination of these eigenvectors,

$$z = a_1 z_1 + a_2 z_2 + \cdots + a_n z_n$$

for suitable coefficients $a_1, \ldots, a_n$. If $a_i \neq 0$, then $y_i = a_i z_i$ is also an eigenvector for B, while if $a_i = 0$, we can drop the term $a_i z_i$ from the sum without loss. In this way, we obtain z as a sum of eigenvectors of B (except for the uninteresting case $z = 0$).

Unfortunately, not every matrix has a complete set of eigenvectors, as we saw earlier in Example 4.10.

Similarity

The fact that not every matrix has a complete set of eigenvectors is an indication of the complications which eigenvalue theory has to offer. It corresponds to the statement that not every square matrix can be written in the form

$$Y \Lambda Y^{-1}$$

for some diagonal matrix Λ. For, $BY = Y\Lambda$ with Λ a diagonal matrix if and only if the columns of the matrix Y consist of eigenvectors of B, while such an $n \times n$ matrix Y is invertible if and only if its columns form a basis for the n-vectors.

One says that two matrices A and B are **similar** if

$$A = C^{-1}BC$$

for some (invertible) matrix C. Similar matrices have the same eigenvalues and related eigenvectors. Indeed, if $(B - \lambda I)x = 0$ for some nonzero vector x, and $A = CBC^{-1}$, then Cx is also nonzero, and $AC = CB$, hence $(A - \lambda I)Cx = C(B - \lambda I)x = C0 = 0$. In short, to each eigenvalue-eigenvector pair $(\lambda, \mathbf{x})$ of B there corresponds the eigenvalue-eigenvector pair $(\lambda, C\mathbf{x})$ of A.

This suggests, as a first step in the calculation of the eigenvalues of B, a similarity transformation of B into a matrix $A = C^{-1}BC$ for which the eigenvalues are easier to calculate, in some sense.

For example, if one could find an upper triangular matrix T similar to B, one would know all the eigenvalues of B, since they would all be found on the diagonal of T. In fact, one can prove

Theorem 4.13: Schur's theorem Every square matrix B can be written as $U^{-1}TU$, with T upper-triangular and U **unitary**, that is, $U^H U = I$.

The fact that U is unitary has the pleasant consequence that $\|U\mathbf{x}\|_2 = \|\mathbf{x}\|_2$ for all $\mathbf{x}$, hence $\|T\|_2 = \|B\|_2$, so that the upper triangular matrix T which is similar to B even has the same size as B. Unfortunately, though, it usually takes an *iterative* process to construct such U and T.

But it is always possible in $\vartheta(2n^3/3)$ floating-point operations to transform B by similarity into a matrix $H = (h_{ij})$ which is almost triangular or **Hessenberg**, that is, for which

$$h_{ij} = 0 \quad \text{for } i > j - 1$$

Thus the lower-triangular part of H is zero except perhaps for the first band below the diagonal. One constructs H from B by a sequence of $n - 2$ simple similarity transformations, each producing one more column of zeros below the first subdiagonal.

For example, one might employ **Householder reflections**, that is, matrices of the form

$$R(\mathbf{y}) = I - \alpha\mathbf{y}\mathbf{y}^T \quad \text{with } \alpha\mathbf{y}^T\mathbf{y} = 2 \tag{4.69}$$

as follows. Suppose that $H^{(k)}$ has already zeros in columns $1, 2, \ldots, k - 1$ below the subdiagonal, as would be the case for $k = 1$ with $H^{(1)} = B$. Then we want to form

$$H^{(k+1)} = (R(\mathbf{y}))^{-1}H^{(k)}R(\mathbf{y})$$

in such a way that the first $k - 1$ columns remain unchanged, while we now have zeros also in column k below the first subdiagonal. For this, one notes first of all that the inverse of $R(\mathbf{y})$ is $R(\mathbf{y})$ itself because

$$(I - \alpha\mathbf{y}\mathbf{y}^T)(I - \alpha\mathbf{y}\mathbf{y}^T) = I - \alpha\mathbf{y}\mathbf{y}^T - \alpha\mathbf{y}\mathbf{y}^T + \alpha^2\mathbf{y}(\mathbf{y}^T\mathbf{y})\mathbf{y}^T$$

and $\alpha\mathbf{y}^T\mathbf{y} = 2$. Hence $H^{(k+1)} = R(\mathbf{y})H^{(k)}R(\mathbf{y})$. One computes similarly that

$$\|R(\mathbf{y})\mathbf{x}\|_2 = \|\mathbf{x}\|_2 \tag{4.70}$$

(recall that $\|\mathbf{z}\|_2^2 = \mathbf{z}^T\mathbf{z}$). This, incidentally, explains the name "reflection." Next, one should realize that the economical way to form the matrix product $AR(\mathbf{y})$ is to take each row $\mathbf{x}^T$ of A and replace it by the row vector

$\mathbf{x}^T - \alpha(\mathbf{x}^T\mathbf{y})\mathbf{y}^T$. Hence, with the choice

$$y_1 = \cdots = y_k = 0 \tag{4.71}$$

the matrix $H^{(k)}R(\mathbf{y})$ has the same first k columns as does $H^{(k)}$. Next, one should realize that the economical way to form the matrix product $R(\mathbf{y})A$ is to take each column $\mathbf{x}$ of A and replace it by the column vector $\mathbf{x} - \alpha(\mathbf{y}^T\mathbf{x})\mathbf{y}$. Since $H^{(k)}$ has zeros in columns 1 through $k-1$ below row $k-1$, this shows that the choice (4.71) also ensures that $R(\mathbf{y})H^{(k)}R(\mathbf{y})$ has the same first $k-1$ columns as $H^{(k)}$. This leaves us with the problem of choosing $y_{k+1}, \ldots, y_n$ in such a way that the kth column of $R(\mathbf{y})H^{(k)}$ has zeros in rows $k+2, \ldots, n$. Because of (4.71), this means that $R(\mathbf{y})$ should map the vector

$$\hat{\mathbf{x}} = \left[0, \ldots, 0, h^{(k)}_{k+1,\,k}, \ldots, h^{(k)}_{n,\,k} \right]^T$$

to the vector $-\beta\mathbf{i}_{k+1}$ for some scalar $-\beta$. [Here, we have written $h^{(k)}_{ij}$ for the (i,j) entry of $H^{(k)}$.] By (4.70), this means that

$$\beta = \pm\|\hat{\mathbf{x}}\|_2 = \left(\left(h^{(k)}_{k+1,\,k} \right)^2 + \cdots + \left(h^{(k)}_{nk} \right)^2 \right)^{1/2}$$

Further,

$$\hat{\mathbf{x}} - (-\beta)\mathbf{i}_{k+1} = \hat{\mathbf{x}} - R(\mathbf{y})\hat{\mathbf{x}} = \hat{\mathbf{x}} - \left(\hat{\mathbf{x}} - \alpha(\mathbf{y}^T\hat{\mathbf{x}})\mathbf{y} \right) = \alpha(\mathbf{y}^T\hat{\mathbf{x}})\mathbf{y}$$

showing that $\mathbf{y}$ must be a scalar multiple of the vector $\hat{\mathbf{x}} + \beta\mathbf{i}_{k+1}$. This indicates that the following choice of $\mathbf{y}$ will do the job:

$$y_i = \begin{cases} \hat{x}_{k+1} + \text{signum}\,(\hat{x}_{k+1})\|\hat{\mathbf{x}}\|_2 & i = k+1 \\ \hat{x}_i & i > k+1 \end{cases} \tag{4.72}$$

i.e., $\beta = \text{signum}\,(\hat{x}_{k+1})\|\hat{\mathbf{x}}\|_2$. Here we have chosen the sign of β so as to avoid loss of significance in the calculation of y_{k+1}. The corresponding α can be written simply as

$$\alpha = 1/(\beta y_{k+1}) \tag{4.73}$$

In this way, one obtains after $n-2$ such steps the matrix

$$H = R^{-1}BR$$

with H Hessenberg, and

$$R = R(\mathbf{y}^{(1)})R(\mathbf{y}^{(2)}) \cdots R(\mathbf{y}^{(n-2)})$$

a product of certain Householder reflections, hence

$$R^{-1} = R(\mathbf{y}^{(n-2)}) \cdots R(\mathbf{y}^{(2)})R(\mathbf{y}^{(1)})$$

A Householder reflection is clearly a real symmetric matrix (if $\mathbf{y}$ is real), therefore H is real symmetric in case B is. Thus, *H is tridiagonal and symmetric in case B is real symmetric.*

For convenience, we now give a formal description.

Algorithm 4.6: Similarity transformation into upper Hessenberg form using Householder reflections Given the matrix A of order n as stored in the first n columns of a workarray H of order $n \times (n + 2)$.

For $k = 1, \ldots, n - 2$, do:

$$\beta := \text{signum} \, (h_{k+1, k}) \left(\sum_{j=k+1}^{n} (h_{jk})^2 \right)^{1/2}$$

$$h_{k+1, k} := h_{k+1, k} + \beta$$

$$\alpha^{-1} := \beta h_{k+1, k}$$

For $j = 1, \ldots, n$, do:

$$\gamma := \left(\sum_{i=k+1}^{n} h_{ik} h_{ji} \right) / \alpha^{-1}$$

For $i = k + 1, \ldots, n$, do:

$$h_{ji} := h_{ji} - \gamma h_{ik}$$

For $j = k + 1, \ldots, n$, do:

$$\gamma := \left(\sum_{i=k+1}^{n} h_{ik} h_{ij} \right) / \alpha^{-1}$$

For $i = k + 1, \ldots, n$, do:

$$h_{ij} := h_{ij} - \gamma h_{ik}$$

$$h_{k+1, n+1} := h_{k+1, k}, \quad h_{k+1, n+2} := \alpha^{-1}$$

$$h_{k+1, k} := -\beta$$

Then H contains the interesting part of an upper Hessenberg matrix similar to the input matrix A in the upper Hessenberg portion of its first n columns and rows. It also contains complete information about the vectors y and the scalars α which determine the various Householder reflections used. This information is needed when the eigenvectors of that upper Hessenberg matrix have to be transformed back into eigenvectors of the original matrix A.

The currently recommended method for finding all the eigenvalues of a general matrix B is the **QR method.** One begins with the reduction to Hessenberg form H as just outlined. Once this is accomplished, the matrix H becomes the first in a sequence

$$A^{(0)} = H, A^{(1)}, A^{(2)}, \ldots$$

with $A^{(k+1)}$ obtained from $A^{(k)}$ as follows: One factors $A^{(k)}$ into a unitary matrix Q and an upper- (or right-) triangular matrix R, $A^{(k)} = QR$, and then forms

$$A^{(k+1)} = RQ = Q^{-1}(QR)Q$$

Thus $A^{(k+1)}$ is similar to $A^{(k)}$. Further, $A^{(k+1)}$ is again a Hessenberg matrix since $A^{(k)}$ is one. This greatly reduces the number of operations necessary to obtain its factorization. Now, in many circumstances, $A^{(k)}$ converges for large k to an upper-triangular matrix whose diagonal entries then necessarily provide all the eigenvalues of B.

The details of, and the theory behind, this calculation are quite tricky, particularly since one factors $(A^{(k)} - s_k I)$ rather than $A^{(k)}$ itself, with the shifts s_k chosen to accelerate convergence. But the reader should be aware of the fact that this method, and other methods particularly suited for special classes of matrices B, have been translated into a package of carefully designed FORTRAN subroutines called EISPACK, available from Argonne National Laboratory, or directly at many scientific computing centers. A complete description of the package, including program listings, can be found in Smith et al. [32].

Localization

At times, one is only interested in a rough estimate of some or all of the eigenvalues of a matrix B. Even if one eventually intends to calculate the eigenvalues, one may have to start with some information about their approximate location. Such information is provided by localization theorems which describe regions in the complex plane in which eigenvalues of B are known to lie.

If $B\mathbf{x} = \lambda\mathbf{x}$, then $|\lambda|\,\|\mathbf{x}\| = \|\lambda\mathbf{x}\| = \|B\mathbf{x}\| \leq \|B\|\,\|\mathbf{x}\|$, which implies that $|\lambda| \leq \|B\|$ in case $\mathbf{x} \neq \mathbf{0}$. This proves that

$$|\lambda| \leq \|B\| \qquad \textit{for every eigenvalue } \lambda \textit{ of } B \tag{4.74}$$

and for every matrix norm.

A more precise statement is the following:

Theorem 4.14: Gershgorin's disks Every eigenvalue λ of the $n \times n$ matrix $B = (b_{ij})$ satisfies

$$|b_{ii} - \lambda| \leq \sum_{\substack{j=1 \\ j \neq i}}^{n} |b_{ij}| \qquad \text{for some } i$$

In other words, all the eigenvalues of B can be found in the union of certain disks in the complex plane. Indeed, if

$$|b_{ii} - \lambda| > \sum_{\substack{j=1 \\ j \neq i}}^{n} |b_{ij}| \qquad \text{for } i = 1, \ldots, n$$

then the matrix $B - \lambda I$ is strictly (row) diagonally dominant; hence, by Exercise 4.6-3, $B - \lambda I$ is then invertible; that is, λ is then not an eigenvalue of B.

Example 4.14 According to (4.74), each eigenvalue of the matrix

$$B = \begin{bmatrix} 1 & 2 & 0 \\ 2 & 1 & 0 \\ 0 & 0 & -1 \end{bmatrix}$$

of Example 4.11 must have absolute value no bigger than $\|B\|_\infty = 3$. Gershgorin's disks provide the more detailed information that every eigenvalue λ of B must satisfy

Either $\quad |1 - \lambda| \le 2 \quad$ or $\quad |-1 - \lambda| \le 0$

A Hermitian matrix, in particular a real symmetric matrix, has all its eigenvalues real. It is similar to a diagonal matrix; that is, it has a complete set of eigenvectors. This is an easy consequence of Schur's theorem; see Exercise 4.8-15. For a Hermitian matrix B, both

$$\max_{\mathbf{x}} \mathbf{x}^H B \mathbf{x} / (\mathbf{x}^H \mathbf{x}) \qquad \text{and} \qquad \min_{\mathbf{x}} \mathbf{x}^H B \mathbf{x} / (\mathbf{x}^H \mathbf{x})$$

are eigenvalues of B, and any other eigenvalue of B lies between these two. Recall that these **Rayleigh quotients** appeared earlier in this section, in the discussion of the power method.

Combination of Lemma 4.4 and Theorem 4.10 produces the following precise localization theorem.

Theorem 4.15 λ is an eigenvalue of the matrix B if and only if λ solves the characteristic equation

$$\det(B - \lambda I) = 0$$

The matrix $(B - \lambda I)$ differs from B only in that λ has been subtracted from each diagonal entry of B. If we use the **Kronecker symbol** δ_{ij} to denote the (i, j) entry of the identity matrix, so that

$$\delta_{ij} = \begin{cases} 1 & \text{if } i = j \\ 0 & \text{if } i \ne j \end{cases}$$

then $\qquad (i, j)$ entry of $(B - \lambda I) = b_{ij} - \lambda \delta_{ij}$

Hence

$$\det(B - \lambda I) = \sum_{\mathbf{p}} \sigma_{\mathbf{p}} (b_{1p_1} - \lambda \delta_{1p_1})(b_{2p_2} - \lambda \delta_{2p_2}) \cdots (b_{np_n} - \lambda \delta_{np_n})$$

$$= \sum_{\mathbf{p}} \sigma_{\mathbf{p}} \left(\prod_{i \ne p_i} b_{ip_i} \right) \left(\prod_{i = p_i} (b_{ip_i} - \lambda) \right)$$

showing $\det(B - \lambda I)$ to be the sum of *polynomials* in the variable λ. Since each summand has n factors, each summand is a polynomial in λ of degree at most n, while the summand corresponding to the identity permutation $\mathbf{p}^T = [1 \quad 2 \quad \cdots \quad n]$ is simply

$$(b_{11} - \lambda)(b_{22} - \lambda) \cdots (b_{nn} - \lambda)$$

hence of exact degree n in λ. If follows that $\det(B - \lambda I)$, considered as a function of λ, is a polynomial in λ of exact degree n,

$$p(\lambda) = \det(B - \lambda I) = (-\lambda)^n + \text{a polynomial of degree} < n$$

This polynomial is called the **characteristic polynomial** of B.

Example 4.15 If

$$B = \begin{bmatrix} 1 & 2 & 0 \\ 2 & 1 & 0 \\ 0 & 0 & -1 \end{bmatrix}$$

then

$$p(\lambda) = \det(B - \lambda I) = \det \begin{bmatrix} 1-\lambda & 2 & 0 \\ 2 & 1-\lambda & 0 \\ 0 & 0 & -1-\lambda \end{bmatrix}$$

and expansion by elements of the last row or column gives

$$p(\lambda) = (-1 - \lambda)\det \begin{bmatrix} 1-\lambda & 2 \\ 2 & 1-\lambda \end{bmatrix} = -(1 + \lambda)[(1 - \lambda)^2 - 4]$$

$$= -(1 + \lambda)(1 - \lambda + 2)(1 - \lambda - 2)$$

Hence the eigenvalues of A, that is, the zeros of $p(\lambda)$, are -1 and 3, as found at the beginning of this Section by different means.

Since a polynomial of degree n can have at most n distinct zeros (see Sec. 2.1), it follows that an $n \times n$ matrix can have at most n eigenvalues. On the other hand, by the fundamental theorem of algebra, every polynomial of positive degree has at least one zero (see Theorem 1.10): hence every square matrix has at least one eigenvalue. These eigenvalues may well be complex even if B is a real matrix.

Theorem 4.15 makes the techniques for finding roots of equations, particularly polynomial equations, as discussed in Chap. 3, available for finding eigenvalues.

The method of quadratic interpolation (Müller's method), for instance, discussed in Sec. 3.7, can be employed to find one or more eigenvalues, real or complex, of a given matrix. To use this method we must be able only to evaluate the polynomial $p(\lambda)$ for any value of λ. Since for a given value of λ, $p(\lambda)$ is simply a determinant of order n, any method for evaluating a determinant can be used. In particular, this can be done by elimination, as explained in Sec. 4.7. But one would do well to bring the matrix into Hessenberg, or, if possible, tridiagonal form first, as discussed earlier, since that brings the cost of one determinant evaluation down to $\mathcal{O}(n^2)$ from $\mathcal{O}(n^3)$. In any event, to apply quadratic interpolation to find a root $\lambda = \xi_1$ of the characteristic polynomial $p(\lambda) = \det(A - \lambda I)$, we proceed as follows:

1. Let λ_0, λ_1, λ_2 be any three approximations to $\lambda = \xi_1$ (or if no information is available, take $\lambda_0 = -1$, $\lambda_1 = 1$, $\lambda_2 = 0$).
2. Evaluate

$$p(\lambda_i) = \det \begin{bmatrix} a_{11} - \lambda_i & a_{12} & \cdots & a_{1n} \\ a_{21} & a_{22} - \lambda_i & \cdots & a_{2n} \\ \cdots\cdots\cdots\cdots\cdots\cdots\cdots\cdots\cdots \\ a_{n1} & a_{n2} & \cdots & a_{nn} - \lambda_i \end{bmatrix} \qquad i = 0, 1, 2$$

3. Apply Algorithm 3.11 until convergence to a root ξ_1 results.
4. To find the next root, repeat this process using, instead of $p(\lambda)$, the deflated function

$$\frac{p(\lambda)}{\lambda - \xi_1}$$

5. Continue as described in Sec. 3.7.

The method of quadratic interpolation is not competitive, relative to computational efficiency, with some of the more advanced methods. However, it is simple to apply, it is completely general, it almost invariably converges, and it provides satisfactory accuracy in most cases. It can also be applied to solve the more general eigenvalue problem

$$\det(A - \lambda B) = 0$$

where A and B are both matrices of order n.

> **Example 4.16: Free vibrations of simple structures** In civil engineering a problem frequently encountered is to determine the natural frequencies λ of the free vibrations of an undamped structure for several masses and degrees of freedom. This problem can be expressed in the form
>
> $$A\mathbf{x} = \lambda M \mathbf{x} \qquad (4.75)$$
>
> where M = mass matrix of system
> A = stiffness of system
> $\mathbf{x}$ = natural mode
>
> Since (4.75) represents a homogeneous system of equations, it will have a nontrivial solution $\mathbf{x}$ if the determinant of the coefficients vanishes, i.e., if
>
> $$\det(A - \lambda M) = 0 \qquad (4.75a)$$
>
> Thus, if the matrices A and M are given, the values of λ for which (4.75a) is satisfied are the required natural frequencies. Müller's method can be applied directly to find these eigenvalues. For example, for a certain system, $M = I$, and the stiffness matrix A is given by
>
> $$A = \begin{bmatrix} 4 & -1 & -1 & -1 \\ -1 & 4 & -1 & -1 \\ -1 & -1 & 4 & -1 \\ -1 & -1 & -1 & 4 \end{bmatrix}$$
>
> Find the natural frequencies λ of this system.

A computer program using the gaussian elimination algorithm 4.2 to evaluate the determinants and the Müller Algorithm 3.11 as a root finder produced the following estimates for the eigenvalues:

$$\lambda_1 = 1.0000000$$
$$\lambda_2 = 5.0000234$$
$$\lambda_3 = 4.9999954$$
$$\lambda_4 = 4.9999973$$

The exact eigenvalues are easily seen to be 1,5,5,5. The effectiveness of Müller's method as a root finder is demonstrated by this example, where a triple root has been found to fairly good accuracy.

Example 4.17 The elements of the tridiagonal matrix B are generated as follows:

$$b_{i,\,i+1} = 0.5 \qquad i = 1, 2, \dots, n-1$$
$$b_{i+1,\,i} = 0.5 \qquad i = 1, 2, \dots, n-1$$
$$b_{ij} = 0 \qquad \text{for all other } i, j$$

Write a computer program to find the eigenvalues of B for $n = 20$.

For $n = 20$, Müller's method produced the following machine results on an IBM 7094:

± 0.074730093	± 0.73305187
± 0.22252094	± 0.82623877
± 0.36534102	± 0.90096886
± 0.50000001	± 0.95557281
± 0.62348980	± 0.98883083

Note that the eigenvalues are all real, are symmetrically placed with respect to the origin, and are all less than one in modulus. For this matrix the eigenvalues are known explicitly (see Exercise 4.8-4) and are given by

$$\lambda_k = \cos \frac{k\pi}{n+1} \qquad k = 1, 2, \dots, n \ .$$

The accuracy of the machine results can be checked from this formula. For $k = 7$ and $n = 20$, $\lambda_7 = \cos(\pi/3) = \frac{1}{2}$, and the machine result underlined above indicates an accuracy of seven significant figures.

The matrix of Example 4.17 is real symmetric and tridiagonal. For such matrices, special methods are available. This is of importance since we saw earlier that any real symmetric matrix can be transformed by similarity into a real symmetric tridiagonal matrix.

It is customary to write such a matrix in the form

$$B = \begin{bmatrix} a_1 & b_1 & & & & \\ b_1 & a_2 & b_2 & & & \\ & b_2 & a_3 & b_3 & & \\ & & b_3 & & \ddots & \\ & & & \ddots & \ddots & b_{n-1} \\ & & & & b_{n-1} & a_n \end{bmatrix}$$

Its characteristic polynomial can be obtained as $\det(B - \lambda I) = p_n(\lambda)$, with

$$p_0(\lambda) = 1, p_1(\lambda) = a_1 - \lambda$$

$$p_j(\lambda) = (a_j - \lambda)p_{j-1}(\lambda) - b_{j-1}^2 p_{j-2}(\lambda) \qquad j = 2, 3, \ldots, n \quad (4.76)$$

Here, $p_j(\lambda)$ is the determinant of the matrix formed by the first j rows and columns of $B - \lambda I$, and one verifies (4.76) using Rule 6, expansion by a row or column, of Sec. 4.7 (see Exercise 4.7-11). The recurrence (4.76) allows the evaluation of $p_n(\lambda)$ in about $3n$ operations. Further, the recurrence is easily differentiated with respect to λ, making it possible to calculate $p_n'(\lambda)$ by recurrence, and so allows for the application of Newton's method.

If $b_i = 0$ for some i, then we see from the recurrence (4.76) that the polynomial $p_{i-1}(\lambda)$ is a factor of $p_n(\lambda) = \det(B - \lambda I)$. The zeros of $p_n(\lambda)$ are then those of the two polynomials $p_{i-1}(\lambda)$ and $p_n(\lambda)/p_{i-1}(\lambda)$ of smaller degree, and we can concentrate on those. Otherwise, *if $b_i \neq 0$ for all i, then B has n distinct eigenvalues.* Also, the sequence $p_0(\lambda), p_1(\lambda), \ldots, p_n(\lambda)$ of values calculated during the evaluation of $p_n(\lambda)$ carries the following additional information: *The number of (strong) sign changes in that sequence equals the number of eigenvalues of B which are less than λ.* This is due to the fact that the polynomials $p_0(\lambda), p_1(\lambda), \ldots, p_n(\lambda)$ form a **Sturm sequence**, which allows the quick construction of intervals containing just one eigenvalue.

Example 4.18 For the matrix of Example 4.17, the recurrence (4.76) simplifies to

$$p_0(\lambda) = 1, p_1(\lambda) = -\lambda, p_j(\lambda) = -(\lambda p_{j-1}(\lambda) + p_{j-2}(\lambda)/4) \qquad j > 1$$

Choosing $n = 10$, and $\lambda = 0$, we get the sequence

$$(p_j(\lambda)) = 1, 0, -\tfrac{1}{4}, 0, \tfrac{1}{16}, 0, -4^{-3}, 0, 4^{-4}, 0, -4^{-5} = -0.000976563$$

which has five sign changes. For $\lambda = 0.2$, we get instead

$$(p_j(\lambda)) = 1, -0.2, -0.21, 0.092, 0.034, -0.029, -0.0025, 0.0079, -0.00095,$$

$$-0.0018, 0.00059857$$

showing six sign changes. [Here we have listed only the first two significant digits, except for the value of $p_{10}(\lambda)$.] It follows that there is exactly one eigenvalue of B in the interval $[0, 0.2]$. Modified regula falsi (Algorithm 3.3) starting with this interval produces in four steps (on a Hewlett-Packard 67) the eigenvalue 0.142314837, corresponding to the correct eigenvalue $0.142314838 = \cos(5\pi/11)$ (see Exercise 4.8-4).

EXERCISES

4.8-1 Let a, b be scalars and A be a square matrix. Prove that, if λ is an eigenvalue of A, then $a\lambda + b$ is an eigenvalue of the matrix $aA + bI$. [*Hint:* Consider $(aA + bI)\mathbf{x}$, where $\mathbf{x}$ is an eigenvector of A belonging to λ.]

4.8-2 Prove that if λ is an eigenvalue of the square matrix A and $p(x)$ is some polynomial, then $p(\lambda)$ is an eigenvalue of $p(A)$ (see Exercise 4.1-12).

4.8-3 Let A be the tridiagonal matrix of order n with diagonal entries equal to zero and $a_{i,i+1} = a_{i+1,i} = 1, i = 1, \ldots, n-1$. For $j = 1, \ldots, n$, let $\mathbf{x}^{(j)}$ be the n-vector whose ith entry is $x_i^{(j)} = \sin[i\,j\pi/(n+1)], i = 1, \ldots, n$. Prove that

$$A\mathbf{x}^{(j)} = 2\cos\left(\frac{j\pi}{n+1}\right)\mathbf{x}^{(j)} \qquad j = 1, \ldots, n$$

4.8-4 Use Exercises 4.8-1 and 4.8-3 to prove that if A is a tridiagonal matrix with $a_{ii} = d$, $a_{i+1,i} = a_{i,i+1} = e$, all i, then the eigenvalues of A consist of the numbers

$$d + 2e\cos\frac{j\pi}{n+1} \qquad j = 1, \ldots, n$$

4.8-5 Use the power method to estimate the eigenvalue of maximum modulus, and a corresponding eigenvector, for the tridiagonal matrix A of order 20 with $a_{ii} = 4$, $a_{i+1,i} = a_{i,i+1} = -1$, all i, and compare with the exact answer obtained from Exercise 4.8-4.

4.8-6 Try to estimate an eigenvalue of maximum modulus for the matrix A of 4.8-3 (with $n = 21$, say) using the power method. Explain any difficulties you encounter.

4.8-7 The power method breaks down if the matrix has two or more eigenvalues of the same maximum modulus. Discuss how one might use Exercise 4.8-1 to circumvent this difficulty. Try your remedy on the problem in Exercise 4.8-6.

4.8-8 Show that the matrix $B = \begin{bmatrix} 1 & 1 \\ 0 & 1 \end{bmatrix}$ does not have a complete set of eigenvectors.

4.8-9 Let $\mathbf{x}$ and $\mathbf{y}$ be two eigenvectors for the matrix A belonging to the eigenvalues λ and μ of A, respectively. Show that if $\lambda \neq \mu$, then $\mathbf{x}$ and $\mathbf{y}$ are linearly independent.

4.8-10 Use 4.8-9 to show that the matrix $\begin{bmatrix} 1 & 2 \\ 0 & 2 \end{bmatrix}$ must have a complete set of eigenvectors.

4.8-11 Find all the eigenvalues of the matrix

$$A = \begin{bmatrix} 4 & -1 & -1 & -1 \\ -1 & 4 & -1 & -1 \\ -1 & -1 & 4 & -1 \\ -1 & -1 & -1 & 4 \end{bmatrix}$$

by determining explicitly its characteristic polynomial, and then the zeros of this polynomial.

4.8-12 Reduce the matrix A of Exercise 4.8-11 to tridiagonal form B by Householder reflections. (Since the characteristic polynomial of A has a triple root, according to Example 4.16, at least two of the b_i's should be zero.) Then find the eigenvalues of B.

4.8-13 Calculate all the eigenvalues of the tridiagonal matrix B of Example 4.17, using the recurrence (4.76), the Sturm sequence property to isolate the eigenvalues, and then Newton's method to obtain the individual eigenvalues. (Consider writing a program for a general symmetric tridiagonal matrix.)

4.8-14 Having done Exercise 4.8-13, use the inverse power method to determine the corresponding eigenvectors.

4.8-15 Verify that a Hermitian matrix is similar to a diagonal matrix, and that all its eigenvalues are real. (*Hint:* Show that the upper-triangular matrix obtained in Schur's theorem is necessarily Hermitian if B is.)

4.8-16 Use Müller's method to find the natural frequencies in Example 4.16 in case

$$A = \begin{bmatrix} -2 & 0 & 1 & 0 \\ 0 & -2 & 0 & 1 \\ 1 & 0 & -2 & 0 \\ 0 & 1 & 0 & -2 \end{bmatrix} \qquad M = \begin{bmatrix} 2 & 1 & 0 & 0 \\ 1 & 2 & 1 & 0 \\ 0 & 1 & 2 & 1 \\ 0 & 0 & 1 & 2 \end{bmatrix}$$

4.8-17 Suppose the matrix A of order n has a complete set of eigenvectors $\mathbf{x}^{(1)}, \ldots, \mathbf{x}^{(n)}$. Prove that then A is similar to a diagonal matrix (whose diagonal entries must be the eigenvalues of A). [*Hint:* Consider the matrix $C^{-1}AC$, where $C\mathbf{i}_j = \mathbf{x}^{(j)}, j = 1, \ldots, n$. Why must C be invertible?]

4.8-18: Deflation for the power method Suppose that we have calculated, by the power method or by any other method, an eigenvalue λ for the matrix A of order n, with corresponding eigenvector $\mathbf{x}$, and assume that $x_n \neq 0$. Let B be the matrix of order $n - 1$ obtained from the matrix $C^{-1}AC$ by omitting its last row and last column, where $C\mathbf{i}_j = \mathbf{i}_j, j = 1, \ldots, n - 1$, and $C\mathbf{i}_n = \mathbf{x}$. Prove that all the eigenvalues of A are also eigenvalues of B, with the possible exception of the eigenvalue λ.

FIVE

*SYSTEMS OF EQUATIONS AND UNCONSTRAINED OPTIMIZATION

A general system of n equations in the n unknowns $x_1, \ldots, x_n$ can always be written in the form

$$f_i(x_1, \ldots, x_n) = 0 \qquad i = 1, \ldots, n \qquad (5.1)$$

with $f_1, \ldots, f_n$ n functions of n variables. We will continue to use vector notation, as introduced in Chap. 4, and so write (5.1) more compactly as

$$\mathbf{f}(\mathbf{x}) = \mathbf{0} \qquad (5.2)$$

Thus, $\mathbf{f}$ is a vector-valued function of a vector. Its value at the n-vector $\mathbf{x} = [x_1 \ x_2 \ \cdots \ x_n]^T$ is the n-vector $\mathbf{f}(\mathbf{x}) = [f_1(\mathbf{x}) \ f_2(\mathbf{x}) \ \cdots \ f_n(\mathbf{x})]^T$.

This notation not only saves some writing, but it is also suggestive of the fact that the iterative methods for solving one equation in one unknown, as discussed in Chap. 3, should be applicable here, too, in some sense. In particular, we will discuss fixed-point iteration, and Newton's method and some of its variants. But we will not be able to get as deeply into the mathematical analysis of those methods. A thorough discussion of the wealth of available material can be found in the monograph of Ortega and Rheinboldt [33]. Also, the solution of systems of equations continues to be an area of active research, particularly in the construction of efficient algorithms.

A particular example of a system (5.1) is the *linear* system

$$A\mathbf{x} - \mathbf{b} = \mathbf{0}$$

We discussed its **direct** solution at some length in Chap. 4. Now, the general system (5.2) usually has to be solved by **iteration**, i.e., by solving an equivalent sequence of linear systems, usually by the direct methods discussed in Chap. 4. But, for some of the iterative methods, especially the relaxation methods, the sequence of linear systems to be solved is so simple that these methods may be (and have been) applied with profit to systems which are themselves linear. We will pay particular attention to such iterative solution of linear systems.

Finally, we stress the close relationship between the solution of systems of equations and the search for extrema of a real-valued function of n variables, as explained further in the first section of this chapter.

*5.1 OPTIMIZATION AND STEEPEST DESCENT

Optimization is a steady source of systems of equations to be solved, and some methods for their solution are directly influenced by this fact. To recall, if a real-valued function $F(\mathbf{x}) = F(x_1, \ldots, x_n)$ of n variables is to be minimized (or maximized), then it is sufficient to look just at its values at its **critical points**, that is, at points $\mathbf{x}$ at which

$$\nabla F(\mathbf{x}) = \mathbf{0}$$

Here, ∇F is the **gradient** of F, that is, the vector

$$\nabla F = [\partial F/\partial x_1 \cdots \partial F/\partial x_n]^T$$

whose entries are the corresponding first partial derivatives

$$f_i := \partial F/\partial x_i \qquad i = 1, \ldots, n$$

of F. We write $\nabla F(\mathbf{x})$ if we want to emphasize the point $\mathbf{x}$ at which the gradient is to be evaluated.

Recall that the gradient ∇F serves as the "first derivative" of the function $F(\mathbf{x})$ of n variables: By Theorem 1.8, the derivative of the function

$$g(t) = F(\mathbf{x} + t\mathbf{u})$$

of the *one* variable t at $t = 0$ is given by

$$g'(0) = \nabla F(\mathbf{x})^T \mathbf{u} = f_1(\mathbf{x})u_1 + \cdots + f_n(\mathbf{x})u_n$$

This number gives information about the behavior of the function F as we strike out from the point $\mathbf{x}$ in the direction $\mathbf{u}$. Thus, F increases in all directions $\mathbf{u}$ which have angle less than 90° with the gradient vector $\nabla F(\mathbf{x})$, with the rate of increase greatest in the direction of the gradient. This is so because

$$(\nabla F)^T \mathbf{u} = \|\nabla F\|_2 \|\mathbf{u}\|_2 \cos\theta \qquad (5.3)$$

with θ the angle between the two vectors. Actually, this is something of a tautology because, on inquiring what the angle θ between the two vectors $\mathbf{u}$ and $\mathbf{v}$ might be, one usually gets the answer that

$$\theta = \cos^{-1}\left(\frac{\mathbf{v}^T\mathbf{u}}{\|\mathbf{v}\|_2\|\mathbf{u}\|_2}\right)$$

But, the point is that, for $\nabla F \neq \mathbf{0}$, roughly half of the possible directions $\mathbf{u}$, namely those for which $(\nabla F)^T\mathbf{u} > 0$, lead to an *increase* for F, with this increase greatest if and only if $\mathbf{u}$ is parallel to ∇F. By the same token, roughly half of all possible directions $\mathbf{u}$ lead to a *decrease* for F, with the decrease greatest when $\mathbf{u}$ is parallel to $-\nabla F$. It follows that $\mathbf{x}$ cannot be a minimum or maximum for F unless $\nabla F = \mathbf{0}$.

Example 5.1 The function $F(\mathbf{x}) = x_1^3 + x_2^3 - 2x_1^2 + 3x_2^2 - 8$ has the gradient

$$\nabla F = [3x_1^2 - 4x_1 \quad 3x_2^2 + 6x_2]^T$$

The equation $\nabla F(\mathbf{x}) = \mathbf{0}$ therefore has the four solutions $(0, 0)$, $(0, -2)$, $(4/3, 0)$ and $(4/3, -2)$, and no others. To understand the nature of these critical points and to get some exercise with gradients, we consider now the various regions into which the (x_1, x_2) plane is cut by the curves

$$(\partial F/\partial x_1)(\mathbf{x}) = 0 \quad \text{and} \quad (\partial F/\partial x_2)(\mathbf{x}) = 0$$

We find that $f_1 = \partial F/\partial x_1$ vanishes at the two straight lines $x_1 = 0$ and $x_1 = \frac{4}{3}$, is negative between these lines and positive elsewhere. Thus the first component of the gradient ∇F is negative between these two lines and positive elsewhere. Also, $f_2 = \partial F/\partial x_2$ vanishes at the two straight lines $x_2 = -2$ and $x_2 = 0$, is negative between these lines and is positive elsewhere. This gives the qualitative picture shown in Fig. 5.1 for the direction of the gradient in the various regions defined by the lines $f_1 = 0$ and $f_2 = 0$. The figure makes apparent that the critical point $(0, -2)$ is a local maximum (since all gradients in its neighborhood point toward it), while the critical point $(\frac{4}{3}, 0)$ is a local minimum (since all gradients in its neighborhood point away from it). The other two critical points are not extrema but saddle points, since in their neighborhood there are both gradients pointing toward them and gradients pointing away from them.

A basic method for finding an extremum is the **method of steepest descent** (or, **ascent**). This method goes back to Cauchy and attempts to solve the problem of finding a minimum of a real-valued function of n variables by finding repeatedly minima of a function of *one* variable. The basic idea is as follows. Given an approximation $\mathbf{x}$ to the minimum $\mathbf{x}^*$ of F, one looks for the minimum of F nearest to $\mathbf{x}$ along the straight line through $\mathbf{x}$ in the direction of $-\nabla F(\mathbf{x})$. This means that one finds the minimum $t^* > 0$ closest to 0 of the *univariate* function

$$g(t) = F(\mathbf{x} - t\,\nabla F(\mathbf{x}))$$

and, having found it, takes the next approximation to the minimum $\mathbf{x}^*$ to

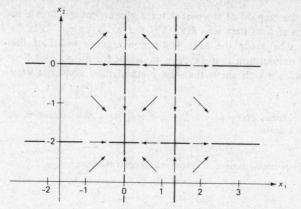

Figure 5.1 Schematic of gradient directions for the function $F(x_1, x_2) = x_1^3 + x_2^3 - 2x_1^2 + 3x_2^2 - 8$.

be the point

$$\mathbf{x} - t^* \, \nabla F(\mathbf{x})$$

Algorithm 5.1: Steepest descent Given a smooth function $F(\mathbf{x})$ of the n-vector $\mathbf{x}$, and an approximation $\mathbf{x}^{(0)}$ to a (local) minimum $\mathbf{x}^*$ of F.

> For $m = 0, 1, 2, \ldots,$ do until satisfied:
> $\quad \mathbf{u} := \nabla F(\mathbf{x}^{(m)})$
> $\quad$ If $\mathbf{u} = \mathbf{0}$, then STOP.
> $\quad$ Else, determine the minimum $t^* > 0$ closest to 0 of
> $\quad\quad$ the function $g(t) = F(\mathbf{x}^{(m)} - t\mathbf{u})$
> $\quad \mathbf{x}^{(m+1)} := \mathbf{x}^{(m)} - t^*\mathbf{u}$

Example 5.2 Given the guess $\mathbf{x}^{(0)} = [1, -1]^T$ for the local minimum $(4/3, 0)$ of the function $F(x_1, x_2) = x_1^3 + x_2^3 - 2x_1^2 + 3x_2^2 - 8$ of Example 5.1, we find

$$\nabla F(\mathbf{x}^{(0)}) = [-1, -3]^T$$

Thus, in the first step of steepest descent, we look for a minimum of the function

$$g(t) = F(1 + t, -1 + 3t) = (1 + t)^3 + (-1 + 3t)^3 - 2(1 + t)^2 + 3(-1 + 3t)^2 - 8$$

Setting $g'(t) = 0$ gives the equation

$$0 = 3(1 + t)^2 + 3(3t - 1)^2 3 - 4(1 + t) + 3 \cdot 2(3t - 1)3$$
$$= 84t^2 + 2t - 10$$

which has the two solutions $t^* = (-2 \pm \sqrt{4 + 3360}\,)/168 = \frac{1}{3}$ or $-\frac{5}{14}$ (using the quadratic formula). We choose the positive root, $t^* = \frac{1}{3}$, since we intend to walk from $\mathbf{x}^{(0)}$ in the direction of $-\nabla F(\mathbf{x}^{(0)})$. This gives $\mathbf{x}^{(1)} = [\frac{4}{3}, 0]^T$, the minimum itself.

It is clear that the method of steepest descent guarantees a decrease in function value from step to step, i.e., $F(\mathbf{x}^{(m+1)}) < F(\mathbf{x}^{(m)})$ (unless $\nabla F(\mathbf{x}^{(m)}) = \mathbf{0}$). This fact can be made the basis for a convergence proof of the method (under the assumption that $\|\mathbf{x}^{(m)}\| \leq$ constant for all m). But it is easy to give examples which show that the method may converge very slowly.

Example 5.3 The function $F(\mathbf{x}) = x_1^2 + \alpha x_2^2$, with $\alpha > 0$, has a global minimum at $\mathbf{x} = \mathbf{0}$. Its gradient is linear,

$$\nabla F = [2x_1, 2\alpha x_2]^T$$

We could therefore determine at once its unique critical point from the system

$$2x_1 = 0$$

$$2\alpha x_2 = 0$$

But, let us use steepest descent instead, to make a point. This requires us to determine the minimum of the function

$$\begin{aligned} g(t) &= F(\mathbf{x} - t \, \nabla F(\mathbf{x})) \\ &= F(x_1(1 - 2t), x_2(1 - 2\alpha t)) \end{aligned}$$

Setting $g'(t) = 0$ gives the equation

$$0 = 2(x(1 - 2t))(-2) + \alpha 2(x(1 - 2\alpha t))(-2\alpha)$$

whose solution is $t^* = \frac{1}{2}(x_1^2 + \alpha^2 x_2^2)/(x_1^2 + \alpha^3 x_2^2)$. Hence, if $\mathbf{x} = [x_1, x_2]^T$ is our current guess, then

$$\frac{x_1 x_2(\alpha - 1)}{x_1^2 + \alpha^3 x_2^2}[\alpha^2 x_2, -x_1]^T$$

is our next guess.

Now take $\mathbf{x}$ in the specific form $c[\alpha, \pm 1]^T$. Then the next guess becomes

$$c\frac{\alpha - 1}{\alpha + 1}[\alpha, \mp 1]^T$$

i.e., the error is reduced by the factor $(\alpha - 1)/(\alpha + 1)$. For example, for $\alpha = 100$, and $\mathbf{x}^{(0)} = [1, 0.01]^T$, we get, after 100 steps of steepest descent, the point

$$\mathbf{x}^{(100)} = \left(\frac{\alpha - 1}{\alpha + 1}\right)^{100}[1, 0.01]^T = [.135 \cdots, 0.00135 \cdots]^T$$

which is still less than $\frac{7}{8}$ of the way from the first guess to the solution.

In Fig. 5.2, we have shown part of the steepest descent iteration for Example 5.2. To understand this figure one needs to realize the following two points: (i) Since $(d/dt)F(\mathbf{x} + t\mathbf{u}) = (\nabla F(\mathbf{x} + t\mathbf{u}))^T\mathbf{u}$, by Theorem 1.8, the gradient of F at the minimum $\mathbf{x} - t^* \, \nabla F(\mathbf{x})$ of F in the negative gradient direction is *perpendicular* to that direction, that is,

$$\nabla F(\mathbf{x}^{(m+1)})^T \nabla F(\mathbf{x}^{(m)}) = 0$$

(ii) A function $F(x_1, x_2)$ of two variables is often described by its level or contour lines in the (x_1, x_2)-plane, i.e., by the curves

$$F(x_1, x_2) = \text{const}$$

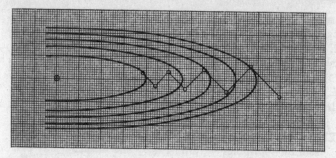

Figure 5.2 The method of steepest descent may shuffle ineffectually back and forth when searching for a minimum in a narrow valley.

Such lines are shown in Fig. 5.2. They give information about gradient direction, since the gradient at a point is necessarily perpendicular to the level line through that point (Exercise 5.1-3).

As the example shows, choice of the direction of steepest descent may be a good tactic, but it is often bad strategy.

One uses today more sophisticated descent methods, in which $x^{(m+1)}$ is found from $x^{(m)}$ in the form

$$x^{(m+1)} = x^{(m)} + t_m u^{(m)} \tag{5.4}$$

Here, $u^{(m)}$ is a **descent direction**, i.e., $\nabla F(x^{(m)})^T u^{(m)} < 0$, and t_m is found by a **line search**, i.e., by approximately minimizing the function

$$g(t) = F(x^{(m)} + t u^{(m)})$$

If the gradient of F is available, then this line search reduces to finding an appropriate zero of the function

$$g'(t) = \nabla F(x^{(m)} + t u^{(m)})^T u^{(m)}$$

and the methods of Chap. 3 may be applied. One should keep in mind, though, that the accuracy with which this zero is determined should depend on how close one is to the minimum of $F(x)$.

If the gradient of F is not available (or is thought to be too expensive to evaluate), then it has been proposed to use **quadratic interpolation** in some form. The following is typical.

Algorithm 5.2: Line search by quadratic interpolation Given a function $g(t)$ with $g'(0) < 0$, a positive number t_{max} and a positive tolerance ε.

1. $s_1 := 0$
2. Choose s_2, s_3 so that $0 \leq s_2 \leq s_3 \leq t_{max}$ and $g[s_1, s_2] \leq 0$
3. IF $s_2 = s_3 = t_{max}$, then $t_m := t_{max}$ and EXIT
   ELSE consider the parabola $p_2(t)$ which agrees with $g(t)$ at s_1, s_2, s_3

4. IF $g[s_1, s_2, s_3] \leq 0$, hence $p_2(t)$ has no minimum,
    then $s_3 := t_{max}$ and GO TO 3
    ELSE calculate the minimum s of $p_2(t)$, i.e.,
    $$s := (s_1 + s_2 - g[s_1, s_2]/g[s_1, s_2, s_3])/2$$
5. IF $s > t_{max}$, then $(s_1, s_2, s_3) := (s_2, s_3, t_{max})$ and GO TO 3
    ELSE
    5.1. IF $|g(s) - \min_i g(s_i)| \leq \varepsilon$ or $|g(s) - p_2(s)| \leq \varepsilon$,
        then $t_m := s$ and EXIT

        ELSE select a new ordered three-point sequence (s_1, s_2, s_3)
        from the four-point set $\{s_1, s_2, s_3, s\}$ and in such a way that
        either $g[s_1, s_2] < 0 < g[s_2, s_3]$ or, if that is not possible, so
        that $\max_i g(s_i)$ is as small as possible and GO TO 4

On EXIT, t_m is taken to be an approximation to the minimum of $g(t)$
on the interval $[0, t_{max}]$.

Note that EXIT at step 5.1. is no guarantee that the t_m so found is
"close" to a minimum of $g(t)$; see Exercise 5.1-5. When Algorithm 5.2 is
used as part of a multivariate minimization algorithm, it is usually started
with $s_1 = s_2 = 0$ [since $g'(0) = \nabla F(x^{(m)})^T u^{(m)}$ is usually available] and $s_3 = t_{max} = 1$, and step 5.1. is simplified to "$t_m := s$ and EXIT". This can be
shown to be allright provided the search direction $u^{(m)}$ is chosen so that
$x^{(m)} + u^{(m)}$ is the local minimum of a quadratic which approximates F near
$x^{(m)}$.

We have made the point that optimization gives rise to systems of
equations, namely systems of the special form

$$\nabla F(x) = 0$$

Conversely, an arbitrary system

$$f(x) = 0$$

of n equations in n unknowns can be solved in principle by optimization,
since, e.g., every minimum of the function

$$F(x) := \|f(x)\|_2^2 = (f_1(x))^2 + \cdots + (f_n(x))^2 \tag{5.5}$$

is a solution of the equation $f(x) = 0$ and vice versa. For this specific
function F,

$$\partial F/\partial x_i = \sum_{j=1}^{n} 2f_j(x)(\partial f_j/\partial x_i)$$

or

$$\nabla F = 2(f')^T f \tag{5.6}$$

with

$$f' := (\partial f_i/\partial x_j)_{i,j=1}^{n}$$

the **Jacobian matrix** of the vector-valued function f.

EXERCISES

5.1-1 Find all critical points of the function

$$F(x_1, x_2) = x_1^3/3 + x_2^2 x_1 + 3$$

by sketching the curves $\partial F/\partial x_1 = 0$ and $\partial F/\partial x_2 = 0$. Then classify them into maxima, minima, and saddle points using the gradient directions in their neighborhood.

5.1-2 Use steepest descent and ascent to find the minima and maxima of the function of Exercise 5.1-1 correct to within 10^{-6}.

5.1-3 Let **u** be the tangent direction to a level line $F(x_1, x_2) = $ const at a point $\mathbf{x} = [x_1, x_2]^T$. Use Theorem 1.8 to prove that $(\nabla F)(\mathbf{x})^T \mathbf{u} = 0$.

5.1-4 Write a FORTRAN subroutine for carrying out Algorithm 5.2, then use it to solve Exercise 5.1-2 above. (*Note:* To find a maximum of the function F is the same as finding a minimum of the function $-F$.)

5.1-5 (S. R. Robinson [34]) Let $h(t)$ be a smooth function on $[a, b]$ with $h''(t) > 0$ and $h(a) = h(b)$.

(*a*) Prove that $h(t)$ has a unique minimum t^* in $[a, b]$.

(*b*) Consider finding t^* by picking some interval $[\alpha, \beta]$ containing t^* and then applying Algorithm 5.2 to the input $g(t) = h(t - \alpha)$, $t_{\max} = \beta - \alpha$, some $\varepsilon > 0$, and the initial choice $(0, t_{\max}/2, t_{\max})$ for (s_1, s_2, s_3). The resulting estimate t_m for t^* then depends on α, β, and ε. Prove: *If, for all such α, β, we get $\lim_{\varepsilon \to 0} t_m = t^*$, then $h(t)$ must be a parabola.* [*Hint:* Choose α, β so that $h(\alpha) = h(\beta)$.]

(*c*) Conclude that Algorithm 5.2 may entirely fail to provide a good estimate for the minimum of g (even if ε is very small), unless g is close to a parabola.

5.1-6: Least-squares approximation A common computational task requires the determination of parameters $a_1, \ldots, a_k$ so that the model $y = R(x; a_1, \ldots, a_k)$ fits measurements (x_i, y_i), $i = 1, \ldots, N$, as well as possible, i.e., so that

$$R(x_i; a_1, \ldots, a_k) = y_i + \varepsilon_i \qquad i = 1, \ldots, N$$

with the N-vector $\boldsymbol{\varepsilon} = [\varepsilon_1 \quad \varepsilon_2 \quad \cdots \quad \varepsilon_N]^T$ as small as possible.

(*a*) Assuming that R depends smoothly on the parameter vector $\mathbf{a} = [a_1 \quad a_2 \quad \cdots \quad a_k]^T$, show that the choice $\mathbf{a}^*$ which minimizes $\|\boldsymbol{\varepsilon}\|_2$ must satisfy the so called **normal equations**

$$A[R(x_1; \mathbf{a}^*), \quad R(x_2; \mathbf{a}^*), \cdots, R(x_N; \mathbf{a}^*)]^T = A\mathbf{y}$$

with the $k \times N$ matrix A given by

$$\left(\frac{\partial R}{\partial a_i}(x_j; \mathbf{a}^*) \right)$$

(*b*) Determine the particular numbers a_1, a_2 in the model

$$y = a_1 e^{a_2 x}$$

which fits best in the above sense the following observations:

x_i	1	2	3	4	5	6	7	8	9	10
y_i	1.48	1.10	0.81	0.61	0.45	0.33	0.24	0.18	0.13	0.10

*5.2 NEWTON'S METHOD

When solving one equation

$$f(\xi) = 0$$

in one unknown ξ in Chap. 3, we derived Newton's method by (*i*) using Taylor's expansion

$$f(x + h) = f(x) + f'(x)h + \mathcal{O}(h^2)$$

for f at the point x, and then (*ii*), ignoring the higher-order term $\mathcal{O}(h^2)$, solving the "linearized" equation

$$0 = f(x) + f'(x)h$$

instead of the full equation $0 = f(x + h)$ for h, getting $h = -f(x)/f'(x)$ and thereby the "improved" approximation

$$x - f(x)/f'(x)$$

Now that we are trying to determine an n-vector ξ satisfying the system

$$\mathbf{f}(\xi) = \mathbf{0}$$

of n equations, we proceed in exactly the same way. From Theorem 1.9, we know that the ith component function f_i of the vector-valued function $\mathbf{f}$ satisfies

$$f_i(\mathbf{x} + \mathbf{h}) = f_i(\mathbf{x}) + (\nabla f_i(\mathbf{x}))^T \mathbf{h} + \mathcal{O}(\|\mathbf{h}\|^2)$$

in case f_i has continuous first and second partial derivatives. Thus

$$\mathbf{f}(\mathbf{x} + \mathbf{h}) = \mathbf{f}(\mathbf{x}) + \mathbf{f}'(\mathbf{x})\mathbf{h} + \mathcal{O}(\|\mathbf{h}\|^2) \qquad (5.7)$$

with the *matrix* $\mathbf{f}'$ called the **Jacobian** matrix for $\mathbf{f}$ at $\mathbf{x}$ and given by

$$\mathbf{f}'(\mathbf{x}) = \left(\partial f_i / \partial x_j\right)_{i,j=1}^n$$

Again we ignore the higher-order term $\mathcal{O}(\|\mathbf{h}\|^2)$ and solve the "linearized" equation

$$0 = \mathbf{f}(\mathbf{x}) + \mathbf{f}'(\mathbf{x})\mathbf{h}$$

instead of the full equation $\mathbf{0} = \mathbf{f}(\mathbf{x} + \mathbf{h})$ for the correction $\mathbf{h}$, getting the solution

$$\mathbf{h} = -\mathbf{f}'(\mathbf{x})^{-1}\mathbf{f}(\mathbf{x})$$

provided the Jacobian $\mathbf{f}'(\mathbf{x})$ is invertible. In this way, we obtain the new approximation

$$\mathbf{x} - \mathbf{f}'(\mathbf{x})^{-1}\mathbf{f}(\mathbf{x})$$

to ξ. This is the basic step of Newton's method for a system. The Newton equation

$$\mathbf{f}'(\mathbf{x})\mathbf{h} = -\mathbf{f}(\mathbf{x})$$

for the correction h to x is, of course, a *linear* system, and is solved by the direct methods described in Chap. 4.

Algorithm 5.3: Newton's method for a system Given the system

$$\mathbf{f}(\xi) = \mathbf{0}$$

of n equations in n unknowns, with $\mathbf{f}$ a vector valued function having smooth components, and a first guess $\mathbf{x}^{(0)}$ for a solution ξ of the system.

For $m = 0, 1, 2, \ldots$, until satisfied, do:
$$\mathbf{x}^{(m+1)} := \mathbf{x}^{(m)} - \mathbf{f}'(\mathbf{x}^{(m)})^{-1}\mathbf{f}(\mathbf{x}^{(m)})$$

It can be shown that Newton's method converges to ξ provided $\mathbf{x}^{(0)}$ is close enough to ξ and provided the Jacobian $\mathbf{f}'$ of $\mathbf{f}$ is continuous and $\mathbf{f}'(\xi)$ is invertible. Further, if also the second partial derivatives of the component functions of $\mathbf{f}$ are continuous, then

$$\|\xi - \mathbf{x}^{(m+1)}\| \le c\|\xi - \mathbf{x}^{(m)}\|^2$$

for some constant c and all sufficiently large m. In other words, Newton's method converges quadratically (see Example 5.6).

Example 5.4 Determine numbers $0 < \xi_1 < \xi_2 < \cdots < \xi_n < 1$ so that

$$G'(\xi_i) = G[\xi_{i-1}, \xi_{i+1}] \qquad i = 1, \ldots, n$$

with $\xi_0 = 0$ and $\xi_{n+1} = 1$, and $G(x) = x^3$.

This requires solution of the system

$$3\xi_i^2 = (\xi_{i+1}^3 - \xi_{i-1}^3)/(\xi_{i+1} - \xi_{i-1}) \qquad i = 1, \ldots, n$$

or
$$\mathbf{f}(\xi) = \mathbf{0}$$

with $0 = \xi_0 < \xi_1 < \cdots < \xi_{n+1} = 1$, and

$$f_i(\mathbf{x}) = x_{i-1}^2 + x_{i-1}x_{i+1} + x_{i+1}^2 - 3x_i^2 \qquad i = 1, \ldots, n$$

Correspondingly, the Jacobian matrix $\mathbf{f}'(\mathbf{x})$ is tridiagonal, of the form

$$\mathbf{f}'(\mathbf{x}) = \begin{bmatrix} -6x_1 & 2x_2 & & & & \\ 2x_1 + x_3 & -6x_2 & x_1 + 2x_3 & & & \\ & 2x_2 + x_4 & -6x_3 & x_2 + 2x_4 & & \\ & & \ddots & \ddots & \ddots & \\ & & & 2x_{n-2} + x_n & -6x_{n-1} & x_{n-2} + 2x_n \\ & & & & 2x_{n-1} + 1 & -6x_n \end{bmatrix}$$

Hence, in solving the Newton equation

$$\mathbf{f}'(\mathbf{x})\mathbf{h} = -\mathbf{f}(\mathbf{x})$$

for the correction $\mathbf{h}$ to $\mathbf{x}$, one would employ Algorithm 4.3 for the solution of a linear system with tridiagonal coefficient matrix.

It can be shown that this problem has exactly one solution. Note that the Jacobian matrix $\mathbf{f}'(\xi)$ at any solution ξ with $\xi_1 < \cdots < \xi_n$ is strictly diagonally dominant (see Exercise 5.2-2), hence $\mathbf{f}'(\xi)$ is invertible. We would therefore expect quadratic convergence if the initial guess $\mathbf{x}^{(0)}$ is chosen sufficiently close to ξ.

We try it with $x^{(0)} = [1 \quad 2 \quad \cdots \quad n]^T/(n + 1)$ and $n = 3$, and get the following iterates and errors.

m		$x^{(m)}$		$\|f(x^{(m)})\|_1$	$\|h\|_1$
0	0.2500000	0.5000000	0.7500000	0.188 + 0	0.889 − 1
1	0.3583333	0.6000000	0.8083333	0.340 − 1	0.135 − 1
2	0.3386243	0.5856949	0.8018015	0.109 − 2	0.426 − 3
3	0.3379180	0.5852901	0.8016347	0.157 − 5	0.512 − 6
4	0.3379171	0.5852896	0.8016345	0.284 − 11	0.823 − 12

The quadratic convergence is evident, both in the decrease of the size of the residual error $f(x^{(m)})$ and in the decrease of the size of the Newton correction h for $x^{(m)}$. The calculations were run on a UNIVAC 1110, in double precision (approximately 17 decimal digits).

Use of Newton's method brings with it certain difficulties not apparent in the above simple example. Chiefly, there are two major difficulties: (1) lack of convergence because of a poor initial guess, and (2) the expense of constructing correctly and then solving the Newton equation for the correction h. We will now discuss both of these in turn.

Two ideas have been used with some success to force, or at least encourage, convergence, viz., continuation or imbedding, and damping. In **continuation**, one views the problem of solving $f(\xi) = 0$ appropriately as the last one in a continuous one-parameter family of problems

$$g(\xi, t) = 0$$

with

$$g(x, 1) = f(x)$$

and $g(x, 0)$ a function for which there is no difficulty in solving

$$g(\xi, 0) = 0$$

Having found $\xi^{(0)}$ so that $g(\xi^{(0)}, 0) = 0$, one chooses a sequence $0 = t_0 < t_1 < \cdots < t_N = 1$ and solves the equation

$$g(\xi^{(i)}, t_i) = 0$$

by Newton's method for $i = 1, 2, \ldots, N$, using as a first guess the vector $\xi^{(i-1)}$ or, perhaps, even the extrapolated vector

$$\xi^{(i-1)} + (t_i - t_{i-2})\frac{\Delta\xi^{(i-2)}}{\Delta t_{i-2}}$$

(if $i > 1$). The hope is that the neighboring problems $g(\xi, t_i) = 0$ and $g(\xi, t_{i-1}) = 0$ are close enough to each other so that a good solution to one provides a good enough first guess for the solution of the other. Customary choice for g are

$$g(x, t) = tf(x) + (1 - t)(f(x) - f(x^{(0)}))$$

$$g(x, t) = tf(x) + (1 - t)(x - x^{(0)})$$

In the **damped** Newton's method, one refuses to accept the next Newton iterate $\mathbf{x}^{(m+1)} = \mathbf{x}^{(m)} + \mathbf{h}$ if this leads to an *increase* in the residual error, i.e., if $\|\mathbf{f}(\mathbf{x}^{(m+1)})\|_2 > \|\mathbf{f}(\mathbf{x}^{(m)})\|_2$. In such a case, one looks at the vectors $\mathbf{x}^{(m)} + \mathbf{h}/2^i$ for $i = 1, 2, \ldots$, and takes $\mathbf{x}^{(m+1)}$ to be the first such vector for which the residual error is less than $\|\mathbf{f}(\mathbf{x}^{(m)})\|_2$.

Algorithm 5.4: Damped Newton's method for a system Given the system $\mathbf{f}(\boldsymbol{\xi}) = \mathbf{0}$ of n equations in n unknowns, with $\mathbf{f}$ a vector-valued function having smooth component functions, and a first guess $\mathbf{x}^{(0)}$ for a solution $\boldsymbol{\xi}$ of the system.

For $m = 0, 1, 2, \ldots$ until satisfied, do:

$$\mathbf{h} := -\mathbf{f}'(\mathbf{x}^{(m)})^{-1}\mathbf{f}(\mathbf{x}^{(m)})$$
$$* \; i := \min\{j : 0 \le j, \|\mathbf{f}(\mathbf{x}^{(m)} + \mathbf{h}/2^j)\|_2 < \|\mathbf{f}(\mathbf{x}^{(m)})\|_2\}$$
$$\mathbf{x}^{(m+1)} := \mathbf{x}^{(m)} + \mathbf{h}/2^i$$

It is not clear, offhand, whether Step * can always be carried out. For i to be defined, it is necessary and sufficient that the Newton direction $\mathbf{h}$ be a *descent* direction at $\mathbf{x} = \mathbf{x}^{(m)}$ for the function

$$F(\mathbf{x}) = \|\mathbf{f}(\mathbf{x})\|_2^2$$

Since

$$\nabla F(\mathbf{x}) = 2\mathbf{f}'(\mathbf{x})^T\mathbf{f}(\mathbf{x})$$

by (5.5) and (5.6), $\mathbf{h}$ is a descent direction for F at $\mathbf{x}$ if and only if

$$\left(\mathbf{f}'(\mathbf{x})^T\mathbf{f}(\mathbf{x})\right)^T\mathbf{h} < 0$$

On the other hand, $\mathbf{h} = -\mathbf{f}'(\mathbf{x})^{-1}\mathbf{f}(\mathbf{x})$. Therefore

$$(\nabla F(\mathbf{x}))^T\mathbf{h} = 2\left(\mathbf{f}'(\mathbf{x})^T\mathbf{f}(\mathbf{x})\right)^T\left(-\mathbf{f}'(\mathbf{x})^{-1}\mathbf{f}(\mathbf{x})\right)$$
$$= -2\mathbf{f}(\mathbf{x})^T\mathbf{f}(\mathbf{x}) = -2\|\mathbf{f}(\mathbf{x})\|_2^2 < 0$$

This shows that the Newton direction is, indeed, a descent direction for $F(\mathbf{x}) = \|\mathbf{f}(\mathbf{x})\|_2^2$, hence the integer i in Step * is well defined.

In practice, though, one would replace Step * by

$$i := \min\{j : 0 \le j \le j_{max}, \|\mathbf{f}(\mathbf{x}^{(m)} + \mathbf{h}/2^j)\|_2 < \|\mathbf{f}(\mathbf{x}^{(m)})\|_2\}$$
IF i is not defined, THEN   FAILURE EXIT
ELSE

with j_{max} chosen a priori, for example, $j_{max} = 10$.

Example 5.5 The system $\mathbf{f}(\boldsymbol{\xi}) = \mathbf{0}$ with

$$f_1(\mathbf{x}) = x_1 + 3\ln|x_1| - x_2^2 \qquad f_2(\mathbf{x}) = 2x_1^2 - x_1x_2 - 5x_1 + 1$$

has several solutions. For that reason, the initial guess has to be picked carefully to ensure convergence to a particular solution, or, to ensure convergence at all.

The Newton equations are

$$\begin{bmatrix} 1 + 3/x_1 & -2x_2 \\ 4x_1 - x_2 - 5 & -x_1 \end{bmatrix} \mathbf{h} = -\mathbf{f}(\mathbf{x})$$

Starting with the initial guess $x^{(0)} = [2 \quad 2]^T$, we obtain the following sequence of iterates.

m	$x^{(m)}$		$\|f(x^{(m)})\|_2$	$\|h\|_2$
0	2.	2.	0.500 + 1	0.238 + 2
1	− 18.1588	− 10.5794	0.572 + 3	0.112 + 2
2	− 8.3710	− 5.2287	0.142 + 3	0.543 + 1
3	− 3.5525	− 2.7191	0.351 + 2	0.266 + 1
4	− 1.2015	− 1.4728	0.860 + 1	0.198 + 1
5	− 0.0004	0.0945	0.234 + 2	0.187 + 4
6	0.0451	− 1866.2415	0.348 + 7	0.933 + 3
7	0.0233	− 933.1179	0.871 + 6	0.467 + 3
8	0.0108	− 466.5520	0.218 + 6	0.233 + 3
		etc.		

Clearly, the iteration is not settling down at all. But now we employ the *damped* Newton's method, starting with the same first guess.

m	$x^{(m)}$		$\|f(x^{(m)})\|_2$	$\|h\|_2$	i
0	2.	2.	0.500 + 1	0.238 + 2	4
1	0.7400698	1.2137849	0.299 + 1	0.160 + 1	1
2	0.5310238	0.4415855	0.205 + 1	0.217 + 1	2
3	0.5178341	− 0.1001096	0.178 + 1	0.372 + 1	3
4	0.5584838	− 0.5637875	0.173 + 1	0.832 + 1	6
5	0.5847026	− 0.6910621	0.172 + 1	0.967 + 1	6
6	0.6215780	− 0.8376443	0.171 + 1	0.937 + 1	6
7	0.6657612	− 0.9772562	0.171 + 1	0.684 + 1	5
8	0.7448782	− 1.1760004	0.169 + 1	0.328 + 1	3
9	0.9489394	− 1.5313175	0.163 + 1	0.676	0
10	1.5501608	− 1.8410875	0.105 + 1	0.315	0
11	1.3892191	− 1.5703845	0.132	0.473 − 1	0
12	1.3735386	− 1.5257440	0.249 − 2	0.781 − 3	0
13	1.3734783	− 1.5249650	0.608 − 6	0.156 − 6	0
14	1.3734783	− 1.5249648	0.843 − 7		

We have listed here also, for each iteration, the integer i determined in Step * of Algorithm 5.4. Initially, the proposed steps h are rather large and are damped by as much as $\frac{1}{2^4} = \frac{1}{64}$. Correspondingly, the size $\|f(x^{(m)})\|_2$ of the residual error barely decreases from step to step. But, eventually, the full Newton step is taken and the iteration converges quadratically, as it should. (It is actually a thrilling experience to watch such an iteration on a computer terminal. One feels like cheering when the quadratic convergence sets in eventually.)

The calculations were run in single precision on a UNIVAC 1110. The error $\|f(x^{(14)})\|_2$ is therefore at noise level.

The second difficulty in the use of Newton's method lies with the construction and solution of the Newton equation for the correction h.

Already the construction of the Jacobian matrix is difficult if $\mathbf{f}$ is of any complexity, because it offers so many opportunities for making mistakes, both in the derivation and in the coding of the entries of $\mathbf{f}'$. Consequence of such mistakes is usually loss of quadratic convergence, or, in extreme cases, loss of convergence. Some computing centers now offer programs for the symbolic differentiation of expressions, and even of functions given by a subroutine. Such programs are of tremendous help in the construction of Jacobian matrices. If such programs are not available, then one might *test* one's coded Jacobian $\mathbf{f}'(\mathbf{x})$ by comparing it at some point $\mathbf{x}$ with simple-minded numerical approximations to its entries, of the form

$$\frac{\partial f_i}{\partial x_j}(\mathbf{x}) \approx \left[f_i(\mathbf{x} + \varepsilon \mathbf{i}_j) - f_i(\mathbf{x}) \right]/\varepsilon \tag{5.8}$$

or
$$\frac{\partial f_i}{\partial x_j}(\mathbf{x}) \approx \left[f_i(\mathbf{x} + \varepsilon \mathbf{i}_j) - f_i(\mathbf{x} - \varepsilon \mathbf{i}_j) \right]/(2\varepsilon) \tag{5.9}$$

familiar from calculus (see Chap. 7).

Alternatively, one might be content to code only the functions $f_1, \ldots, f_n$, and then use formula (5.8) or (5.9) to construct a suitable *approximation J* to $\mathbf{f}'(\mathbf{x})$. This requires proper choice of the step size ε (see Sec. 7.1).

Let J_m be the Jacobian $\mathbf{f}'(\mathbf{x}^{(m)})$ or a suitable approximation for it. Once J_m has been constructed, one must solve the system

$$J_m \mathbf{h} = -\mathbf{f}(\mathbf{x}^{(m)})$$

for the correction $\mathbf{h}$. In general, J_m is a full matrix of order n, so that $\Theta(n^3)$ operations are required to obtain $\mathbf{h}$. On the other hand, if there is convergence and $\mathbf{f}'(\mathbf{x})$ depends continuously on $\mathbf{x}$, then $\mathbf{f}'(\mathbf{x}^{(m+k)})$ will differ little from $\mathbf{f}(\mathbf{x}^{(m)})$. It is then reasonable to use $\mathbf{f}'(\mathbf{x}^{(m)})$ in place of $\mathbf{f}'(\mathbf{x}^{(m+k)})$ for a saving in work, since, having once factored $\mathbf{f}'(\mathbf{x}^{(m)})$, we can solve for additional right sides at a cost of $\Theta(n^2)$ only. This is the **modified** Newton method, in which $J_{m+k} = \mathbf{f}'(\mathbf{x}^{(m)})$ for $k = 0, 1, 2, \ldots$ until or unless a slowdown in convergence signals that J_{m+k} be taken as a more recent Jacobian matrix.

A more extreme departure from Newton's method is proposed in the so-called **matrix-updating** methods, in which J_{m+1} is obtained from J_m by addition of a matrix of rank one or two which depends on J_m, $\mathbf{x}^{(m)}$, $\mathbf{h}$, $\mathbf{f}(\mathbf{x}^{(m)})$, and $\mathbf{f}(\mathbf{x}^{(m+1)})$. The idea is to choose J_{m+1} in such a way that, with

$$\delta \mathbf{x} = \mathbf{x}^{(m+1)} - \mathbf{x}^{(m)} \quad \text{and} \quad \delta \mathbf{f} = \mathbf{f}(\mathbf{x}^{(m+1)}) - \mathbf{f}(\mathbf{x}^{(m)})$$

one gets
$$J_{m+1}(\delta \mathbf{x}) = \delta \mathbf{f}$$

This is reasonable because there should be approximate equality here in case $J_{m+1} = \mathbf{f}'(\mathbf{x})$ for $\mathbf{x}$ near $\mathbf{x}^{(m)}$.

If the matrix added to J_m has rank one or two, then it is possible to express the resulting change in $K_m = J_m^{-1}$ as addition of some easily calculable matrix. Thus, by keeping track of K_m rather than J_m, one can avoid the need to factor the J_m's. A popular scheme of this type is **Broyden's method**. Here, one calculates initially $K_0 = \mathbf{f}'(\mathbf{x}^{(0)})^{-1}$, and then forms K_{m+1} from K_m by

$$K_{m+1} = K_m - \frac{[K_m(\delta\mathbf{f}) - \delta\mathbf{x}](\delta\mathbf{x})^T K_m}{(\delta\mathbf{x})^T K_m(\delta\mathbf{f})} \tag{5.10}$$

with

$$\mathbf{x}^{(m+1)} = \mathbf{x}^{(m)} - K_m \mathbf{f}(\mathbf{x}^{(m)}) \tag{5.11}$$

The corresponding $J_m = K_m^{-1}$ satisfies

$$J_{m+1}(\delta\mathbf{x}) = \delta\mathbf{f}$$

while $\qquad\qquad J_{m+1}\mathbf{z} = J_m\mathbf{z} \qquad$ for all $\mathbf{z}$ perpendicular to $\delta\mathbf{x}$

In practice, one would use damping in this iterative scheme, too.

EXERCISES

5.2-1 Use Newton's method to find solutions of the system $\nabla F(\mathbf{x}) = \mathbf{0}$, with F the function of Exercise 5.1-1. Compare your effort with that required in Exercise 5.1-2.

5.2-2 Prove: If $G'(c) = G[a, b]$ and $a < c < b$, and $G''(x)$, $G'''(x)$ are both positive on $[a, b]$, then $c > (a + b)/2$. [*Hint:* Let $\bar{c} = (a + b)/2$ and show that $G'(\bar{c}) < G[a, b]$ by expanding everything in a Taylor series around $\bar{c}$. Else, use (7.8) directly.]

Conclude that the Jacobian matrix $\mathbf{f}'(\boldsymbol{\xi})$ of Example 5.4 is strictly diagonally dominant, hence invertible.

5.2-3 Use Newton's method to find a solution of the following somewhat complicated system in $0 \le x, y \le 1$.

$$\cos\left[\frac{x^2 - \sqrt{\sin(xy) + 3}}{4 + (xy)^2}\right] + \sin(3xy - 1) = 0.934$$

$$\exp\{\cos[(xy)^3 - 3]\} + \tan\left[\frac{x}{y}(0.08 + \cos x)\right] = 1.79$$

(The arguments of the trigonometric functions here are meant to be measured in radians, of course.)

If you fail to get quadratic convergence, check your coding of the Jacobian matrix, by using (5.8) or (5.9).

5.2-4 Apply damped Newton's method to the solution of the problem discussed in Example 5.5 starting with $\mathbf{x}^{(0)} = [2 \quad 1]^T$.

5.2-5 Try to solve the problem in Example 5.5 by continuation, starting with $\mathbf{x}^{(0)} = [2 \quad 1]^T$, and using $t_0, \ldots, t_N = 0, 0.1, 0.3, 0.6, 1$. (In the early stages, iterate only long enough to detect quadratic convergence.)

5.2-6 Solve the problem in Example 5.4 for $n = 10$ and $G(x) = x^5$.

*5.3 FIXED-POINT ITERATION AND RELAXATION METHODS

Newton's method and some of its variants discussed in Sec. 5.2 are examples of **fixed-point iteration**. Here, one rewrites the equation

$$\mathbf{f}(\boldsymbol{\xi}) = \mathbf{0}$$

into an equivalent one of the form

$$\boldsymbol{\xi} = \mathbf{g}(\boldsymbol{\xi})$$

and then, starting from some initial guess $\mathbf{x}^{(0)}$, generates the sequence

$$\mathbf{x}^{(m+1)} = \mathbf{g}(\mathbf{x}^{(m)}) \qquad m = 0, 1, 2, \ldots$$

which, so one hopes, converges to the fixed point $\boldsymbol{\xi}$ of $\mathbf{g}$.

For example, Newton's method is such a fixed-point iteration, with the **iteration function g** given by

$$\mathbf{g}(\mathbf{x}) = \mathbf{x} - \mathbf{f}'(\mathbf{x})^{-1}\mathbf{f}(\mathbf{x})$$

More generally, the **quasi-Newton** methods use an iteration function of the form

$$g(\mathbf{x}) = \mathbf{x} - C\mathbf{f}(\mathbf{x}) \tag{5.12}$$

with $C = C(\mathbf{x})$ some matrix. **Relaxation**, as discussed later in this section, provides a different idea for constructing iteration functions for solving $\mathbf{f}(\boldsymbol{\xi}) = \mathbf{0}$ by fixed-point iteration.

The analysis of fixed-point iteration for systems differs little from that given for the case of one equation in Chap. 3, the only difference being that we now measure the size of the error $\boldsymbol{\xi} - \mathbf{x}^{(m)}$ in the mth iterate by norms rather than absolute values.

Theorem 5.1 Suppose the iteration function $\mathbf{g}$ maps some closed set S into itself, i.e., $\mathbf{g}(\mathbf{x})$ belongs to S if $\mathbf{x}$ does, and suppose further that $\mathbf{g}$ is contractive on S, i.e.,

$$\|\mathbf{g}(\mathbf{x}) - \mathbf{g}(\mathbf{y})\| \leq K\|\mathbf{x} - \mathbf{y}\|$$

for all $\mathbf{x}$ and $\mathbf{y}$ in S and some $K < 1$. Then

(i) $\mathbf{g}$ has a fixed point in S.
(ii) If $\boldsymbol{\xi}$ is any fixed point of $\mathbf{g}$ in S, then fixed-point iteration starting with any $\mathbf{x}^{(0)}$ in S converges to $\boldsymbol{\xi}$, i.e., $\lim_{m \to \infty}\|\boldsymbol{\xi} - \mathbf{x}^{(m)}\| = 0$ for such a sequence $\mathbf{x}^{(m+1)} = \mathbf{g}(\mathbf{x}^{(m)})$, $m = 0, 1, 2, \ldots$. More explicitly,

$$\|\boldsymbol{\xi} - \mathbf{x}^{(m)}\| \leq \frac{K}{1 - K}\|\mathbf{x}^{(m)} - \mathbf{x}^{(m-1)}\| \tag{5.13}$$

hence
$$\|\boldsymbol{\xi} - \mathbf{x}^{(m)}\| \leq \frac{K^m}{1 - K}\|\mathbf{x}^{(1)} - \mathbf{x}^{(0)}\| \tag{5.14}$$

The assumptions ensure that we can start with any $\mathbf{x}^{(0)}$ in S and continue the iteration $\mathbf{x}^{(m+1)} = \mathbf{g}(\mathbf{x}^{(m)})$, $m = 0, 1, 2, \ldots$, indefinitely, with each $\mathbf{x}^{(m)}$ in S. Further, by an argument which goes beyond the level of this book (namely using the completeness of n-dimensional space), (i) follows. Finally, to get the estimate (5.13) and thereby (5.14), observe that

$$\|\boldsymbol{\xi} - \mathbf{x}^{(m)}\| = \|\mathbf{g}(\boldsymbol{\xi}) - \mathbf{g}(\mathbf{x}^{(m-1)})\|$$
$$\leq K\|\boldsymbol{\xi} - \mathbf{x}^{(m-1)}\| \tag{5.15}$$

since $\mathbf{g}$ is contractive, hence, by the triangle inequality (4.33iii),

$$\|\boldsymbol{\xi} - \mathbf{x}^{(m-1)}\| \leq \|\boldsymbol{\xi} - \mathbf{x}^{(m)}\| + \|\mathbf{x}^{(m)} - \mathbf{x}^{(m-1)}\|$$
$$\leq K\|\boldsymbol{\xi} - \mathbf{x}^{(m-1)}\| + \|\mathbf{x}^{(m)} - \mathbf{x}^{(m-1)}\|$$

or $\quad (1 - K)\|\boldsymbol{\xi} - \mathbf{x}^{(m-1)}\| \leq \|\mathbf{x}^{(m)} - \mathbf{x}^{(m-1)}\|$

Now combine this inequality with (5.15) to get (5.13).

Example 5.6 Newton's method is fixed-point iteration with the iteration function

$$\mathbf{g}(\mathbf{x}) = \mathbf{x} - \mathbf{f}'(\mathbf{x})^{-1}\mathbf{f}(\mathbf{x}).$$

Thus

$$\mathbf{f}'(\mathbf{x})[\mathbf{g}(\mathbf{x}) - \mathbf{x}] = -\mathbf{f}(\mathbf{x})$$

while, by (5.7), we find

$$0 = \mathbf{f}(\boldsymbol{\xi}) = \mathbf{f}(\mathbf{x} + \boldsymbol{\xi} - \mathbf{x})$$
$$= \mathbf{f}(\mathbf{x}) + \mathbf{f}'(\mathbf{x})(\boldsymbol{\xi} - \mathbf{x}) + \Theta(\|\boldsymbol{\xi} - \mathbf{x}\|^2)$$

assuming that $\mathbf{f}$ has continuous first and second partial derivatives. Hence, substituting here $-\mathbf{f}'(\mathbf{x})[\mathbf{g}(\mathbf{x}) - \mathbf{x}]$ for $\mathbf{f}(\mathbf{x})$, we get

$$0 = \mathbf{f}'(\mathbf{x})[- (\mathbf{g}(\mathbf{x}) - \mathbf{x}) + (\boldsymbol{\xi} - \mathbf{x})] + \Theta(\|\boldsymbol{\xi} - \mathbf{x}\|^2)$$

or $\quad \mathbf{f}'(\mathbf{x})[\mathbf{g}(\mathbf{x}) - \boldsymbol{\xi}] = \Theta(\|\boldsymbol{\xi} - \mathbf{x}\|^2)$

This says that

$$\|\mathbf{g}(\mathbf{x}) - \boldsymbol{\xi}\| \leq \|\mathbf{f}'(\mathbf{x})^{-1}\| \cdot c \cdot \|\boldsymbol{\xi} - \mathbf{x}\|^2$$

for some constant c.

If now $\mathbf{f}'(\boldsymbol{\xi})$ is invertible, then, since $\mathbf{f}'(\mathbf{x})$ is continuous by assumption, we can find a positive δ and an M so that $\mathbf{f}'(\mathbf{x})^{-1}$ exists for all $\mathbf{x}$ within δ of $\boldsymbol{\xi}$ and has a matrix norm no bigger than M. But then, choosing ε to be the smaller of δ and $(Mc)^{-1}$, we have, for all $\mathbf{x}$ in the closed set

$$S = \{\mathbf{x} : \|\boldsymbol{\xi} - \mathbf{x}\| \leq \varepsilon\}$$

that $\mathbf{f}'(\mathbf{x})^{-1}$ exists (hence $\mathbf{g}(\mathbf{x})$ is defined) and

$$\|\mathbf{g}(\mathbf{x}) - \boldsymbol{\xi}\| \leq Mc\|\boldsymbol{\xi} - \mathbf{x}\|^2 \leq (Mc\varepsilon)\|\boldsymbol{\xi} - \mathbf{x}\| \leq \|\boldsymbol{\xi} - \mathbf{x}\|$$

Thus $\mathbf{g}$ maps the closed set S into itself. Further, if $\|\boldsymbol{\xi} - \mathbf{x}\| < \varepsilon$, then $K = Mc\|\boldsymbol{\xi} - \mathbf{x}\| < 1$, hence $\boldsymbol{\xi}$ is an attracting fixed point of $\mathbf{g}$, and iteration starting with any $\mathbf{x}^{(0)}$ within less than ε of $\boldsymbol{\xi}$ will converge to $\boldsymbol{\xi}$.

As a further illustration, we now consider the solution of the *linear* system

$$A\boldsymbol{\xi} = \mathbf{b} \tag{5.16}$$

by fixed-point iteration. Such iteration schemes can all be based on the notion of **approximate inverse**. By this we mean any matrix C for which

$$\|I - CA\| < 1 \qquad (5.17)$$

in some matrix norm.

Lemma 5.1 If C is an approximate inverse for the matrix A, i.e., if $\|I - CA\| < 1$ in some matrix norm, then both C and A are invertible.

Indeed, if C or A were not invertible, then neither would the matrix CA be (see Exercise 4.1-8). By Theorem 4.4, we could then find $\mathbf{x} \neq \mathbf{0}$ so that $CA\mathbf{x} = \mathbf{0}$. But then

$$0 \neq \|\mathbf{x}\| = \|(I - CA)\mathbf{x}\| \leq \|I - CA\| \, \|\mathbf{x}\| < \|\mathbf{x}\|$$

which is nonsense.

In particular, (5.16) has exactly one solution if A has an approximate inverse.

Corresponding to an approximate inverse C for A, we consider the iteration function

$$\mathbf{g}(\mathbf{x}) = C\mathbf{b} + (I - CA)\mathbf{x}$$
$$= \mathbf{x} + C(\mathbf{b} - A\mathbf{x})$$

Note that this iteration function is of quasi-Newton type, i.e., of the form $\mathbf{g}(\mathbf{x}) = \mathbf{x} - C\mathbf{f}(\mathbf{x})$, if we take $\mathbf{f}(\mathbf{x}) = A\mathbf{x} - \mathbf{b}$. Also,

$$\mathbf{g}(\mathbf{x}) - \mathbf{g}(\mathbf{y}) = C\mathbf{b} + (I - CA)\mathbf{x} - \left[C\mathbf{b} + (I - CA)\mathbf{y} \right]$$
$$= (I - CA)(\mathbf{x} - \mathbf{y})$$

Consequently,

$$\|\mathbf{g}(\mathbf{x}) - \mathbf{g}(\mathbf{y})\| \leq \|I - CA\| \, \|\mathbf{x} - \mathbf{y}\| \qquad (5.18)$$

showing $\mathbf{g}$ to be contractive, with

$$K = \|I - CA\| < 1$$

Therefore, fixed point iteration

$$\mathbf{x}^{(m+1)} = \mathbf{x}^{(m)} + C(\mathbf{b} - A\mathbf{x}^{(m)}) \qquad m = 0, 1, 2, \ldots$$

starting from *any* $\mathbf{x}^{(0)}$, will converge to the unique solution $\boldsymbol{\xi}$ of (5.16), with the error at each step reduced by at least a factor of $K = \|I - CA\|$.

Example 5.7 Suppose the matrix A is strictly row diagonally dominant, i.e.,

$$|a_{ii}| > \sum_{j \neq i} |a_{ij}| \qquad \text{for } i = 1, \ldots, n$$

Let $D = \text{diag}(a_{11}, a_{22}, \ldots, a_{nn})$ be the diagonal of A. Then

$$\|I - D^{-1}A\|_\infty = \max_i \left\{ 1 - \sum_j |a_{ij}|/|a_{ii}| \right\} = \max_i \sum_{j \neq i} |a_{ij}|/|a_{ii}| < 1$$

Table 5.1

Jacobi				Gauss-Seidel		
$x_1^{(m)}$	$x_2^{(m)}$	$x_3^{(m)}$	m	$x_1^{(m)}$	$x_2^{(m)}$	$x_3^{(m)}$
0	0	0	0	0	0	0
1.2	1.2	1.2	1	1.2	1.08	0.972
0.96	0.96	0.96	2	0.9948	1.0033	1.00019
1.008	1.008	1.008	3	0.99965	1.000016	1.000033
0.9984	0.9984	0.9984	4			
1.00032	1.00032	1.00032	5			
0.999936	0.999936	0.999936	6			

showing that D is then an approximate inverse for A. The corresponding iteration scheme

$$\mathbf{x}^{(m+1)} = \mathbf{x}^{(m)} + D^{-1}(\mathbf{b} - A\mathbf{x}^{(m)}) \qquad m = 0, 1, 2, \ldots \qquad (5.19)$$

is **Jacobi iteration**. Note that $\mathbf{x}^{(m+1)}$ can be obtained from $\mathbf{x}^{(m)}$ by solving, for each i, the ith equation for the ith unknown, giving all the other unknowns their current values. In formulas,

$$x_i^{(m+1)} = \left(b_i - \sum_{j \neq i} a_{ij} x_j^{(m)} \right) / a_{ii} \qquad i = 1, \ldots, n$$

For the particular linear system

$$10x_1 + x_2 + x_3 = 12$$
$$x_1 + 10x_2 + x_3 = 12$$
$$x_1 + x_2 + 10x_3 = 12$$

Jacobi iteration starting with $\mathbf{x}^{(0)} = \mathbf{0}$ produces the vectors $\mathbf{x}^{(1)}, \mathbf{x}^{(2)}, \ldots, \mathbf{x}^{(6)}$ listed above in Table 5.1. The sequence seems to converge nicely to the solution $[1 \quad 1 \quad 1]^T$ of the system. For this example,

$$\|I - D^{-1}A\|_\infty = \max_i \left\{ \tfrac{1}{10} + \tfrac{1}{10} \right\} = 0.2$$

so that we would expect a reduction in error by at least a factor of 0.2 per step, which is borne out by the numbers in Table 5.1.

It is, of course, easy in principle to find an approximate inverse C for A. For example, $C = A^{-1}$ would do, and the corresponding iteration would converge in one step. But, the point of using iteration for solving $A\boldsymbol{\xi} = \mathbf{b}$ in the first place is that one might obtain an approximate solution of acceptable accuracy much faster by iteration than by solving $A\boldsymbol{\xi} = \mathbf{b}$ directly. For this, it is important to choose C so that we can calculate the vector $C\mathbf{r}$ for any particular $\mathbf{r}$ with much less work than it would take to calculate the vector $A^{-1}\mathbf{r}$. Typically, one chooses C as the inverse of a diagonal matrix (as in Jacobi iteration), or the inverse of a triangular matrix (as in Gauss-Seidel iteration discussed below), or as the inverse of the product of two triangular matrices (as in the iterative improvement algorithm 4.5), or even as the inverse of a tridiagonal matrix, etc.

Algorithm 5.5: Fixed-point iteration for linear systems Given the linear system $A\xi = \mathbf{b}$ of order n.

> Pick a matrix C of order n such that
>   (i) For given $\mathbf{r}$, the vector $C\mathbf{r}$ is "easily" calculated
>   (ii) In some matrix norm, $\|I - CA\| < 1$
> Pick an n-vector $\mathbf{x}^{(0)}$, for example, $\mathbf{x}^{(0)} = \mathbf{0}$
> For $m = 0, 1, 2, \ldots$, until satisfied, do:
> $$\quad \mathbf{x}^{(m+1)} := \mathbf{x}^{(m)} + C(\mathbf{b} - A\mathbf{x}^{(m)})$$

In the absence of round-off error, the resulting sequence $\mathbf{x}^{(0)}, \mathbf{x}^{(1)}, \mathbf{x}^{(2)}, \ldots$ converges to the solution of the given linear system.

As in Chap. 3, we employ here the phrase "until satisfied" to stress the incompleteness of the description given. To complete the algorithm, one has to specify precise termination criteria. Typical criteria are:

Terminate if (a): $\|\mathbf{x}^{(m)} - \mathbf{x}^{(m-1)}\| \le \varepsilon$

    or if (b): $\dfrac{\|\mathbf{x}^{(m)} - \mathbf{x}^{(m-1)}\|}{\|\mathbf{x}^{(m)}\|} < \varepsilon$ for some prescribed ε

    or if (c): $m > M$ for some given M

The last criterion should always be present in any program implementing the algorithm. We repeat the warning first voiced in Sec. 1.6: The fact that

$$\|\mathbf{x}^{(m)} - \mathbf{x}^{(m-1)}\| < \varepsilon$$

does not imply that

$$\|\mathbf{x}^{(m)} - \xi\| < \varepsilon$$

But we do know from (5.13) and (5.18) that

$$\|\mathbf{x}^{(m)} - \xi\| \le \frac{K}{1 - K}\|\mathbf{x}^{(m)} - \mathbf{x}^{(m-1)}\| \tag{5.20}$$

with $K = \|I - CA\|$.

> To give an example, we found for the Jacobi iteration in Example 5.7 that $\|I - CA\|_\infty \le 0.2$, and $\|\mathbf{x}^{(6)} - \mathbf{x}^{(5)}\|_\infty = 0.000384$. Therefore, (5.20) gives the estimate
> $$\|\xi - \mathbf{x}^{(6)}\|_\infty \le \frac{0.2}{1 - 0.2}\,0.000384 = 0.000096$$
> In fact, $\|\xi - \mathbf{x}^{(6)}\| = 0.000064$, so that the error is overestimated by *only* 50 percent. Unfortunately, it is usually difficult to obtain good estimates for $\|I - CA\|$, or else the estimate for $\|I - CA\|$ is so close to 1 as to make the denominator $1 - K$ in (5.20) excessively small and the resulting bound on $\|\xi - \mathbf{x}^{(m)}\|$ useless.

It should be pointed out that C may be an approximate inverse for A even though

$$\|I - CA\| > 1$$

for some particular matrix norm. All we require of an approximate inverse C for A (and for the convergence of the corresponding fixed-point iteration) is that $I - CA$ have *some* matrix norm less than one. For example, the matrix $B = \begin{bmatrix} 0.9 & 0.9 \\ 0 & 0 \end{bmatrix}$ satisfies

$$\|B\|_\infty = 1.8 > 1$$

Still, $\|B\| < 1$ in some matrix norm, for example, $\|B\|_1 = 0.9 < 1$. This makes it important to find ways of telling whether $\|B\| < 1$ in some matrix norm (without having to try out all possible matrix norms). The following theorem provides such a way (in principle).

Theorem 5.2 Let $\rho(B)$ be the **spectral radius** of the matrix B, i.e.,

$$\rho(B) = \max\{|\lambda| : \lambda \text{ is an eigenvalue of } B\}$$

Then there exists, for any $\varepsilon > 0$, a vector norm for which the associated matrix norm for B satisfies $\|B\| \le \rho(B) + \varepsilon$.

We conclude that C is an approximate inverse for A if and only if $\rho(I - CA) < 1$. Further, the smaller the spectral radius of $I - CA$ is, the faster ultimately is the convergence of the fixed-point iteration apt to be.

This can also be seen by observing that the error

$$\mathbf{e}^{(m)} = \boldsymbol{\xi} - \mathbf{x}^{(m)}$$

in the mth iterate in fixed-point iteration

$$\mathbf{x}^{(m+1)} = \mathbf{x}^{(m)} + C(\mathbf{b} - A\mathbf{x}^{(m)}) \qquad m = 0, 1, 2, \ldots$$

for the solution $A\boldsymbol{\xi} = \mathbf{b}$ satisfies

$$\mathbf{e}^{(m+1)} = (I - CA)\mathbf{e}^{(m)} \qquad \text{all } m$$

hence $\qquad \mathbf{e}^{(m)} = B^m \mathbf{e}^{(0)} \qquad \text{all } m, \text{ with } B = I - CA$

This shows the sequence $\mathbf{e}^{(0)}, \mathbf{e}^{(1)}, \mathbf{e}^{(2)}, \ldots$ of errors to be of a form discussed in Chap. 4 [see (4.62) through (4.67)] in connection with the power method. We stated there that the corresponding normalized sequence

$$\mathbf{e}^{(m)}/\|\mathbf{e}^{(m)}\| \qquad m = 0, 1, 2, \ldots$$

usually converges to an eigenvector of $B = I - CA$ belonging to the absolutely largest eigenvalue of B, i.e.,

$$\mathbf{e}^{(m+1)} = B\mathbf{e}^{(m)} \approx \lambda \mathbf{e}^{(m)}$$

with $|\lambda| = \rho(B)$. Thus, eventually, the error is reduced at each iteration step by a factor $\rho(B)$ and no faster, in general.

We now discuss specific examples of fixed-point iteration for linear systems. One such example is iterative improvement discussed in the preceding chapter. To recall, one computes the residual $\mathbf{r}^{(m)} = \mathbf{b} - A\mathbf{x}^{(m)}$

for the mth approximate solution $\mathbf{x}^{(m)}$; then, using the triangular factorization of A calculated during elimination, one finds the (approximate) solution $\mathbf{y}^{(m)}$ of the linear system $A\mathbf{y} = \mathbf{r}^{(m)}$ and, adding $\mathbf{y}^{(m)}$ to $\mathbf{x}^{(m)}$, obtains the better (so one hopes) approximate solution $\mathbf{x}^{(m+1)} = \mathbf{x}^{(m)} + \mathbf{y}^{(m)}$. The vector $\mathbf{y}^{(m)}$ is in general not the (exact) solution of $A\mathbf{y} = \mathbf{r}^{(m)}$. This is partially due to rounding errors during forward- and back-substitution. But the major contribution to the error in $\mathbf{y}^{(m)}$ can be shown to come, usually, from inaccuracies in the computed triangular factorization PLU for A, that is, from the fact that PLU is only an approximation to A. If we ignore rounding errors during forward- and back-substitution, we have

$$\mathbf{y}^{(m)} = (PLU)^{-1}\mathbf{r}^{(m)} = (PLU)^{-1}(\mathbf{b} - A\mathbf{x}^{(m)})$$

Hence

$$\mathbf{x}^{(m+1)} = \mathbf{x}^{(m)} + (PLU)^{-1}(\mathbf{b} - A\mathbf{x}^{(m)})$$

This shows *iterative improvement* to be a special case of fixed-point iteration, C being the computed triangular factorization PLU for A. But for certain classes of matrices A, a matrix C satisfying (i) and (ii) of Algorithm 5.5 can be found with far less computational effort than it takes to calculate the triangular factorization for A. For a linear system with such a coefficient matrix, it then becomes more economical to dispense with elimination and to calculate the solution directly by Algorithm 5.5.

To discuss the two most common choices for C, we write the coefficient matrix $A = (a_{ij})$ as the sum of a strictly lower-triangular matrix $\hat{L} = (\hat{l}_{ij})$, a diagonal matrix $\hat{D} = (\hat{d}_{ij})$, and a strictly upper-triangular matrix $\hat{U} = (\hat{u}_{ij})$,

$$A = \hat{L} + \hat{D} + \hat{U}$$

with

$$\hat{l}_{ij} = \begin{cases} a_{ij} & i > j \\ 0 & i \le j \end{cases} \qquad \hat{d}_{ij} = \begin{cases} a_{ij} & i = j \\ 0 & i \ne j \end{cases} \qquad \hat{u}_{ij} = \begin{cases} 0 & i \ge j \\ a_{ij} & i < j \end{cases}$$

Further, we assume that all diagonal entries of A are nonzero; i.e., we assume that $\hat{D}$ is invertible. If this is not so at the outset, we first rearrange the equations so that this condition is satisfied; this can always be done if A is invertible (see Exercise 4.7-5).

In the **Jacobi iteration**, or **method of simultaneous displacements**, one chooses $C = D^{-1}$, as discussed in Example 5.7.

If Jacobi iteration converges, the diagonal part $\hat{D}$ of A is a good enough approximation to A to give

$$\|B\| = \|I - \hat{D}^{-1}A\| < 1$$

But in this circumstance, one would expect the lower-triangular part $\hat{L} + \hat{D}$ of A to be an even better approximation to A; that is, one would expect to have

$$\|I - (\hat{L} + \hat{D})^{-1}A\| \leq \|I - \hat{D}^{-1}A\| < 1$$

Fixed-point iteration with $C^{-1} = \hat{L} + \hat{D}$ would then seem a faster convergent iteration than the Jacobi method. Although this is not true in general, it is true for various classes of matrices A, for example, when A is strictly row-diagonally dominant, or when A is tridiagonal (and more generally, when A is block-tridiagonal with diagonal diagonal blocks), or when A has positive diagonal entries and nonpositive off-diagonal entries.

Fixed-point iteration with $C^{-1} = \hat{L} + \hat{D}$ is called **Gauss-Seidel iteration**, or the **method of successive displacements**. In this method, one has

$$\mathbf{x}^{(m+1)} = \mathbf{x}^{(m)} + (\hat{L} + \hat{D})^{-1}(\mathbf{b} - A\mathbf{x}^{(m)})$$

or

$$(\hat{L} + \hat{D})\mathbf{x}^{(m+1)} = (\hat{L} + \hat{D} - A)\mathbf{x}^{(m)} + \mathbf{b}$$

or

$$\hat{D}\mathbf{x}^{(m+1)} = -\hat{L}\mathbf{x}^{(m+1)} - \hat{U}\mathbf{x}^{(m)} + \mathbf{b}$$

giving the formulas

$$x_i^{(m+1)} = \frac{-\sum_{j<i} a_{ij}x_j^{(m+1)} - \sum_{j>i} a_{ij}x_j^{(m)} + b_i}{a_{ii}} \qquad i = 1, \ldots, n$$

Apparently, we can calculate the ith entry of $\mathbf{x}^{(m+1)}$ once we know $x_1^{(m+1)}, \ldots, x_{i-1}^{(m+1)}$.

Algorithm 5.6: Gauss-Seidel iteration Given the linear system $A\mathbf{x} = \mathbf{b}$ of order n whose coefficient matrix $A = (a_{ij})$ has all diagonal entries nonzero.

Calculate the entries of $B = (b_{ij})$ and of $\mathbf{c} = (c_i)$ by

$$b_{ij} = \begin{cases} -a_{ij}/a_{ii} & i \neq j \\ 0 & i = j \end{cases}$$

$$c_i = \frac{b_i}{a_{ii}} \qquad \text{all } i \text{ and } j$$

Pick $\mathbf{x}^{(0)}$, for example, $\mathbf{x}^{(0)} = \mathbf{0}$
For $m = 1, 2, \ldots,$ until satisfied, do:
   For $i = 1, \ldots, n$, do:
     $x_i^{(m)} := \sum_{j=1}^{i-1} b_{ij}x_j^{(m)} + \sum_{j=i+1}^{n} b_{ij}x_j^{(m-1)} + c_i$

If some matrix norm of $(\hat{L} + \hat{D})^{-1}\hat{U}$ is less than one, then the sequence $\mathbf{x}^{(0)}, \mathbf{x}^{(1)}, \ldots$ so generated converges to the solution of the given system.

The vectors $\mathbf{x}^{(1)}, \mathbf{x}^{(2)}, \mathbf{x}^{(3)}$ resulting from Gauss-Seidel iteration applied to the linear system of Example 5.7 are listed in Table 5.1. Note that, for this example, Gauss-Seidel iteration converges much faster than does Jacobi iteration. After three steps, the accuracy is already better than that obtained at the end of six steps of Jacobi iteration.

In Jacobi iteration, the entries of $\mathbf{x}^{(m)}$ are used only in the calculation of the next iterate $\mathbf{x}^{(m+1)}$, while in Gauss-Seidel iteration, each entry of $\mathbf{x}^{(m)}$ is already used in the calculation of all succeeding entries of $\mathbf{x}^{(m)}$; hence the names simultaneous displacement and successive displacement. In particular, Jacobi iteration requires that *two* iterates be kept in memory, while Gauss-Seidel iteration requires only one vector.

Gauss-Seidel iteration can be shown to converge if the coefficient matrix A is strictly (row) diagonally dominant. It also converges if A is positive definite, i.e., if A is real symmetric and for all nonzero vectors $\mathbf{y}$,

$$\mathbf{y}^T A \mathbf{y} > 0$$

Finally, from among the many acceleration techniques available for speeding up the convergence of fixed-point iteration, we mention **successive overrelaxation** or **SOR**, in which one overshoots the change from $\mathbf{x}^{(m)}$ to $\mathbf{x}^{(m+1)}$ proposed by Gauss-Seidel iteration. Thus, instead of taking

$$x_i^{(m+1)} = x_i^{(m)} - \left(\sum_{j<i} a_{ij} x_j^{(m+1)} + \sum_{j>i} a_{ij} x_j^{(m)} - b_i \right) / a_{ii} \qquad \text{all } i$$

as in Gauss-Seidel iteration, one overshoots and takes

$$x_i^{(m+1)} = x_i^{(m)} - \omega \left(\sum_{j<i} a_{ij} x_j^{(m+1)} + \sum_{j>i} a_{ij} x_j^{(m)} - b_i \right) / a_{ii} \qquad \text{all } i$$

with ω (> 1) the **overrelaxation parameter**. It is possible, though not very illuminating, to write the resulting iteration explicitly in the form

$$\mathbf{x}^{(m+1)} = \mathbf{x}^{(m)} + C_\omega (\mathbf{b} - A \mathbf{x}^{(m)})$$

The corresponding iteration matrix is $I - C_\omega A = (\hat{D} + \omega \hat{L})^{-1}(\hat{D} - \omega \hat{U})$. In theory, the overrelaxation parameter ω is to be chosen so that $\rho(I - C_\omega A)$ is as small as possible. This is, of course, a more difficult task than solving the linear system $A\boldsymbol{\xi} = \mathbf{b}$ in the first place. But, one may have to solve such a linear system for many right-hand sides (and only to a certain accuracy), in which case it would pay to obtain a "good" ω by experiment. Also, for certain matrices A occurring in the numerical solution of standard partial differential equations, one can express $\rho(I - C_\omega A)$ in terms of the spectral radius of the iteration matrix $-\hat{D}^{-1}(\hat{L} + \hat{U})$ of Jacobi iteration, and thus make qualitative statements about the optimal choice of ω. The typical choice for ω is between 1.2 and 1.6.

As pointed out earlier, iterative methods are usually applied to large linear systems with a sparse coefficient matrix. For sparse matrices, the number of nonzero entries is small, and hence the number of arithmetic operations to be performed per step is small. Moreover, iterative methods are less vulnerable to the growth of round-off error. Only the size of the roundoff generated in a single iteration is important. On the other hand, iterative methods will not always converge, and even when they do converge, they may require a prohibitively large number of iterations. For large systems, the total number of iterations required for convergence to four or five places may be of the order of several hundred.

The idea underlying Jacobi and Gauss-Seidel iteration is that of **relaxation**, and this idea makes good sense also in the context of a general system

$$\mathbf{f}(\xi) = \mathbf{0}$$

of n nonlinear equations in n unknowns. In its simplest form, one assumes the equations so ordered that it is possible to solve the ith equation

$$f_i(\xi_1, \ldots, \xi_n) = 0$$

for the ith unknown to get the equivalent equation

$$\xi_i = g_i(\xi_1, \ldots, \xi_{i-1}, \xi_{i+1}, \ldots, \xi_n)$$

Then, given an approximation $\mathbf{x}$ to ξ, one attempts to improve its ith component by changing it to

$$g_i(x_1, \ldots, x_{i-1}, x_{i+1}, \ldots, x_n)$$

The term "relaxation" for this procedure is due to Southwell. In effect, the current guess $\mathbf{x}$ for the solution is the exact solution of the related system

$$x_i = g_i(x_1, \ldots, x_{i-1}, x_{i+1}, \ldots, x_n) + r_i \qquad i = 1, \ldots, n$$

where the error terms r_i are brought in to force the system to have $\mathbf{x}$ as its solution. In relaxation, the ith component of the current guess is then improved by letting it find its new (relaxed) level in response to the removal of the forcing term r_i in equation i.

Relaxation is usually carried out Gauss-Seidel fashion, i.e., the new value of the ith component is immediately used in the subsequent improvement of other components. Further, one goes through all the equations in some systematic fashion, changing all components of $\mathbf{x}$. Each such runthrough constitutes a **sweep**.

There are many useful variants of the basic relaxation idea. For example, it might be more convenient at times to replace the ith equation by an equivalent equation of the form

$$\xi_i = g_i(\xi)$$

in which the right-hand side depends explicitly on ξ_i, too, As another example, one might satisfy the ith equation by changing several components of the current guess at once. In other words, one might determine the new guess $\mathbf{x} + \alpha\mathbf{y}^{(i)}$ so that

$$f_i(\mathbf{x} + \alpha\mathbf{y}^{(i)}) = 0$$

with $\mathbf{y}^{(i)}$ a fixed vector depending on i. In ordinary relaxation, $\mathbf{y}^{(i)} = \mathbf{i}_i$, of course.

Example 5.8 We attempt to solve the nonlinear system of Example 5.4,

$$3\xi_i^2 = \xi_{i-1}^2 + \xi_{i-1}\xi_{i+1} + \xi_{i+1}^2 \qquad i = 1, \ldots, n$$

with $0 = \xi_0 < \xi_1 < \cdots < \xi_{n+1} = 1$, by Gauss-Seidel iteration. Thus, starting with the initial guess $\mathbf{x} = [1 \quad 2 \quad \cdots \quad n]^T/(n + 1)$ and $n = 3$, as in Example 5.4, we carry out the iteration

> For $m = 0, 1, 2, \ldots$, until satisfied, do:
>> For $i = 1, \ldots, n$, do:
>>> $x_i = \sqrt{(x_{i-1}^2 + x_{i-1}x_{i+1} + x_{i+1}^2)/3}$

The table lists the first few iterates, recorded after each sweep.

m	$\mathbf{x}^{(m)}$			$\|\mathbf{x}^{(m)} - \mathbf{x}^{(m-1)}\|_1$
0	0.2500000	0.5000000	0.7500000	
1	0.2886751	0.5361404	0.7796553	0.104
2	0.3095408	0.5612525	0.7908343	$0.572 - 1$
3	0.3240393	0.5734927	0.7963221	$0.322 - 1$
4	0.3311062	0.5794904	0.7990201	$0.158 - 1$
5	0.3345689	0.5824365	0.8003476	$0.774 - 2$
	.	. . .		.
10	0.3378204	0.5852071	0.8015973	$0.223 - 3$
11	0.3378695	0.5852490	0.8016162	$0.110 - 3$
	.	. . .		.
20	0.3379170	0.5852896	0.8016345	$0.190 - 6$
21	0.3379171	0.5852896	0.8016345	$0.931 - 7$

Convergence is linear (hence does not compare with the convergence of Newton's method), but is quite regular, so that convergence acceleration might be tried. Using successive overrelaxation with $\omega = 1.2$ produces the 21st iterate above in just 10 sweeps.

EXERCISES

5.3-1 Solve the system

$$x - \sinh y = 0$$
$$2y - \cosh x = 0$$

by fixed-point iteration. There is a solution near $[0.6 \quad 0.6]^T$.

5.3-2 By experiment, determine a good choice for the overrelaxation parameter to be used in successive overrelaxation for Example 5.8.

Do it also for $n = 10$, and then do it for the related problem 5.2-6.

5.3-3 Try to solve the system

$$x^2 + xy^3 = 9 \qquad 3x^2y - y^3 = 4$$

by fixed-point iteration.

5.3-4 Show that fixed-point iteration with the iteration matrix $B = \begin{bmatrix} 0.9 & 1{,}000 \\ 0 & 0.9 \end{bmatrix}$ converges even though $\|B\|_1 = \|B\|_\infty > 1{,}000$.

5.3-5 Use Schur's theorem to prove that, for any square matrix B and every $\varepsilon > 0$, there is some vector norm for which the corresponding matrix norm satisfies $\|B\| \le \rho(B) + \varepsilon$. (*Hint:* Construct the vector norm in the form $\|\mathbf{x}\| = \|DU\mathbf{x}\|_\infty$, with U chosen by Schur's theorem so that $A = U^{-1}BU$ is upper-triangular, and $D = \text{diag}[1, \delta, \delta^2, \ldots, \delta^{n-1}]$ so chosen that $D^{-1}AD$ has all its off-diagonal entries less than ε/n in absolute value.)

5.3-6 Show that Jacobi iteration and Gauss-Seidel iteration converge in finitely many steps when applied to the solution of the linear system $A\boldsymbol{\xi} = \mathbf{b}$ with A an invertible upper-triangular matrix.

5.3-7 Solve the system

$$\begin{bmatrix} 4 & -1 & 0 & 0 \\ -1 & 4 & -1 & 0 \\ 0 & -1 & 4 & -1 \\ 0 & 0 & -1 & 4 \end{bmatrix} \begin{bmatrix} x_1 \\ x_2 \\ x_3 \\ x_4 \end{bmatrix} = \begin{bmatrix} 1 \\ 1 \\ 1 \\ 1 \end{bmatrix}$$

by Jacobi iteration and by Gauss-Seidel iteration. Also, derive a factorization of the coefficient matrix of the system by Algorithm 4.3; then use iterative improvement to solve the system, starting with the same initial guess. Estimate the work (= floating-point operations) required for each of the three methods to get an approximate solution of absolute accuracy less than 10^{-6}.

5.3-8 Prove that Jacobi iteration converges if the coefficient matrix A of the system is strictly column-diagonally dominant, i.e.,

$$|a_{jj}| > \sum_{i \ne j} |a_{ij}| \qquad j = 1, \ldots, n$$

(*Hint:* Use the matrix norm corresponding to the vector norm $\|\mathbf{x}\| = \sum_{i=1}^n |a_{ii}x_i|$.)

APPROXIMATION

In this chapter, we consider the problem of approximating a general function by a class of simpler functions. There are two uses for approximating functions. The first is to replace complicated functions by some simpler functions so that many common operations such as differentiation and integration or even evaluation can be more easily performed. The second major use is for recovery of a function from partial information about it, e.g., from a table of (possibly only approximate) values. The most commonly used classes of approximating functions are algebraic polynomials, trigonometric polynomials, and, lately, piecewise-polynomial functions. We consider best, and good, approximation by each of these classes.

6.1 UNIFORM APPROXIMATION BY POLYNOMIALS

In this section, we are concerned with the construction of a polynomial $p(x)$ of degree $\leq n$ which approximates a given function $f(x)$ on some interval $a \leq x \leq b$ uniformly well. This means that we measure the error in the approximation $p(x)$ to $f(x)$ by the number or **norm**

$$\|f - p\|_\infty = \max_{a \leq x \leq b} |f(x) - p(x)| \qquad (6.1)$$

Ideally, we would want a **best uniform approximation from** π_n, that is, a polynomial $p_n^*(x)$ of degree $\leq n$ for which

$$\|f - p_n^*\|_\infty = \min_{p \in \pi_n} \|f - p\|_\infty \qquad (6.2)$$

Here, we have used the notation $p \in \pi_n$ as an abbreviation for the statement "p is a polynomial of degree $\leq n$." In other words, p_n^* is a particular polynomial of degree $\leq n$ which is as close to the function f as it is possible to be for a polynomial of degree $\leq n$. We denote the number $\|f - p_n^*\|_\infty$ by

$$\text{dist}_\infty(f, \pi_n)$$

and call it the **uniform distance** on the interval $a \leq x \leq b$ of f from polynomials of degree $\leq n$.

Before discussing the construction of a good or best polynomial approximant, we take a moment to consider ways of *estimating* $\text{dist}_\infty(f, \pi_n)$. If, for example, such an estimate shows that $\text{dist}_\infty(f, \pi_{10}) > 10$ and we are looking for an approximation which is good to two places after the decimal point, then we will not be wasting time and effort on constructing p_{10}^*. For such a purpose, it is particularly important to get **lower bounds** for $\text{dist}_\infty(f, \pi_n)$, and here is one way to get them.

Recall from Chap. 2 that

$$g[x_0, \ldots, x_{n+1}] = \sum_{i=0}^{n+1} g(x_i)/w'(x_i)$$

$$\text{with } w(x) = (x - x_0) \cdots (x - x_{n+1})$$

(see Exercise 2.2-1), and that this $(n + 1)$st divided difference is zero if $g(x)$ happens to be a polynomial of degree $\leq n$ (see Exercise 2.2-5). Thus for any particular polynomial $p \in \pi_n$,

$$
\begin{aligned}
f[x_0, \ldots, x_{n+1}] &= f[x_0, \ldots, x_{n+1}] - p[x_0, \ldots, x_{n+1}] \\
&= (f - p)[x_0, \ldots, x_{n+1}] \\
&= \sum_{i=0}^{n+1} (f(x_i) - p(x_i))/w'(x_i)
\end{aligned}
$$

Consequently, if $x_0, \ldots, x_{n+1}$ are all in $a \leq x \leq b$, then

$$|f[x_0, \ldots, x_{n+1}]| \leq \|f - p\|_\infty \cdot W(x_0, \ldots, x_{n+1})$$

with the positive number $W(x_0, \ldots, x_{n+1})$ given by

$$W(x_0, \ldots, x_{n+1}) = \sum_{i=0}^{n+1} 1/|w'(x_i)| \tag{6.3}$$

Now we choose p to be p_n^*. Then $\|f - p\|_\infty = \text{dist}_\infty(f, \pi_n)$, and we get the lower bound

$$|f[x_0, \ldots, x_{n+1}]|/W(x_0, \ldots, x_{n+1}) \leq \text{dist}_\infty(f, \pi_n) \tag{6.4}$$

Example 6.1 For $n = 1$ and $x_0 = -1$, $x_1 = 0$, $x_2 = 1$, we have

$$f[x_0, x_1, x_2] = \frac{f(x_0)}{(x_1 - x_0)(x_2 - x_0)} + \frac{f(x_1)}{(x_0 - x_1)(x_2 - x_1)} + \frac{f(x_2)}{(x_0 - x_2)(x_1 - x_2)}$$

$$= \quad f(-1)/2 \quad - \quad f(0) \quad + \quad f(1)/2$$

Hence, $W(-1, 0, 1) = 2$, and so, for $a \leq -1$, $1 \leq b$,

$$|f[-1, 0, 1]|/2 \leq \text{dist}_\infty(f, \pi_1)$$

For example, for $f(x) = e^x$, $f[-1, 0, 1] = e^{-1}/2 - e^0 + e^1/2 = 0.54308$; consequently, $\text{dist}_\infty(e^x, \pi_1) \geq 0.27154$.

Use of the lower bound (6.4) requires calculation of the numbers $w'(x_i) = \prod_{j \neq i}(x_i - x_j)$ for the formation of $W(x_0, \ldots, x_{n+1})$. (See Exercise 6.1-14 for an efficient way to accomplish this.) For certain choices of the x_i's, these numbers take on a particularly simple form. For example, if

$$x_i = \cos \frac{i}{n + 1} \pi \qquad i = 0, \ldots, n + 1 \tag{6.5}$$

then $\quad 1/w'(x_i) = \dfrac{2^{n-1}}{n + 1}(-1)^i \begin{cases} 1 & \text{if } i = 0 \text{ or } n + 1 \\ 2 & \text{otherwise} \end{cases} \tag{6.6}$

Hence, $W(x_0, \ldots, x_{n+1}) = 2^n$ (see Exercise 6.1-5) and therefore

$$\frac{1}{2(n + 1)}\left| f(1) - 2f\left(\cos \frac{\pi}{n + 1}\right) \right.$$

$$\left. + 2f\left(\cos \frac{2\pi}{n + 1}\right) - \cdots - (-1)^n f(-1)\right| \leq \text{dist}_\infty(f, \pi_n) \tag{6.7}$$

if the interval $a \leq x \leq b$ contains both 1 and -1. To apply this lower bound to other intervals, one must first carry out a linear change of variables which carries the interval in question to the interval $-1 \leq x \leq 1$.

Example 6.2 Consider approximation to the function $f(x) = \tan \pi/4x$ on the standard interval $-1 \leq x \leq 1$ from π_3. This is an odd function, i.e., $f(-x) = f(x)$; the lower bound (6.7) therefore is equal to zero for odd n, and of no help. Consider, instead, approximation from π_4. Then (6.7) gives

$$\tfrac{1}{10}|f(1) - 2f(\cos\tfrac{\pi}{5}) + 2f(\cos\tfrac{2\pi}{5}) - 2f(\cos\tfrac{3\pi}{5}) + 2f(\cos\tfrac{4\pi}{5}) - f(-1)|$$

$$\leq \text{dist}_\infty(f, \pi_4)$$

or $0.00203 \leq \text{dist}_\infty(f, \pi_4)$. In fact, one can show that $\text{dist}_\infty(f, \pi_4) = 0.0041 \cdots$, hence our lower bound is quite good.

Related to these lower bounds is the following theorem due to de la Vallée-Poussin which avoids computation of the $w'(x_i)$, but requires construction of an approximant $p \in \pi_n$.

Theorem 6.1 Suppose the error $f(x) - p(x)$ in the polynomial approximation $p \in \pi_n$ to f **alternates in sign** at the points $x_0 < x_1$

$$< \cdots < x_{n+1}, \text{ i.e.,}$$

$$(-1)^i [f(x_i) - p(x_i)] \varepsilon \geq 0 \qquad \text{for } i = 0, \ldots, n + 1$$

with $\varepsilon = \text{signum}[f(x_0) - p(x_0)]$. If $a \leq x_i \leq b$, all i, then

$$\text{dist}_\infty(f, \pi_n) \geq \min_i |f(x_i) - p(x_i)|$$

Indeed, if the points x_i are ordered as the theorem assumes, then

$$(-1)^{n+1-i} w'(x_i) > 0 \qquad \text{for } i = 0, \ldots, n + 1$$

and therefore all the summands in the sum

$$(f - p)[x_0, \ldots, x_{n+1}] = \sum_{i=0}^{n+1} [f(x_i) - p(x_i)] / w'(x_i)$$

have the *same sign*. But this means that

$$|f[x_0, \ldots, x_{n+1}]| = \sum_{i=0}^{n+1} |(f(x_i) - p(x_i))/w'(x_i)|$$

$$\geq \min_i |f(x_i) - p(x_i)| \cdot W(x_0, \ldots, x_{n+1})$$

and this, together with (6.4), proves the theorem.

Suppose now that we manage in Theorem 6.1 to have, in addition, that $|f(x_i) - p(x_i)| = \|f - p\|_\infty$ for $i = 0, \ldots, n + 1$. Then we have

$$\|f - p\|_\infty \geq \text{dist}_\infty(f, \pi_n) \geq \min_i |f(x_i) - p(x_i)| = \|f - p\|_\infty$$

and, since the first and last expressions in this string of inequalities coincide, *we must have equality throughout*. In particular, the polynomial p must then be a best uniform approximation to f from π_n. This proves the easy half of the following theorem due to Chebyshev.

Theorem 6.2 A function f which is continuous on $a \leq x \leq b$ has exactly one best uniform approximation on $a \leq x \leq b$ from π_n. The polynomial $p \in \pi_n$ is the best uniform approximation to f on $a \leq x \leq b$ if and only if there are $n + 2$ points $a \leq x_0 < \cdots < x_{n+1} \leq b$ so that

$$(-1)^i [f(x_i) - p(x_i)] = \varepsilon \|f - p\|_\infty \qquad i = 0, \ldots, n + 1 \quad (6.8)$$

with $\varepsilon = \text{signum}[f(x_0) - p(x_0)]$. Here $a = x_0$ and $b = x_{n+1}$ in case $f^{(n+1)}(x)$ does not change sign on $a \leq x \leq b$.

A proof of this basic theorem can be found in any textbook on approximation theory, for example in Rice [17] or Rivlin [35].

Example 6.3 We consider again approximation to $f(x) = e^x$ on the standard interval $-1 \leq x \leq 1$. We saw in Example 6.1 that $\text{dist}_\infty(f, \pi_1) \geq 0.27$. Now choose $p(x) = a + bx$, with $b = (e^1 - e^{-1})/2$, and $a = (e - bx_1)/2$, where $e^{x_1} = f'(x_1) = p'(x_1) = b$, or $x_1 = \ln b$; see Fig. 6.1. Then one verifies that the error $f(x) - p(x)$ satisfies the alternation condition (6.8) with $n = 1$ and $x_0 = -1$, $x_2 = 1$, i.e., $f(-1) - p(-1) = -[f(x_1) - p(x_1)] = f(1) - p(1) = (e^1 + e^{-1})/2 - a = 0.27880 \cdots$. Thus, this particular straight line must be the best uniform approximation to e^x on $-1 \leq x \leq 1$ from π_1, and dist $(e^x, \pi_1) = 0.27880 \cdots$. This shows our lower bound obtained in Example 6.1 to be quite accurate.

A particularly important example is provided by the best uniform approximation on $-1 \leq x \leq 1$ from π_n to the function $f(x) = x^{n+1}$. For the error in this approximation is, as we shall see in a moment, a multiple of $T_{n+1}(x)$, the Chebyshev polynomial of degree $n + 1$.

By definition, the **Chebyshev polynomial of degree** k is given (on $-1 \leq x \leq 1$) by the rule

$$T_k(\cos \theta) = \cos k\theta \tag{6.9}$$

Thus,

$$T_0(x) = 1 \qquad T_1(x) = x \tag{6.10}$$

and, by the addition formula for trigonometric functions,

$$T_{k+1}(x) = 2xT_k(x) - T_{k-1}(x) \qquad k = 1, 2, \ldots \tag{6.11}$$

From this

$$T_2(x) = 2xT_1(x) - T_0(x) = 2x^2 - 1$$

$$T_3(x) = 2xT_2(x) - T_1(x) = 2x(2x^2 - 1) - x = 4x^3 - 3x \qquad \text{etc.}$$

The first eight of these polynomials are listed in Table 6.1. Graphs of the first five are pictured in Figs. 6.2 and 6.3.

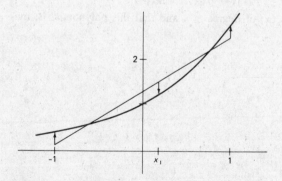

Figure 6.1 Best uniform straight-line approximation to e^x on $-1 \leq x \leq 1$.

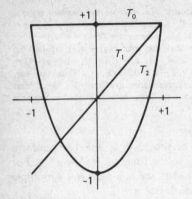

Figure 6.2

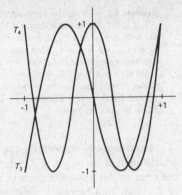

Figure 6.3

The recurrence relation (6.11) makes explicit that $T_k(x)$ as defined by (6.9) is indeed a polynomial, of exact degree k and with leading coefficient 2^{k-1}. Further, it is evident from the definition (6.9) that

$$|T_k(x)| \leq 1 \qquad \text{for all } -1 \leq x \leq 1 \qquad (6.12)$$

and that $T_k(x)$ attains this bound ± 1 alternately at the $k + 1$ points

$$x_j = \cos\frac{k - j}{k}\pi \qquad j = 0, \ldots, k$$

i.e., from (6.9),

$$T_k(x_j) = T_k\left(\cos\frac{k - j}{k}\pi\right) = \cos k\frac{k - j}{k}\pi = (-1)^{k-j} \qquad j = 0, \ldots, k$$

But this shows that, in particular,

$$2^{-n}T_{n+1}(x) = x^{n+1} - p_n(x)$$

for some polynomial $p_n(x)$ of degree $\leq n$ and that this polynomial is, by

Table 6.1

$T_0(x) = 1$
$T_1(x) = x$
$T_2(x) = 2x^2 - 1$
$T_3(x) = 4x^3 - 3x$
$T_4(x) = 8x^4 - 8x^2 + 1$
$T_5(x) = 16x^5 - 20x^3 + 5x$
$T_6(x) = 32x^6 - 48x^4 + 18x^2 - 1$
$T_7(x) = 64x^7 - 112x^5 + 56x^3 - 7x$

Theorem 6.2, the best uniform approximation to x^{n+1} on $-1 \leq x \leq 1$. Also,

$$\text{dist}_\infty\left(x^{n+1}, \pi_n\right) = 1/2^n \tag{6.13}$$

The construction of a best uniform approximation from π_n is, in general, a nontrivial task. Supposing the function $f(x)$ to be differentiable, one would, based on Theorem 6.2, solve the nonlinear system

$$f(x_i) - p_n^*(x_i) = (-1)^i d \qquad i = 0, \ldots, n+1$$

$$\phi(x_i)\left[f'(x_i) - p_n^{*\prime}(x_i)\right] = 0 \qquad i = 0, \ldots, n+1 \tag{6.14}$$

for the points $x_0, \ldots, x_{n+1}$, the $n+1$ coefficients of $p_n^*(x)$ and the (positive or negative) number $d = \pm \|f - p_n^*\|_\infty$, under the restriction that $a \leq x_0 < \cdots < x_{n+1} \leq b$. Here,

$$\phi(x) = \begin{cases} 0 & \text{if } x = a \text{ or } b \\ 1 & \text{otherwise} \end{cases}$$

The function $\phi(x)$ serves to distinguish between an interior extremum of the error $f(x) - p_n^*(x)$, at which the first derivative would have to be zero, and a boundary extremum, at which the derivative need not be zero (though it would have to satisfy some inequality not expressed here). The Remez algorithm and its Murnaghan-Wrench variant (see Rice [17]) attempt to solve this system by Newton's method as discussed in Chap. 5, but adapted to the special structure of (6.14). A first guess is easily obtained from a suitable interpolant $p_n \in \pi_n$ to $f(x)$, using the coefficients of $p_n(x)$ and the local extrema of $f(x) - p_n(x)$.

We will not take the time to discuss construction of a best uniform polynomial approximant in any more detail because it is possible to construct, with less effort, approximations which are *almost best*, by interpolating appropriately.

Indeed, by Theorem 6.2, we know that the error $f(x) - p_n^*(x)$ in the best uniform approximation on $a \leq x \leq b$ to the continuous function $f(x)$ must alternate $n+1$ times; that is, it must satisfy

$$(-1)^i\left[f(x_i) - p_n^*(x_i)\right] = \varepsilon\|f - p_n^*\|_\infty \qquad i = 0, \ldots, n+1$$

with $\varepsilon = \text{signum}[f(x_0) - p_n^*(x_0)]$ and $a \leq x_0 < \cdots < x_{n+1} \leq b$. But then, by the Intermediate Value Theorem for continuous functions (Theorem 1.3), there must exist points $\xi_0 < \cdots < \xi_n$, with $x_i < \xi_i < x_{i+1}$, all i, at which the error $f(x) - p_n^*(x)$ vanishes, i.e., at which the best approximation $p_n^*(x)$ *interpolates* $f(x)$. In principle, then, we could construct even the best approximation by interpolation, if we only knew where to interpolate.

Recall now that the error in the best approximation to x^{n+1} from π_n on the standard interval $-1 \leq x \leq 1$ is a multiple of $T_{n+1}(x)$, the Chebyshev polynomial of degree $n + 1$, which, by its very definition (6.9), vanishes at the $n + 1$ points

$$\xi_{k, n+1} = \cos \frac{2k + 1}{2n + 2} \pi \qquad k = 0, \ldots, n \qquad (6.15)$$

This means that, for the specific function $f(x) = x^{n+1}$, we can obtain its best uniform approximant from π_n by interpolation at the points (6.15), the so-called **Chebyshev points** for the standard interval $-1 \leq x \leq 1$. As it turns out, this procedure produces rather good (if not best) approximations to any continuous function.

To see why this might be so, recall from (2.16) or (2.37) that the error $f(x) - p_n(x)$ in the polynomial interpolant to $f(x)$ at the points $x_0, \ldots, x_n$ satisfies

$$f(x) - p_n(x) = f[x_0, \ldots, x_n](x - x_0) \cdots (x - x_n)$$

Consequently, by (6.4),

$$|f(x) - p_n(x)| \leq |x - x_0| \cdots |x - x_n| \cdot W(x_0, \ldots, x_n, x) \mathrm{dist}_\infty(f, \pi_n)$$

provided $x_0, \ldots, x_n$ and x all lie in the interval of interest. Now, write $x = x_{n+1}$. Then, from (6.3)

$$W(x_0, \ldots, x_n, x) = \sum_{i=0}^{n+1} 1 \bigg/ \prod_{\substack{j=0 \\ j \neq i}}^{n+1} |x_j - x_i|$$

and therefore

$$|x - x_0| \cdots |x - x_n| W(x_0, \ldots, x_n, x)$$
$$= |x_{n+1} - x_0| \cdots |x_{n+1} - x_n| W(x_0, \ldots, x_{n+1})$$
$$= \sum_{i=0}^{n+1} \prod_{\substack{j=0 \\ j \neq i}}^{n+1} \left| \frac{x_{n+1} - x_j}{x_i - x_j} \right|$$
$$= 1 + \sum_{i=0}^{n} |l_i(x_{n+1})|$$

with
$$l_i(x) = \prod_{\substack{j=0 \\ j \neq i}}^{n} \frac{x - x_j}{x_i - x_j} \qquad (6.16)$$

the ith Lagrange polynomial [see (2.5) and (2.6)]. This proves the following theorem.

Theorem 6.3 Let $p_n(x)$ be the polynomial of degree $\leq n$ which interpolates $f(x)$ at the points $x_0 < x_1 < \cdots < x_n$ in the interval $a \leq x \leq b$ of interest. Then

$$\text{dist}_\infty(f, \pi_n) \leq \|f - p_n\|_\infty \leq (1 + \|\Lambda_n\|_\infty)\text{dist}_\infty(f, \pi_n) \quad (6.17)$$

with

$$\Lambda_n(x) = \sum_{i=0}^{n} |l_i(x)|$$

and the Lagrange polynomial $l_i(x)$ given by (6.16).

This makes it desirable to choose the interpolation points $x_0, \ldots, x_n$ in $a \leq x \leq b$ in such a way that the uniform norm $\|\Lambda_n\|_\infty$ of the **Lebesgue function** $\Lambda_n(x)$ be as small as possible. This, as it turns out, is almost accomplished by the **Chebyshev points** (6.15) adjusted to the interval $a \leq x \leq b$ of interest, i.e., by the points

$$x_i = \left[a + b \ + \ (a - b)\cos\frac{2i + 1}{2n + 2}\pi\right]\bigg/ 2 \qquad i = 0, \ldots, n \quad (6.18)$$

In Fig. 6.4, we have plotted $\|\Lambda_n\|_\infty$ for these points as a function of n. We

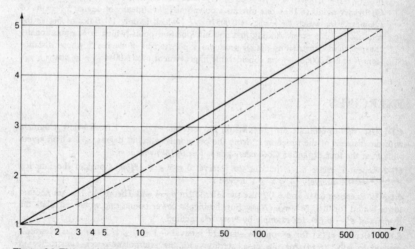

Figure 6.4 The number $\|\Lambda_n\|_\infty$ for the Chebyshev points (solid line) and for the expanded Chebyshev points (dashed line) as a function of n.

have also plotted there the numbers $\|\Lambda_n^e\|_\infty$ corresponding to the so-called **expanded Chebyshev points**

$$x_i^e = \left[a + b \;+\; (a - b)\left(\cos\frac{2i + 1}{2n + 2}\pi\right) \Big/ \left(\cos\frac{\pi}{2n + 2}\right) \right] \Big/ 2$$

$$i = 0, \ldots, n \quad (6.18e)$$

It can be shown that $\|\Lambda_n^e\|_\infty$ is within 0.02 of the smallest possible value for $\|\Lambda_n\|_\infty$ for all n.

We read off from Fig. 6.4 and from Theorem 6.3 that, for $n \leq 47$, the error in the polynomial interpolating $f(x)$ at the expanded Chebyshev points (6.18e) is never bigger than 4 times the best possible error, and is normally smaller than that. If, for example, the best uniform approximation $p_n^*(x)$ would be everywhere on $a \leq x \leq b$ within 10^{-5} of $f(x)$, then the interpolant would be, at worst, only within $4 \cdot 10^{-5}$ of $f(x)$, a loss of less than half a decimal digit in accuracy. Such a loss can usually be made up by interpolating by a polynomial of one or two degrees higher.

By contrast, if Λ_n^u denotes the Lebesgue function for a *uniform* spacing of interpolation points such as occurs when interpolating in a table, then

$$\|\Lambda_n^u\|_\infty \geq e^{n/2} \quad (6.19)$$

which grows very rapidly with n. (See, e.g., Rivlin [35; p. 99] for a result of this kind.)

Example 6.4 We obtained in Example 6.2 the lower bound $0.002 \leq \text{dist}_\infty(f, \pi_4)$ for $f(x) = \tan\frac{\pi}{4}x$ on the standard interval $-1 \leq x \leq 1$, and stated that, actually, $\text{dist}_\infty(f, \pi_4) = 0.0041 \cdots$. If one interpolates to this $f(x)$ at the five expanded Chebyshev points (6.18e), one obtains a polynomial $p(x)$ (ideally of degree 3 because of symmetry) for which $\|f - p\|_\infty = 0.00576 \cdots$, which is only 1.4 times as big as the smallest possible error. Adding just one interpolation point [which is computationally cheaper than constructing $p_4^*(x)$] produces a polynomial of degree 5 whose distance from $f(x)$ is $0.00068 \cdots$, a considerable improvement over $0.0041 \cdots = \text{dist}_\infty(f, \pi_4)$.

EXERCISES

6.1-1 Use (6.7) to estimate $\text{dist}_\infty(e^x, \pi_3)$ on the interval $-1 \leq x \leq 1$ from below. Compare with the distance of the function e^x from the polynomial $p_3(x)$ of degree ≤ 3 which agrees with e^x at the four expanded Chebyshev points [see (6.18e) with $n = 3$].

6.1-2 Repeat Exercise 6.1-1, but for the interval $0 \leq x \leq 1$. (*Hint:* Consider the function $e^{(x+1)/2}$ on the interval $-1 \leq x \leq 1$ instead.)

6.1-3 In Exercises 6.1-1 and 6.1-2, use the interpolant $p_3(x)$ and Theorem 6.1 to get another lower bound for $\text{dist}_\infty(e^x, \pi_3)$. (*Note:* For the biggest lower bound one would calculate the extrema of $e^x - p_3(x)$, for example by Newton's method.)

6.1-4 Calculate $p_3^*(x)$ for e^x on the standard interval $-1 \leq x \leq 1$. [*Hint:* Use Newton's method to solve (6.14) for this case, starting with the interpolant $p_3(x)$, constructed in Exercise 6.1-1, as a first guess for $p_3^*(x)$ and the local extrema $-1 = x_0^{(0)} < x_1^{(0)} < \cdots < x_4^{(0)} = 1$ of the error $e^x - p_3(x)$ as the first guess for the points $x_0 < \ldots < x_4$ of alternation. Note that $x_0 = -1$, $x_4 = 1$, by Theorem 6.2.]

6.1-5 Prove (6.6). [*Hint:* Verify that, with (x_i) given by (6.5), $w(x) = c_n(1 - x^2)T''_{n+1}(x)$ for some appropriate constant c_n, since the x_i's are the local extrema of $T_{n+1}(x)$. Derive the differential equation $(1 - x^2)T''_k(x) = xT'_k(x) - k^2 T_k(x)$ by differentiating (6.9) with respect to θ and use it to eliminate $(1 - x^2)T''_{n+1}(x)$ from your expression for $w'(x)$. Use it also to prove that $xT'_{n+1}(x) = (n + 1)^2 T_{n+1}(x)$ for $x = x_0, x_{n+1}$. Finally, you will need the fact that $T'_{n+1}(x_j) = 0$, $T_{n+1}(x_j) = (-1)^j$, for $j = 1, \ldots, n$.]

6.1-6 Prove that, for a convex function $f(x)$ on some interval $a \leq x \leq b$, the best linear uniform approximation $p_1^*(x)$ to $f(x)$ is of the form $p_1^*(x) = p_1(x) + \frac{1}{2}\min_{a \leq y \leq b}\{f(y) - p_1(y)\}$, with $p_1(x)$ the straight line which agrees with $f(x)$ at a and b.

6.1-7 Let $p_n^*(x)$ be the best uniform approximation to $f(x)$ on the standard interval $-1 \leq x \leq 1$. Use the uniqueness of the $p_n^*(x)$ to prove that $p_n^*(x)$ is odd (even) in case $f(x)$ is odd (even), i.e., in case $f(-x) = -f(x)$ ($f(-x) = f(x)$) for all x.

Conclude that the lower bound obtained in Example 6.2 for $\text{dist}_\infty(\tan\frac{\pi}{4}x, \pi_4)$ is already a lower bound for $\text{dist}_\infty(\tan\frac{\pi}{4}x, \pi_3)$.

6.1-8 Suppose the function $\psi(x)$ is orthogonal to polynomials of degree $\leq n$ on the interval $a \leq x \leq b$, i.e., $\int_a^b \psi(x)p(x)\,dx = 0$ for all $p \in \pi_n$. Prove that then

$$\left| \int_a^b \psi(x)f(x)\,dx \right| \Big/ \int_a^b |\psi(x)|\,dx \leq \text{dist}_\infty(f, \pi_n)$$

for any particular continuous function $f(x)$.

6.1-9 Use the addition formula for the cosine to prove (6.11).

6.1-10 Calculate a good polynomial approximation of degree n on $0 \leq x \leq 1$ to $f(x) = \sqrt{x}$, for $n = 1, 2, 3, \ldots, 10$, and so verify that $\text{dist}_\infty(\sqrt{x}, \pi_n) \approx \text{const } n^{-1}$. From this, estimate the degree n required for which $\text{dist}_\infty(\sqrt{x}, \pi_n) \leq 10^{-6}$.

6.1-11 Repeat Exercise 6.1-10 on the interval $-1 \leq x \leq 1$. Assuming that $\text{dist}_\infty(\sqrt{|x|}, \pi_n) \approx \text{const } n^{-\alpha}$, what is your guess for α?

6.1-12 Repeat the calculations of Example 2.4, but use the expanded Chebyshev points (6.18e) as interpolation points instead of equally spaced interpolation points. Compare your results with those of Example 2.4 and try to explain them in terms of Fig. 6.4 and (6.19).

6.1-13 Repeat 6.1-12, but for the function $f(x) = |x|$. (This is a nice illustration of the fact that, in polynomial approximation, bad behavior in the function *some*where results in a poor approximation *every*where. Use of a *piecewise*-polynomial approximant is a good way to avoid this disagreeable feature of polynomial approximation.)

6.1-14 Prove that the lower bound which is given in (6.4) can be calculated as $|f[x_0, \ldots, x_{n+1}]/g[x_0, \ldots, x_{n+1}]|$, with $g(x)$ any function for which $g(x_i) = (-1)^i$, all i, provided $x_0 < x_1 < \cdots < x_{n+1}$. Then adapt Algorithm 2.3 to carry out the calculation of $g[x_0, \ldots, x_{n+1}]$ simultaneously with that of $f[x_0, \ldots, x_{n+1}]$.

6.2 DATA FITTING

We have so far discussed the approximation of a function $f(x)$ by means of interpolation at certain points. Such a procedure presupposes that the values of $f(x)$ at these points are known. Hence interpolation is of little use (if not outright dangerous) in the following common situation: The function $f(x)$ describes the relationship between two physical quantities x and $y = f(x)$, and, through measurement or other experiment, one has obtained numbers f_n which merely *approximate* the value of $f(x)$ at x_n, that is

$$f(x_n) = f_n + \varepsilon_n \qquad n = 1, \ldots, N$$

where the experimental errors ε_n are unknown. The problem of *data fitting* is to recover $f(x)$ from the given (approximate) data f_n, $n = 1, \ldots, N$.

Strictly speaking, one never *knows* that the numbers f_n are in error. Rather, on the basis of other information about $f(x)$ or even by mere feeling, one decides that $f(x)$ is not as complicated or as quickly varying a function as the numbers f_n would seem to indicate, and therefore believes that the numbers f_n must be in error.

Consider, for example, the data plotted in Fig. 6.5. Here

$$x_n = n \qquad n = 1, \ldots, 11$$

If we have reason to believe that $f(x)$ is a straight line, the given data are most certainly in error. If we only know that $f(x)$ is a convex function, we still can conclude that the data are erroneous. Even if we know nothing about $f(x)$, we might still be tempted to conclude from Fig. 6.5 that $f(x)$ is a straight line, although we would now be on shaky ground. But whether or not we know anything about $f(x)$, we can conclude from the plotted data that most of the information about $f(x)$ contained in the data f_n can be adequately represented by a straight line.

To summarize, data fitting is based on the belief that the given data f_n contain a slowly varying component, the *trend* of, or the **information** about, $f(x)$, and a comparatively fast varying component of comparatively small amplitude, the **error** or **noise** in the data. The task is to approximate or fit the data by some function $F^*(x)$ in such a way that $F^*(x)$ contains or represents most (if not all) the information about $f(x)$ contained in the data and little (if any) of the error or noise.

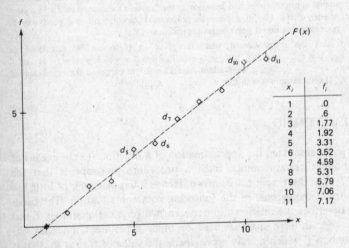

x_i	f_i
1	.0
2	.6
3	1.77
4	1.92
5	3.31
6	3.52
7	4.59
8	5.31
9	5.79
10	7.06
11	7.17

Figure 6.5 Least-squares straight-line approximation to certain data.

This is accomplished in practice by picking a function

$$F(x) = F(x; c_1, \ldots, c_k) \tag{6.20}$$

which depends on certain parameters $c_1, \ldots, c_k$. Normally, one will try to select a function $F(x)$ which depends *linearly* on the parameters, so that $F(x)$ will have the form

$$F(x) = c_1\phi_1(x) + c_2\phi_2(x) + \cdots + c_k\phi_k(x) \tag{6.21}$$

where the $\{\phi_i\}$ are an a priori selected set of functions and the $\{c_i\}$ are parameters which must be determined. The $\{\phi_i\}$ may, for example, be the set of monomials $\{x^{i-1}\}$ or the set of trigonometric functions $\{\sin \pi i x\}$. Normally, k is small compared with the number N of data points. The hope is that k is large enough so that the information about $f(x)$ in the data can be well represented by proper choice of the parameters $c_1, \ldots, c_k$, while at the same time k is too small to also allow for reproduction of the error or noise.

Once practitioners of the art of data fitting have decided on the right form (6.20) for the approximating function, they have to determine particular values $c_1^*, \ldots, c_k^*$ for the parameters c_i to get a "good" approximation $F^*(x) = F(x; c_1^*, \ldots, c_k^*)$. The general idea is to choose $\{c_i\}$ so that the deviations

$$d_n = f_n - F(x_n; c_1, \ldots, c_k) \qquad n = 1, \ldots, N$$

are simultaneously made as small as possible (see Fig. 6.5 for such deviations in a typical example). In the terminology of Chap. 4, one tries to make some *norm* of the N-vector $\mathbf{d} = [d_1 \quad d_2 \quad \cdots \quad d_N]^T$ as small as possible; i.e., one attempts to

$$\text{Minimize } \|\mathbf{d}\|$$

as a function of $c_1, \ldots, c_k$. Popular choices for the norm are
(i) The 1-norm

$$\|\mathbf{d}\|_1 = \sum_{n=1}^{N} |d_n|$$

if one wishes the average deviation to be as small as possible, or
(ii) The ∞-norm

$$\|\mathbf{d}\|_\infty = \max_{1 \le n \le N} |d_n|$$

if one wishes to make all deviations uniformly small.

But, if one attacks these minimization problems in the spirit of Chap. 5 or by some other means, one quickly discovers that they lead to a *nonlinear* system of equations for the determination of the minimum $c_1^*, \ldots, c_k^*$ [see, e.g., the system (6.14) for the related problem of uniform approximation on an interval]. It is therefore customary to choose as the norm to be minimized the 2-norm

$$\|\mathbf{d}\|_2 = \left(\sum_{n=1}^{N} |d_n|^2 \right)^{1/2}$$

for this leads to a *linear* system of equations for the determination of the minimum c_i^*'s. The resulting approximation $F(x; c_1^*, \ldots, c_k^*)$ is then known as a **least-squares approximation** to the given data.

We now derive the system of equations for the c_i^*'s. Since the square-root function is monotone, minimizing $\|\mathbf{d}\|_2$ is the same task as minimizing $\|\mathbf{d}\|_2^2$. For $\mathbf{c}^* = [c_1 \quad \cdots \quad c_k]^T$ to be a minimum of the function

$$E(\mathbf{c}) = E(c_1, \ldots, c_k) = \|\mathbf{d}\|_2^2 = \sum_{n=1}^{N} \left[f_n - F(x_n; \mathbf{c}) \right]^2$$

it is, of course, necessary that the gradient of E vanish at $\mathbf{c}^*$, i.e.,

$$\nabla E(\mathbf{c}^*) = \mathbf{0}$$

(see Sec. 5.1). Therefore, since

$$(\partial/\partial c_i)\left[f_n - F(x_n; \mathbf{c}) \right] = -\phi_i(x_n)$$

because of (6.21), $\mathbf{c}^*$ must satisfy the so-called **normal equations**

$$-2 \sum_{n=1}^{N} \left[f_n - F(x_n; \mathbf{c}^*) \right]\phi_i(x_n) = 0 \qquad i = 1, \ldots, k \qquad (6.22)$$

The epithet "normal" is given to these equations since they specify that the error vector $\mathbf{e} = [e_1 \quad e_2 \quad \cdots \quad e_N]^T$, with $e_n = f_n - F(x_n; \mathbf{c}^*)$, all n, should be normal, or orthogonal, or perpendicular to each of the k vectors

$$\boldsymbol{\phi}_i = \left[\phi_i(x_1) \quad \phi_i(x_2) \quad \cdots \quad \phi_i(x_N) \right]^T \qquad i = 1, \ldots, k$$

Indeed, in terms of these N-vectors, (6.22) reads

$$-2\mathbf{e}^T\boldsymbol{\phi}_i = 0 \qquad i = 1, \cdots, k$$

Since our general approximating function is of the form $F(x) = c_1\phi_1(x) + c_2\phi_2(x) + \cdots + c_k\phi_k(x)$, this says that the error vector should (in this sense) be perpendicular to all possible approximating functions, i.e.,

$$\mathbf{e}^T(c_1\boldsymbol{\phi}_1 + c_2\boldsymbol{\phi}_2 + \cdots + c_k\boldsymbol{\phi}_k) = 0 \qquad \text{for all } c_1, \ldots, c_k$$

This identifies the vector $c_1^*\boldsymbol{\phi}_1 + c_2^*\boldsymbol{\phi}_2 + \cdots + c_k^*\boldsymbol{\phi}_k$ as the **orthogonal projection** of the data vector $\mathbf{f} = [f_1 \quad f_2 \quad \cdots \quad f_N]^T$ onto the hyperplane spanned by the vectors $\boldsymbol{\phi}_1, \boldsymbol{\phi}_2, \ldots, \boldsymbol{\phi}_k$.

We rewrite the normal equations in the form

$$\sum_{j=1}^{k} c_j^*\boldsymbol{\phi}_j^T\boldsymbol{\phi}_i = \mathbf{f}^T\boldsymbol{\phi}_i \qquad i = 1, \ldots, k \qquad (6.23)$$

to make explicit the fact that they form a system of k linear equations in the k unknowns $c_1^*, c_2^*, \ldots, c_k^*$. As it turns out, this system always has at least one solution [regardless of what the $\phi_i(x)$ are]; further, any solution of (6.23) minimizes $E(c_1, \ldots, c_k)$.

To give an example, we now find the least-squares approximation to the data plotted in Fig. 6.5 by a straight line.

In this example, $x_n = n$, $n = 1, \ldots, 11$, and

$$F(x; c_1, c_2) = c_1 + c_2 x$$

so that $k = 2$ and $\phi_1(x) = 1$, $\phi_2(x) = x$. The linear system (6.23) takes the form

$$11c_1^* + 66c_2^* = 41.04$$
$$66c_1^* + 506c_2^* = 328.05$$

which, when solved by Gauss elimination, gives the unique solution

$$c_1^* = -0.7314 \cdots \qquad c_2^* = 0.7437 \cdots$$

The resulting straight line is plotted also in Fig. 6.5.

At this point, all would be well if it were not for the unhappy fact that the coefficient matrix of (6.23) is quite often ill-conditioned, enough so that straightforward application of the elimination algorithm 4.2 produces unreliable results. This is illustrated by the following simple example.

Example 6.5 We are given approximate values $f_n \approx f(x_n)$ with

$$x_n = 10 + \frac{n-1}{5} \qquad n = 1, \ldots, 6$$

and we have reason to believe that these data can be adequately represented by a parabola. Accordingly, we choose

$$\phi_1(x) = 1 \qquad \phi_2(x) = x \qquad \phi_3(x) = x^2$$

For this case, the coefficient matrix A of (6.23) is

$$A = \begin{bmatrix} 6 & 63 & 662.2 \\ 63 & 662.2 & 6,967.8 \\ 662.2 & 6,967.8 & 73,393.5664 \end{bmatrix}$$

It follows that $\|A\|_\infty \approx 8 \cdot 10^4$. On the other hand, with

$$\mathbf{x} = \begin{bmatrix} 10.07 \\ -2. \\ 0.099 \end{bmatrix} \qquad \text{we get} \qquad A\mathbf{x} = \begin{bmatrix} -0.02 \\ -0.18 \\ -1.28 \end{bmatrix}$$

Hence, from the inequality (4.38),

$$\|A\mathbf{x}\| \geq \frac{\|\mathbf{x}\|}{\|A^{-1}\|}$$

we get $\qquad 1.28 = \|A\mathbf{x}\|_\infty \geq \dfrac{10.07}{\|A^{-1}\|_\infty} \qquad \text{or} \qquad \|A^{-1}\|_\infty \geq 7.8$

Therefore the condition number of A is

$$\text{cond}(A) = \|A\|_\infty \|A^{-1}\|_\infty \geq 10^5$$

Actually, the condition number of A is much larger than 10^5, as the following specific results show. We pick

$$f(x) = 10 - 2x + \frac{x^2}{10}$$

and use exact data, $\qquad f_n = f(x_n) \qquad n = 1, \ldots, 6$

Then, since $f(x)$ is a polynomial of degree 2, $F^*(x)$ should be $f(x)$ itself; therefore we should get

$$c_1^* = 10 \qquad c_2^* = -2 \qquad c_3^* = 0.1$$

Using the elimination algorithm 4.2 to solve (6.23) for this case on the CDC 6500 produces the result

$$c_1^* = 9.9999997437 \cdots \qquad c_2^* = -1.9999999511 \cdots \qquad c_3^* = 0.0999999976 \cdots$$

so that 14-decimal-digit floating-point arithmetic for this 3×3 system gives only about 8 correct decimal digits. If we round the $(3,3)$ entry of A to 73,393.6 and repeat the calculation, the computed answer turns out to be an astonishing

$$c_1^* = 6.035 \cdots \qquad c_2^* = -1.243 \cdots \qquad c_3^* = 0.0639 \cdots$$

Similarly, if all calculations are carried out in seven-decimal-digit floating-point arithmetic, the results are

$$c_1^* = 8.492 \cdots \qquad c_2^* = -1.712 \cdots \qquad c_3^* = 0.0863 \cdots$$

This example should make clear that it can be dangerous to rush into solving the normal equations without some preliminary work. This work should consist in choosing the $\phi_i(x)$ carefully.

A seemingly simple way to avoid the condition problem is to choose the $\phi_i(x)$ to be **orthogonal** on the points $x_1, \ldots, x_N$, that is, so that

$$\phi_j^T \phi_i = \sum_{n=1}^{N} \phi_i(x_n)\phi_j(x_n) = 0 \qquad \text{whenever } i \neq j \qquad (6.24)$$

For if (6.24) holds, Eqs. (6.23) reduce to

$$c_i^* \phi_i^T \phi_i = \mathbf{f}^T \phi_i \qquad i = 1, \ldots, k \qquad (6.25)$$

whose solution offers, offhand, no further difficulty.

Of course, this nice way out of the condition problem merely replaces one problem by another, for now we have to get hold of orthogonal functions. If we also want the ϕ_i's to be polynomials, it is possible to construct such orthogonal polynomial functions quite efficiently using a three-term recurrence relation valid for sequences of orthogonal polynomials. This we discuss in Secs. 6.3 and 6.4. If, as is often the case in practice, $f(x)$ cannot be assumed to be of polynomial form, other means for constructing appropriate orthogonal functions have to be used. One such technique, the modified Gram-Schmidt algorithm, is discussed in some texts (see, for example, Rice [17]). Alternatively, one has to be satisfied with choosing $\phi_1(x), \ldots, \phi_k(x)$ to be "nearly" orthogonal. This vague term is meant to describe the fact that the coefficient matrix of (6.23) for such $\phi_i(x)$ is "nearly" diagonal, e.g., diagonally dominant. If the points

$x_1, \ldots, x_N$ are distributed nearly uniformly in some interval (a, b), then $\phi_1(x), \ldots, \phi_k(x)$ tend to be "nearly" orthogonal if each $\phi_i(x)$ changes sign in (a, b) one more time than does $\phi_{i-1}(x)$ (see Exercise 6.2-3).

EXERCISES

6.2-1 Calculate the least-squares approximation to the data plotted in Fig. 6.5 by functions of the form

$$F(x) = c_1 + c_2 x + c_3 \sin[123(x - 1)]$$

by solving the appropriate normal equations. Do you feel that this approximation represents all the information about $f(x)$ contained in the data? Why?

6.2-2 Derive the normal equations for the best c_1^*, c_2^*, in case

$$F(x) = F(x; c_1, c_2) = c_1 e^{c_2 x}$$

following the argument given in the text. Are these normal equations still linear?

6.2-3 Repeat all the calculations in Example 6.5 using the functions

$$\phi_1(x) = 1 \qquad \phi_2(x) = x - 10.5 \qquad \phi_3(x) = (x - 10.3)(x - 10.7)$$

According to the last paragraph of this section, the normal equations should now be much better conditioned. Are they?

*6.3 ORTHOGONAL POLYNOMIALS

In this section, we discuss briefly some pertinent properties and specific examples of sequences of orthogonal polynomials. Although our immediate motivation for this discussion comes from the problem of least-squares approximation by polynomials (to be discussed in the next section), we have use for orthogonal polynomials in different contexts later on, e.g., in Sec. 7.3. In preparation for that section, we use now a notion of orthogonality of functions which is somewhat more general than the one introduced in Sec. 6.2.

In what is to follow, let (a, b) be a given interval and let $w(x)$ be a given function defined (at least) on (a, b) and positive there. Further, we define the **scalar product**

$$\langle g, h \rangle$$

of any two functions $g(x)$ and $h(x)$ [defined on (a, b)] in one of two ways:

$$\langle g, h \rangle = \int_a^b g(x) h(x) w(x) \, dx \tag{6.26}$$

or

$$\langle g, h \rangle = \sum_{n=1}^{N} g(x_n) h(x_n) w(x_n) \tag{6.27}$$

In the first case, we assume that the integral exists (at least as an improper integral) for all functions $g(x)$ and $h(x)$ of interest; in the second case, we assume that we have given N points $x_1, \ldots, x_N$ all in the interval (a, b) which are considered fixed during the discussion. Note that, with $w(x) \equiv 1$, (6.27) reduces to the scalar product $\mathbf{g}^T\mathbf{h} = \mathbf{h}^T\mathbf{g}$ of two functions which appears in the discussion of least-squares approximation in Sec. 6.2.

With the scalar product of two functions defined, we say that the two functions $g(x)$ and $h(x)$ are **orthogonal** (to each other) in case

$$\langle g, h \rangle = 0$$

It is easy to verify, for example, that the functions $g(x) \equiv 1$, $h(x) = x$ are orthogonal if the scalar product is

$$\langle g, h \rangle = \int_{-1}^{1} g(x)h(x) \, dx$$

They are also orthogonal if the scalar product is

$$\langle g, h \rangle = \sum_{n=-10}^{10} g(n)h(n)$$

or if the scalar product is

$$\langle g, h \rangle = \int_{-1}^{1} \frac{g(x)h(x)}{(1 - x^2)^{1/2}} \, dx$$

The functions $g(x) = \sin nx$, $h(x) = \sin mx$ are orthogonal, for n and m integers, if

$$\langle g, h \rangle = \int_{0}^{2\pi} g(x)h(x) \, dx$$

and $n \neq m$, as are the functions $g(x) = \sin nx$, $h(x) = \cos mx$.

Further, we say that $P_0(x)$, $P_1(x)$, $P_2(x)$, $\ldots$ is a (finite or infinite) **sequence of orthogonal polynomials** provided the $P_i(x)$ are all orthogonal to each other and each $P_i(x)$ is a polynomial of exact degree i. In other words,

(i) For each i, $P_i(x) = \alpha_i x^i + $ a polynomial of degree $< i$, with $\alpha_i \neq 0$

(ii) Whenever $i \neq j$, then $\langle P_i, P_j \rangle = 0$

The functions

$$P_0(x) \equiv 1 \qquad P_1(x) = x \qquad P_2(x) = 3x^2 - 1$$

for instance, form a sequence of three orthogonal polynomials if

$$\langle g, h \rangle = \int_{-1}^{1} g(x)h(x) \, dx$$

We mentioned earlier that $\langle P_0, P_1 \rangle = 0$. Also

$$\langle P_0, P_2 \rangle = \int_{-1}^{1} 1(3x^2 - 1) \, dx = x^3 - x \Big|_{-1}^{1} = 0$$

while $\qquad \langle P_1, P_2 \rangle = \int_{-1}^{1} x(3x^2 - 1)\, dx = \frac{3}{4}x^4 - \frac{1}{2}x^2 \Big|_{-1}^{1} = 0$

Let $P_0(x), P_1(x), \ldots, P_k(x)$ be a finite sequence of orthogonal polynomials. Then the following facts can be proved:

Property 1 If $p(x)$ is *any* polynomial of degree $\leq k$, then $p(x)$ can be written

$$p(x) = d_0 P_0(x) + d_1 P_1(x) + \cdots + d_k P_k(x) \qquad (6.28)$$

with the coefficients $d_0, \ldots, d_k$ uniquely determined by $p(x)$. Specifically if

$$p(x) = a_k x^k + \text{a polynomial of degree} < k$$

and if the leading coefficient of $P_k(x)$ is α_k, then

$$d_k = \frac{a_k}{\alpha_k}$$

This property follows from (i), above, by induction on k. For the example above, we can write the general polynomial of degree ≤ 2,

$$p_2(x) = a_0 + a_1 x + a_2 x^2$$

as $\qquad p_2(x) = \left(a_0 + \frac{a_2}{3} \right) P_0(x) + a_1 P_1(x) + \frac{a_2}{3} P_2(x)$

By combining Property 1 with (ii), one gets Property 2.

Property 2 If $p(x)$ is a polynomial of degree $< k$, then $p(x)$ is orthogonal to $P_k(x)$, that is,

$$\langle p, P_k \rangle = 0$$

If in the example above we take $p(x) = 1 + x$, we find that

$$\langle p, P_2 \rangle = \int_{-1}^{1} (1 + x)(3x^2 - 1)\, dx = \frac{3}{4}x^4 + x^3 - \frac{1}{2}x^2 - x \Big|_{-1}^{1} = 0$$

This rather innocuous property has several important consequences.

Property 3 If the scalar product is given by (6.26), then $P_k(x)$ has k simple real zeros, all of which lie in the interval (a, b); that is, $P_k(x)$ is of the form

$$P_k(x) = \alpha_k(x - \xi_{1,k})(x - \xi_{2,k}) \cdots (x - \xi_{k,k}) \qquad (6.29)$$

for certain k distinct points $\xi_{1,k}, \ldots, \xi_{k,k}$ in (a, b).

For our example,

$$P_0(x) \equiv \alpha_0 \equiv 1 \qquad P_1(x) = \alpha_1(x - \xi_{1,1}) = 1 \cdot (x - 0)$$

$$P_2(x) = \alpha_2(x - \xi_{1,2})(x - \xi_{2,2}) = 3\left(x + \frac{1}{\sqrt{3}} \right)\left(x - \frac{1}{\sqrt{3}} \right)$$

A simple proof of Property 3 goes as follows: Let $k > 0$ and let $\xi_{1,k}, \ldots, \xi_{r,k}$ be all the points in the interval (a, b) at which $P_k(x)$ changes sign. We claim that then

$$r \geq k$$

For if r were less than k, then, with $\bar{x} \in (\max_i \xi_{i,k}, b)$,

$$p(x) = P_k(\bar{x})(x - \xi_{1,k})(x - \xi_{2,k}) \cdots (x - \xi_{r,k})$$

would be a polynomial of degree $< k$ which, at every point in (a, b), has the same sign as $P_k(x)$. Hence, on the one hand, by Property 3,

$$\int_a^b p(x) P_k(x) w(x) \, dx = \langle p, P_k \rangle = 0$$

while on the other hand,

$$p(x) P_k(x) w(x) > 0 \qquad \text{for all } x \in (a, b) \text{ except } x = \xi_{1,k}, \ldots, \xi_{r,k}$$

and these two facts certainly contradict each other. Consequently, we must have $r \geq k$: that is, $P_k(x)$ must change sign in (a, b) at least k times. But since $P_k(x)$ is a polynomial of degree k and each $\xi_{i,k}$ is a zero of $P_k(x)$, r cannot be bigger than k (see Sec. 2.1); therefore r must equal k, that is, the k distinct points $\xi_{i,k}$, $i = 1, \ldots, k$, are exactly the zeros of $P_k(x)$.

One proves similarly that (6.29) holds when the scalar product is given by (6.27), provided there are at least k distinct points among the x_n's.

Property 4 The orthogonal polynomials satisfy a **three-term recurrence relation**. If we set

$$A_i = \frac{\alpha_{i+1}}{\alpha_i} \qquad \text{all } i$$

$$P_{-1}(x) \equiv 0$$

and if

$$S_i = \langle P_i, P_i \rangle$$

is not zero for $i = 0, \ldots, k - 1$, then this recurrence relation can be written

$$P_{i+1}(x) = A_i(x - B_i)P_i(x) - C_i P_{i-1}(x) \qquad i = 0, 1, \ldots, k - 1$$

$$(6.30)$$

where

$$B_i = \frac{\langle xP_i(x), P_i(x) \rangle}{S_i} \qquad i = 1, \ldots, k - 1$$

and

$$C_i = \begin{cases} \text{arbitrary} & i = 0 \\ \dfrac{A_i S_i}{A_{i-1} S_{i-1}} & i > 0 \end{cases}$$

This property can be used to generate sequences of orthogonal polynomials (provided the numbers S_i and B_i can be calculated and the S_i are not zero). In such a process, one usually chooses the leading coefficients α_i, or equivalently, the numbers A_i, so that the resulting sequence is particularly simple in some sense.

Table 6.2

k	$P_k(x)$
0	1
1	x
2	$(3/2)(x^2 - 1/3)$
3	$(5/2)[x^3 - (3/5)x]$
4	$(35/8)[x^4 - (6/7)x^2 + 3/35]$

Example 6.6: Legendre polynomials If the scalar product is given by

$$\langle g, h \rangle = \int_{-1}^{1} g(x)h(x)\,dx$$

then the resulting orthogonal polynomials are associated with Legendre's name. Starting with

$$P_0(x) \equiv 1$$

one gets $\qquad S_0 = \int_{-1}^{1} 1\,dx = 2 \qquad S_0 B_0 = \int_{-1}^{1} x \cdot 1\,dx = 0$

Hence, from Property 4, with the choice $A_i = 1$, all i, we get

$$P_1(x) = x$$

Further,

$$S_1 = \int_{-1}^{1} x^2\,dx = \tfrac{2}{3} \qquad S_1 B_1 = \int_{-1}^{1} x \cdot x^2\,dx = 0 \qquad C_1 = \frac{S_1}{S_0} = \tfrac{1}{3}$$

so, again by Property 4,

$$P_2(x) = x^2 - \tfrac{1}{3}$$

Again,

$$S_2 = \int_{-1}^{1} \left(x^2 - \tfrac{1}{3}\right)^2 dx = \tfrac{8}{45} \qquad S_2 B_2 = \int_{-1}^{1} x\left(x^2 - \tfrac{1}{3}\right)^2 dx = 0 \qquad C_2 = \tfrac{4}{15}$$

so $\qquad P_3(x) = x^3 - \tfrac{3}{5}x$

It is customary to normalize the Legendre polynomials so that

$$P_k(1) = 1 \qquad \text{all } k$$

With this normalization, the coefficients in the recurrence relation become

$$A_k = \frac{2k + 1}{k + 1} \qquad B_k = 0 \qquad C_k = \frac{k}{k + 1} \qquad k = 0, 1, 2, \ldots$$

so that $\qquad P_{k+1}(x) = \dfrac{(2k + 1)xP_k(x) - kP_{k-1}(x)}{k + 1}$

Table 6.2 gives the first few Legendre polynomials.

Example 6.7: Chebyshev polynomials If the scalar product is given by

$$\langle g, h \rangle = \int_{-1}^{1} \frac{g(x)h(x)}{(1 - x^2)^{1/2}}\,dx$$

then one gets the Chebyshev polynomials $T_k(x)$ introduced in Sec. 6.1. We already derived there their recurrence relation

$$T_{k+1}(x) = 2xT_k(x) - T_{k-1}(x) \qquad k = 1, 2, \ldots$$

from their defining relation

$$T_k(\cos \theta) \equiv \cos k\theta$$

Example 6.8: Hermite polynomials $H_k(x)$ result when the scalar product

$$\langle g, h \rangle = \int_{-\infty}^{\infty} g(x)h(x)e^{-x^2} dx$$

is used. With the customary normalization, these polynomials satisfy the recurrence relation

$$H_{k+1}(x) = 2xH_k(x) - 2kH_{k-1}(x) \qquad k = 0, 1, 2, \ldots$$

The first few Hermite polynomials are given in Table 6.3.

Table 6.3

k	H(x)
0	1
1	2x
2	$4x^2 - 2$
3	$8x^3 - 12x$
4	$16x^4 - 48x^2 + 12$

Example 6.9 Generalized Laguerre polynomials $L_k^\alpha(x)$ are associated with the scalar product

$$\langle g, h \rangle = \int_0^{\infty} g(x)h(x)x^\alpha e^{-x} dx$$

The coefficients for the recurrence relation are

$$A_k = -\frac{1}{k+1} \qquad B_k = 2k + \alpha + 1 \qquad C_k = \frac{k+\alpha}{k+1}$$

We leave the generation of the first five Laguerre polynomials (with $\alpha = 0$) to the student (see Exercise 6.3-1).

The last two examples are of particular importance in the numerical quadrature over semi-infinite or infinite intervals (see Sec. 7.3).

We conclude this section with the discussion of an algorithm for the evaluation of a polynomial given in terms of orthogonal polynomials. Suppose that $P_0(x), P_1(x), \ldots, P_k(x)$ is a finite sequence of orthogonal polynomials, and suppose that we have given a polynomial $p(x)$ of degree $\leq k$ in terms of the $P_i(x)$, that is, we know the coefficients $d_0, \ldots, d_k$ so that

$$p(x) = d_0 P_0(x) + d_1 P_1(x) + \cdots + d_k P_k(x) \tag{6.31}$$

In evaluating $p(x)$ at a particular point $\bar{x}$, we can make use of the three-term recurrence relation (6.30) for the $P_i(x)$ as follows: By (6.30),

$$P_k(\bar{x}) = A_{k-1}(\bar{x} - B_{k-1})P_{k-1}(\bar{x}) - C_{k-1}P_{k-2}(\bar{x})$$

Therefore

$$p(\bar{x}) = d_0 P_0(\bar{x}) + \cdots + d_{k-3}P_{k-3}(\bar{x}) + (d_{k-2} - d_k C_{k-1})P_{k-2}(\bar{x})$$
$$+ \left[d_{k-1} + d_k A_{k-1}(\bar{x} - B_{k-1}) \right] P_{k-1}(\bar{x})$$

or with the abbreviations

$$\bar{d}_k = d_k \qquad \bar{d}_{k-1} = d_{k-1} + \bar{d}_k A_{k-1}(\bar{x} - B_{k-1})$$

we have

$$p(\bar{x}) = d_0 P_0(\bar{x}) + \cdots + d_{k-3}P_{k-3}(\bar{x}) + \left(d_{k-2} - \bar{d}_k C_{k-1} \right)P_{k-2}(\bar{x})$$
$$+ \bar{d}_{k-1}P_{k-1}(\bar{x}) \quad (6.32)$$

Again by (6.30),

$$P_{k-1}(\bar{x}) = A_{k-2}(\bar{x} - B_{k-2})P_{k-2}(\bar{x}) - C_{k-2}P_{k-3}(\bar{x})$$

and substituting this into (6.32), we get

$$p(\bar{x}) = d_0 P_0(\bar{x}) + \cdots + \left(d_{k-3} - \bar{d}_{k-1}C_{k-2} \right)P_{k-3}(\bar{x}) + \bar{d}_{k-2}P_{k-2}(\bar{x})$$

where we have used the abbreviation

$$\bar{d}_{k-2} = d_{k-2} + \bar{d}_{k-1}A_{k-2}(\bar{x} - B_{k-2}) - \bar{d}_k C_{k-1}$$

Proceeding in this fashion, we calculate sequentially

$$\bar{d}_j = d_j + \bar{d}_{j+1}A_j(\bar{x} - B_j) - \bar{d}_{j+2}C_{j+1} \qquad j = k - 2, \ldots, 0$$

getting finally that $p(\bar{x}) = \bar{d}_0 P_0(\bar{x}) = \bar{d}_0 \alpha_0$

Algorithm 6.1 Nested multiplication for orthogonal polynomials Given the coefficients $A_j, B_j, C_j, j = 0, \ldots, k - 1$, for the three-term recurrence relation (6.30) satisfied by the orthogonal polynomials $P_0(x), \ldots, P_k(x)$; given also the constant $\alpha_0 = P_0(x)$, the coefficients $d_0, \ldots, d_k$ of $p(x)$ in (6.31), and a point $\bar{x}$.

$$\bar{d}_k := d_k$$

If $k = 0$, then EXIT

$$\bar{d}_{k-1} := d_{k-1} + \bar{d}_k A_{k-1}(\bar{x} - B_{k-1})$$

If $k = 1$, then EXIT

For $j = k - 2, k - 3, \ldots, 0$, do:

$$\quad \bar{d}_j := d_j + \bar{d}_{j+1}A_j(\bar{x} - B_j) - \bar{d}_{j+2}C_{j+1}$$

Then, on EXIT, $p(\bar{x})$ is given by

$$p(\bar{x}) = \bar{d}_0 P_0(x)$$

FORTRAN implementations of this algorithm have to contend with the minor difficulty that some FORTRAN dialects do not allow zero subscripts. Also, storage requirements and the number of necessary calculations vary from one set of orthogonal polynomials to another.

Example 6.10 Write a FORTRAN implementation of Algorithm 6.1 in case the orthogonal polynomials are the Chebyshev polynomials.

In this case, the A_i, B_i, C_i need not be stored in arrays since they do not depend on i. Also, the calculation of $\bar{d}_j$ requires only $\bar{d}_{j+1}$ and $\bar{d}_{j+2}$; hence it is not necessary to store the full array $\bar{d}_i$, $i = 0, \ldots, k$.

The FORTRAN FUNCTION CHEB below solves the given problem. NTERMS is the number of terms in $p(x)$; that is, $p(x)$ is of degree $\leq$ NTERMS $-$ 1. Both NTERMS and the coefficients

$$D(i) = d_{i-1} \qquad i = 1, \ldots, \text{NTERMS}$$

are assumed to be in the labeled COMMON POLY.

```
      REAL FUNCTION CHEB (X)
C    RETURNS THE VALUE OF THE POLYNOMIAL OF DEGREE .LT. NTERMS WHOSE
C    CHEBYSHEV COEFFICIENTS ARE CONTAINED IN  D .
      INTEGER NTERMS,   K
      REAL D,X,    PREV,PREV2,TWOX
      COMMON /POLY/ NTERMS,D(30)
      IF ( NTERMS .EQ. 1) THEN
         CHEB = D(1)
                                          RETURN
      END IF
      TWOX = 2.*X
      PREV2 = 0.
      PREV = D(NTERMS)
      IF (NTERMS .GT. 2) THEN
         DO 10 K=NTERMS-1,2,-1
            CHEB = D(K) + TWOX*PREV - PREV2
            PREV2 = PREV
            PREV = CHEB
   10    CONTINUE
      END IF
      CHEB = D(1) + X*PREV - PREV2
                                          RETURN
      END
```

EXERCISES

6.3-1 Using the appropriate recurrence relation, generate the first five Laguerre polynomials (for $\alpha = 0$).

6.3-2 Find the zeros of the Legendre polynomials $P_2(x)$, $P_3(x)$, and $P_4(x)$.

6.3-3 Find the zeros of the Hermite polynomials $H_2(x)$, $H_3(x)$, $H_4(x)$.

6.3-4 Express the polynomial $p(x) = x^4 + 2x^3 + x^2 + 2x + 1$ as a sum of Legendre polynomials.

6.3-5 Verify directly that the Legendre polynomial $P_3(x)$ is orthogonal to any polynomial of degree 2.

6.3-6 Prove that if $P_k(x)$ is the Legendre polynomial of degree k, then

$$\int_{-1}^{1} [P_k(x)]^2 \, dx = \frac{2}{2k+1}$$

Use the three-term recurrence relation satisfied by Legendre polynomials.

6.3-7 Let $P_0(x), P_1(x), \ldots$ be a sequence of orthogonal polynomials and let $x_0, \ldots, x_k$ be the $k + 1$ distinct zeros of $P_{k+1}(x)$. Prove that the Lagrange polynomials $l_i(x) = \amalg_{j \neq i}(x - x_j)/(x_i - x_j)$, $i = 0, \ldots, k$, for these points are orthogonal to each other. [*Hint:* Show that for $i \neq j$, $l_i(x)l_j(x) = P_{k+1}(x)g(x)$, where $g(x)$ is some polynomial of degree $\leq k$.]

*6.4 LEAST-SQUARES APPROXIMATION BY POLYNOMIALS

In this section, we discuss the use of sequences of orthogonal polynomials for the calculation of polynomial (weighted) least-squares approximations.

Let $f(x)$ be a function defined on some interval (a, b), and suppose that we wish to approximate $f(x)$ on (a, b) by a polynomial of degree $\leq k$. If we measure the difference between $f(x)$ and $p(x)$ by

$$\langle f(x) - p(x), f(x) - p(x) \rangle = \begin{cases} \int_a^b [f(x) - p(x)]^2 w(x) \, dx, \text{ or} \\ \sum_{n=1}^{N} [f(x_n) - p(x_n)]^2 w(x_n) \end{cases}$$

(6.33)

where the scalar product is given by (6.26) or (6.27), then it is natural to seek a polynomial of degree $\leq k$ for which (6.33) is as small as possible. Such a polynomial is called a **(weighted) least-squares approximation to** $f(x)$ **by polynomials of degree** $\leq k$.

The problem of finding such a polynomial is solved in Sec. 6.2 for the particular case that the scalar product is given by (6.27) with the weight function $w(x) \equiv 1$. In the general case, one proceeds as follows: Suppose that we can find, for the chosen scalar product, a sequence $P_0(x), \ldots, P_k(x)$ of orthogonal polynomials. By Property 1 of such sequences (see Sec. 6.3), every polynomial $p(x)$ of degree $\leq k$ can be written in the form

$$p(x) = d_0 P_0(x) + \cdots + d_k P_k(x)$$

for suitable coefficients $d_0, \ldots, d_k$. Substituting this into (6.33), it follows that we want to minimize

$$E(d_0, \ldots, d_k) = \langle f(x) - d_0 P_0(x) - \cdots - d_k P_k(x),$$
$$f(x) - d_0 P_0(x) - \cdots - d_k P_k(x) \rangle$$

over all possible choices of $d_0, \ldots, d_k$. Proceeding as in Sec. 6.2, one shows that "best" coefficients $d_0^*, \ldots, d_k^*$ must satisfy the **normal equations**

$$d_0^* \langle P_0, P_i \rangle + d_1^* \langle P_1, P_i \rangle + \cdots + d_k^* \langle P_k, P_i \rangle = \langle f, P_i \rangle \qquad i = 0, \ldots, k$$

which, because of the orthogonality of the $P_j(x)$, reduce to

$$d_i^* \langle P_i, P_i \rangle = \langle f, P_i \rangle \qquad i = 0, \ldots, k$$

Hence, if

$$S_i = \langle P_i, P_i \rangle \qquad i = 0, \ldots, k$$

are all nonzero, then the best coefficients are simply given by

$$d_i^* = \frac{\langle f, P_i \rangle}{S_i} \qquad i = 0, \ldots, k \tag{6.34}$$

Example 6.11 Calculate the polynomial of degree ≤ 3 which minimizes

$$\int_{-1}^{1} [e^x - p(x)]^2 \, dx$$

over all polynomials $p(x)$ of degree ≤ 3.

In this case, $f(x) = e^x$, and the scalar product is given by

$$\langle g, h \rangle = \int_{-1}^{1} g(x) h(x) \, dx$$

From Example 6.6, we find the orthogonal polynomials for this scalar product to be the Legendre polynomials. Using Table 6.2 of these polynomials, we calculate

$$\langle f, P_0 \rangle = \int_{-1}^{1} e^x \, dx = e - \frac{1}{e}$$

$$\langle f, P_1 \rangle = \int_{-1}^{1} e^x x \, dx = \frac{2}{e}$$

$$\langle f, P_2 \rangle = \tfrac{3}{2} \int_{-1}^{1} e^x \left(x^2 - \tfrac{1}{3} \right) dx = e - \frac{7}{e}$$

$$\langle f, P_3 \rangle = \tfrac{5}{2} \int_{-1}^{1} e^x \left(x^3 - \tfrac{3}{5} x \right) dx = -5e + \frac{37}{e}$$

One can show that, for the Legendre polynomials (see Exercise 6.3-6),

$$S_i = \langle P_i, P_i \rangle = \frac{2}{2i + 1} \qquad \text{all } i$$

so that $S_0 = 2$, $S_1 = \tfrac{2}{3}$, $S_2 = \tfrac{2}{5}$, $S_3 = \tfrac{2}{7}$. Using (6.34) to calculate the d_i^* and using $e = 2.71828183$, we find that the least-squares approximation to e^x on $(-1, 1)$ by cubic polynomials is

$$p^*(x) = 1.175201194 P_0(x) + 1.103638324 P_1(x) + 0.3578143506 P_2(x)$$
$$+ 0.07045563367 P_3(x)$$

If we replace $P_i(x)$ by their equivalent expressions in powers of x using Table 6.2 and rearrange, we obtain

$$p^*(x) = 0.9962940183 + 0.9979548730 x + 0.5367215260 x^2 + 0.1761390842 x^3$$

On $(-1, 1)$, this polynomial has a maximum deviation from e^x of about 0.011.

If the appropriate orthogonal polynomials cannot be found in tables, one has to generate them. This can be done with the aid of the three-term recurrence relation (6.30). We now give an algorithmic description of this technique for the practically important case when the scalar product is

$$\langle g, h \rangle = \sum_{n=1}^{N} g(x_n)h(x_n)w(x_n) \tag{6.35}$$

with $x_1, \ldots, x_N$ certain fixed points in (a, b).

Algorithm 6.2: Generation of orthogonal polynomials For simplicity, we elect to get all orthogonal polynomials with leading coefficient 1, so that

$$A_i = \alpha_i = 1 \qquad \text{all } i$$

Step 0 Set $P_0(x) \equiv 1$. Further, calculate

$$S_0 = \langle P_0, P_0 \rangle = \sum_{n=1}^{N} w(x_n)$$

If $N \geq 1$ and $w(x) > 0$, then S_0 is not zero, and we can go on to calculate

$$P_1(x) = (x - B_0)P_0(x) = x - B_0$$

where, by Property 4 of orthogonal polynomials (see Sec. 6.3),

$$B_0 = \frac{\langle xP_0(x), P_0(x) \rangle}{S_0} = \sum_{n=1}^{N} \frac{x_n w(x_n)}{S_0}$$

With $P_0(x), \ldots, P_j(x)$ already constructed, the general, or jth, step proceeds as follows:

Step j Calculate

$$S_j = \langle P_j, P_j \rangle = \sum_{n=1}^{N} \left[P_j(x_n) \right]^2 w(x_n)$$

Since $P_j(x)$ is a polynomial of exact degree j, S_j can be zero only if no more than j of the points $x_1, \ldots, x_N$ are distinct. Hence, if there are more than j distinct points among the x_n's, we can calculate

$$B_j = \frac{\langle xP_j(x), P_j(x) \rangle}{S_j} = \sum_{n=1}^{N} x_n \left[P_j(x_n) \right]^2 \frac{w(x_n)}{S_j}$$

$$C_j = \frac{S_j}{S_{j-1}}$$

and get the next orthogonal polynomial as

$$P_{j+1}(x) = (x - B_j)P_j(x) - C_j P_{j-1}(x) \tag{6.36}$$

Example 6.12 Solve the least-squares approximation problem of Example 6.5 using orthogonal polynomials.

For this example, $f(x) = 10 - 2x + x^2/10$,

$$x_n = 10 + \frac{n-1}{5} \qquad f_n = f(x_n) \qquad n = 1, \ldots, 6$$

and we seek the polynomial of degree ≤ 2 which minimizes

$$\sum_{n=1}^{6} [f_n - p(x_n)]^2$$

i.e., we are dealing with the scalar product (6.27) with $w(x) \equiv 1$. Following the Algorithm 6.2, we calculate

$$P_0(x) \equiv 1 \qquad \text{hence} \qquad S_0 = \sum_{n=1}^{6} 1 = 6$$

$$B_0 = \sum_{n=1}^{6} \left[10 + \frac{n-1}{5} \right] \bigg/ S_0 = \tfrac{63}{6} = 10.5$$

Therefore

$$P_1(x) = x - 10.5 \qquad S_1 = \sum_{n=1}^{6} \left[\frac{n-1}{5} - 0.5 \right]^2 = 0.7$$

and, as $S_1 \neq 0$, we can go on to calculate $P_2(x)$. We get

$$B_1 = \sum_{n=1}^{6} \frac{[10 + (n-1)/5][(n-1)/5 - 0.5]^2}{S_1} = \frac{7.35}{0.7} = 10.5$$

$$C_1 = \frac{S_1}{S_0} = \frac{0.7}{6} = 0.1166667$$

if we carry seven decimal places and round. This gives

$$P_2(x) = (x - 10.5)^2 - 0.1166667 \qquad S_2 = 0.05973332$$

Next, we calculate the best coefficients d_0^*, d_1^*, d_2^* for the least-squares approximation

$$p^*(x) = d_0^* P_0(x) + d_1^* P_1(x) + d_2^* P_2(x)$$

using (6.34) and continuing with seven-decimal-digit floating-point arithmetic. This gives

$$d_0^* = \sum_{n=1}^{6} \frac{f_n}{6} = 0.03666667$$

$$d_1^* = \sum_{n=1}^{6} \frac{f_n P_1(x_n)}{0.7} = 0.1$$

$$d_2^* = \sum_{n=1}^{6} \frac{f_n P_2(x_n)}{0.05973332} = 0.0999999$$

To compare this with the results computed in Example 6.5, we write $p^*(x)$ in terms of $1, x, x^2$. We get

$$p^*(x) = 0.03666667 + 0.1(x - 10.5)$$
$$+ 0.0999999 \big[(x - 10.5)^2 - 0.1166667 \big]$$
$$= 0.03666667 - 1.05 + 0.0999999(110.25 - 0.1166667)$$
$$+ \big[0.1 + 0.0999999(-21) \big] x + 0.0999999 x^2$$

Hence, computed this way, the c_i^* of Example 6.5 become

$$c_1^* = 9.99998 \cdots \qquad c_2^* = -1.9999998 \cdots \qquad c_3^* = 0.0999999 \cdots$$

By contrast, we obtained in Example 6.5

$$c_1^* = 8.492 \cdots \qquad c_2^* = -1.712 \cdots \qquad c_3^* = 0.0863 \cdots$$

when we solved the normal equations (6.23) for the c_i^*'s directly, using seven-decimal-digit floating-point arithmetic. The results using orthogonal polynomials thus show an impressive improvement in this example.

Incidentally, one would normally not go to the trouble of expressing $p^*(x)$ in terms of the powers of x. Rather, one would use Algorithm 6.1 together with the computed d_i^* whenever $p^*(x)$ is to be evaluated, since one has the coefficients B_i and C_i of the recurrence relation available.

In a FORTRAN implementation, the generation of the orthogonal polynomials and the calculation of the best coefficients d_i^* are best combined into one operation to save storage. For the calculation of d_j^* and of $P_{j+1}(x)$, we only need the numbers

$$P_j(x_n) \qquad P_{j-1}(x_n) \qquad n = 1, \ldots, N$$

Hence, if d_j^* is calculated as soon as $P_j(x_n)$, $n = 1, \ldots, N$, become available, then $P_j(x_n)$, $n = 1, \ldots, N$, can safely be forgotten once $P_{j+1}(x)$ and $P_{j+2}(x)$ have been calculated. Again, there is no need to construct the $P_j(x)$ explicitly in terms of the powers of x, say, since we need only their values at the x_n, $n = 1, \ldots, N$.

```
      SUBROUTINE ORTPOL ( X, F, W, NPOINT, PJM1, PJ, ERROR )
C  CONSTRUCTS THE DISCRETE WEIGHTED LEAST SQUARES APPROXIMATION BY POLY-
C  NOMIALS OF DEGREE .LT. NTERMS  TO GIVEN DATA.
C******  I N P U T  ******
C  (X(I), F(I)), I=1,...,NPOINT  GIVES THE ABSCISSAE AND ORDINATES OF
C              THE GIVEN DATA POINTS TO BE FITTED.
C  W  NPOINT-VECTOR CONTAINING THE POSITIVE WEIGHTS TO BE USED.
C  NPOINT  NUMBER OF DATA POINTS.
C******  I N P U T  VIA COMMON BLOCK  P O L Y  ******
C  NTERMS  GIVES THE ORDER (= DEGREE + 1) OF THE POLYNOMIAL APPROXIMANT.
C******  W O R K  A R E A S  ******
C  PJM1, PJ  ARRAYS OF LENGTH  NPOINT  TO CONTAIN THE VALUES AT THE X'S
C            OF THE TWO MOST RECENT ORTHOGONAL POLYNOMIALS.
C******  O U T P U T  ******
C  ERROR  NPOINT-VECTOR CONTAINING THE ERROR AT THE X'S OF THE POLYNOM-
C         IAL APPROXIMANT TO THE GIVEN DATA.
C******  O U T P U T  VIA COMMON BLOCK  P O L Y  ******
C  B, C  ARRAYS CONTAINING THE COEFFICIENTS FOR THE THREE-TERM RECUR-
C        RENCE WHICH GENERATES THE ORTHOGONAL POLYNOMIALS.
C  D  COEFFICIENTS OF THE POLYNOMIAL APPROXIMANT TO THE GIVEN DATA WITH
C     RESPECT TO THE SEQUENCE OF ORTHOGONAL POLYNOMIALS.
C     THE VALUE OF THE APPROXIMANT AT A POINT  Y  MAY BE OBTAINED BY A
C     REFERENCE TO  ORTVAL(Y) .
C******  M E T H O D  ******
C  THE SEQUENCE  P0, P1, ..., PNTERMS-1  OF ORTHOGONAL POLYNOMIALS WITH
C  RESPECT TO THE DISCRETE INNER PRODUCT
C     (P,Q)  =  SUM ( P(X(I))*Q(X(I))*W(I) , I=1,...,NPOINT)
C  IS GENERATED IN TERMS OF THEIR THREE-TERM RECURRENCE
C        PJP1(X) = (X - B(J+1))*PJ(X) - C(J+1)*PJM1(X) ,
C  AND THE COEFFICIENT  D(J)  OF THE WEIGHTED LEAST SQUARES APPROXIMAT-
C  ION TO THE GIVEN DATA IS OBTAINED CONCURRENTLY AS
C        D(J+1) = (F,PJ)/(PJ,PJ) , J=0,...,NTERMS-1 .
```

```
C   ACTUALLY, IN ORDER TO REDUCE CANCELLATION,  (F,PJ)  IS CALCULATED AS
C   (ERROR,PJ),  WITH  ERROR = F  INITIALLY, AND, FOR EACH  J , ERROR RE-
C   DUCED BY  D(J+1)*PJ  AS SOON AS  D(J+1)  BECOMES AVAILABLE.
C
       INTEGER NPOINT,NTERMS,   I,J
       REAL B,C,D,ERROR(NPOINT),F(NPOINT),PJ(NPOINT),PJM1(NPOINT),
      *     W(NPOINT),X(NPOINT),   P,S(20)
       COMMON /POLY/ NTERMS,B(20),C(20),D(20)
C
       DO 9 J=1,NTERMS
         B(J) = 0.
         D(J) = 0.
     9   S(J) = 0.
       C(1) = 0.
       DO 10 I=1,NPOINT
         D(1) = D(1) + F(I)*W(I)
         B(1) = B(1) + X(I)*W(I)
    10   S(1) = S(1) + W(I)
       D(1) = D(1)/S(1)
       DO 11 I=1,NPOINT
    11   ERROR(I) = F(I) - D(1)
       IF (NTERMS .EQ. 1)                    RETURN
       B(1) = B(1)/S(1)
       DO 12 I=1,NPOINT
         PJM1(I) = 1.
    12   PJ(I) = X(I) - B(1)
C
       DO 30 J=2,NTERMS
         DO 21 I=1,NPOINT
           P = PJ(I)*W(I)
           D(J) = D(J) + ERROR(I)*P
           P = P*PJ(I)
           B(J) = B(J) + X(I)*P
    21     S(J) = S(J) + P
         D(J) = D(J)/S(J)
         DO 22 I=1,NPOINT
    22     ERROR(I) = ERROR(I) - D(J)*PJ(I)
         IF (J .EQ. NTERMS)                  RETURN
         B(J) = B(J)/S(J)
         C(J) = S(J)/S(J-1)
         DO 27 I=1,NPOINT
           P = PJ(I)
           PJ(I) = (X(I) - B(J))*PJ(I) - C(J)*PJM1(I)
    27     PJM1(I) = P
    30 CONTINUE
                                             RETURN
       END
```

The calculation of the $D(j)$ as carried out in this subprogram needs perhaps some clarification. Since $D(j) = d_{j-1}^*$, we get from (6.34) that

$$D(j) = \sum_{n=1}^{\text{NPOINT}} \frac{f_n P_{j-1}(x_n) w(x_n)}{S_{j-1}} \tag{6.37}$$

whereas in the program, $D(j)$ is calculated as

$$D(j) = \sum_{n=1}^{\text{NPOINT}} \frac{\text{ERROR}(n) P_{j-1}(x_n) w(x_n)}{S_{j-1}} \tag{6.38}$$

with

$$\text{ERROR}(n) = f_n - D(1)P_0(x_n) - \cdots - D(j-1)P_{j-2}(x_n) \qquad \text{all } n \tag{6.39}$$

If one substitutes (6.39) into (6.38), one gets

$$D(j)$$

$$= \sum_{n=1}^{\text{NPOINT}} \frac{\left[f_n - D(1)P_0(x_n) - \cdots - D(j-1)P_{j-2}(x_n) \right] P_{j-1}(x_n)w(x_n)}{S_{j-1}}$$

$$= \frac{\sum_n f_n P_{j-1}(x_n)w(x_n) - D(1)\langle P_0, P_{j-1} \rangle - \cdots - D(j-1)\langle P_{j-2}, P_{j-1} \rangle}{S_{j-1}}$$

$$= \sum_n \frac{f_n P_{j-1}(x_n)w(x_n)}{S_{j-1}}$$

since P_{j-1} is orthogonal to $P_0(x), \ldots, P_{j-2}(x)$. Hence, in exact or infinite-precision arithmetic, both (6.37) and (6.38) give the same value for $D(j)$. But in finite-precision arithmetic, (6.38) can be expected to be more accurate for the following reason: Since

$$p_r^*(x) = D(1)P_0(x) + \cdots + D(r+1)P_r(x)$$

is the (weighted) least-squares approximation to $f(x)$ by polynomials of degree $\leq r$, it follows that the numbers

$$\text{ERROR}(n) = f_n - p_{j-1}^*(x_n) \qquad n = 1, \ldots, \text{NPOINT}$$

can be expected to be of smaller size than are the numbers f_n, $n = 1, \ldots, \text{NPOINT}$. Hence the calculation of (6.38) is less likely to produce loss of significance due to subtraction of quantities of nearly equal size than is the calculation of (6.37) (see Exercise 6.4-1).

Example 6.13 Given the values f_n of $f(x) = e^x$ at $x_n = (n-1)/10 - 1$ $(n = 1, \ldots, 21)$, rounded to two places after the decimal point. Try to recover the information about $f(x)$ contained in these data.

We attempt to solve this problem by calculating the polynomial $p_3^*(x)$ which minimizes

$$\sum_{n=1}^{21} [f_n - p_3(x_n)]^2$$

over all polynomials $p_3(x)$ of degree ≤ 3. The following FORTRAN program calculates $p_3^*(x)$ with the aid of the subprogram ORTPOL mentioned earlier, then evaluates $p_3^*(x)$ at the x_n using the FUNCTION ORTVAL, which is based on Algorithm 6.1.

```
C   PROGRAM FOR EXAMPLE 6.13 .
      PARAMETER NPMAX=100
      INTEGER NTERMS,   I,J,NPOINT
      REAL B,C,D,ERROR(NPMAX),F(NPMAX),PJ(NPMAX),PJM1(NPMAX),W(NPMAX)
     *    ,X(NPMAX)
      COMMON /POLY/ NTERMS,B(20),C(20),D(20)
      NPOINT = 21
      DO 1 I=1,NPOINT
        W(I) = 1.
        X(I) = -1. + FLOAT(I-1)/10.
```

```
    1    F(I) = FLOAT(IFIX(EXP(X(I))*100. + .5))/100.
         NTERMS = 4
         CALL ORTPOL( X, F, W, NPOINT, PJM1, PJ, ERROR )
         PRINT 601, (J,B(J),C(J),D(J),J=1,NTERMS)
  601    FORMAT(I2,3E16.8)
         DO 60 I=1,NPOINT
           PJM1(I) = EXP(X(I))
   60      PJ(I) = ORTVAL(X(I))
         PRINT 660, (X(I),F(I),PJ(I),ERROR(I),PJM1(I),I=1,NPOINT)
  660    FORMAT(F5.1,F8.3,F10.5,E13.3,F10.5)
                                                      STOP
         END


         REAL FUNCTION ORTVAL (X)
C  RETURNS THE VALUE AT  X  OF THE POLYNOMIAL OF DEGREE .LT. NTERMS
C  GIVEN BY
C             D(1)*P0(X) + D(2)*P1(X) + ... + D(NTERMS)*PNTERMS-1(X),
C  WITH THE SEQUENCE  P0, P1, ...  OF ORTHOGONAL POLYNOMIALS GENERATED
C  BY THE THREE-TERM RECURRENCE
C  PJP1(X) = (X - B(J+1))*PJ(X) - C(J+1)*PJM1(X) , ALL J .
C
         COMMON /POLY/ NTERMS,B(20),C(20),D(20)
         PREV = 0.
         ORTVAL = D(NTERMS)
         IF (NTERMS .EQ. 1)                           RETURN
         DO 10 K=NTERMS-1,1,-1
           PREV2 = PREV
           PREV = ORTVAL
           ORTVAL = D(K) + (X - B(K))*PREV - C(K+1)*PREV2
   10    CONTINUE
                                                      RETURN
         END
```

Table 6.4 Computer results for Example 6.13

x_n	f_n	$p_3^*(x_n)$	$f_n - p_3^*(x_n)$	$p_4^*(x_n)$	$f_n - p_4^*(x_n)$	e^{x_n}
− 1.0	0.370	0.36387	6.130E − 03	0.37115	− 1.154E − 03	0.36788
− 0.9	0.410	0.40874	1.263E − 03	0.40874	1.263E − 03	0.40657
− 0.8	0.450	0.45481	− 4.806E − 03	0.45097	− 9.719E − 04	0.44933
− 0.7	0.500	0.50315	− 3.148E − 03	0.49804	1.964E − 03	0.49659
− 0.6	0.550	0.55484	− 4.836E − 03	0.55021	− 2.134E − 04	0.54881
− 0.5	0.610	0.61094	− 9.436E − 04	0.60789	2.108E − 03	0.60653
− 0.4	0.670	0.67524	− 2.542E − 03	0.67156	− 1.565E − 03	0.67032
− 0.3	0.740	0.74070	− 7.045E − 04	0.74183	− 1.832E − 03	0.74082
− 0.2	0.820	0.81650	3.497E − 03	0.81940	6.029E − 04	0.81873
− 0.1	0.900	0.90101	− 1.010E − 03	0.90507	− 5.070E − 03	0.90484
0.0	1.000	0.99530	4.710E − 03	0.99976	2.358E − 04	1.00000
0.1	1.110	1.10044	9.558E − 03	1.10450	5.499E − 03	1.10517
0.2	1.220	1.21751	2.490E − 03	1.22040	− 4.045E − 04	1.22140
0.3	1.350	1.34758	2.422E − 03	1.34871	1.294E − 03	1.34986
0.4	1.490	1.49172	− 1.717E − 03	1.49074	− 7.399E − 04	1.49182
0.5	1.650	1.65100	− 1.000E − 03	1.64795	2.052E − 03	1.64872
0.6	1.820	1.82650	− 6.499E − 03	1.82188	− 1.876E − 03	1.82212
0.7	2.010	2.01929	− 9.287E − 03	2.01418	− 4.176E − 03	2.01375
0.8	2.230	2.23044	− 4.368E − 04	2.22660	0.397E − 03	2.22554
0.9	2.460	2.46102	− 1.020E − 03	2.46102	− 1.020E − 03	2.45960
1.0	2.720	2.71211	7.890E − 03	2.71939	6.061E − 04	2.71828

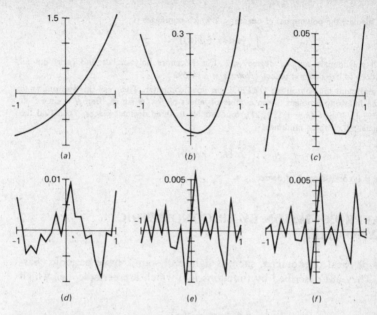

Figure 6.6 The error in the least-squares approximation to the data of Example 6.13 by polynomials of degree (a) zero, (b) one, (c) two, (d) three, (e) four, (f) five.

Table 6.4 gives the results of the calculations which were carried out on a CDC 6500. We have plotted the error, $f_n - p_3^*(x_n)$, in Fig. 6.6d, which shows the error to behave in a somewhat regular fashion, suggesting the $p_3^*(x)$ does not represent *all* the information contained in the given data. We therefore calculate also the least-squares approximation $p_4^*(x)$ to the given data by polynomials of degree ≤ 4. The results are also listed in Table 6.4. The error $f_n - p_4^*(x)$ is plotted in Fig. 6.6e, and is seen to behave quite irregularly. Hence $p_4^*(x)$ can be assumed to represent *all* the information contained in the given data f_n. Increasing the degree of the approximating polynomial any further would only serve to give the approximating function the additional freedom to approximate the noise in the data, too.

EXERCISES

6.4-1 If $f(x) = 6,000 + x$, then any least-squares approximation to $f(x)$ by straight lines is $f(x)$ itself. Calculate the polynomial

$$p_1^*(x) = d_0^* + d_1^* x$$

which minimizes

$$\sum_{n=-2}^{2} [f(n) - p_1(n)]^2$$

Note that 1 and x are already orthogonal, so that one merely has to calculate d_0^* and d_1^*. Show the difference between (6.37) and (6.38) by calculating d_1^* both ways, using four-decimal-digit floating-point arithmetic.

6.4-2 Calculate the polynomial of degree ≤ 2 which minimizes

$$\int_{-1}^{1} [\sin \pi x - p(x)]^2 \, dx$$

over all polynomials $p(x)$ of degree ≤ 2. Use Legendre polynomials and carry out all calculations to five decimal places. (*Note:* $\pi = 3.141593$.)

6.4-3 Implement the subroutine ORTPOL on your computer. Then use this subroutine to solve the following problem. From a table of values of $f(x) = \sin \pi x$, find $f_n = \sin \pi x_n$ at $x_n = (n - 1)/10 - 1$ ($n = 1, \ldots, 21$), rounded off to three decimal places. Then find the polynomial $p_4^*(x)$ which minimizes

$$\sum_{n=1}^{21} [f_n - p_4(x_n)]^2$$

over all polynomials $p_4(x)$ of degree ≤ 4.

*6.5 APPROXIMATION BY TRIGONOMETRIC POLYNOMIALS

Many physical phenomena, such as light and sound, have periodic character. They are described by functions $f(x)$ which are **periodic**, i.e., which satisfy

$$f(x + \tau) = f(x)$$

for all x and some fixed number τ, the **period** of the function. Since the only periodic polynomials are the constant functions, one has to use other function classes for the effective approximation of periodic functions, and the trigonometric polynomials offer themselves as an appropriate alternative.

A **trigonometric polynomial of order** n is, by definition, any function of the form

$$p(x) = a_0/2 + \sum_{j=1}^{n} \left[a_j \cos jx + b_j \sin jx \right] \tag{6.40}$$

with $a_0, \ldots, a_n$ and $b_1, \ldots, b_n$ real or complex constants. Such a trigonometric polynomial is 2π-periodic. We would therefore have to make some adjustment when approximating a τ-periodic function $f(x)$ with $\tau \neq 2\pi$. We agree to consider in such a case the 2π-periodic function $g(x) = f(\tau x/(2\pi))$. Then, having constructed a trigonometric polynomial approximation $p(x)$ to $g(x)$, we obtain from it a τ-periodic approximation for $f(x)$ in the form $p(2\pi x/\tau)$. With this, we will assume from now on that the function $f(x)$ to be approximated is already 2π-periodic.

As it turns out, it is often more convenient to write trigonometric polynomials of order n in the equivalent complex form

$$p(x) = \sum_{j=-n}^{n} c_j e^{ijx} \tag{6.41}$$

Here, and for the remainder of this section and the next, the symbol i stands for the **imaginary unit**,

$$i = \sqrt{-1}$$

and the connection between (6.40) and (6.41) is provided by **Euler's formula**

$$e^{ix} = \cos x + i \sin x \tag{6.42}$$

(a proof of which can be found in Exercise 1.7-9). From Euler's formula, we find [with $\cos(-jx) = \cos jx$, $\sin(-jx) = -\sin jx$] that

$$\sum_{j=-n}^{n} c_j e^{ijx} = \sum_{j=-n}^{n} c_j \big[\cos jx + i \sin jx \big]$$

$$= c_0 + \sum_{j=1}^{n} \Big[(c_j + c_{-j}) \cos jx + i(c_j - c_{-j}) \sin jx \Big]$$

This shows that (6.41) is of the form (6.40) with

$$a_j = c_j + c_{-j} \qquad b_j = i(c_j - c_{-j}) \qquad j = 0, \ldots, n \tag{6.43a}$$

This relationship is easily inverted to give that (6.40) is of the form (6.41) with

$$c_j = (a_j - ib_j)/2 \qquad c_{-j} = (a_j + ib_j)/2 \qquad j = 0, \ldots, n \tag{6.43b}$$

Note that (6.41) represents a real function if and only if it is its own complex conjugate. But, since

$$\overline{\sum_{j=-n}^{n} c_j e^{ijx}} = \sum_{j=-n}^{n} \bar{c}_j e^{-ijx} = \sum_{j=-n}^{n} \bar{c}_{-j} e^{ijx}$$

this means that (6.41) is a real function if and only if

$$c_j = \bar{c}_{-j} \qquad \text{all } j \tag{6.44}$$

Thus, if (6.40) or (6.41) is a real function, then (6.43a) simplifies to

$$a_j = 2 \operatorname{Re} c_j \qquad b_j = -2 \operatorname{Im} c_j \tag{6.45}$$

Approximation by trigonometric polynomials is dominated by the **Fourier series**

$$f(x) \approx \sum_{j=-\infty}^{\infty} \hat{f}(j) e^{ijx} \tag{6.46}$$

with the **Fourier coefficients** $\hat{f}(j)$ calculated by

$$\hat{f}(j) = \frac{1}{2\pi} \int_0^{2\pi} f(x) e^{-ijx} \, dx \tag{6.47}$$

This series converges to $f(x)$ under rather mild conditions [but not for every $f(x)$]. For example, the series converges uniformly if $f(x)$ is continuous with a piecewise-continuous first derivative.

The Fourier series derives from the following fact:

$$\int_0^{2\pi} \overline{e^{ijx}} e^{ikx}\, dx = \int_0^{2\pi} e^{i(k-j)x}\, dx = \begin{cases} \int_0^{2\pi} 1\, dx = 2\pi & \text{if } k = j \\[2mm] \dfrac{1}{i(k-j)} e^{i(k-j)x}\big|_0^{2\pi} = 0 & \text{if } k \neq j \end{cases}$$

This shows that *the functions* $1, e^{\pm ix}, e^{\pm i2x}, \ldots$ *are orthonormal with respect to the scalar or inner product*

$$\langle g, h \rangle = \frac{1}{2\pi} \int_0^{2\pi} \overline{h(x)} g(x)\, dx$$

In other words,

$$\langle e^{ikx}, e^{ijx} \rangle = \begin{cases} 1 & k = j \\ 0 & k \neq j \end{cases}$$

This proves

Theorem 6.4 The partial sum

$$\sum_{j=-n}^{n} \hat{f}(j) e^{ijx}$$

of the Fourier series for $f(x)$ is the best approximation to $f(x)$ by trigonometric polynomials of order n with respect to the norm

$$\|g\| = \|g\|_2 = \left[\frac{1}{2\pi} \int_0^{2\pi} |g(x)|^2\, dx \right]^{1/2}$$

Further, it can be shown that **Parseval's relation**

$$\sum_j |\hat{f}(j)|^2 = \frac{1}{2\pi} \int_0^{2\pi} |f(x)|^2\, dx \tag{6.48}$$

holds.

The Fourier coefficients $\hat{f}(j)$ for the function $f(x)$ are used to "understand" the function $f(x)$, as follows. Suppose $f(x)$ is a real 2π-periodic function. If we think of $f(x)$ as the position at time x of some object moving on a line, then our 2π-periodic function $f(x)$ describes a periodic motion. If now

$$\hat{f}(j) = |\hat{f}(j)| e^{i\theta_j}$$

[the **polar form** for the complex number $\hat{f}(j)$], then we can write the Fourier series for $f(x)$ as

$$f(x) \approx 2 \sum_{j=0}^{\infty} |\hat{f}(j)| \cos(\theta_j + jx)$$

(see Exercise 6.5-7). In this way, we have represented our periodic motion described by $f(x)$ as a sum or superposition of simple harmonic oscillations. The jth such motion,

$$2|\hat{f}(j)| \cos (\theta_j + jx)$$

has **amplitude** $2|\hat{f}(j)|$, **frequency** $j/(2\pi)$, **angular frequency** j, period or **wavelength** $2\pi/j$, and **phase angle** θ_j. The number $|\hat{f}(j)|$ measures the extent to which a simple harmonic motion of angular frequency j is present in the total motion. The entire sequence $|\hat{f}(0)|, |\hat{f}(1)|, \ldots$ (or, perhaps, the sequence of their squares) is called the **power spectrum**, or, simply, the **spectrum** of $f(x)$. Note that, by Parseval's relation (6.48), the spectrum for $f(x)$ is bounded by $\|f\|_2$, but $f(x)$ may have widely differing behavior depending on just how the "total energy" $\|f\|_2^2$ is distributed over the spectrum $|\hat{f}(0)|, |\hat{f}(1)|, \ldots$. A "noisy" function will have sizable $|\hat{f}(j)|$ for larger j, while, for a "smooth" function, the spectrum will decrease rapidly as j increases. See Fig. 6.7.

A favorite method of **smoothing** consists in generating the Fourier coefficients of the given function $f(x)$ from data, **filtering** these coefficients, which means to suppress certain frequencies, usually the high frequencies, in some manner, and then reconstituting the function as a Fourier series with these "purified" or "filtered" coefficients. See Fig. 6.7 for an example.

It can be shown that

$$|\hat{f}(j)| = \mathcal{O}(|j|^{-k-1}) \tag{6.49}$$

in case $f(x)$ has $k - 1$ continuous derivatives (as a periodic function!) and its kth derivative is piecewise continuous (or even only of bounded variation). For example, the "square wave"

$$f(x) = \text{signum} (\sin x) = \begin{cases} 1, & 0 < x < \pi \\ -1 & \pi < x < 2\pi \end{cases}$$

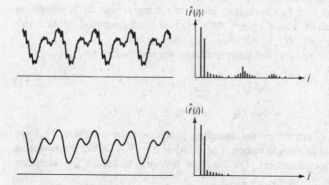

Figure 6.7 Two real 2π-periodic functions and their power spectrum. The second is obtained from the first by suppressing its higher frequencies.

is only piecewise continuous. We therefore expect $|\hat{f}(j)|$ to go to zero as $|j| \to \infty$ no faster than $1/|j|$. This is confirmed by direct calculations:

$$\hat{f}(j) = \frac{1}{2\pi} \int_0^{2\pi} \text{signum} (\sin x) e^{-ijx} \, dx$$

$$= \frac{1}{2\pi} \left\{ \int_0^{\pi} e^{-ijx} \, dx - \int_{\pi}^{2\pi} e^{-ijx} \, dx \right\}$$

$$= \frac{1}{2\pi} \frac{1}{-ij} \{2e^{-ij\pi} + 2\} = i\frac{2}{\pi} \begin{cases} 0 & j \text{ even} \\ 1/j & j \text{ odd} \end{cases}$$

Note that the spectrum for the function

$$f(x) = x$$

decays no faster than $1/j$ even though the function is infinitely often differentiable. This is so because Fourier analysis (as we have described it here) treats this function as a 2π-periodic function whose value for $0 < x < 2\pi$ is x. But this latter function has a jump discontinuity at all multiples of 2π!

It is usually not possible to calculate the Fourier coefficients (6.47) exactly, because the integral cannot be evaluated in closed form or, else, because the function $f(x)$ is not known exactly. In either case, **numerical integration** is used. An introduction to this old and rich subject is given in Chap. 7 in a general context. For the present purpose, the very simple approximation rule

$$\int_0^{2\pi} g(x) \, dx \approx \frac{2\pi}{N} \sum_{n=0}^{N-1} g\left(\frac{2\pi n}{N}\right) \tag{6.50}$$

suffices. This is the composite trapezoid rule (7.49) applied to the present integral, taking into account that the integrand $g(x)$ is 2π-periodic, and therefore, in particular, $g(2\pi) = g(0)$. The rule can be obtained by replacing the 2π-periodic function $g(x)$ under the integral sign by a piecewise-linear interpolant which agrees with $g(x)$ at its equispaced breakpoints $0, \pm 2\pi/N, \pm 2\pi 2/N, \pm 2\pi 3/N, \ldots,$; see Fig. 6.8.

We denote by $\hat{f}_N(j)$ the corresponding approximation to $\hat{f}(j)$:

$$\hat{f}_N(j) = \frac{1}{N} \sum_{n=0}^{N-1} f(x_n) e^{-ix_n} \tag{6.51}$$

with $\qquad x_n = 2\pi n/N \qquad n = 0, \ldots, N-1$

These points x_n are called the **sampling points** and the numbers $f(x_n)$ are the corresponding **sample values**. The number $2\pi/N$ is called the **sampling interval** and its reciprocal, the number $N/(2\pi)$, is called the **sampling frequency**.

How accurate an approximation does $\hat{f}_N(j)$ provide to $\hat{f}(j)$? To answer this question, we now record the fact that the functions $1, e^{\pm ix}, e^{\pm i2x}, \ldots$

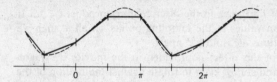

Figure 6.8 A 2π-periodic function (dashed line) and a piecewise-linear interpolant (solid line) on $N = 4$ points per period.

have also certain orthogonality properties with respect to another kind of scalar or inner product, namely the **discrete inner product**

$$\langle g, h \rangle_N = \frac{1}{N} \sum_{n=0}^{N-1} \overline{h(x_n)} g(x_n) \tag{6.52}$$

Explicitly,

$$\langle e^{ikx}, e^{ijx} \rangle_N = \begin{cases} 1 & \text{if } k = j (\text{mod } N) \\ 0 & \text{if } k \neq j (\text{mod } N) \end{cases} \tag{6.53}$$

and a proof of this requires nothing deeper than summing a finite geometric series (see Exercise 6.5-8).

With this, note that

$$\hat{f}_N(j) = \langle f, e^{ijx} \rangle_N$$

Hence, assuming that the Fourier series $\sum \hat{f}(j) e^{ijx}$ converges absolutely to $f(x)$ (this requires nothing more than the existence of the limit $\sum_{-\infty}^{\infty} |\hat{f}(j)|$), we conclude with (6.53) that

$$\hat{f}_N(j) = \langle \sum_{k=-\infty}^{\infty} \hat{f}(k) e^{ikx}, e^{ijx} \rangle_N = \sum_k \hat{f}(k) \langle e^{ikx}, e^{ijx} \rangle_N$$

or

$$\hat{f}_N(j) = \sum_{k=j(\text{mod } N)} \hat{f}(k) \tag{6.54}$$

In words: Our approximate Fourier coefficient $\hat{f}_N(j)$ is made up of all the exact Fourier coefficients $\hat{f}(k)$ whose corresponding function e^{ikx} cannot be distinguished by the inner product (6.52) from the function e^{ijx}.

This phenomenon has been called **aliasing**. If $k = j(\text{mod } N)$, then $k = j + mN$ for some integer m. But then, for any n,

$$e^{ikx_n} = e^{i(j+mN)x_n} = e^{ijx_n} e^{imNx_n}$$

and

$$e^{imNx_n} = e^{(i2\pi)mn} = 1$$

This says that then

$$e^{ikx} = e^{ijx} \qquad \text{for } x = x_n = 2\pi n/N, \text{ and all } n$$

i.e., the two functions e^{ikx} and e^{ijx} agree at every sampling point which is used in the calculation of $\hat{f}_N(j)$, i.e., in the discrete inner product $\langle\ ,\ \rangle_N$. If we only consider function values at the sampling points x_n, all n, then we cannot tell the two functions e^{ikx} and e^{ijx} apart.

A striking example of this effect is provided in the movies by wagon wheels which seem to stand still or even to rotate against the motion of the wagon. Here a periodic motion is sampled every $\frac{1}{20}$ second, and is then identified by the viewer with the *slowest* motion compatible with the evidence.

In the same way, it is customary (when sampling at N uniformly spaced points in $[0, 2\pi)$) to identify the function e^{ijx} with the function $e^{ij'x}$ for which $j' = j(\text{mod } N)$ and whose (angular) frequency $|j'|$ is as small as possible. Note that j' is uniquely defined in this way by j and N, with the following exception: If N is even and j is an odd multiple of $N/2$, then both $N/2$ and $-N/2$ could serve for j'. In this latter case, it has become customary to choose the *average* of the two functions $e^{i(N/2)x}$ and $e^{-i(N/2)x}$, namely the function $\cos(N/2)x$, as the representative of its class.

Correspondingly, although (6.51) provides the approximation $\hat{f}_N(j) = \langle f, e^{ijx} \rangle_N$ to $\hat{f}(j)$ for every j, it is usually taken only as an approximation to $\hat{f}(j)$ with $|j| \leq N/2$. This makes particularly good sense when $f(x)$ is smooth and $|j|$ is much smaller than $N/2$. For then, on combining (6.49) and (6.54), we find that

$$\hat{f}_N(j) = \hat{f}(j) + \mathcal{O}(N^{-k}) \tag{6.55}$$

in case $f(x)$ has $k - 1$ continuous derivatives and its kth derivative is piecewise continuous.

In effect, when we sample a function at N equally spaced points, in the interval $[0, 2\pi)$, the aliasing effect prevents us from seeing periodic phenomena in $f(x)$ with frequencies higher than $(N/2)/(2\pi)$. Put positively, *if we wish to observe a certain periodic phenomenon of frequency ν, then we must sample at a frequency at least as large as 2ν.*

We now discuss briefly the corresponding trigonometric polynomial approximant

$$p(x) = \sum_{|j| < N/2} \hat{f}_N(j)e^{ijx} + \text{Re}\left[\hat{f}_N(N/2)e^{i(N/2)x}\right]$$

Here, the last term is present only when $N/2$ is an integer, i.e., when N is even. But, having mentioned this term for completeness' sake (see Exercise 6.5-11), we will now only discuss the case when N is odd,

$$N = 2n + 1$$

In this case, the $N = 2n + 1$ functions $1, e^{\pm ix}, \ldots, e^{\pm inx}$ are, by (6.53), orthonormal with respect to the discrete inner product $\langle\ ,\ \rangle_N$, i.e.,

$$\langle e^{ikx}, e^{ijx} \rangle_N = \begin{cases} 1 & k = j \\ 0 & k \neq j \end{cases} \qquad k, j = -n, \ldots, n \tag{6.56}$$

By the reasoning of Section 6.2, this implies the following theorem.

Theorem 6.5 For any $m \leq n$, the mth order trigonometric polynomial

$$p_m(x) = \sum_{j=-m}^{m} \hat{f}_N(j) e^{ijx}$$

is the best approximation to $f(x)$ by trigonometric polynomials of order m with respect to the discrete mean-square norm

$$\| g \|_2 = (\langle g, g \rangle_N)^{1/2} = \frac{1}{N} \left(\sum_{j=0}^{N-1} |g(j2\pi/N)|^2 \right)^{1/2}$$

For $m = n$, this means that the nth order trigonometric polynomial

$$p_n(x) = \sum_{j=-n}^{n} \hat{f}_N(j) e^{ijx}$$

interpolates $f(x)$ at the sampling points $x_j = 2\pi j/N$, all j.

If $f(x)$ is a real function, then we can write the interpolating polynomial, according to (6.45), in real form as

$$p_n(x) = a_0/2 + \sum_{m=1}^{n} \left[a_m \cos mx + b_m \sin mx \right] \tag{6.57}$$

with
$$a_m = 2 \operatorname{Re} \hat{f}_N(m) = \frac{2}{N} \sum_{k=0}^{N-1} f(x_k) \cos mx_k \tag{6.58a}$$

$$b_m = -2 \operatorname{Im} \hat{f}_N(m) = \frac{2}{N} \sum_{k=0}^{N-1} f(x_k) \sin mx_k \tag{6.58b}$$

Example 6.14 We construct the trigonometric interpolant of order 1 to $f(x) = \sin x$. Then $N = 3$ and the relevant quantities are:

$$\omega = e^{i2\pi/3} = \cos 2\pi/3 + i \sin 2\pi/3 = \tfrac{1}{2} + i\sqrt{\tfrac{3}{4}}$$

These are important since $\omega^{(m)} := (e^{imx_i}) = (\omega^{mj})$. Further

j	x_j	$f(x_j)$	$w^{(0)}$	$w^{(1)}$	$w^{(-1)}$
0	0	0	1	1	1
1	$2\pi/3$	$\sqrt{\tfrac{3}{4}}$	1	ω	$\omega^{-1} = \bar{\omega}$
2	$4\pi/3$	$-\sqrt{\tfrac{3}{4}}$	1	ω^2	$\omega^{-2} = \bar{\omega}^2$

Now $c_j = \hat{f}_N(j) = (w^{(j)})^H f / M$. Thus $\omega^2 = \omega^{-1} = \bar{\omega}$, we have

$$c_0 = \tfrac{1}{3}\left[0 + \sqrt{3/4} - \sqrt{3/4}\,\right] = 0$$

$$c_1 = \tfrac{1}{3}\left[0 + \sqrt{3/4}\,\omega^{-1} - \sqrt{3.4}\,\omega^{-2}\right] = -\tfrac{1}{3}3/4(\omega - \bar{\omega}) = -\tfrac{2}{3}i\left(\sqrt{3/4}\,\right)^2 = -i/2$$

$$c_{-1} = \tfrac{1}{3}\left[0 + \sqrt{3/4}\,\omega - \sqrt{3/4}\,\omega^2\right] = \bar{c}_1 = i/2$$

Hence $a_1 = 2 \operatorname{Re}(c_1) = c_1 + c_{-1} = 0$, $b_1 = -2 \operatorname{Im}(c_1) = i(c_1 - c_{-1}) = 1$, showing that

$$p_1(x) = 0 + 0 \cdot \cos 1x + 1 \cdot \sin 1x = \sin x$$

as expected.

We mention in passing that it is possible to interpolate uniquely by trigonometric polynomials of order n at any $2n + 1$ distinct points in $[0, 2\pi)$. For the resulting interpolant $p_n(x)$ to $f(x)$, one can show that

$$\|f - p_n\|_\infty \leq \operatorname{const} \operatorname{dist}_\infty(f, \mathring{\pi}_n) \tag{6.59}$$

Here, the max-norm is taken over the interval $[0, 2\pi]$,

$$\|g\|_\infty = \max_{0 \leq x \leq 2\pi} |g(x)|$$

and

$$\operatorname{dist}_\infty(f, \mathring{\pi}_n) = \min_{p \in \mathring{\pi}_n} \|f - p\|_\infty$$

with $p \in \mathring{\pi}_n$ shorthand for the statement "$p(x)$ is a trigonometric polynomial of order n." One shows (6.59) much as the corresponding inequality (6.17) for polynomial interpolation. In particular, the number const depends on the interpolation points. In these terms, the uniformly spaced interpolation points which we have been using here exclusively are **optimal** in that they make the number const in (6.59) as small as possible; see de Boor and Pinkus [39]. The value of this best constant has been calculated by Ehlich and Zeller [38] to be

$$\operatorname{const}_{\text{uniform}} = 1 + \frac{1}{N}\left\{1 + 2\sum_{k=1}^{n} 1/\sin\left(\frac{(2k-1)\pi}{(2n+1)2}\right)\right\} \approx \frac{2}{\pi}\ln N + c \tag{6.60}$$

Thus, for values of n of practical interest, interpolation at uniformly spaced points gives approximations which are not much worse than the best possible uniform approximation from $\mathring{\pi}_n$. There is then usually no need to go through the complicated process of constructing a best uniform approximation, provided the interpolant is easy to obtain. We discuss this last question in the next section.

In this connection, we point out that (6.49) implies

$$\operatorname{dist}_\infty(f, \mathring{\pi}_n) = \mathcal{O}(n^{-k}) \tag{6.61}$$

in case $f(x)$ has k derivatives, with the kth derivative piecewise continuous.

EXERCISES

6.5-1 Calculate the Fourier series for the 2π-periodic function $f(x)$ given by $f(x) = x$ on $[0, 2\pi)$.

6.5-2 Verify that the 2π-periodic function $f(x)$ whose values on $[0, 2\pi)$ are given by

$$f(x) = \begin{cases} (x/\pi)^2 - x/\pi & 0 \leq x \leq \pi \\ (x - \pi)/\pi - ((x - \pi)/\pi)^2 & \pi \leq x \leq 2\pi \end{cases}$$

is continuous and has a continuous first derivative (as a 2π-periodic function), but has jumps in the second derivative. Then construct the spectrum of $f(x)$ and show that it decays like j^{-3} (and no faster) as $j \to \infty$.

6.5-3 Write the Fourier series obtained in Exercise 6.5-2 in terms of sines and cosines. Why would you expect all the a_j's to be zero?

6.5-4 If $f(x)$ is a 2π-periodic function, then so is the function $g_m(x) = f(mx)$, for any integer m. What is the relationship between the $\hat{f}(j)$ and the $\hat{g}_m(j)$?

6.5-5 If $f(x)$ is a 2π-periodic function, then so is the function $g_\alpha(x) = f(x - \alpha)$, for any number α. What is the relationship between the $\hat{f}(j)$ and the $\hat{g}_\alpha(j)$?

6.5-6 Suppose that $f(x)$ is a very smooth function of period τ. But, in converting it to a 2π-periodic function $g(x) = f(\tau x / (2\pi))$, you mistakenly use τ' instead of τ for some $\tau' \neq \tau$. What is the likely effect of this mistake on the computed Fourier coefficients $\hat{g}(j)$?

6.5-7 Prove that, if $f(x)$ is a real function, then $\hat{f}(j)e^{ijx} + \hat{f}(-j)e^{-ijx} = 2|\hat{f}(j)|\cos(\theta_j + jx)$ for an appropriate phase shift θ_j. (*Hint:* Use the fact that any complex number z can be written in **polar form** as $|z|e^{i\theta}$ for an appropriate θ.)

6.5-8 Prove (6.53). (*Hint:* Recall how to sum a geometric series.)

6.5-9 Prove Theorem 6.5.

6.5-10 Derive the addition formulas for $\sin(\alpha + \beta)$ and $\cos(\alpha + \beta)$ from Euler's formula (6.42) and from the law of exponents: $e^{A+B} = e^A e^B$.

6.5-11 Prove that if N is even and $f(x)$ is real, then

$$p(x) = \sum_{|j| < N/2} \hat{f}_N(j)e^{ijx} + \text{Re}\left[\hat{f}(N/2)e^{i(N/2)x} \right]$$

interpolates $f(x)$ at the sampling points x_k, all k.

6.5-12 How would you construct the trigonometric interpolant to $f(x)$ at the points $\alpha + k2\pi/N$, $k = 0, \ldots, N - 1$, with α some positive number less than $2\pi/N$?

*6.6 FAST FOURIER TRANSFORMS

In discrete harmonic, or Fourier, analysis, one calculates the numbers

$$c_j = \hat{f}_N(j) = \frac{1}{N} \sum_{k=0}^{N-1} f(x_k)e^{-ijx_k} \tag{6.62}$$

with
$$x_k = 2\pi k / N \quad \text{all } k \tag{6.63}$$

in order to resolve the 2π-periodic motion described by $f(x)$ into simple harmonics. As we saw in Sec. 6.5,

$$f(x) \approx \sum_{j=-\infty}^{\infty} \hat{f}(j)e^{ijx}$$

with
$$\hat{f}(j) = \hat{f}_N(j) + \Theta(N^{-k})$$

if $f(x)$ has a piecewise continuous kth derivative. One is interested in which frequencies are present in $f(x)$ and in their strength. But, because of the aliasing effect, $\hat{f}_N(j)$ is useless as an approximation to $\hat{f}(j)$ for $|j| > N/2$, and is usually a good approximation only for $|j|$ much smaller than $N/2$. This makes it desirable to calculate $\hat{f}_N(j)$ for "large" N, and so brings up the important question of just how one is to calculate $\hat{f}_N(j)$ efficiently.

It is clear that the evaluation of any particular $\hat{f}_N(j)$ requires $\Theta(N)$ multiplications and additions. The straightforward calculation of N such numbers (e.g., the numbers $\hat{f}_N(j)$ for $|j| \leq N/2$) would therefore take $\Theta(N^2)$ operations. Thus, already for 1000 sample points, we would need millions of operations, and, until recently, this was a major obstacle to the use of discrete Fourier analysis.

This situation changed dramatically when it became well known that the *simultaneous* calculation of N consecutive $\hat{f}_N(j)$'s need only take $\Theta(N \log N)$ arithmetic operations because of the strong interrelations between these numbers. The key word for this has been **fast Fourier transform**, or **FFT**, and it has made calculations with $N \leq 1000$ routine; it has even made it possible to use N's in the tens of thousands.

We are here able only to give an indication of the basic ideas which have led to such a dramatic increase in efficiency. The latest word in 1978 on these matters is to be found in a paper by S. Winograd [36]. In particular, work done before and after publication of Cooley and Tukey's seminal article [37] has long made clear that there are *many* FFTs and that, for greatest efficiency, it is necessary (and profitable) to write a different program for each different value of N one wishes to use.

For the analysis of the computations of the numbers $\hat{f}_N(j)$ for $|j| \leq N/2$ from the numbers $f(x_0), \ldots, f(x_{N-1})$, it is convenient to introduce the **discrete Fourier transform** F_N, which carries the N-vector

$$\mathbf{z} = \begin{bmatrix} z_1 & z_2 & \cdots & z_N \end{bmatrix}^T$$

to the N-vector

$$F_N \mathbf{z} = \hat{\mathbf{z}}$$

given by

$$\hat{z}_j = \sum_{n=1}^{N} z_n \omega_N^{(j-1)(n-1)} \qquad j = 1, \ldots, N \qquad (6.64)$$

with ω_N an Nth root of unity,

$$\omega_N = e^{-i2\pi/N}$$

The connection between the calculation of $\hat{f}_N(j)$ and this discrete Fourier transform is as follows. If we take the particular N-vector

$$\mathbf{z} = \begin{bmatrix} f(x_0) & f(x_1) & \cdots & f(x_{N-1}) \end{bmatrix}^T$$

then

$$\hat{f}_N(j) = \frac{1}{N} \begin{cases} \hat{z}_{j+1} & j = 0, 1, 2, \ldots, \\ \hat{z}_{j+1+N} & j = -1, -2, \ldots \end{cases} \qquad |j| \leq N/2 \qquad (6.65)$$

Thus, it is sufficient to concentrate on the efficient calculation of the discrete Fourier transform.

We begin this discussion with the observation that $\hat{z}_j$ as given by (6.64) is a polynomial of degree $< N$ in the quantity ω_N^{-1}, hence can be evaluated in N operations, by nested multiplication. Here, we count one addition plus one multiplication as one **operation**. It would therefore take N^2 operations for the straightforward evaluation of (6.64) for all j.

The most widely known idea for an FFT has been popularized by Cooley and Tukey. It is applicable whenever N is a product of integers. We now discuss this idea first in the case that

$$N = P \cdot Q$$

Think of the N-vector z as stored FORTRAN-fashion in a one-dimensional array. Then we can interpret the array also FORTRAN-fashion as a two-dimensional array Z, of dimension (P, Q). This means that

$$Z(p, q) = z_{p + P(q-1)}$$

Correspondingly, we factor the sum $\sum z_n \omega_N^{(\nu-1)(n-1)} = \hat{z}_\nu$ into a double sum,

$$\hat{z}_\nu = \sum_{p=1}^{P} \sum_{q=1}^{Q} Z(p, q)\omega_N^{(\nu-1)[p-1+P(q-1)]}$$

$$= \sum_{p=1}^{P} \left[\sum_{q=1}^{Q} Z(p, q)\omega_Q^{(\nu-1)(q-1)} \right] \omega_N^{(\nu-1)(p-1)}$$

Here, we have made use of the fact that $\omega_N^P = \omega_Q$. This makes apparent the crucial fact that *the inner sum* in the last right hand side *is Q-periodic in ν*, i.e., replacing ν by $\nu + Q$ does not change its value, due to the fact that $\omega_Q^Q = 1$. This means that we need only calculate this sum for $\nu = 1, \ldots, Q$ (and each p). Thus, for each $p = 1, \ldots, P$, we calculate from the Q-vector $Z(p, \cdot)$ the Q-vector whose entries are the numbers

$$\sum_{q=1}^{Q} Z(p, q)\omega_Q^{(\nu-1)(q-1)} \qquad \nu = 1, \ldots, Q$$

i.e., we calculate the discrete Fourier transform of the Q-vectors $Z(p, \cdot)$, $p = 1, \ldots, P$, at a total cost of $P \cdot Q^2 = N \cdot Q$ operations.

Now, we could store the transform of $Z(p, \cdot)$ over $Z(p, \cdot)$. But, in anticipation of further developments, we choose to store the transform of $Z(p, \cdot)$ in $Z_1(\cdot, p)$, where Z_1 is a two-dimensional array of size (Q, P), rather than (P, Q).

With this, our calculation of $\hat{z}_\nu$ is reduced to the evaluation of the sum

$$\hat{z}_\nu = \sum_{p=1}^{P} Z_1(\nu_Q, p)\omega_N^{(\nu-1)(p-1)} \qquad \nu = 1, \ldots, N$$

Here, we have used the notation ν_Q to indicate the integer between 1 and Q for which $\nu - \nu_Q$ is divisible by Q. Thus,

$$\nu = \nu_Q + Q(\nu' - 1)$$

for some integer ν' between 1 and P. In effect,

$$\hat{z}_\nu = Z_0(\nu_Q, \nu') \tag{6.66}$$

if we interpret the vector $\hat{z}$ FORTRAN-fashion as a two-dimensional array

Z_0 of size (Q, P). With this, we must calculate

$$Z_0(\nu_Q, \nu') = \sum_{p=1}^{P} Z_1(\nu_Q, p)\omega_N^{(\nu_Q - 1 + Q(\nu' - 1))(p-1)} \qquad \text{all } \nu_Q, \nu'$$

Here, the right-hand side is a polynomial of degree $< P$ in the quantity $\omega_N^{\nu-1} = \omega_N^{\nu_Q - 1 + Q(\nu' - 1)}$. This quantity can be generated step by step, as in the following convenient arrangement of the calculations.

$$
\begin{array}{l}
x := 1 \\
\text{for } \nu' = 1, \ldots, P, \text{do:} \\
\quad \left\lfloor \begin{array}{l}
\text{for } \nu_Q = 1, \ldots, Q, \text{do:} \\
\quad Z_0(\nu_Q, \nu') := \sum_{p=1}^{P} Z_1(\nu_Q, p)x^{p-1} \\
x := x \cdot \omega_N
\end{array} \right.
\end{array}
\qquad (6.67)
$$

The sum in the innermost loop is, of course, to be evaluated by nested multiplication. The total cost of this step is then $Q \cdot P^2 = NP$ operations (if we neglect the N multiplications needed to generate the various x's). In this way, we have obtained in Z_0 the discrete Fourier transform $\hat{z}$ of z at a cost of only $N(P + Q)$ operations compared to the N^2 operations required for the naive way.

If now N is the product of three or more integers greater than 1,

$$N = P_1 \cdots P_m$$

say, then we can calculate the discrete Fourier transform of z even more cheaply, by using the second step (6.67) in a slightly more sophisticated way.

For the description, we need a bit of notation to indicate how a given one-dimensional array is interpreted FORTRAN-fashion equivalently as a two- or a three-dimensional array. If Z is a one-dimensional array of length N, then we denote by Z^A the equivalent two-dimensional array of dimension $(A, N/A)$, and by $Z^{A, B}$ the equivalent three-dimensional array of dimension $(A, B, N/(AB))$. In this way,

$$Z^{A, B}(a, b, c) = Z^A(a, b + B(c - 1)) = Z^{AB}(a + A(b - 1), c)$$
$$= Z(a + A(b - 1 + B(c - 1)))$$

Let now Z be a one-dimensional array containing z, as before, and for $k = 0, \ldots, m$, let Z_k be a one-dimensional array containing the discrete Fourier transform of sections of Z as follows:

$$Z_k^A(\cdot, c) = F_A Z^{BP}(c, \cdot), \qquad c = 1, \ldots, BP \qquad (6.68)$$

with
$$B := B_k := P_1 \cdots P_{k-1}$$
$$P := P_k \qquad\qquad (6.68a)$$
$$A := A_k := P_m \cdots P_{k+1}$$

Note that Z fits the role of Z_m and that Z_0 contains $\hat{z} = F_N z$. To get from Z_k to Z_{k-1}, use the following slightly extended version of (6.67), with B, P, A as given in (6.68a):

$$
\begin{aligned}
&x := 1 \\
&\text{for } p = 1, \ldots, P, \text{ do:} \\
&\quad \text{for } a = 1, \ldots, A, \text{ do:} \\
&\quad\quad \text{for } b = 1, \ldots, B, \text{ do:} \\
&\quad\quad\quad Z_{k-1}^{A, P}(a, p, b) := \sum_{\pi=1}^{P} Z_k^{A, B}(a, b, \pi) \cdot x^{\pi-1} \\
&\quad\quad x := x \cdot \omega_{AP}
\end{aligned}
\tag{6.69}
$$

Indeed, the algorithm produces

$$
Z_{k-1}^{A, P}(a, p, b) = \sum_{\pi=1}^{P} Z_k^{A, B}(a, b, \pi)\omega_{AP}^{[a-1+A(p-1)](\pi-1)}
$$

On the other hand, (6.68) implies that

$$
Z_k^{A, B}(\cdot, b, \pi) = F_A Z^{B, P}(b, \pi, \cdot) = \sum_{\alpha=1}^{A} Z^{B, P}(b, \pi, \alpha)\omega_A^{(\cdot-1)(\alpha-1)}
$$

Therefore,

$$
Z_{k-1}^{A, P}(a, p, b) = \sum_{\pi=1}^{P} \sum_{\alpha=1}^{A} Z^{B, P}(b, \pi, \alpha)\omega_{AP}^{P(a-1)(\alpha-1)+[a-1+A(p-1)](\pi-1)}
$$

But now, since $\omega_{AP}^{AP} = 1$, we may add to the exponent on the right hand side any integer multiple of AP, and this allows the conclusion that

$$
Z_{k-1}^{A, P}(a, p, b) = \sum_{\pi=1}^{P} \sum_{\alpha=1}^{A} Z^{B, P}(b, \pi, \alpha)\omega_{AP}^{[a-1+A(p-1)][\pi-1+P(\alpha-1)]}
$$

and so proves that Z_{k-1}, as produced by (6.69), satisfies (6.68) (with k replaced by $k - 1$).

In particular, Z_0 contains the discrete Fourier transform of z. We reach Z_0 by m applications of the algorithm (6.69), starting with $Z_m = Z$.

The following FORTRAN subprogram implements the algorithm just described.

```
      SUBROUTINE FFT ( Z1, Z2, N, INZEE )
CONSTRUCTS THE DISCRETE FOURIER TRANSFORM OF  Z1 (OR Z2) IN THE COOLEY-
C TUKEY WAY, BUT WITH A TWIST.
      INTEGER INZEE,N,   AFTER,BEFORE,NEXT,NEXTMX,NOW,PRIME(12)
      COMPLEX Z1(N),Z2(N)
C****** I N P U T ******
C  Z1, Z2  COMPLEX N-VECTORS
C  N  LENGTH OF Z1 AND Z2
C  INZEE  INTEGER INDICATING WHETHER  Z1  OR  Z2  IS TO BE TRANSFORMED
C    = 1 , TRANSFORM  Z1
C    = 2 , TRANSFORM  Z2
C****** W O R K  A R E A S ******
C  Z1, Z2  ARE BOTH USED AS WORKARRAYS
```

```
C****** O U T P U T ******
C   Z1 OR  Z2 CONTAINS THE DESIRED TRANSFORM (IN THE CORRECT ORDER)
C   INZEE  INTEGER INDICATING WHETHER  Z1 OR Z2  CONTAINS THE TRANSFORM,
C   = 1 , TRANSFORM IS IN  Z1
C   = 2 , TRANSFORM IS IN  Z2
C****** M E T H O D ******
C      THE INTEGER  N  IS DIVIDED INTO ITS PRIME FACTORS (UP TO A POINT).
C   FOR EACH SUCH FACTOR  P , THE P-TRANSFORM OF APPROPRIATE P-SUBVECTORS
C   OF  Z1 (OR Z2) IS CALCULATED IN  F F T S T P  AND STORED IN A SUIT-
C   ABLE WAY  IN  Z2 (OR Z1).  SEE TEXT FOR DETAILS.
C
      DATA NEXTMX,PRIME / 12, 2,3,5,7,11,13,17,19,23,29,31,37 /
      AFTER = 1
      BEFORE = N
      NEXT = 1
C
   10 IF ((BEFORE/PRIME(NEXT))*PRIME(NEXT) .LT. BEFORE) THEN
         NEXT = NEXT + 1
         IF (NEXT .LE. NEXTMX) THEN
                                           GO TO 10
         ELSE
            NOW = BEFORE
            BEFORE = 1
         END IF
      ELSE
         NOW = PRIME(NEXT)
         BEFORE = BEFORE/PRIME(NEXT)
      END IF
C
      IF (INZEE .EQ. 1)  THEN
         CALL FFTSTP( Z1, AFTER, NOW, BEFORE, Z2 )
      ELSE
         CALL FFTSTP( Z2, AFTER, NOW, BEFORE, Z1 )
      END IF
      INZEE = 3 - INZEE
      IF (BEFORE .EQ. 1)                    RETURN
      AFTER = AFTER*NOW
                                           GO TO 10
      END


      SUBROUTINE FFTSTP ( ZIN, AFTER, NOW, BEFORE, ZOUT )
CALLED IN  F F T .
CARRIES OUT ONE STEP OF THE DISCRETE FAST FOURIER TRANSFORM.
      INTEGER AFTER,BEFORE,NOW,   IA,IB,IN,J
      REAL ANGLE,RATIO,TWOPI
      COMPLEX ZIN(AFTER,BEFORE,NOW),ZOUT(AFTER,NOW,BEFORE),   ARG,OMEGA,
     *                                                        VALUE
      DATA TWOPI / 6.2831 85307 17958 64769 /
      ANGLE = TWOPI/FLOAT(NOW*AFTER)
      OMEGA = CMPLX(COS(ANGLE),-SIN(ANGLE))
      ARG = CMPLX(1.,0.)
      DO 100 J=1,NOW
         DO 90 IA=1,AFTER
            DO 80 IB=1,BEFORE
               VALUE = ZIN(IA,IB,NOW)
               DO 70 IN=NOW-1,1,-1
   70             VALUE = VALUE*ARG + ZIN(IA,IB,IN)
   80          ZOUT(IA,J,IB) = VALUE
   90       ARG = ARG*OMEGA
  100 CONTINUE
                                           RETURN
      END
```

If N is the product of m integers,

$$N = P_1 P_2 \cdots P_m$$

then a program like the above makes it possible to compute the transform

$F_N z = \hat{z}$ in

$$W = N(P_1 + P_2 + \cdots + P_m)$$

operations (rather than N^2). Since, for integers Q, R greater than 1, $Q + R < QR$ unless $Q = R = 2$, this number W is minimized if every factor of N is actually used, except that factors of 2 may be combined to 4 without loss. Further,

$$W/N = P_1 + \cdots + P_m \quad \text{and} \quad \log N = \log P_1 + \cdots + \log P_m$$

so

$$\frac{W}{N \log N} = \frac{P_1 + \cdots + P_m}{\log P_1 + \cdots + \log P_m} = \left(\sum_{j=1}^{m} \frac{P_j}{\log P_j} \log P_j \right) \Big/ \sum_{j=1}^{m} \log P_j$$

This shows $W/(N \log N)$ to be a weighted average of the numbers $P_j/\log P_j$, $j = 1, \ldots, m$. It is easy to see that $P/\log_2 P$, as a function of the integer P, has the minimum value $1.89 \cdots$ at $P = 3$, and has the value 2 at $P = 2$ and $P = 4$, and is only $3.01 \cdots$ at $P = 10$. Hence

$$1.89 N \log_2 N \leq W$$

while, even for factors P_j as big as 10, W is no bigger than $3.02 N \log_2 N$.

Further savings occur in case the data vector z is real, since then

$$\hat{z}_{N+1-j} = \bar{\hat{z}}_{j+1} \tag{6.70}$$

See (6.44) and (6.65).

There are other FFTs available when N is a prime or when N is a product of integers which are pairwise relatively prime; see Winograd's article [36].

EXERCISES

6.6-1 Prove directly from the definition (6.64) that (6.70) holds in case z is real.

6.6-2 Use FFT (with $N = 81$, say) to check your answers for Exercises 6.5-1 and 6.5-2. [This will force you to pay close attention to all the details in (6.65)!]

6.6-3 Use FFT to calculate (approximately) the Fourier coefficients $\hat{f}(j)$ for
    a. $f(x) = \sin 3x$ *b.* $f(x) = \sin(\pi x)$
using, e.g., $N = 81$ or 324 or whatever. Why do the Fourier coefficients for $f(x) = \sin(\pi x)$ fail to decay rapidly as $|j|$ increases?

6.6-4 Tailor the FFT program to the specific case $N = 3 \cdot 4$, making whatever savings in calculations and storage you can.

6.6-5 Improve FFTSTP by adding special coding as a replacement for the range of the DO loop over IB in case NOW = 2, 3, or 4 (say).

6.6-6 Discuss the use of FFT for evaluating the trigonometric sum

$$t(x) = \sum_{j=-n}^{n} a(j) e^{ijx}$$

at the points $x_j = \alpha + 2\pi j/(2n + 1)$, $j = 0, \ldots, n$, for some fixed α in the interval $[0, 2\pi/(2n + 1)]$.

6.6-7 Make use of FFT to construct the trigonometric polynomial interpolant at the $N = 2n + 1$ points $x_j = 2\pi j/N$, $j = 0, \ldots, N - 1$, to the square wave $f(x) = \text{signum}(\sin x)$, using $N = 35$. Then use FFT again to evaluate the interpolant at the 105 points $y_j = 2\pi j/105$, $j = 0, \ldots, 104$. (*Hint:* Use Exercise 6.6-6.)

6.6-8 Use FFT to construct an approximation to the spectrum of a function $f(x)$ whose values at the points $x_j = 2\pi j/N$, $j = 0, \ldots, N - 1$, with $N = 128$ say, are obtained from a (pseudo-)random number generator giving numbers uniformly distributed between 0 and 1. Compare it with the spectrum of the function considered in Exercise 6.5-2.

6.6-9 Using Exercise 6.6-8, discuss how one might use FFT to recover the values $f(x_j)$, $j = 0, \ldots, N - 1$ of a "smooth" 2π-periodic function $f(x)$ from given data $f(x_j) + \varepsilon_j$, all j, with ε_j uniformly distributed noise.

6.6-10 Show that $F_N^{-1}z = \frac{1}{N}(\overline{F_N \bar{z}})$. (This means that you get back the N-vector z from its discrete Fourier transform $\hat{z} = F_N z$ by (*a*) changing all entries of $\hat{z}$ to their complex conjugates, then (*b*) constructing the discrete Fourier transform of the resulting vector $\bar{\hat{z}}$, and then (*c*) dividing each entry of the resulting vector by N.)

6.6-11 Describe how you would use FFT to construct the polynomial interpolant of degree $\leq n$ at the Chebyshev points (6.18) to given data. (*Hint:* Construct the interpolant as a linear combination of the $n + 1$ Chebyshev polynomials $T_0, \ldots, T_n$, using (6.9). Subsequent evaluation would, of course, be via the FUNCTION CHEB.)

6.7 PIECEWISE-POLYNOMIAL APPROXIMATION

A simple and familiar example of piecewise-polynomial approximation is linear interpolation in a table of values $f(x_i)$, $i = 1, \ldots, N + 1$, where $a = x_1 < x_2 < \ldots < x_{N+1} = b$. Here $f(x)$ is approximated at a point $\bar{x}$ by locating the interval $[x_k, x_{k+1}]$ which contains $\bar{x}$ and then taking

$$p_1(\bar{x}) = f(x_k) + f[x_k, x_{k+1}](\bar{x} - x_k)$$

as the approximation to $f(\bar{x})$. In effect, $f(x)$ is approximated over $[a, b]$ by the "broken line" or piecewise-linear function $g_1(x)$ (see Fig. 6.9) with **breakpoints** $x_2, \ldots, x_N$, which interpolates $f(x)$ at $x_1, \ldots, x_{N+1}$. It follows from Example 2.6, applied to each of the subintervals $[x_k, x_{k+1}]$, $k = 1, \ldots, N$, that

For all $x \in [a, b]$: $\quad |f(x) - g_1(x)| \leq \frac{1}{8} \max_k \left\{ (\Delta x_k)^2 \max_{x_k \leq \xi \leq x_{k+1}} |f''(\xi)| \right\}$

$$\leq \max_{a \leq \xi \leq b} |f''(\xi)| \tfrac{1}{8} \left(\max_k \Delta x_k \right)^2 \quad (6.71)$$

provided that $f(x)$ is twice differentiable on $[a, b]$. Note that we can make the interpolation error as small as we wish by making Δx_k small for all k. Note further that such an increase in interpolation points does not complicate further work with $g_1(x)$, since $g_1(x)$ is "locally" a very simple function.

By using a piecewise-polynomial function $g_r(x)$ of degree $r > 1$ instead of the piecewise-linear $g_1(x)$, we can produce approximations to $f(x)$ whose error term contains the $(r + 1)$st power of $\max_k \Delta x_k$; hence goes to zero faster than the error (6.71) for piecewise-linear interpolation as $\max \Delta x_k$

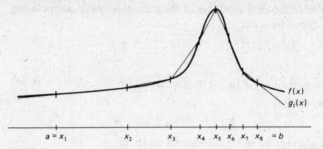

Figure 6.9 Broken-line interpolation.

becomes small. Piecewise-cubic approximation has become particularly popular. We now discuss several piecewise-cubic interpolation schemes.

Let $f(x)$ be a real-valued function defined on some interval $[a, b]$. We wish to construct a piecewise-cubic (polynomial) function $g_3(x)$ which interpolates $f(x)$ at the points $x_1, \ldots, x_{N+1}$, where

$$a = x_1 < x_2 < \cdots < x_{N+1} = b \qquad (6.72)$$

As with piecewise-linear interpolation, we choose the interior interpolation points $x_2, \ldots, x_N$ to be the breakpoints for $g_3(x)$; that is, on each interval $[x_i, x_{i+1}]$, we construct $g_3(x)$ as a certain cubic polynomial $P_i(x)$, $i = 1, \ldots, N$.

To facilitate the use of $g_3(x)$ in subsequent calculations, we write each cubic piece $P_i(x)$ of $g_3(x)$ as

$$P_i(x) = c_{1,i} + c_{2,i}(x - x_i) + c_{3,i}(x - x_i)^2 + c_{4,i}(x - x_i)^3 \quad (6.73)$$

Once we know the coefficients $c_{j,i}$, $j = 1, \ldots, 4$, $i = 1, \ldots, N$, then the following FORTRAN function PCUBIC efficiently evaluates $g_3(x)$ for any particular point $x = \bar{x}$.

```
      REAL FUNCTION PCUBIC ( XBAR, XI, C, N )
C    RETURNS THE VALUE AT  XBAR  OF THE PIECEWISE CUBIC FUNCTION ON  N
C    INTERVALS WITH BREAKPOINT SEQUENCE  XI  AND  COEFFICIENTS  C .
      INTEGER N,    I,J
      REAL C(4,N),XBAR,XI(N+1),    DX
      DATA I /1/
      IF (XBAR .GE. XI(I)) THEN
         DO 10 J=I,N
            IF (XBAR .LT. XI(J+1))        GO TO 30
 10      CONTINUE
         J = N
      ELSE
         DO 20 J=I-1,1,-1
            IF (XBAR .GE. XI(J))          GO TO 30
 20      CONTINUE
         J = 1
      END IF
 30   I = J
      DX = XBAR - XI(I)
      PCUBIC = C(1,I) + DX*(C(2,I) + DX*(C(3,I) + DX*C(4,I)))
                                       RETURN
      END
```

We now turn to the determination of the piecewise-cubic interpolating function $g_3(x)$. Since we want

$$g_3(x_i) = f(x_i) \qquad i = 1, \ldots, N + 1$$

we must have

$$P_i(x_i) = f(x_i) \qquad P_i(x_{i+1}) = f(x_{i+1}) \qquad i = 1, \ldots, N \qquad (6.74)$$

Note that (6.74) implies

$$P_{i-1}(x_i) = P_i(x_i) \qquad i = 2, \ldots, N$$

so that $g_3(x)$ is guaranteed to be continuous on $[a, b]$.

Recall from Theorem 2.1 or 2.4 that we can always interpolate a given function at *four* points by a cubic polynomial. So far, each of the cubic pieces $P_i(x)$ is required to interpolate $f(x)$ only at *two* points. Hence we have still quite a bit of freedom in choosing the $P_i(x)$. Different interpolation methods differ only in how this freedom is used.

In **piecewise-cubic Hermite** interpolation, one determines $P_i(x)$ so as to interpolate $f(x)$ at $x_i, x_i, x_{i+1}, x_{i+1}$, that is, so that also

$$P_i'(x_i) = f'(x_i) \qquad P_i'(x_{i+1}) = f'(x_{i+1}) \qquad i = 1, \ldots, N \qquad (6.75)$$

It then follows from the Newton formula (2.32) that, for $i = 1, \ldots, N$,

$$P_i(x) = f(x_i) + f[x_i, x_i](x - x_i) + f[x_i, x_i, x_{i+1}](x - x_i)^2$$
$$+ f[x_i, x_i, x_{i+1}, x_{i+1}](x - x_i)^2(x - x_{i+1})$$

Since $(x - x_{i+1}) = (x - x_i) + (x_i - x_{i+1})$, this gives

$$P_i(x) = f(x_i) + f'(x_i)(x - x_i) + \left(f[x_i, x_i, x_{i+1}] - f[x_i, x_i, x_{i+1}, x_{i+1}]\Delta x_i \right)$$
$$\times (x - x_i)^2 + f[x_i, x_i, x_{i+1}, x_{i+1}](x - x_i)^3$$

where $\Delta x_i = x_{i+1} - x_i$, from which we can read off directly the coefficients $c_{1,i}, c_{2,i}, c_{3,i}, c_{4,i}$ for $P_i(x)$. Using the abbreviations

$$f_i = f(x_i) \qquad s_i = f'(x_i) \qquad i = 1, \ldots, N + 1 \qquad (6.76)$$

we get

$$c_{1,i} = f_i \qquad c_{2,i} = s_i$$

$$c_{3,i} = f[x_i, x_i, x_{i+1}] - f[x_i, x_i, x_{i+1}, x_{i+1}]\Delta x_i$$

$$= \frac{f[x_i, x_{i+1}] - s_i}{\Delta x_i} - c_{4,i}\Delta x_i \qquad (6.77)$$

$$c_{4,i} = \frac{f[x_i, x_{i+1}, x_{i+1}] - f[x_i, x_i, x_{i+1}]}{\Delta x_i}$$

$$= \frac{s_{i+1} + s_i - 2f[x_i, x_{i+1}]}{(\Delta x_i)^2}$$

With f_i stored in $c_{1,i}$ and s_i stored in $c_{2,i}$, $i = 1, \ldots, N + 1$, the following FORTRAN subroutine utilizes (6.77) to calculate $c_{3,i}, c_{4,i}, i = 1, \ldots, N$.

```
      SUBROUTINE CALCCF ( XI, C, N )
      INTEGER N,    I
      REAL C(4,N+1),XI(N+1),    DIVDF1,DIVDF3,DX
C******  I N P U T  ******
C  XI(1), ..., XI(N+1) STRICTLY INCREASING SEQUENCE OF BREAKPOINTS.
C  C(1,I), C(2,I), VALUE AND FIRST DERIVATIVE AT  XI(I), I=1,...,N+1,
C    OF THE PIECEWISE CUBIC FUNCTION.
C******  O U T P U T  ******
C  C(1,I), C(2,I), C(3,I), C(4,I)  POLYNOMIAL COEFFICIENTS OF THE FUNC-
C    TION ON THE INTERVAL  (XI(I), XI(I+1))   I=1,...,N .
C
      DO 10 I=1,N
         DX = XI(I+1) - XI(I)
         DIVDF1 = (C(1,I+1) - C(1,I))/DX
         DIVDF3 = C(2,I) + C(2,I+1) - 2.*DIVDF1
         C(3,I) = (DIVDF1 - C(2,I) - DIVDF3)/DX
   10    C(4,I) = DIVDF3/(DX*DX)
                                      RETURN
      END
```

Example 6.15 Solve the interpolation problem of Example 2.4 using piecewise-cubic Hermite interpolation; i.e., for $N = 2, 4, \ldots, 16$, choose

$$x_i = \frac{(i-1)10}{N} - 5 \qquad i = 1, \ldots, N + 1$$

and interpolate $\qquad\qquad f(x) = (1 + x^2)^{-1}$

at these points, estimating as before the maximum interpolation error in $[-5, 5]$.

The following FORTRAN program solves this problem:

```
C  PROGRAM FOR EXAMPLE 6.15 .
      INTEGER I,J,K,N
      REAL C(4,17),ERRMAX,H,X(17),Y
C  PIECEWISE CUBIC HERMITE INTERPOLATION AT EQUALLY SPACED POINTS
C  TO THE FUNCTION
          F(Y) = 1./(1. + Y*Y)
C
      PRINT 600
  600 FORMAT('1  N',5X,'MAXIMUM ERROR')
      DO 40 N=2,16,2
         H = 10./FLOAT(N)
         DO 10 I=1,N+1
            X(I) = FLOAT(I-1)*H - 5.
            C(1,I) = F(X(I))
C           C(2,I) = F'(X(I))
   10       C(2,I) = -2.*X(I)*C(1,I)**2
         CALL CALCCF ( X, C, N )
C              ESTIMATE MAXIMUM INTERPOLATION ERROR ON (-5,5).
         ERRMAX = 0.
         DO 30 I=1,101
         Y =.1*I - 5.
            ERRMAX = MAX(ERRMAX, ABS(F(Y)-PCUBIC(Y,X,C,N)))
   30    CONTINUE
   40    PRINT 640, N,ERRMAX
  640 FORMAT(I5,E18.7)
                                      STOP
      END
```

COMPUTER OUTPUT FOR EXAMPLE 6.15

N	MAXIMUM ERROR
2	4.9188219E − 01
4	2.1947326E − 01
6	9.1281965E − 02
8	3.5128250E − 02
10	1.2705882E − 02
12	4.0849234E − 03
14	1.6011164E − 03
16	1.6953134E − 03

In contrast to polynomial interpolation (see Example 2.4), the maximum error now decreases quite nicely as N increases.

The error in piecewise-cubic Hermite interpolation is easily estimated. Since, for $x \in [x_i, x_{i+1}]$, $g_3(x) = P_i(x)$, where $P_i(x)$ interpolates $f(x)$ at x_i, x_i, x_{i+1}, x_{i+1}, it follows from (2.37) that, for $x \in [x_i, x_{i+1}]$,

$$f(x) - g_3(x) = f[x_i, x_i, x_{i+1}, x_{i+1}, x](x - x_i)^2 (x - x_{i+1})^2$$

$$= \frac{1}{4!} f^{(4)}(\xi_x)(x - x_i)^2 (x - x_{i+1})^2 \qquad \text{some } \xi_x \in (x_i, x_{i+1})$$

provided $f(x)$ is four times continuously differentiable. Further,

$$\max_{x \in [x_i, x_{i+1}]} |(x - x_i)^2 (x - x_{i+1})^2| = \left(\tfrac{1}{2} \Delta x_i\right)^4 \le \frac{(\max_j \Delta x_j)^4}{16}$$

Therefore

For $a \le x \le b$:
$$|f(x) - g_3(x)| \le \frac{1}{384} \max_k \left\{ (\Delta x_k)^4 \max_{x_k \le \xi \le x_{k+1}} |f^{(4)}(\xi)| \right\}$$

$$\le \max_{\xi \in [a, b]} |f^{(4)}(\xi)| \frac{(\max_i \Delta x_i)^4}{384} \qquad (6.78)$$

Piecewise-cubic Hermite interpolation requires knowledge of $f'(x)$. In practice, it is often difficult, if not impossible, to acquire the needed numbers $f'(x_i)$, $i = 1, \ldots, N + 1$. In such a case, one uses for s_i some reasonable approximation to $f'(x_i)$, $i = 1, \ldots, N + 1$. Thus, in **piecewise-cubic Bessel** interpolation, one uses

$$s_i = \frac{\Delta x_{i-1} f[x_i, x_{i+1}] + \Delta x_i f[x_{i-1}, x_i]}{\Delta x_{i-1} + \Delta x_i} \qquad (6.79)$$

instead of $s_i = f'(x_i)$, but proceeds otherwise as before, determining the coefficients $c_{j,i}$ for the cubic pieces by (6.77). Note that (6.79) requires the two additional points x_0, x_{N+2} to give some number for the boundary derivatives s_1, s_{n+1} of $g_3(x)$. One chooses these points somehow, e.g.,

$$x_0 = x_3 \qquad x_{N+2} = x_{N-1}$$

Or, corresponding to the choice $x_0 = a$, $x_{N+2} = b$, one uses

$$s_1 = f'(a) \qquad s_{N+1} = f'(b) \tag{6.80}$$

if these numbers are available. Yet another possibility is to choose s_1 and s_{N+1} in such a way that $g_3(x)$ satisfies the "free-end" conditions

$$g_3''(a) = g_3''(b) = 0 \tag{6.81}$$

If we continue to use $f_i = f(x_i)$, $i + 1, \ldots, N + 1$, in (6.77), then regardless of the particular choice of numbers s_i, $i = 1, \ldots, N + 1$, the resulting piecewise-cubic function $g_3(x)$ interpolates $f(x)$ at $x_1, \ldots, x_{N+1}$. Further, $g_3(x)$ is not only continuous, but also continuously differentiable on $[a, b]$, since (6.77) implies that

$$P_{i-1}'(x_i) = s_i = P_i'(x_i) \qquad i = 2, \ldots, N$$

As we now show, it is always possible to determine the numbers $s_1, \ldots, s_{N+1}$ in such a way that the resulting $g_3(x)$ is even *twice* continuously differentiable. This method of determining $g_3(x)$ is known as **cubic spline interpolation**. The name "spline" has been given to the interpolant $g_3(x)$ in this case, since its graph approximates the position which a draftman's spline (i.e., a thin flexible rod) would occupy if it were constrained to pass through the points $\{x_i, f_i\}$, $i = 1, \ldots, N + 1$.

The requirement that $g_3(x)$ be twice continuously differentiable is equivalent to the condition that

$$P_{i-1}''(x_i) = P_i''(x_i) \qquad i = 2, \ldots, N$$

or with (6.73),

$$2c_{3, i-1} + 6c_{4, i-1} \Delta x_{i-1} = 2c_{3, i} \qquad i = 2, \ldots, N$$

Hence, with (6.77) we want

$$\frac{2(f[x_{i-1}, x_i] - s_{i-1})}{\Delta x_{i-1}} + 4c_{4, i-1} \Delta x_{i-1} = \frac{2(f[x_i, x_{i+1}] - s_i)}{\Delta x_i} - 2c_{4, i} \Delta x_i$$

$$i = 2, \ldots, N$$

If we use (6.77) to express $c_{4, i-1}$ and $c_{4, i}$ in terms of the f_j's and s_j's, and simplify, we get

$$(\Delta x_i)s_{i-1} + 2(\Delta x_{i-1} + \Delta x_i)s_i + (\Delta x_{i-1})s_{i+1}$$
$$= 3(f[x_{i-1}, x_i] \Delta x_i + f[x_i, x_{i+1}] \Delta x_{i-1}) \qquad i = 2, \ldots, N \tag{6.82}$$

This is a system of $N - 1$ linear equations in the $N + 1$ unknowns $s_1, \ldots, s_{N+1}$. If we somehow choose s_1 and s_{N+1}, for example, by (6.79) or (6.80), we can solve (6.82) for $s_2, \ldots, s_N$ by Gauss elimination (see Chap. 4). The coefficient matrix of (6.82) is then strictly row diagonally dominant, hence (see Exercise 4.6-3) invertible, so that (6.82) has then a unique solution. Once we obtain the solution $s_2, \ldots, s_N$ of the linear system

(6.82), we use it, together with the boundary slopes s_1 and s_{N+1}, in CALCCF to construct the local polynomial coefficients of the interpolating cubic spline.

It can be shown (see, e.g., de Boor [40; V(6)]) that the error in the cubic spline interpolant satisfies

$$\text{For } a \leq x \leq b: \quad |f(x) - g_3(x)| \leq \max_{\xi \in [a,\, b]} |f^{(4)}(\xi)| \frac{5(\max_i \Delta x_i)^4}{384}$$

$$(6.83)$$

This error bound is only 5 times as big as the error bound (6.78) for cubic Hermite interpolation, even though cubic Hermite interpolation uses twice as much information about the function $f(x)$, viz., the values $f'(x_i)$, $i = 2, \ldots, N$ in addition to the function values. This suggests that the slopes $g_3'(x_i)$ of the interpolating spline must be good approximations to the corresponding slopes $f'(x_i)$ of $f(x)$. One can show (see, e.g., de Boor [40; V(11)–(12)]) that

$$\text{For } a \leq x \leq b: \quad |f'(x) - g_3'(x)| \leq \max_{\xi \in [a,\, b]} |f^{(4)}(\xi)| \frac{(\max_i \Delta x_i)^3}{24}$$

$$(6.84)$$

while, in case of a uniform point sequence, $x_i = x_0 + ih$, all i, one even has

$$\text{For } i = 2, \ldots, N: \quad |f'(x_i) - g_3'(x_i)| \leq \max_{\xi \in [a,\, b]} |f^{(5)}(\xi)| h^4 / 60$$

$$(6.85)$$

This has made cubic-spline interpolation popular as a means for **numerical differentiation** (see Chap. 7).

The FORTRAN subprogram SPLINE below uses Gauss elimination adapted to take advantage of the tridiagonal character of the coefficient matrix of (6.82) (see Algorithm 4.3) to calculate $c_{2,\, i} = s_i$, $i = 2, \ldots, N$, as the solution of (6.82), given the numbers $c_{1,\, i} = f_i$, $i = 1, \ldots, N + 1$, and $c_{2,\, 1} = s_1$, $c_{2,\, N+1} = s_{N+1}$.

```
      SUBROUTINE SPLINE ( XI, C, N )
      PARAMETER NP1MAX=50
      INTEGER N,   M
      REAL C(4,N+1),XI(N+1),   D(NP1MAX),DIAG(NP1MAX),G
C******  I N P U T  ******
C  XI(1), ..., XI(N+1) STRICTLY INCREASING SEQUENCE OF BREAKPOINTS
C  C(1,I), C(2,I), VALUE AND FIRST DERIVATIVE AT  XI(I), I=1,...,N+1,
C  OF THE CUBIC SPLINE.
C******  O U T P U T  ******
C  C(1,I), C(2,I), C(3,I), C(4,I) POLYNOMIAL COEFFICIENTS OF THE SPLINE
C  ON THE INTERVAL (XI(I), XI(I+1)) , I=1,...,N .
      DATA DIAG(1),D(1) /1.,0./
      DO 10 M=2,N+1
         D(M) = XI(M) - XI(M-1)
   10    DIAG(M) = (C(1,M) - C(1,M-1))/D(M)
      DO 20 M=2,N
         C(2,M) = 3.*(D(M)*DIAG(M+1) + D(M+1)*DIAG(M))
```

```
20    DIAG(M) = 2.*(D(M) + D(M+1))
   DO 30 M=2,N
      G = -D(M+1)/DIAG(M-1)
      DIAG(M) = DIAG(M) + G*D(M-1)
30    C(2,M) = C(2,M) + G*C(2,M-1)
   DO 40 M=N,2,-1
40    C(2,M) = (C(2,M) - D(M)*C(2,M+1))/DIAG(M)
                                       RETURN
   END
```

Example 6.16: Approximating a design curve by a cubic spline We are given a design curve, a cross section of part of a car door, say, as pictured in Fig. 6.10a. The curve has a slope discontinuity at $x = 6.1$. Measurements have been taken and end slopes have been estimated graphically, as indicated in Fig. 6.10a and c. The problem is to find a function $s(x)$ which fits the data and "looks smooth."

A solution to this problem is easily provided by cubic spline interpolation to the given data, using two cubic splines which join continuously, but with differing slopes, at

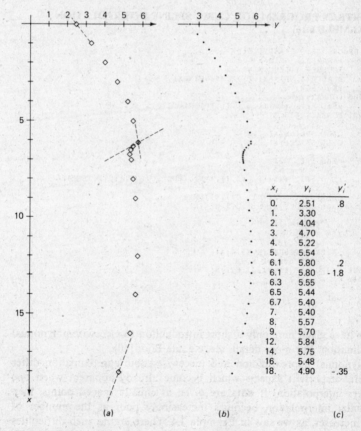

x_i	y_i	y_i'
0.	2.51	.8
1.	3.30	
2.	4.04	
3.	4.70	
4.	5.22	
5.	5.54	
6.1	5.80	.2
6.1	5.80	-1.8
6.3	5.55	
6.5	5.44	
6.7	5.40	
7.	5.40	
8.	5.57	
9.	5.70	
12.	5.84	
14.	5.75	
16.	5.48	
18.	4.90	-.35

(a)　　　　　(b)　　　　　(c)

Figure 6.10 Cubic spline approximation to a design curve.

$x = 6.1$. The following FORTRAN program accomplishes this, using the subprograms SPLINE and CALCCF discussed earlier. The program reads in the data up to $x = 6.1$, including the two given end slopes, and stores the calculated polynomial coefficients of the first six polynomial pieces in

$$C(J, I), J = 1, \ldots, 4 \quad I = 1, \ldots, 6$$

Then the data from $x = 6.1$ to $x = 18$ are read in, together with the two end slopes, and using SPLINE and CALCCF once again, the coefficients

$$C(J, I), J = 1, \ldots, 4 \quad I = 7, \ldots, 16$$

of the remaining 10 polynomial pieces are found. Finally, the calculated piecewise-cubic function $s(x)$ is evaluated, using PCUBIC, for various values of x; some of these values are plotted in Fig. 6.10b. Even without the slope discontinuity, polynomial interpolation to these data would produce an "unsmooth," i.e., oscillatory, approximation because the region of relatively high curvature near 6.1 is followed by a rather flat and enigmatic section (see Exercise 6.7-2).

FORTRAN PROGRAM FOR CUBIC SPLINE INTERPOLATION (EXAMPLE 6.16)

```
C   PROGRAM FOR EXAMPLE 6.16
        PARAMETER NP1MAX = 50
        INTEGER I,IEND,N,N1,N2
        REAL C(4,NP1MAX),FX,X,XI(NP1MAX)
        READ 500, N1
  500 FORMAT(I2)
        READ 501, (XI(I),C(1,I),I=1,N1),C(2,1),C(2,N1)
  501 FORMAT(2E10.3)
        N = N1 - 1
        CALL SPLINE(XI,C,N)
        CALL CALCCF(XI,C,N)
C
        READ 500, N2
        IEND = N + N2
        READ 501, (XI(I),C(1,I),I=N1,IEND),C(2,N1),C(2,IEND)
        N = N2 - 1
        CALL SPLINE(XI(N1),C(1,N1),N)
        CALL CALCCF(XI(N1),C(1,N1),N)
C
        N = IEND - 1
        X = XI(1)
        DO 10 I=1,40
        FX = PCUBIC(X,XI,C,N)
        PRINT 600, I,X,FX
  600   FORMAT(I5,F10.1,E20.9)
   10   X = X + .5
                                    STOP
        END
```

We have given here only a short introduction to piecewise-polynomial approximation. For more detail, see, e.g., de Boor [40].

Polynomial approximation and piecewise-cubic approximation differ in several important aspects which become already apparent when one considers interpolation. If data are given at equally spaced points, then polynomial interpolation becomes increasingly poor as the number of points increases, as we saw in Example 2.4. There are no such difficulties even in cubic-spline interpolation. (Note that there are also no difficulties in trigonometric polynomial interpolation.) Also, as the number of points increases, the polynomial (and the trigonometric polynomial) becomes more and more complex in the sense that it becomes more costly to evaluate it. Also, because of the illcondition of the power form, one has to use double precision or write the polynomial in some other form, e.g., in terms of Chebyshev polynomials, when the degree exceeds 10 or so. No such difficulties are encountered in piecewise-cubic interpolation. For, no matter how large the number of interpolation points, the interpolant is locally always a very simple function, a cubic polynomial. Finally, if the function to be approximated is badly behaved somewhere, then the best polynomial approximant is apt to be a poor approximation everywhere (see Exercises 6.1-10 and 6.1-11). In piecewise-polynomial approximation, it is possible, by proper choice of the breakpoints, to confine such effects to an interval close to the points of bad behavior, allowing good approximation everywhere else.

EXERCISES

6.7-1 In the notation employed in this section, derive the equation which f_1, f_2, s_1, s_2 must satisfy in order for the "free-end" condition

$$g_3''(a) = 0$$

to hold.

6.7-2 Calculate the polynomial of appropriate degree which interpolates the design curve of Example 6.16 at all the given data points from 6.1 to 18 (including slopes), and compare it with the spline approximation calculated in Example 6.16.

6.7-3 Interpolate the data of Example 6.16 by cubic Bessel interpolation and compare.

6.7-4 Cubic Bessel interpolation is **local** in the sense that the value of the interpolating function $g_3(x)$ at any point $\bar{x}$ depends only on the four given function values nearest $\bar{x}$. By contrast, cubic spline interpolation is **global**; i.e., the value of $g_3(x)$ at any given point depends on all the given information about $f(x)$. Prove these two assertions.

6.7-5 Try to construct a reasonable scheme of interpolating a given function by a piecewise-parabolic function $g_2(x)$. Can you make $g_2(x)$ continuously differentiable?

DIFFERENTIATION AND INTEGRATION

In Chap. 2, we developed some techniques for approximating a given function by a polynomial, typically by interpolation. In this chapter, we consider a major use of such approximating polynomials—that of **analytic substitution**. Here we are concerned with replacing a complicated, or a merely tabulated, function by an approximating polynomial so that the fundamental operations of calculus can be performed more easily, or can be performed at all. These operations include

$$I(f) = \int_a^b f(x)\,dx \qquad D(f) = f'(a) \qquad S_n(f) = \frac{1}{2\pi}\int_{-\pi}^{\pi} f(x)\sin nx\,dx$$

and even
$$Z(f) = \lim_{h \to 0} f(h)$$

Abstractly, if L denotes one of these operations on functions (or a similar one), we approximate the number $L(f)$ by the number $L(p)$, where, for given $f(x)$, $p(x)$ is an approximation to $f(x)$. The hope is that the operation L can be carried out easily on $p(x)$, and this hope is justified if $p(x)$ is a polynomial and L is any one of the above operations.

In estimating the error $L(f) - L(p)$, it is of some help that the operation L is usually **linear** (as are the operations mentioned above). This means that

$$L(f(x) + g(x)) = L(f) + L(g)$$
$$L(af(x)) = aL(f)$$

where $f(x)$ and $g(x)$ are functions and a is a number. The linearity implies that

$$L(f) - L(p) = L(e)$$

where $e(x)$ is the error in the approximation $p(x)$ to $f(x)$, that is,

$$f(x) = p(x) + e(x)$$

We will usually choose $p(x)$ to be an interpolating polynomial; say, $p(x)$ is the polynomial of degree $\leq k$ which interpolates $f(x)$ at the points $x_0, \ldots, x_k$. If these points are distinct, then, by (2.7),

$$p(x) = \sum_{i=0}^{k} f(x_i) l_i(x)$$

where the $l_i(x)$ are the Lagrange polynomials for the points $x_0, \ldots, x_k$. If now the operation L is linear, it follows that

$$L(p) = \sum_{i=0}^{k} f(x_i) w_i$$

where the numbers w_i are given by

$$w_i = L(l_i) \qquad i = 0, \ldots, k$$

and *do not depend on* $f(x)$; hence can be calculated once for all (for any particular point set $x_0, \ldots, x_k$). In this form, the approximation $L(p)$ is usually called a **rule** [for the approximation of $L(f)$], the points $x_0, \ldots, x_k$ are its **nodes**, and the numbers w_i are called its **weights**, or coefficients. We obtain an expression for the error

$$E(f) = L(f) - L(p)$$

in such a rule by applying the operation L to the error function of polynomial interpolation as given by (2.18) or (2.37), making use of the fact that the divided difference is a well-behaved function of its arguments.

7.1 NUMERICAL DIFFERENTIATION

We consider first some numerical techniques for approximating the derivative $f'(x)$ of a given function. The resulting rules are of prime importance in the numerical solution of differential equations, and this is the major reason for describing them here. They can also be used to obtain numerical approximations to a derivative from function values. But, we should point out that numerical differentiation based on the interpolating polynomial is basically an unstable process and that we cannot expect good accuracy even when the original data are known to be accurate. As we shall see, the error $f'(x) - p'(x)$ may be very large, especially when the values of $f(x)$ at the interpolating points are "noisy." These comments will be made more precise in what follows.

Let $f(x)$ be a function continuously differentiable on the interval $[c, d]$. If $x_0, \ldots, x_k$ are distinct points in $[c, d]$, we can write $f(x)$ according to (2.37) as

$$f(x) = p_k(x) + f[x_0, \ldots, x_k, x]\psi_k(x) \tag{7.1}$$

where $p_k(x)$ is the polynomial of degree $\leq k$ which interpolates $f(x)$ at $x_0, \ldots, x_k$, and

$$\psi_k(x) = \prod_{j=0}^{k} (x - x_j)$$

By (2.38),

$$\frac{d}{dx} f[x_0, \ldots, x_k, x] = f[x_0, \ldots, x_k, x, x]$$

if $f(x)$ is sufficiently smooth. Hence, in such a case, we can differentiate (7.1) to get

$$f'(x) = p_k'(x) + f[x_0, \ldots, x_k, x, x]\psi_k(x) + f[x_0, \ldots, x_k, x]\psi_k'(x) \tag{7.2}$$

Define the operator D as

$$D(f) = f'(a)$$

with a some point in $[c, d]$. If we approximate $D(f)$ by $D(p_k)$, then by (7.2), the error in this approximation is

$$E(f) = D(f) - D(p_k)$$

$$= f[x_0, \ldots, x_k, a, a]\psi_k(a) + f[x_0, \ldots, x_k, a]\psi_k'(a)$$

or

$$E(f) = \frac{f^{(k+2)}(\xi)\psi_k(a)}{(k + 2)!} + \frac{f^{(k+1)}(\eta)\psi_k'(a)}{(k + 1)!} \tag{7.3}$$

for some $\xi, \eta \in (c, d)$.

The expression (7.3) for the error $E(f)$ in numerical differentiation tells us in general very little about the true error, since we will seldom know the derivatives $f^{(k+1)}$ and $f^{(k+2)}$ involved in $E(f)$ and we will almost never know the arguments ξ, η. In some cases this error term can be simplified greatly either by choosing the point a at which the derivative is to be evaluated or by choosing the interpolating points $x_0, \ldots, x_k$ appropriately.

We consider first the case when a is one of the interpolation points. Let $a = x_i$ for some i. Then, since $\psi_k(x)$ contains the factor $(x - x_i)$, it follows that $\psi_k(a) = 0$ and the first term in the error (7.3) drops out. Moreover, $\psi_k'(a) = q(a)$, where

$$q(x) = \frac{\psi_k(x)}{x - x_i} = (x - x_0) \cdots (x - x_{i-1})(x - x_{i+1}) \cdots (x - x_k)$$

Therefore, if we choose $a = x_i$, for some i, then (7.3) reduces to

$$E(f) = \frac{1}{(k+1)!} f^{(k+1)}(\eta) \prod_{\substack{j=0 \\ j \neq i}}^{k} (x_i - x_j) \qquad \text{some } \eta \in (c, d) \quad (7.4)$$

Another way to simplify the error expression (7.3) is to choose a so that $\psi_k'(a) = 0$, for then the second term in (7.3) will vanish. If k is an odd number, we can achieve this by placing the x_i's *symmetrically around* a, that is, so that

$$x_{k-j} - a = a - x_j \qquad j = 0, \ldots, \frac{k-1}{2} \qquad (7.5)$$

For then

$$(x - x_j)(x - x_{k-j}) = (x - a + a - x_j)(x - a + a - x_{k-j})$$

$$= (x - a)^2 - (a - x_j)^2 \qquad j = 0, \ldots, \frac{k-1}{2}$$

Hence

$$\psi_k(x) = \prod_{j=0}^{(k-1)/2} \left[(x - a)^2 - (a - x_j)^2 \right]$$

Since

$$\frac{d}{dx} \left[(x - a)^2 - (a - x_j)^2 \right] \big|_{x=a} = 2(x - a) \big|_{x=a} = 0 \qquad \text{all } j$$

it then follows that $\psi_k'(a) = 0$. To summarize, if (7.5) holds, then (7.3) reduces to

$$E(f) = \frac{1}{(k+2)!} f^{(k+2)}(\xi) \prod_{j=0}^{(k-1)/2} \left[- (a - x_j)^2 \right] \qquad (7.6)$$

Note that the derivative of $f(x)$ in (7.6) is of one order higher than the one in (7.4).

We now consider specific examples. If $k = 0$, then $D(p_k) = 0$, which is a safe but (usually) not very good approximation to $D(f) = f'(a)$. We choose therefore $k \geq 1$. For $k = 1$,

$$p_k(x) = f(x_0) + f[x_0, x_1](x - x_0)$$

Hence

$$D(p_k) = f[x_0, x_1]$$

regardless of a. If $a = x_0$, then (7.2) and (7.4) give, with $h = x_1 - x_0$, the **forward-difference** formula

$$\boxed{f'(a) \approx f[a, a + h] = \frac{f(a + h) - f(a)}{h}} \qquad \boxed{E(f) = -\tfrac{1}{2} h f''(\eta)}$$

$$(7.7)$$

On the other hand, if we choose $a = \frac{1}{2}(x_0 + x_1)$, then x_0, x_1 are symmetric around a, and (7.6) gives, with $x_0 = a - h$, $x_1 = a + h$, $h = \frac{1}{2}(x_1 - x_0)$, the very popular **central-difference** formula

$$f'(a) \approx f[a - h, a + h] = \frac{f(a + h) - f(a - h)}{2h} \tag{7.8}$$

$$E(f) = -\frac{h^2}{6} f'''(\eta)$$

Hence, if x_0, x_1 are "close together," then $f[x_0, x_1]$ is a much better approximation to $f'(a)$ at the midpoint $a = \frac{1}{2}(x_0 + x_1)$ than at either end point $a = x_0$ or $a = x_1$. This is not surprising since we know by the mean-value theorem for derivatives (see Sec. 1.7) that

$$f[x_0, x_1] = f'(a) \qquad \text{for } some\ a \text{ between } x_0 \text{ and } x_1$$

This is also illustrated in Fig. 7.1.

Next, we consider using three interpolation points so that $k = 2$. Then

$$p_k(x) = f(x_0) + f[x_0, x_1](x - x_0) + f[x_0, x_1, x_2](x - x_0)(x - x_1)$$

so that $\qquad p_k'(x) = f[x_0, x_1] + f[x_0, x_1, x_2](2x - x_0 - x_1)$

Hence, if $a = x_0$, then (7.2) and (7.4) give

$$f'(a) = f[a, x_1] + f[a, x_1, x_2](a - x_1) + \frac{1}{6}(a - x_1)(a - x_2)f'''(\eta) \tag{7.9}$$

Let now, in particular, $x_1 = a + h$, $x_2 = a + 2h$. Then (7.9) reduces to

$$f'(a) \approx \frac{-3f(a) + 4f(a + h) - f(a + 2h)}{2h} \tag{7.10}$$

$$E(f) = \frac{h^2}{3} f'''(\xi), \text{ some } \xi \text{ between } a \text{ and } a + 2h$$

On the other hand, if we choose $x_1 = a - h$, $x_2 = a + h$, then we get

$$f'(a) \approx \frac{f(a + h) - f(a - h)}{2h}$$

$$E(f) = -\frac{h^2}{6} f'''(\xi) \qquad \text{with } |\xi - a| < |h| \tag{7.11}$$

which is just (7.8).

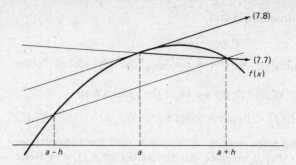

Figure 7.1 Numerical differentiation.

Formulas for approximating higher derivatives of $f(x)$ can be obtained in a similar manner. Thus, on differentiating (7.1) twice, one gets

$$f''(x) = p_k''(x) + 2f[x_0, \ldots, x_k, x, x, x]\psi_k(x)$$
$$+ 2f[x_0, \ldots, x_k, x, x]\psi_k'(x)$$
$$+ f[x_0, \ldots, x_k, x]\psi_k''(x) \tag{7.12}$$

With $k = 2$ and $a = x_0$, this gives

$$f''(a) = 2f[a, x_1, x_2] + 2f[a, x_1, x_2, a, a](a - x_1)(a - x_2)$$
$$+ f[a, x_1, x_2, a]2(a - x_1 + a - x_2)$$

Hence, with $x_1 = a + h$, $x_2 = a + 2h$,

$$\boxed{f''(a) \approx \frac{f(a) - 2f(a + h) + f(a + 2h)}{h^2}}$$

$$\boxed{E(f) = \frac{h^2}{6}f^{iv}(\xi) - hf'''(\eta)} \tag{7.13}$$

By choosing $x_1 = a - h$, $x_2 = a + h$ instead, so that the interpolation points are symmetric around a, we get

$$\boxed{f''(a) \approx \frac{f(a - h) - 2f(a) + f(a + h)}{h^2}}$$

$$\boxed{E(f) = -\frac{h^2}{12}f^{iv}(\xi)} \qquad \text{with } |\xi - a| < |h| \tag{7.14}$$

Note that placing the interpolation points symmetrically around a has resulted once again in a higher-order formula.

Finally, we infer from (2.17) that

$$k! f[x_0, \ldots, x_k]$$

is a "good" approximation to $f^{(k)}(a)$ provided the x_i's are all "close enough" to a.

Formulas (7.7), (7.8), and (7.10) are all of the general form

$$D(f) = D(p_k) + \text{const } h^r f^{(r+1)}(\xi) \tag{7.15}$$

with $D(f) = f'(a)$, and h the spacing of the points used for interpolation. Further, the number $D(p_k)$ involves just the values of $f(x)$ at a finite number of discrete points. The process of replacing $D(f)$ by $D(p_k)$ is therefore known as **discretization**, and the error-term const $h^r f^{(r+1)}(\xi)$ is called the **discretization error**.

It follows from (7.15) that we should be able to calculate $D(f)$ to any desired accuracy merely by calculating $D(p_k)$ for small enough h. However, the fact that computers have limited word length, together with loss of significance caused when nearly equal quantities are subtracted, combine to make high accuracy difficult to obtain. Indeed, for a computer with fixed word length and for a given function, there is an optimum value of h below which the approximation will become worse. Consider, for instance, the values given in Table 7.1. These were computed using the IBM 7094 computer in single-precision floating-point arithmetic.

In this table, the column headed D_h gives $f'(a)$ as estimated by (7.8), while the column with D_h^2 gives $f''(a)$ as estimated by (7.14). The function $f(x)$ is e^x, and with $a = 0$, the exact values of $f'(a)$ and $f''(a)$ are obviously one. We see from the table that the D_h and D_h^2 continue to improve as h diminishes until $h = 0.01$. After this, the results worsen. For $h = 0.0001$, there is a loss of four significant figures in D_h and of seven significant figures in D_h^2. The only remedy for this loss of significance is to increase the number of significant digits to which $f(x)$ is computed as h becomes smaller. This will normally be impossible on most computers. Moreover, $f(x)$ will itself normally be the result of other computations which have introduced other numerical errors.

Table 7.1

h	EXP(h)	EXP($-h$)	D_h	D_h^2
1.0	0.27182817E 01	0.36787944E 00	0.11752012E 01	0.10861612E 01
0.1	0.11051708E 01	0.90483743E 00	0.10016673E 01	0.10008334E 01
0.01	0.10100501E 01	0.99004984E 00	0.10000161E 01	0.10000169E 01
0.001	0.10010005E 01	0.99900050E 00	0.99999458E 00	0.99837783E 00
0.0001	0.10000999E 01	0.99990001E 00	0.99994244E 00	0.14901161E 01

To analyze this phenomenon, consider formula (7.11), which gives

$$f'(a) = \frac{f(a + h) - f(a - h)}{2h} - \frac{h^2 f'''(\xi)}{6}$$

In calculations, we will in fact use the numbers $f(a + h) + E_+$ and $f(a - h) + E_-$ instead of the numbers $f(a + h)$ and $f(a - h)$, because of roundoff. Therefore we compute

$$f'_{comp} = \frac{f(a + h) + E_+ - f(a - h) - E_-}{2h}$$

$$= \frac{f(a + h) - f(a - h)}{2h} + \frac{E_+ - E_-}{2h}$$

Hence, with (7.11),

$$f'(a) = f'_{comp} - \frac{E_+ - E_-}{2h} - \frac{h^2 f'''(\xi)}{6} \qquad (7.16)$$

The error in the computed approximation f'_{comp} to $f'(a)$ is therefore seen to consist of two parts, one part due to roundoff, and the other part due to discretization. If $f'''(x)$ is bounded, then the discretization error goes to zero as $h \to 0$, but the round-off error grows if we assume (as we must in practice) that $E_+ - E_-$ does not decrease (but see Exercise 7.1-5).

We define the **optimum** value of h as that value for which the sum of the magnitudes of the round-off error and of the discretization error is minimized. To illustrate the procedure for finding an optimum value of h, let us consider the problem above of computing $f'(0)$ when $f(x) = e^x$. Let us assume that the error in computing e^x is $\pm 1 \cdot 10^{-8}$ and that $E_+ - E_-$ remains finite and equal approximately to $\pm 2 \cdot 10^{-8}$. Then, from (7.16), the round-off error R is approximately

$$R = \pm \frac{2 \cdot 10^{-8}}{2h}$$

The discretization error T is approximately

$$T = -\tfrac{1}{6} h^2$$

since $f'''(\xi)$ is approximately one. To find the optimum h we must therefore minimize

$$|R| + |T| = \frac{10^{-8}}{h} + \tfrac{1}{6} h^2 = g(h)$$

To find the value of h for which $g(h)$ is a minimum, we differentiate $g(h)$ with respect to h and find its zero. Thus

$$g'(h) = \frac{-10^{-8}}{h^2} + \frac{h}{3} = 0$$

and its positive solution is

$$h^3 = 3 \cdot 10^{-8}$$

or

$$h = 10^{-3}\sqrt[3]{30} \approx 0.003$$

This is the optimum value of h. The student can verify by examining Table 7.1 that the best value of h falls between 0.01 and 0.001.

Formulas for numerical differentiation as derived in this section are very useful in the study of methods for the numerical solution of differential equations (see Chaps. 8 and 9). But the above analysis shows these formulas to be of limited utility for the approximate calculation of derivatives. The analysis shows that we can combat the round-off-error effect by using "sufficiently" high precision arithmetic. But this is impossible when $f(x)$ is known only approximately at finitely many points.

If the numerical calculation of derivatives cannot be avoided, it is usually more advantageous to estimate $D(f)$ by $D(p_k)$, with $p_k(x)$ the least-squares approximation to $f(x)$ by polynomials of low degree (see Sec. 6.4). A very promising alternative is the approximation of $D(f)$ by $D(g_3)$, where $g_3(x)$ is the cubic spline interpolating $f(x)$ at a number of points, or best approximating $f(x)$ in the least-squares sense.

EXERCISES

7.1-1 From the following table find $f'(1.4)$, using (7.7), (7.8), and (7.10). Also find $f''(1.4)$, using (7.14). Compare your results with the results $f'(1.4) = \cosh 1.4 = 2.1509$ and $f''(1.4) = \sinh 1.4 = 1.9043$, which are correct to the places given.

x	$f(x)$
1.2	1.5095
1.3	1.6984
1.4	1.9043
1.5	2.1293
1.6	2.3756

7.1-2 From the following table of values of $f(x) = \sinh x$, find $f'(0.400)$, using (7.8) with $h = 0.001$ and $h = 0.002$. Which of these is the more accurate? The correct result is $f'(0.4) = \cosh 0.4 = 1.081072$.

x	$f(x)$
0.398	0.408591
0.399	0.409671
0.400	0.410752
0.401	0.411834
0.402	0.412915

7.1-3 In Eq. (7.16) let $f(x) =$ sinh x and assume that the round-off error in computing sinh x remains constant, so that $E_+ - E_- = 0.5 \cdot 10^{-7}$. Determine the optimum value of h to be used if formula (7.8) is used to compute $f'(0)$.

7.1-4 Derive a formula for $f'''(a)$ by differentiating (7.1) three times, choosing $k = 3$ and setting $a = x_0$, $x_1 = a - h$, $x_2 = a + h$, $x_3 = a + 2h$. Also derive the error term for this formula.

7.1-5 On your computer, calculate the sequence of numbers

$$a_n = f[2 - 2^{-n}, 2 + 2^{-n}] \qquad n = 1, 2, 3, \ldots$$

where $f(x) =$ ln x. Without round-off effects,

$$\lim_{n \to \infty} a_n = f'(2) = 0.5$$

According to the discussion in this section,

$$\lim_{n \to \infty} |a_n| = \infty$$

because of roundoff. Does this really happen? If not, why not? Does this invalidate the discussion in the text?

7.1-6 Verify the formula (7.8) by expanding $f(a + h)$ and $f(a - h)$ into Taylor series about the point a.

7.1-7 Derive the formula (7.14) for $f''(a)$ using Taylor series expansions.

7.2 NUMERICAL INTEGRATION: SOME BASIC RULES

The problem of numerical integration, or numerical quadrature, is that of estimating the number

$$I(f) = \int_a^b f(x) \, dx \tag{7.17}$$

This problem arises when the integration cannot be carried out exactly or when $f(x)$ is known only at a finite number of points.

For this, we follow the outline given at the beginning of this chapter. We approximate $I(f)$ by $I(p_k)$, where $p_k(x)$ is the polynomial of degree $\leq k$ which agrees with $f(x)$ at the points $x_0, \ldots, x_k$. The approximation is usually written as a rule, i.e., as a weighted sum

$$I(p_k) = A_0 f(x_0) + A_1 f(x_1) + \cdots + A_k f(x_k)$$

of the function values $f(x_0), \ldots, f(x_k)$. The weights could be calculated as $A_i = I(l_i)$, with $l_i(x)$ the ith Lagrange polynomial.

Assume now that the integrand $f(x)$ is sufficiently smooth on some interval $[c, d]$ containing a and b so that we can write, as in (2.37),

$$f(x) = p_k(x) + f[x_0, \ldots, x_k, x] \psi_k(x)$$

where
$$\psi_k(x) = \prod_{j=0}^{k} (x - x_j)$$

Then the error in our estimate $I(p_k)$ for $I(f)$ is

$$E(f) = I(f) - I(p_k) = \int_a^b f[x_0, \ldots, x_k, x] \psi_k(x) \, dx \tag{7.18}$$

$f[x_0, \ldots, x_k, x]$ being a continuous, hence integrable, function of x, by Theorem 2.5.

This error term can, at times, be simplified. If, for example, $\psi_k(x)$ is *of one sign* on (a, b), then, by the mean-value theorem for integrals (see Sec. 1.7),

$$\int_a^b f[x_0, \ldots, x_k, x]\psi_k(x)\, dx = f[x_0, \ldots, x_k, \xi]\int_a^b \psi_k(x)\, dx$$

$$\text{some } \xi \in (a, b) \quad (7.19)$$

If, in addition, $f(x)$ is $k + 1$ times continuously differentiable on (c, d), we get from (7.18) and (7.19) that

$$E(f) = \frac{1}{(k+1)!} f^{(k+1)}(\eta)\int_a^b \psi_k(x)\, dx \qquad \text{some } \eta \in (c, d) \quad (7.20)$$

Even if $\psi_k(x)$ is not of one sign, certain simplifications in the error term (7.18) are possible. A particularly desirable instance of this kind occurs when

$$\int_a^b \psi_k(x)\, dx = 0 \tag{7.21}$$

In such a case, we can make use of the identity

$$f[x_0, \ldots, x_k, x] = f[x_0, \ldots, x_k, x_{k+1}] + f[x_0, \ldots, x_{k+1}, x](x - x_{k+1})$$

which is valid for arbitrary x_{k+1}, to get that

$$E(f) = \int_a^b f[x_0, \ldots, x_{k+1}]\psi_k(x)\, dx$$

$$+ \int_a^b f[x_0, \ldots, x_{k+1}, x](x - x_{k+1})\psi_k(x)\, dx$$

$$= \int_a^b f[x_0, \ldots, x_{k+1}, x]\psi_{k+1}(x)\, dx$$

since

$$\int_a^b f[x_0, \ldots, x_{k+1}]\psi_k(x)\, dx = f[x_0, \ldots, x_{k+1}]\int_a^b \psi_k(x)\, dx = 0$$

If we now can choose x_{k+1} in such a way that $\psi_{k+1}(x) = (x - x_{k+1})\psi_k(x)$ is of one sign on (a, b), and if $f(x)$ is $(k + 2)$ times continuously differentiable, then it follows (as before) that

$$E(f) = \frac{1}{(k+2)!} f^{(k+2)}(\eta)\int_a^b \psi_{k+1}(x)\, dx \qquad \text{some } \eta \in (c, d) \quad (7.22)$$

Note that the derivative of $f(x)$ appearing in (7.22) is of one order higher than the one in (7.20). As in numerical differentiation, this indicates that (7.22) is of higher order than (7.20).

We now consider specific examples. Let $k = 0$. Then

$$f(x) = f(x_0) + f[x_0, x](x - x_0)$$

Hence

$$I(p_k) = (b - a)f(x_0)$$

If $x_0 = a$, then this approximation becomes

$$\boxed{I(f) \approx R = (b - a)f(a)} \tag{7.23}$$

the so-called **rectangle rule** (see Fig. 7.2). Since, in this case, $\psi_0(x) = x - a$ is of one sign on (a, b), the error E^R of the rectangle rule can be computed from (7.20). One gets

$$\boxed{E^R = f'(\eta) \int_a^b (x - a)\, dx = \frac{f'(\eta)(b - a)^2}{2}} \tag{7.24}$$

If $x_0 = (a + b)/2$, then $\psi_0(x)$ fails to be of one sign. But then

$$\int_a^b (x - x_0)\, dx = 0$$

while $(x - x_0)^2$ is of one sign. Hence, in this case, the error in $I(p_k)$ can be computed from (7.22), with $x_1 = x_0$. One gets

$$\boxed{I(f) \approx M = (b - a)f\!\left(\frac{a + b}{2}\right)} \qquad \boxed{\begin{aligned} E^M &= \frac{f''(\eta)(b - a)^3}{24} \\ &\text{some } \eta \in (a, b) \end{aligned}}$$

$$\tag{7.25}$$

the **midpoint rule**.

Next, let $k = 1$. Then

$$f(x) = f(x_0) + f[x_0, x_1](x - x_0) + f[x_0, x_1, x]\psi_1(x)$$

To get $\psi_1(x) = (x - x_0)(x - x_1)$ of one sign on (a, b), we choose $x_0 = a$, $x_1 = b$. Then, by (7.20),

$$I(f) = \int_a^b \{f(a) + f[a, b](x - a)\}\, dx + \tfrac{1}{2}f''(\eta)\int_a^b (x - a)(x - b)\, dx$$

or

$$\boxed{I(f) \approx T = \tfrac{1}{2}(b - a)[f(a) + f(b)]} \qquad \boxed{\begin{aligned} E^T &= -\frac{f''(\eta)(b - a)^3}{12} \\ &\text{some } \eta \in (a, b) \end{aligned}}$$

$$\tag{7.26}$$

the **trapezoid(al) rule** (see Fig. 7.2).

Now let $k = 2$. Then

$$f(x) = p_2(x) + f[x_0, x_1, x_2, x]\psi_2(x)$$

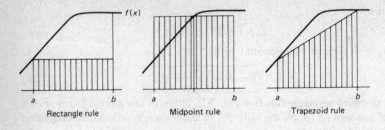

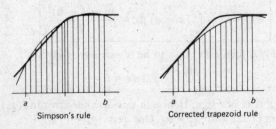

Figure 7.2 Numerical integration.

Note, for distinct x_0, x_1, x_2 in (a, b), $\psi_2(x) = (x - x_0)(x - x_1)(x - x_2)$ is not of one sign on (a, b). But if we choose $x_0 = a$, $x_1 = (a + b)/2$, $x_2 = b$, then one can show by direct integration or by symmetry arguments that

$$\int_a^b \psi_2(x)\, dx = \int_a^b (x - a)(x - (a + b)/2)(x - b)\, dx = 0$$

The error is of the form (7.22). If we now choose $x_3 = x_1 = (a + b)/2$, then

$$\psi_3(x) = (x - a)\left(x - \frac{a + b}{2}\right)^2 (x - b)$$

is of one sign on (a, b). Hence it then follows from (7.18) and (7.22) that

$$I(f) = I(p_2) + \frac{1}{4!} f^{iv}(\eta) \int_a^b \psi_3(x)\, dx$$

One calculates directly

$$\int_a^b \psi_3(x)\, dx = \int_a^b (x - a)\left(x - \frac{a + b}{2}\right)^2 (x - b)\, dx = -\frac{4}{15}\left(\frac{b - a}{2}\right)^5$$

so that the error for this formula becomes

$$E^S(f) = \frac{-1}{90}\left(\frac{b - a}{2}\right)^5 f^{iv}(\eta) \qquad \eta \in [a, b]$$

We now calculate $I(p_2)$ directly to obtain the formula corresponding to the case $k = 2$ with the choice of interpolating points $x_0 = a$, $x_1 = (a + b)/2$, $x_2 = b$. It is convenient to write the interpolating polynomial in the form

$$p_2(x) = f(a) + f[a, b](x - a) + f\left[a, b, \frac{a + b}{2}\right](x - a)(x + b)$$

Then

$$\int_a^b p_2(x)\, dx = f(a)(b - a) + f[a, b](b - a)^2/2$$

$$+ f\left[a, b, \frac{a + b}{2}\right]\int_a^b (x - a)(x - b)\, dx$$

But $\int_a^b (x - a)(x - b)\, dx = -(b - a)^3/6$, as we just found out when deriving (7.26). So

$$\int_a^b p_2(x)\, dx = f(a)(b - a) + f[a, b](b - a)^2/2$$

$$- f\left[a, \frac{a + b}{2}, b\right](b - a)^3/6 \qquad (7.27)$$

using the fact that by symmetry of the divided difference

$$f\left[a, b, \frac{a + b}{2}\right] = f\left[a, \frac{a + b}{2}, b\right]$$

But now,

$$f[a, b](b - a) = f(b) - f(a)$$

while

$$f\left[a, \frac{a + b}{2}, b\right](b - a)^2 = \left(f\left[\frac{a + b}{2}, b\right] - f\left[a, \frac{a + b}{2}\right]\right)(b - a)$$

$$= 2\left(f(b) - f\left(\frac{a + b}{2}\right) - \left(f\left(\frac{a + b}{2}\right) - f(a)\right)\right)$$

Substituting these expressions into (7.27) gives us

$$\int_a^b p_2(x)\, dx = (b - a)\left\{ f(a) + (f(b) - f(a))/2 \right.$$

$$\left. - 2\left(f(b) - 2f\left(\frac{a + b}{2}\right) + f(a)\right)/6 \right\}$$

$$= \frac{b - a}{6}\left\{ f(a) + 4f\left(\frac{a + b}{2}\right) + f(b) \right\}$$

We thus arrive at the justly famous **Simpson's rule** together with its associated error

$$I(f) \approx S = \frac{b-a}{6}\left\{ f(a) + 4f\left(\frac{a+b}{2}\right) + f(b) \right\}$$

$$E^S = -\frac{f^{iv}(\eta)[(b-a)/2]^5}{90} \qquad (7.28)$$

Finally let $k = 3$. Then

$$f(x) = p_3(x) + f[x_0, x_1, x_2, x_3, x]\psi_3(x)$$

By choosing $x_0 = x_1 = a$, $x_2 = x_3 = b$ we can be assured that $\psi_3(x) = (x-a)^2(x-b)^2$ is of one sign on (a, b) and hence from (7.20) that the error can be expressed as

$$E(f) = \frac{1}{4!}f^{iv}(\eta)\int_a^b (x-a)^2(x-b)^2\, dx = \frac{f^{iv}(\eta)(b-a)^5}{720}$$

To derive the integration formula corresponding to the choice of points $x_0 = x_1 = a$, $x_2 = x_3 = b$ we first observe that

$$p_3(x) = f[a] + f[a, a](x-a) + f[a, a, b](x-a)^2$$
$$+ f[a, a, b, b](x-a)^2(x-b)$$

so that

$$\int_a^b p_3(x)\, dx = f(a)(b-a) + f[a, a]\frac{(b-a)^2}{2} + f[a, a, b]\frac{(b-a)^3}{3}$$

$$+ f[a, a, b, b]\left\{ \frac{(b-a)^4}{4} - \frac{(b-a)^4}{3} \right\} \qquad (7.29a)$$

From Sec. 2.7 on Osculatory Interpolation we find that

$$f[a, a] = f'(a)$$
$$f[a, a, b] = \{f[a, b] - f'(a)\}/(b-a)$$
$$f[a, a, b, b] = \{f'(b) - 2f[a, b] + f'(a)\}/(b-a)^2$$

Substituting, into (7.29a) and simplifying we have

$$\int_a^b p_3(x)\, dx = f(a)(b-a) + f'(a)\frac{(b-a)^2}{2} + \{f[a, b] - f'(a)\}\frac{(b-a)^2}{3}$$

$$- \{f'(b) - 2f[a, b] + f'(a)\}\frac{(b-a)^2}{12}$$

Finally replacing $f[a, b]$ by $(f(b) - f(a))/(b - a)$ and rearranging in powers of $(b - a)$ we arrive at the formula

$$I(f) \approx CT = \frac{(b - a)}{2} \left[f(a) + f(b) \right] + \frac{(b - a)^2}{12} \left[f'(a) - f'(b) \right]$$

(7.29*b*)

which, for obvious reasons, is known as the **corrected trapezoid rule**. The error of the corrected trapezoid rule is

$$E^{CT} = \frac{f^{iv}(\eta)(b - a)^5}{720}$$

If the above-mentioned rules for numerical integration do not give a satisfactory approximation to $I(f)$, we could, of course, increase the degree k of the interpolating polynomial used. We discussed the dangers of such an action in Sec. 6.7 and proposed there the use of piecewise-polynomial interpolation as a more reasonable and certain means for achieving high accuracy. Accordingly, we approximate $I(f)$ by $I(g_k)$, where $g_k(x)$ is a piecewise-polynomial function of "low" degree k which interpolates $f(x)$. We discuss the resulting integration rules, usually called **composite rules**, in Sec. 7.4.

We have derived in this section five basic integration rules. These are the rectangle rule (7.24), the midpoint rule (7.25), the trapezoid rule (7.26), Simpson's rule (7.28), and the corrected trapezoid rule (7.29). The corrected trapezoid rule is the only one of these requiring knowledge of the derivative of $f(x)$, and this is an obvious disadvantage of this particular method. The error terms of these rules suggest that Simpson's rule or the corrected trapezoid rule should be preferred whenever the function $f(x)$ is sufficiently smooth. There are, nevertheless, some functions for which lower-order formulas yield better results than do higher-order formulas [see Exercise 7.2-2].

Example 7.1 Apply each of the five rules given above to find estimates for

$$I = \int_0^1 e^{-x^2} dx$$

We set $a = 0$, $b = 1$, $(a + b)/2 = \frac{1}{2}$, and from a table of values find that

$$f(0) = 1 \quad f(1) = e^{-1} = 0.36788 \quad f\left(\tfrac{1}{2}\right) = e^{-1/4} = 0.77880$$

We will also need

$$f'(0) = 0 \quad f'(1) = -2e^{-1} = -0.73576$$

We can then calculate from the appropriate formulas

$$R = 1 \cdot e^0 = 1$$

$$M = 1 \cdot e^{-1/4} = 0.77880$$

$$T = \tfrac{1}{2}[e^0 + e^{-1}] = 0.68394$$

$$S = \tfrac{1}{6}[e^0 + 4e^{-1/4} + e^{-1}] = 0.74718$$

$$CT = \tfrac{1}{2}[e^0 + e^{-1}] + 1/12[0 + 2e^{-1}] = 0.74525$$

The value of the integral correct to five decimal places is $I = 0.74682$. The corrected trapezoid (CT) rule and Simpson's (S) rule clearly give the best results, as might be expected from a consideration of the error terms and the fact that the first few derivatives of the function e^{-x^2} do not vary much in size.

EXERCISES

7.2-1 Verify by direct integration that $\int_a^b \psi_2(x)\, dx = 0$ if

$$\psi_2(x) = (x - a)(x - (a + b)/2)(x - b)$$

7.2-2 Apply each of the five rules given in this section to find an approximation to $I = \int_0^1 x \sin x\, dx$. Compare the results with the correct value $I = \sin 1 - \cos 1 = 0.301169$.

7.2-3 The function $f(x)$ is defined on the interval $[0, 1]$ as follows:

$$f(x) = x \qquad 0 \le x \le \tfrac{1}{2}$$

$$= 1 - x \qquad \tfrac{1}{2} \le x \le 1$$

Calculate the results of applying the following rules to find $\int_0^1 f(x)\, dx$:

    (a) The trapezoid rule over the interval $[0, 1]$
    (b) The trapezoid rule first over the interval $[0, \tfrac{1}{2}]$ and then over the interval $[\tfrac{1}{2}, 1]$
    (c) Simpson's rule over the interval $[0, 1]$
    (d) The corrected trapezoid rule over the interval $[0, 1]$

Account for the differences in the results.

7.2-4 The corrected trapezoid rule can be derived more simply by observing that since $p_3(x)$ is a polynomial of degree 3, $p_3^{iv}(x) = 0$, and hence that Simpson's rule (7.28) can be used to evaluate $I(p_3)$ exactly. Hence

$$I(p_3) = \frac{b - a}{6}\left\{ p_3(a) + 4p_3\left(\frac{a + b}{2}\right) + p_3(b) \right\}$$

Since $p_3(x)$ interpolates $f(x)$ at a, a, b, b we must have $p_3(a) = f(a), p_3(b) = f(b)$. Show using the results of Sec. 2.7 on osculatory interpolation that

$$p_3\left(\frac{a + b}{2}\right) = \tfrac{1}{2}[f(a) + f(b)] + \frac{b - a}{8}[f'(a) - f'(b)]$$

Then substitute into the expression for $I(p_3)$ above to derive the corrected trapezoid rule (7.29b).

7.2-5 Use Simpson's rule to estimate the value of the integral

$$I = \int_0^1 (1 - x^2)^{3/2}\, dx$$

7.2-6 Use the trapezoid rule to estimate the value of the integral $I = \int_0^1 x e^{-x^2}\, dx$. Obtain a bound on the error of the trapezoid rule (7.26) and compare with the actual error.

7.3 NUMERICAL INTEGRATION: GAUSSIAN RULES

All the rules derived in Sec. 7.2, except for the corrected trapezoid rule, can be written in the form

$$I(g) \approx A_0 g(x_0) + A_1 g(x_1) + \cdots + A_k g(x_k) \qquad (7.30)$$

where the weights $A_0, \ldots, A_k$ do not depend on the particular function $g(x)$. We have, so far, picked the nodes $x_0, \ldots, x_k$ somehow, for example, equispaced as in a table, and have then calculated the weights A_i as $I(l_i)$, all i. This guarantees that the rule is exact for polynomials of degree $\leq k$. But it is possible to make such a rule exact for polynomials of degree $\leq 2k - 1$, by choosing also the nodes appropriately. This is the basic idea of gaussian rules.

The resulting rules look more complicated than the rules derived in Sec. 7.2. Both nodes and weights for gaussian rules are, in general, irrational numbers. This fact may have deterred people from using these rules when calculations were done by hand. But, on a computer, it usually makes no difference whether one evaluates a function at $x = 3$ or at $x = 1/\sqrt{3} \approx 0.57735\ 02690$. Once the nodes and weights of such a rule are stored in some form (for example, as in the subroutine LGNDRE below), these rules are as easily used as the trapezoid rule or Simpson's rule. At the same time, these gaussian rules are usually much more accurate when compared with the rules of Sec. 7.2 on the basis of number of function values used.

We discuss these gaussian rules in the more general context of an integral $\int_a^b f(x)\, dx$ in which the integrand $f(x)$ may not be often enough differentiable to justify application of the rules of Sec. 7.2. For example, $f(x)$ may behave like $(x - a)^\alpha$ near a, for some $\alpha > -1$, or a and/or b may be infinite. In such situations, it is often possible to rewrite the integral as

$$\int_a^b f(x)\, dx = \int_a^b g(x) w(x)\, dx$$

where $w(x)$ is a nonnegative integrable function, and

$$g(x) = \frac{f(x)}{w(x)}$$

is smooth. In the above example, this is the case with $w(x) = (x - a)^\alpha$. Other choices for $w(x)$ are discussed below. The situation of a trouble-free integrand is also covered in this setup, by the simple choice $w(x) \equiv 1$.

Consider now the approximate evaluation of the weighted integral

$$I(g) = \int_a^b g(x) w(x)\, dx \qquad (7.31)$$

by a rule of the form (7.30). We say that the rule (7.30) is **exact** for the particular function $p(x)$ if substitution of $p(x)$ for $g(x)$ into (7.30) makes (7.30) an equality. The trapezoid rule

$$\int_a^b g(x)\, dx \approx \frac{b-a}{2} g(a) + \frac{b-a}{2} g(b)$$

for instance, is exact for all polynomials of degree ≤ 1. To check this, we only have to look at the error term for this rule,

$$E^T = \frac{g''(\eta)(b-a)^3}{12}$$

Since this error term involves the second derivative of $g(x)$, and the second derivative of any polynomial of degree ≤ 1 is identically zero, it follows that the error is zero whenever $g(x)$ is a polynomial of degree ≤ 1. More generally, if the error term of (7.30) is of the form

$$E = \text{const } g^{(r+1)}(\eta) \cdot (\text{some function of } x_0, \ldots, x_k) \qquad (7.32)$$

then the rule (7.30) must be exact for all polynomials of degree $\leq r$.

Hence, if we wish to construct a rule of the form (7.30) which, for fixed k, is exact for polynomials of as high a degree as possible, we should construct the rule in such a way that it has an error term of the form (7.32), with r as large an integer as possible. This we can do, using a trick already employed in Sec. 7.2.

As in Sec. 7.2, we use analytic substitution, picking points $x_0, \ldots, x_k$ in (a, b) and writing

$$g(x) = p_k(x) + g[x_0, \ldots, x_k, x]\psi_k(x)$$

where $p_k(x)$ is the polynomial of degree $\leq k$ which interpolates $g(x)$ at $x_0, \ldots, x_k$, and

$$\psi_k(x) = (x - x_0) \cdots (x - x_k)$$

This gives

$$I(g) = I(p_k) + \int_a^b g[x_0, \ldots, x_k, x]\psi_k(x)w(x)\, dx$$

The approximation $I(p_k)$ to $I(g)$ is clearly of the form (7.30). For if we write $p_k(x)$ in Lagrange form (see Sec. 2.2),

$$p_k(x) = g(x_0)l_0(x) + g(x_1)l_1(x) + \cdots + g(x_k)l_k(x)$$

with

$$l_i(x) = \prod_{\substack{j=0 \\ j \neq i}}^{k} \frac{x - x_j}{x_i - x_j} \qquad i = 0, \ldots, k$$

then

$$I(p_k) = \int_a^b p_k(x)w(x)\, dx$$

$$= g(x_0)\int_a^b l_0(x)w(x)\, dx + \cdots + g(x_k)\int_a^b l_k(x)w(x)\, dx$$

Hence

$$I(p_k) = A_0 g(x_0) + A_1 g(x_1) + \cdots + A_k g(x_k) \tag{7.33}$$

where

$$A_i = \int_a^b l_i(x)w(x)\,dx \qquad i = 0, \ldots, k \tag{7.34}$$

Next, consider the error

$$I(g) - I(p_k) = \int_a^b g[x_0, \ldots, x_k, x]\psi_k(x)w(x)\,dx$$

Suppose that

$$\int_a^b \psi_k(x)w(x)\,dx = 0$$

Then, as argued in Sec. 7.2,

$$I(g) - I(p_k) = \int_a^b g[x_0, \ldots, x_k, x_{k+1}, x]\psi_{k+1}(x)w(x)\,dx$$

for any choice of x_{k+1}. If now also

$$\int_a^b \psi_{k+1}(x)w(x)\,dx = 0$$

then, by the same reasoning,

$$I(g) - I(p_k) = \int_a^b g[x_0, \ldots, x_{k+2}, x]\psi_{k+2}(x)w(x)\,dx$$

Hence, in general, if for certain $x_0, \ldots, x_{k+m}$,

$$\int_a^b \psi_k(x)(x - x_{k+1}) \cdots (x - x_{k+1+i})w(x)\,dx = 0$$

$$i = 0, \ldots, m-1 \tag{7.35}$$

then, for any choice of x_{k+m+1}

$$I(g) - I(p_k) = \int_a^b g[x_0, \ldots, x_{k+m+1}, x]\psi_{k+m+1}(x)w(x)\,dx$$

$$\tag{7.36}$$

Now recall from Sec. 6.6 that we can find, for many $w(x)$, a polynomial $P_{k+1}(x)$ such that

$$\int_a^b P_{k+1}(x)q(x)w(x)\,dx = 0 \tag{7.37}$$

for all polynomials $q(x)$ of degree $\leq k$ (see Property 3 of orthogonal polynomials in Sec. 6.6). Further, by Property 2 of orthogonal polynomials, we can write

$$P_{k+1}(x) = \alpha_{k+1}(x - \xi_0)(x - \xi_1) \cdots (x - \xi_k)$$

where $\xi_0, \ldots, \xi_k$ are the $k+1$ distinct points in the interval (a, b) at which P_{k+1} vanishes. Hence, if we set

$$x_j = \xi_j \qquad j = 0, \ldots, k \tag{7.38}$$

and let x_{k+j} be arbitrary points in (a, b), $j = 1, \ldots, k+1$, then (7.35), and therefore (7.36), is satisfied for $m = k$. For then (7.35) is of the form (7.37), with

$$q(x) = \frac{(x - x_{k+1}) \cdots (x - x_{k+1+i})}{\alpha_{k+1}} \qquad i = 0, \ldots, m-1$$

which, for $m \le k$, are all polynomials of degree $\le k$. Therefore

$$I(g) - I(p_k) = \int_a^b g[x_0, \ldots, x_{2k+1}, x]\psi_{2k+1}(x)w(x)\,dx \tag{7.39}$$

To get this error into the form (7.32), we pick the x_{k+j}'s as

$$x_{k+j} = \xi_{j-1} \qquad j = 1, \ldots, k+1$$

Then

$$\begin{aligned}
\psi_{2k+1}(x) &= (x - x_0) \cdots (x - x_{2k+1}) \\
&= (x - \xi_0) \cdots (x - \xi_k)(x - \xi_0) \cdots (x - \xi_k) \\
&= \left[\frac{P_{k+1}(x)}{\alpha_{k+1}}\right]^2
\end{aligned}$$

so that $\psi_{2k+1}(x)w(x)$ is of one sign, i.e., nonnegative, on (a, b). Hence we can apply the mean-value theorem for integrals (see Sec. 1.7) to get

$$I(g) - I(p_k) = g[x_0, \ldots, x_{2k+1}, \eta]\int_a^b\left[\frac{1}{\alpha_{k+1}}P_{k+1}(x)\right]^2 w(x)\,dx$$

Finally, if $g(x)$ is $2k + 2$ times continuously differentiable, we can make use of Theorem 2.5 to express the error in the form

$$I(g) - I(p_k) = \frac{1}{(2k+2)!}g^{(2k+2)}(\xi)\frac{S_{k+1}}{\alpha_{k+1}^2} \tag{7.40}$$

where

$$S_{k+1} = \int_a^b\left[P_{k+1}(x)\right]^2 w(x)\,dx$$

To summarize, we have shown that if we choose the points $x_0, \ldots, x_k$ in (7.33) as the zeros of the polynomial $P_{k+1}(x)$ of degree $k + 1$ which is orthogonal with respect to the weight function $w(x)$ over the interval (a, b) to any polynomial of degree $\le k$, and if the coefficients A_i $(i = 0, \ldots, k)$ in (7.33) are chosen according to (7.34), the resulting gaussian formula (7.33) will then be exact for all polynomials of degree $\le 2k + 1$. Quadrature rules of this type are said to be "best possible" in the sense defined, and under the conditions given above.

We now give some examples. First, let $w(x) = 1$. If (a, b) is a finite interval, then the linear change of variables $x = [(b - a)t + (b + a)]/2$

can be used to change the limits of integration from (a, b) to $(-1, 1)$. With this,

$$\int_a^b f(x)\,dx = \int_{-1}^1 f(x(t))x'(t)\,dt = \int_{-1}^1 f(x(t))\frac{b-a}{2}\,dt \qquad (7.41)$$

Assuming that this transformation has already been made, we consider the integral (7.31) to be in the form

$$I(g) = \int_{-1}^1 g(x)w(x)\,dx$$

Since $w(x) = 1$, the appropriate orthogonal polynomials are the Legendre polynomials (see Example 6.6). In this case

$$P_1(x) = x \qquad\qquad \xi_0 = 0$$

$$P_2(x) = \tfrac{3}{2}(x^2 - \tfrac{1}{3}) \qquad \xi_0 = -\frac{1}{\sqrt{3}}, \xi_1 = \frac{1}{\sqrt{3}}$$

$$P_3(x) = \tfrac{5}{2}(x^3 - \tfrac{3}{5}x) \qquad \xi_0 = -\sqrt{\tfrac{3}{5}}, \xi_1 = 0, \xi_2 = \sqrt{\tfrac{3}{5}}$$

etc. If we choose $k = 1$, then $x_0 = \xi_0 = -1/\sqrt{3}$, $x_1 = \xi_1 = 1/\sqrt{3}$, and substituting into (7.33) and (7.40), we obtain

$$\int_{-1}^1 g(x)\,dx \approx A_0 g\left(\frac{-1}{\sqrt{3}}\right) + A_1 g\left(\frac{1}{\sqrt{3}}\right) \qquad (7.42)$$

$$E = Cg^{iv}(\eta)$$

where

$$A_1 = \int_{-1}^1 \frac{x - (-1/\sqrt{3})}{1/\sqrt{3} - (-1/\sqrt{3})}\,dx = 1$$

$$A_0 = \int_{-1}^1 \frac{x - 1/\sqrt{3}}{(-1/\sqrt{3}) - 1/\sqrt{3}}\,dx = 1$$

$$C = \frac{1}{4!}\frac{S_2}{\alpha_2^2} = \frac{1}{24}\cdot\frac{2}{5}\cdot\frac{4}{9} = \frac{1}{135}$$

since

$$S_2 = \int_{-1}^1 [P_2(x)]^2\,dx = \tfrac{2}{5} \qquad \alpha_2 = \tfrac{3}{2}$$

Substituting these constants into (7.42), we obtain the gaussian two-point quadrature formula

$$\int_{-1}^1 g(x)\,dx \approx g\left(\frac{-1}{\sqrt{3}}\right) + g\left(\frac{1}{\sqrt{3}}\right) \qquad (7.43)$$

with the error

$$E = \frac{1}{135}g^{iv}(\eta) \qquad (7.44)$$

For $k > 1$, both the points ξ_i and the weights A_i become irrational. Their calculation, however, is straightforward. We record these nodes and weights for $k = 0, \ldots, 5$ in the following FORTRAN subroutine LGNDRE. Note that (former) FORTRAN restrictions have forced us to number nodes and weights from 1 through $NP = k + 1$ rather than from 0 through k. Thus, the input parameter NP specifies the number of points rather than the degree of the underlying polynomial.

```
      SUBROUTINE LGNDRE ( NP , POINT, WEIGHT )
C  SUPPLIES POINTS AND WEIGHTS FOR GAUSS-LEGENDRE QUADRATURE
C  INTEGRAL(F(X), -1 .LE. X .LE. 1)  IS APPROXIMATELY EQUAL TO
C            SUM(F(POINT(I))*WEIGHT(I), I=1,...,NP) .
      INTEGER NP,    I
      REAL POINT(NP),WEIGHT(NP)
      IF (NP .GT. 6) THEN
         PRINT 600,NP
 600     FORMAT(' THE GIVEN NUMBER NP =',I2,' IS GREATER THAN 6.'
     *        /' EXECUTION STOPPED IN SUBROUTINE  L G N D R E .')
                                                  STOP
      END IF
                                 GO TO (1,2,3,4,5,6),NP
  1 POINT(1) = 0.
    WEIGHT(1) = 2.
                                 GO TO 99
  2 POINT(2) = .57735 02691 89626 D0
    WEIGHT(2) = 1.
                                 GO TO 95
  3 POINT(2) = 0.
    POINT(3) = .77459 66692 41483 D0
    WEIGHT(2) = .88888 88888 88888 9 D0
    WEIGHT(3) = .55555 55555 55555 6 D0
                                 GO TO 95
  4 POINT(3) = .33998 10435 84856 D0
    POINT(4) = .86113 63115 94053 D0
    WEIGHT(3) = .65214 51548 62546 D0
    WEIGHT(4) = .34785 48451 37454 D0
                                 GO TO 95
  5 POINT(3) = 0.
    POINT(4) = .53846 93101 05683 D0
    POINT(5) = .90617 98459 38664 D0
    WEIGHT(3) = .56888 88888 88888 9 D0
    WEIGHT(4) = .47862 86704 99366 D0
    WEIGHT(5) = .23692 68850 56189 D0
                                 GO TO 95
  6 POINT(4) = .23861 91860 83197 D0
    POINT(5) = .66120 93864 66265 D0
    POINT(6) = .93246 95142 03152 D0
    WEIGHT(4) = .46791 39345 72691 D0
    WEIGHT(5) = .36076 15730 48139 D0
    WEIGHT(6) = .17132 44923 79170 D0
C
 95 DO 96 I=1,NP/2
       POINT(I) = -POINT(NP+1-I)
 96    WEIGHT(I) = WEIGHT(NP+1-I)
 99                                      RETURN
    END
```

Example 7.2 For comparison purposes, we again wish to evaluate $I = \int_0^1 \exp(-x^2)\, dx$, but using the gaussian five-point formula $(k = 4)$.

The required change of variables (7.41) here is $x = (t + 1)/2$, so

$$I = \int_0^1 e^{-x^2}\, dx = \int_{-1}^1 \tfrac{1}{2} e^{-(t+1)^2/4}\, dt = \sum_{i=0}^4 A_i \exp\big(-(\xi_i + 1)^2/4\big)/2$$

Naturally, we use a program to carry out the calculation.

```
EXAMPLE 7.2 GAUSSIAN INTEGRATION
REAL INTGRL,P(5),WEIGHT(5)
F(T) = EXP(-(1.+T)**2/4.)/2.
CALL LGNDRE ( 5, P, WEIGHT )
INTGRL = WEIGHT(1)*(F(P(1))+F(P(5))) + WEIGHT(2)*(F(P(2))+F(P(4)))
*          + WEIGHT(3)*F(P(3))
PRINT 600,INTGRL
600 FORMAT(' EXAMPLE 7.2. GAUSS QUADRATURE'/' INTEGRAL = ',1PE14.7)
STOP
END
```

This gives the output

$$\text{INTEGRAL} = 7.4682413\text{-}001$$

To achieve comparable accuracy with the trapezoidal rule would require some 2,800 subdivisions, whereas Simpson's rule would require about 20 subdivisions.

Example 7.3 Find an approximation to

$$I = \int_1^3 \frac{(\sin x)^2}{x} \, dx$$

using gaussian quadrature with $k = 3$. (The correct value is $I = 0.79482518 \ldots$.)

We again transform to the interval $[-1, 1]$, this time by the change of variable $x = t + 2$. This yields

$$I = \int_{-1}^1 \frac{(\sin(t + 2))^2}{t + 2} \, dt$$

After changing the body of the program for Example 7.2 appropriately to

```
F(T) = SIN(T + 2.)**2/ (T + 2.)
CALL LGNDRE ( 4, P, WEIGHT )
INTGRL = WEIGHT (1)*(F(P(1)) + F(P(4))) + WEIGHT(2)*(F(P(2)) + F(P(3)))
```

we obtain the output

$$\text{INTEGRAL} = 7.9482833\text{-}001$$

Gaussian-type formulas are especially useful in dealing with singular integrals. If, for example, $\int_a^b f(x) \, dx$ is to be calculated, where $f(x)$ has an algebraic singularity at a and/or b, then one transforms the integral into

$$\int_{-1}^1 g(x)w(x) \, dx$$

where

$$w(x) = (1 - x)^\alpha (1 + x)^\beta$$

for appropriate exponents α and β. In this case, the ξ_i's are the zeros of the appropriate **Jacobi** polynomial. In the special case $\alpha = \beta = -\frac{1}{2}$, these are just the **Chebyshev** polynomials introduced in Example 6.7 and discussed in Sec. 6.1. For this special case, one gets the very attractive rule

$$\int_{-1}^1 \frac{g(x)}{(1 - x^2)^{1/2}} \, dx \approx \frac{\pi}{k + 1} \sum_{i=0}^k g(\xi_i) \tag{7.45}$$

for which all the weights A_i coincide, and for which the ξ_i's are the

Chebyshev points [see (6.18)]

$$\xi_i = \cos\left(\frac{2i + 1}{k + 1}\frac{\pi}{2}\right) \qquad i = 0, \ldots, k \qquad (7.46)$$

If the interval of integration is semi-infinite, it is at times of help to transform the integral into

$$\int_0^\infty g(x)w(x)\, dx$$

with
$$w(x) = x^\alpha e^{-x}$$

In this case, the ξ_i's are the zeros of the appropriate **Laguerre** polynomial; see Example 6.9. Finally, integrals of the form

$$\int_{-\infty}^\infty g(x)e^{-x^2}\, dx$$

can often be successfully estimated using the zeros of the appropriate **Hermite** polynomial (see Example 6.8).

For all these examples (and others), tables are available both for the ξ_i's and the weights A_i, the most recent, and probably most extensive, being Stroud and Secrest's "Gaussian Quadrature Formulas" [20]. See also [27].

EXERCISES

7.3-1 For which polynomials is Simpson's rule exact?

7.3-2 Construct a rule of the form

$$I(f) = \int_{-1}^1 f(x)\, dx \approx A_0 f\left(-\tfrac{1}{2}\right) + A_1 f(0) + A_2 f\left(\tfrac{1}{2}\right)$$

which is exact for all polynomials of degree ≤ 2.

7.3-3 Calculate

$$\int_0^1 \frac{\sin \pi x}{[x(1 - x)]^{3/2}}\, dx$$

correct to four significant digits. [*Hint:* Transform the integral appropriately and use (7.45) and (7.46).]

7.3-4 Find an estimate for $\int_0^\infty e^{-x^2}\, dx$

7.3-5 Derive the weights A_i for the gaussian formula with $k = 3$, using the zeros ξ_i given in LGNDRE.

7.3-6 Use the gaussian five-point formula to obtain an estimate for the integrals given in Exercises 7.4-3 and 7.4-4.

7.3-7 Use Exercise 6.3-7 to show that (7.34) can also be written $A_i = \int_a^b [l_i(x)]^2 w(x)\, dx$, $i = 0, \ldots, k$. Conclude that gaussian weights are always positive.

7.3-8 Lobatto's rule is a gaussian formula for integrating $I = \int_{-1}^1 f(x)\, dx$ except that it includes ± 1 as two *fixed* abscissas. It has the form [see (7.31)]

$$I(f) \approx A_0 f(-1) + A_1 f(x_1) + \cdots + A_{k-1} f(x_{k-1}) + A_k f(1)$$

Derive the Lobatto rule for the case $k = 2$ and show that it is exact for all polynomials of degree ≤ 3.

7.3-9 Check out the subroutine LGNDRE by using it to calculate

$$\int_{-1}^{1} x^n \, dx = \frac{1}{(n + 1)}(1 - (-1)^{n+1}) \qquad \text{for } n = 0, 1, 2, \ldots$$

For what values of n should the Gauss-Legendre rule on NP points give the integral exactly?

7.4 NUMERICAL INTEGRATION: COMPOSITE RULES

The simple quadrature rules developed in the preceding sections to estimate

$$I = \int_{a}^{b} f(x) \, dx$$

will usually not produce sufficiently accurate estimates, particularly when the interval $[a, b]$ is reasonably large. It is customary in practice to divide the given interval $[a, b]$ into N smaller intervals and to apply the simple quadrature rules to each of these subintervals. We therefore subdivide the interval $[a, b]$ in such a way that

$$a = x_0 < x_1 < x_2 < \cdots < x_N = b$$

and we denote by $g_k(x)$ a piecewise-polynomial function (see Sec. 6.7) with breakpoints $\{x_i\}$ $(i = 1, \ldots, N - 1)$. Furthermore, let $P_{i,k}(x)$ $(i = 1, \ldots, N)$ denote the polynomial of degree $\leq k$ which agrees with $g_k(x)$ on (x_{i-1}, x_i). By the rules of integration we know that

$$I(f) = \int_{a}^{b} f(x) \, dx = \sum_{i=1}^{N} \int_{x_{i-1}}^{x_i} f(x) \, dx$$

and that

$$I(g_k) = \sum_{i=1}^{N} \int_{x_{i-1}}^{x_i} g_k(x) \, dx = \sum_{i=1}^{N} \int_{x_{i-1}}^{x_i} P_{i,k}(x) \, dx$$

Hence, approximating $I(f)$ by $I(g_k)$ amounts to approximating

$$\int_{x_{i-1}}^{x_i} f(x) \, dx \qquad \text{by} \qquad \int_{x_{i-1}}^{x_i} P_{i,k}(x) \, dx \qquad i = 1, \ldots, N$$

and summing the results. Evidently, on each subinterval (x_{i-1}, x_i), we are proceeding just as in Secs. 7.2 and 7.3. In particular, we can apply any of the rules derived in Secs. 7.2 and 7.3 by substituting some polynomial for the integrand, on each subinterval, and then summing the results.

In the absence of any reason to do otherwise, we choose the x_i's to be equally spaced,

$$x_i = a + ih \qquad i = 0, \ldots, N, \text{ with } h = \frac{b - a}{N}$$

We also use, as in Sec. 2.6, the abbreviation

$$f_s = f(a + sh)$$

so that $f_i = f(x_i)$, $i = 0, \ldots, N$.

We now consider specific examples. If we apply the rectangle rule (7.23) on each subinterval, we get

$$\int_{x_{i-1}}^{x_i} f(x) \, dx = (x_i - x_{i-1}) f(x_{i-1}) + \frac{f'(\eta_i)(x_i - x_{i-1})^2}{2}$$

$$= h f(x_{i-1}) + \frac{f'(\eta_i) h^2}{2}$$

for the subinterval (x_{i-1}, x_i). Summing, we obtain

$$\boxed{I(f) \approx R_N = h \sum_{i=1}^{N} f_{i-1}} \qquad (7.47a)$$

the composite rectangle rule (on N intervals). Its error is just the sum of the errors committed in each subinterval,

$$E_N^R = \sum_{i=1}^{N} \frac{f'(\eta_i) h^2}{2}$$

where $\eta_i \in (x_{i-1}, x_i)$. If $f'(x)$ is continuous (as we assume), this can be simplified, using Theorem 1.2 in Sec. 1.7, as follows:

$$\sum_{i=1}^{N} \frac{f'(\eta_i) h^2}{2} = f'(\eta) \sum_{i=1}^{N} \frac{h^2}{2} = \frac{f'(\eta) N h^2}{2}$$

so that, with $Nh = b - a$,

$$\boxed{E_N^R = \frac{f'(\eta)(b - a)h}{2}} \qquad \text{some } \eta \in (a, b) \qquad (7.47b)$$

We derive next the composite Simpson rule. Letting $a = x_{i-1}$, $b = x_i$, and $x_i - x_{i-1} = h$ in (7.28), we obtain for a single subinterval

$$\int_{x_{i-1}}^{x_i} f(x) \, dx = \frac{h}{6} \left[f_{i-1} + 4 f_{i-1/2} + f_i \right] - \frac{f^{iv}(\eta_i)(h/2)^5}{90} \qquad x_{i-1} < \eta_i < x_i$$

Summing for $i = 1, \ldots, N$, we obtain

$$I(f) = \sum_{i=1}^{N} \int_{x_{i-1}}^{x_i} f(x) \, dx = \frac{h}{6} \sum_{i=1}^{N} \left[f_{i-1} + 4 f_{i-1/2} + f_i \right] - \sum_{i=1}^{N} \frac{f^{iv}(\eta_i)(h/2)^5}{90}$$

$$= S_N + E_N^S$$

The composite Simpson approximation S_N can be simplified to yield

$$\boxed{S_N = \frac{h}{6} \left[f_0 + f_N + 2 \sum_{i=1}^{N-1} f_i + 4 \sum_{i=1}^{N} f_{i-1/2} \right]} \qquad (7.48a)$$

while the error term can be simplified, again using Theorem 1.2 of Sec. 1.7, to

$$E_N^S = -\frac{f^{iv}(\xi)(h/2)^4(b-a)}{180} \qquad a < \xi < b \qquad (7.48b)$$

Note that in Simpson's rule we must be able to evaluate the function at the midpoints $x_{i-1/2}$ $(i = 1, \ldots, N)$ as well as at the breakpoints x_i $(i = 0, 1, \ldots, N)$. This implies in particular that we always need an *odd* number of equally spaced points at which we know the value of the integrand.

In the same manner, one gets the composite midpoint rule

$$I(f) \approx M_N = h \sum_{i=1}^{N} f_{i-1/2} \qquad E_N^M = \frac{f''(\xi)h^2(b-a)}{24} \qquad (7.49a)$$

from the midpoint rule (7.25), and the composite trapezoid rule

$$I(f) \approx T_N = h \sum_{i=1}^{N-1} f_i + \frac{h}{2}(f_0 + f_N)$$

$$E_N^T = -\frac{f''(\eta)h^2(b-a)}{12} \qquad (7.49b)$$

from (7.26).

From the corrected trapezoid rule (7.29), one obtains

$$I(f) \approx CT_N = h \sum_{i=1}^{N-1} f_i = \frac{h}{2}(f_0 + f_N) + \frac{h^2}{12}\big[f'(a) - f'(b)\big] \quad (7.50)$$

$$E_N^{CT} = \frac{f^{iv}(\eta)h^4(b-a)}{720}$$

Note that all the interior derivatives $f'(x_i)$, $i = 1, \ldots, N - 1$, cancel each other when the results of applying the corrected trapezoid rule on each subinterval are summed. Hence the composite corrected trapezoid rule is, in fact, a corrected composite trapezoid rule, i.e.,

$$CT_N = T_N + \frac{h^2[f'(a) - f'(b)]}{12} \qquad (7.51)$$

The corrected trapezoid rule has, of course, the disadvantage that the derivative of $f(x)$ must be known or calculable [except when $f(x)$ happens to be $(b - a)$-periodic].

If any of these composite rules are to be applied, one has to determine first an appropriate N, or equivalently, an appropriate $h = (b - a)/N$. If some information about the size of the derivative appearing in the error term is available, one simply determines h or N so as to guarantee an error less than a prescribed tolerance.

Example 7.4 Determine N so that the composite trapezoid rule (5.33) gives the value of

$$\int_0^1 e^{-x^2} \, dx$$

correct to six digits after the decimal point, assuming that e^{-x^2} can be calculated accurately, and compute the approximation.

In this example, $f(x) = e^{-x^2}$, $a = 0$, $b = 1$, $h = 1/N$; hence the error in the composite trapezoid rule is $-f''(\eta)N^{-2}/12$, for some $\eta \in (a, b)$. Since we do not know η, the best statement we can make is that the error is in absolute value no bigger than

$$\max_{0 \le \eta \le 1} \frac{|f''(\eta)|N^{-2}}{12}$$

We compute

$$f''(x) = e^{-x^2}(4x^2 - 2)$$

Further, $f'''(x) = e^{-x^2}4x(3 - 2x^2)$, which vanishes at $x = 0$ and $x = \pm \sqrt{2.5}$. Hence $\max|f''(x)|$ on $[0, 1]$ must occur at $x = 0$ or at the end points $x = 0$, 1: thus

$$\max_{0 \le \eta \le 1} |f''(\eta)| = \max\{|f''(0)|, |f''(1)|\} = \max\{2, 2e^{-1}\} = 2$$

We are therefore guaranteed six-place accuracy (after the decimal point) if we choose N such that

$$\frac{2N^{-2}}{12} < 5 \cdot 10^{-7}$$

or

$$N^2 > \frac{10^6}{3} = \frac{10^7}{6 \cdot 5}$$

or

$$N > \frac{10^3}{\sqrt{3}} \approx 578$$

The computer output below shows this to be a slight overestimate for N.

As computed on an IBM 7094 in both single precision (SP) and double precision (DP), the results for various values of N are:

N	$I(SP)$	$I(DP)$	ERROR(SP)	ERROR(DP)
50	7.4679947E-01	7.4670061D-01	2.466E-05	2.452D-05
100	7.4681776E-01	7.4681800D-01	6.37 E-06	6.13 D-06
200	7.4682212E-01	7.4682260D-01	2.01 E-06	1.53 D-06
400	7.4682275E-01	7.4682375D-01	1.56 E-06	3.8 D-07
800	7.4682207E-01	7.4682404D-01	2.06 E-06	9. D-08

The value of I correct to eight significant figures is $I = 0.74682413$. It thus appears that in single-precision arithmetic we cannot obtain six-place accuracy, no matter how many subdivisions we take. Indeed, for $N = 800$, the results are worse than those for $N = 400$. This shows that round-off error has affected the last three figures. The double-precision results show that for $N = 400$ we have six-decimal-place accuracy, somewhat earlier than predicted above.

The FORTRAN program is:

FORTRAN PROGRAM FOR EXAMPLE 7.4 (SINGLE PRECISION)

```
C   EXAMPLE 7.4 . TRAPEZOID RULE .
        INTEGER I,N
        REAL A,B,H,T
        F(X) = EXP(-X*X)
      1 PRINT 601
    601 FORMAT(' EXAMPLE 7.4 TRAPEZOIDAL INTEGRATION')
        READ 501,  A,B,N
    501 FORMAT(2E20.0,I5)
        IF (N .LT. 2)                        STOP
        T = F(A)/2.
        H = (B - A)/FLOAT(N)
        DO 2 I=1,N-1
      2    T = F(A + FLOAT(I)*H) + T
        T = (F(B)/2. + T)*H
        PRINT 602, A,B,N,T
    602 FORMAT(' INTEGRAL FROM A = ',1PE14.7,' TO B = ',E14.7,
       *        ' FOR N = ',I5,' IS ',E14.7)
                                             GO TO 1
        END
```

If we use the corrected trapezoid rule (7.50) instead, the required N drops dramatically. We now have the error bounded by

$$\max_{0 \le \eta \le 1} \frac{|f^{iv}(\eta)|N^{-4}}{720}$$

One calculates $f^{iv}(x) = 4e^{-x^2}(3 - 12x^2 + 4x^4)$; hence

$$\max_{0 \le \eta \le 1} |f^{iv}(\eta)| = |f^{iv}(0)| = 12$$

For six-place accuracy, it is therefore sufficient that

$$\frac{12N^{-4}}{720} < 5 \cdot 10^{-7}$$

or

$$N^4 > (10/3)10^4 = \frac{10^7}{300}$$

or

$$N > 13.5 \approx \sqrt[4]{(10/3)}\,(10)$$

so that only 14 subintervals are required as compared with 578 for the composite trapezoid rule without the differential end correction.

As this example illustrates, higher-order formulas can reduce the necessary number of function evaluations tremendously over lower-order rules *if* the higher-order derivatives of the integrand are approximately the same size as the lower-order derivatives. Gaussian rules, in particular, can be very effective.

In the absence of information about the size of the appropriate derivative of $f(x)$, it is possible only to apply the composite rules for various values of N, thus producing a sequence I_N of approximations to $I(f)$ which, theoretically, converges to $I(f)$ as $N \to \infty$, if $f(x)$ is sufficiently smooth. One terminates this process when the difference between successive estimates becomes "sufficiently small." The dangers of such a procedure have been discussed in Sec. 1.6. An added difficulty arises in this case from round-off effects, which increase with increasing N. The computer results in Example 7.4 show this very clearly.

Example 7.5 Write a program for the corrected trapezoid rule and solve the problem of Example 7.4 using this program.

FORTRAN PROGRAM

```
C      EXAMPLE 7.5 . CORRECTED TRAPEZOID RULE
       INTEGER I,N
       REAL A,B,CORTRP,H,TRAP
       F(X) = EXP(-X*X)
       FPRIME(X) = -2.*X*F(X)
       DATA A,B /0., 1. /
       PRINT 600
 600   FORMAT(9X,'N',7X,'TRAPEZOID SUM',7X,'CORR.TRAP.SUM')
       DO 10 N = 10,15
         H = (B - A)/FLOAT(N)
         TRAP = (F(A) + F(B))/2.
         DO 1 I=1,N-1
   1        TRAP = TRAP + F(A + FLOAT(I)*H)
         TRAP = H*TRAP
         CORTRP = TRAP + H*H*(FPRIME(A) - FPRIME(B))/12.
  10     PRINT 610, N,TRAP,CORTRP
 610   FORMAT(I10,2E20.7)
                                            STOP
       END
```

Single precision output

N	TRAPEZOID SUM	CORR.TRAP.SUM
10	0.7462108E 00	0.7468239E 00
11	0.7463173E 00	0.7468240E 00
12	0.7463983E 00	0.7468240E 00
13	0.7464612E 00	0.7468240E 00
14	0.7465112E 00	0.7468240E 00
15	0.7465516E 00	0.7468241E 00

Double precision output

N	TRAPEZOID SUM	CORR.TRAP.SUM
10	7.4621080E-01	7.4682393E-01
11	7.4631727E-01	7.4682399E-01
12	7.4639825E-01	7.4682403E-01
13	7.4646126E-01	7.4682406E-01
14	7.4651126E-01	7.4682408E-01
15	7.4655159E-01	7.4682409E-01

Example 7.6 Write a program for Simpson's rule and solve the problem of Example 7.4 using this program in both single precision and double precision.

The FORTRAN program and the results obtained on an IBM 7094 are given below for $N = 25$, 50, and 100 subdivisions. Note that the results in single precision are again worse for $N = 50$, 100 than for $N = 25$, indicating round-off-error effects. The double-precision results are all correct to the number of figures given. On comparing these results with those of Examples 7.4 and 7.5, we see that both Simpson's rule and the corrected trapezoid rule are much more efficient than the trapezoid rule.

```
C  PROGRAM FOR EXAMPLE 7.6 . SIMPSON'S RULE .
      INTEGER I,N
      REAL A,B,H,HALF,HOVER2,S,X
      F(X) = EXP(-X*X)
      PRINT 600
 600  FORMAT(' EXAMPLE 7.6 SIMPSON''S RULE'/)
   1  READ 501, A,B,N
 501  FORMAT(2E20.0,I5)
      IF (N .LT. 2)              STOP
      H = (B - A)/FLOAT(N)
      HOVER2 = H/2.
      S = 0.
      HALF = F(A + HOVER2)
      DO 2 I=1,N-1
        X = A + FLOAT(I)*H
        S = S + F(X)
   2    HALF = HALF + F(X+HOVER2)
      S = (H/6.)*(F(A) + 4.*HALF + 2.*S + F(B))
      PRINT 602, A,B,N,S
 602  FORMAT(' INTEGRAL FROM A = ',1PE14.7,' TO B = ',E14.7,
     *       ' FOR N = ',I5,' IS ',E14.7)
                                  GO TO 1
   4  FORMAT(2E20.0,I5)
      END
```

COMPUTER RESULTS FOR EXAMPLE 7.6

N	$I(SP)$	ERROR (SP)	$I(DP)$	ERROR (DP)
25	7.4682406E-01	7. E-07	7.4682413D-01	0.
50	7.4682400E-01	1.3E-06	7.4682413D-01	0.
100	7.4682392E-01	2.1E-06	7.4682413D-01	0.

Finally, composite rules based on gaussian formulas can also be derived. To be consistent with the composite rules already discussed, we restrict ourselves to definite integrals of the form

$$I = \int_a^b f(x)\, dx$$

We again subdivide the interval (a, b) into N equally spaced panels so that

$$x_i = a + ih \qquad i = 0, 1, \ldots, N \quad \text{with} \quad h = (b - a)/N$$

We wish to apply gaussian quadrature to the integral over the ith interval, i.e., to

$$I_i = \int_{x_{i-1}}^{x_i} f(x)\, dx \tag{7.52}$$

The gaussian weights and points based on Legendre polynomials given in Sec. 7.3 assume that the limits of integration are from -1 to $+1$. Hence we first make the linear change of variables

$$x = \frac{h}{2} t + x_{i-1/2} \qquad \text{with } x_{i-1/2} = (x_i + x_{i-1})/2$$

and substitute into (7.52) to obtain

$$I_i = \frac{h}{2} \int_{-1}^{1} f\left(\frac{ht}{2} + x_{i-1/2}\right) dt = \int_{-1}^{1} g_i(t) \, dt$$

where

$$g_i(t) = \frac{h}{2} f\left(\frac{ht}{2} + x_{i-1/2}\right)$$

We now approximate the integral I_i with the gaussian formula on $k + 1$ points to obtain

$$I_i \approx A_0 g_i(\xi_0) + A_1 g_i(\xi_1) + \cdots + A_k g_i(\xi_k) \tag{7.53}$$

where the weights and abscissas are taken from LGNDRE in Sec. 7.3.

Finally, on summing over the N subintervals we obtain

$$I = \sum_{i=1}^{N} \int_{x_{i-1}}^{x_i} f(x) \, dx = \sum_{i=1}^{N} \int_{-1}^{1} g_i(t) \, dt = \sum_{i=1}^{N} I_i$$

which from (7.53) gives the approximation

$$I \approx \sum_{i=1}^{N} \left\{ A_0 g_i(\xi_0) + A_1 g_i(\xi_1) + \cdots + A_k g_i(\xi_k) \right\}$$

$$= \frac{h}{2} \sum_{i=1}^{N} \left\{ A_0 f\left(\frac{h}{2}\xi_0 + x_{i-1/2}\right) + \cdots + A_k f\left(\frac{h}{2}\xi_k + x_{i-1/2}\right) \right\} \tag{7.54a}$$

Notice that the weights are independent of i.

According to the error equation (7.40), the error over the single panel (x_{i-1}, x_i) is expressible in the form

$$E_i = C_k g_i^{(2k+2)}(\eta_i) \qquad \text{for some } \eta_i \text{ in } [-1, 1]$$

but this means that

$$E_i = C_k \left(\frac{h}{2}\right)^{2k+3} f^{(2k+2)}(\eta_i') \qquad x_{i-1} < \eta_i' < x_i$$

Hence the error over the interval (a, b) can be expressed as

$$E_N^G = \tfrac{1}{2} C_k \left(\frac{h}{2}\right)^{2k+2} f^{(2k+2)}(\eta) \tag{7.54b}$$

Example 7.7 Evaluate the integral $I = \int_1^3 (\sin x)^2 / x \, dx$ using gaussian quadrature with $k = 3$ and $N = 2$ subdivisions of the interval $[1, 3]$. See Example 7.3.

```
C  PROGRAM FOR EXAMPLE 7.7. COMPOSITE FOUR-POINT GAUSS-LEGENDRE .
      INTEGER I,N
      REAL A,B,H,HOVER2,P1,P2,POINT(2),S,S1,S2,WEIGHT(2),X
      DATA POINT,WEIGHT / .33998 10436, .86113 63116,
     *                    .65214 51549, .34785 48451 /
      F(X) = SIN(X)**2/X
      PRINT 600
  600 FORMAT(' EXAMPLE 7.7  FOUR-POINT GAUSS-LEGENDRE'/)
    1 READ 501, A,B,N
```

```
501 FORMAT(2E20.0,I5)
    IF (N .LT. 1)                        STOP
    H = (B - A)/FLOAT(N)
    HOVER2 = H/2.
    P1 = POINT(1)*HOVER2
    P2 = POINT(2)*HOVER2
    S1 = 0.
    S2 = 0.
    DO 2 I=1,N
       X = A + FLOAT(I)*H - HOVER2
       S1 = S1 + F(-P1+X) + F(P1+X)
  2    S2 = S2 + F(-P2+X) + F(P2+X)
    S = HOVER2*(WEIGHT(1)*S1 + WEIGHT(2)*S2)
    PRINT 602, A,B,N,S
602 FORMAT(' INTEGRAL FROM A = ',1PE14.7,' TO B = ',E14.7,
   *        ' FOR N = ',I3,' IS ',E14.7)
                                         GO TO 1
    END
```

The answer, as obtained on a UNIVAC 1110 in single precision, is 0.79482517, which is in error by less than 3 in the last place.

EXERCISES

7.4-1 Derive the composite trapezoid rule T_N (7.49) and the composite midpoint rule M_N (7.48).

7.4-2 Derive the composite corrected trapezoid rule CT_N (7.50) and verify that the interior derivatives $f'(x_i)$ $(i = 1, \ldots, N - 1)$ cancel out in the sum.

7.4-3 Write a program for the composite Simpson rule. Inputs to the program should be $f(x)$, the interval $[a, b]$ and the number of subdivisions N. Use this program to calculate

$$I = \int_1^2 x \ln x \, dx$$

with $N = 10$ and $N = 20$ subdivisions.

7.4-4 Use the program for Simpson's rule to calculate an approximation to the integrals

$$I = \int_0^1 xe^{-x}dx \qquad I = \int_0^1 x \cos x \, dx \qquad I = \int_0^1 (1 + x^2)^{3/2}dx$$

which are correct to six decimal places. Do this by starting with $N = 10$ and doubling N until you are satisfied that you have the required accuracy.

7.4-5 Write a program for the corrected trapezoid rule. In this case input will consist of $f(x)$, $f'(x)$, $[a, b]$, and N. Apply this program to the integral in Exercise 7.4-3 and compare the results with those given by Simpson's rule.

7.4-6 Write a program for the composite gaussian rule (7.54a) using $k = 3$. Use it to evaluate the integral in Exercise 7.4-3 first with $N = 2$ and then with $N = 4$ subdivisions. Compare the amount of computational effort and the accuracy obtained with those required by Simpson's rule.

7.4-7 The error function erf(x) is defined by

$$\text{erf}(x) = \frac{2}{\sqrt{\pi}} \int_0^x e^{-t^2} \, dt$$

Use the gaussian composite rule for $k = 3$ to evaluate erf(0.5) again with $N = 2$ and $N = 4$ subdivisions. Estimate the accuracy of your result and compare with the correct value erf(0.5) = 0.520499876.

7.4-8 The determination of the condensation of a pure vapor on the outside of a cooled horizontal tube requires that the mean heat-transfer coefficient Q be computed. This coefficient requires, along with other parameters, the evaluation of the integral

$$I = \int_0^\pi (\sin x)^{1/3} \, dx$$

Find the value of this integral using Simpson's rule with $N = 5, 10, 15, 20$ subdivisions. *Answer:* For $N = 5$, $I \approx 2.5286949$.

7.5 ADAPTIVE QUADRATURE

The composite rules discussed so far are all based on N subintervals of *equal* size. Such a choice of subintervals is quite natural, and at times even necessary, if the integrand is known only at a sequence of equally spaced points, e.g., if $f(x)$ is given only in the form of a table of function values. But if $f(x)$ can be evaluated with equal ease for every point in the interval of integration, it is usually more economical to use subintervals whose length is determined by the local behavior of the integrand. In other words, it is usually possible to calculate $I(f)$ to within a prescribed accuracy with fewer function evaluations if the subintervals are of properly chosen unequal size than if one insists on equal-length subintervals.

Consider, for example, the general composite trapezoid rule

$$I(f) = \sum_{i=1}^{N} \frac{x_i - x_{i-1}}{2} \left[f(x_{i-1}) + f(x_i) \right] - \sum_{i=1}^{N} \frac{f''(\eta_i)(x_i - x_{i-1})^3}{12}$$

where the breakpoints $a = x_0 < x_1 < \cdots < x_N = b$ are not necessarily equally spaced. The contribution

$$-\frac{f''(\eta_i)(x_i - x_{i-1})^3}{12} \qquad \text{some } \eta_i \in (x_{i-1}, x_i)$$

from the interval (x_{i-1}, x_i) to the overall error depends on both the size of $f''(x)$ on the interval (x_{i-1}, x_i) and the size $|x_i - x_{i-1}|$ of the subinterval. Hence, in those parts of the interval of integration (a, b) where $|f''(x)|$ is "small," we can take subintervals of "large" size, while in regions where $|f''(x)|$ is "large," we have to take "small" subintervals, if we want the contribution to the overall error from each subintervals to be about equal. It can be shown that such a policy is best if the goal is to minimize the number of subintervals, and hence the number of function evaluations, necessary to calculate $I(f)$ to a given accuracy.

Integration schemes which adapt the length of subintervals to the local behavior of the integrand are called **adaptive**. The major difficulty such schemes have to face is lack of knowledge about the derivative appearing in the error term. This means that such schemes have to *guess* the local behavior of the integrand from its values at a few points.

We shall describe briefly an adaptive quadrature scheme based on the use of Simpson's rule as a basic integration formula. We assume that we are given a function $f(x)$, an interval $[a, b]$ and an error criterion ε. The objective is to compute an approximation P to the integral $I = \int_a^b f(x)\, dx$ so that

$$|P - I| \leq \varepsilon \tag{7.55}$$

and to do this using as small a number of function evaluations as possible.

We begin by dividing the interval $[a, b]$ into N subintervals, usually, but not necessarily, equally spaced. Let x_i, x_{i+1} be the endpoints of one such subinterval and let $x_{i+1} - x_i = h$. We now obtain two Simpson rule approximations to the integral

$$I_i = \int_{x_i}^{x_{i+1}} f(x)\, dx$$

One of these, which we denote by S, is based on the use of two panels; the other, denoted by $\bar{S}$, is based on the use of four panels. According to the formula (7.28) these approximations are given by

$$S_i = \frac{h}{6}\left\{ f(x_i) + 4f\left(x_i + \frac{h}{2}\right) + f(x_{i+1}) \right\} \tag{7.56a}$$

$$\bar{S}_i = \frac{h}{12}\left\{ f(x_i) + 4f\left(x_i + \frac{h}{4}\right) + 2f\left(x_i + \frac{h}{2}\right) + 4f\left(x_i + \frac{3h}{4}\right) + f(x_{i+1}) \right\} \tag{7.56b}$$

From these two approximations we can estimate the error in the more accurate approximation $\bar{S}_i$ as follows. According to the error term in Simpson's rule (7.28), we have

$$I_i - S_i = -\frac{f^{iv}(\eta)}{90}\left(\frac{h}{2}\right)^5 \tag{7.57a}$$

$$I_i - \bar{S}_i = -\frac{2 \cdot f^{iv}(\eta)}{90}\left(\frac{h}{4}\right)^5 \tag{7.57b}$$

In (7.57b) the factor 2 comes from the fact that we are integrating over two subintervals, each of width $h/2$. Assuming that the derivative $f^{iv}(x)$ is approximately constant over the interval $[x_i, x_{i+1}]$, we can subtract (7.57b) from (7.57a) and simplify to obtain

$$\bar{S}_i - S_i = \frac{f^{iv} \cdot h^5}{2^5 \cdot 90}\left(\frac{1 - 2^4}{2^4}\right)$$

from which we find that

$$\frac{f^{iv} \cdot h^5}{2^5 \cdot 90} = \frac{2^4(\bar{S}_i - S_i)}{1 - 2^4} \tag{7.58}$$

Substituting (7.58) into the right-hand side of (7.57b) we obtain the error estimate

$$I_i - \bar{S}_i = \frac{\bar{S}_i - S_i}{2^4 - 1} = \tfrac{1}{15}\left(\bar{S}_i - S_i\right) \tag{7.59}$$

In words, the error in the more accurate approximation $\bar{S}_i$ is approximately $\tfrac{1}{15}$ times the difference between the two approximations $\bar{S}_i$ and S_i, a quantity which is easily computable.

If the interval $[a, b]$ is covered by N subintervals, and if on each of these subintervals we arrange that the error estimate satisfies

$$E_i = \tfrac{1}{15}|\bar{S}_i - S_i| \le \frac{h}{b - a}\,\varepsilon \tag{7.60}$$

then it can be shown that the approximation to the integral I obtained by summing

$$P = \sum_{i=1}^{N} \bar{S}_i$$

will satisfy the required error criterion (7.55) over the entire interval $[a, b]$. In (7.60) it is important to note that $h = x_{i+1} - x_i$ will change as the subinterval width changes.

Adaptive quadrature essentially consists of applying the formulas (7.56a) and (7.56b) to each of the subintervals covering $[a, b]$ until the inequality (7.60) is satisfied. If the inequality (7.60) is not satisfied on one or more of the subintervals, then those subintervals must be further subdivided and the entire process repeated.

Any subroutine based on adaptive quadrature must keep track of all subintervals to ensure that the interval $[a, b]$ is covered, and it must properly select the subinterval widths h needed in formulas (7.56a), (7.56b), and (7.60). The complexity of adaptive quadrature subroutines arises from the extensive bookkeeping needed to keep track of nested subintervals, and on the need for alternative courses of action when difficulties are encountered. Adaptive subroutines based on Simpson's rule can also be made more efficient by noting in the formulas (7.56a) and (7.56b) that the points at which $f(x)$ is evaluated in (7.56a) also occur in (7.56b). Hence these values of $f(x)$ can be saved. The following example will clarify the procedure described here.

Example 7.8 Using adaptive quadrature based on Simpson's rule find an approximation to the integral

$$I = \int_0^1 \sqrt{x}\ dx$$

correct to an error $\varepsilon = 0.0005$.

The correct answer is easily calculated to be $I = \tfrac{2}{3}$. It is revealing, however, to attempt to solve it by an adaptive Simpson rule procedure. By drawing a graph of the function $f(x) = \sqrt{x}$, the student will observe that the curve is very steep in the vicinity of the origin [indeed $f'(0) = \infty$], while it is fairly flat as $x \to 1$. Hence we would expect to have more difficulty in integrating over an interval near the origin than over an interval near $x = 1$.

We begin by dividing the interval $[0, 1]$ into two subintervals $[0, \frac{1}{2}]$ and $[\frac{1}{2}, 1]$. We apply the formulas (7.56a) and (7.56b) over the interval $[\frac{1}{2}, 1]$ first. Here $h = \frac{1}{2}$ and hence

$$S\left[\tfrac{1}{2}, 1\right] = \tfrac{1}{12}\left\{ \sqrt{1/2} + 4\sqrt{3/4} + \sqrt{1} \right\} = 0.43093403$$

$$\overline{S}\left[\tfrac{1}{2}, 1\right] = \tfrac{1}{24}\left\{ \sqrt{1/2} + 4\sqrt{5/8} + 2\sqrt{3/4} + 4\sqrt{7/8} + \sqrt{1} \right\} = 0.43096219$$

We use here a slightly different notation to make clear the subinterval being considered. From the error formula (7.60) we have

$$E\left[\tfrac{1}{2}, 1\right] = \tfrac{1}{15}(\overline{S} - S) = 0.0000018775 < \tfrac{1/2}{1}(0.0005) = 0.00025$$

Since the error criterion is satisfied, we accept the value $\overline{S}[\frac{1}{2}, 1]$ and set it aside in a SUM register. Next we apply the formulas (7.56a) and (7.56b) to the interval $[0, \frac{1}{2}]$. We find again with $h = 1/2$ that

$$S\left[0, \tfrac{1}{2}\right] = \tfrac{1}{12}\left\{ 0 + 4\sqrt{1/4} + \sqrt{1/2} \right\} = 0.22559223$$

$$\overline{S}\left[0, \tfrac{1}{2}\right] = \tfrac{1}{24}\left\{ 0 + 4\sqrt{1/8} + 2\sqrt{1/4} + 4\sqrt{3/8} + \sqrt{1/2} \right\} = 0.23211709$$

and $$E\left[0, \tfrac{1}{2}\right] = 0.00043499 \not< 0.00025$$

Here the error test fails so that we must subdivide the interval $[0, \frac{1}{2}]$. On halving this interval we obtain the two intervals $[0, 1/4]$ and $[1/4, 1/2]$. Applying formulas (7.56a) and (7.56b) with $h = 1/4$, we obtain

$$S\left[\tfrac{1}{4}, \tfrac{1}{2}\right] = 0.15235819$$

$$\overline{S}\left[\tfrac{1}{4}, \tfrac{1}{2}\right] = 0.15236814$$

$$E\left[\tfrac{1}{4}, \tfrac{1}{2}\right] = 0.664 \cdot 10^{-6} < \tfrac{1/4}{1}(0.0005) = 0.000125$$

The error criterion is clearly satisfied, hence we add the value of $\overline{S}[1/4, 1/2]$ to the SUM register to obtain the partial approximation

$$\text{SUM}\left[\tfrac{1}{4}, 1\right] = 0.43096219 + 0.15236814 = 0.58333033.$$

Applying again the basic formulas (7.56) to the interval $[0, \frac{1}{4}]$ with $h = 1/4$, we find

$$S\left[0, \tfrac{1}{4}\right] = 0.07975890$$

$$\overline{S}\left[0, \tfrac{1}{4}\right] = 0.08206578$$

$$D\left[0, \tfrac{1}{4}\right] = (0.0001537922) \not< 0.000125$$

The error test is not satisfied and hence we subdivide the interval $[0, \frac{1}{4}]$ into the two intervals $[0, \frac{1}{8}]$ and $[\frac{1}{8}, \frac{1}{4}]$. Proceeding as above with $h = \frac{1}{8}$ we find that

$$S\left[\tfrac{1}{8}, \tfrac{1}{4}\right] = 0.05386675$$

$$\overline{S}\left[\tfrac{1}{8}, \tfrac{1}{4}\right] = 0.05387027$$

$$E\left[\tfrac{1}{8}, \tfrac{1}{4}\right] = 0.0000002346 < 1/8(0.0005) = 0.0000625$$

and that

$$S\left[0, \tfrac{1}{8}\right] = 0.02819903$$

$$\bar{S}\left[0, \tfrac{1}{8}\right] = 0.02901464$$

$$E\left[0, \tfrac{1}{8}\right] = 0.00005437 < 0.0000625$$

Since the error test is passed on both intervals, we can add these values into the SUM register to get

$$P = \text{SUM } [0, 1] = 0.58331033 + 0.05387027 + 0.02901464$$
$$= 0.66621524$$

Since the exact value of I is $.66666666$ we see that the approximation P to I satisfies the required error criterion

$$|P - I| = 0.00045142 < 0.0005$$

over the entire interval $[0, 1]$.

As this example shows, adaptive quadrature schemes use large spacings where the curve $f(x)$ is changing slowly; where the curve is changing rapidly, e.g., near sharp peaks or near points of singularity, the interval spacing will have to be much finer to achieve a required accuracy.

We do not include here a subroutine based on adaptive quadrature. As already noted, such a subroutine is certain to be very complex if it is to handle large classes of functions. There are some excellent adaptive quadrature routines available on most modern computers.

EXERCISES

7.5-1 Using a pocket calculator verify the results given in Example 7.8 for $\bar{S}[\tfrac{1}{4}, \tfrac{1}{2}]$, $\bar{S}[\tfrac{1}{8}, \tfrac{1}{4}]$ and $\bar{S}[0, \tfrac{1}{8}]$.

7.5-2 Change the error criterion in Example 7.8 to $\varepsilon = 0.0001$. Which of the interval estimates already obtained will satisfy the required error criterion and which will not? Subdivide the interval $[0, \tfrac{1}{8}]$ and compute the integral as in the example until the new error criterion is satisfied.

7.5-3 Using adaptive Simpson-rule-based quadrature, find an approximation to the integral

$$I = \int_0^1 (1 - x^2)^{3/2} \, dx$$

correct to three decimal places. First draw a curve of $f(x)$ and try to determine where you will expect to encounter difficulties.

7.5-4 Find an approximation to

$$I = \int_0^1 \frac{\sin x}{x^{3/2}} \, dx$$

good to six decimal places using adaptive quadrature.

7.5-5 Write a program for an adaptive Simpson-rule-based quadrature routine subject to the restrictions given below.

    1. User input will consist of the function $f(x)$, a finite interval $[a, b]$, and an absolute error criterion ε.

2. The subroutine should divide the interval $[a, b]$ into two equal parts and apply formulas (7.56a), (7.56b), and (7.60) to obtain S, $\bar{S}$, and E for each part.
3. If E satisfies the required error conditions on a subinterval, store $\bar{S}$; otherwise halve that interval and repeat step 2.
4. Continue subdividing as necessary up to a maximum of four nested subdivisions.
5. Output should consist of
   (i) An integer variable IFLAG = 1 if the error test was satisfied on a set of intervals covering $[a, b]$, and IFLAG = 2 if the error test was not satisfied on one or more subintervals.
   (ii) If IFLAG = 1, print $P = \Sigma \bar{S}_i$
   If IFLAG = 2, print the partial sum PP = $\Sigma \bar{S}_i$ on those intervals where the error test was satisfied and a list of intervals $[x_i, x_{i+1}]$ on which the test was not satisfied.

7.5-6 Verify the statement in the text that if the error (7.60) is satisfied on each of the N subintervals which cover the interval $[a, b]$, then $P = \Sigma_{i-1}^{N} \bar{S}_i$ will satisfy the required error condition (7.55) over the whole interval $[a, b]$.

*7.6 EXTRAPOLATION TO THE LIMIT

In the preceding sections, we spent considerable effort in deriving expressions for the error of the various rules for approximate integration and differentiation. To summarize: With $L(f)$ the integral of $f(x)$ over some interval $[a, b]$, or the value of some derivative of $f(x)$ at some point a, we constructed an approximation $L_h(f)$ to $L(f)$, which depends on a parameter h and which satisfies

$$\lim_{h \to 0} L_h(f) = L(f)$$

More explicitly, we usually proved that

$$L(f) = L_h(f) + ch^r f^{(s)}(\xi)$$

where c is some constant, r and s are positive integers, and $\xi = \xi(h)$ is an unknown point in some interval. We pointed out that a direct bound for the size of the error term requires knowledge of the size of $|f^{(s)}(\xi)|$, which very often cannot be obtained accurately enough (if at all) to be of any use.

Nevertheless, such an error term tells us at what rate $L_h(f)$ approaches $L(f)$ (as $h \to 0$). This knowledge can be used at times to estimate the error from successive values of $L_h(f)$. The possibility of such estimates was briefly mentioned in Sec. 1.6; in Sec. 3.4, we discussed a specific example, the Aitken Δ^2 process, and another example is given in the preceding Sec. 7.5.

As a simple example, consider the approximation

$$D_h(f) = \frac{f(a + h) - f(a - h)}{2h}$$

to the value

$$D(f) = f'(a)$$

of the first derivative of $f(x)$ at $x = a$. If $f(x)$ has three continuous derivatives, then, according to (7.8) or (7.11),

$$D(f) = D_h(f) - \tfrac{1}{6}h^2 f'''(\xi) \qquad \text{some } \xi \text{ with } |\xi - a| < |h|$$

Since $\xi(h) \to a$ as $h \to 0$, and $f'''(x)$ is continuous, we have

$$f'''(\xi) \to f'''(a) \qquad \text{as } h \to 0$$

Hence

$$\frac{[f'''(\xi) - f'''(a)]h^2}{6}$$

goes to zero faster than h^2. Using the order notation introduced in Sec. 1.6, we therefore get that

$$D(f) = D_h(f) + C_1 h^2 + o(h^2) \tag{7.61}$$

where the constant $C_1 = -f'''(a)/6$ does not depend on h.

A numerical example might help to bring out the significance of Eq. (7.61). With $f(x) = \sin x$ and $a = 1$, we get

$$D(f) = 0.540402$$
$$C_1 = 0.090050$$

In Table 7.2, we have listed $D_h(f)$, the error $E_h(f) = -h^2 f'''(\xi)/6$, and its two components, $C_1 h^2$ and $o(h^2)$, for various values of h. (To avoid round-off-error noise interference, all entries in this table were computed in double-precision arithmetic, then rounded.) As this table shows, $C_1 h^2$ becomes quickly the dominant component in the error since, although $C_1 h^2$ goes to zero (with h), the $o(h^2)$ component goes to zero faster. But this implies that we can get a good estimate for the dominant error component $C_1 h^2$ as follows: Substitute $2h$ for h in (7.61) to get

$$D(f) = D_{2h}(f) + 4C_1 h^2 + o(h^2)$$

On subtracting this equation from (7.61), we obtain

$$0 = D_h(f) - D_{2h}(f) - 3C_1 h^2 + o(h^2)$$

or

$$C_1 h^2 = \frac{D_h(f) - D_{2h}(f)}{3} + o(h^2) \tag{7.62}$$

This last equation states that, for sufficiently small h, the computable number

$$\frac{D_h(f) - D_{2h}(f)}{3} \tag{7.63}$$

is a good estimate for the usually unknown dominant error component $C_1 h^2$. This is nicely illustrated in Table 7.2, where we have also listed the numbers (7.63).

Table 7.2

h	$D_h(f)$	$E_h(f)$	C_1h^2	$o(h^2)$	$(D_h - D_{2h})/3$	R_h
6.4	0.009839	0.530463	3.688464	−3.158001		
3.2	−0.009856	0.550158	0.922116	−0.371957	−0.065652	−0.57
1.6	0.337545	0.202757	0.230529	−0.027772	0.115800	2.37
0.8	0.484486	0.055816	0.057632	−0.001816	0.048980	3.54
0.4	0.526009	0.014293	0.014408	−0.000115	0.013841	3.88
0.2	0.536707	0.003594	0.003602	−0.000007	0.003566	3.97
0.1	0.539402	0.000900	0.000901	−0.0000005	0.000898	

The catch in these considerations is, of course, the phrase "for sufficiently small h." Indeed, we see from Table 7.2 that, in our numerical example, $(D_h - D_{2h})/3$ is good only as an order-of-magnitude estimate when $h = 1.6$, while for $h = 3.2$, $(D_h - D_{2h})/3$ is not even in the ball park. Hence the number (7.63) should not be accepted indiscriminately as an estimate for the error. Rather, one should protect oneself against drastic mistakes by a simple check, based on the following argument: If C_1h^2 is indeed the dominant error component, i.e., if the $o(h^2)$ is "small" compared with C_1h^2, then, from (7.62),

$$C_1h^2 \approx \frac{D_h - D_{2h}(f)}{3}$$

Hence also

$$C_1\left(\frac{h}{2}\right)^2 \approx \frac{D_{h/2}(f) - D_h(f)}{3}$$

Therefore

$$\frac{D_h(f) - D_{2h}(f)}{D_{h/2}(f) - D_h(f)} \approx \frac{C_1h^2}{C_1h^2/4} = 4$$

In words, if C_1h^2 is the dominant error component, then the computable ratio of differences

$$R_h = \frac{D_h(f) - D_{2h}(f)}{D_{h/2}(f) - D_h(f)} \tag{7.64}$$

should be about 4. This is quite evident, for our numerical example, in Table 7.2, where we have also listed the ratios R_h.

Once one believes that (7.63) is a good estimate for the error in $D_h(f)$, having reassured oneself by checking that $R_h \approx 4$, then one can expect

$$D_h^1(f) = D_h(f) + \frac{D_h(f) - D_{2h}(f)}{3} \tag{7.65}$$

to be a much better approximation to $D(f)$ than is $D_h(f)$. In particular, one then believes that

$$|D(f) - D_h^1(f)| < \frac{|D_h(f) - D_{2h}(f)|}{3} \qquad (7.66)$$

In order to see how much better an approximation $D_h^1(f)$ might be, we now obtain a more detailed description of the error term

$$E_h(f) = -\tfrac{1}{6}h^2 f'''(\xi)$$

for $D_h(f)$. For the sake of variety, we use Taylor series rather than divided differences for this. If $f(x)$ has five continuous derivatives, then, on expanding both $f(a + h)$ and $f(a - h)$ in a partial Taylor series around $x = a$, we get

$$f(a + h) = f(a) + f'(a)h + \frac{f''(a)h^2}{2} + \frac{f'''(a)h^3}{6} + \frac{f^{iv}(a)h^4}{24}$$
$$+ \frac{f^v(a)h^5}{120} + o(h^5)$$

$$f(a - h) = f(a) - f'(a)h + \frac{f''(a)h^2}{2} - \frac{f'''(a)h^3}{6} + \frac{f^{iv}(a)h^4}{24}$$
$$- \frac{f^v(a)h^5}{120} + o(h^5)$$

Subtract the second equation from the first; then divide by $2h$ to get

$$D_h(f) = f'(a) + \frac{f'''(a)h^2}{6} + \frac{f^v(a)h^4}{120} + o(h^4)$$

Hence

$$D(f) = D_h(f) + C_1 h^2 + C_2 h^4 + o(h^4) \qquad (7.67)$$

where the constants

$$C_1 = \frac{-f'''(a)}{6} \qquad C_2 = \frac{-f^v(a)}{120}$$

do not depend on h. Therefore, on substituting $2h$ for h in (7.67), we get

$$D(f) = D_{2h}(f) + 4C_1 h^2 + 16C_2 h^4 + o(h^4) \qquad (7.68)$$

Subtracting $\tfrac{1}{3}$ of (7.68) from $\tfrac{4}{3}$ of (7.67) now gives

$$D(f) = D_h^1(f) + C_2^1 h^4 + o(h^4) \qquad (7.69)$$

with

$$C_2^1 = -4C_2 = \frac{f^v(a)}{30}$$

since, by (7.65),

$$D_h^1(f) = \frac{4D_h(f) - D_{2h}(f)}{3}$$

A comparison of (7.69) with (7.67) shows that $D_h^1(f)$ is a *higher-order* approximation to $D(f)$ than is $D_h(f)$: If $C_1 \neq 0$, then $D(f) - D_h(f)$ goes to zero (with h) only as fast as h^2, while $D(f) - D_h^1(f)$ goes to zero at least as fast as h^4.

This process of obtaining from two lower-order approximations a higher-order approximation is usually called **extrapolation to the limit**, or **to zero-grid size**. (See Exercise 7.6-3 for an explanation of this terminology.)

Extrapolation to the limit is in no way limited to approximations with $\mathcal{O}(h^2)$ error. We get, for example, from (7.69), by setting $h = 2h$, that

$$D(f) = D_{2h}^1(f) + 16C_2^1 h^4 + o(h^4)$$

Hence, on subtracting this from (7.69) and rearranging, we obtain

$$C_2^1 h^4 = \frac{D_h^1(f) - D_{2h}^1(f)}{15} + o(h^4)$$

Therefore, setting

$$D_h^2(f) = D_h^1(f) + \frac{D_h^1(f) - D_{2h}^1(f)}{15}$$

we get that

$$D(f) = D_h^2(f) + o(h^4)$$

showing $D_h^2(f)$ to be an even higher order approximation to $D(f)$ than is $D_h^1(f)$. More explicitly, it can be shown that

$$D(f) = D_h^2(f) + C_3^2 h^6 + o(h^6) \qquad (7.70)$$

if $f(x)$ is sufficiently smooth. But note that, for any particular value of h, $D_h^2(f)$ cannot be expected to be a better approximation to $D(f)$ than is $D_h^1(f)$ unless

$$\frac{D_h^1(f) - D_{2h}^1(f)}{15}$$

is a good estimate for the error in $D_h^1(f)$, that is, unless $C_2^1 h^4$ is the dominant part of the error in $D_h^1(f)$. This will be the case only if

$$R_h^1 = \frac{D_h^1(f) - D_{2h}^1(f)}{D_{h/2}^1(f) - D_h^1(f)} \approx \frac{C_2^1 h^4}{C_2^1 (h/2)^4} = 16$$

Hence this condition should be checked before believing that

$$|D(f) - D_h^2(f)| < \frac{|D_h^1(f) - D_{2h}^1(f)|}{15}$$

We have listed in Table 7.3 the results of applying extrapolation to the limit twice to the sequence of $D_h^1(f)$ calculated for Table 7.2. We have also listed the various values of R_h^1. All calculations were carried out with rounding to six places after the decimal point.

Table 7.3

h	$D_h(f)$	R_h	$D_h^1(f)$	R_h^1	$D_h^2(f)$
6.4	0.009839				
3.2	−0.009856	−0.57	−0.075508		
1.6	0.337545	2.37	0.453345	6.1	0.488602
0.8	0.484486	3.54	0.533466	12.5	0.538807
0.4	0.526009	3.88	0.539850	15.1	0.540276
0.2	0.536707	3.97	0.540273	15.7	0.540301
0.1	0.539402		0.540300		0.540302

Finally, there is nothing sacred about the number 2 used above for all extrapolations. Indeed, if q is any fixed number, then we get, for example, from (7.67) that

$$D(f) = D_{qh}(f) + q^2 C_1 h^2 + q^4 C_2 h^4 + o(h^4)$$

Subtracting this from (7.67) and rearranging then gives

$$C_1 h^2 = \frac{D_h(f) - D_{qh}(f)}{q^2 - 1} - (1 + q^2) C_2 h^4 + o(h^4)$$

Hence, with

$$D_{h,q}(f) = D_h(f) + \frac{D_h(f) - D_{qh}(f)}{q^2 - 1}$$

we find that

$$D(f) = D_{h,q}(f) - q^2 C_2 h^4 + o(h^4)$$

showing $D_{h,q}(f)$ to be an $\mathcal{O}(h^4)$ approximation to $D(f)$. For example, we calculate from Table 7.2 that

$$D_{0.1,4}(f) = 0.539402 + \frac{0.539402 - 0.526009}{16 - 1} = 0.540295$$

which is in error by only seven units in the last place.

We have collected the salient points of the preceding discussion in the following algorithm.

Algorithm 7.1: Extrapolation to the limit Given the means of calculating an approximation $L_h(f)$ to the number $L(f)$ for every $h > 0$, where $L_h(f)$ is known to satisfy

$$L(f) = L_h(f) + Ch^r + o(h^r) \qquad \text{all } h > 0$$

with C a constant independent of h, and r a positive number.

Pick an h, and a number $q > 1$ (for example, $q = 2$) and calculate

$$L_{h,q}(f) = L_h(f) + \frac{L_h(f) - L_{qh}(f)}{q^r - 1}$$

from the two numbers $L_h(f)$ and $L_{qh}(f)$. Then

$$L(f) = L_{h,q}(f) + o(h^r)$$

so that, for sufficiently small h,

$$|L(f) - L_{h,q}(f)| < |L_{h,q}(f) - L_h(f)| \tag{7.71}$$

Before putting any faith in (7.71), ascertain that, at least,

$$\frac{L_h(f) - L_{qh}(f)}{L_{h/p}(f) - L_h(f)} \approx \frac{Ch^r(q^r - 1)}{Ch^r(1 - p^{-r})} = p^r \frac{q^r - 1}{p^r - 1}$$

for some $p > 1$ (for example, $p = q$).

EXERCISES

7.6-1 With $f(x) = x + x^2 + x^5$ and $a = 0$, calculate $D_h(f)$ and $D_h^1(f)$ for various values of h. Why is $D_h^1(f)$ *always* a worse approximation to $D(f) = f'(0)$ than is $D_h(f)$? (Use high enough precision arithmetic to rule out roundoff as the culprit or get an explicit expression for D_h and D_h^1 in terms of h.)

7.6-2 Using extrapolation to the limit, find $f'(0.4)$ for the data given.

x	$\sinh x = f(x)$
0.398	0.408591
0.399	0.409671
0.400	0.410752
0.401	0.411834
0.402	0.412915

In this case the extrapolated value is a poorer approximation. Explain why this is so. [*Note:* The correct value of $f'(0.4)$ is 1.081072.]

7.6-3 Show that extrapolation to the limit can be based on analytic substitution. Specifically, with the notation of Algorithm 7.1, show that

$$L_{h,q}(f) = \lim_{x \to 0} p(x) \approx \lim_{x \to 0} L_x(f) = L(f)$$

where the approximation $p(x)$ to $g(x) = L_x(f)$ is obtained by finding A and B such that

$$p(x) = A + Bx^r$$

agrees with $g(x)$ at $x = h$ and $x = qh$. How does this explain the name "extrapolation to the limit"?

*7.7 ROMBERG INTEGRATION

Extrapolation to the limit is probably best known for its use with the composite trapezoid rule where it is known as **Romberg integration**. We start out with the composite trapezoid rule approximation (see Sec. 7.4)

$$T_N = T_N(f) = h \sum_{i=1}^{N-1} f_i + \frac{h(f_0 + f_N)}{2} \tag{7.72}$$

to the number
$$I = I(f) = \int_a^b f(x)\, dx$$

Here N is a positive integer related to h by

$$h = \frac{b - a}{N}$$

and
$$f_i = f_{i, N} = f(a + ih) \quad i = 0, \ldots, N$$

If $f(x)$ is four times continuously differentiable, we infer from (7.50) and (7.51) that

$$I(f) = T_N(f) + C_1 h^2 + \mathcal{O}(h^4) \tag{7.73}$$

where the constant $C_1 = [f'(a) - f'(b)]/12$ is independent of h. Hence extrapolation to the limit is applicable. We get that

$$T_{N, q}(f) = T_N + \frac{T_N(f) - T_{N/q}(f)}{q^2 - 1}$$

is an $\mathcal{O}(h^4)$ approximation to $I(f)$, while in general, $T_N(f)$ has only an error of $\mathcal{O}(h^2)$.

Note that the choice of q or N is restricted by the condition that N/q be an integer. One usually chooses $q = 2$ (so that N must be even). This choice for q has the computationally important advantage that all function values used for the calculation of $T_{N/q}$ can also be used for the calculation of T_N. Specifically, we prove that for even N,

$$T_N(f) = \frac{T_{N/2}(f)}{2} + h \sum_{i=1}^{N/2} f(a + (2i - 1)h) \tag{7.74}$$

For by (7.72),

$$T_N(f) = h \sum_{i=1}^{N-1} f(a + ih) + \frac{h(f(a) + f(b))}{2}$$

$$= h \sum_{i=1}^{N/2} f(a + (2i - 1)h) + h \sum_{i=1}^{N/2-1} f(a + 2ih) + \frac{h(f(a) + f(b))}{2}$$

Here the first sum extends over the "odd" points and the second sum over the "even" points. The last two terms can be written

$$\left[2h \sum_{j=1}^{N/2-1} f(a + j(2h)) + \frac{2h(f(a) + f(b))}{2} \right] \bigg/ 2$$

Hence, since

$$2h = \frac{2(b - a)}{N} = \frac{b - a}{N/2}$$

these last two terms add up to $T_{N/2}(f)/2$. This proves (7.74). Note that (7.74) can be written more simply

$$T_N(f) = \frac{T_{N/2}(f) + M_{N/2}(f)}{2}$$

with M denoting the composite midpoint rule (7.49a).

If the integrand has $2k + 2$ continuous derivatives, it can be shown that, more explicitly than (7.73),

$$I(f) = T_N(f) + C_1 h^2 + C_2 h^4 + C_3 h^6 + \cdots + C_k h^{2k} + \mathcal{O}(h^{2k+2})$$

where the constants $C_1, \ldots, C_k$ do not depend on h. Hence, with

$$T_N^1(f) = T_N(f) + \frac{T_N(f) - T_{N/2}(f)}{3}$$

we get that

$$I(f) = T_N^1(f) + C_2^1 h^4 + C_3^1 h^6 + \cdots + C_k^1 h^{2k} + \mathcal{O}(h^{2k+2})$$

with the constants $C_2^1, \ldots, C_k^1$ independent of h. Further extrapolation is therefore meaningful. Setting

$$T_N^2(f) = T_N^1(f) + \frac{T_N^1(f) - T_{N/2}^1(f)}{15}$$

we get that

$$I(f) = T_N^2(f) + C_3^2 h^6 + \cdots + C_k^2 h_k^{2k} + \mathcal{O}(h^{2k+2})$$

More generally, it is seen that, for $m = 1, \ldots, k$,

$$T_N^m(f) = T_N^{m-1}(f) + \frac{T_N^{m-1}(f) - T_{N/2}^{m-1}(f)}{4^m - 1}$$

is an $\mathcal{O}(h^{2m+2})$ approximation to $I(f)$.

Note that the calculation of T_N^m involves $T_{N/2}^{m-1}$ and T_N^{m-1}; hence $T_{N/4}^{m-2}$, $T_{N/2}^{m-2}$, and T_N^{m-2}; $\ldots$, and finally, $T_{N/2^m}, \ldots, T_{N/2}$, and T_N. $N/2^m$ must therefore be an integer,

$$\frac{N}{2^m} = M$$

say, for T_N^m to be defined. It is convenient to visualize these various approximations to $I(f)$ as entries of a triangular array, the so-called T table:

$$
\begin{array}{lllll}
T_M^0 & & & & \\
T_{2M}^0 & T_{2M}^1 & & & \\
T_{4M}^0 & T_{4M}^1 & T_{4M}^2 & & \\
\cdots\cdots & \cdots\cdots & \cdots\cdots & \cdots\cdots & \\
T_{2^mM}^0 & T_{2^mM}^1 & T_{2^mM}^2 & \cdots & T_{2^mM}^m
\end{array}
$$

Here we have written T_N^0 for T_N.

Algorithm 7.2: Romberg integration Given a function $f(x)$ defined on $[a, b]$ and a positive integer M (usually, $M = 1$).

$h := (b - a)/M$
Calculate $T_M^0 = h\sum_{i=1}^{M-1} f(a + ih) + h(f(a) + f(b))/2$
For $k = 1, 2, 3, \ldots$, do:

> $h := h/2$
> Calculate $T_{2^kM}^0 = \frac{1}{2}T_{2^{k-1}M}^0 + h\sum_{i=1}^{2^{k-1}M} f(a + (2i - 1)h)$
> For $m = 1, \ldots, k$, do:
>> Calculate $T_{2^kM}^m = T_{2^kM}^{m-1} + (T_{2^kM}^{m-1} - T_{2^{k-1}M}^{m-1})/(4^m - 1)$

If $f(x)$ has $2m + 2$ continuous derivatives, then

$$
I(f) = \int_a^b f(x)\,dx = T_{2^kM}^m + \mathcal{O}\!\left(\left[\frac{b - a}{2^kM}\right]^{2m+2}\right) \qquad k = m, m + 1, \cdots
$$

Also, if k is sufficiently large, then

$$
|I(f) - T_{2^kM}^m| < |T_{2^kM}^m - T_{2^kM}^{m-1}|
$$

But before putting any faith in this inequality, check that at least

$$
R_k^{m-1} = \frac{T_{2^{k-1}M}^{m-1} - T_{2^{k-2}M}^{m-1}}{T_{2^kM}^{m-1} - T_{2^{k-1}M}^{m-1}} \approx 4^m
$$

Example 7.9 Use Romberg integration for Example 7.1.

The integral in question is

$$
I(f) = \int_0^1 e^{-x^2}\,dx
$$

The FORTRAN program below has been set up to produce the first six rows of the T table and the corresponding table of ratios R_k^m, as follows:

Romberg T table

0.7313700E 00				
0.7429838E 00	0.7468551E 00			
0.7458653E 00	0.7468258E 00	0.7468238E 00		
0.7465842E 00	0.7468238E 00	0.7468237E 00	0.7468237E 00	
0.7467639E 00	0.7468237E 00	0.7468237E 00	0.7468237E 00	0.7468237E 00
0.7468069E 00	0.7468212E 00	0.7468210E 00	0.7468210E 00	0.7468209E 00

Table of ratios

4.03			
4.01	14.88		
4.00	16.50	0.0	
4.17	0.05	0.0	0.0

M was chosen to be 2, so that the first entry in the T table is $T_2(f)$. Note that the first column of ratios converges very nicely to 4, but then begins to move away from 4. This effect is even more pronounced in the second column of ratios, which approach 16 (as they should), and then, as the last entry shows, become erratic. Conclusion: The error in the entries of the last row of the T table is mainly due to roundoff (rather than discretization). Hence

$$0.7468237$$

seems to be the best estimate for $I(f)$ to be gotten with the particular arithmetic used. Since

$$R_4^1 = 16.5 \approx 16 = 4^2$$

and

$$T_{2 \cdot M}^1 = T_{2 \cdot M}^2 = 0.7468237$$

to the number of places shown, we conclude that this estimate is accurate to the number of places shown. Actually,

$$\int_0^1 e^{-x^2}\, dx = 0.74682413279 \cdots$$

The discrepancy between this number and our "accurate" estimate is due to the fact that we are not dealing with the integrand

$$f(x) = e^{-x^2}$$

in our calculations, but rather with a rounded version of $f(x)$, that is, with the function

$$F(X) = EXP(-X*X)$$

All calculations were carried out in single precision on an IBM 360, which has particularly poor rounding characteristics.

FORTRAN PROGRAM FOR EXAMPLE 7.9

```
      REAL T(100)
      EXTERNAL FERR
      CALL RMBERG( FERR, 0., 1., 2, T, 6 )
                                          STOP
      END
      SUBROUTINE RMBERG ( F, A, B, MSTART, T, NROW )
C  CONSTRUCTS AND PRINTS OUT THE FIRST   NROW  ROWS OF THE ROMBERG T-
C  TABLE FOR THE INTEGRAL OF   F(X)   FROM   A   TO  B  , STARTING WITH THE
C  TRAPEZOIDAL SUM ON  MSTART  INTERVALS.
      INTEGER MSTART,NROW,   I,K,M
      REAL A,B,T(NROW,NROW),   H,SUM
      M = MSTART
      H = (B-A)/M
      SUM = (F(A) + F(B))/2.
      IF (M .GT. 1) THEN
         DO 10 I=1,M-1
10          SUM = SUM + F(A+FLOAT(I)*H)
      END IF
      T(1,1) = SUM*H
      PRINT 610
```

```
    610 FORMAT('1',10X,'ROMBERG T-TABLE'//)
        PRINT 611, T(1,1)
    611 FORMAT(7E15.7)
        IF (NROW .LT. 2)                        RETURN
C
        DO 20 K=2,NROW
           H = H/2.
           M = M*2
           SUM = 0.
           DO 11 I=1,M,2
    11        SUM = SUM + F(A+FLOAT(I)*H)
           T(K,1) = T(K-1,1)/2. + SUM*H
           DO 12 J=1,K-1
C                   SAVE DIFFERENCES FOR LATER CALC. OF RATIOS
              T(K-1,J) = T(K,J) - T(K-1,J)
    12        T(K,J+1) = T(K,J) + T(K-1,J)/(4.**J - 1.)
    20     PRINT 611, (T(K,J),J=1,K)
        IF (NROW .LT. 3)                        RETURN
C                    CALCULATE RATIOS
        PRINT 620
    620 FORMAT(///11X,'TABLE OF RATIOS'//)
        DO 30 K=1,NROW-2
           DO 25 J=1,K
              IF (T(K+1,J) .EQ. 0.) THEN
                 RATIO= 0.
              ELSE
                 RATIO = T(K,J)/T(K+1,J)
              END IF
    25        T(K,J) = RATIO
    30     PRINT 630, (T(K,J),J=1,K)
    630 FORMAT(8F10.2)
                                                RETURN
        END
        REAL FUNCTION FERR(X)
        REAL X
        FERR = EXP(-X*X)
                                                RETURN
        END
```

EXERCISES

7.7-1 Prove that, in Romberg integration, $T_{2M}^1 = S_M$, where S_M is the composite Simpson's rule; see (7.48).

7.7-2 Try to estimate $I(f) = \int_a^b f(x)\,dx$ to within 10^{-6}, using Romberg integration, for each of the following cases:

(a) $f(x) = x^2$	$a = 0, b = 1$, M arbitrary
(b) $f(x) = \sin 101\pi x$	$a = 0, b = 1$, $M = 1$
(c) $f(x) = 1 + \sin 10\pi x$	$a = 0, b = 1$, $M = 1$
(d) $f(x) = |x - \frac{1}{3}|$	$a = 0, b = 1$, $M = 1$ and $M = 3$
(e) $f(x) = \sqrt{x}$	$a = 0, b = 1$, M arbitrary

$$(f)\ f(x) = \begin{cases} \dfrac{\sin x}{x} & x \neq 0 \\ 1 & x = 0 \end{cases} \qquad a = 0, b = 1$$

7.7-3 From the data below calculate $\int_1^{1.8} f(x)\,dx$ as accurately as possible using Romberg integration. Construct a T table starting with $M = 1$.

x	f(x)
1.0	0.36787944
1.1	0.36615819
1.2	0.36143305
1.3	0.35429133
1.4	0.34523574
1.5	0.33469524
1.6	0.32303443
1.7	0.31056199
1.8	0.29753800

7.7-4 Obtain Simpson's rule for $I_h(f) = \int_{-h}^{h} f(x)\, dx$ by extrapolating from the midpoint rule and the trapezoid rule. (*Hint:* Form the appropriate linear combination of the two equations

$$I_h(f) = T(f) + C_T h^2 + \Theta(h^4) \qquad I_h(f) = M(f) + C_M h^2 + \Theta(h^4)$$

to eliminate the h^2 terms. This requires you to find out what the constants C_T and C_M are.

EIGHT

THE SOLUTION OF DIFFERENTIAL EQUATIONS

Many problems in engineering and science can be formulated in terms of differential equations. A large part of the motivation for building the early computers came from the need to compute ballistic trajectories accurately and quickly. Today computers are used extensively to solve the equations of ballistic-missile and artificial-satellite theory, as well as those of electrical networks, bending of beams, stability of aircraft, vibration theory, and others.

It is assumed that the student is familiar with the elementary theory of differential equations. In a first course one learns various techniques for solving in closed form some selected classes of differential equations. The vast majority of equations encountered in practice cannot, however, be solved analytically, and recourse must necessarily be made to numerical methods. Fortunately, there are many good methods available for solving differential equations on computers. In this chapter we shall derive several classes of methods, and we shall evaluate them for computational efficiency.

8.1 MATHEMATICAL PRELIMINARIES

It will be useful to review some elementary definitions and concepts from the theory of differential equations. An equation involving a relation between the values of an unknown function and one or more of its derivatives is called a **differential equation**. We shall always assume that the equation can be solved explicitly for the derivative of highest order. An ordinary differential equation of order n will then have the form

$$y^{(n)}(x) = f(x, y(x), y'(x), \ldots, y^{(n-1)}(x)) \tag{8.1}$$

By a solution of (8.1) we mean a function $\phi(x)$ which is n times continuously differentiable on a prescribed interval and which satisfies (8.1); that is $\phi(x)$ must satisfy

$$\phi^{(n)}(x) = f(x, \phi(x), \phi'(x), \phi''(x), \ldots, \phi^{(n-1)}(x))$$

The general solution of (8.1) will normally contain n arbitrary constants, and hence there exists an n-parameter family of solutions. If $y(x_0)$, $y'(x_0), \ldots, y^{(n-1)}(x_0)$ are prescribed at one point $x = x_0$, we have an **initial-value problem**. We shall always assume that the function f satisfies conditions sufficient to guarantee a unique solution to this initial-value problem. A simple example of a first-order equation is $y' = y$. Its general solution is $y(x) = Ce^x$, where C is an arbitrary constant. If the initial condition $y(x_0) = y_0$ is prescribed, the solution can be written $y(x) = y_0 e^{(x-x_0)}$.

Differential equations are further classified as **linear** and **nonlinear**. An equation is said to be linear if the function f in (8.1) involves y and its derivatives linearly. Linear differential equations possess the important property that if $y_1(x), y_2(x), \ldots, y_m(x)$ are any solutions of (8.1), then so is $C_1 y_1(x) + C_2 y_2(x) + \cdots + C_m y_m(x)$ for arbitrary constants C_i. A simple second-order equation is $y'' = y$. It is easily verified that e^x and e^{-x} are solutions of this equation, and hence by linearity the following sum is also a solution:

$$y(x) = C_1 e^x + C_2 e^{-x} \tag{8.2}$$

Two solutions y_1, y_2 of a second-order linear differential equation are said to be **linearly independent** if the Wronskian of the solution does not vanish, the **Wronskian** being defined by

$$W(y_1, y_2) = y_1 y_2' - y_2 y_1' = \begin{vmatrix} y_1 & y_1' \\ y_2 & y_2' \end{vmatrix} \tag{8.3}$$

The concept of linear independence can be extended to the solutions of equations of higher order. If $y_1(x), y_2(x), \ldots, y_n(x)$ are n linearly independent solutions of a homogeneous differential equation of order n, then

$$y(x) = C_1 y_1(x) + C_2 y_2(x) + \cdots + C_n y_n(x)$$

is called the **general solution**.

Among linear equations, those with constant coefficients are particularly useful since they lend themselves to a simple treatment. We write the nth-order linear differential equation with constant coefficients in the form

$$Ly = y^{(n)} + a_{n-1} y^{(n-1)} + \cdots + a_0 y^{(0)} = 0 \tag{8.4}$$

where the a_i are assumed to be real. If we seek solutions of (8.4) in the form $e^{\beta x}$, then direct substitution shows that β must satisfy the polynomial equation

$$\beta^n + a_{n-1}\beta^{n-1} + \cdots + a_0 = 0 \qquad (8.5)$$

This is called the **characteristic equation** of the nth-order differential equation (8.4). If the equation (8.5) has n distinct roots β_i $(i = 1, \ldots, n)$, then it can be shown that

$$y(x) = C_1 e^{\beta_1 x} + C_2 e^{\beta_2 x} + \cdots + C_n e^{\beta_n x} \qquad (8.6)$$

where the C_i are arbitrary constants, is the general solution of (8.4). If $\beta_1 = \alpha + i\beta$ is a complex root of (8.5), so is its conjugate, $\beta_2 = \alpha - i\beta$. Corresponding to such a pair of conjugate-complex roots are two solutions $y_1 = e^{\alpha x} \cos \beta x$ and $y_2 = e^{\alpha x} \sin \beta x$, which are linearly independent. When (8.5) has multiple roots, special techniques are available for obtaining linearly independent solutions. In particular, if β_1 is a double root of (8.5), then $y_1 = e^{\beta_1 x}$ and $y_2 = xe^{\beta_1 x}$ are linearly independent solutions of (8.4). For the special equation $y'' + a^2 y = 0$, the characteristic equation is $\beta^2 = -a^2$; its roots are $\beta_{1,2} = \pm ia$, and its general solution is $y(x) = C_1 \cos ax + C_2 \sin ax$.

Finally, if Eq. (8.1) is linear but nonhomogeneous, i.e., if

$$Ly = g(x) \qquad (8.7)$$

and if $\zeta(x)$ is a particular solution of (8.7), i.e., if

$$L\zeta = g(x)$$

then the general solution of (8.7), assuming that the roots of (8.5) are distinct, is

$$y = \zeta(x) + C_1 e^{\beta_1 x} + C_2 e^{\beta_2 x} + \cdots + C_n e^{\beta_n x} \qquad (8.8)$$

Example Find the solution of the equation

(a) $y'' - 4y' + 3y = x$

satisfying the initial conditions

(b) $y(0) = \frac{4}{9}$ $y'(0) = \frac{7}{3}$

1. To find a particular solution $\zeta(x)$ of (a), we try $\zeta(x) = ax + b$, since the right side is a polynomial of degree ≤ 1 and the left side is such a polynomial whenever $y = y(x)$ is. Substituting into (a), we find that $a = \frac{1}{3}$, $b = \frac{4}{9}$. Hence

$$\zeta(x) = \tfrac{1}{3}x + \tfrac{4}{9}$$

2. To find solutions of the homogeneous equation

$$y'' - 4y' + 3y = 0$$

we examine the characteristic equation

$$\beta^2 - 4\beta + 3 = 0$$

Its roots are $\beta_1 = 3$, $\beta_2 = 1$. Hence the two linearly independent solutions of the homogeneous system are

$$y_1(x) = e^{3x} \qquad y_2(x) = e^x$$

3. The general solution of equation (a) is

$$y(x) = \frac{x}{3} + \frac{4}{9} + C_1 e^{3x} + C_2 e^x$$

4. To find the solution satisfying conditions (b), we must have

$$y(0) = \tfrac{4}{9} + C_1 + C_2 = \tfrac{4}{9}$$

$$y'(0) = \tfrac{1}{3} + 3C_1 + C_2 = \tfrac{7}{3}$$

The solution of this system is $C_1 = 1$, $C_2 = -1$. Hence the desired solution is

$$y(x) = \frac{x}{3} + \frac{4}{9} + e^{3x} - e^x$$

EXERCISES

8.1-1 Find the general solution of the equations

(a) $y' = -2y$

(c) $y''' - 2y'' - y' + 2y = 0$

(e) $y' - xy = e^x$

(b) $y'' - 4y' + 4y = 0$

(d) $y' - ay = x$

(f) $y'' - 2y' + 2y = 0$

8.1-2 Find the solution of the following initial-value problems:

(a) $y' + 2y = 1$ $y(0) = 1$

(b) $y'' - a^2y = 0$ $y(0) = 0$ $y'(0) = 1$

(c) $y'' - 4y' + 4y = x$ $y(0) = 0$ $y'(0) = 1$

8.2 SIMPLE DIFFERENCE EQUATIONS

To analyze numerical methods for the solution of differential equations, it is necessary to understand some simple theory of difference equations. A difference equation of order N is a relation between the differences $y_n = \Delta^0 y_n, \Delta^1 y_n, \Delta^2 y_n, \ldots, \Delta^N y_n$ of a number sequence, i.e.,

$$\Delta^N y_n = f(n, y_n, \Delta y_n, \ldots, \Delta^{N-1} y_n) \tag{8.9}$$

A solution of such a difference equation is a sequence $y_m, y_{m+1}, y_{m+2}, \cdots$ of numbers such that (8.9) holds for $n = m, m + 1, m + 2, \ldots$. Hence, whereas a differential equation involves functions defined on some interval of real numbers, and their derivatives, a difference equation involves functions defined on some "interval" of integers, and their differences.

If (8.9) is a **linear** difference equation, so that the right side of (8.9) depends linearly on $y_n, \ldots, \Delta^{N-1} y_n$, then it is possible and customary to write (8.9) explicitly in terms of the y_j's as

$$y_{n+N} + a_{n,N-1} y_{n+N-1} + a_{n,N-2} y_{n+N-2} + \cdots + a_{n,0} y_n = b_n$$

Evidently, a linear difference equation of order N can be viewed as a (finite or infinite) system of linear equations whose coefficient matrix is a banded matrix of bandwidth $N + 1$.

Simple examples of linear difference equations are

$$y_{n+1} - y_n = 1 \qquad \text{all } n \qquad\qquad (8.10a)$$

$$y_{n+1} - y_n = n \qquad \text{all } n \geq 0 \qquad\qquad (8.10b)$$

$$y_{n+1} - (n + 1)y_n = 0 \qquad \text{all } n \geq 0 \qquad\qquad (8.10c)$$

$$y_{n+2} - (2 \cos \gamma)y_{n+1} + y_n = 0 \qquad \text{all } n \qquad\qquad (8.10d)$$

By direct substitution, these equations can be shown to have the solutions

$$y_n = n + c \qquad \text{all } n \qquad\qquad (8.11a)$$

$$y_n = \frac{n(n - 1)}{2} + c \qquad \text{all } n \geq 0 \qquad\qquad (8.11b)$$

$$y_n = cn! \qquad \text{all } n \geq 0 \qquad\qquad (8.11c)$$

$$y_n = c \cos \gamma n \qquad \text{all } n \qquad\qquad (8.11d)$$

with c an arbitrary constant.

We consider in detail a homogeneous linear difference equation of order N with *constant* coefficients

$$y_{n+N} + a_{N-1}y_{n+N-1} + \cdots + a_0 y_n = 0 \qquad\qquad (8.12)$$

As with homogeneous linear differential equations with constant coefficients, we seek solutions of the form $y_n = \beta^n$, all n. Substituting into (8.12) yields

$$\beta^{n+N} + a_{N-1}\beta^{n+N-1} + \cdots + a_0 \beta^n = 0$$

Dividing by β^n, we obtain the characteristic equation

$$p(\beta) = \beta^N + a_{N-1}\beta^{N-1} + \cdots + a_0 = 0 \qquad\qquad (8.13)$$

The **characteristic polynomial** is of degree N. We assume, first, that its zeros $\beta_1, \beta_2, \ldots, \beta_N$ are distinct. Then $\beta_1^n, \beta_2^n, \ldots, \beta_N^n$ are all solutions of (8.12), and by linearity it follows that

$$y_n = c_1\beta_1^n + c_2\beta_2^n + \cdots + c_N\beta_N^n \qquad \text{all } n \qquad\qquad (8.14)$$

for arbitrary constants c_i is also a solution of (8.12). Moreover, in this case it can be shown that (8.14) is the general solution of (8.12).

As an example, the difference equation

$$y_{n+3} - 2y_{n+2} - y_{n+1} + 2y_n = 0 \qquad\qquad (8.15)$$

is of third order, and its characteristic equation is

$$\beta^3 - 2\beta^2 - \beta + 2 = 0$$

The roots of this polynomial equation are $+1$, -1, 2, and the general solution of (8.15) is

$$y_n = c_1(1)^n + c_2(-1)^n + c_3(2)^n$$
$$= c_1 + (-1)^n c_2 + 2^n c_3 \tag{8.16}$$

If the first $N - 1$ values of y_n are given, the resulting **initial-value** difference equation can be solved explicitly for all succeeding values of n. Thus in (8.15), if $y_0 = 0, y_1 = 1, y_2 = 1$, then y_3 as computed from (8.15) is

$$y_3 = 2(1) + 1 - 0 = 3$$

Continuing to use (8.15), we find that $y_4 = 5, y_5 = 11$, etc. This does not yield a closed formula for y_n. However, using (8.16) and imposing the initial conditions for $n = 0, 1, 2$, we obtain the following system of equations for c_1, c_2, c_3:

$$0 = c_1 + c_2 + c_3$$
$$1 = c_1 - c_2 + 2c_3$$
$$1 = c_1 + c_2 + 4c_3$$

Its solution is $c_1 = 0, c_2 = -\frac{1}{3}, c_3 = \frac{1}{3}$, so that the closed-form solution of the initial-value problem is

$$y_n = -\tfrac{1}{3}(-1)^n + \frac{2^n}{3}$$

If the characteristic polynomial in (8.13) has a pair of conjugate-complex zeros, the solution can still be expressed in real form. Thus, if $\beta_1 = \alpha + i\beta$ and $\beta_2 = \alpha - i\beta$, we first express $\beta_{1,2}$ in polar form,

$$\beta_1 = re^{i\theta}$$
$$\beta_2 = re^{-i\theta}$$

where $r = \sqrt{\alpha^2 + \beta^2}$, and $\theta = \arctan(\beta/\alpha)$. Then the solution of (8.12) corresponding to this pair of zeros is

$$c_1\beta_1^n + c_2\beta_2^n = c_1 r^n e^{in\theta} + c_2 r^n e^{-in\theta}$$
$$= r^n[c_1(\cos n\theta + i \sin n\theta) + c_2(\cos n\theta - i \sin n\theta)]$$
$$= r^n(C_1 \cos n\theta + C_2 \sin n\theta)$$

where $C_1 = c_1 + c_2$ and $C_2 = i(c_1 - c_2)$. As a simple example, we consider the difference equation

$$y_{n+2} - 2y_{n+1} + 2y_n = 0 \tag{8.17}$$

Its characteristic equation is $\beta^2 - 2\beta + 2 = 0$, and the roots of this equation are $\beta_{1,2} = 1 \pm i$. Hence $r = \sqrt{2}$ and $\theta = \pi/4$, so that the general solution of (8.17) is

$$y_n = (\sqrt{2})^n \left(C_1 \cos \frac{n\pi}{4} + C_2 \sin \frac{n\pi}{4} \right)$$

If β_1 is a double root of the characteristic equation (8.13), then a second solution of (8.13) is $n\beta_1^n$. To verify this, we note first that if β_1 is a double zero of $p(\beta)$, then $p(\beta_1) = 0$ and also $p'(\beta_1) = 0$. Now on substituting $y_n = n\beta_1^n$ in (8.12) and rearranging, we find that

$$(n + N)\beta_1^{n+N} + a_{n-1}(n + N - 1)\beta_1^{n+N-1} + \cdots + a_0 n\beta_1^n$$
$$= \beta_1^n\{n(\beta_1^n + a_{N-1}\beta_1^{N-1} + \cdots + a_0)$$
$$+ \beta_1[N\beta_1^{N-1} + a_{N-1}(N - 1)\beta_1^{N-2} + \cdots + a_1]\}$$
$$= \beta_1^n[np(\beta_1) + \beta_1 p'(\beta_1)] = 0$$

since $p(\beta_1) = p'(\beta_1) = 0$. It can, moreover, be shown that these two solutions β_1^n and $n\beta_1^n$ are linearly independent.

As an illustration, for the difference equation

$$y_{n+3} - 5y_{n+2} + 8y_{n+1} - 4y_n = 0$$

the roots of the characteristic equation are 2, 2, 1, and the general solution is

$$y_n = 2^n(c_1 + nc_2) + c_3$$

We consider, finally, the solution of the nonhomogeneous linear difference equation with constant coefficients. The general solution of the equation

$$y_{n+N} + a_{N-1}y_{n+N-1} + \cdots + a_0 y_n = b_n \qquad (8.18)$$

can be written in the form

$$y_n = y_n^G + y_n^P$$

where y_n^G is the general solution of the homogeneous system (8.12), and y_n^P is a particular solution of (8.18). In the special case when $b_n = b$ is a constant, a particular solution can easily be obtained by setting $y_n^P = A$ (a constant) in (8.18). Substitution of $y_n = A$ in (8.18) leads to the determination

$$A = \frac{b}{1 + a_{N-1} + \cdots + a_0}$$

provided that the sum of the coefficients does not vanish.

For example, the general solution of the nonhomogeneous equation

$$y_{n+2} - 2y_{n+1} + 2y_n = 1$$

is
$$y_n = (\sqrt{2})^n\left(C_1 \cos\frac{n\pi}{4} + C_2 \sin\frac{n\pi}{4}\right) + 1$$

The simple properties of difference equations considered here will be sufficient for the applications in the remainder of this chapter.

Example Show that the general solution of the difference equation

(a) $y_{n+2} - (2 + h^2)y_{n+1} + y_n = h^2$

can be expressed in the form

$$(b) \quad y_n = c_1 \left[1 + h + \frac{h^2}{2} + \Theta(h^3) \right]^n + c_2 \left[1 - h + \frac{h^2}{2} + \Theta(h^3) \right]^n - 1$$

SOLUTION

1. A particular solution of (a), obtained by trying $y_n^P = C$ in (a), is found to be

$$y_n^P = -1$$

2. The characteristic equation of the homogeneous equation of (a) is

$$\beta^2 - (2 + h^2)\beta + 1 = 0$$

By the quadratic formula the roots are

$$\beta_{1,2} = \frac{2 + h^2 \pm \sqrt{4h^2 + h^4}}{2}$$

$$= \frac{2 + h^2 \pm 2h\sqrt{1 + h^2/4}}{2}$$

$$= 1 + \frac{h^2}{2} \pm h\left(1 + \frac{h^2}{4}\right)^{1/2}$$

On expanding $(1 + t)^{1/2}$ around $t = 0$ into a Taylor series and substituting $h^2/4$ for t, we obtain

$$\beta_{1,2} = 1 + \frac{h^2}{2} \pm h\left[1 + \frac{h^2}{8} + \Theta(h^4)\right]$$

$$\beta_1 = 1 + h + \frac{h^2}{2} + \Theta(h^3)$$

$$\beta_2 = 1 - h + \frac{h^2}{2} + \Theta(h^3)$$

Hence the general solution of the homogeneous system is

$$y_n^G = c_1\beta_1^n + c_2\beta_2^n$$

3. The solution of (a) is therefore

$$y_n = y_n^P + y_n^G$$

which establishes the solution in the form (b).

EXERCISES

8.2-1 Find the general solution of the difference equations

    (a) $y_{n+1} - 3y_n = 5$

    (b) $y_{n+2} - 4y_{n+1} + 4y_n = n$

(*Hint:* To find a particular solution, try $y_n^P = an + b$.)

    (c) $y_{n+2} + 2y_{n+1} + 2y_n = 0$

    (d) $y_{n+3} - y_{n+2} + 2y_{n+1} - 2y_n = 0$

    (e) $y_{n+2} - y_{n+1} - y_n = 0$

8.2-2 Find the solution of the initial-value difference equations

    (a) $y_{n+2} - 4y_{n+1} + 3y_n = 2^n$ $y_0 = 0$ $y_1 = 1$

    (b) $y_{n+2} - y_{n+1} - y_n = 0$ $y_0 = 0$ $y_1 = 1$

[*Hint:* To find a particular solution of (a), try $y_n^P = A2^n$.]

8.2-3 Show that the general solution of the difference equation

$$y_{n+2} + 4hy_{n+1} - y_n = 2h$$

where h is a positive constant, can be expressed in the form

$$y_n = c_1[1 - 2h + \Theta(h^2)]^n + c_2(-1)^n[1 + 2h + \Theta(h^2)]^n + \tfrac{1}{2}$$

8.2-4 Show that if $y_0 = 1$, $y_1 = x$, then the nth term, $y_n = y_n(x)$, of the solution of

$$y_{n+2} - 2xy_{n+1} + y_n = 0$$

is a polynomial of degree n in x with leading coefficient 2^{n-1}. [*Note:* The $y_n(x)$ are the Chebyshev polynomials considered in Sec. 6.1.]

8.3 NUMERICAL INTEGRATION BY TAYLOR SERIES

We are now prepared to consider numerical methods for integrating differential equations. We shall first consider a first-order initial-value differential equation of the form

$$y' = f(x, y) \qquad y(x_0) = y_0 \tag{8.19}$$

The function f may be linear or nonlinear, but we assume that f is sufficiently differentiable with respect to both x and y. It is known that (8.19) possesses a unique solution if $\partial f/\partial y$ is continuous on the domain of interest. If $y(x)$ is the exact solution of (8.19), we can expand $y(x)$ into a Taylor series about the point $x = x_0$:

$$y(x) = y_0 + (x - x_0)y'(x_0) + \frac{(x - x_0)^2}{2!}y''(x_0) + \cdots \tag{8.20}$$

The derivatives in this expansion are not known explicitly since the solution is not known. However, if f is sufficiently differentiable, they can be obtained by taking the total derivative of (8.19) with respect to x, keeping in mind that y is itself a function of x (see Sec. 1.7). Thus we obtain for the first few derivatives:

$$y' = f(x, y)$$
$$y'' = f' = f_x + f_y y' = f_x + f_y f$$
$$y''' = f'' = f_{xx} + f_{xy}f + f_{yx}f + f_{yy}f^2 + f_y f_x + f_y^2 f$$
$$= f_{xx} + 2f_{xy}f + f_{yy}f^2 + f_x f_y + f_y^2 f \tag{8.21}$$

Continuing in this manner, we can express any derivative of y in terms of $f(x, y)$ and its partial derivatives. It is already clear, however, that unless $f(x, y)$ is a very simple function, the higher total derivatives become increasingly complex. For practical reasons then, one must limit the number of terms in the expansion (8.20) to a reasonable number, and this restriction leads to a restriction on the value of x for which (8.20) is a reasonable approximation. If we assume that the truncated series (8.20) yields a good approximation for a step of length h, that is, for $x - x_0 = h$, we can then evaluate y at $x_0 + h$; reevaluate the derivatives y', y'', etc., at $x = x_0 + h$; and then use (8.20) to proceed to the next step. If we continue in this manner, we will obtain a discrete set of values y_n which are approximations to the true solution at the points $x_n = x_0 + nh$ ($n = 0, 1, 2, \ldots$). In this chapter we shall always denote the value of the exact solution at a point x_n by $y(x_n)$ and of an approximate solution by y_n.

In order to formalize this procedure, we first introduce the operator

$$T_k(x, y) = f(x, y) + \frac{h}{2!} f'(x, y) + \cdots + \frac{h^{k-1}}{k!} f^{(k-1)}(x, y)$$

$$k = 1, 2, \ldots \quad (8.22)$$

where we assume that a fixed step size h is being used, and where $f^{(j)}$ denotes the jth total derivative of the function $f(x, y(x))$ with respect to x. We can then state Algorithm 8.1.

Algorithm 8.1: Taylor's algorithm of order k To find an approximate solution of the differential equation

$$y' = f(x, y)$$
$$y(a) = y_0$$

over an interval $[a, b]$:

1. Choose a step $h = (b - a)/N$. Set
$$x_n = a + nh \qquad n = 0, 1, \ldots, N$$

2. Generate approximations y_n to $y(x_n)$ from the recursion
$$y_{n+1} = y_n + hT_k(x_n, y_n) \qquad n = 0, 1, \ldots, N - 1$$
where $T_k(x, y)$ is defined by (8.22).

Taylor's algorithm, and other methods based on this algorithm, which calculate y at $x = x_{n+1}$ by using only information about y and y' at a single point $x = x_n$, are frequently called **one-step** methods.

Taylor's theorem with remainder shows that the **local error** of Taylor's algorithm of order k is

$$E = \frac{h^{k+1} f^{(k)}(\xi, y(\xi))}{(k + 1)!} \qquad x_n < \xi < x_n + h$$

$$= \frac{h^{k+1}}{(k + 1)!} y^{(k+1)}(\xi)$$

The Taylor algorithm is said to be of **order** k if the local error E as defined above is $\mathcal{O}(h^{k+1})$.

On setting $k = 1$ in Algorithm 8.1 we obtain **Euler's method** and its local error,

$$\boxed{y_{n+1} = y_n + hf(x_n, y_n)} \qquad \boxed{E = \frac{h^2}{2} y''(\xi)} \qquad (8.23)$$

To illustrate Euler's method, consider the initial-value problem

$$y' = y \qquad y(0) = 1$$

On applying (8.23) with $h = 0.01$ and retaining six decimal places, we obtain

$$y(0.01) \approx y_1 = 1 + 0.01 = 1.01$$
$$y(0.02) \approx y_2 = 1.01 + 0.01(1.01) = 1.0201$$
$$y(0.03) \approx y_3 = 1.0201 + 0.01(1.0201) = 1.030301$$
$$y(0.04) \approx y_4 = 1.030301 + 0.01(1.030301) = 1.040606$$

Since the exact solution of this equation is $y = e^x$, the correct value at $x = 0.04$ is 1.0408. It is clear that, to obtain more accuracy with Euler's method, we must take a considerably smaller value for h.

If we take $h = 0.005$, we obtain the values

$$y(0.005) \approx y_1 = 1.0050$$
$$y(0.010) \approx y_2 = 1.0100$$
$$y(0.015) \approx y_3 = 1.0151$$
$$y(0.020) \approx y_4 = 1.0202$$
$$y(0.025) \approx y_5 = 1.0253$$
$$y(0.030) \approx y_6 = 1.0304$$
$$y(0.035) \approx y_7 = 1.0356$$
$$y(0.040) \approx y_8 = 1.0408$$

These results are correct to four decimal places after the decimal point.

Because of the relatively small step size required, Euler's method is not commonly used for integrating differential equations.

We could, of course, apply Taylor's algorithm of higher order to obtain better accuracy, and in general, we would expect that the higher the order of the algorithm, the greater the accuracy for a given step size. If $f(x, y)$ is a relatively simple function of x and y, then it is often possible to generate the required derivatives relatively cheaply on a computer by employing symbolic differentiation, or else by taking advantage of any particular properties the function $f(x, y)$ may have (see Exercise 8.3-4). However, the necessity of calculating the higher derivatives makes Taylor's algorithm completely unsuitable on high-speed computers for general integration purposes. Nevertheless, it is of great theoretical interest because most of the practical methods attempt to achieve the same accuracy as a Taylor algorithm of a given order without the disadvantage of having to calculate the higher derivatives. Although the general Taylor algorithm is hardly ever used for practical purposes, the special case of Euler's method will be considered in more detail for its theoretical implications.

Example 8.1 Using Taylor's series, find the solution of the differential equation

$$xy' = x - y \qquad y(2) = 2$$

at $x = 2.1$ correct to five decimal places.

The first few derivatives and their values at $x = 2, y = 2$ are

$$y' = 1 - \frac{y}{x} \qquad\qquad\qquad y_0' = 0$$

$$y'' = \frac{-y'}{x} + \frac{y}{x^2} \qquad\qquad y_0'' = \tfrac{1}{2}$$

$$y''' = \frac{-y''}{x} + \frac{2y'}{x^2} - \frac{2y}{x^3} \qquad y_0''' = -\tfrac{3}{4}$$

$$y^{iv} = \frac{-y'''}{x} + \frac{3y''}{x^2} - \frac{6y'}{x^3} + \frac{6y}{x^4} \qquad y_0^{iv} = \tfrac{3}{2}$$

The Taylor series expansion about $x_0 = 2$ is

$$y(x) = y_0 + (x - 2)y_0' + \tfrac{1}{2}(x - 2)^2 y_0'' + \tfrac{1}{6}(x - 2)^3 y_0''' + \tfrac{1}{24}(x - 2)^4 y_0^{iv} + \cdots$$

$$= 2 + (x - 2)0 + \tfrac{1}{4}(x - 2)^2 - \tfrac{1}{8}(x - 2)^3 + \tfrac{1}{16}(x - 2)^4 + \cdots$$

At $x = 2.1$ we obtain

$$y(2.1) = 2 + 0.0025 - 0.000125 + 0.0000062 - \cdots$$

$$\approx 2.00238$$

Since the terms in this Taylor series decrease in magnitude and alternate (see Exercise 8.3-4) in sign, this result is correct to five decimal places. If we now wished to find $y(2.2)$ to the same accuracy, we would have to carry the series through two additional terms. Alternatively, we could now make a new expansion about $x = 2.1$, reevaluate the first four derivatives at $x = 2.1$, and then compute $y(2.2)$.

Example 8.2 Solve the equation

$$y' = \frac{1}{x^2} - \frac{y}{x} - y^2$$

$$y(1) = -1$$

from $x = 1$ to $x = 2$. Use Taylor's algorithm of order 2. Solve the problem with $h = \tfrac{1}{16}$, $\tfrac{1}{32}$, $\tfrac{1}{64}$, $\tfrac{1}{128}$, and estimate the accuracy of the results.

SOLUTION Since

$$f(x, y) = \frac{1}{x^2} - \frac{y}{x} - y^2$$

$$f'(x, y) = \frac{-2}{x^3} - \frac{y'}{x} + \frac{y}{x^2} - 2yy'$$

then
$$T_2(x, y) = f + \frac{h}{2} f'$$

and
$$y_{n+1} = y_n + h\left[f(x_n, y_n) + \frac{h}{2} f'(x_n, y_n) \right]$$

The results as computed on the IBM 7094 are given below. The step size h is given in the first column, and the values of $y(1.5)$, $y'(1.5)$, $y(2.0)$, $y'(2.0)$, respectively, are given in the next four columns. The exact solution of this equation is $y = -1/x$, so that the exact value of $y(1.5)$ is $-\frac{2}{3}$, and the exact value of $y(2.0)$ is $-\frac{1}{2}$. We may estimate the total discretization error as follows: The local error of Taylor's algorithm of order 2 is $(h^3/6)y'''$. Since $y''' = 6/x^4$, its maximum value on the interval $[1, 2]$ is 6, and hence the local error is for each step, at most, h^3. With $h = \frac{1}{128}$, we will take 128 integration steps so that the accumulated error will be, at most, $128h^3 = (\frac{1}{128})^2 \approx 0.00006$. The actual error at $x = 2.0$ appears to be 0.00003, in close agreement with this estimate. In general, we will not know the solution to check against. Even without knowing the solution, however, we can estimate from the number of places of agreement as $h \to 0$, the accuracy of the solution. Since each halving of h appears to produce almost one additional digit of accuracy, it appears that in the absence of round-off error, a step of $1/1,024$ should produce at least seven places of accuracy. This same problem will be solved later by two other methods. For comparison purposes, the results for all three methods are included here.

COMPUTER RESULTS FOR EXAMPLE 8.2

Method 1—Taylor expansion method of order 2

H	Y(1.5)	YPRM(1.5)	Y(2.)	YPRM(2.)
0.62500000E-01	−0.66787238E 00	0.44363917E-00	−0.50187737E 00	0.24905779E-00
0.31250000E-01	−0.66696430E 00	0.44424593E-00	−0.50046334E 00	0.24976812E-00
0.15625000E-01	−0.66674034E 00	0.44439532E-00	−0.50011456E 00	0.24994271E-00
0.78125000E-02	−0.66668454E 00	0.44443253E-00	−0.50002744E 00	0.24998628E-00

Method 2—Simplified Runge-Kutta order 2

H	Y(1.5)	YPRM(1.5)	Y(2.)	YPRM(2.)
0.62500000E-01	−0.66552725E 00	0.44520275E-00	−0.49822412E-00	0.25088478E-00
0.31250000E-01	−0.66637699E 00	0.44463748E-00	−0.49954852E-00	0.25022554E-00
0.15625000E-01	−0.66659356E 00	0.44449317E-00	−0.49988601E-00	0.25005698E-00
0.78125000E-02	−0.66664808E 00	0.44445683E-00	−0.49997083E-00	0.25001458E-00

Method 3—Classical Runge-Kutta order 4

H	Y(1.5)	YPRM(1.5)	Y(2.)	YPRM(2.)
0.62500000E-01	−0.66666625E 00	0.44444472E-00	−0.49999941E-00	0.25000029E-00
0.31250000E-01	−0.66666664E 00	0.44444446E-00	−0.49999997E-00	0.25000001E-00
0.15625000E-01	−0.66666666E 00	0.44444444E-00	−0.50000000E 00	0.25000000E-00
0.78125000E-02	−0.66666667E 00	0.44444444E-00	−0.50000001E 00	0.24999999E-00

EXERCISES

8.3-1 For the equation

$$y' = -xy + \frac{1}{y^2} \qquad y(1) = 1$$

derive the difference equation corresponding to Taylor's algorithm of order 3. Carry out by hand one step of the integration with $h = 0.01$. Write a program for solving this problem, and carry out the integration from $x = 1$ to $x = 2$, using $h = \frac{1}{64}$ and $h = \frac{1}{128}$.

8.3-2 For the equation

$$y' = 2y \qquad y(0) = 1$$

obtain the exact solution of the difference equation obtained from Euler's method. Estimate a value of h small enough to guarantee four-place accuracy in the solution over the interval $[0, 1]$. Carry out the solution with an appropriate value of h for 10 steps.

8.3-3 From the Taylor series for $y(x)$, find $y(0.1)$ correct to six decimal places if $y(x)$ satisfies

$$y' = xy + 1 \qquad y(0) = 1$$

8.3-4 Prove that, for the function $f(x, y) = 1 - y/x$ of Example 8.1, $y'' = (1 - 2y')/x$, $y^{(k)} = -ky^{(k-1)}/x$, $k = 3, 4, \ldots$. Based on this, write a FORTRAN program which finds the value $y(3)$ of the solution $y(x)$ of the problem in Example 8.1 to within 10^{-6}, using Algorithm 8.1.

8.4 ERROR ESTIMATES AND CONVERGENCE OF EULER'S METHOD

To solve the differential equation $y' = f(x, y)$, $y(x_0) = y_0$ by Euler's method, we choose a constant step size h, and we apply the formula

$$y_{n+1} = y_n + hf(x_n, y_n) \qquad n = 0, 1, \ldots \tag{8.23}$$

where $x_n = x_0 + nh$. We denote the true solution of the differential equation at $x = x_n$ by $y(x_n)$, and the approximate solution obtained by applying (8.23) as y_n. We wish to estimate the magnitude of the **discretization** error e_n defined by

$$e_n = y(x_n) - y_n \tag{8.24}$$

We note that, if y_0 is exact, as we shall assume, then $e_0 = 0$. Assuming that the appropriate derivatives exist, we can expand $y(x_{n+1})$ about $x = x_n$, using Taylor's theorem with remainder:

$$y(x_{n+1}) = y(x_n) + hy'(x_n) + \frac{h^2}{2}y''(\xi_n) \qquad x_n \le \xi_n \le x_{n+1} \tag{8.25}$$

The quantity $(h^2/2)y''(\xi_n)$ is called the **local discretization** error, i.e., the error committed in the single step from x_n to x_{n+1}, assuming that y and y' were known exactly at $x = x_n$. On a computer there will also be an error in computing y_{n+1} using (8.23), due to roundoff. Round-off errors will be neglected in this section.

On subtracting (8.23) from (8.25) and using (8.24), we obtain

$$e_{n+1} = e_n + h\left[f(x_n, y(x_n)) - f(x_n, y_n) \right] + \frac{h^2}{2} y''(\xi_n) \qquad (8.26)$$

By the mean-value theorem of differential calculus, we have

$$f(x_n, y(x_n)) - f(x_n, y_n) = f_y(x_n, \bar{y}_n)(y(x_n) - y_n)$$
$$= f_y(x_n, \bar{y}_n) e_n$$

where $\bar{y}_n$ is between y_n and $y(x_n)$. Hence (8.26) becomes

$$e_{n+1} = e_n + h f_y(x_n, \bar{y}_n) e_n + \frac{h^2}{2} y''(\xi_n) \qquad (8.27)$$

We now assume that over the interval of interest,

$$|f_y(x,y)| < L \qquad |y''(x)| < Y$$

where L and Y are fixed positive constants. On taking absolute values in (8.27), we obtain

$$|e_{n+1}| \le |e_n| + hL|e_n| + \frac{h^2}{2} Y = (1 + hL)|e_n| + \frac{h^2}{2} Y \qquad (8.28)$$

We will now show by induction that the solution of the difference equation

$$\xi_{n+1} = (1 + hL)\xi_n + \frac{h^2}{2} Y \qquad (8.29)$$

with $\xi_0 = 0$ dominates the solution of (8.27); i.e., we will show that

$$\xi_n \ge |e_n| \qquad n = 0, 1, \ldots \qquad (8.30)$$

Since $e_0 = \xi_0 = 0$, (8.30) is certainly true for $n = 0$. Assuming the truth of (8.30) for an integer n, it then follows from (8.29), since $\xi_n \ge |e_n|$ and $(1 + hL) > 1$, that

$$\xi_{n+1} \ge |e_{n+1}|$$

completing the induction.

The solution ξ_n of the nonhomogeneous difference equation (8.29) therefore provides an upper bound for the discretization error e_n. From the theory of difference equations given in Sec. 8.2, the solution of (8.29) is

$$\xi_n = c(1 + hL)^n - B \qquad (8.31)$$

where c is an arbitrary constant, and

$$B = \frac{hY}{2L}$$

To satisfy the condition $\xi_0 = 0$, we see that we must choose $c = + B$, so that (8.31) becomes

$$\xi_n = B(1 + hL)^n - B$$

We infer from Sec. 1.7 that $e^x = 1 + x + e^\xi x^2/2$; hence $e^x \geq 1 + x$, for all x. It follows that $1 + hL \leq e^{hL}$ and therefore also that $(1 + hL)^n \leq e^{nhL}$. Using this in (8.31), we can therefore assert that

$$\xi_n \leq B(e^{nhL} - 1)$$

$$= \frac{hY}{2L}(e^{nhL} - 1)$$

$$= \frac{hY}{2L}(e^{(x_n - x_0)L} - 1)$$

where we have used the fact that $nh = x_n - x_0$. Since $|e_n| \leq \xi_n$, we have proved the following theorem.

Theorem 8.2 Let y_n be the approximate solution of (8.19) generated by Euler's method (8.23). If the exact solution $y(x)$ of (8.19) has a continuous second derivative on the interval $[x_0, b]$, and if on this interval the inequalities

$$|f_y(x, y)| \leq L \qquad |y''(x)| < Y$$

are satisfied for fixed positive constants L and Y, the error $e_n = y(x_n) - y_n$ of Euler's method at a point $x_n = x_0 + nh$ is bounded as follows:

$$|e_n| \leq \frac{hY}{2L}(e^{(x_n - x_0)L} - 1) \tag{8.32}$$

This theorem shows that the error is $\Theta(h)$; that is, the error tends to zero as $h \to 0$, like ch for some constant c if $x = x_n$ is kept fixed. It must be emphasized that the estimate (8.32) provides an upper bound rather than a realistic bound. Its primary importance is to establish convergence of the method rather than to provide us with a realistic a priori error estimate.

Example 8.3 Determine an upper bound for the discretization error of Euler's method in solving the equation $y' = y$, $y(0) = 1$ from $x = 0$ to $x = 1$.

SOLUTION Here $f(x, y) = y$, $\partial f/\partial y = 1$; hence we can take $L = 1$. Also since $y = e^x$, then $y'' = e^x$ and $|y''(x)| \leq e$ for $0 \leq x \leq 1$. To find a bound for the error at $x = 1$, we have $x_n - x_0 = 1$, $y = e^1$, and from (8.32)

$$|e(1)| \leq \frac{he}{2}(e - 1)$$

$$< 2.4h$$

Thus the error $e(1)$ at $x = 1$ is bounded by $2.4h$. To see how realistic this bound is, we shall obtain the exact solution of Euler's method for this problem. Thus

$$y_{n+1} = y_n + hf(x_n, y_n)$$

$$= (1 + h)y_n$$

The solution of this difference equation satisfying $y(0) = 1$ is

$$y_n = (1 + h)^n$$

Now if $h = 0.1$, $n = 10$, we find on expanding $(1.1)^{10}$ that Euler's method gives $y_{10} \approx y(1) = 2.5937$. On subtracting this from the exact solution $y(1) = e = 2.71828$, we find the error to be 0.1246, compared with the bound of 0.24 obtained by using (8.32).

EXERCISES

8.4-1 For the equation $y' = -2y$, $0 \le x \le 1$, $y(0) = 1$:

(a) Find an upper bound on the error at $x = 1$ in terms of the step size h, using (8.32).

(b) Solve the difference equation which results from Euler's method.

(c) Compare the bound obtained from (a) with the actual error as obtained from (b) at $x = 1$ for $h = 0.1$, $h = 0.01$.

(d) How small a step size h would have to be taken to produce six significant figures of accuracy at $x = 1$, using Euler's method (assuming no round-off error)?

8.4-2 The error e_n of an integration method is known to satisfy a difference inequality

$$|e_{n+2}| \le a_1|e_{n+1}| + a_2|e_n| + A$$

where a_1, a_2, A are positive constants with $e_1 = e_0 = 0$. Let ξ_n be a solution of the difference equation

$$\xi_{n+2} = a_1\xi_{n+1} + a_2\xi_n + A$$

with $\xi_1 = \xi_0 = 0$. Show by induction that

$$|e_n| \le \xi_n \qquad \text{for all } n$$

8.5 RUNGE-KUTTA METHODS

As mentioned previously, Euler's method is not very useful in practical problems because it requires a very small step size for reasonable accuracy. Taylor's algorithm of higher order is unacceptable as a general-purpose procedure because of the need to obtain higher total derivatives of $y(x)$. The Runge-Kutta methods attempt to obtain greater accuracy, and at the same time avoid the need for higher derivatives, by evaluating the function $f(x, y)$ at selected points on each subinterval. We shall derive here the simplest of the Runge-Kutta methods. A formula of the following form is sought:

$$y_{n+1} = y_n + ak_1 + bk_2 \tag{8.33}$$

where

$$k_1 = hf(x_n, y_n)$$

$$k_2 = hf(x_n + \alpha h, y_n + \beta k_1)$$

and a, b, α, β are constants to be determined so that (8.33) will agree with the Taylor algorithm of as high an order as possible. On expanding $y(x_{n+1})$

in a Taylor series through terms of order h^3, we obtain

$$y(x_{n+1}) = y(x_n) + hy'(x_n) + \frac{h^2}{2}y''(x_n) + \frac{h^3}{6}y'''(x_n) + \cdots$$

$$= y(x_n) + hf(x_n, y_n) + \frac{h^2}{2}(f_x + ff_y)_n$$

$$+ \frac{h^3}{6}\left(f_{xx} + 2ff_{xy} + f_{yy}f^2 + f_x f_y + f_y^2 f\right)_n + \mathcal{O}(h^4) \quad (8.34)$$

where we have used the expansions (8.21), and the subscript n means that all functions involved are to be evaluated at $\{x_n, y_n\}$.

On the other hand, using Taylor's expansion for functions of two variables (see Sec. 1.7), we find that

$$\frac{k_2}{h} = f(x_n + \alpha h, y_n + \beta k_1) = f(x_n, y_n) + \alpha h f_x + \beta k_1 f_y$$

$$+ \frac{\alpha^2 h^2}{2}f_{xx} + \alpha h \beta k_1 f_{xy} + \frac{\beta^2 k_1^2}{2}f_{yy} + \mathcal{O}(h^3)$$

where all derivatives are evaluated at $\{x_n, y_n\}$.

If we now substitute this expression for k_2 into (8.33) and note that $k_1 = hf(x_n, y_n)$, we find upon rearrangement in powers of h that

$$y_{n+1} = y_n + (a + b)hf + bh^2(\alpha f_x + \beta ff_y)$$

$$+ bh^3\left(\frac{\alpha^2}{2}f_{xx} + \alpha\beta ff_{xy} + \frac{\beta^2}{2}f^2 f_{yy}\right) + \mathcal{O}(h^4) \quad (8.34a)$$

On comparing this with (8.34), we see that to make the corresponding powers of h and h^2 agree we must have

$$\begin{aligned} a + b &= 1 \\ b\alpha = b\beta &= \tfrac{1}{2} \end{aligned} \quad (8.35)$$

Although we have four unknowns, we have only three equations, and hence we still have one degree of freedom in the solution of (8.35). We might hope to use this additional degree of freedom to obtain agreement of the coefficients in the h^3 terms. It is obvious, however, that this is impossible for all functions $f(x, y)$.

There are many solutions to (8.35), the simplest perhaps being

$$a = b = \tfrac{1}{2} \qquad \alpha = \beta = 1$$

Algorithm 8.2: Runge-Kutta method of order 2 For the equation

$$y' = f(x, y) \qquad y(x_0) = y_0$$

generate approximations y_n to $y(x_0 + nh)$, for h fixed and $n =$

0, 1, . . . , using the recursion formula

$$y_{n+1} = y_n + \tfrac{1}{2}(k_1 + k_2) \quad \text{with} \quad k_1 = hf(x_n, y_n)$$
$$k_2 = hf(x_n + h, y_n + k_1)$$

(8.36)

Algorithm 8.2 may be pictured geometrically as in Fig. 8.1. Euler's method yields an increment $P_1P_0 = hf(x_n, y_n)$ to y_n; $P_2P_0 = hf(x_n + h, y_n + hf(x_n, y_n))$ is another increment based on the slope obtained at x_{n+1}. Taking the average of these increments leads to formula (8.36).

The local error of (8.36) is of the form

$$y(x_{n+1}) - y_{n+1} = \frac{h^3}{12}\left(f_{xx} + 2ff_{xy} + f^2f_{yy} - 2f_xf_y - 2ff_y^2\right) + \Theta(h^4)$$

The complexity of the coefficient in this error term is characteristic of all Runge-Kutta methods and constitutes one of the least desirable features of such methods since local error estimates are very difficult to obtain. The local error of (8.36), is, however, of order h^3, whereas that of Euler's method is h^2. We can therefore expect to be able to use a larger step size with (8.36). The price we pay for this is that we must evaluate the function $f(x, y)$ twice for each step of the integration. Formulas of the Runge-Kutta type for any order can be derived by the method used above. However, the derivations become exceedingly complicated. The most popular and most commonly used formula of this type is contained in Algorithm 8.3.

Algorithm 8.3: Runge-Kutta method of order 4 For the equation $y' = f(x, y)$, $y(x_0) = y_0$, generate approximations y_n to $y(x_0 + nh)$ for h fixed and for $n = 0, 1, 2, \ldots ,$ using the recursion formula

$$y_{n+1} = y_n + \tfrac{1}{6}(k_1 + 2k_2 + 2k_3 + k_4)$$

(8.37)

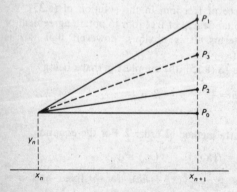

Figure 8.1

where

$$k_1 = hf(x_n, y_n)$$

$$k_2 = hf\left(x_n + \frac{h}{2}, y_n + \frac{1}{2}k_1\right)$$

$$k_3 = hf\left(x_n + \frac{h}{2}, y_n + \frac{1}{2}k_2\right)$$

$$k_4 = hf(x_n + h, y_n + k_3)$$

The local discretization error of Algorithm 8.3 is $\Theta(h^5)$. Again the price we pay for the favorable discretization error is that four function evaluations are required per step. This price may be considerable in computer time for those problems in which the function $f(x, y)$ is complicated. The Runge-Kutta methods have additional disadvantages, which will be discussed later. Formula (8.37) is widely used in practice with considerable success. It has the important advantage that it is self-starting: i.e., it requires only the value of y at a point $x = x_n$ to find y and y' at $x = x_{n+1}$.

A general-purpose FORTRAN program based on Algorithm 8.2 for a single differential equation is given below. To use this program, the user must include a subroutine for evaluating the function $f(x, y)$, and must specify the initial value $y(x_0) = y_0$, the final point x_{NSTEP}, and the total number of steps NSTEPS.

FORTRAN PROGRAM FOR ALGORITHM 8.2

```
C   FORTRAN PROGRAM TO SOLVE THE FIRST ORDER DIFFERENTIAL EQUATION
C        Y'(X) = F(X,Y)
C   WITH INITIAL CONDITION OF
C        Y(XBEGIN) = YBEGIN
C   TO THE POINT  XEND , USING THE SECOND ORDER RUNGE-KUTTA METHOD.
C   A FUNCTION SUBPROGRAM CALLED 'F' MUST BE SUPPLIED.
      INTEGER I,N,NSTEPS
      REAL DERIV,H,K1,K2,XBEGIN,XN,XEND,YBEGIN,YN
    1 READ 501, XBEGIN,YBEGIN,XEND,NSTEPS
  501 FORMAT(3F10.5,I3)
      IF (NSTEPS .LT. 1)                   STOP
      H = (XEND - XBEGIN)/NSTEPS
      XN = XBEGIN
      YN = YBEGIN
      DERIV = F(XN,YN)
      N = 0
      PRINT 601, N,XN,YN,DERIV
  601 FORMAT(1X,I3,3E21.9)
      DO 10 N=1,NSTEPS
         K1 = H*F(XN,YN)
         K2 = H*F(XN+H,YN+K1)
         YN = YN + .5*(K1+K2)
         XN = XBEGIN + N*H
         DERIV = F(XN,YN)
   10    PRINT 601, N,XN,YN,DERIV
                                       GO TO 1
      END
      REAL FUNCTION F(X,Y)
      REAL X,Y
      F = (1./X - Y)/X - Y*Y
                                       RETURN
      END
```

Example 8.4 Solve the problem of Example 8.2 by the second-order Runge-Kutta method (8.36) and by the fourth-order Runge-Kutta method (8.37).

In the machine results given in Sec. 8.3, (8.36) is called method 2 and (8.37) method 3. We see that the second-order Runge-Kutta method gives results which are entirely comparable with the Taylor algorithm of order 2 (method 1). The fourth-order Runge-Kutta method, however, yields remarkably improved results correct to six decimal places for $h = \frac{1}{16}$ and to seven or eight places for other values of h. The computational efficiency of methods 2 and 3 may be compared by considering the number of function evaluations required for each. Method 2 requires two function evaluations per step and for $h = \frac{1}{128}$ requires in all 256 evaluations. Method 3 requires four function evaluations and for $h = \frac{1}{16}$ a total of only 64 function evaluations and yet produces considerably more accurate results. The fourth-order Runge-Kutta method is clearly a more efficient method to use for this problem, and this is generally true.

EXERCISES

8.5-1 For the equation $y' = x + y$, $y(0) = 1$, calculate the local error of method (8.36). Compare this with the error of Taylor's algorithm of order 2. Which would you expect to give better results over the interval $[0, 1]$?

8.5-2 Carry out a few steps of the integration of $y' = x + y$, $y(0) = 1$, using (8.36) and a step size of $h = 0.01$; then write a program to solve this problem on a computer from $x = 0$ to $x = 1$.

8.5-3 To Eqs. (8.35) add the additional condition that the coefficients of f_{xx} in (8.34) and (8.34a) must agree. Solve the resulting system of equations for a, b, α, β. Determine the error term of the second-order Runge-Kutta method obtained from this choice of a, b, α, β.

8.5-4 It can be shown that the error of the fourth-order Runge-Kutta method satisfies for a step size h a relation of the form

$$y_{n(h)} - y(b) = A(b)h^4 + \Theta(h^5)$$

as h goes to zero, where $b = x_0 + nh$, hence $n(h) = (b - x_0)/h$ and the constant $A(b)$ does not depend on h. Use an extrapolation procedure as in the case of Romberg integration to obtain an approximation to $y(b)$ for which the error is $\Theta(h^5)$.

8.6 STEP SIZE CONTROL WITH RUNGE-KUTTA METHODS

In Section 8.5 we considered two Runge-Kutta (RK) methods, one of order 2 and one of order 4. Runge-Kutta methods of any order can be derived, although the derivation can become exceedingly complicated. An important consideration in using one-step methods of Runge-Kutta type is that of estimating the local error and of selecting the proper step size to achieve a required accuracy. There is no reason why the step size h needs to be kept fixed over the entire interval as we did in Example 8.4. Estimating the accuracy using different fixed step sizes as we did in Example 8.4 may be very inefficient. In this section we will examine methods for estimating the local error and for varying the step size according to some error criterion.

The first method is based on interval halving. Let us assume that we are using an RK method of order p and that we have arrived at a point x_n with $h = x_n - x_{n-1}$. We now integrate from x_n to $x_{n+1} = x_n + h$ twice, once using the current step h and again using two steps of length $h/2$. We will thus obtain two estimates $y_h(x_{n+1})$ and $y_{h/2}(x_{n+1})$ of the value of $y(x)$ at $x = x_{n+1}$ and a comparison of these two estimates will yield an estimate of the error. To derive the estimate we first note that a Runge-Kutta method of order p has a local asymptotic error expansion of the form

$$y_h(x_n + mh) = y(x_n + mh) + C(x_n + mh)h^p + \mathcal{O}(h^{p+1}) \quad (8.38)$$

Here, $y_h(x_n + mh)$ denotes the approximation to the solution $y(x)$ at the point $x = x_n + mh$ obtained after m h-steps of the Runge-Kutta method, starting from the exact value $y_n = y(x_n)$. Further, the constant $C(x_n + mh)$ does not depend on h, though it does depend on $f(x, y)$ and on the point $x = x_n + mh$. Therefore,

$$y_h(x_{n+1}) = y(x_{n+1}) + C(x_{n+1})h^p + \mathcal{O}(h^{p+1}) \quad (8.39a)$$

$$y_{h/2}(x_{n+1}) = y(x_{n+1}) + C(x_{n+1})(h/2)^p + \mathcal{O}(h^{p+1}) \quad (8.39b)$$

On subtracting (8.39a) from (8.39b) we find that the principal part of the error in (8.39b) can be estimated as

$$C_n \left(\frac{h}{2} \right)^p \approx \frac{y_{h/2}(x_{n+1}) - y_h(x_{n+1})}{1 - 2^p}$$

The quantity

$$D_n = \frac{|y_{h/2}(x_{n+1}) - y_h(x_{n+1})|}{2^p - 1} \quad (8.40)$$

thus provides us with a computable estimate of the error in the approximation $y_{h/2}(x_{n+1})$ and it can be used to help us decide whether the step h being used is just right, too big, or too small.

Suppose now that we are given some local error tolerance ε and that we wish to keep the estimated error D_n below the local error tolerance **per unit step**, i.e., we want

$$D_n \le \varepsilon h \quad (8.41)$$

Assume that we have computed $y_h(x_{n+1}), y_{h/2}(x_{n+1})$, and D_n. We must now decide on whether to accept the value $y_{h/2}(x_{n+1})$ and on what step h to use for the next integration. From the given error tolerance ε, we compute a lower error bound $\varepsilon' < \varepsilon$ in a manner to be described later. We have the following possibilities:

(i) $\varepsilon' < \dfrac{D_n}{h} < \varepsilon$

In this case we accept the value $y_{h/2}(x_{n+1})$, and continue the integration from x_{n+1} using the same step size h.

(ii) $\dfrac{D_n}{h} > \varepsilon$

In this case the error is too large, hence we must reduce h—say to $h/2$—and integrate again from the point $x = x_n$.

(iii) $\dfrac{D_n}{h} < \varepsilon'$

In this case we are getting more accuracy than required. We accept the value $y_{h/2}(x_{n+1})$, replace h—by say $2h$—and integrate from x_{n+1}.

If we restrict the interval step size to halving or doubling, then the lower bound ε' can be set to

$$\varepsilon' = \varepsilon/2^{p+1}$$

for a pth order method since halving the step size reduces the error by approximately $1/2^{p+1}$. For the Runge-Kutta method of order 4 we have $p = 4$, hence $\varepsilon' = \varepsilon/32$. Actually it is not advisable to change the step size too often, and to be safe one might use $\varepsilon' = \varepsilon/50$.

A more sophisticated form of step size control, which does not restrict h to doubling or halving, takes the following form. From (8.40) we have

$$D_n \approx 2C_n\left(\frac{h}{2}\right)^{p+1} \tag{8.42a}$$

Our goal is to choose a step size $\bar{h}$ for the next step. Since the principal part of the error at the next step will be $2C_n(\bar{h}/2)^{p+1}$ we must choose $\bar{h}$ so that the error tolerance (8.41) is satisfied, hence we must have

$$2C_n\left(\frac{\bar{h}}{2}\right)^{p+1} \le \varepsilon\bar{h} \tag{8.42b}$$

Assuming again that C_n does not change much, we can eliminate C_n between (8.42a) and (8.42b) as follows: From (8.42b) we have

$$2C_n\left(\frac{h}{2}\right)^{p+1}\left(\frac{\bar{h}}{2}\right)^{p+1} \le \varepsilon\bar{h}\left(\frac{h}{2}\right)^{p+1}$$

$$D_n\frac{(\bar{h})^p}{2^{p+1}} \le \frac{\varepsilon h \cdot h^p}{2^{p+1}}$$

$$\bar{h}^p \le h^p \varepsilon h / D_n$$

$$\bar{h} \approx h(\varepsilon h / D_n)^{1/p} \tag{8.42c}$$

Thus if we have already successfully integrated with a step h, the next integration step size should be $\bar{h}$ or perhaps, to be safe, a little smaller. As an example suppose that we have a method with $p = 4$, that $\varepsilon = 10^{-6}$, $h = 0.1$ and D_n is computed to be 10^{-5}. Then

$$\bar{h} \approx 0.1(0.01)^{1/4} = 0.01(.32) = 0.032$$

These conditions would thus require a much smaller value of h. On the other hand, if again $p = 4$, $h = 0.1$, $\varepsilon = 10^{-6}$ and we compute $D_n = 10^{-8}$, then

$$\bar{h} \approx 0.1(10)^{1/4} \approx 0.1(1.8) = 0.18,$$

so that the step size can be almost doubled. The use of variable step sizes adds considerably to the complexity of a program and leads to results at a set of nonuniformly spaced points which to a user may be disconcerting. Halving and doubling intervals is generally more acceptable to the user. On the other hand, programs with automatic step size control provide the user with very good estimates of accuracy, and are overall quite efficient.

The major disadvantage of this method of error control is the substantial additional effort required. In recent years several new variations of Runge-Kutta methods suitable for step size control have been introduced. Some names associated with these new variations are Merson, Verner, and Fehlberg. We describe briefly the method proposed by Fehlberg which we denote by RKF 45 [28]. This method requires six function evaluations per step but it provides an automatic error estimate and at the same time produces better accuracy than the standard fourth-order method. Fehlberg showed that four of these function values combined with one set of coefficients could be used to produce a fourth-order method while all six values combined with another set of coefficients could be used to produce a fifth-order method. Comparison of the values produced by the fourth-order and fifth-order methods then leads to an estimate of the error which can be used for step size control.

We describe very briefly the approach taken by Fehlberg. We assume that we have integrated the equation $y' = f(x, y)$ up to a point x_n with a step size h_n and we now wish to find an estimate of $y(x)$ at $x = x_{n+1}$. One estimate will be given by the formula

$$y_{n+1} = y_n + \sum_{i=1}^{6} c_i k_i \tag{8.43a}$$

for certain coefficients c_i and a second estimate will be given by

$$y_{n+1}^* = y_n + \sum_{i=1}^{6} c_i^* k_i \tag{8.43b}$$

for another set of coefficients c_i^*. The error estimate for step size control is then computed as follows:

$$D_n = \sum_{i=1}^{6} (c_i - c_i^*) k_i$$

and it can be used as described earlier to estimate the proper step h for the next integration. The functions k_i are the same in both formulas and can be expressed in the form

$$k_i = h_n f\left(x_n + \alpha_i h_n, y_n + \sum_{j=1}^{i-1} \beta_{ij} k_i \right) \qquad i = 1, \ldots, 6$$

There are many possible choices of the coefficients α_i and β_{ij} that will lead to Runge-Kutta methods of order 5. Fehlberg proposed one particular set of coefficients which we will not reproduce here. The interested reader is referred to [28] for further details about this method.

Another Runge-Kutta method with step size control, due to Verner, is the basis of a very successful differential-equation-solving subroutine named DVERK which is widely available in subroutine libraries. Verner's method, which we denote by RKV 56, requires eight function evaluations per step, and from these, two estimates of $y(x)$ are obtained, one based on a fifth-order approximation and one based on a sixth-order approximation. A comparison of these two estimates then provides a basis for step size selection. Some of the initial testing of this method was done at the University of Toronto [29]. The method was later incorporated into the subroutine DVERK and disseminated by IMSL Inc., Houston, Texas. IMSL, which stands for **International Mathematical and Statistical Library**, is a collection of thoroughly tested subroutines for a wide variety of mathematical and statistical problems. The library is available on a subscription basis and is available for almost all medium- and large-scale computers, including those of IBM, CDC, UNIVAC, Burroughs, and Honeywell. Since most computing installations now subscribe to the IMSL collection, we shall not reproduce the code for DVERK here. Since we will use this subroutine to solve several problems in this chapter, we will describe briefly the parameters in the call statement and the various available options.

In normal usage under default options and after initialization, the heart of the program to solve a first-order differential equation $y' = f(x, y)$ from $x = $ XBEGIN to $x = $ XM consists of a DO loop of the form:

```
      X = XBEGIN
      Y = YBEGIN
      DO 10 K=1,M
         XEND = XBEGIN + FLOAT(K)*(XM - XBEGIN)/FLOAT(M)
         CALL DVERK ( N, FCN1, X, Y, XEND, TOL, IND, C, NW, W, IER )
         PRINT 600, XEND, Y(1), C(24)
  600    FORMAT(F19.6,E21.8,F16.0)
   10 CONTINUE
```

The parameters in the subroutine have the following meanings:

> $N \equiv$ the number of equations to be solved (here $N = 1$)
> $FCN1 \equiv$ the name of the subroutine for $f(x, y)$; to be supplied by the user as an external subprogram
> $X \equiv$ the initial value of the independent variable

Y ≡ the initial value of the dependent variable

XEND ≡ the value of x at which the solution is to be output

TOL ≡ tolerance for error control; while different types of error tolerance specifications are possible, the default option tries to keep the relative global error less than TOL

IND ≡ 1 causes all default options to be used

≡ 2 allows options to be selected

C ≡ communications vector of length 24; some of these can be set by the user if IND was set to 2; these choices allow different types of error control, minimum or maximum step sizes, limits on the number of function evaluations, etc.

NW ≡ the first dimension of the workspace matrix W, must be at least as large as N

W ≡ workspace matrix whose first dimension is NW and whose second dimension must be greater than or equal to 9

IER ≡ an error flag, used to denote various types of errors encountered

In the DO loop above, the points XEND are those values of x at which the solution is outputted. In this case the solution will be output at the M equally spaced points XBEGIN + $k \Delta X$ where ΔX = (XM-XBEGIN)$/M$. Internally, DVERK will automatically select the proper step sizes so as to achieve the required accuracy. The step size normally will vary as the integration proceeds. The subroutine also keeps track of the number of function evaluations required to find the solution at XEND. DVERK is a high-order-accuracy routine which requires a minimum of eight function evaluations per integration step. The number of function evaluations actually used is stored in C(24) and can on option be outputted as we have done above.

As applied to the differential equation

$$y'(x) = \frac{1}{x^2} - \frac{y(x)}{x} - y^2(x)$$

$$y(1) = -1$$

which we considered in Example 8.2; the complete program and the results are given below.

```
C  USE OF  D V E R K  TO SOLVE EXAMPLE 8.2 .
      INTEGER IER,IND,K,N,NW
      REAL C(24),TOL,W(1,9),X,XEND,Y(1)
      DATA N , X ,Y(1), TOL ,IND,NW
     *    / 1 , 1.,-1. ,1.E-7, 1 , 1 /
      EXTERNAL FCN1
      DO 10 K=1,4
        XEND = 1. + FLOAT(K)/4.
        CALL DVERK ( N, FCN1, X, Y, XEND, TOL, IND, C, NW, W, IER )
        PRINT 600, XEND,Y(1),C(24)
  600   FORMAT(11X,F8.6,5X,E16.8,5X,F11.0)
   10 CONTINUE
```

```
                                        STOP
      END
      SUBROUTINE FCN1 ( N, X, Y, YPRIME )
      REAL X,Y(1),YPRIME(1)
      YPRIME(1) = (1./X - Y(1))/X - Y(1)*Y(1)
                                        RETURN
      END
```

OUTPUT

X	Y(1)	FCN EVALS
1.25	−0.79999999	16.
1.50	−0.66666664	24.
1.75	−0.57142854	32.
2.00	−0.49999996	40.

The results are comparable in accuracy with those obtained using the classical fourth-order method with a fixed step size of $h = 1/32$. Since the classical fourth-order method requires four function evaluations per step, a total of 128 function evaluations was required to achieve about seven-decimal-place accuracy. By contrast, DVERK requires only 40 function evaluations for the same accuracy. Note that 16 function evaluations were required for the output at $x = 1.25$, indicating that the step $h = \frac{1}{4}$ was too large and apparently had to be halved to achieve 1.10^{-7} accuracy.

In Sec. 8.12 we will illustrate the use of DVERK to solve a system of first-order differential equations.

EXERCISES

8.6-1 Suppose we are using a Runge-Kutta method of order 2 and step size control based on interval halving to solve a differential equation. If we are using a step $h = 0.1$ and the error criterion $e = 10^{-6}$, and we find that $D_n = 10^{-4}$ at a point $x = x_n$, what step $\bar{h}$ should be used for the next integration step?

8.6-2 Write a program for the Runge-Kutta method of order 2 with step size control restricted to doubling or halving. Apply this program to solve the equation of Example 8.2 with $e = 10^{-6}$.

8.6-3 Check with your computing center to see whether they carry the IMSL collection of subroutines. Use subroutine DVERK to solve the following differential equations. In each case set TOL $= 10^{-7}$ and request output at the XEND values

$$\text{XEND} = \text{XO} + K(\text{XM-XO})/10 \qquad K = 1, 2, \ldots, 10$$

(a) $y' = x - 1 + y/x$
    XO $= 1$, XM $= 2$, $y(\text{XO}) = 2$

(b) $y' = xy^2$
    XO $= 1$, XM $= 4$, $y(\text{XO}) = 1$

8.7 MULTISTEP FORMULAS

The Taylor algorithm of order k and the Runge-Kutta methods are both examples of one-step methods. They require information about the solution at a single point $x = x_n$, from which the methods proceed to obtain y at the next point $x = x_{n+1}$. **Multistep methods** make use of information about the solution at more than one point. Let us assume that we have already obtained approximations to y' and y at a number of equally spaced points, say $x_0, x_1, \ldots, x_n$. One class of multistep methods is based on the principle of numerical integration. If we integrate the differential equation $y' = f(x, y)$ from x_n to x_{n+1}, we will have

$$\int_{x_n}^{x_{n+1}} y' \, dx = \int_{x_n}^{x_{n+1}} f(x, y(x)) \, dx$$

or

$$y_{n+1} = y_n + \int_{x_n}^{x_{n+1}} f(x, y(x)) \, dx \qquad (8.44)$$

To carry out the integration in (8.44) we now approximate $f(x, y(x))$ by a polynomial which interpolates $f(x, y(x))$ at the $(m + 1)$ points $x_n, x_{n-1}, x_{n-2}, \ldots, x_{n-m}$. If we use the notation

$$f(x_k, y(x_k)) = f_k$$

we can use the Newton backward formula (see Exercise 2.6-8) of degree m for this purpose:

$$p_m(x) = \sum_{k=0}^{m} (-1)^k \binom{-s}{k} \Delta^k f_{n-k} \qquad s = \frac{x - x_n}{h}$$

Inserting this into (8.44) and noting that $dx = h \, ds$, we obtain

$$y_{n+1} = y_n + h \int_0^1 \sum_{k=0}^{m} (-1)^k \binom{-s}{k} \Delta^k f_{n-k} \, ds$$

$$= y_n + h \{ \gamma_0 f_n + \gamma_1 \, \Delta f_{n-1} + \cdots + \gamma_m \, \Delta^m f_{n-m} \} \qquad (8.45)$$

where

$$\gamma_k = (-1)^k \int_0^1 \binom{-s}{k} \, ds \qquad (8.45a)$$

From the definition of the binomial function given in Chap. 2 we can easily compute the γ_k, the first few of which are

$$\gamma_0 = 1 \qquad \gamma_1 = \tfrac{1}{2} \qquad \gamma_2 = \tfrac{5}{12} \qquad \gamma_3 = \tfrac{3}{8} \qquad \gamma_4 = \tfrac{251}{720}$$

Formula (8.45) is known as the **Adams-Bashforth** method. The simplest case, obtained by setting $m = 0$ in (8.45), again leads to Euler's method. In general, the use of (8.45) requires the value of $y' = f$ at the $m + 1$ points $x_n, x_{n-1}, \ldots, x_{n-m}$. From these we can form the differences $\Delta f_{n-1}, \Delta^2 f_{n-2}, \ldots, \Delta^m f_{n-m}$; from (8.45) we can compute y_{n+1}; from the differential equation we can compute $f_{n+1} = f(x_{n+1}, y_{n+1})$. We now relabel the point x_{n+1} as x_n, form a new line of differences, and repeat the process. For $m = 3$, which is commonly used in practice, the difference table is

$$
\begin{array}{ccccccc}
x_{n-3} & y_{n-3} & f_{n-3} & & & & \\
& & & \Delta f_{n-3} & & & \\
x_{n-2} & y_{n-2} & f_{n-2} & & \Delta^2 f_{n-2} & & \\
& & & \Delta f_{n-2} & & \Delta^3 f_{n-3} & \\
x_{n-1} & y_{n-1} & f_{n-1} & & \Delta^2 f_{n-2} & & \\
& & & \Delta f_{n-1} & & & \\
x_n & y_n & f_n & & & &
\end{array}
$$

and (8.45) specializes to

$$
\boxed{y_{n+1} = y_n + h\left(f_n + \tfrac{1}{2} \Delta f_{n-1} + \tfrac{5}{12} \Delta^2 f_{n-2} + \tfrac{3}{8} \Delta^3 f_{n-3}\right)} \tag{8.46}
$$

In practice, it is more convenient computationally to work with ordinates instead of differences. From the definition of the forward-difference operator Δ we find that

$$
\Delta f_{n-1} = f_n - f_{n-1}
$$

$$
\Delta^2 f_{n-2} = f_n - 2f_{n-1} + f_{n-2}
$$

$$
\Delta^3 f_{n-3} = f_n - 3f_{n-1} + 3f_{n-2} - f_{n-3}
$$

Substituting in (8.46) and regrouping, we obtain

$$
\boxed{y_{n+1} = y_n + \frac{h}{24}(55f_n - 59f_{n-1} + 37f_{n-2} - 9f_{n-3})} \tag{8.47}
$$

The local error of (8.46) may be derived as follows: From Exercise 2.6-8 we know that the error of Newton's backward formula with $n = 3$ and $k = 0$ is

$$
h^4 f^{(4)}(\eta)\binom{-s}{4}
$$

The error of (8.46) is then given by

$$
E_{AB} = h\int_0^1 h^4 f^{(4)}(\eta)\binom{-s}{4}\,ds
$$

Since $\binom{-s}{4}\,ds$ does not change sign on the interval $[0, 1]$, there exists a point ξ between x_{n-3} and x_{n+1} such that

$$
E_{AB} = h^5 f^{(4)}(\xi)\int_0^1 \binom{-s}{4}\,ds
$$

$$
\boxed{E_{AB} = h^5 y^v(\xi)\tfrac{251}{720}} \tag{8.48}
$$

To use (8.47) we must have four starting values. These starting values must be obtained from some independent source. To illustrate how (8.47) is used, we carry out a few steps of the integration of the equation

$$y' = -y^2$$
$$y(1) = 1$$

with $h = 0.1$. The exact solution of this problem is $y = 1/x$. In the table below, the first four starting values are obtained from the exact solution, and the remaining entries by (8.47).

x_n	y_n	$f_n = -y_n^2$	$y(x_n) = 1/x_n$
1.0	1.00000000	−1.00000000	
1.1	0.90909091	−0.82644628	0.90909091
1.2	0.83333333	−0.69444444	0.83333333
1.3	0.76923077	−0.59171598	0.76923077
1.4	0.71443632	−0.51041926	0.71428571
1.5	0.66686030	−0.44470266	0.66666667
1.6	0.62524613	−0.39093272	0.62500000

The values y_n computed by formula (8.47) are seen to be in error by about two units in the fourth decimal place. Using the local error estimate (6.43) and the fact that

$$|y^v(x)| = \left| \frac{5!}{x^6} \right| \le 120 \qquad 1 < x < 2$$

we obtain the error bound

$$|E_{AB}| \le \tfrac{251}{720}(120)(10^{-5}) \approx 0.0004$$

This bound is about twice as large as the errors encountered in going from one step to the next.

A number of other formulas of the multistep type can be derived similarly, using numerical integration. Instead of integrating $f(x, y)$ in (8.43) from x_n to x_{n+1}, we could, for example, integrate from x_{n-p} to x_{n+1} for some integer $p \ge 0$. If we again interpolate at the $m + 1$ points $x_n, x_{n-1}, \ldots, x_{n-m}$ with Newton's backward formula, we obtain

$$y_{n+1} = y_{n-p} + h \int_{-p}^{1} \sum_{k=0}^{m} (-1)^k \binom{-s}{k} \Delta^k f_{n-k} \, ds \qquad (8.49)$$

The case $p = 0$ yields the Adams-Bashforth formula (8.44). Some especially interesting formulas of this type are those corresponding to $m = 1$, $p = 1$ and to $m = 3$, $p = 3$. These formulas together with their local-error terms are

$$y_{n+1} = y_{n-1} + 2hf_n \qquad E = \frac{h^3}{3} y'''(\xi) \tag{8.50}$$

$$y_{n+1} = y_{n-3} + \frac{4h}{3}(2f_n - f_{n-1} + 2f_{n-2}) \qquad E = \tfrac{14}{45} h^5 y^{v}(\xi) \tag{8.51}$$

Formula (8.50), which is comparable in simplicity to Euler's method, has a more favorable discretization error. Similarly (8.51), which requires knowledge of $f(x, y)$ at only three points, has a discretization error comparable with that of the Adams-Bashforth method (8.47). It can be shown that all formulas of the type (8.49) with m odd and $m = p$ have the property that the coefficient of the mth difference vanishes, thus yielding a formula of higher order than might be expected. On the other hand, these formulas are subject to greater instability, a concept which will be developed later.

A major disadvantage of multistep formulas is that they are not self-starting. Thus, in the Adams-Bashforth method (8.47), we must have four successive values of $f(x, y)$ at equally spaced points before this formula can be used. These starting values must be obtained by some independent method. We might, for example, use Taylor's algorithm or one of the Runge-Kutta methods to obtain these starting values. We must also be assured that these starting values are as accurate as necessary for the overall required accuracy. A second disadvantage of the Adams-Bashforth method is that, although the local discretization error is $\Theta(h^5)$, the coefficient in the error term is somewhat larger than for formulas of the Runge-Kutta type of the same order. Runge-Kutta methods are generally, although not always, more accurate for this reason. On the other hand, the multistep formulas require only one derivative evaluation per step, compared with four evaluations per step with Runge-Kutta methods, and are therefore considerably faster and require less computational work.

Example 8.5 Solve the equation

$$y' = x + y \qquad y(0) = 0$$

from $x = 0$ to $x = 1$, using the Adams-Bashforth method.

A FORTRAN program and the results for this problem are given below. The exact solution of this problem is $y = e^x - 1 - x$. The first four starting values are computed, using this solution. The first column of the results gives the values of x_n with $h = \frac{1}{32}$, the second column gives y_n as computed by formula (8.47), the third column gives the value $y(x_n)$ as computed from the solution, and the fourth column gives the error $e_n = y_n - y(x_n)$.

The results are correct to about six significant figures, which is approximately what would be expected from the error formula (8.48). Since the accumulated discretization error is $\Theta(h^4)$, we would expect to reduce the error by $\frac{1}{16}$ if the step size h were halved.

FORTRAN PROGRAM FOR EXAMPLE 8.5

```
C  ADAMS-BASHFORTH METHOD
       INTEGER I,N,NSTEPS
       REAL ERROR,F(4),H,XBEGIN,XN,YBEGIN,YN
C
       SOLN(X) = EXP(X) - 1. - X
C
C  ** INITIALIZE
       PRINT 600
  600 FORMAT('1ADAMS-BASHFORTH METHOD'/
     * '0',4X,'N',13X,'XN',15X,'YN',13X,'Y(XN)',12X,'ERROR'/)
       NSTEPS = 32
       H = 1./NSTEPS
       YBEGIN = 0.
       XBEGIN = 0.
C
C  ** COMPUTE FIRST FOUR POINTS USING EXACT SOLUTION
       F(1) = XBEGIN + YBEGIN
       N = 0
       ERROR = 0.
       PRINT 601, N,XBEGIN,YBEGIN,YBEGIN,ERROR
  601 FORMAT(' ',I3,4X,4E17.8)
       DO 20 N=1,3
          XN = XBEGIN + N*H
          YN = SOLN(XN)
          F(N+1) = XN + YN
          PRINT 601, N,XN,YN,YN,ERROR
   20 CONTINUE
C
C  ** BEGIN ITERATION
       DO 50 N=4,NSTEPS
          YN = YN + (H/24.)*(55.*F(4)-59.*F(3)+37.*F(2)-9.*F(1))
          XN = XBEGIN + N*H
          F(1) = F(2)
          F(2) = F(3)
          F(3) = F(4)
          F(4) = XN + YN
          YOFXN = SOLN(XN)
          ERROR = YN - YOFXN
          PRINT 601, N,XN,YN,YOFXN,ERROR
   50 CONTINUE
                                              STOP
       END
```

COMPUTER RESULTS FOR EXAMPLE 8.5

N	XN	YN	Y(XN)	ERROR
0	0.	0.	0.	0.
1	0.31250000E-01	0.49340725E-03	0.49340725E-03	0.
2	0.62500000E-01	0.19944459E-02	0.19944459E-02	0.
3	0.93750000E-01	0.45351386E-02	0.45351386E-02	0.
4	0.12500000E-00	0.81484411E-02	0.81484467E-02	$-0.55879354E-08$
5	0.15625000E-00	0.12868421E-01	0.12868434E-01	$-0.12922101E-07$
6	0.18750000E-00	0.18730211E-01	0.18730238E-01	$-0.26309863E-07$
7	0.21875000E-00	0.25770056E-01	0.25770098E-01	$-0.41676685E-07$
8	0.25000000E-00	0.34025350E-01	0.34025416E-01	$-0.65192580E-07$
9	0.28125000E-00	0.43534677E-01	0.43534756E-01	$-0.78696758E-07$
10	0.31250000E-00	0.54337843E-01	0.54337934E-01	$-0.90803951E-07$
11	0.34375000E-00	0.66475919E-01	0.66476032E-01	$-0.11269003E-06$
12	0.37500000E-00	0.79991280E-01	0.79991400E-01	$-0.12014061E-06$
13	0.40625000E-00	0.94927646E-01	0.94927788E-01	$-0.14156103E-06$

COMPUTER RESULTS FOR EXAMPLE 8.5 (continued)

N	XN	YN	Y(XN)	ERROR
14	0.43750000E-00	0.11133012E-00	0.11133029E-00	-0.16111881E-06
15	0.46875000E-00	0.12924525E-00	0.12924545E-00	-0.19185245E-06
16	0.50000000E 00	0.14872105E-00	0.14872126E-00	-0.21234155E-06
17	0.53125000E 00	0.16980705E-00	0.16980730E-00	-0.24400651E-06
18	0.56250000E 00	0.19255438E-00	0.19255446E-00	-0.26822090E-06
19	0.59375000E-00	0.21701577E-00	0.21701607E-00	-0.29988587E-06
20	0.62500000E 00	0.24324562E-00	0.24324594E-00	-0.31664968E-06
21	0.65625000E 00	0.27130008E-00	0.27130044E-00	-0.34645200E-06
22	0.68750000E 00	0.30123707E-00	0.30123746E-00	-0.39115548E-06
23	0.71875000E 00	0.33311634E-00	0.33311677E-00	-0.42840838E-06
24	0.75000000E 00	0.36699954E-00	0.36700001E-00	-0.46566129E-06
25	0.78125000E 00	0.40295030E-00	0.40295079E-00	-0.49173832E-06
26	0.81250000E 00	0.44103424E-00	0.44103476E-00	-0.52526593E-06
27	0.84375000E 00	0.48131907E-00	0.48131964E-00	-0.56624413E-06
28	0.87500000E 00	0.52387466E 00	0.52387527E 00	-0.61094761E-06
29	0.90625000E 00	0.56877308E 00	0.56877375E 00	-0.66310167E-06
30	0.93750000E 00	0.61608872E 00	0.61608934E 00	-0.71525574E-06
31	0.96875000E 00	0.66589829E 00	0.66589907E 00	-0.77486038E-06
32	0.09999999E 01	0.71828098E 00	0.71828181E 00	-0.82701445E-06

EXERCISES

8.7-1 Using (8.45a), derive the coefficients γ_k ($k = 1, \ldots, 4$) in the Adams-Bashforth formula (8.45).

8.7-2 Set $m = 4$ in (8.45) and derive the corresponding Adams-Bashforth formula in terms of ordinates as in formula (8.47). Also derive the error term for this formula.

8.7-3 Derive Milne's formula (8.51) and its corresponding error term.

8.7-4 Write a program using Milne's formula for integrating a differential equation with equally spaced points. Assume that the first three starting values are known.

8.7-5 Solve the equation of Example 8.5 using the Milne program with $h = \frac{1}{32}$ and compare your results with those given in Example 8.5.

8.7-6 Solve the equation $xy' = x - y$, $y(2) = 2$ from $x = 2$ to $x = 3$ with $h = 0.05$ using the Adams-Bashforth method (8.47). Obtain the starting values from the exact solution

$$y(x) = \frac{x}{2} + \frac{2}{x}$$

8.7-7 Using the Adams-Bashforth method (8.47) solve the equation $y' + y = e^{-x}$ from $x = 0$ to $x = 1$ using $h = \frac{1}{64}$ and $h = \frac{1}{128}$. Estimate the accuracy of your results. Starting values can be obtained from the exact solution $y = xe^{-x}$.

8.7-8 Derive the formulas in (8.51) using (8.49) with $m = 2$ (not 3) and the error (2.18) in polynomial interpolation. In this the discussion at the beginning of Sec. 7.2 will be helpful.

8.7-9 Verify (8.50) by expanding y_{n+1} and y_{n-1} about $x = x_n$ through third-order terms, assuming that the starting values are exact.

8.8 PREDICTOR-CORRECTOR METHODS

The multistep methods of Sec. 8.7 were derived using polynomials which interpolated at the point x_n and at points backward from x_n. These are sometimes known as formulas of **open** type. Formulas of **closed** type are derived by basing the interpolating polynomial on the point x_{n+1}, as well as on x_n and points backward from x_n. The simplest formula of this type is obtained if we approximate the integral in (8.43) by the trapezoidal formula (7.26). This leads to the formula

$$\boxed{y_{n+1} = y_n + \frac{h}{2} \left[f(x_n, y_n) + f(x_{n+1}, y_{n+1}) \right]} \qquad n = 0, 1, \ldots$$

$$(8.52)$$

The error of this formula is $-(h^3/12)y'''$ and thus represents an improvement over Euler's method. However, (8.52) is an *implicit* equation for y_{n+1} since y_{n+1} appears as an argument on the right-hand side.

If $f(x, y)$ is a nonlinear function, we will, in general, not be able to solve (8.52) for y_{n+1} exactly. We can, however, attempt to obtain y_{n+1} by means of iteration. Thus, keeping x_n fixed, we obtain a first approximation $y_{n+1}^{(0)}$ to y_{n+1} by means of Euler's formula

$$y_{n+1}^{(0)} = y_n + hf(x_n, y_n) \tag{8.53}$$

We then evaluate $f(x_{n+1}, y_{n+1}^{(0)})$ and substitute in the right-hand side of (8.52) to obtain the approximation

$$y_{n+1}^{(1)} = y_n + \frac{h}{2} \left[f(x_n, y_n) + f(x_{n+1}, y_{n+1}^{(0)}) \right]$$

Next we evaluate $f(x_{n+1}, y_{n+1}^{(1)})$ and again use (8.52) to obtain a next approximation. In general, the iteration is defined by

$$y_{n+1}^{(k)} = y_n + \frac{h}{2} \left[f(x_n, y_n) + f(x_{n+1}, y_{n+1}^{(k-1)}) \right] \qquad k = 1, 2, \ldots \tag{8.54}$$

The iteration is terminated when two successive iterates agree to the desired accuracy. This iteration for obtaining improved values of y_{n+1} at a fixed point x_{n+1} is sometimes called an **inner iteration** to distinguish it from (8.52), which is used to generate values of y_n at $n = 0, 1, \ldots$. We shall summarize this procedure in Algorithm 8.4.

Algorithm 8.4: A second-order predictor-corrector method For the differential equation $y' = f(x, y)$, $y(x_0) = y_0$ with h given and $x_n = x_0 + nh$, for each fixed $n = 0, 1, \ldots$:

1. Compute $y_{n+1}^{(0)}$, using (8.53).

2. Compute $y_{n+1}^{(k)}$ $(k = 1, 2, \ldots)$, using (8.54), iterating on k until

$$\frac{|y_{n+1}^{(k)} - y_{n+1}^{(k-1)}|}{|y_{n+1}^{(k)}|} < \varepsilon \qquad \text{for a prescribed } \varepsilon$$

In specifying ε in Algorithm 8.4, we must keep in mind that the accuracy that can be expected on each step is limited by the error of the basic formula (8.52) and by the step size h.

To adapt this algorithm to the solution of a specific problem, we would have to specify (a) the number N of steps desired; (b) a maximum number K of inner iterations; (c) what to do in case k exceeds K.

It is customary to call an explicit formula such as Euler's formula an open-type formula, while an implicit formula such as (8.52) is said to be of closed type. When they are used as a pair of formulas, the open-type formula is also called a **predictor**, while the closed-type formula is called a **corrector**. A corrector formula is generally more accurate than a predictor formula, even when both have a discretization error of the same order, primarily because the coefficient in the error term is smaller. Two questions arise naturally in connection with corrector formulas. The first is, "Under what conditions will the inner iteration on k converge?," and the second, "How many iterations will be needed to produce the required accuracy?" The answer to the latter question will depend on many factors. However, if the predictor and corrector formulas are of the same order, experience has shown that only one or two applications of the corrector are sufficient, provided that the step size h has been properly selected. If we find that one or two corrections are not sufficient, it is better to reduce the step size h than to continue to iterate. The answer to the first question is contained in Theorem 8.2.

Theorem 8.2 If $f(x, y)$ and $\partial f / \partial y$ are continuous in x and y on the closed interval $[a, b]$ the inner iteration defined by (8.54) will converge, provided h is chosen small enough so that, for $x = x_n$, and all y with $|y - y_{n+1}| \leq |y_{n+1}^{(0)} - y_{n+1}|$,

$$\left| \frac{\partial f}{\partial y} \right| h < 2 \qquad (8.55)$$

To prove this, we first observe that in the iteration (8.54) x_n is fixed. Hence, if we set $y_{n+1}^{(k)} =: Y^{(k)}$, we can write (8.54) in the form

$$Y^{(k)} = F(Y^{(k-1)})$$

where $$F(Y) = \frac{h}{2} f(x_{n+1}, Y) + C$$

and where C depends on n but not on Y. This can be viewed as an instance of fixed-point iteration considered in Sec. 3.3. In a corollary to Theorem 3.1 we proved that such an iteration will converge provided that $F'(Y)$ is continuous and satisfies

$$|F'(Y)| < 1$$

for all Y with $|Y - y_{n+1}| \leq |Y^{(0)} - y_{n+1}|$, where y_{n+1} is the fixed point of $F(Y)$. Since $F'(Y) = (h/2)\partial f/\partial y$, and since $\partial f/\partial y$ is bounded and non-vanishing by assumption, the iteration (8.54) will converge if

$$|F'(Y)| = \left|\frac{h}{2}\frac{\partial f}{\partial y}\right| < 1$$

i.e., if

$$h < \frac{2}{|\partial f/\partial y|}$$

Since $F'(Y) = (h/2) \partial f/\partial y$, this proves the theorem.

Example 8.6 Solve the equation

$$y' = x - \frac{1}{y} \qquad y(0) = 1$$

from $x = 0$ to $x = 0.2$, using Algorithm 8.4 with $h = 0.1$.

Since the error of (8.54) is $-(h^3/12)y'''$, and since by differentiating above we find that $y'''(0) \approx -2$, the error will be approximately 0.0002. We cannot therefore expect much more than three decimal places of accuracy in the results.

Step 1

By Euler's method: $y_1^{(0)} = 0.9$
By (8.54): $y_1^{(1)} = 0.8994$
     $y_1^{(2)} = 0.8994$

Since $y_1^{(1)}$ and $y_1^{(2)}$ agree to four places, we accept this answer, and we compute $y_1' = f(x_1, y_1) = -1.0118$.

Step 2 By Euler's method,

$$y_2^{(0)} = 0.8994 + 0.1(-1.0118) = 0.7982$$

By (8.54),

$$y_2^{(1)} = 0.8994 + 0.05\left[-1.0118 + \left(0.2 - \frac{1}{0.7982}\right)\right] = 0.7962$$

$$y_2^{(2)} = 0.8994 + 0.05\left[-1.0118 + \left(0.2 - \frac{1}{0.7962}\right)\right] = 0.7960$$

$$y_2^{(3)} = 0.7960$$

We accept $y_2 = 0.7960$, compute y_2', and proceed to the next step.

As the computation proceeds, we can expect a gradual loss of accuracy. It appears here that for $h = 0.1$ we need two or three applications of the corrector. This is primarily due to the fact that we are using a predictor which is of lower order than the corrector.

To verify that the inner iterations for this example will converge for $h = 0.1$, we compute $\partial f/\partial y = 1/y^2$, and hence, from Theorem 8.2, we want h to be less that $2y^2$. We do not know the solution y, but it is clear from the above steps that $y > 0.7$ on the interval [0, 0.2]. Hence the inner iterations will converge if $h < 2(0.7)^2 = 0.98$.

EXERCISES

8.8-1 For the special equation $y' = Ay$, $y(0) = 1$, show that the trapezoidal corrector formula (8.52) leads to a difference equation whose solution is

$$y_n = \left[\frac{(1 + Ah/2)}{(1 - Ah/2)} \right]^n$$

provided that $|Ah/2| < 1$.

8.8-2 For the solution obtained in Exercise 8.8-1 show that

$$\lim_{h \to 0} y_n = e^{Ax_n}$$

for a fixed value of $x = x_n = nh$.

8.8-3 Solve the equation $y' = x^2 + y$, $y(0) = 1$, from $x = 0$ to $x = 0.5$, using Euler's method as a predictor and (8.54) as a corrector. Determine the step h so that four decimal places of accuracy are obtained at $x = 0.5$. Start with $h = 0.05$.

8.9 THE ADAMS-MOULTON METHOD

Corrector formulas of higher order can be obtained by using a polynomial which interpolates at $x_{n+1}, x_n, \ldots, x_{n-m}$ for an integer $m > 0$. The Newton backward formula which interpolates at these $m + 2$ points in terms of $s = (x - x_n)/h$ is

$$P_{m+1}(s) = \sum_{k=0}^{m+1} (-1)^k \binom{1-s}{k} \Delta^k f_{n+1-k} \tag{8.56}$$

These differences are based on the values $f_{n+1}, f_n, \ldots, f_{n-m}$. If we integrate (8.56) from x_n to x_{n+1} and use (8.43), we obtain

$$y_{n+1} = y_n + h(\gamma_0' f_{n+1} + \gamma_1' \Delta f_n + \cdots + \gamma_{m+1}' \Delta^{m+1} f_{n-m}) \tag{8.57}$$

where $\gamma_k' = (-1)^k \int_0^1 \binom{1-s}{k} ds \qquad k = 0, 1, \ldots, m + 1$

The first few values of γ_k' are

$$\gamma_0' = 1 \qquad \gamma_1' = -\tfrac{1}{2} \qquad \gamma_2' = -\tfrac{1}{12} \qquad \gamma_3' = -\tfrac{1}{24} \qquad \gamma_4' = -\tfrac{10}{720}$$

The error of (8.57), based on the error of the interpolating polynomial, is

$$E = \gamma_{m+2}' h^{m+3} y^{(m+3)}(\xi) \tag{8.58}$$

The case $m = 2$ is frequently used. If the differences in (8.57) are expressed in terms of ordinates for $m = 2$, we obtain

$$y_{n+1} = y_n + \frac{h}{24}(9f_{n+1} + 19f_n - 5f_{n-1} + f_{n-2}) \tag{8.59}$$

with the error

$$E_{AM} = -\tfrac{19}{720} h^5 y^{v}(\xi) \tag{8.60}$$

The formula (8.57) is known as the **Adams-Moulton formula**. The fourth-order Adams-Moulton formula (8.59) is clearly a corrector formula of closed type since $f_{n+1} = f(x_{n+1}, y_{n+1})$ involves the unknown quantity y_{n+1}. It must therefore be solved by iteration. It can be shown that the iteration based on (8.59) will converge, provided that h is small enough so that the condition $9h/24|\partial f/\partial y| < 1$ is satisfied. A convenient predictor to use with this corrector is the Adams-Bashforth fourth-order formula (8.47). In this case the predictor is of the same order as the corrector. If h is properly chosen, then one application of the corrector will yield a significant improvement in accuracy.

Specifications for a fourth-order predictor-corrector method are given in Algorithm 8.5.

Algorithm 8.5: The Adams-Moulton predictor-corrector method For the differential equation $y' = f(x, y)$ with h fixed and $x_n = x_0 + nh$ and with (y_0, f_0), (y_1, f_1), (y_2, f_2), (y_3, f_3) given, for each fixed $n = 3, 4, \ldots$:

1. Compute $y_{n+1}^{(0)}$, using the formula

$$y_{n+1}^{(0)} = y_n + \frac{h}{24}(55f_n - 59f_{n-1} + 37f_{n-2} - 9f_{n-3})$$

2. Compute $f_{n+1}^{(0)} = f(x_{n+1}, y_{n+1}^{(0)})$.
3. Compute

$$y_{n+1}^{(k)} = y_n + \frac{h}{24}\left[9f(x_{n+1}, y_{n+1}^{(k-1)}) + 19f_n - 5f_{n-1} + f_{n-2}\right]$$

$$k = 1, 2, \ldots$$

4. Iterate on k until

$$\frac{|y_{n+1}^{(k)} - y_{n+1}^{(k-1)}|}{|y_{n+1}^{(k)}|} < \varepsilon \qquad \text{for } \varepsilon \text{ prescribed}$$

Again this algorithm is not complete unless we specify what to do in case of nonconvergence in step 4. A subroutine like DVERK contains a more complete specification for a general-purpose subroutine to solve differential equations.

Besides yielding improved accuracy, the corrector formula serves another useful function. It provides an estimate of the local discretization error, which can then be used to decide whether the step h is adequate for the required accuracy. To examine this error estimation procedure for the predictor-corrector pair consisting of the Adams-Bashforth and Adams-Moulton fourth-order formulas, we write the local-error estimate for each:

$$E_{AB} = \tfrac{251}{720}h^5 y^{\nu}(\xi_1)$$

$$E_{AM} = -\tfrac{19}{720}h^5 y^{\nu}(\xi_2)$$

(8.61)

Let $y_{n+1}^{(0)}$ represent the value of y_{n+1} obtained from (8.47), and $y_{n+1}^{(1)}$ the result obtained with one application of Algorithm 8.5. If the values of f are assumed to be exact at all points up to and including x_n, and if $y(x_{n+1})$ represents the exact value of y at x_{n+1}, then from (8.61) we obtain the error estimates

$$y(x_{n+1}) - y_{n+1}^{(0)} = \tfrac{251}{720} h^5 y^v(\xi_1) \tag{8.62a}$$

$$y(x_{n+1}) - y_{n+1}^{(1)} = -\tfrac{19}{720} h^5 y^v(\xi_2) \tag{8.62b}$$

In general, $\xi_1 \neq \xi_2$. However, if we assume that over the interval of interest $y^v(x)$ is approximately constant, then on subtracting (8.62b) from (8.62a), we obtain the following estimate for y^v:

$$h^5 y^v = \tfrac{720}{270}\left(y_{n+1}^{(1)} - y_{n+1}^{(0)}\right)$$

Substituting this into (8.62b), we find that

$$y(x_{n+1}) - y_{n+1}^{(1)} = -\tfrac{19}{270}\left(y_{n+1}^{(1)} - y_{n+1}^{(0)}\right)$$

$$\approx -\tfrac{1}{14}\left(y_{n+1}^{(1)} - y_{n+1}^{(0)}\right) = D_{n+1} \tag{8.63}$$

Thus the error of the corrected value is approximately $-\tfrac{1}{14}$ of the difference between the corrected and predicted values.

As mentioned before, it is advisable to use the corrector only once. If the accuracy as determined by (8.63) is not sufficient, it is better to reduce the step size than to correct more than once.

In a general-purpose routine for solving differential equations, the error estimate is used in the following manner: Let us assume that we wish to keep the local error per unit step bounded as in (8.41) so that

$$E_1 \leq \frac{|D_{n+1}|}{h} \leq E_2$$

and that starting values have been provided. We proceed as follows:

1. Use (8.47) to obtain $y_{n+1}^{(0)}$. Compute $f_{n+1}^{(0)}$.
2. Use (8.59) to obtain $y_{n+1}^{(1)}$. Compute $f_{n+1}^{(1)}$.
3. Compute $|D_{n+1}|$ from (8.63).
4. If $E_1 \leq |D_{n+1}|/h \leq E_2$, proceed to the next integration step, using the same value of h.
5. If $|D_{n+1}|/h > E_2$, the step size h is too large and should be reduced. It is customary to replace h by $h/2$, recompute four starting values, and then return to step 1.
6. If $|D_{n+1}|/h < E_1$, more accuracy is being obtained than is necessary. Hence we can save computer time by replacing h by $2h$, recomputing four new starting values at intervals of length $2h$, and returning to step 1.

In using predictor-corrector methods with variable step size as outlined above, it is necessary to (*a*) have a method for obtaining the necessary starting values initially; (*b*) have a method for obtaining the necessary values of *y* at half steps when the interval is halved; and (*c*) have a method for obtaining the necessary values of *y* when the interval is doubled. Special formulas can be worked out for each of these three situations. These formulas add considerably to the complexity of a program. However, a fairly ideal combination is to use the fourth-order Runge-Kutta method (8.37), together with a fourth-order predictor-corrector pair such as (8.47) and (8.59). The Runge-Kutta method can then be used for starting the solution initially, for halving, and for doubling, while the predictor-corrector pair can be used for normal continuation when the step size is kept fixed.

Before leaving this section, it should be pointed out that there are many other predictor-corrector formulas, and in particular that the following formulas due to Milne are often used:

$$y_{n+1}^{(0)} = y_{n-3} + \frac{4h}{3}(2f_n - f_{n-1} + 2f_{n-2}) \qquad E_M^0 = \frac{28}{90}h^5 y^{\text{v}}(\xi_1) \quad (8.64a)$$

$$y_{n+1}^{(1)} = y_{n-1} + \frac{h}{3}(f_{n+1}^{(0)} + 4f_n + f_{n-1}) \qquad E_M^1 = -\frac{1}{90}h^5 y^{\text{v}}(\xi_2)$$
$$(8.64b)$$

Equation (8.64*a*) was derived in Sec. 8.6, and (8.64*b*) is based on Simpson's rule for numerical integration. Proceeding as in the Adams-Moulton formulas, we can show that a local-error estimate is provided by

$$D_{n+1} = -\frac{1}{29}(y_{n+1}^{(1)} - y_{n+1}^{(0)}) \qquad (8.65)$$

The error estimate for the Milne method appears to be somewhat more favorable than for the Adams-Moulton method, but as we shall see, (8.64*b*) is subject to numerical instability in some cases.

While the literature is abundant with methods for integrating differential equations, the most popular in the United States are the fourth-order Runge-Kutta method and predictor-corrector methods such as those of Adams-Moulton or Milne (8.64). Although no one method will perform uniformly better than another method on all problems, it is appropriate to point out the advantages and disadvantages of each of these types for general-purpose work.

Runge-Kutta methods have the important advantage that they are self-starting. In addition, they are stable, provide good accuracy, and, as a computer program, occupy a relatively small amount of core storage. Standard RK methods provide no estimate of the local error, so that the user has no way of knowing whether the step *h* being used is adequate. One can, of course, use the step size control methods described in Sec. 8.6, but this is expensive in machine time. The second major disadvantage of the fourth-order Runge-Kutta method is that it requires four function evaluations per integration step, compared with only two using the fourth-order predictor-corrector methods. On some problems Runge-Kutta methods will require almost twice as much computing time.

Predictor-corrector methods provide an automatic error estimate at each step, thus allowing the program to select an optimum value of h for a required accuracy. They are also fast since they require only two function evaluations per step. On the other hand, predictor-corrector subroutines are very complicated to write, they require special techniques for starting and for doubling and halving the step size, and they may be subject to numerical instability (see Sec. 8.11).

For many years Runge-Kutta methods were used almost exclusively in the United States for general-purpose work, but recently predictor-corrector methods have been gaining in popularity.

In the past few years much more sophisticated general-purpose methods using both variable orders and variable steps have been developed. The Adams methods described previously are the most widely used in variable-order–variable-step methods. The objective of these methods is to automatically select the proper order and the proper step which will minimize the amount of work required to achieve a specified accuracy for a given problem. Other important advantages of these methods are that they are self-starting since a low-order method can be used at the start, and they can easily be adjusted to supply missing values when the step size is changed. A complete description of a subroutine called DIFSUB based on an Adams variable-order–variable-step method is given in Gear [30, pp. 158–167]. A subroutine called DVOGER, also based on Gear's method, is available in the IMSL programs and has been adapted to run on most modern computers.

Example 8.7 Solve the problem of Example 8.5 with $h = \frac{1}{32}$, using the Adams-Moulton predictor-corrector formulas. Compare the results with those of Example 8.5.

The program and the machine results are given below. In this case we list x_n, y_n (corrected value); the local-error estimate D_n; and the actual error e_n. On comparing these results with those of Example 8.5, we notice a decided improvement in accuracy, particularly as x approaches 1, where the results are correct to seven or eight significant figures. The local-error estimate D_n appears to be relatively constant and in general somewhat smaller than the actual error e_n. On closer examination, however, we find that in steps 5 to 13 the results are correct to only six significant figures. The explanation for this is that the values of y_n for these steps are an order of magnitude smaller than they are as $x \to 1$. Since D_n is an absolute error test, it does not indicate the number of significant digits of accuracy in the result. This is a typical situation when working in floating-point arithmetic. When working with numbers which are either very large or very small compared with 1, a better indicator of the number of significant digits of accuracy is provided by a relative test than by an absolute test. A relative error test for the Adams-Moulton formula, for instance, would be

$$\bar{D}_{n+1} = \frac{1}{14} \frac{|y_{n+1}^{(0)} - y_{n+1}^{(1)}|}{|y_{n+1}^{(1)}|}$$

in place of (8.63).

FORTRAN PROGRAM FOR EXAMPLE 8.7

```
C  ADAMS-MOULTON METHOD
      INTEGER I,N,NSTEPS
      REAL ERROR,F(4),H,XBEGIN,XN,YBEGIN,YN
C
      SOLN(X) = EXP(X) - 1. - X
C
C  ** INITIALIZE
      PRINT 600
  600 FORMAT('1ADAMS-MOULTON METHOD'/
     *'0',3X,'N',14X,'XN',15X,'YN',9X,'DN = YN - YNP',8X,'ERROR'/)
      NSTEPS = 32
      H = 1./NSTEPS
      YBEGIN = 0.
      XBEGIN = 0.
C
C  ** COMPUTE FIRST FOUR POINTS USING EXACT SOLUTION
      F(1) = XBEGIN + YBEGIN
      N = 0
      ERROR = 0.
      DIFF = 0.
      PRINT 601,N,XBEGIN,YBEGIN,DIFF,ERROR
  601 FORMAT(' ',I3,4X,4E17.8)
      DO 20 N=1,3
         XN = XBEGIN + N*H
         YN = SOLN(XN)
         F(N+1) = XN + YN
         PRINT 601, N,XN,YN,DIFF,ERROR
   20 CONTINUE
C
C  ** BEGIN ITERATION
      DO 50 N=4,NSTEPS
C        PREDICT USING ADAMS-BASHFORTH FORMULA
         YNPRED = YN + (H/24.)*(55.*F(4)-59.*F(3)+37.*F(2)-9.*F(1))
         XN = XBEGIN + N*H
         FNPRED = XN + YNPRED
C        CORRECT USING ADAMS-MOULTON FORMULA
         YN = YN + (H/24.)*(9.*FNPRED + 19.*F(4) - 5.*F(3) + F(2))
         DIFF = (YN - YNPRED)/14.
         F(1) = F(2)
         F(2) = F(3)
         F(3) = F(4)
         F(4) = XN + YN
         YOFXN = SOLN(XN)
         ERROR = YN - YOFXN
         PRINT 601, N,XN,YN,DIFF,ERROR
   50 CONTINUE
                                          STOP
      END
```

COMPUTER RESULTS FOR EXAMPLE 8.7

N	XN	YN	DN	ERROR
0	0.	0.	0.	0.
1	0.31250000E-01	0.49340725E-03	0.	0.
2	0.62500000E-01	0.19944459E-02	0.	0.
3	0.93750000E-01	0.45351386E-02	0.	0.
4	0.12500000E-00	0.81484520E-02	0.78164571E-09	0.53551048E-08
5	0.15625000E-00	0.12868445E-01	0.90637643E-09	0.11408702E-07
6	0.18750000E-00	0.18730249E-01	0.88143028E-09	0.11175871E-07
7	0.21875000E-00	0.25770108E-01	0.91469178E-09	0.10011718E-07
8	0.25000000E-00	0.34025417E-01	0.93132257E-09	0.13969839E-08

COMPUTER RESULTS FOR EXAMPLE 8.7 (*continued*)

N	XN	YN	DN	ERROR
9	0.28125000E-00	0.43534759E-01	0.96458407E-09	0.37252903E-08
10	0.31250000E-00	0.54337924E-01	0.99784564E-09	0.83819032E-08
11	0.34375000E-00	0.66476036E-01	0.99784564E-09	0.37252903E-08
12	0.37500000E-00	0.79991416E-01	0.10643686E-08	0.15832484E-07
13	0.40625000E-00	0.94927801E-01	0.11308917E-08	0.13969839E-07
14	0.43750000E-00	0.11133030E-00	0.11308917E-08	0.14901161E-07
15	0.46875000E-00	0.12924545E-00	0.10643686E-08	0.55879354E-08
16	0.50000000E 00	0.14872127E-00	0.11974147E-08	0.74505806E-08
17	0.53125000E 00	0.16980730E-00	0.13304609E-08	0.18626451E-08
18	0.56250000E 00	0.19255465E-00	0.13304609E-08	0.37252903E-08
19	0.59375000E 00	0.21701607E-00	0.13304609E-08	0.
20	0.62500000E 00	0.24324595E-00	0.13304609E-08	0.11175871E-07
21	0.65625000E 00	0.27130044E-00	0.13304609E-08	0.11175871E-07
22	0.68750000E 00	0.30123746E-00	0.13304609E-08	0.
23	0.71875000E 00	0.33311676E-00	0.13304609E-08	−0.37252903E-08
24	0.75000000E 00	0.36700001E-00	0.15965530E-08	−0.74505806E-08
25	0.78125000E 00	0.40295079E-00	0.15965530E-08	0.37252903E-08
26	0.81250000E 00	0.44103477E-00	0.15965530E-08	0.74505806E-08
27	0.84375000E 00	0.48131964E-00	0.18626451E-08	0.74505806E-08
28	0.87500000E 00	0.52387527E 00	0.15965530E-08	0.74505806E-08
29	0.90625000E 00	0.56877375E 00	0.21287372E-08	0.
30	0.93750000E 00	0.61608943E 00	0.21287372E-08	0.
31	0.96875000E 00	0.66589906E 00	0.21287372E-08	−0.74505806E-08
32	0.09999999E 01	0.71828180E 00	0.21287372E-08	−0.74505806E-08

EXERCISES

8.9-1 Show that the iteration defined by

$$y_{n+1}^{(k)} = y_n + \frac{h}{24}\left[9f(x_{n+1}, y_{n+1}^{(k-1)}) + 19f_n - 5f_{n-1} + f_{n-2}\right] \qquad \begin{matrix} k = 1, 2, \ldots \\ x_n \text{ fixed} \end{matrix}$$

will converge, provided that $|(9h/24)(\partial f/\partial y)| < 1$ (see Sec. 8.8).

8.9-2 Derive the error (8.60) for the Adams-Moulton method, using (8.57) and (8.58).

8.9-3 Derive the local-error estimate (8.65) for the Milne predictor-corrector formulas (8.64).

8.9-4 Solve the equation $y' = y + x^2$, $y(0) = 1$, from $x = 0$ to $x = 2$ with $h = 0.1$, using the Adams-Moulton predictor-corrector formulas. The starting values correct to six decimal places are

$$y(0) = 1.000000$$
$$y(0.1) = 1.105513$$
$$y(0.2) = 1.224208$$
$$y(0.3) = 1.359576$$

Compute D_{n+1}, and estimate the error at $x = 2$.

*8.10 STABILITY OF NUMERICAL METHODS

When computers first became widely used for solving differential equations, it was observed that some of the commonly used integration formulas, such as Milne's formulas (8.64), led to errors in the solution much larger than would be expected from the discretization error alone. Moreover, as the step size was made smaller, these errors for a fixed value of x actually became larger rather than smaller. To illustrate this behavior, let us consider the method derived in Sec. 8.7,

$$y_{n+1} = y_{n-1} + 2hf_n \qquad (8.66)$$

for which the discretization error is $\frac{1}{6}h^3 y'''(\xi)$. We would expect this method to give more accurate results for h fixed than Euler's method, whose error is $\mathcal{O}(h^2)$. Consider, however, the following simple problem,

$$y' = -2y + 1 \qquad y(0) = 1 \qquad (8.67)$$

whose exact solution is $y = \frac{1}{2}e^{-2x} + \frac{1}{2}$.

The results given in Table 8.1 were obtained by the computer, using a step size of $h = \frac{1}{32}$. The first column gives selected values of x at which the solution is printed, Y(N) denotes the exact solution, Y1(N) denotes the solution obtained by Euler's method, Y2(N) the solution obtained by (8.66), and E1(N), E2(N) their respective errors. Method (8.66) requires

Table 8.1

X(N)	Y(N)	Y1(N)	Y2(N)	E1(N)	E2(N)
0.	1.0000000	1.0000000	1.0000000	0.	0.
0.0312500	0.9697065	0.9687500	0.9697065	−0.0009565	−0.0000000
0.5000000	0.6839397	0.6780370	0.6840817	−0.0059027	0.0001420
1.0000000	0.5676676	0.5633943	0.5678247	−0.0042733	0.0001571
1.5000000	0.5248935	0.5225730	0.5251328	−0.0023205	0.0002392
2.0000000	0.5091578	0.5080376	0.5097007	−0.0011202	0.0005429
2.2500000	0.5055545	0.5047962	0.5064264	−0.0007583	0.0008719
2.5000000	0.5033690	0.5028620	0.5047904	−0.0005070	0.0014214
3.0000000	0.5012394	0.5010190	0.5050759	−0.0002203	0.0038365
3.5000000	0.5004559	0.5003628	0.5108669	−0.0000931	0.0104110
3.7500000	0.5002765	0.5002165	0.5174337	−0.0000601	0.0171571
3.7812500	0.5002598	0.5002029	0.4819995	−0.0000568	−0.0182603
3.8125000	0.5002440	0.5001903	0.5196837	−0.0000538	0.0194397
3.8437500	0.5002293	0.5001784	0.4795391	−0.0000509	−0.0206902
3.8750000	0.5002154	0.5001672	0.5222413	−0.0000482	0.0220260
3.9062500	0.5002023	0.5001568	0.4767589	−0.0000456	−0.0234434
3.9375000	0.5001901	0.5001470	0.5251465	−0.0000431	0.0249564
3.9687500	0.5001785	0.5001378	0.4736156	−0.0000408	−0.0265630
4.0000000	0.5001677	0.5001292	0.5284445	−0.0000386	0.0282768

two starting values y_0 and y_1. For y_1 we take the exact value as computed from the exact solution.

The error columns show that E2(N) is considerably smaller than E1(N) for the first few steps but grows rapidly, so that at $x = 2.25$, E2(N) is greater than E1(N). As $x \to 4$, the solution approaches the steady-state value $y = \frac{1}{2}$. Euler's method actually approaches this steady-state solution with monotonically decreasing error, whereas for method (8.66) the error is growing exponentially. Moreover, as the last few steps (where the results are printed at every integration step) show, the errors E2(N) oscillate in sign. Beyond $x = 4$, Y2(N) would have no significant digits of accuracy. The phenomenon exhibited in this example is known as **numerical instability**.

To help us understand this behavior, let us examine the difference equation (8.66) more closely. For the example being considered, $f_n = -2y_n + 1$, and hence (8.66) becomes

$$y_{n+1} + 4hy_n - y_{n-1} = 2h \qquad y_0 = 1 \tag{8.68}$$

We can solve this difference equation explicitly, using the methods of Sec. 8.2. The general solution of (8.68) is

$$y_n = C_1 \beta_1^n + C_2 \beta_2^n + \tfrac{1}{2} \tag{8.69}$$

where β_1, β_2 are the roots of the characteristic equation

$$\beta^2 + 4h\beta - 1 = 0$$

These roots are

$$\beta_{1,2} = -2h \pm \sqrt{1 + 4h^2}$$

If we expand $\sqrt{1 + 4h^2}$ in a Taylor's series through linear terms, these roots can be expressed in the form

$$\beta_1 = 1 - 2h + \mathcal{O}(h^2)$$
$$\beta_2 = -(1 + 2h) + \mathcal{O}(h^2)$$

Substituting into (8.69), we have

$$y_n = C_1(1 - 2h + \mathcal{O}(h^2))^n + C_2(-1)^n(1 + 2h + \mathcal{O}(h^2))^n + \tfrac{1}{2} \tag{8.70}$$

In the calculus it is shown that

$$\lim_{\varepsilon \to 0} (1 + \varepsilon)^{1/\varepsilon} = e$$

Using this limit and the fact that $n = x_n/h$, it follows for x_n fixed that

$$\lim_{h \to 0} (1 + 2h)^n = \lim_{h \to 0} (1 + 2h)^{(1/2h)(2x_n)} = e^{2x_n}$$

and similarly that

$$\lim_{h \to 0} (1 - 2h)^n = e^{-2x_n}$$

Hence, as $h \to 0$, the solution (8.70) approaches

$$y_n = \left(C_1 e^{-2x_n} + \tfrac{1}{2} \right) + C_2(-1)^n e^{2x_n} \qquad (8.71)$$

Thus the first term tends to the true solution of the differential equation. The second term is extraneous and arises only because we have replaced a first-order differential equation by a second-order difference equation. Imposing the initial conditions will, if all arithmetic operations are exact, result in choosing $C_2 = 0$ so that the correct solution will be selected from (8.71). In practice, however, some errors will be introduced, primarily due to roundoff or to inexact starting values, and hence C_2 will not be exactly zero. A small error will therefore be introduced at each step of the integration, and this error will subsequently be magnified because it is being multiplied by the exponentially increasing factor $(-1)^n e^{2x_n}$. Because the major part of the true solution is exponentially decreasing, the error introduced from the extraneous solution will eventually dominate the true solution and lead to completely incorrect results.

Loosely speaking, we can say that a method is unstable if errors introduced into the calculations grow at an exponential rate as the computation proceeds.

One-step methods like those of the Runge-Kutta type do not exhibit any numerical instability for h sufficiently small. Multistep methods may, in some cases, be unstable for all values of h, and in other cases for a range of values of h. To determine whether a given multistep method is stable, we can proceed as follows: If the multistep method leads to a difference equation of order k, find the roots of the characteristic equation corresponding to the homogeneous difference equation. Call these β_i ($i = 1, \ldots, k$). The general solution of the homogeneous difference equation is then

$$y_n = c_1 \beta_1^n + c_2 \beta_2^n + \cdots + c_k \beta_k^n \qquad (8.72)$$

One of these solutions, say β_1^n, will tend to the exact solution of the differential equation as $h \to 0$. All the other solutions are extraneous. A multistep method is defined to be **strongly stable** if the extraneous roots satisfy as $h \to 0$ the condition

$$|\beta_i| < 1 \qquad i = 2, 3, \ldots, k$$

Under these conditions any errors introduced into the computation will decay as n increases, whereas if any of the extraneous β_i are greater than one in magnitude, the errors will grow exponentially.

For the general differential equation $y' = f(x, y)$, it will be impossible to obtain the roots β_i of the characteristic equation. A consideration of the special equation $y' = \lambda y$, λ constant, is usually considered sufficient, however, to give an indication of the stability of a method.

We consider first the Adams-Bashforth fourth-order method. If in (8.47) we set $f(x, y) = \lambda y$ we obtain

$$y_{n+1} - y_n - \frac{h\lambda}{24}(55y_n - 59y_{n-1} + 37y_{n-2} - 9y_{n-3}) = 0 \qquad (8.73)$$

The characteristic equation for this difference equation is

$$\beta^4 - \beta^3 - \frac{h\lambda}{24}(55\beta^3 - 59\beta^2 + 37\beta - 9) = 0$$

The roots of this equation are of course functions of $h\lambda$. It is customary to write the characteristic equation in the form

$$\rho(\beta) + h\lambda\sigma(\beta) = 0 \qquad (8.74)$$

where $\rho(\beta)$ and $\sigma(\beta)$ are polynomials defined by

$$\rho(\beta) = \beta^4 - \beta^3$$

$$\sigma(\beta) = -\frac{1}{24}(55\beta^3 - 59\beta^2 + 37\beta - 9)$$

We see that as $h \to 0$, (8.74) reduces to $\rho(\beta) = 0$, whose roots are $\beta_1 = 1$, $\beta_2 = \beta_3 = \beta_4 = 0$. For $h \neq 0$, the general solution of (8.73) will have the form

$$y_n = c_1 \beta_1^n + c_2 \beta_2^n + c_3 \beta_3^n + c_4 \beta_4^n$$

where the β_i are solutions of (8.74). It can be shown that β_1^n approaches the desired solution of $y' = \lambda y$ as $h \to 0$ while the other roots correspond to extraneous solutions. Since the roots of (8.74) are continuous functions of h, it follows that for h small enough, $|\beta_i| < 1$ for $i = 2, 3, 4$, and hence from the definition of stability that the Adams-Bashforth method is strongly stable. All multistep methods lead to a characteristic equation in the form (8.74) whose left-hand side is sometimes called the **stability polynomial**. The definition of stability can be recast in terms of the stability polynomial. A method is **strongly stable** if all the roots of $\rho(\beta) = 0$ have magnitude less than one except for the simple root $\beta = 1$.

We investigate next the stability properties of Milne's method (8.64b) given by

$$y_{n+1} = y_{n-1} + \frac{h}{3}(f_{n+1} + 4f_n + f_{n-1}) \qquad (8.75)$$

Again setting $f(x, y) = \lambda y$ we obtain

$$y_{n+1} - y_{n-1} - \frac{h\lambda}{3}(y_{n+1} + 4y_n + y_{n-1}) = 0$$

and its characteristic equation becomes

$$\rho(\beta) + h\lambda\sigma(\beta) = 0 \qquad (8.76)$$

with
$$\rho(\beta) = \beta^2 - 1$$
$$\sigma(\beta) = \beta^2 + 4\beta + 1$$

This time $\rho(\beta) = 0$ has the roots $\beta_1 = 1$, $\beta_2 = -1$, and hence by the definition above, Milne's method is not strongly stable. To see the implications of this we compute the roots of the stability polynomial (8.76). For h small we have

$$\beta_1 = 1 + \lambda h + \mathcal{O}(h^2)$$
$$\beta_2 = -(1 - \lambda h/3) + \mathcal{O}(h^2) \tag{8.77}$$

Hence the general solution of (8.75) is

$$y_n = c_1(1 + \lambda h + \mathcal{O}(h^2))^n + c_2(-1)^n(1 - \lambda h/3 + \mathcal{O}(h^2))^n$$

If we set $n = x_n/h$ and let $h \to 0$, this solution approaches

$$y_n = c_1 e^{\lambda x_n} + c_2(-1)^n e^{-\lambda x_n/3} \tag{8.78}$$

In this case stability depends upon the sign of λ. If $\lambda > 0$ so that the desired solution is exponentially increasing, it is clear that the extraneous solution will be exponentially decreasing so that Milne's method will be stable. On the other hand if $\lambda < 0$, then Milne's method will be unstable since the extraneous solution will be exponentially increasing and will eventually swamp the desired solution. Methods of this type whose stability depends upon the sign of λ for the test equation $y' = \lambda y$ are said to be **weakly stable**. For the more general equation $y' = f(x, y)$ we can expect weak stability from Milne's method whenever $\partial f/\partial y < 0$ on the interval of integration.

In practice all multistep methods will exhibit some instability for some range of values of the step h. Consider, for example, the Adams-Bashforth method of order 2 defined by

$$y_{n+1} = y_n + \frac{h}{2}\{3f_n - f_{n-1}\}$$

If we apply this method to the test equation $y' = \lambda y$, we will obtain the difference equation

$$y_{n+1} - y_n - \frac{h\lambda}{2}\{3y_n - y_{n-1}\} = 0$$

and from this the stability polynomial

$$\beta^2 - \beta - \frac{h\lambda}{2}\{3\beta - 1\}$$

or the equation

$$\beta^2 - \left(1 + \frac{3h\lambda}{2}\right)\beta + \frac{h\lambda}{2} = 0$$

If $\lambda < 0$, the roots of this quadratic equation are both less than one in magnitude provided that $-1 < h\lambda < 0$. In this case we will have absolute stability since errors will not be magnified because of the extraneous solution. If, however, $|h\lambda| > 1$, then one of these roots will be greater than one in magnitude and we will encounter some instability. The condition that $-1 < h\lambda < 0$ effectively restricts the step size h that can be used for this method. For example, if $\lambda = -100$, then we must choose $h < 0.01$ to assure stability. A multistep method is said to be **absolutely stable** for those values of $h\lambda$ for which the roots of its stability polynomial (8.74) are less than one in magnitude. Different methods have different regions of absolute stability. Generally we prefer those methods which have the largest region of absolute stability. It can be shown, for example, that the Adams-Moulton implicit methods have regions of stability that are more than 10 times larger than those for the Adams-Bashforth methods of the same order. In particular, the second-order Adams-Moulton method given by

$$y_{n+1} = y_n + h\left(f_{n+1} - \tfrac{1}{2}f_n + \tfrac{1}{2}f_{n-1} \right)$$

is absolutely stable for $-\infty < h\lambda < 0$ for the test equation $y' = \lambda y$ with $\lambda < 0$.

For equations of the form $y' = \lambda y$ where $\lambda > 0$, the required solution will be growing exponentially like $e^{h\lambda}$. Any multistep method will have to have one root, the principal root, which approximates the required solution. All other extraneous roots will then have to be less in magnitude than this principal root. A method which has the property that all extraneous roots of the stability polynomial are less than the principal root in magnitude is said to be **relatively stable**. Stability regions for different multistep methods are discussed extensively in Gear [30].

EXERCISES

8.10-1 Show that the corrector formula based on the trapezoidal rule (8.52) is stable for equations of the form $y' = \lambda y$ (see Exercise 8.8-1).

8.10-2 Show that the roots of the characteristic equation (8.76) can be expressed in the form (8.77) as $h \to 0$, and that the solution of the difference equation (8.75) approaches (8.78) as $h \to 0$.

8.10-3 Write a computer program to find the roots of the characteristic equation (8.73) for the Adams-Bashforth formula. Take $\lambda = -1$ and $h = 0(0.1)\bar{h}$. Determine an approximate value of $\bar{h}$ beyond which one or more roots of this equation will be greater than one in magnitude. Thus establish an upper bound on h, beyond which the Adams-Bashforth method will be unstable.

8.10-4 Solve Eq. (8.67) by Milne's method (8.64) from $x = 0$ to $x = 6$ with $h = \tfrac{1}{2}$. Take the starting values from Table 8.1. Note the effect of instability on the solution.

*8.11 ROUND-OFF-ERROR PROPAGATION AND CONTROL

In Sec. 8.4 we defined the discretization error e_n as

$$e_n = y(x_n) - y_n$$

where $y(x_n)$ is the true solution of the differential equation, and y_n is the exact solution of the difference equation which approximates the differential equation. In practice, because computers deal with finite word lengths, we will obtain a value $\tilde{y}_n$ which will differ from y_n because of round-off errors. We shall denote by

$$r_n = y_n - \tilde{y}_n$$

the **accumulated round-off error**, i.e., the difference between the exact solution of the difference equation and the value produced by the computer at $x = x_n$. At each step of an integration, a round-off error will be produced which we call the **local round-off error** and which we denote by ε_n. In Euler's method, for example, ε_n is defined by

$$\tilde{y}_{n+1} = \tilde{y}_n + hf(x_n, \tilde{y}_n) + \varepsilon_n$$

The accumulated round-off error is not simply the sum of the local round-off errors, because each local error is propagated and may either grow or decay as the computation proceeds. In general, the subject of round-off-error propagation is poorly understood, and very few theoretical results are available. The accumulated roundoff depends upon many factors, including (1) the kind of arithmetic used in the computer, i.e., fixed point or floating point; (2) the way in which the machine rounds; (3) the order in which the arithmetic operations are performed; (4) the numerical procedure being used.

As shown in Sec. 8.10, where numerical instability was considered, the effect of round-off propagation can be disastrous. Even with stable methods, however, there will be some inevitable loss of accuracy due to rounding errors. This was illustrated in Chap. 7, where the trapezoidal rule was used to evaluate an integral. Over an extended interval the loss of accuracy may be so serious as to invalidate the results completely.

It is possible to obtain estimates of the accumulated rounding error by making some statistical assumptions about the distribution of local round-off errors. These possibilities will not be pursued here. We wish to consider here a simple but effective procedure for reducing the loss of accuracy due to round-off errors when solving differential equations.

Most of the formulas discussed in this chapter for solving differential equations can be written in the form

$$y_{n+1} = y_n + h\,\Delta y_n$$

where $h\,\Delta y_n$ represents an increment involving combinations of $f(x, y)$ at selected points. The increment is usually small compared with y_n itself. In forming the sum $y_n + h \Delta y_n$ in floating-point arithmetic, the computer will therefore shift $h \Delta y_n$ to the right until the exponent of $h \Delta y_n$ agrees with that of y_n dropping bits at the right end as it does so. The addition is then performed, but because of the bits which were dropped, there will be a rounding error. To see this more clearly, let us attempt to add the two floating-point numbers $(0.5472)(10^4)$ and $(0.3856)(10^2)$, assuming a word length of four decimal places. If we shift the second number two places to the right, drop the last two digits, and add to the first number, we will obtain $(0.5510)(10^4)$, whereas with proper rounding the result should be $(0.5511)(10^4)$. This is, of course, an exaggerated example, since the computer will be working with binary bits and longer word lengths, but even then the cumulative effects can be serious.

We shall now describe a simple procedure which will significantly reduce errors of this type. First, each computed value of y_n is stored in double-precision form; next $h \Delta y_n$ is computed in single precision, and only the single-precision part of any value of y_n needed in forming $h \Delta y_n$ is used; the sum $y_n = h \Delta y_n$ is formed in **double precision**; and $y_{n+1} = y_n + h \Delta y_n$ is stored in double precision. This procedure may be called **partial double-precision accumulation.** On some computers double-precision arithmetic is available as an instruction, but even when it is not, only one double-precision sum must be formed per integration step. The major part of the computation is determining $h \Delta y_n$, and this is performed in single precision. The extra amount of work as well as the extra storage is quite minor. On the other hand, the possible gain in accuracy can be very significant, especially when great accuracy over an extended interval is required. Indeed, this procedure is so effective in reducing round-off-error accumulation that no general-purpose library routine for solving differential equations should ever be written which does not provide for some form of partial double-precision accumulation.

A final word of caution is in order at this point. The accuracy of a numerical integration will depend upon the discretization error and the accumulated rounding error. To keep the discretization error small, we will normally choose the step size h small. On the other hand, the smaller h is taken, the more integration steps we shall have to perform, and the greater the rounding error is likely to be. There is, therefore, an optimum value of the step size h which for a given machine and a given problem will result in the best accuracy. This optimum is in practice very difficult to find without the use of extensive amounts of computer time. The existence of such an optimum does show, however, that there is some danger in taking too small a step size.

Example 8.8 Solve the equation

$$y' = \frac{1}{x^2} - \frac{y}{x} - y^2 \qquad y(1) = -1$$

from $x = 1$ to $x = 3$, using the Adams-Bashforth method, with and without partial double-precision accumulation, for $h = \frac{1}{256}$.

The machine results are given below. The step size is purposely chosen small enough so that the discretization error is negligible. The results are printed every 16 steps. The exact solution of this problem is $y = -1/x$. The accuracy can therefore be easily checked. At $x = 3$ the partial double-precision results are correct to three units in the eighth decimal place; the single-precision results are correct to 253 units in the eighth decimal place. Since all this error is due to roundoff, this example clearly demonstrates the effectiveness of partial double precision in reducing round-off-error accumulation.

COMPUTER RESULTS FOR EXAMPLE 8.8

X	SINGLE PRECISION	PARTIAL DOUBLE PRECISION
0.99999999	−0.99999999	−0.99999999
1.06250000	−0.94117642	−0.94117647
1.12500000	−0.88888878	−0.88888889
1.18750000	−0.84210509	−0.84210526
1.24999990	−0.79999977	−0.80000000
1.31249990	−0.76190444	−0.76190476
1.37500000	−0.72727232	−0.72727273
1.42750000	−0.69565168	−0.69565218
1.50000000	−0.66666608	−0.66666667
1.56249990	−0.63999934	−0.64000001
1.62499990	−0.61538386	−0.61538462
1.68750000	−0.59259175	−0.59259260
1.75000000	−0.57142763	−0.57142858
1.81250000	−0.55172310	−0.55172415
1.87499990	−0.53333220	−0.53333335
1.93749990	−0.51612781	−0.51612905
2.00000000	−0.49999869	−0.50000001
2.06250000	−0.48484711	−0.48484850
2.12500000	−0.47058678	−0.47058825
2.18749990	−0.45714134	−0.45714287
2.24999990	−0.44444284	−0.44444446
2.31250000	−0.43243076	−0.43243245
2.37500000	−0.42105088	−0.42105265
2.43750000	−0.41025458	−0.41024643
2.49999990	−0.39999810	−0.40000002
2.56249990	−0.39024193	−0.39024393
2.62500000	−0.38095033	−0.38095240
2.68750000	−0.37209089	−0.37209304
2.75000000	−0.36363416	−0.36363639
2.81249990	−0.35555328	−0.35555558
2.87499990	−0.34782372	−0.34782612
2.92750000	−0.34042308	−0.34042556
3.00000000	−0.33333080	−0.33333336

EXERCISES

8.11-1 Write a program based on the Adams-Bashforth method which uses both single-precision and partial-double-precision accumulation.

8.11-2 Use the program of Exercise 8.11-1 to solve the equation

$$y' = -2y \qquad y(0) = 1$$

from $x = 0$ to $x = 2$ using a fixed step size $h = 0.01$. The starting values can be obtained from the exact solution $y = e^{-2x}$. What is the error due to roundoff?

8.11-3 Write a program for the classical fourth-order Runge-Kutta method which uses both single-precision and double-precision accumulation. Use it to solve the equation of Exercise 8.11-2 with the same value of h.

*8.12 SYSTEMS OF DIFFERENTIAL EQUATIONS

Most general-purpose differential-equation subroutines assume that an Nth-order differential equation has been expressed as a system of N first-order equations. For an Nth-order equation given in the form

$$y^{(N)} = f(x, y(x), y'(x), \ldots, y^{(N-1)}(x)) \qquad (8.79)$$

this reduction can always be accomplished as follows: With $y_1 = y$, we set

$$
\begin{aligned}
y_1' &= y_2 \\
y_2' &= y_3 \\
y_3' &= y_4 \\
&= \cdots \\
y_{N-1}' &= y_N \\
y_N' &= f(x, y_1, y_2, \ldots, y_N)
\end{aligned}
\qquad (8.80)
$$

The system (8.80) is equivalent to (8.79). Not every system of equations will be expressible in the simple form of (8.80). More generally, a system of N first-order equations will have the form

$$
\begin{aligned}
y_1' &= f_1(x, y_1, y_2, \ldots, y_N) \\
y_2' &= f_2(x, y_1, y_2, \ldots, y_N) \\
&\cdots\cdots\cdots\cdots\cdots\cdots \\
y_N' &= f_N(x, y_1, y_2, \ldots, y_N)
\end{aligned}
\qquad (8.81)
$$

All the numerical methods considered in this chapter can be adapted to the system (8.81). The system (8.81) can be expressed more compactly in vector form,

$$\mathbf{y}' = \mathbf{f}(x, \mathbf{y})$$

where $\mathbf{y}'$, $\mathbf{f}$, and $\mathbf{y}$ are vectors with N components.

We illustrate the procedure for the Runge-Kutta method for two equations, which we write in the form

$$y' = f(x, y, z)$$
$$z' = g(x, y, z) \tag{8.82}$$

The Runge-Kutta formulas corresponding to (8.37) will now be

$$y_{n+1} = y_n + \frac{1}{6}(k_1 + 2k_2 + 2k_3 + k_4)$$

$$z_{n+1} = z_n + \frac{1}{6}(l_1 + 2l_2 + 2l_3 + l_4) \tag{8.83}$$

where

$$k_1 = hf(x_n, y_n, z_n)$$

$$l_1 = hg(x_n, y_n, z_n)$$

$$k_2 = hf\left(x_n + \frac{h}{2}, y_n + \frac{k_1}{2}, z_n + \frac{l_1}{2}\right)$$

$$l_2 = hg\left(x_n + \frac{h}{2}, y_n + \frac{k_1}{2}, z_n + \frac{l_1}{2}\right)$$

$$k_3 = hf\left(x_n + \frac{h}{2}, y_n + \frac{k_2}{2}, z_n + \frac{l_2}{2}\right)$$

$$l_3 = hg\left(x_n + \frac{h}{2}, y_n + \frac{k_2}{2}, z_n + \frac{l_2}{2}\right)$$

$$k_4 = hf(x_n + h, y_n + k_3, z_n + l_3)$$

$$l_4 = hg(x_n + h, y_n + k_3, z_n + l_3)$$

Extension to a system of equations is obvious. Note that all the increments with lower subscript must be computed before proceeding to those of next higher subscript.

The Adams-Moulton formulas adapted to the pair of equations (8.82) proceed as follows:

$$y_{n+1}^{(0)} = y_n + \frac{h}{24}\left[55f(x_n, y_n, z_n) - 59f(x_{n-1}, y_{n-1}, z_{n-1})\right.$$
$$\left. + 37f(x_{n-2}, y_{n-2}, z_{n-2}) - 9f(x_{n-3}, y_{n-3}, z_{n-3})\right]$$

$$z_{n+1}^{(0)} = z_n + \frac{h}{24}\left[55g(x_n, y_n, z_n) - 59g(x_{n-1}, y_{n-1}, z_{n-1})\right.$$
$$\left. + 37g(x_{n-2}, y_{n-2}, z_{n-2}) - 9g(x_{n-3}, y_{n-3}, z_{n-3})\right] \tag{8.84}$$

$$y_{n+1}^{(1)} = y_n + \frac{h}{24}\left[9f(x_{n+1}, y_{n+1}^{(0)}, z_{n+1}^{(0)}) + 19f(x_n, y_n, z_n)\right.$$
$$\left. - 5f(x_{n-1}, y_{n-1}, z_{n-1}) + f(x_{n-2}, y_{n-2}, z_{n-2})\right]$$

$$z_{n+1}^{(1)} = z_n + \frac{h}{24}\left[9g(x_{n+1}, y_{n+1}^{(0)}, z_{n+1}^{(0)}) + 19g(x_n, y_n, z_n)\right.$$
$$\left. - 5g(x_{n-1}, y_{n-1}, z_{n-1}) + g(x_{n-2}, y_{n-2}, z_{n-2})\right]$$

In Sec. 8.6 we described a subroutine named DVERK from the IMSL programs and used it to solve a single differential equation. Here we will use this subroutine to solve a system of first-order differential equations. In DVERK, X will denote the independent variable while Y(K), K = 1, ..., N is used to denote the vector of dependent variables of length N assuming that we have a system of N first-order equations in the form (8.81). YPRIME(K), K = 1, ..., N is used to denote the vector of functions $f_1, \ldots, f_N$ in the right-hand side of (8.81). The subroutine FCN is used to define YPRIME(K). Usage of DVERK for a system of equations is otherwise identical to its usage for a single equation. The example below illustrates this usage.

Example 8.9 Express the following system of equations as a system of first-order equations and solve it from $x = 0$ to $x = 1$ using the subroutine DVERK:

$$\frac{d^2z}{dx^2} = z^2 - y + e^x$$

$$\frac{d^2y}{dx^2} = z - y^2 - e^x \qquad (8.85)$$

$$z(0) = z'(0) = 0 \qquad y(0) = 1 \qquad y'(0) = -2$$

In this example x is the independent variable while $z(x)$ and $y(x)$ are the dependent variables. To express this as a first-order system we set $z(x) = y_1(x)$, $y(x) = y_2(x)$ and then the first-order system together with the initial conditions becomes

$$
\begin{aligned}
y_1'(x) &= y_3(x) & y_1(0) &= 0.0 \\
y_2'(x) &= y_4(x) & y_2(0) &= 1.0 \\
y_3'(x) &= y_1^2(x) - y_2(x) + e^x & y_3(0) &= 0.0 \\
y_4'(x) &= y_1(x) - y_2^2(x) - e^x & y_4(0) &= -2.0
\end{aligned}
\qquad (8.86)
$$

The FORTRAN program and partial results are given below. The values are correct to at least eight significant digits. It appears that 16 function evaluations per output step were required to achieve this accuracy. This implies that an internal step of roughly $h = 0.05$ was used.

```
C    PROGRAM TO SOLVE EXAMPLE 8.9 USING  D V E R K  (IMSL) .
     INTEGER IER,IND,K,N,NW
     REAL C(24),TOL,W(5,9),X,XEND,Y(4)
     DATA N , X ,        Y        , TOL ,IND,NW
    *     / 4 , 0.,   0.,1.,0.,-2.  ,1.E-9, 1 , 5 /
     EXTERNAL FCN2
     DO 12 K=1,10
     XEND = FLOAT(K)/10.
     CALL DVERK ( N, FCN2, X, Y, XEND, TOL, IND, C, NW, W, IER )
     PRINT 600, XEND,Y(1),Y(2),C(24)
600  FORMAT(3X,F3.1,3X,2(E16.8,3X),F4.0)
  12 CONTINUE
                                        STOP
     END
     SUBROUTINE FCN2 ( N, X, Y, YPRIME )
     INTEGER N
     REAL X, Y(N), YPRIME(N)
     YPRIME(1) = Y(3)
     YPRIME(2) = Y(4)
     YPRIME(3) = Y(1)**2 - Y(2) + EXP(X)
     YPRIME(4) = Y(1) - Y(2)**2 - EXP(X)
                                        RETURN
     END
```

COMPUTER RESULTS FOR EXAMPLE 8.9

X	Y(1)	Y(2)	FCN EVALS
.1	5.12342280E − 04	7.90476884E − 01	16
.2	4.19528369E − 03	5.63595308E − 01	32
.3	1.44796017E − 02	3.21283135E − 01	48
.4	3.50756908E − 02	6.44861308E − 02	64
.5	6.99842327E − 02	−2.07035152E − 01	80
.6	1.23532042E − 01	−4.94906488E − 01	96
.7	2.00446026E − 01	−8.02372169E − 01	112
.8	3.05983760E − 01	−1.13460479E + 00	128
.9	4.46147292E − 01	−1.49915828E + 00	144
1.0	6.28019076E − 01	−1.90666076E + 00	160

As this example illustrates, DVERK is a very simple subroutine to use, and it is extremely efficient when high accuracy is required.

EXERCISES

8.12-1 Write the second-order equation

$$y''(x) = 2(e^{2x} - y^2)^{1/2}$$
$$y(0) = 0 \qquad y'(0) = 1$$

as a system of first-order equations and solve it from $x = 0$ to $x = 1$ using the classical fourth-order Runge-Kutta method with fixed step sizes of $h = \frac{1}{64}$ and $h = \frac{1}{128}$. Estimate the accuracy of your results.

8.12-2 Solve the following second-order equation from $x = 1$ to $x = 2$ using the Adams-Moulton formulas (8.84) with a fixed step size of $h = 0.1$:

$$y''(x) = 2y^3$$
$$y(1) = 1 \qquad y'(1) = -1$$

You will need four starting values for $y(x)$ and $f(x, y) = 2y^3$. Generate these from the exact solution $y(x) = 1/x$ and then compare your results with the exact solution.

8.12-3 Check with your computing center to see if they subscribe to the IMSL programs. If they do, solve the equation in Exercise 8.12-1 using DVERK with the XEND values K/10. with K = 1, ..., 10.

*8.13 STIFF DIFFERENTIAL EQUATIONS

Applications in a number of important areas, including chemical reactions, control systems, and electronic networks, lead to systems of differential equations which are especially difficult to solve because different processes in the system behave with significantly different time scales. If, for example, the solution of a differential equation is given by $y(x) = C_1 e^{-x} + C_2 e^{-100x}$, the second component of the solution will decay much more rapidly than the first component as x increases. Most of the methods we have described for solving differential equations exhibit extreme instability when applied to problems which have solutions of this type. Problems with solution components containing widely different time scales are said to be *stiff problems*.

Consider for instance the second order equation

$$\frac{d^2y}{dx^2} + 1001\frac{dy}{dx} + 1000y = 0 \qquad (8.87)$$

The general solution of (8.87) is

$$y(x) = Ae^{-x} + Be^{-1000x}$$

If we impose the initial conditions $y(0) = 1$, $y'(0) = -1$, the exact solution is

$$y(x) = e^{-x}$$

We now try to solve (8.87) with these initial conditions using the RK 4 method. The system rewritten as a first-order system (see Sec. 8.12) is

$$\frac{dy_1}{dx} = y_2 \qquad\qquad y_1(0) = 1$$
$$\frac{dy_2}{dx} = -1001y_2 - 1000y_1 \quad y_2(0) = -1 \qquad (8.88)$$

For steps $h < 0.002$, the Runge-Kutta method yields solutions which approximate e^{-x} very nicely. However, $h = 0.002$ means that we must take 500 integration steps per unit interval. Since the desired solution is $y(x) = e^{-x}$, it would appear safe to take a much larger step h. However, if we take $h = 0.003$, still quite small, the numerical solution essentially explodes to ∞. The explanation for this behavior is related to the stability requirements of the method being used. For the RK 4 method, the region of stability is such that we must have (see Gear [30])

$$1000h < 2.8$$

or $h < 0.0028$. That is, the step h is for stability reasons restricted by the most rapidly changing component of the solution, namely e^{-1000y}, for the problem above. Adams-Moulton and other standard multistep methods would similarly restrict the step h.

Extensive research is still going on to find suitable methods for solving stiff differential equations. The most successful methods apparently are implicit. The trapezoidal method (8.52), for example, has been used with some success. For this method the region of stability is the entire negative half-plane, so that h is unrestricted by stability requirements (see Gear [30]). As applied to a system of two equations in two unknowns of the form

$$y_1' = f_1(x, y_1, y_2)$$
$$y_2' = f_2(x, y_1, y_2)$$

the trapezoidal method becomes

$$y_{1,n+1} = y_{1n} + \frac{h}{2}\{f_1(x_n, y_{1n}, y_{2n}) + f_1(x_{n+1}, y_{1,n+1}, y_{2,n+1})\}$$

$$y_{2,n+1} = y_{2n} + \frac{h}{2}\{f_2(x_n, y_{1n}, y_{2n}) + f_2(x_{n+1}, y_{1,n+1}, y_{2,n+1})\}$$

$$(8.89)$$

Specializing these to the system (8.88), which is linear, leads to

$$y_{1,n+1} = y_{1n} + \frac{h}{2}\{y_{2n} + y_{2,n+1}\}$$

$$y_{2,n+1} = y_{2n} + \frac{h}{2}\{-1001y_{2n} - 1000y_{1n} + (-1001y_{2,n+1} - 1000y_{1,n+1})\}$$

Normally, these equations are solved by iteration but because of the linearity we can obtain an explicit system for the unknowns $y_{1,n+1}$ and $y_{2,n+1}$:

$$y_{1,n+1} - \frac{h}{2}y_{2,n+1} = y_{1n} + \frac{h}{2}y_{2n}$$

$$\frac{h}{2}(1000)y_{1,n+1} + \left(1 + \frac{1001h}{2}\right)y_{2,n+1} = y_{2n} - \frac{h}{2}\{1001y_{2n} + 1000y_{1n}\}$$

$$(8.90)$$

We now choose $h = 0.1$ so that (8.90) becomes

$$y_{1,n+1} - 0.05y_{2,n+1} = y_{1n} + .05y_{2n}$$
$$50y_{1,n+1} + 51.05y_{2,n+1} = -49.05y_{2n} - 50y_{1n} \qquad (8.91)$$

For $n = 0$ we have $y_{10} = 1$, $y_{20} = -1$, and from (8.91) we obtain

$$y_{11} = 0.904762 \qquad y_{21} = -0.904762$$

which is a reasonable approximation to the exact solution $y(0.1) = e^{-0.1} = 0.904837$, considering the large step size being used. After 10 steps with $h = 0.1$ we obtain $y_1(1.0) \approx 0.367573$ which compares very favorably with the exact result $y(1.0) = e^{-1.0} = 0.367879$.

In using the trapezoidal method for stiff nonlinear problems, however, there is one essential modification which must be used. For the single equation $y' = f(x, y)$ the trapezoidal method is implicit and defined by

$$y_{n+1} = y_n + \frac{h}{2}\{f(x_n, y_n) + f(x_{n+1}, y_{n+1})\} \qquad (8.92)$$

With n fixed, this is an implicit equation which must be solved for y_{n+1} by some iterative method. Normally, one uses fixed-point iteration defined by

$$y_{n+1}^{(m+1)} = y_n + \frac{h}{2}\{f(x_n, y_n) + f(x_{n+1}, y_{n+1}^{(m)})\} \qquad m = 0, 1, \ldots$$

where $y_{n+1}^{(0)}$ is an approximation to y_{n+1} obtained by some other method such as Euler's method. This fixed-point iteration will converge as shown in Sec. 8.8 if $\left| \dfrac{h}{2} \dfrac{\partial f}{\partial y} \right| < 1$, and since $|\partial f/\partial y|$ for stiff problems is very large, this requires very small step sizes for convergence. We can, however, solve (8.92) for y_{n+1} by Newton's iteration method as follows. We set $\bar{y} = y_{n+1}$ and rewrite (8.92) in the form

$$F(\bar{y}) = \bar{y} - y_n - \frac{h}{2} f(x_n, y_n) - \frac{h}{2} f(x_{n+1}, \bar{y}) = 0 \qquad (8.93)$$

If $\bar{y}^{(0)} = y_{n+1}^{(0)}$ is an initial approximation to $\bar{y}$, then successive approximations are generated according to Newton's method by the iteration

$$\bar{y}^{(m+1)} = \bar{y}^{(m)} + \frac{F(\bar{y}^{(m)})}{F'(\bar{y}^{(m)})} \qquad m = 0, 1, \ldots$$

where from (8.93)

$$F'(\bar{y}) = 1 - \frac{h}{2} \frac{\partial f}{\partial \bar{y}} (x_{n+1}, \bar{y})$$

In this case there is no difficulty with convergence when $\partial f/\partial y$ is large and negative, which is the typical situation with stiff problems. Newton's method does, however, require the computation of $\partial f/\partial y$ for a single equation and of the elements of the Jacobian matrix for a system of equations. Subroutines for solving stiff differential equations can therefore be expected to be somewhat complicated.

For a system of linear equations of the form

$$y' = Ay$$

where A is a constant matrix, the stiffness of the problem is determined by the eigenvalues of the matrix A. If the eigenvalues of A are negative and widely separated, then the system is stiff and we can expect difficulty in solving it by ordinary methods. For the example (8.88) the matrix A is

$$A = \begin{bmatrix} 0 & 1 \\ -1000 & -1001 \end{bmatrix}$$

and its eigenvalues are -1000, -1.

For more general nonlinear systems of the form

$$y' = f(x, y)$$

stiffness is determined by the eigenvalues of the Jacobian matrix

$$\left(\frac{\partial f}{\partial y} \right)$$

The reader is referred to Gear [30] for a more complete discussion of stiff problems and for other methods for handling them.

EXERCISES

8.13-1 Try to solve the system (8.88) from $x = 0$ to $x = 2$ using the Runge-Kutta method of order 4 for the step-sizes $h = 0.001, 0.002, 0.003, 0.01$. Verify that the solution explodes for $h = 0.003$ and $h = 0.01$ while for $h = 0.001$ and $h = 0.002$ we obtain reasonable approximations to the exact solution $y = e^{-x}$.

8.13-2 For the system

$$y_1' = \qquad\qquad y_2$$
$$y_2' = -200y_1 - 102y_2$$

show that the eigenvalues of the coefficient matrix are -2 and -100 and hence that the general solution is given by

$$y_1(x) = y(x) = Ae^{-2x} + Be^{-100x}$$

Under the conditions $y(0) = 1, y'(0) = -2$ which corresponds to $y_1(0) = 1, y_2(0) = -2$, the exact solution is $y(x) = e^{-2x}$. Solve this system from $x = 0$ to $x = 1$ using the trapezoidal method with a step $h = 0.1$ and compare your results with the exact solution.

BOUNDARY-VALUE PROBLEMS IN ORDINARY DIFFERENTIAL EQUATIONS

In Chap. 8 we considered numerical methods for solving initial-value problems. In such problems all the initial conditions are given at a single point. In this chapter we consider problems in which the conditions are specified at more than one point. A simple example of a second-order boundary-value problem is

$$y''(x) = y(x) \qquad y(0) = 0 \qquad y(1) = 1 \tag{9.1}$$

An example of a fourth-order boundary-value problem is

$$y^{iv}(x) + ky(x) = q \tag{9.2a}$$

$$y(0) = y'(0) = 0 \tag{9.2b}$$

$$y(L) = y''(L) = 0 \tag{9.2c}$$

Here y may represent the deflection of a beam of length L which is subjected to a uniform load q. Condition (9.2b) states that the end $x = 0$ is built in, while (9.2c) states that the end $x = L$ is simply supported. We shall consider three methods for solving such problems: the method of **finite differences** and an adaptation of the methods of Chap. 8, which we shall call "shooting" methods, and the method of **collocation**.

9.1 FINITE-DIFFERENCE METHODS

We assume that we have a linear differential equation of order greater than one, with conditions specified at the end points of an interval $[a, b]$. We divide the interval $[a, b]$ into N equal parts of width h. We set $x_0 = a$,

$x_N = b$, and we define

$$x_n = x_0 + nh \qquad n = 1, 2, \ldots, N - 1$$

as the **interior mesh points**. The corresponding values of y at these mesh points are denoted by

$$y_n = y(x_0 + nh) \qquad n = 0, 1, \ldots, N$$

We shall sometimes have to deal with points outside the interval $[a, b]$. These will be called **exterior mesh points**, those to the left of x_0 being denoted by $x_{-1} = x_0 - h$, $x_{-2} = x_0 - 2h$, etc., and those to the right of x_N being denoted by $x_{N+1} = x_N + h$, $x_{N+2} = x_N + 2h$, etc. The corresponding values of y at the exterior mesh points are denoted in the obvious way as $y_{-1}, y_{-2}, y_{N+1}, y_{N+2}$, etc.

To solve a boundary-value problem by the method of finite differences, every derivative appearing in the equation, as well as in the boundary conditions, is replaced by an appropriate difference approximation. Central differences are usually preferred because they lead to greater accuracy. Some typical central-difference approximations are the following (see Chap. 7):

$$y'(x_n) \approx \frac{y_{n+1} - y_{n-1}}{2h}$$

$$y''(x_n) \approx \frac{y_{n+1} - 2y_n + y_{n-1}}{h^2} \tag{9.3}$$

$$y^{\mathrm{iv}}(x_n) \approx \frac{y_{n+2} - 4y_{n+1} + 6y_n - 4y_{n-1} + y_{n-2}}{h^4}$$

In each case the finite-difference representation is an $\mathcal{O}(h^2)$ approximation to the respective derivative. To illustrate the procedure, we consider the linear second-order differential equation

$$y''(x) + f(x)y' + g(x)y = q(x) \tag{9.4}$$

under the boundary conditions

$$y(x_0) = \alpha \tag{9.5}$$

$$y(x_N) = \beta \tag{9.6}$$

The finite-difference approximation to (9.4) is

$$\frac{y_{n-1} - 2y_n + y_{n+1}}{h^2} + \frac{f(x_n)(y_{n+1} - y_{n-1})}{2h} + g(x_n)y_n = q(x_n)$$

$$n = 1, 2, \ldots, N - 1$$

Multiplying through by h^2, setting $f(x_n) = f_n$, etc., and grouping terms, we have

$$\left(1 - \frac{h}{2}f_n\right)y_{n-1} + (-2 + h^2g_n)y_n + \left(1 + \frac{h}{2}f_n\right)y_{n+1} = h^2q_n$$

$$n = 1, 2, \ldots, N - 1 \quad (9.7)$$

Since y_0 and y_N are specified by the conditions (9.5) and (9.6), (9.7) is a linear system of $N - 1$ equations in the $N - 1$ unknowns y_n ($n = 1, \ldots, N - 1$). Writing out (9.7) and replacing y_0 by α and y_N by β, the system takes the form

$$(-2 + h^2g_1)y_1 + \left(1 + \frac{h}{2}f_1\right)y_2 = h^2q_1 - \left(1 - \frac{h}{2}f_1\right)\alpha$$

$$\left(1 - \frac{h}{2}f_2\right)y_1 + (-2 + h^2g_2)y_2 + \left(1 + \frac{h}{2}f_2\right)y_3 = h^2q_2$$

$$\left(1 - \frac{h}{2}f_3\right)y_2 + (-2 + h^2g_3)y_3 + \left(1 + \frac{h}{2}f_3\right)y_4 = h^2q_3$$

$$\cdots\cdots\cdots\cdots\cdots\cdots\cdots\cdots\cdots\cdots\cdots\cdots\cdots\cdots\cdots\cdots$$

$$\left(1 - \frac{h}{2}f_{N-2}\right)y_{N-3} + (-2 + h^2g_{N-2})y_{N-2} + \left(1 + \frac{h}{2}f_{N-2}\right)y_{N-1} = h^2q_{N-2}$$

$$\left(1 - \frac{h}{2}f_{N-1}\right)y_{N-2} + (-2 + h^2g_{N-1})y_{N-1} = h^2q_{N-1} - \left(1 + \frac{h}{2}f_{N-1}\right)\beta$$

$$(9.8)$$

The coefficients in (9.8) can, of course, be computed since $f(x)$, $g(x)$, and $q(x)$ are known functions of x. This linear system can now be solved by any of the methods discussed in Chap. 4. In matrix form we have $A\mathbf{y} = \mathbf{b}$, $\mathbf{y} = [y_1, y_2, \ldots, y_{N-1}]^T$, representing the vector of unknowns; $\mathbf{b}$ representing the vector of known quantities on the right-hand side of (9.8); and A, the matrix of coefficients. The matrix A in this case is tridiagonal and of order $N - 1$. It has the special form

$$A = \begin{bmatrix} d_1 & c_1 & & & & \\ a_2 & d_2 & c_2 & & & \\ & a_3 & d_3 & c_3 & & \\ & & \cdots & \cdots & \cdots & \\ & & & a_{N-2} & d_{N-2} & c_{N-2} \\ & & & & a_{N-1} & d_{N-1} \end{bmatrix}$$

The system $A\mathbf{y} = \mathbf{b}$ can be solved directly using Algorithm 4.3 of Sec. 4.2. We need only replace n by $N - 1$, identify $\mathbf{x}$ and $\mathbf{y}$, and apply the recursion formulas of Algorithm 4.3.

Returning to the boundary conditions, let us see how the system (9.8) is affected if in place of (9.5) we prescribe the following condition at

$x = x_0$:

$$y'(x_0) + \gamma y(x_0) = 0 \qquad (9.9)$$

If we replace $y'(x_0)$ by a forward difference, we will have

$$\frac{y(x_0 + h) - y(x_0)}{h} + \gamma y(x_0) = 0$$

or on rearranging,

$$y_1 + (-1 + \gamma h)y_0 = 0 \qquad (9.9a)$$

If we now write out (9.7) for $n = 1$ and then replace y_0 by $y_1/(1 - \gamma h)$, we will have

$$\left[(-2 + h^2 g_1) + \frac{1 - (h/2)f_1}{1 - \gamma h}\right]y_1 + \left(1 + \frac{h}{2}f_1\right)y_2 = h^2 q_1 \qquad (9.10)$$

The first equation of (9.8) can now be replaced by (9.10). All other equations of (9.8) will remain unchanged, and the resulting system can again be solved, using Algorithm 4.3. We note, however, that (9.9a) is only an $\mathcal{O}(h)$ approximation to the boundary condition (9.9) (see Sec. 7.1).

The accuracy of the solution will then also be of order h. To obtain a solution which is everywhere of order h^2, we replace (9.9) by the approximation

$$\frac{y(x_0 + h) - y(x_0 - h)}{2h} + \gamma y(x_0) = 0$$

or on rearranging,

$$y_1 - y_{-1} + 2h\gamma y_0 = 0 \qquad (9.11)$$

Since we have introduced an exterior point y_{-1}, we must now consider y_0 as well as $y_1, y_2, \ldots, y_{N-1}$ as unknowns. Since we now have N unknowns, we must have N equations. We can obtain an additional equation by taking $n = 0$ in (9.7). If we then eliminate y_{-1} using (9.11), we will have for the first two equations

$$\left[2h\gamma\left(1 - \frac{h}{2}f_0\right) + (-2 + h^2 g_0)\right]y_0 + 2y_1 = h^2 q_0 \qquad n = 0$$

$$\left(1 - \frac{h}{2}f_1\right)y_0 + (-2 + h^2 g_1)y_1 + \left(1 + \frac{h}{2}f_1\right)y_2 = h^2 q_1 \qquad n = 1$$

The remaining equations will be the same as those appearing in (9.8). The system is still tridiagonal but now of order N. It can again be solved explicitly with the aid of Algorithm 4.3.

The accuracy attainable with finite-difference methods will clearly depend upon the fineness of the mesh and upon the order of the finite-difference approximation. As the mesh is refined, the number of equations to be solved increases. As a result, the amount of computer time required may become excessive, and good accuracy may be difficult to achieve. The use of higher-order approximations will yield greater accuracy for the same mesh size but results in considerable complication, especially near the end points of the interval where the exterior values will not be known.

In practice, it is advisable to solve the linear system for several different values of h. A comparison of the solutions at the same mesh points will then indicate the accuracy being obtained. In addition, the extrapolation process, described in Sec. 7.5, can usually be applied to yield further improvement. As adapted to the solution of finite-difference systems, extrapolation to the limit proceeds as follows. Let $y_h(x)$ denote the approximate solution at one of the mesh points x of the boundary-value problem based on $N = (b - a)/h$ subdivisions of the interval $[a, b]$. Let $y_{h/2}(x)$ be the approximate solution of the same problem based on $2N = (b - a)/(h/2)$ subdivisions of the interval $[a, b]$. At the $N - 1$ points $x_1 = a + h$, $x_2 = a + 2h, \ldots, x_{N-1} = a + (N - 1)h$, we now have two approximations, $y_h(x_n)$ and $y_{h/2}(x_n)$. Applying extrapolation to these, we obtain

$$y(x_n) \approx y_n^{(1)} := \frac{4y_{h/2}(x_n) - y_h(x_n)}{3} \qquad n = 1, 2, \ldots, N - 1$$

This extrapolation will usually produce a significant improvement in the approximation.

Example 9.1 Solve the boundary-value problem (9.1), using finite-difference methods.

Taking $f(x) = 0$, $g(x) = -1$, $q(x) = 0$, and setting $y_0 = 0$, $y_N = 1$ in (9.8), we obtain the system

$$\begin{aligned}
(-2 - h^2)y_1 + y_2 &= 0 \\
y_{n-1} + (-2 - h^2)y_n + y_{n+1} &= 0 \qquad n = 2, 3, \ldots, N - 2 \\
y_{N-2} + (-2 - h^2)y_{N-1} &= -1
\end{aligned}$$

This is a system of $N - 1$ equations in the $N - 1$ unknowns: $y_1, y_2, \ldots, y_{N-1}$. This system was solved on the IBM 7090 with $h = 0.1$ and $h = 0.05$, using a subroutine based on Algorithm 4.3. The results are given on page 411. The fourth column gives the extrapolated values at intervals of 0.1 obtained from the formula

$$y_n^{(1)} = \frac{4y_{h/2}(x_n) - y_h(x_n)}{3}$$

The values in the last column are obtained from the exact solution to the problem,

$$y(x) = \frac{\sinh x}{\sinh 1}$$

These results show that for $h = 0.1$ the solution is correct to three to four significant figures and for $h = 0.05$ to four to five significant figures, while the extrapolated solution is correct to about seven significant figures. To obtain seven significant figures of accuracy without extrapolation would require a subdivision of the interval $[0, 1]$ into approximately 100 mesh points ($h = 0.01$).

COMPUTER RESULTS FOR EXAMPLE 9.1

XN	YN(H = 0.05)	YN(H = 0.10)	YN(1)	Y(XN)
0	0	0	0	0
0.05	.04256502			.04256363
0.10	.08523646	.08524469	.08523372	.08523369
0.15	.12812098			.12811689
0.20	.17132582	.17134184	.17132048	.17132045
0.25	.21495896			.21495239
0.30	.25912950	.25915240	.25912187	.25912183
0.35	.30394787			.30393920
0.40	.34952610	.34955449	.34951663	.34951659
0.45	.39597815			.39596794
0.50	.44342014	.44345213	.44340946	.44340942
0.55	.49197068			.49195965
0.60	.54175115	.54178427	.54174010	.54174004
0.65	.59288599			.59287506
0.70	.64550304	.64553425	.64549263	.64549258
0.75	.69973386			.69972418
0.80	.75571401	.75573958	.75570550	.75570543
0.85	.81358345			.81357635
0.90	.87348684	.87350228	.87348166	.87348163
0.95	.93557395			.93557107
1.00	1	1	1	1

EXERCISES

9.1-1 Solve by difference methods the boundary-value problem

$$\frac{d^2 y}{dx^2} + y = 0 \qquad y(0) = 0 \qquad y(1) = 1$$

Take $h = \frac{1}{4}$, and solve the resulting system, using a pocket calculator.

Answer: $y_1 = 0.2943$, $y_2 = 0.5702$, $y_3 = 0.8104$.

Compare this solution with the exact solution $y = (\sin x)/(\sin 1)$.

9.1-2 Solve the boundary-value problem (9.1) with the condition $y(0) = 0$ replaced by the condition $y'(0) + y(0) = 0$, using a mesh $h = 0.1$.

9.1-3 Write an $\mathcal{O}(h^2)$ finite-difference system for approximating the solution of the boundary-value problem

$$y'' + xy' + y = 2x \qquad y(0) = 1 \qquad y(1) = 0$$

Let $h = 0.1$, and write the system in matrix form. Then solve this system, using a computer program based on Algorithm 4.3.

9.1-4 Show that the Gauss-Seidel iterative method can also be used to solve the system of Example 9.1, and obtain this solution by iteration to four significant figures of accuracy. For this problem, is the direct method more efficient than the iterative method?

9.1-5 Solve by difference methods the boundary-value problem

$$y'' + 2y' + y = x \qquad y(0) = 0 \qquad y(1) = 0$$

using $h = \frac{1}{8}$, $h = \frac{1}{16}$, and improve the results by extrapolation.

9.2 SHOOTING METHODS

For linear boundary-value problems, a number of methods can be used. The method of differences described above works reasonably well in such cases. Other methods attempt to obtain linearly independent solutions of the differential equation and to combine them in such a way as to satisfy the boundary conditions. For nonlinear equations, the latter method cannot be used. Difference methods can be adapted to nonlinear problems, but they require guessing at a tentative solution and then improving this by an iterative process. In addition to the complexity of the programming required, there is no guarantee of convergence of the iterations. The shooting method to be described in this section applies equally well to linear and nonlinear problems. Again, there is no guarantee of convergence, but the method is easy to apply, and when it does converge, it is usually more efficient than other methods.

Consider again the problem given in (9.1). We wish to apply the initial-value methods discussed in Chap. 8, but to do so, we must know both $y(0)$ and $y'(0)$. Since $y'(0)$ is not prescribed, we consider it as an unknown parameter, say α, which must be determined so that the resulting solution yields the prescribed value $y(1)$ to some desired accuracy. We therefore guess at the initial slope and set up an iterative procedure for converging to the correct slope. Let α_0, α_1 be two guesses at the initial slope $y'(0)$, and let $y(\alpha_0; 1)$, $y(\alpha_1; 1)$ be the values of y at $x = 1$ obtained from integrating the differential equation. Graphically, the situation may be presented as in Figs. 9.1 and 9.2.

In Fig. 9.1 the solutions of the initial-value problems are drawn, while in Fig. 9.2, $y(\alpha; 1)$ is plotted as a function of α. A normally better approximation to α can now be obtained by linear interpolation. The intersection of the line joining P_0 to P_1 with the line $y(1) = 1$ has its α coordinate given by

$$\alpha_2 = \alpha_0 + (\alpha_1 - \alpha_0) \frac{y(1) - y(\alpha_0; 1)}{y(\alpha_1; 1) - y(\alpha_0; 1)} \tag{9.12}$$

We now integrate the differential equation, using the initial values $y(0) = 0$, $y'(0) = \alpha_2$, to obtain $y(\alpha_2; 1)$. Again, using linear interpolation based on α_1, α_2, we can obtain a next approximation α_3. The process is repeated

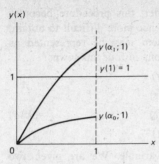

Figure 9.1   **Figure 9.2**

until convergence has been obtained, i.e., until $y(\alpha_i; 1)$ agrees with $y(1) = 1$ to the desired number of places. There is no guarantee that this iterative procedure will converge. The rapidity of convergence will clearly depend upon how good the initial guesses are. Estimates are sometimes available from physical considerations, and sometimes from simple graphical representations of the solution.

For a general second-order boundary-value problem

$$y'' = f(x, y, y') \qquad y(0) = y_0 \qquad y(b) = y_b \qquad (9.13)$$

the procedure is summarized in Algorithm 9.1.

Algorithm 9.1: The shooting method for second-order boundary-value problems

1. Let α_k be an approximation to the unknown initial slope $y'(0) = \alpha$. (Choose the first two α_0, α_1, using physical intuition.)
2. Solve the initial-value problem

$$y'' = f(x, y, y') \qquad y(0) = y_0 \qquad y'(0) = \alpha_k$$

from $x = 0$ to $x = b$, using any of the methods of Chap. 8. Call the solution $y(\alpha_k; b)$ at $x = b$.
3. Obtain the next approximation from the linear interpolation

$$\alpha_{k+1} = \alpha_{k-1} + (\alpha_k - \alpha_{k-1}) \frac{y_b - y(\alpha_{k-1}; b)}{y(\alpha_k; b) - y(\alpha_{k-1}; b)}$$

$$k = 1, 2, \ldots$$

4. Repeat steps 2 and 3 until $|y(\alpha_k; b) - y_b| < \varepsilon$ for a prescribed ε.

The iteration used in Algorithm 9.1 is an application of the secant method described in Chap. 3.

For systems of equations of higher order, this procedure becomes considerably more complicated, and convergence more difficult to obtain. The general situation for a nonlinear system may be represented as follows. We consider a system of four equations in four unknowns:

$$x' = f(x, y, z, w, t)$$
$$y' = g(x, y, z, w, t)$$
$$z' = h(x, y, z, w, t) \qquad (9.14)$$
$$w' = l(x, y, z, w, t)$$

where now t represents the independent variable. We are given two conditions at $t = 0$, say

$$x(0) = x_0$$
$$y(0) = y_0$$

and two conditions at $t = T$, say

$$z(T) = z_T$$
$$w(T) = w_T$$

Let $z(0) = \alpha$, $w(0) = \beta$ be the correct initial values of $z(0)$, $w(0)$, and let α_0, β_0 be guesses for these initial values. Now integrate the system (9.14), and denote the values of z and w obtained at $t = T$ by $z(\alpha_0, \beta_0; T)$ and $w(\alpha_0, \beta_0; T)$.

Since z and w at $t = T$ are clearly functions of α and β, we may expand $z(\alpha, \beta; T)$ and $w(\alpha, \beta; T)$ into a Taylor series for two variables through linear terms:

$$z(\alpha, \beta; T) = z(\alpha_0, \beta_0; T) + (\alpha - \alpha_0)\frac{\partial z}{\partial \alpha}(\alpha_0, \beta_0; T)$$
$$+ (\beta - \beta_0)\frac{\partial z}{\partial \beta}(\alpha_0, \beta_0; T) \quad (9.15)$$

$$w(\alpha, \beta; T) = w(\alpha_0, \beta_0; T) + (\alpha - \alpha_0)\frac{\partial w}{\partial \alpha}(\alpha_0, \beta_0; T)$$
$$+ (\beta - \beta_0)\frac{\partial w}{\partial \beta}(\alpha_0, \beta_0; T)$$

We may set $z(\alpha, \beta, T)$ and $w(\alpha, \beta; T)$ to their desired values z_T and w_T, but before we can solve (9.15) for the corrections $\alpha - \alpha_0$ and $\beta - \beta_0$, we must obtain the partial derivatives in (9.15). We do not know the solutions z and w and therefore cannot find these derivatives analytically. However, we can find approximate numerical values for them. To do so, we solve (9.14) once with the initial conditions $x_0, y_0, \alpha_0, \beta_0$, once with the conditions $x_0, y_0, \alpha_0 + \Delta\alpha_0, \beta_0$, and then with the conditions $x_0, y_0, \alpha_0, \beta_0 + \Delta\beta_0$, where $\Delta\alpha_0$ and $\Delta\beta_0$ are small increments. Omitting the variables x_0, y_0

which remain fixed, we then form the difference quotients:

$$\frac{z(\alpha_0, \beta_0 + \Delta\beta_0; T) - z(\alpha_0, \beta_0; T)}{\Delta\beta_0} \approx \frac{\partial z}{\partial \beta}(\alpha_0, \beta_0; T)$$

$$\frac{w(\alpha_0, \beta_0 + \Delta\beta_0; T) - w(\alpha_0, \beta_0; T)}{\Delta\beta_0} \approx \frac{\partial w}{\partial \beta}(\alpha_0, \beta_0; T)$$

$$\frac{z(\alpha_0 + \Delta\alpha_0, \beta_0; T) - z(\alpha_0, \beta_0; T)}{\Delta\alpha_0} \approx \frac{\partial z}{\partial \alpha}(\alpha_0, \beta_0; T)$$

$$\frac{w(\alpha_0 + \Delta\alpha_0, \beta_0; T) - w(\alpha_0, \beta_0; T)}{\Delta\alpha_0} \approx \frac{\partial w}{\partial \alpha}(\alpha_0, \beta_0; T)$$

After replacing $z(\alpha, \beta; T)$ by z_T and $w(\alpha, \beta; T)$ by w_T, we can then solve (9.15) for the corrections $\delta\alpha_0 = \alpha - \alpha_0$ and $\delta\beta_0 = \beta - \beta_0$, to obtain new estimates $\alpha_1 = \alpha_0 + \delta\alpha_0$, $\beta_1 = \beta_0 + \delta\alpha_0$ for the parameters α and β. The entire process is now repeated, starting with x_0, y_0, α_1, β_1 as the initial conditions.

Each iteration thus consists in solving the system (9.14) three times. In general, if there are n unknown initial parameters, each iteration will require $n + 1$ solutions of the original system. The method used here is equivalent to a modified Newton's method for finding the roots of equations in several variables (see Sec. 5.2).

Boundary-value problems constitute one of the most difficult classes of problems to solve on a computer. Convergence is by no means assured, good initial guesses must be available, and considerable trial and error, as well as large amounts of machine time, are usually required.

Example 9.2 Solve the problem (9.1), using the shooting method. Start with the initial approximations $\alpha_0 = 0.3$ and $\alpha_1 = 0.4$ to $y'(0)$ and $h = 0.1$.

The solution given below was obtained using the standard RK4 differential equation solver described in Chap. 8, combined with linear interpolation based on (9.12). The iteration was stopped by the condition $|\alpha_{k+1} - \alpha_k| < 1 \cdot 10^{-6}$.

k	α_k	$y(\alpha_k; 1)$
0	0.30000000	0.35256077
1	0.40000000	0.47008103
2	0.85091712	0.99999999
3	0.85091712	0.99999999

The correct value of y' at $x = 0$ is $\sinh^{-1} 1 = 0.85091813$. Convergence for this problem is very rapid. Moreover, the indicated accuracy is exceptionally good, considering the coarse step size used. To obtain comparable accuracy using the finite-difference methods of Sec. 9.1 would require a step size $h = 0.01$. Nevertheless, the finite-difference method might still be computationally more efficient.

Example 9.3 Solve the nonlinear boundary-value problem

$$yy'' + 1 + y'^2 = 0 \qquad y(0) = 1 \qquad y(1) = 2 \tag{9.16}$$

by the shooting method.

SOLUTION Let $\alpha_0 = 0.5$, $\alpha_1 = 1.0$ be two approximations to the unknown slope $y'(0)$. Using again the RK4 package and linear interpolation with a step size $h = \frac{1}{64}$, the following results were obtained:

α_i	$y(\alpha_i; 1)$
0.5000000	0.9999999
0.9999999	1.4142133
1.7071071	1.8477582
1.9554118	1.9775786
1.9982968	1.9991463
1.9999940	1.9999952
2.0000035	2.0000000

The correct slope at $x = 0$ is $y'(0) = 2$. After seven iterations, the initial slope is seen to be correct to six significant figures, while the value of y at $x = 1$ is correct to at least seven significant figures. After the first three iterations, convergence could have been speeded up by using quadratic interpolation.

The required number of iterations will clearly depend upon the choice of the initial approximations α_0 and α_1. These approximations can sometimes be obtained from graphical or physical considerations.

EXERCISES

9.2-1 Find a numerical solution of the equation

$$2yy'' - y'^2 + 4y^2 = 0 \qquad y\left(\frac{\pi}{6}\right) = \frac{1}{4} \qquad y\left(\frac{\pi}{2}\right) = 1$$

Take $\alpha_0 = 0.5$, $\alpha_1 = 0.8$ as initial approximations to $y'(\pi/6)$, and iterate until the condition at $x = \pi/2$ is satisfied to five places.

SOLUTION $y = (\sin x)^2$; and the initial slope is $y'(\pi/6) = \sqrt{3}/2$.

9.2-2 In Example 9.3 use quadratic interpolation based on α_0, α_1, α_2 to obtain the next approximation. How many iterations would have been saved?

9.2-3 Solve the following problems, using the shooting method:

(a) $y'' = 2y^3$, $y(1) = 1$, $y(2) = \frac{1}{2}$, taking $y'(1) = 0$ as a first guess. (*Exact solution:* $y = 1/x$.)

(b) $y'' = e^y$, $y(0) = y(1) = 0$, taking $y'(0) = 0$ as a first guess.

9.3 COLLOCATION METHODS

In recent years a great deal of interest has focused on approximation methods for solving boundary-value problems in both one- and higher-dimensional cases. In those approximation methods, rather than seeking a solution at a discrete set of points, an attempt is made to find a linear combination of linearly independent functions which provide an approximation to the solution. Actually the basic ideas are very old, having originated with Galerkin and Ritz [31], but more recently they have taken new shape under the term "finite element" methods (see Strang and Fix [31]), and they have been refined to the point where they are now very competitive with finite-difference methods.

We shall sketch very briefly the basic notions behind these approximation methods focusing on the so-called **collocation method** (see Strang and Fix [31]).

For simplicity we assume that we have a second-order linear boundary-value problem which we write in the form

$$Ly \equiv -y'' + p(x)y' + q(x)y = r(x) \qquad a \le x \le b \qquad (9.17a)$$

$$a_0 y(a) - a_1 y'(a) = \alpha \qquad (9.17b)$$

$$b_0 y(b) + b_1 y'(b) = \beta \qquad |a_0| + |b_0| \ne 0$$

Let $\{\psi_j(x)\}, j = 1, \ldots, N$, be a set of linearly independent functions to be chosen in a manner to be described later. An approximate solution to (9.17) is then sought in the form

$$U_N(x) = \sum_{j=1}^{N} c_j \psi_j(x) \qquad (9.18)$$

The coefficients $\{c_j\}$ in this expansion are to be chosen so as to minimize some measure of the error in satisfying the boundary-value problem. Different methods arise depending on the definition of the measure of error.

In the **collocation method** the coefficients are chosen so that $U_N(x)$ satisfies the boundary conditions (9.17b) and the differential equation (9.17a) exactly at selected points interior to the interval $[a, b]$. Thus the $\{c_j\}$ satisfy the equations

$$a_0 U_N(a) - a_1 U_N'(a) = \alpha$$

$$b_0 U_N(b) + b_1 U_N'(b) = \beta \qquad (9.19)$$

$$L U_N(x_i) - r(x_i) = 0 \qquad i = 1, \ldots, N - 2$$

where the x_i are a set of distinct points on the interval $[a, b]$. When written out (9.19) is a linear system of N equations in the N unknowns $\{c_j\}$. Once (9.19) is solved, by, for example, the methods of Chap. 4, its solution $\{c_j\}$ is substituted into (9.18) to obtain the desired approximate solution. The error analysis for this method is very complicated and beyond the scope of this book. In practice one can obtain a sequence of approximations by increasing the number N of basis functions. An estimate of the accuracy can then be obtained by comparing these approximate solutions at a fixed set of points on the interval $[a, b]$.

We turn now to a consideration of the choice of the basis functions $\{\psi_j(x)\}$. They are usually chosen so as to have one or more of the following properties:

(i) The $\psi_j(x)$ are continuously differentiable on $[a, b]$
(ii) The $\psi_j(x)$ are orthogonal over the interval $[a, b]$, i.e.,

$$\int_a^b \psi_j(x)\psi_k(x)\, dx = 0 \qquad \text{for } j \neq k$$

(iii) The $\psi_j(x)$ are "simple" functions such as polynomials or trigonometric functions
(iv) The $\psi_j(x)$ satisfy those boundary conditions (if any) which are homogeneous.

One commonly used basis is the set $\{\psi_j(x)\} = \{\sin j\pi x\}, j = 1, \ldots, N$ which is orthogonal over the interval $[0, 1]$. Note that $\sin j\pi x = 0$ at $x = 0$ and at $x = 1$ for all j. Another important basis set is $\{\psi_j(x)\} = \{P_j(x)\}$, $j = 0, \ldots, N$ where $P_j(x)$ are the Legendre polynomials described in Chap. 6. These polynomials are orthogonal over the interval $[-1, 1]$. Finally the $\psi_j(x)$ can be chosen to be piecewise-cubic polynomials (see Chap. 6).

As an example we apply the collocation method to the equation (9.1) which we rewrite as

$$U''(x) - U(x) = 0 \qquad\qquad (9.20a)$$
$$U(0) = 0 \qquad\qquad (9.20b)$$
$$U(1) = 1$$

We select polynomials for our basis functions and we seek an approximate solution $U_N(x)$ in the form

$$U_N(x) = c_1 x + c_2 x^2 + c_2 x^3 \qquad\qquad (9.21)$$

we see that $U_N(0) = 0$ regardless of the choice of the c_i's. Since there are three coefficients we must impose three conditions on $U_N(x)$. One condition is that $U_N(x)$ must satisfy the boundary condition at $x = 1$, hence one equation for the c_i's is

$$U_N(1) = c_1 + c_2 + c_3 = 1 \qquad\qquad (9.22)$$

We can impose two additional conditions by insisting that $U_N(x)$ satisfy the equation (9.20a) exactly at two points interior to the interval $[0, 1]$. We choose, for no special reason, $x_0 = \frac{1}{4}$ and $x_1 = \frac{3}{4}$. One computes directly that

$$U_N''(x) - U_N(x) = -c_1 x + (2 - x^2)c_2 + (6x - x^3)c_3$$

and hence that

$$U_N''\left(\tfrac{1}{4}\right) - U_N\left(\tfrac{1}{4}\right) = -\tfrac{1}{4}c_1 + \tfrac{31}{16}c_2 + \tfrac{95}{64}c_3 = 0$$
$$U_N''\left(\tfrac{3}{4}\right) - U_N\left(\tfrac{3}{4}\right) = -\tfrac{3}{4}c_1 + \tfrac{23}{16}c_2 + \tfrac{261}{64}c_3 = 0 \qquad (9.23)$$

The system of equations (9.22) through (9.23) can be solved directly to yield the solution

$$c_1 = 0.852237 \cdots \qquad c_2 = -0.0138527 \cdots \qquad c_3 = 0.161616 \cdots$$

Substituting these into (9.21) yields the approximate solution

$$U_N(x) = 0.852237x - 0.0138527x^2 + 0.161616x^3 \qquad (9.24)$$

This approximate solution can now be used to find an approximate value for $U(x)$, or even for $U'(x)$, at any point of the interval $[0, 1]$.

To see how good an approximation $U_N(x)$ is to the exact solution $U(x) = \sinh x / \sinh 1$, we list below a few comparative values (see Table 9.1).

x	$U_N(x)$	$U(x)$
0.10	0.085247	0.085337
0.25	0.214719	0.214952
0.50	0.424675	0.443409
0.75	0.699567	0.699724
0.90	0.873611	0.873481

We thus seem to have two to three digits of agreement, with the worst values occurring near the midpoint of the interval. Considering the small number of basis functions used in $U_N(x)$, the results appear to be quite good. To obtain more accurate results we would simply increase the number of basis functions.

EXERCISES

9.4-1 Solve the boundary-value problem

$$U''(x) - U(x) = x \qquad U(0) = 0 \qquad U(1) = 1$$

by the collocation method. For the trial functions use the polynomial basis

$$U_N(x) = c_1 x + c_2 x^2 + c_3 x^3 + \cdots + c_N x^N$$

Take $N = 3$ first and then $N = 4$ and compare the results at selected points on the interval. Also compare the approximate results with the exact solution

$$U(x) = \frac{\sinh x}{\sinh 1} - x$$

9.4-2 Try to solve the boundary-value problem

$$U''(x) + U(x) = x$$
$$U(0) = 0 \qquad U(1) = 1$$

by the collocation method. Start with the trial function

$$U_N(x) = x + \sum_{j=1}^{N} c_j \sin j\pi x$$

which automatically satisfies the boundary conditions for all c_j's. Try $N = 2$ and $N = 4$ and compare the results.

APPENDIX

SUBROUTINE LIBRARIES

Listed below are brief descriptions of some major software packages which contain tested subroutines for solving all of the major problems considered in this book. Further information as to availability can be obtained from the indicated source.

1. IMSL (INTERNATIONAL MATHEMATICAL AND STATISTICAL LIBRARY)

This is probably the most complete package commercially available. It contains some 235 subroutines which are applicable to all of the problem areas discussed in this book and to other areas such as statistical computations and constrained optimization as well. All of them are written in ANSI FORTRAN and have been adapted to run on all modern large-scale computers.
SOURCE: IMSL, Inc. GNB Building, 7500 Bellaire Blvd., Houston, Texas 77036.

2. PORT

A fairly complete set of thoroughly tested subroutines for all of the commonly encountered problems in numerical analysis. It was written in

PFORT, a portable subset of ANSI FORTRAN, and was designed to be easily portable from one machine to another.

SOURCE: Bell Telephone Laboratories, Murray Hill, New Jersey.

3. EISPACK

A package for solving the standard eigenvalue-eigenvector problem. It is coded in ANSI FORTRAN in a completely machine-independent form. This is a very high quality software package; it is extremely reliable and contains numerous diagnostic aids for the user (see [32]).

SOURCE: National Energy Software Center, Argonne National Laboratories, 9700 S. Cass Ave., Argonne, Illinois 60439.

4. LINPACK

A software package for solving linear systems of equations as well as least-squares problems. It is written in ANSI FORTRAN, is machine independent, and is available in real, complex, and double-precision arithmetic. It has been widely tested at many different computer sites.

SOURCE: National Energy Software Center, Argonne National Laboratories, 9700 S. Cass Ave., Argonne, Illinois 60439.

REFERENCES

1. Hamming, R. W.: *Numerical Methods for Scientists and Engineers*, McGraw-Hill, New York, 1962.
2. Henrici, P. K.: *Elements of Numerical Analysis*, John Wiley, New York, 1964.
3. Traub, J. F.: *Iterative Methods for the Solution of Equations*, Prentice-Hall, New Jersey, 1963.
4. Scarborough, J. B.: *Numerical Mathematical Analysis*, Johns Hopkins, Baltimore, 1958.
5. Hildebrand, F. B.: *Introduction to Numerical Analysis*, McGraw-Hill, New York, 1956.
6. Müller, D. E.: "A method of solving algebraic equations using an automatic computer," *Mathematical Tables and Other Aids to Computation (MTAC)*, vol. 10, 1956, pp. 208–215.
7. Hastings, C. Jr.: *Approximations for Digital Computers*, Princeton University Press, New Jersey, 1955.
8. Milne, W. E.: *Numerical calculus*, Princeton University Press, New Jersey, 1949.
9. Lanczos, C.: *Applied Analysis*, Prentice-Hall, New Jersey, 1956.
10. Householder, A. S.: *Principles of Numerical Analysis*, McGraw-Hill, New York, 1953.
11. Faddeev, D. K., and V. H. Faddeeva: *Computational Methods of Linear Algebra*, Freeman, San Francisco, 1963.
12. Carnahan, B., et al.: *Applied Numerical Methods*, John Wiley, New York, 1964.
13. *Modern Computing Methods*, Philosophical Library, New York, 1961.
14. McCracken, D., and W. S. Dorn: *Numerical Methods and Fortran Programming*, John Wiley, New York, 1964.
15. Henrici, P. K.: *Discrete Variable Methods for Ordinary Differential Equations*, John Wiley, New York, 1962.
16. Hamming, R. W.: "Stable Predictor-Corrector Methods for Ordinary Differential Equations," *Journal of the Association for Computing Machinery (JACM)*, vol. 6, no. 1, 1959, pp. 37–47.

17. Rice, J. R.: *The Approximation of Functions*, vols. 1 and 2, Addison-Wesley, Reading, Mass., 1964.

18. Forsythe, G., and C. B. Moler; *Computer Solution of Linear Algebraic Systems*, Prentice-Hall, New Jersey, 1967.

19. Isaacson, E., and H. Keller: *Analysis of Numerical Methods*, John Wiley, New York, 1966.

20. Stroud, A. H., and D. Secrest: *Gaussian Quadrature Formulas*, Prentice-Hall, New Jersey, 1966.

21. Johnson, L. W., and R. D. Riess: *Numerical Analysis*, Addison-Wesley, Reading, Mass, 1977.

22. Forsythe, G. E., M. A. Malcolm, and C. D. Moler: *Computer Methods for Mathematical Computations*, Prentice-Hall, New Jersey, 1977.

23. Stewart, G. W., *Introduction to Matrix Computation*, Academic Press, New York, 1973.

24. Wilkinson, J. H.: *The Algebraic Eigenvalue Problem*, Clarendon Press, Oxford, 1965.

25. Ralston, A.: *A First Course in Numerical Analysis*, McGraw-Hill, New York, 1965.

26. Shampine, L. and R. Allen: *Numerical Computing*, Saunders, Philadelphia, 1973.

27. Gautschi, W.: "On the Construction of Gaussian Quadrature Rules from Modified Moments," *Math. Comp.*, vol. 24, 1970, pp. 245–260.

28. Fehlberg, E.: "Klassische Runge-Kutta-Formeln vierter und niedriger Ordnung mit Schrittweitenkontrolle und ihre Anwendung auf Wärmeleitungsprobleme," *Computing*, vol. 6, 1970, pp. 61–71.

29. Hull, T. E., W. H. Enright, and R. K. Jackson: *User's Guide for DVERK—A Subroutine for Solving Non-Stiff ODE's*, TR 100, Department of Computer Science, University of Toronto, October, 1976.

30. Gear, C. W.: *Numerical Initial Value Problems in Ordinary Differential Equations*, Prentice-Hall, New Jersey, 1971.

31. Strang, G., and G. Fix: *An Analysis of the Finite Element Method*, Prentice-Hall, New Jersey, 1973.

32. Smith, B. T., J. M. Boyle, J. J. Dongerra, B. S. Garbow, Y. Ikebe, V. C. Klema, and C. B. Moler: "Matrix Eigensystem routines—EISPACK Guide," *Lecture Notes in Computer Science*, vol. 6, Springer-Verlag, Heidelberg, 1976.

33. Ortega, J. M., and W. C. Rheinboldt: *Iterative Solution of Nonlinear Equations in Several Variables*, Academic Press, New York, 1970.

34. Robinson, S. R.: "Quadratic Interpolation Is Risky," *SIAM J. Numer. Analysis*, vol. 16, 1979, pp. 377–379.

35. Rivlin, T. J.: *An Introduction to the Approximation of Functions*, Blaisdell, Waltham, Mass., 1969.

36. Winograd, S.: "On Computing the Discrete Fourier Transform," *Math. Comp.*, vol. 32, 1978, pp. 175–199.

37. Cooley, J. W., and J. W. Tukey: "An Algorithm for the Machine Calculation of Complex Fourier Series," *Math. Comp.*, vol. 19, 1965, pp. 297–301.

38. Ehlich, H., and K. Zeller: "Auswertung der Normen von Interpolationsoperatoren," *Math. Annalen*, vol. 164, 1966, pp. 105–112.

39. de Boor, C., and A. Pinkus: "Proof of the Conjectures of Bernstein and Erdös," *J. Approximation Theory*, vol. 24, 1978, pp. 289–303.

40. de Boor, C.: *A Practical Guide to Splines*, Springer-Verlag, New York, 1978.

41. Wendroff, B.: *Theoretical Numerical Analysis*, Academic Press, New York, 1966.

42. Wilkinson, J. H.: *Rounding Errors in Algebraic Processes*, Prentice-Hall, New Jersey, 1963.

INDEX

INDEX